Microsoft® Forefront®
Threat Management
Gateway (TMG)

Administrator's Companion

Jim Harrison, Yuri Diogenes,
and Mohit Saxena from the
Microsoft Forefront TMG Team
with Dr. Tom Shinder

PUBLISHED BY
Microsoft Press
A Division of Microsoft Corporation
One Microsoft Way
Redmond, Washington 98052-6399

Library of Congress Control Number: 2009943415

Printed and bound in the United States of America.

2 3 4 5 6 7 8 9 10 11 QGT 5 4 3 2 1 0

Distributed in Canada by H.B. Fenn and Company Ltd.

A CIP catalogue record for this book is available from the British Library.

Microsoft Press books are available through booksellers and distributors worldwide. For further information about international editions, contact your local Microsoft Corporation office or contact Microsoft Press International directly at fax (425) 936-7329. Visit our Web site at www.microsoft.com/mspress. Send comments to mspinput@microsoft.com.

Microsoft, Microsoft Press, Access, Active Directory, ActiveX, Forefront, Internet Explorer, Jscript, MS, Windows, Windows NT, and Windows Server are either registered trademarks or trademarks of Microsoft Corporation in the United States and/or other countries. Other product and company names mentioned herein may be the trademarks of their respective owners.

The example companies, organizations, products, domain names, e-mail addresses, logos, people, places, and events depicted herein are fictitious. No association with any real company, organization, product, domain name, e-mail address, logo, person, place, or event is intended or should be inferred.

This book expresses the author's views and opinions. The information contained in this book is provided without any express, statutory, or implied warranties. Neither the authors, Microsoft Corporation, nor its resellers, or distributors will be held liable for any damages caused or alleged to be caused either directly or indirectly by this book.

Acquisitions Editor: Martin DelRe
Developmental Editor: Karen Szall
Project Editor: Carol Vu
Editorial Production: Christian Holdener, S4Carlisle Publishing Services
Technical Reviewer: Dr. Tom Shinder; Technical Review services provided by Content Master, a member of CM Group, Ltd.
Cover: Tom Draper Design

Body Part No. X16-38617

Contents at a Glance

Introduction   *xxxi*

PART I   A NEW ERA FOR THE MICROSOFT FIREWALL

CHAPTER 1   What's New in TMG   3
CHAPTER 2   What Are the Differences Between TMG and UAG?   21

PART II   PLANNING FOR TMG

CHAPTER 3   System Requirements   35
CHAPTER 4   Analyzing Network Requirements   47
CHAPTER 5   Choosing the Right Network Topology   65
CHAPTER 6   Migrating to TMG   87
CHAPTER 7   Choosing a TMG Client Type   107

PART III   IMPLEMENTING A TMG DEPLOYMENT

CHAPTER 8   Installing TMG   141
CHAPTER 9   Troubleshooting TMG Setup   169
CHAPTER 10   Exploring the TMG Console   185

PART IV   TMG AS YOUR FIREWALL

CHAPTER 11   Configuring TMG Networks   209
CHAPTER 12   Understanding Access Rules   241
CHAPTER 13   Configuring Load-Balancing Capabilities   263
CHAPTER 14   Network Inspection System   307

PART V   TMG AS YOUR CACHING PROXY

CHAPTER 15   Web Proxy Auto Discovery for TMG   345
CHAPTER 16   Caching Concepts and Configuration   387

PART VI   TMG CLIENT PROTECTION

CHAPTER 17	Malware Inspection	427
CHAPTER 18	URL Filtering	465
CHAPTER 19	Enhancing E-Mail Protection	487
CHAPTER 20	HTTP and HTTPS Inspection	529

PART VII   TMG PUBLISHING SCENARIOS

CHAPTER 21	Understanding Publishing Concepts	573
CHAPTER 22	Publishing Servers	599
CHAPTER 23	Publishing Microsoft Office SharePoint Server	661
CHAPTER 24	Publishing Exchange Server	697

PART VIII   REMOTE ACCESS

CHAPTER 25	Understanding Remote Access	733
CHAPTER 26	Implementing Dial-in Client VPN	747
CHAPTER 27	Implementing Site-to-Site VPN	773

PART IX   LOGGING AND REPORTING

CHAPTER 28	Logging	797
CHAPTER 29	Enhanced NAT	817
CHAPTER 30	Scripting TMG	829

PART X   TROUBLESHOOTING

CHAPTER 31	Mastering the Art of Troubleshooting	851
CHAPTER 32	Exploring HTTP Protocol	869
CHAPTER 33	Using Network Monitor 3 for Troubleshooting TMG	891

	Appendix A: From Proxy to TMG	*911*
	Appendix B: TMG Performance Counters	*937*
	Appendix C: Windows Internet Libraries	*967*
	Appendix D: WPAD Script CARP Operation	*973*
	Index	*981*

Contents

Introduction   *xxxi*

PART I   A NEW ERA FOR THE MICROSOFT FIREWALL

Chapter 1   What's New in TMG   3

Introducing TMG. 3

    New Feature Comparisons   4

    Management Console   5

    Deployment   5

    Traffic Filtering   6

Beyond the Firewall 8

    Integration: The Security Challenge   8

    Types of Firewalls   9

    Where TMG Fits In   10

What's New?. 11

    Windows Server 2008, Windows Server 2008 R2,
    and Native 64-Bit Support   12

    Web Antivirus and Anti-Malware Support   12

    Enhanced User Interface, Management, and Reporting   14

    URL Filtering   16

    HTTPS Inspection   16

    E-Mail Anti-Malware and Anti-Spam Support   16

    Network Intrusion Prevention   17

What do you think of this book? We want to hear from you!

Microsoft is interested in hearing your feedback so we can continually improve our
books and learning resources for you. To participate in a brief online survey, please visit:

microsoft.com/learning/booksurvey

The Session Initiation Protocol (SIP) Filter 18

TFTP Filter 18

Network Functionality Enhancements 18

Feature Comparison Summary 19

Summary. 20

Chapter 2   What Are the Differences Between TMG and UAG?   21

Enabling Anywhere Access 22

Understanding IAG 2007. 23

IAG 2007 Integration with ISA Server 2006 24

Forefront UAG: The Next Generation of IAG 2007 .25

What's New in UAG?. 25

Aligning UAG with Security Needs 26

Designing Network Protection. 27

When Do You Deploy UAG?   27

When Do You Deploy TMG?   27

Network Designs for TMG and UAG   28

Summary. 32

PART II   PLANNING FOR TMG

Chapter 3   System Requirements   35

Hardware Requirements 35

Software Requirements 36

General Recommendations. 37

Network Infrastructure   37

Performance Monitoring   41

Behavioral Monitoring   43

Deploying in Virtual Environments 44

Summary. 45

Chapter 4   Analyzing Network Requirements   47

Determining Your Traffic Profile. 47

    Network Mapping   48

    Application Mapping   49

    Protocol Mapping   50

TMG Deployment Options 51

    Edge Firewall   52

    Back Firewall   52

    Single Network Adapter   52

    Domain Isolation   53

Addressing Complex Networks 53

Configuring TMG Networks 54

Understanding How Name Resolution Impacts TMG. 58

    Reviewing How Windows Resolves Names   58

    Recommendations for DNS Configuration on TMG   59

    Side Effects of DNS Issues   62

    DNS Cache in TMG   63

Summary. 64

Chapter 5   Choosing the Right Network Topology   65

Choosing the Network Template. 65

    Edge Firewall Network Template   66

    3-Leg Perimeter Network Template   67

    Back Firewall Network Template   68

    Single NIC Network Template   69

Examining High Availability. 71

    Designing High Availability for Publishing Rules   76

    Designing High Availability for Access Rules   80

Joining the Firewall to a Domain or Workgroup. 82

Summary. 85

Chapter 6   Migrating to TMG   87

General Considerations 87

    Go No Further Until You Understand This!   87

    Base Software   88

    Service Level   88

    If It Breaks   89

    Practice, Practice, Practice!   89

Scenarios. 90

    Publishing   90

    Dial-In VPN   91

    Site-to-Site (S2S) VPN   92

    Proxy   92

    Common Points   94

Example Checklists 96

Example Migration from ISA 2006 SE to TMG 2010 EE Forward
    Proxy Scenario 99

Summary. 105

Chapter 7   Choosing a TMG Client Type   107

Web Proxy Client. 107

    How the Web Proxy Client Works   109

    Server-Side Configuration   111

    When to Use the Web Proxy Client   112

SecureNET Client. 113

    How the SecureNET Client Works   115

    Name Resolution for SecureNET Clients   115

    SecureNET Client Advantages   117

    SecureNET Client Disadvantages   118

Forefront TMG Client 119

    Winsock: A Primer   119

    Winsock Service Providers   122

    The TMGC as a Layered Service Provider   125

    TMGC Configuration Data   126

    Example Winsock Usage without TMGC   130

Winsock Usage with the TMGC   131

Web Proxy Client with TMGC   132

TMG Client Authentication   132

Choosing the Right Client for Your Environment .132

Ease of Deployment   132

Support for Heterogeneous Operating Systems   133

Protocol Support   133

Authentication Requirements and User- or Group-Based
Access Control   133

Security   133

Summary. 137

PART III   IMPLEMENTING A TMG DEPLOYMENT

Chapter 8   Installing TMG   141

Final Considerations Before Installing TMG 141

Additional Recommendations   142

Installing TMG MBE 145

Manual Installation   146

Installing TMG 2010 156

Manual Installation   156

Unattended Installation   168

Summary. 168

Chapter 9   Troubleshooting TMG Setup   169

Understanding Setup Architecture 169

Setup Goals   169

Setup Architecture   170

Setup Process   172

Setup Options 172

Applying Security Updates and Service Packs   173

Installing TMG with Updates   174

What to Look for When Setup Fails. 174

Understanding the Setup Log Files   175

Reading Log Files 176

Setup Failed—Now What? 181

Summary. 184

Chapter 10 Exploring the TMG Console   185

TMG Medium Business Edition. 185

Monitoring 186

Update Center 187

Firewall Policy 188

Web Access Policy 188

Networking 191

System 191

Updates for TMG 2010. 192

Monitoring 193

Firewall Policy 194

Web Access Policy 194

E-Mail Policy 194

Intrusion Prevention System 196

Networking 197

Logs and Reports 199

Update Center 199

New Wizards 199

The Getting Started Wizard 200

The Network Setup Wizard 201

The System Configuration Wizard 202

The Deployment Wizard 202

The Web Access Policy Wizard 203

The Join Array and Disjoin Array Wizards (TMG 2010 only) 203

The Connect to Forefront Protection Manager 2010 Wizard
(TMG 2010 only) 204

The Configure SIP Wizard (TMG 2010 only) 205

The Configure E-Mail Policy Wizard (TMG 2010 only) 205

The Enable ISP Redundancy Wizard (TMG 2010 only) 206

Summary. 206

PART IV   TMG AS YOUR FIREWALL

Chapter 11 Configuring TMG Networks   **209**

    Understanding Network Relationships 209

        Basic IP Routing   210

        Route Relationships   215

        NAT Relationships   215

        NAT Address Selection   218

        Network Rules   220

    Creating Networks 222

        Built-In Networks   222

        Creating a New Network   224

        Creating a Network Rule   226

    Configuring Your Protected Networks 231

        Authenticating Traffic from Protected
        Networks   233

    Summary. 240

Chapter 12 Understanding Access Rules   **241**

    Traffic Policy Behavior 241

        Policy Engine Rule Basics   241

        Ping Access Rule Example   242

        CERN Proxy HTTP Example   245

    Understanding Policy Re-Evaluation. 249

        Policy Enforcement   250

        Exemptions in Policy Enforcement   252

        Policy Enforcement in Certain
        Scenarios   253

    Troubleshooting Access Rules. 253

        Basic Internet Access   254

        Authentication   256

        Name Resolution   259

        Using the Traffic Simulator   259

    Summary. 262

Chapter 13 Configuring Load-Balancing Capabilities 263

Multiple Paths to the Internet. 263

What Is ISP Redundancy? 263

How ISP Redundancy Works 265

Link Availability Testing 265

Implementing ISP Redundancy 267

Planning for ISP-R 267

ISP-R Constraints 268

Enabling ISP-R 269

Failover Mode 269

Load-Balancing Mode 276

Understanding and Implementing NLB 284

NLB Architecture 285

Considerations When Enabling NLB
on TMG 288

Configuring NLB on TMG 293

Post-Installation Best Practices 298

Considerations When Using TMG NLB in
Virtual Environments 300

Troubleshooting NLB on TMG 301

Summary. 306

Chapter 14 Network Inspection System 307

Understanding Network Inspection System 307

Implementing Network Inspection System 309

Configuring NIS 311

Customizing Individual Signatures 316

Monitoring NIS 319

NIS Update 322

IPS Compared to IDS 322

Implementing Intrusion Detection. 323

Configuring Intrusion Detection 324

Configuring DNS Attack Detection 326

Configuring IP Preferences 327

Configuring Flood Mitigation   330

TMG Preconfigured Attack Protection   337

Summary. 341

PART V   TMG AS YOUR CACHING PROXY

Chapter 15   Web Proxy Auto Discovery for TMG   345

WPAD as Protocol and Script 345

WPAD Protocol   345

WPAD Script   352

Configuring Automatic Discovery in the Network 364

Preparing for Automatic Discovery   365

Configuring Client Applications 374

Configuring Internet Explorer for Automatic
Discovery   375

Automatic Proxy Cache   379

Troubleshooting Issues with Auto Discovery
and IE   381

Configuring TMG Client for Automatic
Discovery   381

Configuring Windows Media Player   382

Using AutoProxy in Managed Code   384

Summary. 385

Chapter 16   Caching Concepts and Configuration   387

Understanding Proxy Cache 387

How Caching Works   388

Cache Storage   389

Caching Scenarios   390

Cache Rules   391

Caching Web Objects   392

Caching Compressed Content   393

Monitoring Cache   394

Cache Array Routing Protocol (CARP)   395

How CARP Works   396

Configuring the Forefront TMG 2010 Cache 397

    Enable Web Caching   397

    Add a Cache Rule   400

    Add a Content Download Job   407

    CARP Configuration   413

    Configuring the Intra-Array Address   415

    Configuring the CARP Load Factor   416

Troubleshooting Cache 417

    Analyzing Cache Behavior   417

    Using CacheDir   420

    Using FetchURL   421

    Rebuilding the Cache   421

Summary. 424

PART VI   TMG CLIENT PROTECTION

Chapter 17 Malware Inspection   427

Understanding Malware Inspection
  in TMG. 427

Configuring Malware Inspection 431

    Configuring Malware Inspection for
    Your Environment   431

    Defining Per-Rule Malware Inspection   442

    Testing Internet Access with Malware
    Inspection   443

Creating Reports with Malware Statistics 446

    Configuring a One-Time Report   447

    Configuring a Recurring Report   451

    Generating and Viewing Malware Inspection
    Reports   455

    Customizing Malware Inspection Content in
    Reports   462

Summary. 463

Chapter 18 URL Filtering   465

    How URL Filtering Works 465

        Components Involved in URL Filtering   469

    Configuring URL Filtering 470

        Global URL Filtering Configuration   472

        Rule-Based URL Filtering Configuration   475

        Testing URL Filtering   476

        URL Category Overrides   477

    Update Center 478

        How Update Center Works   479

        Configuring Update Center   481

    Summary 485

Chapter 19 Enhancing E-Mail Protection   487

    Understanding E-Mail Threats 487

        E-Mail Attack Methods   488

    How SMTP Protection Works in TMG 490

    Configuring SMTP Protection on TMG 493

        Running the E-Mail Protection Wizard   494

        Configuring Spam Filtering   502

        Configuring Virus and Content Filtering   518

    Summary 527

Chapter 20 HTTP and HTTPS Inspection   529

    The Web Proxy Application Filter 529

        Troubleshooting Web Proxy Traffic
        in TMG   532

        HTTP Filter   533

    Configuring HTTPS Inspection 534

        Configuring HTTPS Inspection   538

        Common HTTPS Inspection Errors   548

Configuring the HTTP Filter 550

    General Options   550

    HTTP Methods   553

    Extensions   555

    Headers   557

    Signatures   561

Summary. 570

PART VII   TMG PUBLISHING SCENARIOS

Chapter 21 Understanding Publishing Concepts   573

Core Publishing Scenarios. 573

    Server Publishing   574

    Server Publishing and Network
    Relationships   576

    Server Publishing vs. Access Rules   577

    Web Publishing   578

Publishing Rule Elements. 580

    Elements in a Web Publishing Rule   580

    Elements in a Server Publishing Rule   588

Planning Publishing Rules 591

    Evaluating System Capacity   592

    Protocol Considerations   593

    Certificate Considerations   595

    Load Balancing   595

Summary. 598

Chapter 22 Publishing Servers   599

How to Publish a Web Server 599

    Publishing a Web Server Using
    HTTP Protocol   600

    Publishing a Web Server Using HTTPS   618

Publishing a Non-Web Server. 637

    Creating a Non-Web Server Publishing Rule   637

Troubleshooting Publishing Rules 647

Web Publishing Rules   647

Web Publishing Test Button   656

Non-Web Publishing Rules   657

Summary. 660

Chapter 23 Publishing Microsoft Office SharePoint Server   661

Planning to Publish SharePoint. 661

Security Considerations   662

Authentication   663

Alternate Access Mapping   664

Configuring SharePoint Publishing 665

Troubleshooting 689

Review Your Publishing Rule First   689

Summary. 696

Chapter 24 Publishing Exchange Server   697

Planning 697

Understanding Exchange Server
Roles   697

Planning Client Access   698

Certificates   699

Authentication   700

Using the Wizards   702

Capacity Planning   703

Specific Client Considerations   706

Configuring Exchange Client Access through
Forefront TMG 707

Troubleshooting 719

General Troubleshooting Rules   720

Exchange ActiveSync (EAS) and Office Mobile
Access (OMA)   721

Outlook Web Access (OWA)   721

Exchange Web Services (EWS)   723

Outlook Anywhere (OA)   724

Using the Test Rule Button   725

Summary. 730

PART VIII   REMOTE ACCESS

Chapter 25   Understanding Remote Access   **733**

Understanding VPN Concepts 733

Tunnel Types   734

Protocols   734

Authentication   735

VPN Technology Comparison   736

Planning VPN Access 737

Selecting the VPN Protocol   738

Hardware Requirements   739

Authentication   741

VPN Access Policy   741

Supportability   742

NAP Integration. 743

Considerations When Planning NAP
Integration   745

Summary. 745

Chapter 26   Implementing Dial-in Client VPN   **747**

Configuring VPN Client Access. 747

Configure VPN Client Access with NAP Integration 756

Configuring Forefront TMG for NAP Integration   758

Configuring NPS to Use Forefront TMG as
a RADIUS Client   762

Configuring VPN Client Access Using SSTP 763

Planning SSTP   766

Enabling SSTP on Forefront TMG   767

Changing Client Configuration   770

Summary. 771

Chapter 27 Implementing Site-to-Site VPN   **773**

Configuring L2TP Over IPsec Site-to-Site VPN 774

Configuring PPTP Site-to-Site VPN 782

Troubleshooting VPN Client Connections 788

PPTP   788

L2TP over IPsec   790

SSTP   792

Common Errors and Likely Causes   793

Summary. 794

PART IX   LOGGING AND REPORTING

Chapter 28 Logging   **797**

Why Logging Is Important 797

New Firewall and Web Proxy Log Fields   798

Configuring TMG Logging 800

Common Logging Options   800

Log File and Disk Space Controls   803

SQL Express   804

SQL Database   805

Local Text Logging   807

Logging Queue   809

Logging Best Practices. 809

Collecting Information about Your Environment   810

Logging Options   810

General Guidelines   812

Summary. 815

Chapter 29 Enhanced NAT   **817**

Understanding Enhanced NAT. 817

Configuring Enhanced NAT. 820

Troubleshooting Enhanced NAT. 826

Summary. 828

Chapter 30 Scripting TMG   **829**

Understanding the TMG Component Object Model (COM)..........829

Forefront TMG COM hierarchy   830

New COM Elements in TMG   831

Administering TMG with VBScript or JScript 834

TMG Scripting Best Practices   834

TMG Task Automation Example   836

Administering TMG with Windows PowerShell.....................842

Windows PowerShell Automation Examples   845

Summary...848

PART X   TROUBLESHOOTING

Chapter 31 Mastering the Art of Troubleshooting   **851**

General Troubleshooting Methodology...........................851

You've Defined the Problem—What's Next?   853

Time to Analyze the Data   854

Got It, Now I'm Going to Fix It!   854

Troubleshooting Tools   855

TMG Troubleshooting Tab   858

Best Practices Analyzer   860

Network Monitor   861

Performance Monitor   861

Windows Event Logs   862

Putting It All Together 862

Real Life Case Study   862

Summary...868

Chapter 32 Exploring HTTP Protocol   **869**

Understanding the HTTP Protocol...............................869

HTTP Transaction   870

How HTTP Authentication Works 874

Rules of the Game   874

HTTP Authentication in Action   876

Understanding HTTPS 884

    Negotiation Phase   885

    Client Acknowledgement   888

    Server Acknowledgement   889

Summary. 890

**Chapter 33 Using Network Monitor 3
for Troubleshooting TMG   891**

Using Network Monitor to Capture Traffic. 891

    Data Gathering with Network Monitor   892

Reading a Network Monitor Capture 897

Troubleshooting TMG Using Network Monitor 903

Summary. 909

    Appendix A: From Proxy to TMG   *911*

    Appendix B: TMG Performance Counters   *937*

    Appendix C: Windows Internet Libraries   *967*

    Appendix D: WPAD Script CARP Operation   *973*

    Index   *981*

What do you think of this book? We want to hear from you!

Microsoft is interested in hearing your feedback so we can continually improve our
books and learning resources for you. To participate in a brief online survey, please visit:

microsoft.com/learning/booksurvey

Foreword

As the Product Unit Manager for the Forefront Threat Management Gateway (TMG) 2010 release, I was able to take advantage of a unique opportunity to change the industry regarding how we protect small business users and enterprise customers when connecting to the Internet in a world of ever-evolving threats, malicious software, and dynamic criminal activities. It was a challenge I could not pass up and I jumped at the opportunity to see how we could simplify the secure Web gateway (SWG) experience for customers and still provide the flexibility and security that hardcore security professionals have grown to love with the existing Internet Security and Acceleration (ISA) Server platform.

TMG has introduced a new era not only for Microsoft but also for the industry in how we create a comprehensive network protection solution for both small and large enterprise customers. Customers have told us that they love the Microsoft infrastructure integrated firewall and proxy that allows configuration and management using the tools and management infrastructure they are familiar with, such as Active Directory. But as we saw the threats and the workforce evolve, we realized that our customers needed something more to protect their users when accessing the Internet.

I wish I could summarize the full set of capabilities and potential in a short foreword for this book, but it proved to be impossible. The simple answer comes in the product name itself: Threat Management Gateway. The name deservedly implies the dynamic and integrated nature of the product and its extensible capability as it integrates with the Forefront Protection Suite. When you put it all together, the product really has six unique value propositions that emphasize our comprehensive approach to network protection:

- **Enforce network policy access at the edge** (Firewall)
- **Protect users from Web browsing threats** (Web Client Protection)
- **Protect users from e-mail threats** (E-mail Protection)
- **Protect desktops and servers from intrusion attempts** (Network Intrusion System)
- **Enable users to remotely access corporate resources** (VPN, Secure Web Publishing)
- **Simplify management** (Deployment)

In the end, the quality and the value proposition of the product speak for themselves. Throughout the beta program, we have had more downloads and production deployments than all the other betas of the ISA platform combined. The breadth of the new features has driven new customers and new deployments never possible with the ISA product line. On the firewall side, we have added key components such as VoIP traversal (SIP), Enhanced NAT, and ISP Link Redundancy. Combined with our NAP (Network Access Protection) integration with the VPN functionality, the firewall and remote access capabilities are richer than ever. On the Web client protection area, we now have integrated URL filtering, HTTP anti-virus/spyware scanning, and HTTPS forward inspection. The new secure e-mail relay deployment option enables a hardened edge–based anti-virus and anti-spam solution not previously available. And last but not least, the fully integrated and new Forefront Network Inspection System (NIS) has changed the game of network intrusion prevention and detection. Not only does the NIS provide the capability for administrators to provide threat management in the face of zero-day attacks, but it also enables security assessment and responses when deployed in conjunction with the Forefront Protection Suite.

What's next for the future of secure Web gateways and the threat landscape? If I were to be an oracle and predict the future, I would expect first that the trend of more complex malware and malicious attacks will continue to grow in volume and in criminal intent. I would also suspect that we will see a demand from the marketplace for further integration of information protection and control (IPC) with access and protection. We will see consolidation not only of solutions, but we'll also see the management and policy capabilities being integrated and unified across solution verticals. I believe TMG 2010 will be a product foreshadowing the future when it comes to network and virtualized datacenter protection.

In summary, this book is a must-have for the Forefront Threat Management Gateway administrator—it embodies the core of the product team development knowledge, the best practices from the Microsoft consultants around the world, and the learning from our customer deployments to date, and it distills this all into a one-stop resource kit of knowledge. Jim Harrison is known throughout Microsoft and the broader industry as the foremost ISA—and now TMG—expert. His in-depth understanding of the product internals combined with real-world deployment and operational experience provide a perspective unlike any other expert in the community. Yuri Diogenes and Mohit Saxena have not only been on the front lines of the top ISA deployments around the world, but have also been on the forefront (no pun intended) of the TMG beta program. Their firsthand guidance and best practices will help you ensure a smooth and easy deployment by avoiding mistakes in advance and suggesting the most secure configuration from the start. Tom Shinder, a recognized Microsoft security professional and widely known ISA expert, brings his extended ISA experience to bear as a valued technical reviewer for this book.

The availability of this book helps to achieve the goal that we set with the original inception of the TMG project: to enable customers to deploy protection easily in a cost-effective and manageable way to achieve their security and application-protection requirements in an ever-changing threat landscape. I believe we have achieved that goal with our upcoming release and with security experts such as Jim, Yuri, and Mohit evangelizing the knowledge.

David B. Cross
Product Unit Manager
Microsoft Corporation

Acknowledgments

This book took more than a year to write; starting in April 2008 with our final content submission in September of 2009. Although the authors get lots of credit for a book, there can be little doubt that we could not have even begun, much less completed this book, without the cooperation (not to mention the permission) of an incredibly large number of people. We'd like to take a few moments of your time here to express our gratitude to the folks that made it all possible.

From "The Collective"

To Dr. Tom Shinder for adding his deep and broad technical and writing experience as a technical reviewer. Much of what you read herein is the result of Tom's willingness to ask us, "Wachootawkinbout, Willis?"

To the folks at Microsoft Press who made the process as smooth as they possibly could: Carol Vu and her team of crack editors, Karen Szall, and Martin DelRe, who helped us get this project off the ground.

To David Cross and the Forefront Edge marketing team, who approved and supported us in this effort, and especially to David for writing the foreword.

To the TMG Core and CS teams, who responded immediately and in painstaking detail to our unending stream of e-mails. You folks built an extremely fine product and we sincerely hope we did your efforts justice.

To Bala Natarajan and the whole TMG TAP team who continually asked us, "Are you dealing with this in your book?" (causing several chapter rewrites), but never failed to make the book better in the process.

To Paul Long and the Network Monitor Team for producing Network Monitor and reviewing Chapter 33, "Using Network Monitor 3 for Troubleshooting TMG."

To Mark Stanfill for assisting during the creation of the Windows PowerShell script—your assistance was very much appreciated.

To the Security Content Review Board participants: We may not always agree with what you offer, but we always took your review comments seriously.

From Jim

First and foremost, to my wife, Lois, who in an apparent fit of extreme silliness responded, "Sure—go ahead!" when I asked her permission to collaborate with Yuri and Mohit on this book. Neither she nor I had a clue what lay before us, but she never wavered and more than anything else her support helped keep me on track.

To Yuri and Mohit, who must have wondered if "my head was with me all day" (three social points for that quote) when they read some of my review comments. You guys made this far easier and much more fun than it might have been otherwise. I'm all little-girl-giggly to see my name printed alongside yours on this book.

To Tom: It took me almost 10 years (yes, we've been "ISA-lated" that long), but I finally had a chance to give you "your props" in my book. Thanks so much for helping—the book is that much better as a result of your participation!

To "Da Boyz"; Tom, Tim (Thor), Steve, and Greg—there's nothing like a group of solid bros that's willing to call me to task for my cranial effluvium.

From Yuri

Above all, thanks to God for blessing my life and leading my way. I also couldn't have even thought about writing this book if I didn't have such a great family. They have always supported me and understood my long days away working on this long project: I love you, Yanne and Ysis. Thanks to my wife, Alexsandra, for all your comprehension and love. Without you this wouldn't be possible.

To Jim and Mohit, I have a simple sentence to define those months working on this project with y'all: It was an honor to share so many great moments. Each of you contributed to my personal growth with your thoughts, advice, and guidance. Without a doubt these long months writing this book were worth it because of this amazing partnership that we had. The same applies to Tom, who jumped on this project at the right moment and used his vast writing experience in guiding all of us to write this content better.

Last but not least I would like to say thanks to all my friends from Microsoft CSS Security (Texas, North Carolina, Washington, EMEA, and India) for sharing your experiences every day and to my direct managers for supporting my passion to write and giving me so many opportunities to do so. To Nathan Bigman: You were responsible for this writing dream that became true. To my buddies Alexandre Hollanda and Mohit Kumar: Thanks, guys, for always being there when I need you.

From Mohit

First and foremost I would like to thank my wife, Anusha, for being extremely supportive during the time I was working on this book and for being my strength during times when I really felt I couldn't write anymore. I still remember times when I was up late into the night, trying to meet deadlines for the book along with my regular work and feeling completely frustrated. A cup of hot coffee along with a gentle reminder from her that no matter how much hard work it was I could still do it took all the frustration away. I really couldn't have done this without her love and support and without my little puppy, Mojo, who stayed up with me as long as I worked. I would also like to thank my parents and my brother, who have always inspired me to take on more challenges in life and remind me that the only change that is constant in life is knowledge, and by sharing your knowledge you gain more.

To Jim and Yuri: I still remember the day when I jokingly mentioned the idea to Yuri. I understood later that joking about any idea about writing to Yuri is always dangerous. The whole idea of writing a book was a dream that soon turned into reality when Jim joined us. I will always be thankful to you two for helping this dream come true for me. Thank you for bearing with me when I was late on the schedule (which I always was) and for always being there to cover for me whenever I couldn't complete my part. We would have never been able to complete this book so soon if it hadn't been for Yuri making sure we stuck to our deadlines and for Jim making sure to correct me technically if I had wandered off into my own ideas. A big thank you to Tom for helping us make this book a masterpiece with his participation and guidance.

Finally, I would like to thank all my teammates in Bangalore, Charlotte, Las Colinas, and Redmond along with my managers for being supportive of my passion to write this book. Thanks to Bala Natarajan, Dan Herzog, Mohit Kumar, and Tarun Sachdeva for always being patient with me and helping me with all my questions, but above all being great friends.

Introduction

Welcome to the *Microsoft Forefront Threat Management Gateway (TMG) Administrator's Companion*. This book was written over the course of more than a year to help you design, deploy, and maintain TMG in multiple scenarios as well as to help you understand the history and design goals of TMG. The functionality descriptions and examples in this book are based on actual deployment and testing in the authors' labs, so you can rest assured that what we describe is a demonstrated fact, not simply a "feature description."

Forefront TMG was designed and tested to provide the best possible security for Internet access for your users and to provide you with the means to more easily understand and manage the ever-increasing Internet threat landscape. Network Inspection, HTTPS Inspection, Enhanced Malware Protection, and URL Filtering are all designed to help you provide greater security for your users. The built-in troubleshooting tools are included to help you keep your TMG deployments running at peak performance and effectiveness.

The Target Audience

The person we tried to keep in mind while writing this book is someone with at least a year of experience deploying and troubleshooting networks with at least 2 to 10 routed subnets. Ideally, you would have some experience configuring switches, routers, and basic firewalls and also have had some experience with ISA Server 2004 or ISA Server 2006. You should also have some basic understanding of common Internet protocols such as HTTP, SMTP, IMAP, IPsec, PPTP, and so on, and be familiar with the OSI network model.

This book is written by technical people for technical people; the goal is to inform and educate. The primary product focus of the book is TMG 2010. ISA Server is included to provide historical comparison and to illustrate improvements TMG offers over ISA Server. TMG (MBE), IAG, and UAG are included to illustrate differences between TMG 2010 and these other products and to help you decide which product best serves your needs.

One thing to bear in mind as you work your way through this book is that many of the descriptions and screen shots were written using pre-release versions of the product—from early beta up to the first release candidate. We performed a review of all chapters just before TMG was released in order to ensure that the information and screen shots were as current as we could possibly make them.

Organization and Usage

In general, we've organized the book so that you get some background on a feature set as well as introducing the feature to you. With the exception of those chapters that required reevaluation as the product evolved over the past year, we were able to keep with the planned layout. You may notice those that seem out of place as you use the book.

We wrote this book with an eye toward functional usage. The first section provides an introduction to TMG as a single product and in the context of other Forefront Edge products. Each section collects chapters into functional groups that are related by an overarching concept, such as protected clients, publishing, and so on, and within each chapter that addresses specific action, we've tried to include some basic troubleshooting methodology and examples.

Part 1 A New Era for the Microsoft Firewall

Part 1 includes discussions on TMG features, design goals, and their relationship to the Microsoft Forefront Edge product line.

Chapter 1 What's New in TMG

Chapter 1 summarizes the design goals and scenarios for TMG in comparison to ISA Server, Internet Access Gateway (IAG), and Universal Access Gateway (UAG).

Chapter 2 What Are the Differences Between TMG and UAG?

Chapter 2 details the design goals and scenarios for TMG in comparison to Universal Access Gateway (UAG). It provides comparisons between IAG and UAG for historical reference.

Part 2 Planning for TMG

Part 2 includes discussions on planning for TMG deployments, including product requirements, client traffic considerations, and virtual deployments.

Chapter 3 System Requirements

Chapter 3 details and discusses the hardware and software requirements for TMG. This chapter also covers considerations for deploying on a virtual environment.

Chapter 4 Analyzing Network Requirements

Chapter 4 discusses the methodology for determining the traffic profile and client load for TMG deployments. This chapter also addresses distributed and remote traffic paths related to client traffic profiles.

Chapter 5 Choosing the Right Network Topology

Chapter 5 discusses the methodology for determining the correct network topology for TMG. This chapter also deals with the question of domain membership versus workgroup deployments for TMG as well as high-availability scenarios and solutions.

Chapter 6 Migrating to TMG

Chapter 6 discusses how to plan, coordinate, and test migrating from an ISA Server deployment to a Forefront TMG deployment.

Chapter 7 Choosing a TMG Client Type

Chapter 7 discusses the various client request types supported by TMG as well as the deployment choices that impact the use of these clients.

Part 3 Implementing a TMG Deployment

Part 3 covers installing and configuring TMG Medium Business edition and TMG 2010 and provides an introduction to the new management console.

Chapter 8 Installing TMG

Chapter 8 covers installing TMG MBE separately from Windows Essential Business Server as well as installing TMG 2010. This chapter provides checklists that refer to concepts provided in the planning chapters.

Chapter 9 Troubleshooting TMG Setup

Chapter 9 discusses the methodology for troubleshooting TMG setup failures. This chapter provides details on how the setup mechanisms are constructed and how they interrelate as well as guidance on using the setup logs to solve TMG installation problems.

Chapter 10 Exploring the TMG Console

Chapter 10 introduces you to the TMG management MMC and provides comparisons to ISA 2006 and TMG Medium Business edition (MBE). This chapter also outlines new wizards provided by TMG.

Part 4 TMG as Your Firewall

Part 4 includes discussions on TMG network concepts as well as configuring and troubleshooting network and access rules. This section also includes a discussion on NIS.

Chapter 11 Configuring TMG Networks

Chapter 11 discusses TMG logical network configurations and the impact these choices have on TMG behavior. This chapter includes a basic discussion on IP routing to help you understand how TMG networks operate.

Chapter 12 Understanding Access Rules

Chapter 12 discusses how the TMG policy engine processes traffic in the context of access rules and includes guidance on basic troubleshooting.

Chapter 13 Configuring Load-Balancing Capabilities

Chapter 13 discusses load-balancing concepts in general, including Network Load Balancing (NLB), DNS Round-Robin (DNS-RR), and ISP Redundancy (ISP-R). This chapter also provides comparisons of each solution and how they interact.

Chapter 14 Network Inspection System

Chapter 14 discusses how TMG implements Generic Application Protocol Analysis (GAPA) in the Network Inspection System (NIS) to protect computers that send their traffic through TMG.

Part 5 TMG as Your Caching Proxy

Part 5 introduces general caching concepts as well as TMG caching mechanism and controls.

Chapter 15 Web Proxy Auto Discovery for TMG

Chapter 15 covers WPAD as the discovery protocol and the configuration script provided by TMG. This chapter includes general network requirements and steps to ensure proper WPAD behavior.

Chapter 16 Caching Concepts and Configuration

Chapter 16 discusses Web caching as implemented within TMG. This chapter includes TMG cache configuration and troubleshooting methodology.

Part 6 TMG Client Protection

Part 6 introduces protection mechanisms provided by TMG for clients in protected networks.

Chapter 17 Malware Inspection

Chapter 17 discusses TMG Malware Inspection, including how to configure it for your organization's needs and how to produce reports that summarize EMP detection actions.

Chapter 18 URL Filtering

Chapter 18 discusses URL Filtering concepts, including the relationship with Microsoft Reputation Services (MRS). You'll also learn how to configure URLF to meet your organization's requirements.

Chapter 19 Enhancing E-mail Protection

Chapter 19 discusses the threat landscape presented by e-mail and how TMG works with Exchange Edge and Forefront Protection 2010 for Exchange Server to minimize the threats presented to your organization.

Chapter 20 HTTP and HTTPS Inspection

Chapter 20 discusses how TMG handles inspection for HTTP traffic and how the new HTTPS Inspection (HTTPSi) feature helps to improve this functionality.

Part 7 TMG Publishing Scenarios

Part 7 discusses publishing concepts in general as well as specific publishing scenarios.

Chapter 21 Understanding Publishing Concepts

Chapter 21 discusses the functional concepts related to publishing scenarios. This chapter also discusses how to properly plan your publishing scenarios and the resulting TMG policy configuration.

Chapter 22 Publishing Servers

Chapter 22 discusses how to publish Web and non-Web services to best take advantage of TMG functionality and security mechanisms.

Chapter 23 Publishing Microsoft Office SharePoint Server

Chapter 23 discusses how to plan and publish Windows SharePoint services. This chapter includes publishing concepts specific to SharePoint, publishing steps, and troubleshooting hints.

Chapter 24 Publishing Exchange Server

Chapter 24 discusses the concepts and methodology for publishing Exchange mail services, such as Outlook Web Access and SMTP. This chapter also includes discussions about proper certificate construction and installation as well as troubleshooting guidance.

Part 8 Remote Access

Part 8 discusses remote access concepts including the protocols involved. This part also details configuring TMG for dial-in and Site-to-Site VPN access.

Chapter 25 Understanding Remote Access

Chapter 25 discusses VPN concepts, including detailed, comparative discussions on various VPN tunnel technologies and related protocols. Network Access Protection (NAP) integration is also introduced in this chapter.

Chapter 26 Implementing Dial-in Client VPN

Chapter 26 includes detailed instructions on how to configure TMG to provide dial-in VPN access using classic VPN, SSTP, and NAP.

Chapter 27 Implementing Site-to-Site VPN

Chapter 27 includes detailed instructions on how to configure TMG to support Site-to-Site VPN networks using classic L2TP/IPsec and PPTP. This chapter also includes troubleshooting guidance for common issues.

Part 9 Logging and Reporting

Part 9 discusses logging, reporting, administrative scripting for TMG, and Enhanced NAT.

Chapter 28 Logging

Chapter 28 discusses firewall logging in general as well as what TMG logging provides you. This chapter also includes discussions on logging best practices.

Chapter 29 Enhanced NAT

Chapter 29 discusses Enhanced Network Address Translation (ENAT) concepts, configuration, and troubleshooting.

Chapter 30 Scripting TMG

Chapter 30 provides a discussion of the TMG Component Object Model (COM) and changes to the COM since ISA 2006 and also provides scripting examples in VBScript, Jscript, and Windows PowerShell.

Part 10 Troubleshooting

Part 10 covers general troubleshooting, as well as techniques and tools useful for troubleshooting TMG scenarios.

Chapter 31 Mastering the Art of Troubleshooting

Chapter 31 discusses the habits and techniques understood by all good troubleshooters. This chapter includes discussions of problem recognition, methodology, and tools.

Chapter 32 Exploring the HTTP Protocol

Chapter 32 provides a detailed discussion on the HTTP protocol; the authentication methods it includes; and how adding Secure Sockets Layer (SSL) to the protocol changes client, proxy, and server expectations.

Chapter 33 Using Network Monitor 3 for Troubleshooting TMG

Chapter 33 uses Network Monitor 3 to discuss the concepts and methodology behind TMG troubleshooting using a network capture and analysis tool.

Appendices

The appendices include content providing expanded explanations as well as historical references.

Appendix A From Proxy to TMG

This section includes discussions on TMG features, design goals, and the relationship between TMG and the Forefront product line.

Appendix B TMG Performance Counters

This section includes discussions on TMG performance counters and how they may be used together and separately to monitor TMG behavior and identify problems as well as the need to scale up or out.

Appendix C Windows Internet Libraries

This section includes discussions on two Windows Internet libraries (WinInet and WinHTTP). We provide special considerations for each with regard to CERN proxy behavior and limitations.

Appendix D WPAD Script CARP Operation

This section includes a detailed discussion on the TMG CFILE and includes some test scripts for use by the TMG administrator to test client-side CARP behavior.

Terminology

While writing this book, we strove to maintain the standard terms in describing general networking concepts as well as specific technologies, mechanisms, and protocols. In particular, and because there is so much argument on this point, our use of the terms *firewall*, *server*, *computer*, and *proxy* are described below:

- **Firewall** This term may be used in reference to TMG in the context of its function as a firewall—a network entity that controls traffic flow between two or more unique networks.

- **Proxy** This term may be used in reference to TMG in the context of its function as a proxy server. This includes the following use cases:

  - CERN proxy (AKA forward proxy) and Web Publishing (AKA reverse proxy)

  - SOCKS proxy as defined in *http://en.wikipedia.org/wiki/SOCKS*

  - Winsock proxy (AKA TMG Clients) as described in *http://technet.microsoft.com/en-us/library/ee291341.aspx*

- **Server** This term may be used in reference to TMG in the context of any function normally provided by Windows Server mechanisms, such as file shares, authentication, and so on. This term may also be used to refer to TMG in the general sense, such as *array server* or *the TMG server*.

- **Computer**   This term may be used in reference to TMG in the context of any physical or logical configuration related specifically to Windows or the underlying server hardware itself, such as CPU, memory, network interfaces, and so on.

Companion CD

The companion CD is a valuable addition to this book and includes the following items:

- Sample scripts written in Visual Basic Scripting edition (VBScript), Java Script (Jscript), or Windows PowerShell for TMG administration. These scripts can be used either as is or customized to meet your administrative needs.

- SOCKS parser for Network Monitor 3.3. Instructions for the use of this parser are included on the CD.

- An electronic version of the entire *Microsoft Forefront Threat Management Gateway (TMG) Administrator's Companion*.

 Full documentation of the contents and structure of the companion media can be found in the Readme.txt file on the CD.

> **Digital Content for Digital Book Readers:** If you bought a digital-only edition of this book, you can enjoy select content from the print edition's companion CD.
> Visit **http://go.microsoft.com/fwlink/?LinkId=178779** to get your downloadable content. This content is always up-to-date and available to all readers.

System Requirements

You'll need the following hardware and software to work with the companion content included with this book:

- Microsoft Windows Vista, Windows Server 2008, or Windows 7. Server Core is not supported for TMG or these tools.

- Microsoft Forefront TMG (for server installation) or Remote Administration (for client operating systems).

- 1 gigahertz (GHz) or faster 32-bit (x86) or 64-bit (x64) processor.

- 1 GB of available, physical RAM.

- Video (800 × 600 or higher resolution) monitor with at least 256 colors.

- CD-ROM or DVD-ROM drive.

- Microsoft mouse or compatible pointing device.

- Adobe Reader for viewing the eBook (Adobe Reader is available as a download at *http://adobe.com*).

Feedback and Support for This Book

Although we always strive for perfect content, the fact that humans are involved in the process from start to finish (no, really—we have flesh and bones and bad breath and everything) pretty much guarantees that we won't achieve that lofty goal. Because you will no doubt discover mistakes, or something we've said may raise more questions than answers, please feel free to contact us collectively at *authors@mstmgbook.org*. We will respond as soon as possible with an answer appropriate to the question or comment.

Every effort has been made to ensure the accuracy of this book and companion content. As corrections or changes are collected, they will be added to a Microsoft Knowledge Base article accessible via the Microsoft Help and Support site. Microsoft Press provides support for books, including instructions for finding Knowledge Base articles, at the following Web site:

http://www.microsoft.com/learning/support/books/

If you have questions regarding the book that are not answered by visiting the site above or viewing a Knowledge Base article, send them to Microsoft Press via e-mail to *mspinput@microsoft.com.*

Please note that Microsoft software product support is not offered through these addresses.

We Want to Hear from You

We welcome your feedback about this book. Please share your comments and ideas via the following short survey:

http://www.microsoft.com/learning/booksurvey/

Your participation will help Microsoft Press create books that better meet your needs and your standards.

> **NOTE** We hope that you will give us detailed feedback via our survey. If you have questions about our publishing program, upcoming titles, or Microsoft Press in general, we encourage you to interact with us via Twitter at *http://twitter.com/MicrosoftPress*. For support issues, use only the e-mail address shown in the previous section.

## PART I

A New Era for the Microsoft Firewall

CHAPTER 1 What's New in TMG **3**

CHAPTER 2 What Are the Differences Between TMG and UAG? **21**

What's New in TMG

- Introducing TMG   **3**

- Beyond the Firewall   **8**

- What's New?   **11**

- Summary   **20**

The Microsoft Forefront Threat Management Gateway 2010 (TMG) is a firewall that has application-layer intelligence and anti-malware capabilities that can be used to identify and mitigate many of the threats facing modern networks. Forefront TMG is the successor to Microsoft ISA Server and includes all of the ISA Server functionality you're accustomed to while improving usability, security, and functionality. All the feature changes and troubleshooting updates included in the ISA Server 2006 Supportability Update are included in TMG.

> **MORE INFO**   You can find the ISA Server 2006 Supportability Update at the Microsoft Download Center: *http://www.microsoft.com/downloads/details .aspx?FamilyID=6F629EAC-D8C6-4437-9D20-B47B02DB413A*.

Introducing TMG

Along with Forefront Unified Access Gateway (UAG), TMG is a new addition to the Forefront Edge product suite. The name Threat Management Gateway was chosen to help illustrate the separation of duties between the two Forefront Edge products. TMG is primarily targeted at outbound traffic scenarios, such as those generated by hosts on protected networks; UAG is primarily targeted at inbound traffic scenarios, as in the case of Microsoft SharePoint or Exchange Web publishing. We'll discuss the finer points of these differences in Chapter 2, "What Are the Differences Between TMG and UAG?"

Although the new functionality of TMG is targeted primarily at securing hosts in a protected network, TMG still provides all of the functionality with which an ISA Server administrator is already familiar.

The two versions of the TMG are:

- TMG Medium Business Edition (MBE), which is available in a stand-alone version or with Windows Essential Business Server (EBS)

- TMG 2010 for all other deployments

TMG MBE was released with Windows EBS in late 2008. TMG 2010 is expected to be released at the end of 2009. Because of this split, the feature set and design goals for each TMG version are somewhat different.

You might ask "Why is there no version of TMG for Windows Small Business Server 2008?" The answer lies in the fact that Windows Small Business Server would be a third scenario differing greatly in requirements and behavior. As is often the case in software development, choices had to be made to optimize the available resources and meet a set quality level.

> **MORE INFO** The "Microsoft Essential Business Server Overview" is available at *http://www.microsoft.com/presspass/presskits/ServerSolutions/businessserver.mspx*.

New Feature Comparisons

TMG adds some interesting new features that were not available with ISA Server. It's worth noting that this functionality also differs between TMG releases. Table 1-1 compares the features of the two TMG releases. This chapter discusses the details of each feature.

TABLE 1-1 Main TMG Features by Version

FEATURE COMPARISONS	TMG MBE	TMG FULL
Windows Server 2008 x64 **	X	X
Windows Filtering Platform (WFP) Integration	X	X
Web Proxy anti-malware	X	X
Web Access Policy	X	X
Enhanced management	X	X
SQL Reporting Services	X	X
SSTP VPN and NAP		X
ISP Load-balancing and sharing		X
NAT Enhancements		X
E-Mail anti-malware *		X
Subscription URL Filtering		X

* TMG MBE e-mail malware is provided by the EBS installation.

** TMG MBE components run as 32-bit processes

Management Console

The Forefront TMG Management Console (Figure 1-1) was reorganized to simplify TMG configuration and monitoring. Many task-oriented controls have been relocated closer to one another for ease of access and task simplification. For example, the General node in the left pane of the ISA 2004 and ISA 2006 management console (Figure 1-2) has been eliminated, and the functions that were once grouped within it have been relocated to more task-relevant locations. You'll get all the details in Chapter 10, "Exploring the TMG Console."

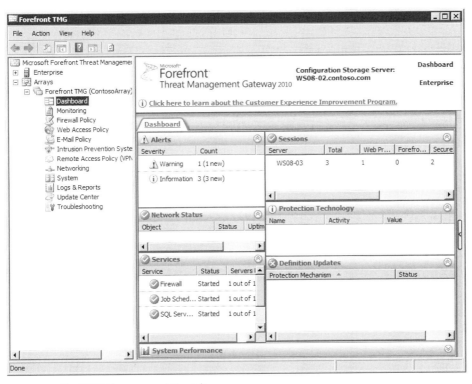

FIGURE 1-1 The TMG Management Console

Deployment

TMG 2010 was designed for use with Windows Server 2008 and Windows Server 2008 R2 and is available only in 64-bit editions. TMG includes 32-bit versions of the management components to facilitate remote management using computers running Windows 32-bit operating systems.

TMG Medium Business Edition

Because TMG MBE is designed specifically for Windows EBS deployments that provide a single TMG server joined to the domain, TMG MBE does not support installation in a workgroup or array membership. As with ISA Server on Windows Small Business Server, initial deployment and configuration of TMG is performed using installation wizards.

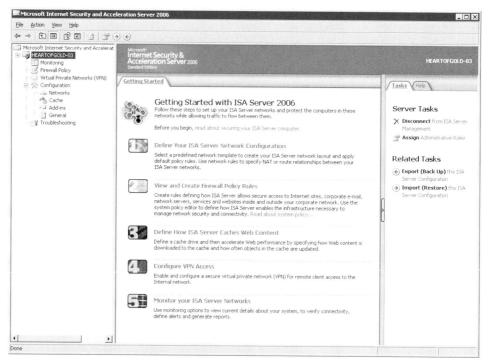

FIGURE 1-2 ISA Server 2006 Management Console

TMG 2010

TMG continues the distinction between Enterprise and Standard versions as well as the *Array* and *Standalone* deployments for Enterprise edition. All the features relevant to each scenario are identical except for the following, which are limited to array deployment:

- Integrated Network Load Balancing (NLB)
- Cache Array Routing Protocol (CARP)
- Enterprise Management

Traffic Filtering

Since ISA Server 2000, ISA Server has provided network traffic filtering at network layer 3 (IP) and above, but only for IP Protocol version 4 (IPv4). Although ISA server performed quite well as an application-level firewall in a great many deployments, the lack of support for IPv6 or non-IP protocol filtering at network layer 3 caused many firewall administrators to consider ISA 2006 an incomplete firewall solution. TMG improves on this by extending the traffic filtering mechanisms to layer 2 through the use of a Network Driver Interface Specification (NDIS) driver. TMG 2010 will support IPv6 only as far as is necessary for UAG direct access (DA) functionality.

Windows Filtering Platform (WFP) Integration

One important change for TMG is that it operates in cooperation with the Windows Filtering Platform (WFP) mechanism. The combination of Windows Server 2003 and ISA Server, Windows Internet Connection Firewall (ICF) and Internet Connection Sharing (ICS) functionality were disabled in favor of ISA Server traffic filtering and routing.

In fact, if you attempted to enable either of these Windows features, you would receive warning messages informing you that this functionality is unavailable because of dependencies created by another program or component. The ISA Server installation and control service made sure that the ICS service was dependent on the firewall service and remained disabled as well. This was done to prevent resource and traffic control conflicts resulting from ISA and ICF/ICS running concurrently.

> **MORE INFO**   For more information, see "Windows Filtering Platform" at *http://www.microsoft .com/whdc/device/network/WFP.mspx.*

With TMG on Windows Server 2008, the Windows Firewall is functional and even allows the administrator to create traffic policies within it. This may seem like an odd choice, but this level of cooperation is required for TMG to participate correctly as a WFP registrant. One advantage to this integration with WFP is that if a custom application or Web proxy filter misbehaves and changes TMG policies, WFP policies can be employed to selectively lock the computer out of the network until the problem is resolved.

Conversely, because WFP policies can be controlled through Active Directory Group Policies, it's equally possible to render your TMG firewall inoperative from a network flow perspective. This fact will require much more communication between the teams that manage your TMG arrays and Active Directory policies to prevent unexpected traffic blocking. The simplest way to avoid such an event is to place your TMG firewalls in an organizational unit (OU), which is defined as exempt from Group Policy–imposed firewall rules.

> **IMPORTANT**   If your group policies specify any Windows Firewall state—whether enabled or disabled—TMG installation will be blocked because TMG needs to disable the Windows Firewall to register. In this case, the TMG computer should be placed in an Organizational Unit (OU) that does not specify any Windows Firewall state.

> **MORE INFO**   You can find information about Active Directory and administering Group Policy in *Active Directory Administrator's Pocket Consultant* and *Windows Group Policy Administrator's Pocket Consultant,* both by William R. Stanek (Microsoft Press, 2009).

Network Driver Interface Specification Miniport

TMG further improves network security and traffic flow efficiency by inserting a network driver interface specification (NDIS) filter into the network stack. This component provides traffic filtering at network layer 2 and, when TMG policies allow, also provides a fast-path for traffic directly between network interfaces. Although TMG policies are extended to this protocol layer, MAC-address filtering is not part of the traffic policy extension. Note that although the NDIS filter driver exists in TMG MBE, the fast-path functionality is not included. Appendix A includes a block diagram that illustrates TMG functional design.

Beyond the Firewall

The edge of your network is like the door to your house. You don't leave your door wide open all day and night long, do you? This concern is something that all network and security administrators have. They realize that every environment needs to include elements that can protect the internal environment against external threats. In addition, they need to protect the external world against a compromised network. In both scenarios, one core component that addresses this issue can be placed on the edge of those networks: the firewall. The firewall provides traffic filtering for all networks defined as "protected" to the Internet as well as between the hosts in different protected networks that communicate to each other through TMG.

The best place to start a discussion about firewalls is to look back to 1989 and RFC 1135, which discusses viruses on the Internet. This RFC illustrates what could happen in an environment without any protection on the edge. Although overall network security has improved since RFC 1135 was published, the threats have become more intelligent and they can spread out more rapidly and inflict more damage than ever before. Therefore, having a firewall that can offer functionality beyond the limits of simply "locking the door" through port-blocking methods is something needed in today's networks. The Microsoft Forefront TMG is a firewall that has application-layer intelligence and anti-malware capabilities that can be used to identify and mitigate many of the threats facing modern networks.

In October 2000, the Internet Engineering Task Force (IETF) created RFC 2979, which defines the behavioral characteristics of and interoperability requirements for Internet firewalls. This RFC represents an important step forward in allowing companies to develop their own firewall solutions while keeping to an expected standard.

It is important to understand the evolution of the firewall, as well as the most common types of firewalls. A proper understanding of this technology will allow you to see why TMG is a firewall that meets today's network security challenges.

Integration: The Security Challenge

In the past, the firewall was a device that only large companies implemented, mainly because only large companies were concerned about security. Today we live in a connected world whose main feature is the connection between your own private network and the Internet;

this connection drives firewall deployments on small and medium networks and even in a home user environment.

The challenge of balancing usability and security affects every firewall administrator. The challenge resides in the phrase "Satisfy the user's business needs in a secure manner." This need will be satisfied by the Microsoft Forefront family of products and the way they are integrated. When Forefront Protection Manager (FPM) ships, TMG will receive a feature pack allowing it to integrate with this environment.

Types of Firewalls

The first generation of firewall—and likely the most simplistic—was the *packet-filtering firewall* that first appeared in the 1980s. As shown in Figure 1-3, this firewall was simplistic in that it just used access lists for allowing or denying traffic based on the following elements:

- Transport protocols such as TCP or UDP
- Source and destination IP address
- Other IP protocols, such as GRE (Protocol 47)

MORE INFO For a complete list of IP protocols, see the Internet Assigned Numbers Authority (IANA) Web site at *http://www.iana.org/assignments/protocol-numbers.*

Because no consideration was given to whether the traffic was valid in the context of the protocol conversation, this device could not evaluate the validity of the traffic based on anything more than connection state.

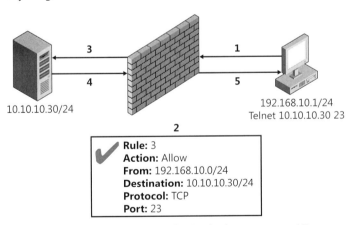

FIGURE 1-3 A packet-filtering firewall using basic access control lists

The traffic flows in a packet-filtering firewall through the following steps:

1. The client sends the connection attempt to the destination host.

2. The packet-filtering firewall evaluates this request and looks for a matching rule in the access control list (ACL).

3. Assuming that the traffic was allowed, the request arrives at the destination server.

4. The destination server replies to the request made by the source computer.

5. The packet traverses the firewall again, which re-evaluates it. Assuming that the traffic is allowed, it reaches the source computer.

> **NOTE** The term *firewall generation* is a de facto standard used in the industry to identify firewall capabilities. The Internet Draft Document "Authenticated Firewall Traversal with IPsec" from IETF classifies the main aspects of the firewall generations. You can find this document at *http://en.wikipedia.org/wiki/Firewall_(networking)*.

The second-generation firewalls were *circuit-level* firewalls. They were smarter than the first generation in that they incorporated the capability to understand and track the conversation state between the source and destination. This feature is also called *stateful inspection* because the firewall is actually aware of the connection state between source and destination. A memory-based session table in the device maintained the state of the connection.

A state table has the following common components:

- Source IP address
- Source port
- Destination IP address
- Destination port
- IP protocol
- State (such as TCP connection state per RFC 793)
- Time

If you think about the TCP/IP architecture, you notice that the first and second generation only protected the lower-level layers (part of the transport layer and all network layer). What about the application layer? The answer came with the third generation of firewall, with application-layer inspection. The *application-layer* firewall can understand commands at the application layer and determine whether they are valid. Third-generation firewalls also include all capabilities previous generation firewalls implemented.

The parameters and the intelligence of these devices changed over the years. These changes were made to provide more security and awareness of the data crossing the device. Application-layer firewalls include the functionality of previous generation firewalls while adding more protocol intelligence. Figure 1-4 summarizes the three firewall generations and where each one fits in the TCP/IP architecture.

Where TMG Fits In

Microsoft implemented stateful packet and application-layer inspection features with ISA Server 2000, and the evolution of this product with ISA Server 2004 and 2006 brought more capabilities to the application-layer inspection feature set.

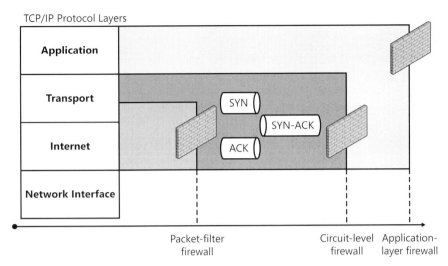

FIGURE 1-4 The three main firewall generations

ISA Server 2004 and ISA Server 2006 are Common Criteria EAL4+ (Evaluation Assurance Level 4+)–certified. TMG will be submitted for testing with the goal being EAL4+ certification as well.

> **MORE INFO** You can see the updated list and more information about ISA Server Common Criteria process at *http://www.microsoft.com/isaserver/commoncriteria/default.mspx*.

TMG builds on previous ISA Server versions with new capabilities that make TMG a more intelligent firewall that can help protect against attackers of increasing sophistication. And while ISA Server 2006 has third-generation firewall capabilities, the TMG firewall has more comprehensive application-layer inspection capabilities than its predecessors. TMG's enhanced application-layer inspection features set is designed to help the edge firewall administrator combat threats that are much more complex than when ISA Server 2000 was released.

TMG includes new features such as Web Antivirus and Anti-Malware, which allow real-time inspection for malware (worms, viruses, and spyware) while the client is browsing the Internet. (This feature is covered in more detail in Chapter 17, "Malware Inspection.") The E-Mail Anti-Malware and Anti-Spam feature adds a deeper traffic inspection for e-mail. (This feature is covered in more detail in Chapter 19, "Enhancing E-Mail Protection.")

What's New?

TMG has carried forward all the features from ISA Server 2006 and has introduced some impressive features of its own. TMG Medium Business Edition (MBE), which is included with Windows Essential Business Server (EBS), also contains some new features, but these represent only a subset of those that are included in the TMG 2010. The main features included in the

MBE release improve security by including features such as Web and e-mail anti-malware and virus protection.

TMG represents a significant change in the approach to firewall design. Recognition that the attack focus is now concentrated at the higher network layers (primarily in the presentation and application layers of the OSI model) has forced firewall designers to include more application-level intelligence in the core design, rather than providing it as an add-on.

Windows Server 2008, Windows Server 2008 R2, and Native 64-Bit Support

Because of the increase in the number of users in all major networks, it is essential to have fast devices to process traffic. ISA Server is a "software" firewall that relies on the Windows operating system for its own performance. Any performance limitation to the Windows operating system also applies to the firewall residing on it. A known limitation of ISA Server is that it could not be installed on a 64-bit platform.

TMG firewalls do not have this limitation; you must install them on 64-bit operating systems. Windows Server 2008 and Windows EBS also support 64-bit environments. With the introduction of native 64-bit support, TMG firewalls can use more than 4 gigabytes (GB) of RAM. This is important because it also increases the amount of non-paged pool memory, a critical performance and stability consideration that is improved in 64-bit environments.

Windows Server 2008 introduces new TCP features with the Next Generation TCP/IP stack. Improvements included in the Next Generation TCP/IP stack help address high-loss environments with features such as Receive Auto Tuning, which continuously adjusts the TCP receive window depending on the fluctuations in the network conditions by measuring the bandwidth delay product and application retrieve rate.

In addition, the Next Generation TCP/IP stack includes Explicit Congestion Notification support. This feature enables routers experiencing congestion to send a notification by marking packets so that when the client receives the marked packet it lowers its transmission rate to prevent further congestion and segment losses and improve overall throughput between the two computers exchanging data.

The Windows Server 2008 networking stack also includes support for default gateway failover and failback. If the first default gateway goes down, the alternate gateway is used in conjunction with the failing one so that as soon as the first gateway is back up, it can be used as the primary gateway again.

Web Antivirus and Anti-Malware Support

To improve the end-user experience and edge security, TMG firewalls can detect and isolate malicious content in HTTP traffic before it reaches the client. This feature provides an additional layer of protection and enhanced security for all hosts on TMG-protected networks.

The HTTP Malware filter is a Web filter that intercepts traffic between the client and Web server. The content of this traffic is stored in memory or on disk, depending on the size of the content. The TMG MPEngine (Microsoft Malware Protection Engine) scans the content before it is delivered to the client.

To ensure that the antivirus scanning engine and signatures are up to date, the MPEngine and signature updates can be downloaded from Microsoft Update and installed by the Edge Malware Protection (EMP) Scanner without any service interruption.

To better understand this process, Figure 1-5 illustrates how the request from the client is fetched from the Web server, intercepted by the TMG firewall, passed to the MPEngine and, finally, returned to the client after processing.

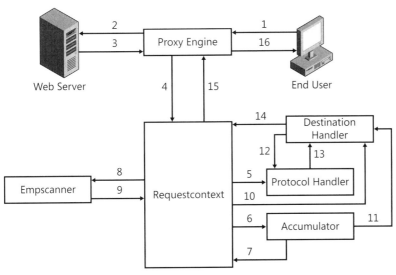

FIGURE 1-5 A request is intercepted by the TMG Server and inspected.

Figure 1-5 illustrates the following steps:

1. The original request from the client is intercepted by the TMG Firewall Engine.
2. The request is forwarded from the TMG to the Web Server.
3. The response from the Web server is returned to the TMG.
4. The traffic is forwarded from the TMG Firewall Engine to the Web Filter.
5. The traffic is sent to the protocol handler to parse the HTTP traffic before inspection.
6. The traffic is sent to the ACCUMULATOR, where the content is accumulated on disk or memory, depending on size.
7. Once the content is accumulated it is sent back to the filter.
8. The filter sends the content to the Edge Malware Protection (EMP) Scanner for inspection.
9. The EMP Scanner inspects the traffic and sends it back to the Web filter.
10. The traffic is sent to the destination handler.
11. The destination handler retrieves the accumulated content.

12. The traffic is sent to the protocol handler again to encapsulate it back in HTTP.

13. Once traffic is encapsulated in HTTP, it is sent back to the destination handler.

14. The destination handler sends the traffic to the Web filter to respond back to the client.

15. The filter sends the traffic to the Firewall Engine.

16. The TMG Firewall Engine sends the final response back to the client.

IMPORTANT The end-user experience varies when the content is being inspected based on the size of the file that is being downloaded.

When the user attempts to browse a site and download a file, TMG accumulates the contents, checks how much time it will take to complete the download, and then inspects the content. If the content is downloaded and inspected within 10 seconds, TMG passes the file to the end user. If downloading and inspecting the file takes more than 10 seconds, TMG either sends an HTML progress page (see Figure 1-6) to the client showing the progress of the download, or shows a trickled response depending on the type of content being downloaded. A trickled response is the same kind of response one would see when copying files from one folder to another. The Edge Malware Protection process is covered in depth in Chapter 17.

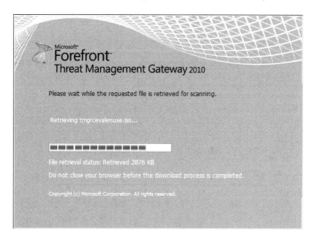

FIGURE 1-6 An HTML page displayed to the client while inspection takes place

Enhanced User Interface, Management, and Reporting

TMG includes a new reporting engine: SQL Server Reporting Services (SRS). SRS can generate reports from SQL databases. SRS comes with an extensive framework that allows report design and definition, report storage, rendering to several formats, a programmable Web service interface, and more. SRS includes a Database Service and, in the case of SRS 2005 a Web Service hosted by IIS, making IIS a requirement on the TMG computer for this reason. IIS is also required for Windows EBS management remote reporting. IIS is not a required role for TMG 2010.

 SECURITY ALERT   The default SRS-enabled instance of IIS listens on TCP port 8008 and not on TCP port 80 to provide a lower-profile attack surface.

TMG's new reports include information related to malware inspection, URL filtering, and intrusion prevention. TMG reports include information not available in previous versions of the firewall. The following questions are among those answered by the new TMG firewall reports:

- Which Web site or which user caused the most malware incidents?
- What was the most common malware encountered?
- How many users browse the Internet based on popular categories (such as news-, sports-, entertainment-, or work-related)?
- How many intrusions were prevented?
- Which downloaded virus signatures were the most frequently identified?

When Forefront Protection Manager 2010 ships, TMG 2010 will integrate completely with FPM to provide an end-to-end protection solution. TMG reports can be viewed or controlled from the FPM reporting interface, but will require that TMG reporting be made available to FPM by default.

TMG also includes new user interface features to improve report creation and management. Table 1-2 shows the functionality included in the TMG firewall for Windows Essential Business Server and TMG 2010.

TABLE 1-2 TMG MBE and TMG 2010 Reporting Functionality

FUNCTIONALITY	TMG MBE	TMG 2010
New reports	Antivirus only	IPS, URL, and more
Improved user interface	YES	YES
SRS-based	YES	YES
Array support	NO	YES
Workgroup support	NO	YES
Integration with FPM reports	NO	YES

TMG also includes the following new user interface changes:

- A new Getting Started Wizard.
- Active Directory in Application Mode (ADAM) storage (new in the standard version).
- Removal of the General node in the left pane of the TMG management console.

- The Firewall Policy node in the left pane of the TMG management console now contains settings for configuring intrusion detection, DNS attack detection, IP preferences, flood mitigation, and global link translation.
- The Network Node in the left pane of the TMG management console now contains settings for configuring the TMG Client.
- A New Web access policy configures Web access and malware inspection.
- Web proxy settings are now located in the Web Access Policy node in the left pane of the TMG management console.

URL Filtering

The URL Filtering feature allows you to enforce security and productivity policies. Using URL Filtering, you can block access to sites that might pose a security risk or are prohibited according to your company's browsing policy.

As the administrator, you can define URL categories such as malware, adult, religion, news, and so on or select category sets such as Security and Bandwidth from more than 90 categories without having to manually specify a URL list. You can then use the Web Access Wizard to create allow or deny policies for these categories. You can also specify custom deny messages for the denied sites. You can configure deny rules to have exemptions that allow users access to these sites if certain conditions exist.

When a user tries to access a blocked site, he receives an HTML notification that browsing to the site is prohibited according to company policy. The HTML notification is configurable. The custom message can also advise users to contact the administrator to dispute the categorization of the sites. By prohibiting access to these sites, you are reducing the number of potential infections resulting from malicious content. This feature is covered in detail in Chapter 18, "URL Filtering."

HTTPS Inspection

The HTTPS Inspection feature allows visibility into Secure Sockets Layer (SSL) sessions initiated from computers in protected networks. This feature plays a major role in malware inspection and helps provide protection from downloading viruses from Web-based e-mail servers such as Outlook Web Access (OWA) and other HTTPS sites. For HTTPS inspection, it is necessary to push the Root Certification Authority certificate to all domain clients and set the TMG firewall to be trusted as an Intermediate Certification Authority. When a client requests a secure page on the Internet, TMG intercepts the response from the Web server, creates a certificate with the same subject name, and responds back to the client. In this way all HTTPS traffic can be inspected by TMG before it is passed between client and server.

E-Mail Anti-Malware and Anti-Spam Support

TMG provides an interface to control mail flow, anti-spam, and anti-malware features. For Web-based e-mail servers, content can be inspected using HTTPS inspection before the response is passed to the client. For SMTP, you can define an SMTP route, which is an entity that represents a link between TMG and internal or external mail servers. The purpose of SMTP routes is to simplify edge configuration and provide a link between TMG and the Internet and between TMG and the published mail server. The new user interface makes it easier to manage the published mail server configuration; you simply enable antivirus (AV) scanning on the SMTP route.

Using the new reporting and logging features, you can monitor traffic and get reports for any spam or malicious content sent through e-mail.

Network Intrusion Prevention

An Intrusion Prevention System (IPS) is a very popular tool, mainly because it can be used as a proactive measure to detect intrusions. An IPS is a device that tries to protect systems from exploitation. An IPS is generally considered to be an extension of an Intrusion Detection System (IDS), but can also be seen as a form of access control, similar to an application-layer firewall that not only detects suspicious activity, but also takes preventive measures to stop intrusions and only allow selected traffic to pass through.

TMG uses a Generic Network Intrusion System (NIS) to provide IPS functionality (see Figure 1-7). This mechanism is based on the Generic Application Protocol Analysis (GAPA) research performed by Microsoft Research and includes signatures that, when matched, trigger an event to the firewall engine to block the requested traffic. TMG 2010 also provides subscription-based URL and malware signature filtering.

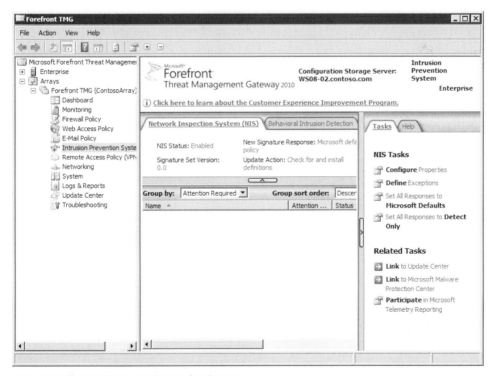

FIGURE 1-7 The TMG Intrusion Prevention System

The Session Initiation Protocol (SIP) Filter

The Session Initiation Protocol (SIP) Filter, which is included with TMG, supports audio and video streams through TMG firewalls and also allows users to transfer files and share applications and whiteboards. The TMG firewall pre-authenticates traffic for users external to TMG and analyzes the SIP protocol traffic. It is now possible to securely publish a SIP service through the TMG firewall.

TFTP Filter

TMG includes a new Trivial File Transfer Protocol (TFTP) Filter. TFTP is generally used by BootP clients to download an operating system. In addition, because many Voice Over IP (VoIP) phones use TFTP to download configuration files, the TMG firewall provides TFTP support to facilitate these requests using the TFTP Filter.

Many client and server deployments are automated using one of several methods, and many of these methods involve multiple protocols. One point they have in common is the use of TFTP to move the data to the newly deployed computer. TFTP is a file transfer protocol similar to the File Transfer Protocol (FTP), but operates quite a bit differently and uses different IP-layer protocols than FTP. Because ISA Server was frequently used to isolate networks from one another and didn't understand how to manage TFTP communications, automated deployment of Windows and disk images typically failed. TMG resolves this issue by adding a TFTP filter to provide better management of, and security for, TFTP traffic across TMG network boundaries.

Network Functionality Enhancements

In all previous versions of ISA Server, when a Network Address Translation (NAT) relationship existed between networks, ISA did not allow specifying the external IP address, even when the external interface had multiple IP addresses. Instead, ISA always used the primary IP address associated with the interface, making this IP address the source address for all outbound traffic. Likewise, ISA was unable to make use of more than one ISP connection, causing many customers to purchase a separate device to satisfy this need.

NAT Address Selection

The TMG firewall has new NAT enhancements that allow you to specify which address to use for outbound requests when there is a NAT relationship between network entities. In addition, if TMG has multiple external IP addresses, you can specify which address is seen by the remote SMTP Server. This is particularly useful if any IP address restrictions are in place for spam protection at the remote SMTP Server. NAT address selection is set through the New Network Rule Wizard, as shown in Figure 1-8.

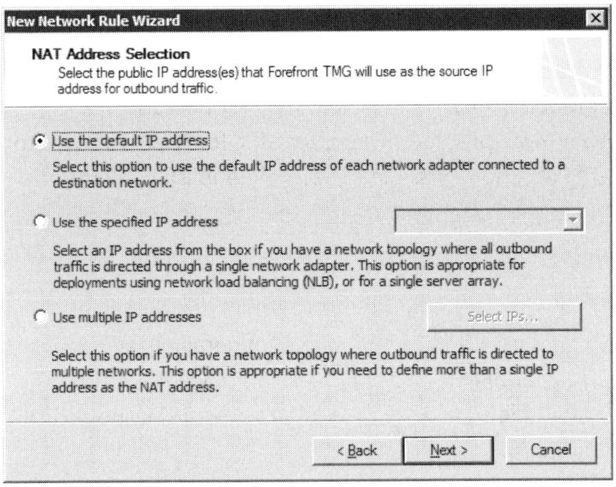

FIGURE 1-8 The New Network Rule Wizard

ISP Sharing/Failover

TMG also supports dual ISP connections (External Links) that can operate in one of two modes: ISP failover or ISP sharing. In ISP failover mode, if one ISP connection fails, TMG can provide fault tolerance by automatically switching to the other ISP connection. This helps TMG provide dynamic load balancing between multiple ISPs with fallback and failover capabilities. In ISP load-sharing mode, you can assign a load percentage to each of two ISP connections and TMG will route new traffic based on the current traffic flow through each ISP connection. These features will be covered in greater detail in Chapter 13.

Feature Comparison Summary

Table 1-3 compares new features between TMG MBE and TMG 2010 and changes from ISA 2006.

TABLE 1-3 ISA 2006, TMG MBE, and TMG Feature Comparison

FEATURES	ISA 2006	TMG MBE	TMG 2010
Network Firewall	X	X	X
Application Firewall	X	X	X
Web Access Protection (Proxy)	X	X	X
Basic OWA and SharePoint Publishing	X	X	X
Exchange Publishing (RPC over HTTP)	X	X	X
IPsec VPN (Remote and Site-to-Site)	X	X	X

FEATURES	ISA 2006	TMG MBE	TMG 2010
Web Caching, HTTP Compression	X	X	X
Windows Server 2008, Native 64-bit *		X	X
Web Antivirus, Anti-Malware		X	X
Enhanced UI, Management, Reporting		X	X
E-Mail Anti-Malware, Anti-Spam **		X	X
URL Filtering			X
Network Intrusion Prevention			X
ISP Redundancy			X

* TMG MBE runs as a 32-bit process

** TMG MBE offers e-mail protection only when deployed as part of Windows EBS

Summary

Although TMG is the Microsoft firewall solution, you need to think in multiple layers when you are talking about security. Security solutions need to address the threats at each layer to be effective; otherwise, your weakest point might expose you to threats that are beyond the control of the firewall. The next chapter goes into more depth, examining the use of Unified Access Gateway (UAG) as your main point for application publishing and helping you to understand how TMG and UAG can be a combined solution for your edge protection.

## CHAPTER 2

What Are the Differences Between TMG and UAG?

- Enabling Anywhere Access   **22**

- Understanding IAG 2007   **23**

- IAG 2007 Integration with ISA Server 2006   **24**

- Forefront UAG: The Next Generation of IAG 2007   **25**

- What's New in UAG?   **25**

- Aligning UAG with Security Needs   **26**

- Designing Network Protection   **27**

- Summary   **32**

I n May of 2006, Microsoft officially announced the acquisition of Whale Communications, Ltd. At that time, Secure Sockets Layer Virtual Private Network (SSL VPN) gateways were gaining increased visibility for organizations of all sizes. Microsoft did not have an SSL VPN gateway product at the time and decided to acquire Whale to provide an SSL VPN solution to include in its Forefront product suite. One year after this acquisition, Microsoft changed the product's name to Intelligent Application Gateway 2007 (IAG 2007).

IAG 2007 was offered as an appliance-based solution that customers could purchase from different Original Equipment Manufacturers (OEM) vendors. IAG 2007 has capabilities that vary based on OEM feature additions and management capabilities. However, all OEM versions of IAG 2007 include the same core IAG 2007 features. Microsoft plans to rename IAG 2007 to *Unified Access Gateway (UAG)* in a subsequent release. UAG will be a mature product with features and stability based largely on IAG 2007 customer feedback.

This chapter covers the best practices for designing a network topology that takes full advantage of both UAG and TMG. In addition, it covers the key differences between the products and the evolution from IAG 2007 to UAG.

Enabling Anywhere Access

The traditional method of allowing users at remote locations access to internal resources over the Internet is through network layer Virtual Private Networks (VPNs). Network-layer VPN technology traditionally works with either of the main two tunneling protocols: PPTP or L2TP. These protocols enable encrypted tunnels to be established between either a client and server or between two network-layer VPN gateways (also known as VPN routers).

The problem is that sometimes the client is behind an edge firewall that allows only HTTP and HTTPS traffic outbound, as shown in Figure 2-1. This often results in end-user frustration because outbound PPTP or L2TP/IPsec connections are denied. Therefore, the term *anywhere access* really doesn't apply when speaking of network-layer VPN connectivity.

> **NOTE** We provide a more detailed discussion of VPN technology in Chapter 26, "Implementing Dial-in Client VPN."

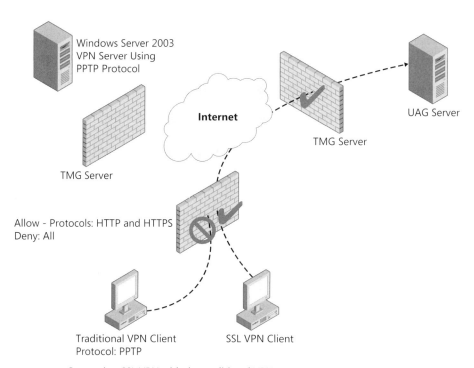

FIGURE 2-1 Comparing SSL VPN with the traditional VPN

Figure 2-1 shows that SSL VPN technology does not suffer from the connectivity issues inherent in network-layer VPN connections. The figure shows an edge firewall that allows only HTTP and HTTPS traffic outbound and two clients behind this firewall. The client using a traditional VPN protocol (such as PPTP) to connect to the VPN Server is blocked by the firewall, whereas the SSL VPN client is not. This illustrates the greater flexibility of SSL VPN technology, allowing enhanced security access to resources without having to deal with connectivity issues that can be imposed by restrictive firewalls. SSL VPN technology makes it possible for the remote client workstation to easily connect to the HTTPS portal and from there connect to the internal resources (server, workstation, and so on) from a number of different locations without having to worry about connectivity issues that were commonly encountered in the past.

SSL VPN technology is now an industry standard for allowing remote access. Windows Server 2008 allows you to configure RRAS as an SSL VPN server using the new Secure Socket Tunneling Protocol (SSTP) VPN protocol. Given that Windows Server 2008 provides SSL VPN capabilities, we need to figure out where the UAG fits in. In the following sections we consider some possible answers to this question and discuss how you can most effectively integrate IAG 2007 and UAG SSL VPN technology into your existing network infrastructure.

Understanding IAG 2007

IAG 2007 is a server application that runs as an Internet Server Application Programming Interface (ISAPI) filter and ISAPI Extension on Internet Information Services (IIS) 6.0. IAG 2007 requires IIS 6.0 and Windows Server 2003. To protect the IAG 2007 application from attacks that might emanate from either outside or inside the network, ISA Server 2006 Standard edition was added to IAG 2007. This means that when you purchase an IAG 2007 appliance, ISA Server 2006 is already installed on the same computer. Figure 2-2 illustrates the core IAG 2007 architecture.

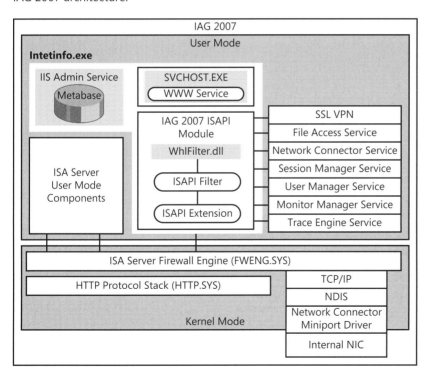

FIGURE 2-2 IAG 2007 software layers

IAG 2007 was built as an IIS ISAPI Filter and Extension; therefore, it is heavily dependent on IIS to work properly. Figure 2-2 shows that the IAG 2007 ISAPI Filter and the ISAPI Extension run under the context of the Inetinfo.exe process in user mode. The only kernel mode process directly correlated with IIS is HTTP.SYS (HTTP protocol stack).

You might ask, "What is the advantage of having only the HTTP.SYS in kernel mode if everything else is running in user mode?" The answer lies in improved performance in the following areas:

- Requests for IIS that are located in cache are answered more quickly because IIS doesn't have to switch to user mode.

- When IIS queues requests, those requests are in kernel mode. Sending to user mode is not delayed if no worker process is available to accept the request.

IAG 2007 Integration with ISA Server 2006

ISA 2006 provides network-layer protection for IAG 2007. When you publish applications and portals, IAG 2007 automatically creates the firewall rules in ISA 2006 that allow traffic to and from IAG. IAG 2007 supports both HTTP and HTTPS, and for each protocol you can have multiple trunks, including the following:

- Basic, which provides access to a single application

- Portal, which provides access to multiple applications

- Webmail, for a single mail application

The following steps summarize what happens behind the scenes when a new trunk is created:

1. The trunk is created and configured in the IAG 2007 Configuration Console.

2. The configuration is saved and activated in the IAG 2007 Configuration Console.

3. IAG creates a Web site in IIS that corresponds with the trunk.

4. IAG creates the needed rules to access the trunk and the trunk's applications in ISA Server 2006.

The IAG configuration creates firewall rules required for the portals and applications you define. In the ISA Server 2006 Management Console, all of the rules created by IAG are prefaced with *Whale::* and are always grouped together. If you need to create additional rules, ensure that they are placed above any of the rules created by IAG or they might be deleted by the IAG Configuration when you manage the IAG configuration. Be aware that in the event of a conflict between the rules you create and the rules created by IAG 2007 the rules higher in the list will be evaluated and enforced unless you place them before or after the rules created by IAG. The rules created by IAG are prefaced by *Whale::*.

Forefront UAG: The Next Generation of IAG 2007

Forefront Unified Access Gateway (UAG) represents a big step forward in integration and security awareness of applications as well as in improving the end user's anywhere access experience. UAG represents the maturity of the original Whale software and includes major improvements in management, administration, and integration with TMG.

UAG operates in collaboration with a collocated instance of TMG. Because UAG runs on Windows Server 2008 R2, it also takes advantage of the IIS 7.0 architecture that provides security improvements over IIS 6.0. An example of a core security change on IIS 7.0 is that now the HTTP.SYS protocol stack is also responsible in pre-processing the security filtering for requests (such as HTTP Kerberos authentication).

What's New in UAG?

While IAG is an appliance-only solution, UAG extends this offering with a software-only, server-installed deployment option. The UAG will provide you with two options: a pre-installed version of UAG on an OEM hardware appliance and a downloadable .vhd file that you can use to deploy UAG in a virtual environment, using Microsoft Hyper-V or any SVVP-validated virtualization platform. UAG is also able to be installed in a virtual environment using any SVVP-validated virtualization platform.

> **MORE INFO** You can read more about SVVP (Server Virtualization Validation Program) at *http://www.windowsservercatalog.com/svvp.aspx?svvppage=svvp.htm.*

The best way to understand the differences between IAG and UAG is through a brief comparison of the two products, as illustrated in Table 2-1.

TABLE 2-1 IAG and UAG Feature Comparison

FEATURE	IAG	UAG
Application Intelligence and Publishing	X	X
End Point Security	X	X
SSL Tunneling	X	X
Information Leakage Prevention	X	X
Robust Authentication Support (KCD, ADFS, OTP)	X	X
Windows Server 2008 R2, Native 64-Bit		X
NAP Integration		X

FEATURE	IAG	UAG
Terminal Services Gateway Integration		X
Web Farm Load Balancing		X
Array Management		X
Enhanced Management and Monitoring (SCOM Pack)		X
Enhanced Mobile Solutions		X
New and Customizable User Portal		X
Wizard Driven Configuration		X

The new features that make a big difference when comparing IAG with UAG include the following:

- **Native 64-bit**   UAG will be delivered in a 64-bit version.
- **Integration with Network Access Protection (NAP)**   This integration provides an additional layer of protection for internal network access by unsecured endpoint devices.
- **Web farm load-balancing**   This feature allows you to publish a farm of Web servers and distribute requests evenly among these servers. This is a major improvement in that you don't have to purchase separate load-balancing devices to achieve this task.

Aligning UAG with Security Needs

Many businesses, both medium and large, have started to invest more in security by using a top-down approach. To do this effectively, they need tools that enable them to smoothly implement policies and procedures defined by the company. When companies create security policies, areas of major concern are confidentiality, integrity, and availability. You must consider each of these issues when you create a UAG portal that allows access to internal resources from anywhere.

How can you use UAG to address confidentiality, integrity, and availability concerns? Here are some examples:

- **Confidentiality**   Endpoint policies offered by UAG allow you to specify a minimum security profile for remote computers that attempt access to the portal. You can configure security policies for portal access and also for access to specific applications. These policies help to prevent data leakage, which can lead to a loss of confidentiality. Security policies also enable you to implement need-to-know and least-privilege rules for applications published in the UAG portal.
- **Integrity With UAG**   You can control the level of access to applications. UAG uses the concept of authentication and authorization separately from the Windows system, adding an additional layer of control.
- **Availability**   You can have multiple UAGs in an array that enables service redundancy.

Designing Network Protection

This section addresses deployment design for UAG and TMG and provides some examples of network topology scenarios.

When Do You Deploy UAG?

UAG is designed to provide the following:

- Universal access to your applications from the Internet
- Broader support for a single sign-on (SSO) experience
- Deeper trust of the user and the user's computer
- Increased application awareness and enhanced control over application behavior
- Broader range of authentication providers
- SSL VPN remote access

UAG allows the network and security teams to serve the mobile user's need to access company resources from Internet-connected locations, while simultaneously meeting the company's need to control access based on a definition of trustworthiness and security for the connected user and computer.

UAG is designed and tested to operate as the Internet-facing gateway. Placing another firewall between the UAG and the Internet can cause problems that cannot be solved by changing the UAG configuration. Because UAG takes advantage of TMG's firewall functionality, it presents much less of a concern for the company security team and obviates the need to put a firewall in front of or behind the UAG.

UAG is also able to take advantage of the TMG multi-network model so that published applications can be isolated from other networks. This enables you to increase your overall level of security by implementing a layered network security model.

When Do You Deploy TMG?

TMG is designed to serve deployments where security requirements might include:

- General application-level firewall and proxy
- Simplified access to application services, such as SMTP, POP3, and others
- Assessment of client computer trustworthiness
- Protected Internet access to and from your networks
- SSTP, PPTP, and L2TP/IPsec VPN connectivity

Unlike UAG, TMG is designed to serve the broader needs imposed by both external and internal application access. Although TMG lacks the level of application awareness for Web-based applications provided by UAG, it makes up for this with its malware inspection and subscription URL filtering capabilities.

Table 2-2 summarizes the decision table for answering the question of whether to use TMG or UAG. Features and functionality shared by both products have been omitted because they can't help the decision process.

TABLE 2-2 TMG vs. UAG Decision Table

FUNCTIONALITY	NEED	TMG	UAG
Generic single sign-on (SSO)			X
SSL VPN			X
Endpoint security			X
Deep application awareness			X
Broader authentication options			X
Outbound Web and Winsock proxy		X	
Windows EBS deployment		X	
E-mail (SMTP/POP3/IMAP4) publishing		X	
Malware inspection		X	
Intrusion Detection		X	
Integrated E-mail Filtering		X	
Total			

For each item in the Functionality column that you require in your deployment, place a check in the Need column. Under the TMG and UAG columns, add up the number of checks that also appear in the Need column.

Network Designs for TMG and UAG

Unlike TMG, which you can deploy almost anywhere on your network, UAG was specifically designed to be an edge network device. However, in some circumstances legacy policies might in place, making it difficult for you to place IAG on the edge of the network. As shown in Figure 2-3, if your network policy requires an edge firewall in front of UAG, you will have to allow inbound TCP port 443 (HTTPS) to the UAG.

> **MORE INFO**   A discussion of the details of UAG functionality impacted by various network deployments is beyond the scope of this book and is addressed in related UAG articles on TechNet at *http://technet.microsoft.com/en-us/library/dd861463.aspx.*

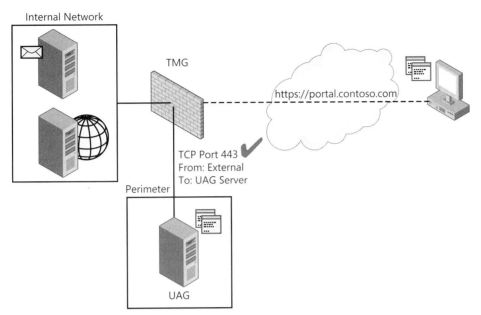

FIGURE 2-3 Example network topology with UAG in the back end

On the other hand, TMG is specifically designed to operate in any of four basic network designs (and many variations on these themes):

- Edge firewall
- 3-leg perimeter firewall
- Back firewall
- Single NIC Web proxy server

Each of these designs can be associated with a TMG network template. A network template is a wizard-based solution that automatically configures several components of TMG based on the deployment model you choose. You can use a network template to get you up and running quickly and then fine-tune the configuration created by the wizard at a later time.

Edge Firewall

When deployed as an edge firewall, TMG's main task is to act as a layer-2 and layer-3 firewall for traffic sent to and from the Internet. Even if TMG is also deployed to provide higher-level, application-layer inspection protection (such as IDS, URL filtering, malware inspection, and so on), TMG's primary task is still as a stateful packet inspection firewall. As an edge firewall, the external interface faces the Internet and the internal interface faces the protected LAN. All of TMG's network wizards and related functionality operate based on this assumption.

The biggest advantage of using TMG as an edge firewall is that it gives TMG direct access to the network traffic it is designed to control. With fewer additional devices in the network path, TMG is better able to evaluate and make proper control decisions. This is also the default deployment configuration for UAG. Figure 2-4 illustrates a typical firewall deployment.

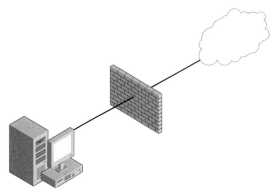

FIGURE 2-4 TMG as edge firewall

3-leg Perimeter

A 3-leg perimeter deployment, as shown in Figure 2-5, is often referred to as a *trihomed perimeter network* because a single device (TMG, in this case) has three NICs, each associated with a different network security zone, one of which is a perimeter network segment. TMG is ideally suited to this task because it combines all of the control mechanisms you would normally employ at different locations into a single network control point.

Unlike ISA 2006, where it was assumed that you would use a NAT relationship between the default internal network and the trihomed perimeter network segment, the TMG trihomed perimeter network template is aware that the networks defined as *perimeter* and *internal* cannot have pre-defined route or NAT relationships. For this reason, the Network Setup Wizard offers you the opportunity to define the relationships as part of the configuration process. The advantage of the 3-leg perimeter deployment is similar to that of the edge firewall deployment: TMG has unfettered access to the traffic produced at all networks.

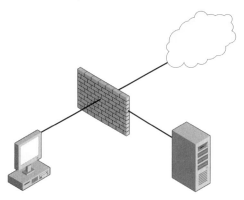

FIGURE 2-5 TMG as 3-leg perimeter firewall

Back Firewall

The back firewall network template is essentially a variation on the edge firewall template except that the TMG firewall's external interface is connected to a perimeter network segment between itself and the internal interface of an upstream firewall. As such, the network template wizards have been updated to give you the option to define the network relationship between the internal and perimeter networks as either route or NAT. The advantage to the back firewall deployment is that with a separate device handling the low-level traffic decisions, TMG has more resources to apply to higher-level traffic control filtering. Figure 2-6 illustrates the back firewall deployment.

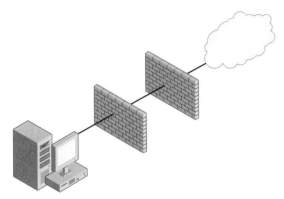

FIGURE 2-6 TMG as a back firewall

Single-NIC

Except for the additional HTTP intelligence provided by TMG, the single-NIC (often referred to as *unihomed*) deployment is exactly as it was for ISA 2006. This deployment option provides firewall functionality only for the computer on which TMG operates. Like ISA 2006, a unihomed TMG can only provide support for HTTP-based traffic (CERN proxy or Web Publishing) and dial-in VPN clients. As with ISA 2006, the only valid networks for a unihomed TMG are:

- **Local Host**   This network includes all IP addresses assigned to the TMG computer, not just the 127/8 network.
- **Internal**   This network includes all IP addresses not assigned to dial into either of the VPN client networks.
- **VPN Clients**   This network includes only those addresses that have been defined for use by the TMG administrator by non-quarantined VPN clients.
- **Quarantined VPN Clients**   This network includes only the IP addresses defined for use by VPN clients that have not satisfied the security requirements defined for VPN connectivity.

One advantage of a single-NIC deployment, as shown in Figure 2-7, is that TMG resources can be dedicated to processing only HTTP-associated traffic. Another advantage of the unihomed deployment is you never need to renumber networks to support a unihomed TMG firewall.

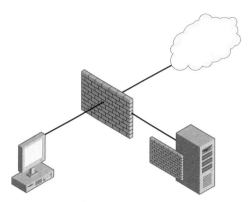

FIGURE 2-7 Single-NIC deployment

MORE INFO   Chapter 4, "Analyzing Network Requirements," discusses how and why to choose each of the network templates discussed here.

Summary

The Forefront UAG is an SSL VPN gateway that helps you enable a more secure, access-anywhere solution for your users. The UAG SSL VPN server has an advantage over the RRAS network-level VPN server: It doesn't suffer from connectivity issues because of restrictive firewalls. In addition, the UAG SSL VPN gateway allows you to configure powerful access-control policies so that clients of variable levels of trust are allowed variable levels of access based on their assessed security configuration.

A UAG SSL VPN gateway and the TMG firewall can exist on the same network. Both the UAG SSL VPN and the TMG firewall are designed to be edge security devices. However, if legacy security policies make it difficult for you to deploy the UAG and TMG as edge security devices, a number of alternative options are available to you. The TMG firewall includes a network template wizard that simplifies deploying the TMG firewall in a number of network scenarios.

The combination of UAG SSL VPN gateways and TMG network firewalls can offer multiple layers of protection for your network. In the next chapter you will learn about network and system requirements that should be in place before deploying a TMG firewall.

PART II

Planning for TMG

CHAPTER 3   System Requirements   **35**

CHAPTER 4   Analyzing Network Requirements   **47**

CHAPTER 5   Choosing the Right Network Topology   **65**

CHAPTER 6   Migrating to TMG   **87**

CHAPTER 7   Choosing a TMG Client Type   **107**

System Requirements

- Hardware Requirements **35**

- Software Requirements **36**

- General Recommendations **37**

- Deploying in Virtual Environments **44**

- Summary **45**

We strongly recommend that you determine the computer and network requirements that will enable you to achieve the best performance, stability, and security for your deployment before installing TMG. Because TMG can be your gateway to multiple networks, time spent planning for your deployment is fundamental. Failure to do so could result in an underperforming firewall or proxy.

This chapter discusses the process for determining system and network requirements for TMG installation. In addition, we will discuss general considerations regarding the supporting network infrastructure that can impact TMG performance.

> **IMPORTANT** Prior to installing TMG, ensure that you can support the recommended configuration. This configuration includes minimum requirements and best practices. Even though requirements vary for different scenarios, the configuration described in this chapter defines the minimum requirements for a TMG installation.

Hardware Requirements

TMG is a critical component of your network infrastructure. Because of this, it is important that the device on which TMG is installed has sufficient memory and redundant components, such as RAID hardware mirroring. Certain scenarios, such as reverse Web proxy for RPC over HTTP publishing, require more processor utilization than outbound Web proxy, and for this reason it is important to have a computer that can handle the load for a given deployment.

Minimum requirements for TMG 2010 are:

- A 64-bit version of Windows Server 2008 Standard, Enterprise, or Datacenter editions; RTM with Service Pack 2 (SP2) or R2
- 2 GB of RAM
- One dual-core CPU
- One local hard disk partition formatted with NTFS file system
- 150 MB hard disk space
- At least one network card compatible with the operating system and able to communicate with the internal network (at least two network interfaces are required to support full firewall functionality)
- One network card for each physical network TMG will be connected to

> **MORE INFO** See *http://technet.microsoft.com/en-us/library/cc441727.aspx* for the most current requirements.

Note that these are the minimum requirements. They are not best practice recommendations for TMG firewalls or Web proxy servers, nor do they address the need for additional drive space for logging, Web caching, and other key TMG activities. In scenarios where you have a large number of users connecting through TMG for reverse Web proxy or for remote access VPN, memory requirements can increase precipitously. Similarly, disk space requirements can be much greater if you plan to take advantage of TMG's Web caching capabilities. In other scenarios, one TMG firewall or Web proxy server may not be sufficient, so capacity planning is not only an important factor when sizing a specific computer, but also in terms of how many computers you may need in your TMG solution.

From a disk management perspective, TMG is typically installed on a single hard disk with two or more logical partitions. At a minimum, all components can be installed on the same partition. However, depending on TMG's role, and to ensure that the disk doesn't fill up quickly, the log file and cache file directories can be stored on separate physical drives.

Software Requirements

TMG has very few software pre-requisites. TMG must be installed on a 64-bit edition of Windows Server 2008. You cannot install TMG on a 32-bit version of Windows Server 2008.

You should update the Windows Server 2008 operating system using Windows Update or your preferred updating mechanism prior to installing the TMG software. This helps ensure that TMG features will work with the updated system components and decrease the overall attack surface prior to TMG software installation.

When TMG is installed on a Windows Server 2008 operating system, it also installs the following:

- The Active Directory Lightweight Directory Services Server Role
- The Network Policy and Access Services Server Role
- Windows Powershell 1.0
- The Web Server (IIS) Server Role (for SRS 2005 only)
- Microsoft SQL Express (Microsoft Forefront TMG logging instance)
- Microsoft SQL Express (Microsoft Forefront TMG reporting instance)
- Microsoft SQL Server backward compatibility
- Microsoft SQL Server Native Client
  - Microsoft SQL Server Setup Support Files
  - Microsoft SQL Server Volume Shadow Copy Service (VSS) Writer
- Microsoft Office 2003 Web Components (as part of the SQL Server Express installation)

The default instance of IIS on TMG MBE binds to TCP port 8008. You should not modify this value because the standard reporting links are pre-configured to use TCP port 8008. When TMG is uninstalled, the IIS Server and Office Web Components are not uninstalled. You must remove these components manually.

General Recommendations

As with ISA Server, the combination of traffic profile, network infrastructure, network services, and the underlying server configuration impact TMG performance. As with any other network service, extended monitoring and periodic performance analyses are required to ensure optimal operational efficiency, effectiveness, and security.

Network Infrastructure

TMG performance is affected by the network infrastructure in which it operates. If any component of the network infrastructure performs at less than optimal efficiency, TMG tries to compensate through use of the traffic buffering (backlog) mechanisms built into it. The more TMG must compensate for traffic inefficiencies, the less efficient TMG traffic processing becomes.

You need to address several issues when designing your TMG deployments; all of these can have a significant impact on TMG performance, stability, and security:

- Name resolution
- Authentication
- Traffic control devices (IDS and IPS)

Name Resolution

TMG is highly dependent on functioning name resolution and a supporting DNS infrastructure. Any inefficiency introduced by an incorrectly configured name-resolution infrastructure can lead to impaired TMG performance. Consider the following when assessing your name resolution infrastructure prior to deploying TMG:

- **Policy evaluation**   When TMG policies refer to destinations as names (frequently the case for HTTP traffic), TMG must perform name and IP address resolution to ensure that the rules can be properly evaluated for both cases (IP address- or name-based requests). Although TMG maintains its own name cache to improve name and IP address lookup performance, TMG must depend on Windows to perform the initial name or IP address resolution. Thus, traffic evaluation efficiency is directly proportional to the efficiency of the underlying Windows name-resolution mechanisms.

- **Windows name resolution configuration**   TMG depends on Windows name-resolution mechanisms. Because Windows is designed to be deployed in multiple network configurations, the default is designed to accommodate as many of these configurations as possible. Although this provides the most flexible configuration, it may do so at the expense of efficiency. Because the majority of traffic handled by TMG is HTTP-based and destined for the Internet, Windows is configured as a NetBIOS hybrid node by default. This means that if Windows has DNS and WINS services available to it and DNS and WINS queries fail to provide an authoritative success or failure response, Windows falls back to NetBIOS name broadcasts. The following points affect any TMG deployment:

  - The majority of TMG name resolution requests are for Internet hosts.
  - Internet reverse-lookups tend to fail because less attention is paid to updating reverse lookup zones.
  - NetBIOS broadcasts are the default fallback mechanism.
  - TMG blocks broadcast traffic by default.

  Because broadcast traffic is not functional on the Internet and because TMG blocks broadcast traffic by default, NetBIOS broadcasts will fail. Because of the way the NetBIOS name broadcast mechanism operates, it can take up to a full minute to report failure, causing very high delays or outright failure for TMG traffic processing. Because TMG also logs these broadcast packets, additional processing overhead is incurred for traffic that has already caused traffic processing delays.

  BEST PRACTICES   The best way to prevent NetBIOS broadcast traffic (and dramatically improve TMG performance) is to configure Windows as a peer-node host using the following registry value:

  ```
  Path: HKEY_LOCAL_MACHINE\System\CurrentControlSet\Services\NetBT\
  Parameters
  Name: NodeType
  Type: REG_DWORD
  Value: 2
  ```

  Because this change affects a Windows kernel-mode networking component (NetBIOS over TCP/IP), it does not take effect until the computer is rebooted.

- **Name services configuration** Although most network administrators recognize the value of reliable and fast name-resolution services, the ability to perform reverse DNS name resolution (IP address to name resolution) is frequently overlooked for edge services (such as those provided by TMG). An unfortunate fact of life for Internet name resolution is that few sites actually provide reverse-lookup zones in their public DNS structure. This is unfortunate because this limits TMG's ability to accurately evaluate name-based traffic policies when the request is issued using an IP address. Although it's true that you can't control Internet services that you don't own or lease, you can help TMG and your TMG-served hosts make accurate name-to-IP comparisons by building accurate reverse-lookup zones in your internal DNS structure.

- **Name services load** When TMG is required to evaluate traffic based on the destination name, the resulting name lookups may place a heavier-than-expected load on the name-resolution services in the network. TMG's internal name cache helps reduce this, but in cases where name resolution fails, TMG has no choice but to issue the name-resolution query for each request where it has no entry in the name cache. In many cases, it's preferable to provide a DNS server that is dedicated to resolving names for TMG. This has the benefit of reducing the request load on name servers used by the internal network hosts while simultaneously decreasing the response time for TMG name queries. This DNS server should be installed on the internal or perimeter network and allowed outbound access to Internet based DNS servers.

- **Non-TMG effects** If the name-lookup load presented by TMG is high enough, it may cause name resolution for internal resources to be delayed or even fail outright, causing failures for connections to applications or services for which TMG is not part of the traffic path. These errors may be difficult to isolate; these situations are best avoided by providing a DNS resolver dedicated to TMG queries. Although it may be tempting to install DNS services on the TMG server itself, you should not do this without careful evaluation of the increased processing overhead and attack surface incurred by this combination.

> *MORE INFO* Chapter 4, "Analyzing Network Requirements," covers name-resolution recommendations.

Authentication

One of the primary benefits of TMG deployments is the ability to control traffic based on the user context. Because all client requests are initially sent without this information, TMG must request credentials and then refer those credentials to an authentication provider for validation. Delays or errors encountered in the authentication process also adversely affect TMG performance. You should understand the following points about authentication for TMG:

- **Policy evaluation** When TMG policies refer to users, groups, or both, TMG must request user credentials and defer these to a credentials authority for validation. This process necessarily incurs a traffic delay proportional to the delay experienced in the credentials acquisition and validation process. As with name resolution, TMG employs a local credentials cache to reduce the load presented to the credentials authority and thus improve TMG authentication and traffic processing performance.

- **Windows Authentication**   In an environment where TMG must authenticate requests using Windows credentials, TMG must use Windows authentication methods. If the user accounts are part of a domain structure, TMG must be a member of the same domain or a trusting domain. Otherwise, the user accounts must be mirrored in TMG's local SAM database. Firewall client authentication is limited to using NTLM and Kerberos authentication, which require a Windows credentials authority.

- **Non-Windows Authentication**   TMG has multiple authentication options available, depending on the network from which the request is received and the context in which it is sent. For authentication of Web Proxy traffic sourcing from a protected network listener (typically referred to as outbound Web proxy traffic), TMG is able to authenticate users based on Windows or RADIUS credentials authorities. When TMG uses RADIUS authentication, the request for authentication from TMG to the client is seen as HTTP-Basic.

- **Authentication load**   Any authentication process can place a high traffic load on TMG and the credentials authority. For Windows authentication, this is typically a domain controller. For non-Windows authentication, this is likely to be either a RADIUS or Active directory–based LDAP server. If the credentials authority cannot respond quickly to the authentication load presented by TMG, the resulting request backlog will impair TMG performance and produce an unacceptable user experience typically expressed as "the Internet is awfully slow today."

- **Non-TMG effects**   Because Windows authentication requires access to domain controllers, and domain controllers are typically shared with other network services and hosts, the authentication load placed on them by TMG can adversely affect authentication services provided to other network clients. In such cases, user application mishandling of resulting authentication errors may cause troubleshooting efforts to be misdirected. As with name resolution, it may be advantageous to provide dedicated credentials authority for TMG use. For a domain controller, this is more difficult because any host in the same site will see this domain controller. By placing TMG and its associated domain controller in a separate site, you can help prevent use of the domain controller by hosts other than TMG firewalls and Web proxy servers and thus limit the authentication load presented to it.

> **MORE INFO**   Chapter 32, "Exploring HTTP Protocol," covers the benefits and pitfalls of authentication types.

Traffic Control Devices

TMG might be deployed in an environment where other traffic monitoring devices, such as intrusion detection and protection systems, perform traffic analysis and control traffic flow. If these devices are unable to process traffic as quickly as TMG, TMG attempts to buffer the traffic until the device allows TMG to send it. As with name resolution and authentication delays, this buffering action produces traffic processing delays and a poor end-user experience.

Network traffic control devices see the traffic coming from TMG as sourcing from a single IP address, which can lead to these devices incorrectly concluding that TMG is flooding the network. This can lead the network traffic control device to block or reject traffic sent by TMG. In addition, this can lead to network conditions that generate "connection reset" or "no response" errors, even though the requested server is responding to other requests.

Unless network administrators understand the traffic control device's behavioral characteristics and configuration parameters, determining the cause of the problem becomes very difficult when individual tests from TMG or from a separate host fail to produce the same error. Discovering the root cause of the problem often involves analyzing large network captures taken concurrently from multiple locations along the traffic path. This process takes a significant amount of time, especially if you are not familiar with the traffic path or application behavior observed on the network. For this reason, you must ensure that any IDS or IPS device in the traffic path is aware that the TMG is a valid high-traffic generator. Because TMG offers significant IDS and IPS capabilities, you might consider replacing or relocating existing devices that monitor edge traffic.

Performance Monitoring

Performance monitoring is an important management activity that you need to carry out on TMG throughout its service lifetime. If TMG is tasked beyond capacity, the resulting denial-of-service may not only make your users unhappy, but can also result in significant losses in employee productivity and increased administrative overhead, as well as lost sales opportunities resulting from the inability to connect with partners and customers.

Although you can choose from a lot of performance counters, this discussion centers on a set of counters specific to evaluating TMG performance and stability.

> **IMPORTANT** In general, it's accurate to say "lower is better" or "higher is better" for a given performance counter, but these must never be taken as absolutes. Accurate performance analysis is an ongoing exercise and any counter value must be evaluated in the context of other performance indicators.

If you have not established a performance baseline for your environment, you cannot determine whether a specific performance counter represents poor performance, excellent performance, or something in between. A detailed list of the TMG performance counters is included in Appendix B.

Disk Performance

TMG uses local drive resources for log storage and content caching. When evaluating disk subsystem problems, you need to watch disk-related performance counters over an extended period of time. A single point-in-time snapshot of disk performance cannot provide the information you need to correctly assess disk subsystem issues.

The following list is a sampling of common disk-related performance counters used to analyze overall firewall performance and the relationship of these counters to specific TMG performance characteristics:

- **\\.\LogicalDisk\Avg. Disk Write Queue Length and \\.\PhysicalDisk\Avg. Disk Write Queue Length**   These counters are used to monitor TMG logging and caching drives, providing indicators of the relative drive write efficiency. In general, disk queue length should be less than the number of spindles of the disk. Occasional values near 2 are not necessarily a cause for concern, but if they happen frequently, it may indicate poor disk performance. Resolving this may involve separating the Firewall, Malware, and Web Proxy log destinations to separate physical drives.

- **\\.\Forefront TMG Firewall Packet Engine\Log Items enqueued/sec**   This counter value indicates the number of unwritten log items generated per second by the packet filter engine. This counter provides a relative indication of TMG logging destination responsiveness. A higher value indicates lower logging performance.

- **\\.\Forefront TMG Firewall Service\Log queue size on disk**   This counter indicates the amount of disk space consumed by the log queue. A higher value indicates lower logging performance.

- **\\.\Forefront TMG Web Proxy\Malware Inspection - Disk Errors**   This value indicates the total number of disk errors encountered by the malware inspection disk caching mechanism. An increase in this value correlating with an increase in the \Forefront TMG Firewall Packet Engine\Log Items enqueued/sec and \Forefront TMG Firewall Service\Log queue size on disk counters indicates an underperforming disk subsystem or poor disk allocation for TMG services.

- **\\.\Forefront TMG Cache\Total Disk Failures**   This value indicates the total number of disk I/O failures encountered since the firewall service started. This value is of interest when TMG is configured to use the same logical or physical disk for logging and content caching. If this counter increases over time, it indicates a potential need for separation of the cache to a separate physical drive.

- **\\.\Forefront TMG Cache\Disk Failure Rate (Fail/sec)**   This value indicates the total number of disk I/O failures per second encountered since the firewall service started. Although this counter is not specifically related to TMG logging, an increase in this value indicates problems with the disk subsystem for the TMG cache drives. This could have a significant performance impact because TMG is forced to wait for disk timeouts before the error can be determined and reported.

Network Performance

Network performance analysis for any firewall or proxy is a difficult process, made more so by the complexities introduced by the protocols used on the network. In general, it's best to start such troubleshooting at the lowest network layer possible. The following counters represent good starting points for evaluating network performance at layer 1:

- **\\.\Network Interface\Output Queue Length**   This counter provides an indicator of the number of packets waiting to be sent on the network. If this value is greater than 2 for more than short periods of time, it indicates a traffic bottleneck that should be investigated and resolved.

- **\\.\Network Interface\Bytes Sent/sec and \\.\Network Interface\Bytes Received/sec**   These counters indicate the amount of data sent and received per second on a specific network interface. Because this value represents bytes, you should multiply this number by 8 to determine whether the network is reaching saturation. Most Ethernet networks can pass approximately 80 percent of their specified maximum bandwidth. For 100-base-T networks, this value would be around 80 Mb/s; for Gb networks, this value would be about 800 Mb/s. Depending on the quality of the network interfaces, cables, and network devices, you may see different values.

Behavioral Monitoring

In addition to performance counters, TMG provides a number of behavioral indicators collectively referred to as *alerts*. Alerts are designed to provide the administrator with near-instantaneous insight into TMG behavioral characteristics. Although this feature has been available since ISA Server 2000, the number of alert triggers has increased dramatically in TMG.

Alerts provide information about specific problems or actions. All alerts provide the same options for announcing the fact that they were triggered. Figure 3-1 shows only a few of the total alerts available with TMG.

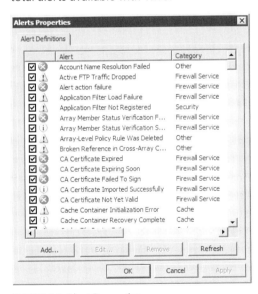

FIGURE 3-1 Alert Properties

Figure 3-2 shows the actions available for use with TMG alerts. As with ISA Server, you have the option to write to the application event log, send e-mail, run a program, or manage specific services.

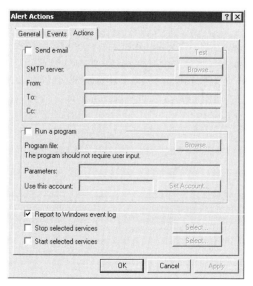

FIGURE 3-2 Configuring the Alert Actions dialog box

Another option for TMG monitoring is System Center Operations Manager 2007 or System Center Operations Manager 2008. System Center Operations Manager provides you the tools necessary for detailed monitoring and reporting for multiple servers from a single control console.

Deploying in Virtual Environments

TMG is supported in virtual environments. When planning such deployments, you must consider security, functionality, and manageability issues unique to a virtualized deployment.

- **Networks**   Because of network designs typically employed in virtualized environments, virtual network traffic is frequently invisible to physical network monitoring and management systems. Therefore, you must take extra care to provide some form of visibility into the virtual networks.

- **Performance**   Because all hosts in a virtual environment are sharing the resources of the host computer, the performance of a given application is unlikely to meet the performance characteristics of a physical deployment. Because of the time shift inherent in a virtualized server, the performance monitoring of a virtualized server using its own time-based performance counters is likely to be inaccurate.

- **Security** Strict access controls and change management policies and procedures on the virtual host and the virtual machines are paramount to ensuring a secure virtual deployment. This is especially true in the case of virtual edge or perimeter networks, such as those where TMG would operate.

> **MORE INFO** See *http://technet.microsoft.com/library/cc891502.aspx* for a deeper discussion on virtual deployments for TMG. Please see *http://blogs.msdn.com/tvoellm/archive/2008/05/12/hyper-v-performance-counters-part-four-of-many-hyper-v-hypervisor-virtual-processor-and-hyper-v-hypervisor-root-virtual-processor-counter-set.aspx* for more information on Hyper-V performance counters clock skew.

Summary

One of the key elements that can directly impact the user's experience while browsing the Internet is firewall performance. When using TMG as your gateway to the Internet and other networks, system performance is a key issue that you need to monitor and evaluate regularly. TMG is the first Microsoft firewall designed to take advantage of a 64-bit Windows platform. Other elements that can impact performance are name resolution, network topology, authentication, and firewall placement. TMG also can be installed and fully supported in a virtual environment, but special planning is required to provide the same level of performance and security that you expect from a similarly configured non-virtual environment.

In the next chapter, you will learn more about how to analyze and evaluate the network requirements for TMG.

## CHAPTER 4

Analyzing Network Requirements

- Determining Your Traffic Profile **47**

- TMG Deployment Options **51**

- Addressing Complex Networks **53**

- Configuring TMG Networks **54**

- Understanding How Name Resolution Impacts TMG **58**

- Summary **64**

Before you begin sizing your TMG deployment, you need to understand the network and traffic patterns that TMG will be required to support. This involves several steps, each of which may require repeated cycles of testing and analysis. In this chapter, you will learn how to evaluate your network and your network's traffic patterns so that your TMG deployment can proceed as smoothly as possible.

Determining Your Traffic Profile

A traffic profile is a map of the application protocols used within your network. These may include simple protocols such as the Simple Mail Transfer Protocol (SMTP) or complex protocols such as the Remote Procedure Call (RPC) or Distributed Component Object Model (DCOM) protocols. Perhaps the hardest thing for any network or firewall administrator to define and maintain is a reliable, accurate list of the traffic profile for his network. The following discussion will provide the building blocks of how to think through your TMG deployment in terms of the network traffic and protocols, sometimes referred to as your network's *traffic profile*. To determine your network's traffic profile, you'll perform the following types of mapping:

- Network mapping
- Application mapping
- Protocol mapping

Network Mapping

The first thing you must do is gain a better understanding of the network infrastructure that will be served by TMG. If your first reaction is "You've got to be kidding me; we're a global organization!" you most certainly want to consider separating your TMG deployments into geographic regions that would be served by their own TMG deployment (or, ideally, a TMG array). The point of this exercise is to help you define the boundaries that define supportable network regions within your organization and thus help you to better plan your TMG deployment.

For instance, your company may be a distributed organization, with the majority of your offices in Houston and satellite offices in Budapest, Eilat, and Buenos Aires. You need to have a clear understanding of how these networks are connected, as well as any backup routes or split routing infrastructure. In particular, split routing (where response traffic takes a different path than the origination traffic takes) is something TMG cannot handle properly. Because TMG is a stateful, application-aware firewall and proxy, any traffic deemed to be out of context is dropped. Figure 4-1 provides an example of a simplified network map.

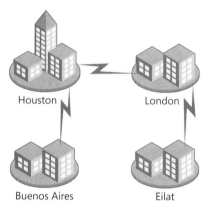

FIGURE 4-1 Sample network diagram

A review of the network in Figure 4-1 seems to suggest that the TMG should be located near the routes serving each geographical location. However, these might not be the only locations where TMG could serve as a firewall or proxy.

In cases where the wide area network (WAN) is well connected, the temptation to direct all of your Internet-destined traffic to a single portal may seem like a good way to simplify traffic management and policy enforcement. What you must remember when considering such a deployment is how to handle the inevitable cases when TMG is unavailable to remote networks for any number of reasons. For instance, if the users in Buenos Aires are normally directed to their local proxy for Internet access and that proxy fails, they should be routed to the next-closest proxy as a backup path. In Figure 4-1, the closest alternate path would be Houston.

Application Mapping

After you've defined the network infrastructure, you use it to help define the application map for your organization. Because line-of-business services are more likely to be centralized, you need to consider whether you can deploy TMG to help manage traffic load for those applications or help improve security of those same applications.

At this point you're not trying to map network protocols used by these applications; that comes later. For now, you only want to identify the application servers' network location and the network location of the clients that use the application servers. By performing this task immediately after mapping the network structure, you can identify the areas where application bottlenecks or areas requiring additional analysis or testing may exist. By identifying these points early in the traffic profile mapping process, you're better able to accommodate them later when you deploy TMG between the client and server networks.

Because many internal applications tend to be Web-based or support HTTP-based access as well as their native protocols (for example, Microsoft Exchange Server and Microsoft Office SharePoint Server), you can use TMG to provide security for internal as well as external access to these applications by creating a network structure that forces all client requests for these applications through TMG.

> **NOTE** One critical point here is to identify cases where the client and server communicate across the Internet rather than by using your private network structure. Such traffic paths are used in plenty of cases, for a great many reasons. This may be a good opportunity to re-examine the motivations for this traffic flow design and decide whether this traffic path should remain as-is or be rerouted internally.

Don't forget to include any management or monitoring applications used within your organization. The last thing you need is to deploy TMG only to discover that your Network Operations Center can no longer "see" the servers on the other side of TMG. Table 4-1 provides an example of an application mapping table. Of course, you may have additional criteria to consider for your table, such as reporting, auditing, and so on. You need to evaluate all these aspects of your line-of-business applications when considering whether TMG can provide value in that traffic path.

This map provides the baseline data from which you will build the next part of the traffic profile: the protocol map. Once you're satisfied with the application map's contents, you should store it somewhere safe and set a schedule for your team to review and update it regularly. This is especially true if your organization makes application changes often for upgrades, product changeover, and so on.

TABLE 4-1 Application Map

APPLICATION	OWNER	SERVER NETS	CLIENT NETS	SLA	SECURITY
Exchange Internal	Messaging	Houston	Houston Buenos Aires	95%	2
		London	London Eilat		
Exchange External		Houston	Houston Buenos Aires	95%	2
		London	London Eilat		
Team Sites	Business Applications	Houston London	All Internal	90%	3
Active Directory	Active Directory Group	Houston	Houston Buenos Aires	98%	1
		London	London Eilat		
Certificate Services	Auth Group	Houston	Houston Buenos Aires	90%	1
		London	London Eilat	90%	1

Protocol Mapping

After the network infrastructure and application maps are defined, you need to determine which protocols are in use on your network. Luckily, the Microsoft Knowledge Base (KB) article 832017 (*http://support.microsoft.com/kb/832017*) lists the ports and protocols used by most Microsoft server applications.

This Microsoft TechNet article also provides several examples of how to describe these so that the communication between the client and server are clear without including so much detail that it becomes difficult to understand at a glance: *http://technet.microsoft.com/en-us/library/cc891503.aspx*.

Two related protocols that are difficult to map accurately are RPC and DCOM. These are complex, negotiated protocols. Typically, they both begin with a connection to the server's RPC Endpoint Mapper at TCP port 135. This is followed by connections to the server application's listening ports. This complexity makes RPC and DCOM difficult to follow and equally difficult to pass across a firewall. TMG includes an application filter that understands RPC protocols, but because of the packet signing and encryption used in most DCOM communications, TMG is unable to support DCOM across its borders.

Other complex, negotiated protocols that TMG's application filters support include FTP, TFTP, SIP, Streaming Media (RTSP, MMS), and PPTP, just to name a few. Figure 4-2 illustrates the application filters provided with TMG.

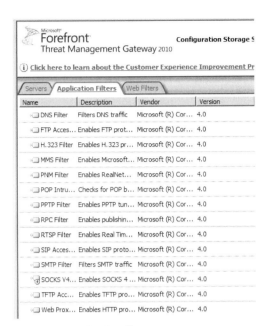

FIGURE 4-2 Application filters

If your applications are custom-built for your business or organization, you need to contact the vendor to gain a detailed understanding of the protocols used by the application if you expect them to cross TMG borders. You also need to bear in mind that it's not unusual for an application development team to be almost completely ignorant of the full protocol requirements for their application—or for that matter to have actually tested their application across a firewall.

For example, many applications built on Microsoft Management Console (MMC) technology often use many protocols to accomplish their tasks. In addition to any custom protocols defined by the application, MMC-based applications frequently incur a dependency on RPC, DCOM, Server Message Block (SMB), or NetBIOS protocols for remote service or state monitoring. Frequently, these are hinted at in the application documentation when such terms as *Windows remote services* are used to describe the application functionality. Table 4-2 provides an example of such a protocol map.

TMG Deployment Options

Now that you have a better understanding of your traffic profile, you can start examining the question of where to deploy TMG. The goals of a given network deployment differ based on your network security requirements. The goal is to define your network security requirements and then choose the TMG deployment option that works best to meet your requirements.

TABLE 4-2 Application Protocol Map

| APPLICATION PROTOCOL | PRIMARY CONNECTION | | SECONDARY CONNECTION | | | |
	SOURCE TRANSPORT /PORT	DEST TRANSPORT /PORT	SOURCE TRANSPORT /PORT	DEST TRANSPORT /PORT	DESTINATION	NOTES
MAPI	TCP:Dyn	TCP:135	TCP:Dyn	TCP:6001 TCP:6002 TCP:6004	Exchange	Outlook Clients
SMTP	TCP:Dyn	TCP:25			Exchange	In/Out Mail
HTTP	TCP:Dyn	TCP:80			Web Server	
Management	TCP:Dyn	TCP:1234	TCP:Dyn	TCP:666	Servers	System Monitoring

Edge Firewall

In an edge firewall deployment, TMG serves as the primary protection mechanism between the Internet and the organization's perimeter or internal network. Protocols that should not be seen passing through TMG in this deployment include anything specific to intradomain communications or any application traffic you do not wish external entities to see.

If you find yourself creating policies that allow application traffic beyond an edge-deployed TMG, you may wish to reconsider the application traffic path.

Another use of the edge deployment is providing access to specific internal applications from the Internet, such as Exchange Web Access, SharePoint, SMTP, IMAP, or specific line-of-business applications.

Back Firewall

The TMG's primary purpose as the back firewall is typically to separate a perimeter network from an internal network. The Internet is only accessible from TMG through an upstream device, which could be another TMG firewall or a third-party firewall or router.

In a back firewall deployment, TMG might need to allow domain trust traffic, or if your network policies are especially restrictive, allow only IPsec between specific hosts across the back-end TMG firewall.

Single Network Adapter

The single network adapter deployment option limits the protocols that can be passed through TMG. Specifically, only protocols handled by the Web proxy filter (HTTP, HTTPS, FTP) and dial-in VPN (PPTP, L2TP, IPsec, and SSTP) to TMG itself are usable.

NOTE VPN traffic in this deployment scenario must be terminated by TMG; TMG cannot publish VPN protocols in single network adapter deployments. TMG can filter all IP protocols passing through the VPN tunnel because the traffic effectively originates in a TMG local host network.

Typically, because it cannot function as a network firewall, when TMG is deployed in a single network adapter configuration, it is isolated from the Internet by another TMG or a third-party firewall. TMG can still provide all of the forward and reverse Web Proxy functionality it offers in all other deployments.

Domain Isolation

When used to separate internal networks, TMG can provide traffic controls based on individual protocols or by allowing only IPsec between hosts on the networks and the TMG. Although IPsec may seem daunting at first, it actually makes your access control design more effective because hosts that cannot communicate using IPsec to TMG can't even begin to send data using any other IP protocol.

MORE INFO You can read more about the details of domain isolation using ISA Server at *http://technet.microsoft.com/en-us/library/dd835480.aspx*.

Addressing Complex Networks

As an administrator, you know it can be difficult to describe a complex network structure in a way that makes sense to the firewall. In many cases, the firewall actually serves traffic to and from networks that are not local to the firewall. An instance of such a network topology is show in Figure 4-3.

In this diagram, TMG serves hosts in three networks: Houston, operating in subnet 192.168.1.0/24; Buenos Aires, operating in subnet 192.168.2.0/24; and London, operating in subnet 192.168.3.0/24. All branch offices are using TMG (located in the main office) as Web proxy, because for this example the only office that has direct Internet connection is the main office in Houston.

Like ISA Server, TMG defines networks based on the addresses located behind a particular network interface. In Figure 4-3, addresses in three different network IDs are located behind a single NIC in the TMG in the Houston office. You would use all of these addresses when defining the TMG Network located behind that NIC.

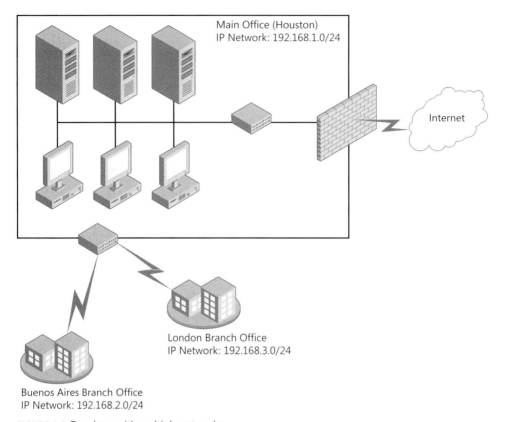

Main Office (Houston)
IP Network: 192.168.1.0/24

Internet

London Branch Office
IP Network: 192.168.3.0/24

Buenos Aires Branch Office
IP Network: 192.168.2.0/24

FIGURE 4-3 Topology with multiple networks

Configuring TMG Networks

When you install TMG, part of what you provide to the installer are the addresses that belong to the default internal network (we call this the default internal network because you can create multiple "internal" networks). This is necessary so that TMG can evaluate where the traffic is coming from and determine whether it is valid for the network definition as understood by TMG. If the address does not meet the network definition you provided, TMG treats the traffic as invalid, drops the traffic, and logs a spoofed packet alert.

The default internal network is defined during TMG installation and also when using the Getting Started Wizard. To configure the default internal network, complete the following steps:

1. On the TMG computer, open the Forefront TMG Management Console.
2. Click Forefront TMG (Server Name) in the left pane.
3. In the task pane, click Launch The Getting Started Wizard on the Tasks tab of the task pane to open the wizard shown in Figure 4-4.

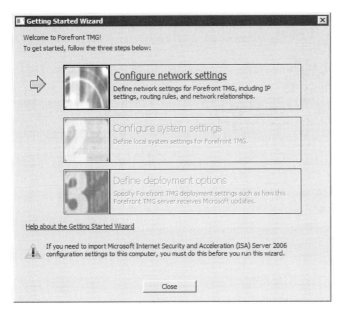

FIGURE 4-4 The Getting Started Wizard

4. Click Configure Network Settings, then click Next on the Welcome page to open the Network Template Selection page.

5. Choose Edge Firewall template, as shown in Figure 4-5, and then click Next.

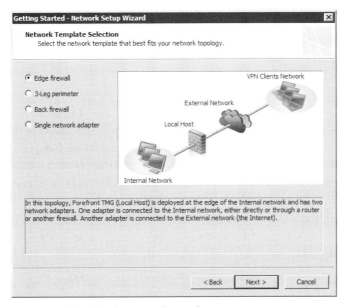

FIGURE 4-5 Choosing the network template

6. In the Local Area Network (LAN) Settings dialog box, select the name of the interface representing the internal interface on the TMG from the Network Adapter Connected To The LAN drop-down list as shown in Figure 4-6. When you choose this option, TMG automatically populates the fields (IP address, Subnet Mask, Default Gateway, and DNS Server) based on your internal adapter configuration. Note that for the internal interface, a default gateway should not be configured. Click Next. In the Specify Additional Routes For The Network Adapter text box you can add other networks that belong to your internal environment. As discussed previously, in some situations TMG is located in one network but more networks behind it are considered internal. Use the Add option to included those networks so that TMG knows how to handle requests coming from those networks.

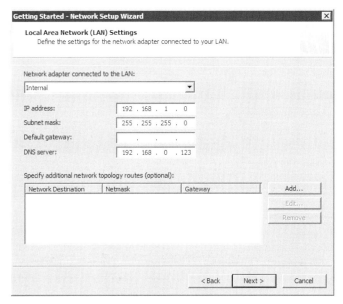

FIGURE 4-6 Selecting the internal network

The default internal network is defined to use only the local on-subnet IP address ranges, but because we're using the scenario described in Figure 4-3, there are other networks behind this on-subnet network that you need to add manually. This is where you need to have a good understanding of how your own network is numbered. For example, in the scenario specified in Figure 4-4 you would need to add the subnets for network IDs 192.168.2.0/24 and 192.168.3.0/24 to the default internal network.

To add these addresses, complete the following steps:

1. In the Local Area Network (LAN) Settings page, click Add.

2. In the Network Topology Route Properties dialog, enter the information as shown in Figure 4-7 and click OK.

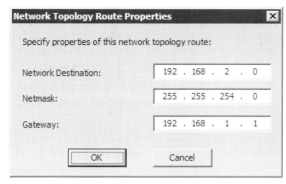

FIGURE 4-7 Additional routes entry dialog

3. Verify that the data in the Local Area Networks (LAN) Settings page appears as shown in Figure 4-8 and then click Next.

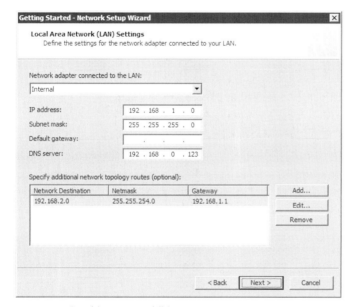

FIGURE 4-8 Resulting route additions

4. Continue through the Network configuration wizard.

5. When prompted by TMG, click Apply to commit the changes.

With this configuration in place, when users from a remote office try to access the Internet, TMG evaluates the source address and identifies that the address belongs to the default internal network.

> **MORE INFO** Chapter 11, "Configuring TMG Networks," covers possible issues you might encounter if the internal network is not configured correctly.

Understanding How Name Resolution Impacts TMG

Chapter 3, "System Requirements," covered the main aspects of how name resolution can impact the overall user experience. It all starts with how Domain Name System (DNS) is configured on TMG. Remember that TMG relies on Windows for name resolution and thus any configuration mistakes in Windows name resolution adversely affect TMG.

Reviewing How Windows Resolves Names

Windows name resolution uses DNS as the preferred method of name resolution; however, if the name cannot be resolved by DNS, the operating system tries to perform a NetBIOS name resolution. For NetBIOS name resolution, two methods can be used to resolve a name: Windows Internet Name Service (WINS) and broadcast. If your network does not have a WINS server, Windows will try to resolve the name by sending a broadcast for the NetBIOS portion of the name (the host name portion of the fully qualified domain name, or FQDN). For example, when you run the command *ping srv1.contoso.com,* Windows tries the following default steps:

1. Checks whether the local host name is the same as the name it is trying to resolve (srv1).

2. Checks whether the local HOSTS file has a match for this name.

3. Queries the first DNS server in the TCP/IP stack.

   The operating system sends a query to the first server on the preferred adapter's search list—which is why it is important to have the internal adapter at the top of the list—and waits one second for a response. If the operating system does not receive a response from the first server within one second, it sends the query to the first DNS servers on all adapters and waits two seconds for a response. This process repeats in cycles of two, four, and eight seconds respectively.

   If Windows receives a positive response from the DNS server, it stops querying for the name, adds the response to the DNS cache, and returns the response to the client.

> **IMPORTANT** You can monitor the number of name resolution failures by opening Performance Monitor, adding the Microsoft Firewall Service object, and monitoring the Failed DNS Resolutions counter.

4. Performs NetBIOS name resolution if no match is found.

   Windows uses NetBIOS name resolution if all attempts to resolve the host name by DNS fail. Windows is compliant with RFCs 1001 and 1002, which define NetBIOS service for TCP and UDP. One way in which the operating system is compliant is by defining how the name will be resolved by setting the node type. By default, Windows uses broadcast node type (*BNode*); however, this setting can be changed in the registry as explained in the Chapter 3. The possible values are:

- **Peer Node Type (*PNode*)**   Sends a direct query to a NetBIOS name server (for example, WINS).
- **Mixed Node Type (*MNode*)**   Sends a broadcast first and if doesn't resolve the name it will send a direct query to the NetBIOS name server (WINS). This is also called B + P (*BNode + PNode*).
- **Hybrid Node Type (*HNode*)**   Sends a query directly to the NetBIOS name server and if it does not resolve, sends a broadcast. This is also called P + B.

5. If the hybrid node type is used, the name resolution process continues in the following way:

   a. Windows checks the local NetBIOS name cache. Up to 16 names (by default) are held in this cache for 10 minutes.

   b. If Windows can't resolve the name from the local NetBIOS name cache, it sends a NetBIOS name query to the primary WINS server configured in the Advanced TCP/IP options of the network interface on the top of the interface list. If the primary WINS server fails to respond, Windows tries to contact all other configured WINS servers (in top-down order).

   c. If the preceding step does not succeed, Windows checks the lmhosts file if LMHOSTS lookup is enabled on the WINS tab in the Advanced TCP/IP Properties dialog box. This dialog box is found in the TCP/IP properties of a network interface on the firewall.

   d. Windows sends a NetBIOS broadcast to the local segment (255.255.255.255) because, by default, routers do not allow NetBIOS broadcasts to pass.

Name resolution can be a long and difficult process if you don't have the correct configuration in place.

MORE INFO   For more information on the name resolution process, review Chapter 7 of *Windows Server 2008 Networking and Network Access Protection (NAP)* by Joseph Davies and Tony Northrup (Microsoft Press, 2008).

Recommendations for DNS Configuration on TMG

Windows name resolution always follows the steps outlined in the previous section. However, the way that you configure TMG (workgroup or domain member) and the template that you use (Edge, Single NIC, or 3-Leg Perimeter) can directly affect how you configure the DNS settings on TMG.

IMPORTANT Regardless of environment and configuration, you must remember one key rule of thumb for TMG DNS configuration: Never configure TMG with a DNS server address on more than one physical network interface. If you have two network interface cards (internal and external), DNS server IP addresses should be configured on only one interface and that interface should be on top of the network interface list.

Edge or Perimeter in a Workgroup

When you have TMG in a workgroup, you still need to resolve names for internal hosts, and the general DNS recommendations remain the same: configure DNS in one interface, as shown in Figure 4-9. In this case, you can configure DNS to point to an internal DNS server and this DNS server should be configured to use forwarders or root hints.

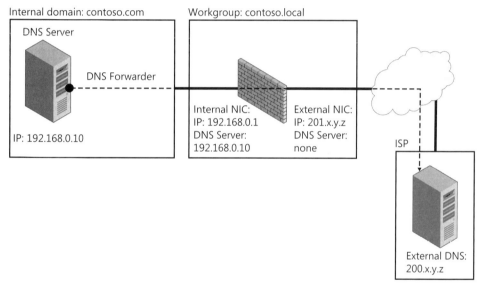

FIGURE 4-9 DNS Configuring TMG in a workgroup

Although this is the most common scenario and general recommendation for workgroup, in some other scenarios access to the internal DNS is not allowed by the company's security policy. In these situations, you can implement some alternate methods:

- **Use another DNS server** Allow full name resolution for internal and external resources by adding a DNS server that can use conditional forwarders. A *conditional forwarder* is a DNS server that can be used to forward DNS queries according to the DNS domain name received in the query. For example, a DNS server can be configured to forward all the queries it receives for names ending with contoso.com to the IP address of a specific DNS server—for example, to the IP of the internal DNS.

- **Install DNS services on TMG** In this setup, TMG has a the DNS service installed and can be configured to use a conditional forwarder for the internal domain and forwarders for external domains. Another option is to create a secondary zone for the internal domain and use forwarders (or root hints) for external domains. Although this is an viable alternative, it is not commonly used because of the separation of duties and increased administrative overhead. For many reasons, you don't want to add another service to your firewall. The main reason is that you will now have two components that might not have the same maintenance window. For example, if you plan to update your DNS service with the latest security updates, you might need to restart the server; therefore, your firewall would also be offline during that time.

Table 4-3 summarizes the benefits and drawbacks of each option.

TABLE 4-3 Pros and Cons of Configuration Options

DNS CONFIGURATION	PROS	CONS
Use another DNS server	■ Separation of duties: TMG should be a dedicated network firewall. ■ Availability: if the DNS server becomes unavailable, TMG will still be up and running. ■ Fewer services running on TMG reduces the number of services to maintain.	■ You need to install an additional server. ■ You need to maintain another server.
Install DNS on TMG	No need to build a new server.	■ One more service to harden and maintain. ■ If this single computer is unavailable, two main services will also be down (DNS and Firewall).

Another scenario includes a network that doesn't have internal DNS services and relies on broadcasts for internal name resolution. In this case TMG relies on an ISP's DNS server for external name resolution. This is the only situation where you configure TMG to use an external DNS server.

Edge or Perimeter in a Domain

In a domain environment, you have internal DNS services used by your Active Directory infrastructure. TMG should be configured to use internal DNS servers and the addresses of the internal DNS server should be configured on TMG's internal interface. The same recommendations for how the internal DNS resolves external names still apply, which means you should use forwarders or root hints.

Single NIC Scenario (Workgroup or Domain)

In a TMG Single NIC environment, you need to configure the preferred DNS server to point to your internal DNS servers and not use external DNS servers. The recommendations remain the same: use forwarders or root hints in your DNS Server configuration.

REAL WORLD Common DNS Configuration Mistakes

We are often called on to assist the Microsoft CSS security team to resolve network security problems. However, we are typically called after an incident has taken place. Although working with Microsoft CSS Security Team allows us to assist customers in a reactive manner, it also allows us to advise them about the best practices for configurations prior to the final deployment. In one break-fix incident, a customer was experiencing slow browsing performance and sometimes even timeouts when attempting to access some Web sites. The server's performance was looking good with no indication of a network bottleneck.

Using Microsoft Network Monitor, we were able to discover that the delay was related to name resolution issues. After some troubleshooting we determined that the problem was due to the DNS configuration on the ISA Server (yes, that was back in the days of ISA Server 2006). After reviewing the configuration, we noticed that the customer had configured both NICs to use internal and external DNS server addresses. In addition, the configuration was crossing out, where the internal NIC was using internal DNS as preferred server and external DNS as alternate, whereas the external NIC was using the external DNS as preferred and internal DNS as alternate.

Administrators sometimes set up Windows to configure the internal DNS server to be the preferred DNS server and then use an external DNS server as an alternate. This is not recommended. KB article 825036 (*http://support.microsoft.com/ kb/825036/*) discusses best practices for DNS configuration on member servers. The root cause of the problem is that if the preferred DNS server fails, the operating system uses the alternate DNS server and never goes back to the preferred DNS server unless the alternate DNS server fails (or the server is restarted). The other problem in the customer's case was that the customer configured an external DNS server on the external network interface. ISA ended up trying to resolve internal names by sending queries to the external DNS server.

Side Effects of DNS Issues

The main side effect of having name resolution issues in TMG is decreased performance. The Web browsing experience is slower, as well as user authentication. The two main issues when dealing with name resolution in TMG are:

- **Name Resolution Delay**   When TMG sends a query and DNS does not answer in a timely manner, TMG's worker threads are blocked pending DNS responses, causing the number of backlogged packets to increase.
- **Authentication Delay**   The wrong DNS configuration can also cause TMG to delay or fail to authenticate when firewall rules require authentication.

DNS Cache in TMG

TMG keeps its own DNS cache within the user mode process wspsrv.exe, which is the Firewall Service. This component is built on top of Windows DNS resolver and is used to reduce the number of DNS queries TMG has to make to resolve a name. Figure 4-10 shows the DNS Cache components in TMG.

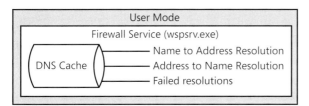

FIGURE 4-10 DNS cache in TMG

TMG employs a mechanism to determine when the entries should be removed from the DNS cache. The mechanism uses the following parameters:

- **DnsCacheNegativeTtl**   Verifies whether the TTL (given by the DNS server) for that entry has been reached.
- **DnsCacheRecordMaxKB**   Verifies whether the cache size reaches some maximum threshold which is by default 10,000. If this is true, the oldest 25 percent of the entries will be removed from the cache.
- **DnsCacheSize**   TMG checks whether the previous two events have not occurred and then the firewall service scans the three caches once every 30 minutes (by default) to remove cache entries where the TTL has been reached.

You can retrieve and change these values by running the script specified in Microsoft KB article 843127 (*http://support.microsoft.com/kb/843127/*).

> **BEST PRACTICES**   While troubleshooting name-resolution issues, it is common to run the command *ipconfig /flushdns* to clear the local computer DNS cache. Because TMG has its own cache you need to remember that to have a clean cache you also need to restart the Firewall Service. You can do this by running the command net stop fwsrv && net start fwsrv.

Summary

To better control your network, you should know which applications are running and the protocols they use; this allows you to create your traffic profile. By defining the applications, defining who owns the applications, and defining the protocols and the network topology, you can better define where TMG should be installed and what rules you need to create.

Defining the IP addresses on your network is a key element that needs to be documented before installing TMG. The network topology map should include all IP addresses used by local and remote networks in your organization. Those addresses should be included as internal address in TMG configuration if the clients from the remote network plan to use the TMG firewall for Internet access.

Part of the network topology and firewall placement planning also includes assessment of your TMG's DNS requirements. Name resolution is done by the operating system and it affects the way that TMG answers browsing requests as well as how well TMG will perform authentication.

## CHAPTER 5

Choosing the Right Network Topology

■ Choosing the Network Template **65**

■ Examining High Availability **71**

■ Joining TMG to a Domain or Workgroup **82**

■ Summary **85**

You may have the challenging task of designing the network infrastructure TMG will serve. If this is the case, or even if you're just trying to decide which TMG network topology best applies to your network infrastructure, you'll want to read through this chapter carefully so that you make the right decision the first time. Changing this decision after deploying TMG can present some difficult challenges.

Choosing the Network Template

After establishing your traffic profile and identifying the IP address ranges that belong to your networks, it is time for you to determine which network template you will apply to TMG. The template you choose should match your current TMG configuration and satisfy your network needs.

In Chapter 4, "Analyzing Network Requirements," you identified TMG placement considerations, and during this process you saw that TMG can be placed at the edge of your network as a front-end firewall, behind another firewall in a back-end firewall configuration, or as a single NIC Web proxy (forward and reverse Web proxy). TMG network templates can assist you in reflecting the physical configuration into a logical firewall or Web proxy configuration. TMG includes four network templates:

■ Edge Firewall

■ 3-Leg Perimeter

■ Back Firewall

■ Single Network Adapter

You can choose the network template when you run the Getting Started Wizard by choosing Configure Network Settings. But before we apply the template it is important to understand what each template does.

Edge Firewall Network Template

You need a firewall on the edge regardless of your deployment; this adds the first layer of protection for your internal assets. By using the Edge Firewall network template for this scenario, you apply a configuration that reflects the main goal of your edge TMG placement.

This template assumes that you have two interfaces: one connected to the internal network and one connected to the external network. Usually the external interface is the one connected directly to the Internet (through a router for instance), but it can also be behind another firewall or NAT device. Most often, the external interface is the NIC configured with a default gateway.

When you run the Getting Started Wizard, choose the Edge Firewall template, as shown in Figure 5-1.

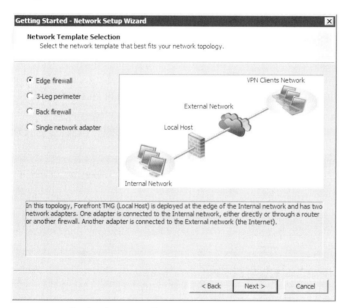

FIGURE 5-1 The Getting Started Wizard–Edge Firewall template selection

This template provides the following benefits:

- TMG blocks all unauthorized attempts to gain access to the default Internal Network from the default External Network.

- TMG hides the default Internal Network from the outside.

- You have the ability to provide secure access to internal servers by publishing them.
- The template carries little overhead and has an easy configuration.

MORE INFO   For more information about how to run the Getting Started Wizard, read Chapter 4 of this book.

3-Leg Perimeter Network Template

The 3-Leg Perimeter template can assist you in implementing a perimeter network, also known as demilitarized zone, or DMZ. This perimeter network is used to securely expose resources that are shared by users coming from untrusted networks (such as the Internet) and trusted networks (TMG-protected networks).

This template involves setting up TMG with three network interfaces. One network adapter is connected to the Internet (external network), one is connected to the internal network, and the third is connected to a perimeter network. The 3-Leg Perimeter option is not available if you have fewer than three NICs installed on TMG.

When you run the Getting Started Wizard you can choose the 3-Leg Perimeter template, as shown in Figure 5-2.

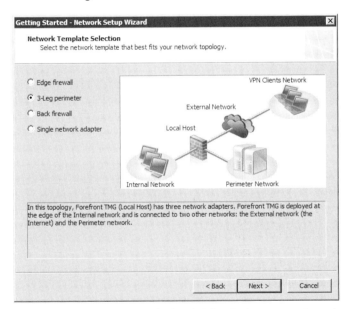

FIGURE 5-2 The Getting Started Wizard–3-Leg Perimeter template selection

By selecting this template in the Getting Started Wizard, you will have to specify later which adapter is connected to the perimeter as shown in Figure 5-3.

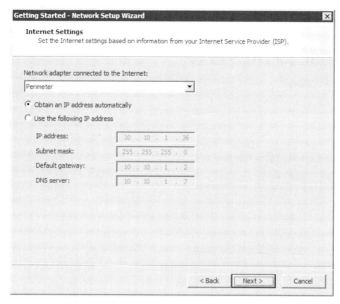

FIGURE 5-3 Selecting the perimeter adapter

During this selection you need to specify whether the IP addresses used on the perimeter network are public or private. This is a key determination because it also affects the network relationship between the perimeter network with the default Internal and External networks. The perimeter network usually uses private IP addresses, which is the typical scenario because you want to hide the real IP address of the resource from Internet.

This template provides the following benefits:

- It protects the default Internal Network from external attacks.
- Allows you to securely publish services to the Internet by placing them in a perimeter zone.
- External users can access resources located in the perimeter network while still being prevented from accessing internal resources.

Back Firewall Network Template

Scenarios involving the Back Firewall template include the deployment of TMG in between a perimeter network and the default Internal network. TMG acts as the back-end line of defense for the internal resources. Another firewall is necessary between the external network and perimeter network. Use this scenario when you want to provide two lines of defense and also gain the following benefits:

- Granular access control
- Multiple layers of protection
- Separation of duties (Each firewall is responsible for different traffic profiles.)

When you run the Getting Started Wizard you can choose the Back Firewall template, as shown in Figure 5-4.

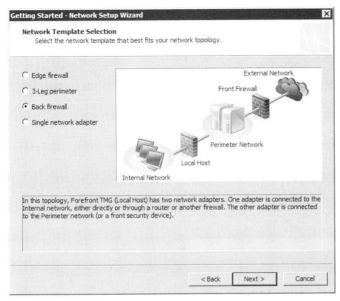

FIGURE 5-4 The Getting Started Wizard–Back Firewall template selection

When you select this template using the Getting Started Wizard, you have to specify which adapter is connected to the default Internal Network and which adapter is connected to the perimeter network.

Single NIC Network Template

You use the Single NIC template when you want to limit the firewall to one or more of the following roles:

- A forward Web proxy server
- A Web caching server
- A reverse Web proxy (Web publishing—HTTP/HTTPs, RPC over HTTPs, and FTP)
- A VPN remote-access client server

You cannot use a single NIC TMG to protect the edge of your network. The single NIC scenario assumes that TMG will provide these limited services and that another firewall will provide edge security.

The Single NIC template introduces a number of limitations to TMG functionality. The single NIC TMG has no concept of an external network, because it has only one network interface and the default gateway that connects you to anything beyond your own network lies on the same network card. Therefore, the only networks available are localhost (TMG itself) and internal. All firewall policies need to be created by using those elements.

Additionally, using the Single NIC template creates a number of unsupported scenarios, including:

- **Application filtering**   Although the TMG has built-in application-layer inspection, the Single NIC template limits what can be inspected. Application-layer inspection is done only for HTTP/HTTPS and FTP over HTTP traffic.

- **Server Publishing**   The Server Publishing feature requires two network interface cards (NICs); this template supports only a single NIC deployment.

- **TMG Client**   TMG client requests are not supported.

- **SecureNET Client**   SecureNET client requests are not supported.

Even if you configure a network adapter to use two or more IP addresses or you add a second network adapter and later disable it in an attempt to work around some of those limitations, this configuration still does not add support for the above scenarios.

When you run the Getting Started Wizard, you can choose the Single NIC template as shown in Figure 5-5.

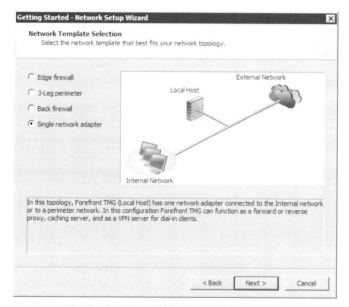

FIGURE 5-5 The Getting Started Wizard—Single NIC template selection

After you apply the single NIC template the following addresses are excluded from the network:

- 0.0.0.0
- 255.255.255.255
- 127.0.0.0 – 127.255.255.255
- 224.0.0.0 – 254.255.255.255

REAL WORLD   Cannot Access Some Web Sites

The following real-world example is based on a support incident regarding a recent deployment of TMG using the Single NIC template. The user was trying to access a Web site that gave him access to a payroll system. Unfortunately, this company didn't really communicate how the Web site worked, and according to the basic manual the only traffic required was HTTPS (SSL).

The user was able to access the first page and log in to the system, but when he tried to retrieve data from the payroll system, the page never loaded completely. The user argued that TMG was at fault because everything worked fine when TMG was bypassed. We had to do some reverse engineering to understand how this application worked. By using Network Monitor 3.2 we were able to view the details of the client/server traffic and we could see that the application indeed used HTTPS, but it also tried to open some Winsock connections using a non-HTTP port.

That was the problem: to use this application, the customer needed support for both Web and non-Web protocols. To get support for non-Web protocols (and require client authentication), the user needed to use the TMG Client on his workstations to handle Winsock requests. But the problem was that the user was running a single NIC environment and the TMG Client requests are not supported in this configuration.

The bottom line was that the user had to add a second NIC and reconfigure TMG to use the Edge Firewall template. The lesson is that you really need to determine your traffic profile and define the type of traffic you need to support when you are purchasing a service from a third party. Make sure to ask what protocols are required. By defining this prior to implementing the application, you might avoid long support calls that end up being due to an unsupported scenario.

NOTE   The Single NIC template can be very useful if you clearly understand the limitations it imposes. However, regardless of the template you choose, it is important to mention that you should not use more than one default gateway on the external interface. This is also an unsupported scenario and can cause connectivity problems for your Forefront TMG.

Examining High Availability

Implementing a highly available network service frequently means different things to different people depending on their experiences in the IT community. In general, all network and application administrators agree that the term *high availability* means "uninterrupted service availability to the user." In other words, if the service has to defer a user's traffic path from one server to another, the user should not be aware that this action has occurred.

For example, some network or application administrators consider the goals of load-balancing and failover/failback to be completely different tasks, but they usually agree that they can both be employed to provide a more robust service to the user. In fact, if you choose to use load-balancing and failover/failback in combination, it's in your best interest to deploy these mechanisms in a way that allows them to be compatible rather than conflicting. Otherwise, you could spend a great deal of your time chasing ghosts in the machine caused by conflicting traffic management mechanisms.

One thing all high-availability solutions have in common is that they try to use one or more aspects of the traffic definition to determine how the traffic should be handled in the course of traffic balancing across a server farm and in case of server failure. The use of one or more aspects of the conversation to control traffic flow is called *affinity*.

Most IP traffic is defined by a combination of five unique identifiers, known as a *5-tuple*:

- **Source IP address**   The IP address of the sending host.
- **Destination IP address**   The IP address of the receiving host.
- **Transport**   The IP protocol (TCP, UDP, GRE, and so on) that carries the higher-level protocol, such as SSL or HTTP. Note that only TCP and UDP provide source and destination ports.
- **Source port**   A number identifying the transport socket used by the sending host.
- **Destination port**   A number identifying the transport socket used by the receiving host.

In network protocol layer order, the following list describes some common high-availablity techniques:

- **Source IP affinity**   High-availability solutions that use this technique build a map of the traffic flow in the context of the host IP addresses that started the conversation (the client). The primary advantage to this technique is that it guarantees all traffic from a specific IP address is always sent to a specific server, regardless of the higher-level protocols in use. This also represents the greatest disadvantage of this technique: When traffic from multiple clients is sourced from behind a remote NAT or proxy device, the source IP for all clients is likely to be the same. This is the primary traffic management method used by NLB. TMG offers IP affinity for Web Publishing Load Balancing (WPLB).
- **Source port affinity**   This technique builds a map of the traffic flow in the context of the transport and source port. This is one method by which a high-availability mechanism can get around a case where multiple clients are behind a NAT or proxy device that makes them all appear as a single source IP. The primary advantage to this technique is that it is independent of the source or destination addresses. The primary disadvantage is that this technique can only be applied to protocols that make use of ports (TCP and UDP). Where protocols that do not use ports (such as GRE) are used, this method cannot be employed. When NLB is configured for *no affinity*, it is actually configured to use source port affinity.

- **SSL-ID affinity**   SSL is a session layer protocol because it operates a layer above the transport protocols in the network protocol stack. Although it doesn't fall into the 5-tuple definition we described, it provides a statistically unique identifier that can be used to build the traffic flow map. The primary advantage of this technique is that it is a better identifier than IP addresses or ports, because it is cryptographically defined at the server side of the conversation and therefore unique to all traffic served by that host. The primary disadvantage to this technique is that although many third-party vendors use this, their management of the traffic in this context varies and occasionally conflicts when these techniques are used together. Neither TMG nor NLB support SSL-ID affinity.

- **HTTP cookie affinity**   Because much of the traffic crossing the Internet is HTTP, and because HTTP offers the concept of cookies as a unique session identifier for the client application itself, many high-availability solutions make use of cookie affinity. TMG also offers this when configured for WPLB. The primary advantage to this technique is that it is independent of the lower-layer protocols and can be used to uniquely identify a user's browser session. This technique has a couple of disadvantages: The high-availability device must terminate SSL sessions; otherwise, it cannot insert the cookie in the response headers or read the cookies created by the server in the response headers. In addition, in some cases, such as Microsoft Office Outlook Anywhere and Terminal Services Gateway, cookies are not handled by the client application as the high-availability solution expects (if at all). TMG provides cookie affinity for WPLB; NLB does not support cookie-affinity.

- **DNS Round-Robin**   This method takes advantage of the ability to define more than one IP address for a host name in a DNS zone. In most cases, when a client queries a host name for which multiple IP addresses are defined, the DNS server will respond with all of the IP addresses defined for that host. Depending on the capabilities and configuration of the DNS server, it may apply IP filtering or ordering according to the subnet structure it determines based on the requesting host's IP address.

> **IMPORTANT**   DNS Round-Robin functionality varies between DNS server implementations and is referred to as *netmask ordering*. You can read more about Microsoft DNS netmask ordering at *http://technet.microsoft.com/en-us/library/cc787373.aspx*.

Although not strictly a high-availability mechanism, this is a very cheap (almost free) method for providing client connection load-sharing and failover. Neither TMG nor NLB have any effect on DNS Round-Robin, although the combination of DNS RR with NLB can produce interesting (read: confusing) results and are best not used in combination.

> **IMPORTANT**   Although DNS Round-Robin is a very popular high-availability method because of its low cost and ease of deployment and management, it doesn't come highly recommended because its effectiveness is entirely dependent on how the client operating system or application handles such responses. A high-availability solution that depends almost entirely on client operating system or application behavior is not a high-availability solution that you can exert much influence over.

- **Bidirectional affinity**   This affinity requires that the high-availability solution have a monitor and control point on opposite sides of the traffic path across a NAT device, and that both sides of this high-availability solution must intercommunicate to maintain proper traffic flow across it. NLB and some third-party high-availability solutions support this mechanism, although some of the third-party solutions require that you purchase duplicate units to have a functional bi-directional high-availability mechanism. The primary purpose of this mechanism is to ensure that traffic related to this connection is guaranteed to take the same path between the two endpoints. We discuss this in more detail in Chapter 8, "Installing TMG."

Figure 5-6 depicts a simplified view of the traffic flow between multiple clients and a TMG array using an IP affinity–based high-availability solution such as NLB. The funnel represents the virtual-IP (VIP) address used by the high-availability mechanism. The critical point in this scenario is that all traffic—regardless of transport, port, or other criteria—is directed to a specific TMG array member. In this example, TMG 1 receives traffic from client 2, TMG 2 receives traffic from client 3, and TMG 3 receives traffic from client 1.

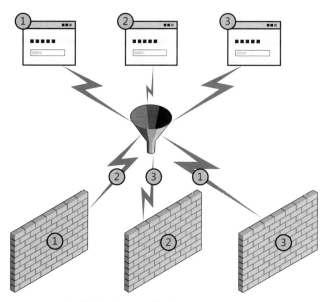

FIGURE 5-6 IP-affinity from multiple sources

> **NOTE**   If all three clients were behind a NAT or proxy, they might all appear to come from the same source IP address and would all be directed to the same TMG array member. This is where non-IP-based high-availability may be beneficial.

Figure 5-7 illustrates the typical behavior of a high-availability solution that uses non-IP-affinity, such as source-port or SSL-ID affinity. In this case, the client application opens multiple connections to the VIP and thus these connections are distributed across the TMG array. If all the TMG array members are publishing the same application server or back-end VIP, this technique may work well. If not, the results could be unpredictable.

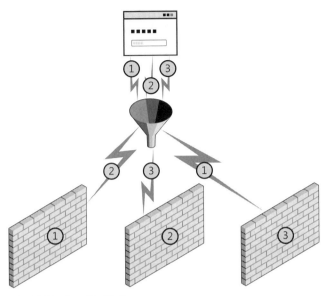

FIGURE 5-7 Non-IP-affinity

NOTE Figure 5-7 illustrates how multiple clients would appear to a high-availability solution if they were isolated by a NAT device or proxy. Because they all use the same source-IP, you must use a non-IP-based affinity method to ensure the best traffic balance across the TMG farm.

Figure 5-8 depicts the behavior of an application that is aware of multiple IP addresses used by a single host. In such cases, the high-availability solution may choose to connect to different destination IP addresses, depending on how the application was designed and tested. This is one reason DNS Round-Robin is not used where predictable client behavior is important. In most cases where the client applications are multi-IP-aware, they will typically use the IP addresses received in the same order they were provided. To provide the best distribution across the TMG array, the order of IP addresses must change in each DNS server response.

At this point you might be asking, "Why didn't you include the remainder of the 5-tuple in the affinity set?" The answer is that at the server end of the conversation, the destination IP, transport, and destination port is the same for all conversations. Thus, they offer nothing of value to the task of traffic affinity for high availability.

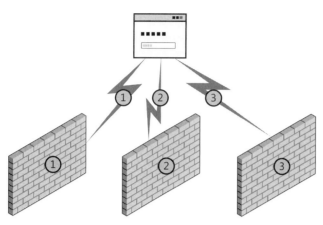

FIGURE 5-8 DNS Round-Robin

In the context of traffic sent through TMG arrays, two basic scenarios impact the high-availability design:

- Traffic handled by publishing rules
- Traffic handled by access rules

In each of these scenarios, you may have the ability to choose between two design options for the TMG network where the client request is seen:

- Integrated NLB
- Third-party solution

We can't address all third-party solutions in this book, but you should be able to use the concepts provided here to compare the functionality and limits of any third-party device you evaluate. Each of the high-availability scenarios also includes the need to evaluate the use of ISP Failover, a new feature introduced in the TMG firewall. We'll examine the considerations for this option in each of the following sections.

Designing High Availability for Publishing Rules

In most cases, publishing scenarios allow TMG to operate as the network service itself as far as the client is concerned. In this scenario, the client communicates with TMG, which then processes, filters, and forwards the traffic to the application server.

Web Publishing

Although typically used to serve requests from the Internet, Web Publishing is also useful for intranet scenarios. The most common use of intranet Web Publishing is to serve Exchange Outlook Web Access (OWA) users. In this scenario, you configure DNS so that connections for the OWA Web site are directed to the TMG Web Listener rather than the Exchange server. You also configure the Exchange server's OWA listener so that it accepts traffic only from TMG. This allows you to accomplish four goals:

- Provide a consistent login experience for all OWA users.
- Take advantage of customized TMG log on forms.
- Limit the maintenance of the login forms to the TMG.
- Use TMG to protect Exchange from common attacks against OWA.

Intranet Web publishing is also a useful technique to reduce the traffic overhead between branch offices and the central office through the use of TMG HTTP compression and DiffServ traffic prioritization (if your network infrastructure supports it).

On first consideration, Web Publishing appears to impose a fairly well-defined set of constraints for high-availability deployment design. For instance, you only need to consider three protocols for the traffic to the Web Listener; TCP, HTTP, and SSL (TLS). Because the TCP, SSL, and HTTP traffic will always be terminated at the TMG Web Listeners, the traffic is always handled by TMG in a routed context. This is because the traffic operates in the context of "to Local Host," causing the firewall to process the traffic according to Network Rule #1: Local Host Access, which defines this relationship as *route*. Because Network Rules, which define a routed context, are bi-directional, any traffic sourced from TMG to anywhere is also handled in a routed context.

You also need to consider Web Chaining rules for Web Publishing because these are part of any traffic processed by the Web proxy filter. Web Chaining rules are processed after the Web Publishing rule has completed its task. Although Web Chaining rules don't necessarily affect how the high-availability solution for traffic to the Web listener should be designed, they may affect how you design high availability between the TMG array and the published servers.

Because of the way they create and manage connections to the Web application server, some Web applications may not be well suited to some high-availability implementations. To make matters worse, the abuse of the HTTP protocol imposed by some Web applications makes it extremely difficult for many high-availability mechanisms to provide proper handling of this traffic. In particular, Exchange Outlook Anywhere Services and Terminal Service Gateway tend to stretch the HTTP protocol to its limits because of the way RPC is channeled through HTTP.

RPC over HTTP transforms a protocol that was originally designed to handle single-channel simplex traffic into a two-channel, full-duplex transport for each RPC connection between the Outlook client and Exchange server. Because an Outlook client session may incur between 5 and 10 RPC (and thus TCP) connections, this translates to 10 to 20 TCP connections and corresponding HTTP channels for each RPC send/receive context. Unless IP-affinity can be successfully employed, no high-availability current solution can collect all of these connections and sessions into a single context, so these sessions may be split across the TMG array and thus across the Exchange farm as well. Remember that because RPC over HTTP is unable to manage HTTP cookies, we cannot use cookie-affinity to work around this limitation.

Server (non-Web) Publishing

Because most deployments that use Server Publishing do so against a NAT network relationship, NLB and external high-availability solutions are generally equally effective when compared to their use with Web Publishing scenarios. The biggest difference between Web- and Server-Publishing high-availability solutions is that Server Publishing is typically used for non–HTTP protocols, which effectively eliminates the use of application protocol–specific load balancing techniques such as cookie-based affinity and WPLB.

When Server Publishing is configured in a route relationship, the destination IP address in the traffic sent by the client is the actual IP address of the published server and not TMG itself. Because the destination IP address is not owned by TMG, and because NLB functions only for traffic destined to the local computer, you can't use NLB to provide high availability at the TMG array when the network relationship for a Server Publishing Rule is *route*. In this case, only an external third-party high-availability solution is functional.

ISP Redundancy

Whether you use Web or Server Publishing, the configuration chosen for ISP Redundancy dictates how your publishing rules and the related high-availability solution must operate. ISP redundancy offers two operating modes: ISP failover and ISP load balancing. Both options include two distinct public subnets; the DNS structure that serves the remote clients must be configured according to the ISP Redundancy mode you've chosen so that hosts use the proper route to reach your rule listeners. TMG Integrated NLB and WPLB functionality is effectively unchanged by the ISP Redundancy configuration. Your planning considerations deal strictly with the DNS configuration for each ISP Redundancy option.

When ISP Redundancy is configured for ISP failover, it operates in what is commonly referred to as *active-passive* mode, meaning that only one ISP link is operating at any time. In this mode, your publishing rules may have listeners configured to listen on one or both ISP connections, but only one ISP connection actually processes incoming traffic. Because only one ISP connection accepts traffic at any time, the DNS structure serving those clients must be agile enough to change the responses it provides when the ISP connection changes. The primary concern for this scenario is the time it takes for DNS record changes to be recognized by the rest of the Internet. Contrary to popular belief, DNS records do not "propagate" across the Internet. Instead, each DNS server that holds a copy of the record will query the DNS server that is authoritative for that record (or the nearest forwarding DNS server) for updates to that record. If the Time-To-Live (TTL) for that record is long (for instance, 1 day), it can take several days for the Internet to realize that this record has changed. This is one reason host TTL is made extremely short for those hosting companies that use DNS Round-Robin for their high-availability or geographic-targeting solution.

When ISP Redundancy is configured for ISP load-balancing, it operates in what is commonly referred to as *active-active* mode, meaning both links are operating at the same time and traffic is shared between them according to the load factor you assigned. In this mode, your publishing rules may have listeners operating on one or both ISP connections. The DNS records relevant to the Forefront TMG listeners determine which listeners receive traffic from remote clients. Figure 5-9 illustrates ISP load-balancing.

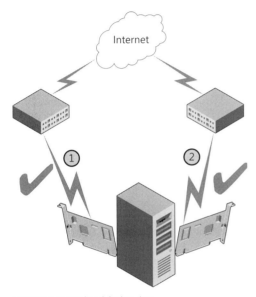

FIGURE 5-9 ISP load-balancing

High Availability from TMG to Published Web Servers

Although the Forefront TMG firewall integrates with NLB to provide an out-of-box high-availability solution for traffic destined to TMG itself, you cannot configure NLB at the TMG server array to provide high availability for traffic that TMG originates. For traffic sourced from TMG itself, other means of high availability are required, such as WPLB, NLB at the published server farm, or third-party solutions deployed between the TMG array and the destination server farm. We'll discuss NLB deployment and configuration in more detail in Chapter 8.

As noted previously, WPLB can use either IP-affinity or HTTP-cookie affinity, but not both simultaneously. Unlike NLB, WPLB does not provide *no-affinity* functionality. The effectiveness of cookie-affinity is completely dependent on the client's ability to process cookies properly. If the client application cannot process cookies properly, WPLB can only be effective if IP-affinity is used. Because WPLB deals with handling traffic to the published applications and

NLB is handling traffic sent to the TMG array, the two are generally compatible when properly configured and all points in the communication (client to TMG to server) can participate properly.

> **NOTE** Because WPLB is provided by a Web filter, and this Web filter is built and configured only for incoming Web requests, WPLB functionality is only available for traffic handled by Web Publishing Rules.

Designing High Availability for Access Rules

When TMG operates as a forward Web proxy for hosts on protected networks, the question of client- versus server-based high availability becomes even more complex, especially when dynamic proxy configuration is employed. Many articles, blogs, and forum postings tout the use of client-side Cache Array Routing Protocol (CARP) as a cheap load-balancing technique, but this is actually much less effective or reliable than DNS Round-Robin and may even create additional problems if you have chosen to use other high-availability techniques for this traffic.

> **MORE INFO** CARP will be discussed in detail in Chapter 16, "Caching Concepts and Configuration."

External Network

Although it's not generally a best practice from a security standpoint, many IT administrators will co-locate a server application on the firewall in an effort to save deployment costs. Most often, this sort of deployment is seen in a branch office scenario where cost containment is a higher priority than network security best practices or application isolation. In these cases, Access Rules can be used to allow traffic from remote hosts to the application hosted on TMG. In some cases, Access Rules do not provide the same level of traffic protection as do server- or Web-Publishing rules due to the way TMG application filters process the traffic. Therefore, if you wish to co-locate server applications on TMG, you're better off if you Web or Server publish the application.

That being said, you configure, maintain, and troubleshoot high availability for access rules on the external network exactly as you would for that high-availability technique when used with Web Publishing and Server Publishing across a NAT relationship.

Protected Networks

Traffic on protected networks offers a very different traffic context for TMG and the connecting clients. As such, your high-availability solutions need to be designed with these facts in mind during the design process.

Hosts communicating through TMG from protected networks use three distinct traffic contexts:

- **SecureNET client**   This client is the simplest to design high availability for because it is effectively unaware that the TMG array even exists in the traffic path.

- **Web proxy client**   This client is aware that a CERN proxy exists in the network and communicates to it in a specific way.

- **TMG client**   This client is aware that TMG exists on the network and uses a complex control protocol set to serve Winsock application requests.

SecureNET clients offer the simplest traffic flow management scenario for the high-availability designer. This client communicates to hosts in remote subnets using its local routing table. One problem you may encounter with this client traffic is that unless you use IP-affinity, each new connection created by this client may be sent to a different member of the TMG array. If the remote server uses source-IP as a security factor (many banking sites do this), and the application creates multiple connections to the remote server, those connections may be seen by the remote server as coming from multiple IP addresses and they all could be disconnected. Needless to say, this behavior can cause your users to apply some creative alternative definitions to the term *high availability*. Some third-party high-availability offerings are smart enough to match the destination IP to existing client connections and thus avoid this problem, but they are not common. NLB does not offer this functionality.

Web proxy clients complicate the high-availability scenario even further because they can operate in one of three ways:

- **Automatic detection**   This client configuration uses the WPAD protocol to discover the location of a proxy script. Once the WPAD client acquires the script, this client uses the script to determine how each individual request should be handled.

- **Configuration URL**   This client configuration is similar to the automatic detection in that it uses a proxy script acquired from TMG; the primary difference is that it does not use the WPAD protocol to discover the location of this script.

- **Static proxy**   This client configuration makes every request to a proxy as specified in the static configuration. Depending on the application, it may make all requests to a specific proxy, or it may communicate with different proxies depending on the protocol in use, such as HTTP, HTTPS (HTTP over SSL/TLS), FTP, and so on. This client configuration does not use a proxy script to determine which proxy to use for individual requests.

> **IMPORTANT**   Many Web applications may be configured as any or all of the preceding configurations. In some cases, as with Internet Explorer, Windows Media Player, and many applications based on WinHTTP (Outlook, RDP client, Windows Media, and many others), you can use Group Policy to provide standardized configuration of these applications across all clients in an organization. The Firefox browser even offers an .adm file that allows the Group Policy management of the browser configuration. This template is available from *http://sourceforge.net/projects/firefoxadm/*.

When a Web proxy client uses auto-detection or a configuration URL, the script provided by TMG provides data and code that allows the Web client application to decide whether a destination is local or remote and—if TMG is deployed in a CARP-enabled array—which array member should be contacted to provide the desired content according to the client-side CARP algorithm. What this boils down to is the fact that a Web proxy client application using client-side CARP may make requests to more than one host in the TMG array. Because by default the script lists the array members by IP address, the client-side CARP mechanism should never communicate to a Virtual IP address (VIP) in an NLB-enabled TMG array. In fact, it's best if you don't try to make your high-availability solution work in opposition to the client-side CARP; this creates additional intra-array traffic because the array member that receives the client's request uses the same CARP algorithm to acquire the content from the same server the client tried to contact in the first place. IP-specific load-balancing techniques are a poor choice for these client configurations.

When a client uses a static Web proxy client configuration, IP-specific high-availability solutions tend to work better since each Web proxy application will use the same configuration and so you can direct them to the (VIP) assigned. NLB enabled on the TMG internal network works well for these clients.

TMG clients complicate matters even further, since they acquire a configuration file regardless of whether they are configured for automatic or manual operation. This file tells the TMG client how it should communicate with TMG and which applications require special handling. Because traffic is handled on a per-application basis, it's entirely possible that one application could be operating as a SecureNET client, whereas another is handled as a Web proxy client and still another is handled as a TMG client.

When the TMG client operates with a TMG array, you should use DNS Round-Robin to spread the TMG client load across the array. Each time the TMG client needs to connect to the array, it will ask Windows to resolve the server name, and if the DNS server provides multiple IP addresses for the array FQDN, the TMG client will cycle through those IP addresses for each new application connection. Other high-availability solutions should use IP-affinity to ensure that TMG client traffic does not get split between multiple TMG array members.

ISP Failover

High availability for access rules that serve ISP connections should be handled exactly as you would with Web and Server Publishing across a NAT relationship. For all intents and purposes, they operate exactly the same way.

Joining the Firewall to a Domain or Workgroup

Over the years, administrators have discussed whether ISA Server should operate as domain members. This discussion now applies to the TMG as well. Some conservative, "old guard" firewall administrators think that having a firewall joined to the domain can compromise the security of the environment. No real proof exists regarding the unsecure state that a firewall domain membership could cause. The good news is that the debate that has been going on and on over the years is becoming less relevant and thus less important.

However, you might still hear statements such as: "If an attacker gains access to the firewall it owns your directory service." This is an untrue statement. No instances of an ISA firewall being compromised in a production environment have been reported, and we expect the same to apply to TMG. Attackers are focused on gaining access to the application services, not gaining access to firewall itself. Table 5-1 outlines the advantages and disadvantages of having TMG operating in the domain or workgroup.

TABLE 5-1 Domain vs. Workgroup

FOREFRONT TMG INSTALLATION	PROS	CONS
Domain–Joined	▪ More granular control for user access in forward and reverse proxy scenario. ▪ Full support for client certificate authentication as the primary authentication method. ▪ No need to have a certificate for connectivity with CSS. ▪ Support for Active Directory Group Policy. This can add another layer of protection when hardening the TMG computer by using Group Policy. ▪ Enhanced security while publishing services, such as Exchange Server by using Kerberos Constrained Delegation.	▪ If your TMG Server is located in a Perimeter network in front of another firewall, you need to allow more protocols through it to allow communication with the domain.
Workgroup	▪ If the firewall is compromised, the directory services might not be affected.	▪ Requires additional overhead for administration because a certificate is required if CSS is installed in Workgroup.

FOREFRONT TMG INSTALLATION	PROS	CONS
	■ Even if Active Directory is compromised, the firewall might not be compromised because it isn't part of the domain.	■ Doesn't have the same flexibility to use domain users and groups for outbound access. ■ Can't use client certificates as the primary authentication method. ■ User accounts are created on the firewall itself to allow intra-server communication. ■ Doesn't support Active Directory Group Policy. ■ TMG client authentication requires account mirroring on TMG

Although this table gives you a set of comparative parameters, in some scenarios you will see TMG implemented in a workgroup. Most of the time this happens because of one of the following reasons:

■ A lack of information about the real benefits of having the TMG as a domain member

■ A back-to-back firewall scenario where TMG (firewall and CSS) is placed between two third-party firewalls and the firewall administrator wants to avoid opening RPC and other port from Forefront TMG to the internal network

■ A company security policy that determines that no device that faces an untrusted network can be part of the corporate domain

Among the preceding arguments, the most understandable one from a political and sociological perspective is the last one, because it involves something that usually comes from management and is not based on technical facts. You can work around the other two arguments if the security administrator has a good understanding of the benefits of deploying the TMG as a domain member.

Summary

When you plan your TMG deployment, you have two choices: Design the network around the TMG deployment or fit TMG into an existing network structure. Because the highest probability is that TMG will have to fit an existing structure, you've most likely already had the opportunity to think through the requirements of your network and high-availability needs and match your TMG deployment to them. Now that you know the elements that you need to address prior to choosing your network template, you can start planning your migration. In the next chapter you will learn how to migrate from ISA Server 2004 or ISA Server 2006 to TMG.

## CHAPTER 6

Migrating to TMG

- General Considerations **87**

- Scenarios **90**

- Example Checklists **96**

- Example Migration from ISA 2006 SE to TMG 2010 EE Forward Proxy Scenario **99**

- Summary **105**

As with any change in network services, a plan that guides you through the migration process must be created and vetted before any changes can actually take place. The TMG product team placed a high priority on making this process as smooth and logical as possible. This chapter will help guide you through your deployment migration planning.

General Considerations

Anyone who has made the change from Proxy 2 to ISA 2000, from ISA 2000 to ISA 2004, or from ISA 2004 to ISA 2006 can probably regale you with tales of incomplete tools, failed results, and a general dislike for the overall process. In particular, an in-place upgrade was the most painful because of incompatibilities between storage locations or schema, operating system requirements, and so on.

Go No Further Until You Understand This!

Regardless of the starting and ending scenarios, if the current ISA or TMG deployment is displaying problems of any kind, you *must* resolve those problems before you attempt to migrate to the new deployment. Fully 80 percent of all cases answered by Microsoft Forefront Edge Customer Support Services are PICNIC problems indicated by computer, network, or traffic policy configuration errors. If the problem is duplicated to the new deployment (and the odds are very good that it will be), you will have only spent the time moving the problem from one deployment to the other. I'm sure this is not what you have planned for your migration goals.

This is also a good time to review your current traffic policies to determine whether you have duplications, inefficiencies, or "chaff" lying around from previous efforts. Performing this task before you start your migration can only help make your resulting deployment that much more efficient and predictable.

Base Software

You may recall from Chapter 3, "System Requirements," that TMG runs only on Windows 2008 SP2 or R2 x64. Because ISA Server only runs on Windows 2000 (ISA 2004 SE) or Windows 2003 x86, a complete server rebuild (or replacement if the processor is 32-bit) is required before TMG can be installed on it. Because the migration from ISA Server to TMG requires a completely new operating system, *an in-place upgrade to TMG is simply not possible.*

You must satisfy the following conditions for your migration plans:

- All array members must use the same operating system update level, beginning with Windows Server 2008 Service Pack 2.

- All array members must use the same Windows version. You may not mix computers running Windows Server 2008 (SP2) and Windows Server 2008 R2 in the same array.

Also, before you can begin your migration, you have to bring your ISA servers to the latest supported update level, as detailed in Table 6-1.

TABLE 6-1 Minimum update versions

ORIGINAL PRODUCT	REQUIRED UPDATE LEVEL
ISA Server 2004	Service Pack 3 (SP3)
ISA Server 2006	Service Pack 1 (SP1)
TMG MBE	RTM

Service Level

Because it's highly unlikely that any ISA deployment that is currently serving an organization's business needs can be out of service for an extended period, the best migration process is a rolling upgrade. A bare summary of this process is as follows:

- Build the base environment required.
- Configure the environment so that the new and old servers share the traffic load.
- Replace old array members with new ones as they are built.

We'll cover this in more detail later in this chapter.

If you don't have the resources to perform a rolling upgrade, you'll have to schedule downtime so that you can replace the current service with the new one. This process incurs greater risk than the rolling upgrade for two reasons:

- An in-place replacement requires that the service go offline. Because you will be time-limited by business needs, any problems encountered during the upgrade are potentially magnified if they cause you to exceed the defined service window.
- Any service outage that impedes business costs the organization money. How much money is lost depends on many factors, but in all cases, the net result will be a negative value. Regardless of the reason for the outage extension, it will be viewed negatively (and likely very loudly) by your users (and manager).

Granted, a rolling upgrade requires you to have at least one extra computer on hand for the duration of the upgrade, but the cost of this computer can be compared favorably to the cost of lost or delayed business transactions that this deployment currently serves—especially when it hosts organization communication services such as Exchange, Office SharePoint, or instant messaging.

If It Breaks

Although the TMG product team took all possible precautions to prevent installation or migration failure, stuff happens that even the most well-designed and well-executed code can't resolve. In any case, you should have a rollback plan in place for those situations where problem resolution is not successful and you need to revert to the old environment.

In the migration process descriptions that follow, critical reversal points are called out. You should define your plan of action for these points ahead of time so that if you should fall victim to Murphy's Law, you will have a clear idea how to get around it, or back off to your previous state.

Practice, Practice, Practice!

Nothing gets you prepared for a task like time spent thinking through the fine details of the process and most importantly, engaging in task simulation. For instance, one of the most commonly asked questions of any team responsible for performing backups is "How often do you simulate an emergency restore event?" As with validating a backup process by performing an emergency restoration, your migration plans must include repeated lab simulation with your partner teams so that you can identify weak or missing spots in the plan as well as any places in the process where failure can potentially render either or both deployments inoperable. Only by actually performing the migration can you truly understand how it needs to work.

Scenarios

Although the common use of the term *scenario* with respect to firewall deployments generally refers to egress versus ingress scenarios, in the context of migration, it also includes the starting and ending combinations. Table 6-2 summarizes the supported migration paths you can follow.

TABLE 6-2 Direct Migration Paths

FROM	TO			BASIC PROCESS
	TMG 2010 SE	**TMG 2010 EE***	**TMG 2010 EE**	
ISA 2004 SE SP3 ISA 2006 SE SP1	Yes	Yes		
ISA 2004 EE SP3 ISA 2006 EE SP1			Yes	export / import
TMG MBE	Yes	Yes		
TMG MBE (EBS)#	Yes			EBS R2 Wizards
TMG 2010 SE		Yes		EE PID entry

Note: An asterisk (*) indicates TMG 2010 Enterprise Edition Standalone Array. The pound sign (#) indicates Windows Essential Business Server (EBS).

You may notice from Table 6-2 that you cannot migrate directly from ISA Server Standard Edition (SE), TMG Medium Business Edition (MBE), or TMG 2010 SE directly to TMG Enterprise Edition (EE) EMS-managed arrays. This is because to migrate to an EMS-managed array, you must first upgrade to TMG Enterprise or Standard Edition; then you can join TMG to an Enterprise Edition EMS-managed array. There is no upgrade from TMG MBE on Windows Essential Business Server (EBS) without the use of the WEBS R2 upgrade wizards.

Publishing

Publishing scenarios present a unique set of challenges to a migration effort. You have to understand the traffic flow, the networking structure that allows it, and any configuration dependencies the rules and listeners present. The following migration criteria are the most interesting for migrating publishing scenarios.

Listeners

Collect the complete list of IP addresses used by each listener. Although it's true that the export/import process will carry these to the new deployment, you'll need to have this list handy for the DNS updates.

> **IMPORTANT** Although Server Publishing rules do not use explicitly defined *listeners* in the same way as Web Publishing rules, each Server Publishing rule does define a listener.

Certificates

Export any certificates currently used by Web listeners, Web Publishing rules, and Web Chaining rules. If the currently installed certificates or their private keys are not exportable, you will need to acquire the original (or identical) certificates with a private key so that you can satisfy the certificate requirements for those rules in the new deployment.

Network Structure

Make sure the network routing structure allows the published servers to respond to the client traffic sent through the new deployment. This may mean changing the network routing structure or modifying the routing tables at the published servers (or both). If the publishing rules are defined so that the published server sees the traffic as sourced from the originating client IP address, your rules will fail if the published servers cannot use the new deployment as their default route back to the client.

Dial-In VPN

DoD VPN scenarios require extra consideration because although the VPN services in Windows 2008 are very similar to those provided in Windows 2000 and Windows 2003, they are also very different from their predecessors in some significant ways.

Network Access Protection (NAP) vs. Quarantine Scripts

With ISA Server Dial-in VPN, you may have opted for using quarantine scripts to help mitigate threats posed by VPN users. This mechanism is still functional with Windows 2008 and TMG, but you also have the ability to take advantage of Network Access Protection (NAP) to perform the same task in a much more secure and granular way. You are not forced to change your VPN deployment to use NAP-based connections as a mandatory step in the migration process, but you may want to consider this as a post-migration change to increase your VPN connection security.

IP Assignments

Because you will create traffic conflicts if different VPN servers are assigning identical IP addresses to connecting clients, you will have to provide unique IP sets to each VPN server in the new deployment. If you have any rules that are IP-specific for VPN clients, you will need to change them in the new deployment to accommodate the IP differences for those clients. If you are changing subnets for VPN clients, you should also verify that users who are assigned an IP address based on their Active Directory configuration are assigned an IP address within the new subnet.

Network Structure

Make sure the network structure allows the VPN clients to reach the VPN servers as well as the hosts in the protected networks. Also, you need to ensure that the hosts in the protected network can respond to the VPN clients. As with other scenarios, this may mean changing the routing tables at the VPN clients, computers in protected networks, or both.

Name Services

Make sure that the DNS or WINS services used by the VPN clients direct them to the proper destinations. If they are directed to the old proxy deployment, or to services that have not yet been updated to understand the new routing structure, those users will get a nasty surprise (and you will get an angry call) when they try to reach those destinations.

Site-to-Site (S2S) VPN

S2S VPN scenarios require extra consideration for exactly the same reasons as Dial-in VPN scenarios. Additionally, you have to coordinate the migration to the new deployment with the remote sites so that you impact their service as little as possible.

Network Structure

Make sure the network structure allows the VPN clients to reach the VPN servers as well as the hosts in the protected networks. Also, you need to ensure that the hosts in the protected network can respond to the VPN clients. As with other scenarios, this may mean changing the routing tables at the VPN clients, computers in protected networks, or both.

IP Assignments

You should decide whether you want to duplicate the IP assignments used for each S2S connection or to create new assignments. If you choose to use new subnet assignments, you must ensure that the remote site is aware of and activates these changes or the connection to the new VPN servers may fail.

Name Services

As with Dial-in VPN clients, you must ensure that the DNS or WINS services used by the clients in each site direct them to the proper destinations. If they are directed to services that have not yet been updated to understand the new routing structure, those connections will fail or at the very least, produce incorrect results.

Proxy

Odds are good that because TMG is targeted at protecting clients from the evil bits on the Internet that you are planning to use TMG to replace an existing proxy service.

Network Structure

Make sure the network routing structure allows the clients to reach the new deployment. If you have SecureNET clients that need to reach destinations in a network isolated by TMG, you need to ensure that they can reach their destination through the new deployment. As with publishing scenarios, this may mean changing the network routing structure or modifying the routing tables at the published servers (or both).

WPAD

If your current deployment makes use of automatic discovery, you will need to change the relevant DNS, DHCP, or perhaps even WINS records to send your clients to the new deployment. As noted in Chapter 15, "Web Proxy Auto Discovery for TMG," the TMG client is able to discover the TMG deployment through the use of an Active Directory "Winsock Proxy" attribute (AD Marker). The planning phase of your migration efforts is a good time to define those attributes. You also need to remember that the WPAD script itself is cached by the clients for at least one hour (ISA and TMG deliver it with a "cache-control: max-age=3000" directive). If you want to ensure that all clients use the new deployment after you change the network WPAD configuration, you may want to consider using a temporary logon script that deletes all WPAD scripts on the user's computer.

> **NOTE** The *delete wpad* command to use in a logon or startup script is *del \wpad*.dat /s*.

Certificates

Make a list of any certificates currently used by Web Chaining rules. If the currently installed certificates or a private key is not exportable, acquire the original (or identical) certificates with a private key so that you can satisfy the certificate requirements for those rules.

TMG Client (TMGC)

If you are currently using the ISA Server 2004 or ISA Server 2006 Firewall Client in your deployment, you can continue to use it after you migrate to TMG. The time frame and priority for migrating from the FWC to the TMGC should be determined by the importance you place on HTTPS inspection notification and improved WPAD security offered by the AD marker feature included in the TMGC.

> **MORE INFO** The functional and supported combinations for ISA Server, Forefront TMG, Firewall Client, and TMG Client are discussed in *http://blogs.technet.com/isablog/archive/2009/11/03/forefront-tmg-client.aspx*.

Common Points

Regardless of the scenarios involved, some points are relevant to each and must be accounted for in your migration plans.

Domain Membership vs. Workgroup

Because TMG incurs exactly the same requirements for user authentication as ISA does, if your migration plans include changes in the authentication requirements for publishing or proxy traffic, you must determine whether the new deployment must act as part of the domain. If domain membership is required, you must join the computer to the domain before you install TMG on the computer. If TMG is to face the Internet directly, you should wait to make that connection until after TMG is installed.

Coordination

Unless you own the whole network and all of the services it provides (you don't sleep much, do you?), you will have to collaborate with other people to ensure that the migration occurs as smoothly as possible. This means that you should build a test lab to evaluate your plan, and you need to include all related teams in the planning and testing process. Also, you need to ensure that the executive suite is included in defining the migration process and schedule. It's quite likely that one or more of them has plans that interfere with your schedule, and the last thing you need is an angry CFO breathing down your neck as you try to restore a much-needed service.

Performance and Scale

Although it's true that 64-bit Windows Server 2008 offers much better performance and scalability than 32-bit Windows Server 2003, and TMG is expected to improve on ISA performance and scale, you should not assume any specific value for this difference. You need to perform testing to gain some idea of the capacity of *your* proposed TMG deployment based on the intended traffic profile and the TMG features you use. Enhanced Malware Protection (EMP), Network Inspection System (NIS), and URL Filtering all increase the requirements on the CPU, memory, and in the case of EMP, the disk for content caching during scanning. Each of these adds latency to the overall throughput, so a TMG computer given the same CPU and memory resources as the previous ISA computer may actually perform less well under high demand.

> **NOTE** At the time this chapter was written the TMG performance team was still perfecting the guidance and tools for TMG. These should be available on TechNet at or shortly following TMG release.

Name Resolution

More often than not, the applications trying to reach the published services have to resolve a name to an IP address. One thing you may want to do prior to changing the DNS entries to represent the new deployment is to change the time-to-live (TTL) in the current DNS records. Doing so will allow you to realize a faster changeover from the old service to the new because the client computers will need to refresh their local name caches faster. In general, a TTL of 10 to 30 minutes is preferable. Any less than that, and you greatly increase the number of queries to your DNS servers. Any more than that and you will have to wait that much longer before you can even consider examining the deployments for connection changes. After you're satisfied that the migration is complete, you can change the DNS-relevant DNS records to their former TTL.

Load-Balancing (LB)

In general, the easiest way to migrate services from one load-balanced deployment to another is to add the new service to the LB technology, then slowly remove the old deployment from the LB until only the new deployment is servicing connections. Depending on the LB technology, additional methods may be required.

HARDWARE LB

Unless you manage this service, you will have to coordinate this part of the migration with the team that manages this service. You should collaborate with this team to create the migration plan, the testing criteria, and the test lab. Exactly how you perform this planning and testing will depend on the devices used and the availability of the team that manages them.

WINDOWS NETWORK LOAD BALANCING (NLB)

Although it is technically possible to configure non-integrated NLB across disjoint arrays, doing so is not supported and actually provides inaccurate (if not service-debilitating) results. The best way to migrate from one NLB deployment to another is to do the following:

- "Merge" the two deployment VIPs using DNS RR.
- Drainstop each server in the old deployment one by one.
- Remove the old service VIP from the DNS RR set once the new array is taking load.

DNS ROUND-ROBIN (RR)

DNS RR is the easiest form of LB to migrate because it's a simple matter of changing DNS records to reflect the new service hosts. This LB technique is also the slowest to drainstop because it depends on the client's ability to update the DNS cache.

Example Checklists

The scenario depicted in Figure 6-1 defines the simplified traffic profile for the example migration scenario. The SIP protocol path is an addition to the services deployment because TMG supports this protocol while ISA Server does not.

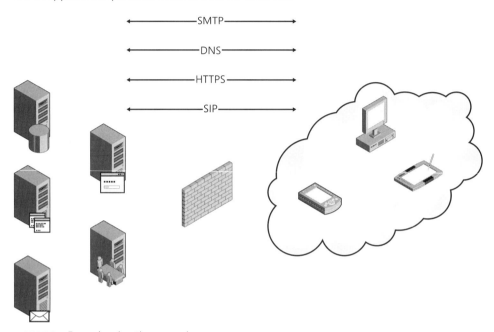

FIGURE 6-1 Example migration scenario

Tables 6-3, 6-4, and 6-5 illustrate basic ownership relationships and a typical scheduling order for some of the migration tasks.

TABLE 6-3 Example Owner Checklist

TEAMS AND SERVICES					
TEAM AND LEAD		**WEB SERVICES AND OWNER**		**NON-WEB SERVICES AND OWNER**	
Networking	Kim				
Name Services	Carol			DNS	Markus
AD	Tad				
Mail	Alice	OWA, EAS, OA	Dil	SMTP	Sven
Web	Jesper	SharePoint	Sandeep		
Communications	Patrick	OCS	Phil		

TEAMS AND SERVICES			
TEAM AND LEAD		**WEB SERVICES AND OWNER**	**NON-WEB SERVICES AND OWNER**
Human Resources	Zwie	HRWeb	Liz	
Accounting	Tommy	Expense Tool	Maria	
Simulation Lab	Josh		Lori	Yun-Feng
ISA/TMG	Gary		Dorena	Arno
Executive	Diliana			

TABLE 6-4 Example Global Task Checklist

SUMMARY PROCESS (NOT NECESSARILY IN ORDER)				
TASK	**OWNERS**	**EST. TIME**	**DEPENDENCIES**	**COMMENTS**
Export ISA configuration	Gary	1 hour	None	Occurs nightly using script.
Collect certificates	Gary	2 hours	Off-hours	Prefer to avoid service outage.
Build Test lab	Josh, Lori, Yun-Feng	1 week	Hardware, licenses for virtual deployments, certificates	Service owners must be responsive to queries.
Validate test lab	All service owners	4 days	Services team availability	Blocking issues to be raised immediately.
Lab service testing	All service owners	3 weeks	Network Duplication	Perform TMG testing first.
Order dependency begins here				
Build TMG array	Gary, Dorena, Arno	1–2 days	Lab test 50 percent complete, certificates, IP assignments	Use lab TMG config export; adjust IPs as necessary.
Migrate Web mail	Gary, Tommy	1 day	TMG lab 100 percent TMG deployment 100 percent	50 percent of users migrated.
Migrate OCS, SharePoint	Gary, Phil, Sandeep	1 day	Web mail 100 percent	50 percent of users migrated.
Migrate HRWeb, Expense tool	Gary, Maria, Liz	2 days	OCS, SharePoint 100 percent	50 percent of users migrated.

SUMMARY PROCESS (NOT NECESSARILY IN ORDER)

TASK	OWNERS	EST. TIME	DEPENDENCIES	COMMENTS
Migrate DNS	Gary, Markus	1 day	HRWeb, Expense 100 percent	DNS Load to 50 percent.
Migrate SMTP	Gary, Sven	1 day	DNS load 100 percent	Update SPF, MX records.
Change DNS records	Markus	4 days	New Services load 50 percent	
Monitor new services	All service owners	3 weeks	Services migration	Errors require preventive action plan or exec exception.
Decommission old array	Gary, Arno, Dorena	2 days	Lab test 50 percent complete	Use lab TMG config export; adjust IPs as necessary.
Party time	All	All day and night	Migration completed	

TABLE 6-5 Example TMG Buildout Checklist

FIREWALL MIGRATION PROCESS – IN PROCESS ORDER

TASK	OWNERS	EST. TIME	DEPENDENCIES	COMMENTS
Build EMS computer	Dorena	1 hour	Active Directory, hardware	Perform state backup, join to Active Directory.
Install EMS role	Dorena	1/2 hour	Computer state	
Build TMG computers	Arno	1 hr per server	IP assignments, certificates imported	Perform state backup, join to Active Directory.
Install TMG firewall roles	Arno	1/2 hr per server	License keys	Join to EMS array.
Import lab config	Arno	1 hour	EMS, lab sim	Verify state.
Verify deployment	Dorena, Arno	1 day	Build, import	**Blocking state**

This sample migration only examines a few publishing scenarios without any form of load balancing or redundancy and does not examine the potential for concurrent proxy and VPN services. You should perform the same sort of service and ownership devolution for those scenarios to determine process dependencies.

Each point in each one of the sample checklists could (and probably should) be expanded to a process checklist of its own so that the fine details of each process can be clearly examined for unexpected issues and potential blocking states that may require process reversal.

Example Migration from ISA 2006 SE to TMG 2010 EE Forward Proxy Scenario

In this example, the contoso.com forward proxy service is being migrated from an ISA Server 2006 Standard Edition (SE) deployment to a Forefront TMG Enterprise Edition deployment. Because the current servers are x32-based hardware, they must be replaced completely to deploy Windows Server 2008 and Forefront TMG. Figure 6-2 illustrates the deployment as it currently operates.

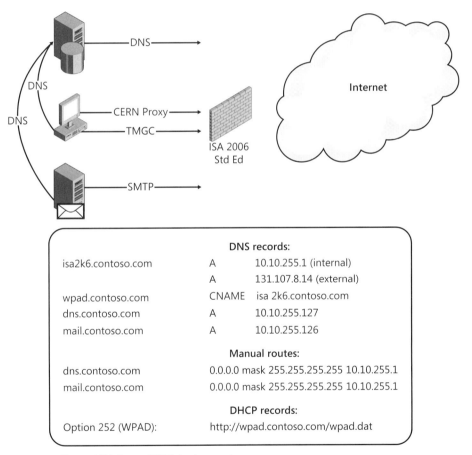

FIGURE 6-2 Current ISA Server 2006 deployment

Contoso management has decreed that the new deployment must improve in terms of service availability as well as traffic capacity and security versus the current ISA Server 2006 deployment. You also have the task of migrating to the new service with no user impact.

Because the TMG deployment design and migration methodology must improve on the current Internet access service availability and security while simultaneously minimizing the impact to users, you decide to:

- Deploy an array of three TMG computers using TMG 2010 Enterprise Edition.
- Include Integrated NLB as part of the service design.
- Use a rolling upgrade method.

You must consider the following client factors as part of this migration strategy:

- Web Proxy client automatic discovery and CFILE caching
- TMG Client automatic discovery and policy update cycle
- dns.contoso.com and mail.contoso.com service outage during default route reassignment

The client traffic must be transferred as smoothly as possible from the ISA 2006 service to the TMG 2010 service, so you will have to have both deployments operating concurrently. The migration major tasks checklist appears as defined in Table 6-6.

TABLE 6-6 Contoso firewall migration major steps

CONTOSO FIREWALL MIGRATION MAJOR STEPS				
TASK	OWNERS	ESTIMATED TIME	DEPENDENCIES	COMMENTS
Export ISA 2006 policies	Dorena	15 minutes	none	Must include password, server information
Build EMS computer	Dorena	1 hour	Active Directory, hardware, IP assignments	Perform state backup, join to Active Directory
Build TMG computers	Arno	3 hours	Active Directory, hardware, IP assignments	Perform state backup, join to Active Directory
Install EMS role; create TMG array	Dorena	1/2 hour	EMS computer state	Verify state
Import ISA 2006 policies	Dorena	1/2 hour	EMS installation	Verify state
Install TMG firewall roles	Arno	1/2 hour per server	Computer build, license keys	Verify state

CONTOSO FIREWALL MIGRATION MAJOR STEPS

TASK	OWNERS	ESTIMATED TIME	DEPENDENCIES	COMMENTS
Join TMG computers to EMS array	Dorena, Arno	2 hours	EMS, firewall role verification	
Verify deployment	Dorena, Arno	1 day	Build, Join, import	
Change default routes to 10.10.255.2	Gary, Markus, Sven	1/2 hour	TMG deployment	
Update WPAD DNS records	Gary, Markus	1/2 hour, 2 days *	SMTP, DNS validation	**Blocking states**
Decommission ISA 2006	Gary	1/2 hour	ISA2K6 carrying no traffic	
Enable NLB on Internal network; VIP = 10.10.255.1	Gary	1 hour	ISA 2006 removed	
Change default routes to 10.10.255.1	Gary, Markus, Sven	1/2 hour	NLB validation	
Configure URLF, EMP, HTTPSi	Gary	1 hour	DNS, SMTP traffic flow	

NOTE "2 days *" indicates that you should allow at least 2 days for the DNS WPAD record changes to take effect. This is especially true if you have a lot of users moving in and out of your environment on a daily basis. By allowing two or more days, you ensure that the majority of your clients are using the latest information.

The following processes may occur independently:

- ISA 2006 policy export
- EMS computer build and EMS role installation
- TMG computer build and TMG firewall role installation

All other tasks are process state–dependent. In other words, the dependency specification must be completed before that step may be taken. Although it's true that the default route, NLB, and DNS changes could occur simultaneously, it's equally true that the fewer changes you make at one time, the easier it is to identify and resolve problems you encounter during those changes.

Your interim deployment state is represented in Figure 6-3.

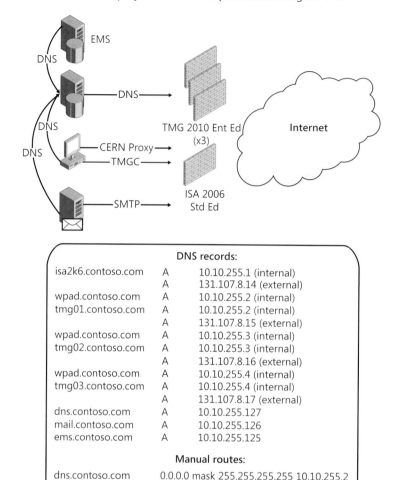

FIGURE 6-3 Interim TMG deployment state

To provide the best service availability, each TMG computer is registered in DNS with two names: wpad.contoso.com and tmg##.contoso.com, where ## represents the computer itself (01, 02, 03). Additionally, the internal network TMG client configuration was configured as shown in Figure 6-4.

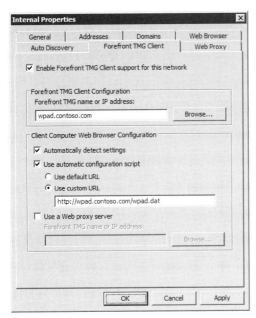

FIGURE 6-4 Internal network configuration

This technique was chosen because TMG clients only receive a single computer name as part of the wspad.dat and TMG client configuration data. Recall that when DNS holds multiple host records for a name, it will provide all of those IP addresses in response to that name query. When a computer requests resolution for the name wpad.contoso.com, the response from dns.contoso.com will include 10.10.255.2, 10.10.255.3, and 10.10.255.4. By mapping wpad.contoso.com to multiple IP addresses and configuring the TMGC settings to use the name wpad.contoso.com, the TMG client can take advantage of a small measure of redundancy across the TMG firewall array through DNS round-robin.

> **NOTE** Because the target name used by the TMGC when authenticating to the TMG computer will not represent the actual TMG computer account in Active Directory, authentication between the TMGC and the TMG computer will use NTLM, not Kerberos. You can read more about this limitation at *http://blogs.technet.com/isablog/archive/2008/06/26/understanding-by-design-behavior-of-isa-server-2006-using-kerberos-authentication-for-web-proxy-requests-on-isa-server-2006-with-nlb.aspx.*

No change to the DHCP WPAD record was necessary (or desired) because it specified a fully qualified name. The total changes to the domain DNS records are illustrated in Figure 6-5 and include:

1. Addition of each EMS and TMG computer IP addresses
2. Replacement of the isa2k6.contoso.com with the tmgnlb.contoso.com IP address

3. Replacement of the wpad.contoso.com CNAME record with one wpad.contoso.com record for each TMG firewall computer

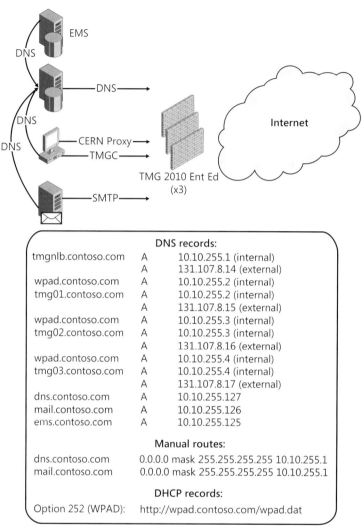

FIGURE 6-5 Final TMG deployment

By using DNS round-robin for wpad.contoso.com and configuring the TMG array to specify *wpad.contoso.com* in the TMGC configuration, you have satisfied the requirement to improve the firewall service availability for user traffic.

By using the TMG array NLB VIP as the default route for dns.contoso.com and mail.contoso.com, firewall availability for both DNS and outbound E-Mail services is increased threefold.

Because the ISA Server 2006 policies you imported cannot define the URL Filtering configuration, HTTPS Inspection, and Enhanced Malware Protection feature configuration, you must run the Web Policy Wizard. When this step is completed, you will have satisfied the final requirement for improving the overall security of the firewall/proxy service.

Summary

You've seen some examples of the considerations involved in planning a migration from one service deployment to another. Yours may be as simple as a single ISA SE deployment with a single Exchange and SharePoint publishing and outbound Internet services, or it may be multiple arrays separately serving outbound proxy, publishing, and VPN roles. Regardless of the scale, the main point is that if you spend the majority of your time in collaboration and planning, the execution will be much smoother as a result. The more time you put into the planning part of the process, the better you can react when (not if) something goes awry during actual execution. Chapter 7, "Choosing a TMG Client Type," will help you understand which client types are best suited for your environment and what changes you may need to create to support them.

## CHAPTER 7

Choosing a TMG Client Type

- Web Proxy Client   **107**

- SecureNET Client   **113**

- Forefront TMG Client   **119**

- Choosing the Right Client for Your Environment   **132**

- Summary   **137**

One important step during the planning phase of Forefront TMG is to identify your environment's TMG client-type requirements. Choosing the appropriate TMG client type involves many considerations, such as network topology and the types of software deployed in your organization. This chapter will help you understand the three TMG client types—the Web proxy client, the SecureNET client, and the Forefront TMG client—and how to use them in your production environment.

Web Proxy Client

The most popular Internet client application is the Web browser, and one of the most common enterprise deployment scenarios for this application is configuring it to use a Web proxy device for Internet access. Any client that sends CERN proxy requests to TMG is considered a Web proxy client.

A number of today's Web applications are Web proxy–aware. This means that you can configure these applications to use a CERN-compliant Web proxy device for Internet access. Windows applications that need Internet access through a Web proxy can use the *WinHTTP* application programming interface (API) to allow access through CERN-compliant Web proxies.

> **MORE INFO**   For more information about the *WinHTTP* API, see the following MSDN
> page: *http://msdn.microsoft.com/en-us/library/aa382925(VS.85).aspx.*

WinHTTP is not the only API that you can use to develop a CERN-compliant, Web proxy–aware application; applications can use many mechanisms to take advantage of Web proxy functionality. For example, the Microsoft .NET Framework provides the *WebProxy* class, which you can use to configure Web proxy settings. This class contains proxy settings used by the *WebRequest* class to determine whether a Web proxy is used to send requests to it.

The following code offers an example of using the *WebProxy* class in the C# language, where you can manually specify the proxy server for the application:

```
WebProxy proxyObject = new WebProxy("http://proxy:8080/",true);
WebRequest req = WebRequest.Create("http://www.fabrikam.com");
req.Proxy = proxyObject;
```

In the preceding example, the Web proxy address is manually specified. However, in a real application it is not a good idea to hard-code the proxy server address—that can cause problems for the end user because the Web proxy name can change. You should create a graphical interface where the user can specify Web proxy settings or retrieve Web proxy settings from Internet Explorer.

> **MORE INFO**   To understand how to use WinINet API to set proxy settings use the code sample from KB226473, which can be found at *http://support.microsoft.com/kb/226473*

In the Windows operating system, WinINet stores settings that are used for Web proxy purposes in the registry. If you change Internet Explorer settings, WinINet updates the following registry key:

HKEY_CURRENT_USER\SOFTWARE\Microsoft\windows\CurrentVersion\Internet Settings.

For example, the registry is updated when you change the following settings, as shown in Figure 7-1.

- **ProxyEnable**   If this DWORD value is 0, the browser should access the Internet directly. If the value is 1, the browser is using a proxy for Internet access.
- **ProxyServer**   This REG_SZ value specifies the name and port used by the proxy server.
- **ProxyOverride**   Use this REG_SZ value to manage the addresses that are consider local and should not pass through the proxy server.

If *ProxyEnable* is 0, the application uses the WinINet function *INTERNET_OPEN_TYPE_DIRECT*, which means the application won't use a Web proxy and will access the Internet directly. If the developer doesn't want to deal with manual proxy configuration, the application can also use the current registry settings for proxy by using the *INTERNET_OPEN_TYPE_PRECONFIG* access type.

> **MORE INFO**   For more information on WinINet functions and how they work, see *http://msdn.microsoft.com/en-us/library/aa383630(VS.85).aspx.*

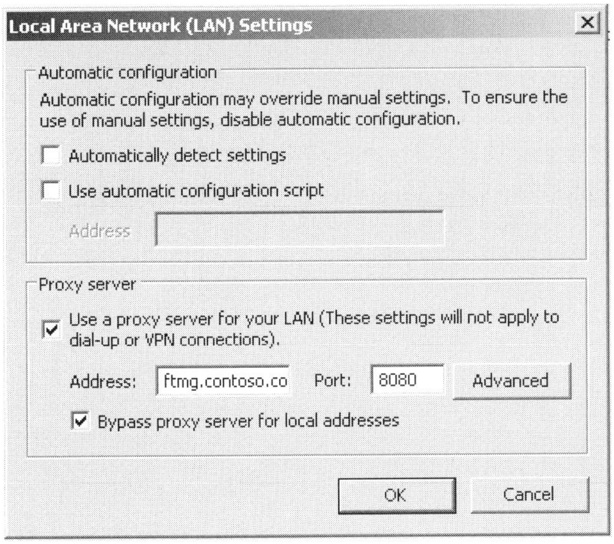

FIGURE 7-1 Internet Explorer proxy settings

How the Web Proxy Client Works

Many applications can act as a Web proxy client. However, the Web browser is the most commonly used application configured to do so. The following example uses a Web browser to demonstrate how a Web proxy client sends an HTTP request to TMG. In this example, the Web browser is configured to use TMG as a Web proxy and a user tries to access *http://www.contoso.com*.

The client sends an HTTP GET request to TMG on the listening port for Web proxy client requests. By default, TMG is configured to enable Web proxy client connections on TCP port 8080. After TMG receives the connection from the Web proxy client, the Microsoft Firewall service checks its access rules to determine which rules apply to the predefined HTTP protocol definition (port 80). This determines whether a request is allowed or denied from the source to the destination host.

> **MORE INFO** For more information about HTTP Protocol see Chapter 32, "Exploring the HTTP Protocol."

While performing this check against firewall policy, the Firewall service may perform forward DNS name resolution to determine whether an IP address–based rule applies to the request. If the request is allowed, the Firewall service forwards the request to the Web proxy filter, which connects to the destination server on the port specified in the URL (port 80 by default).

TMG performs application-layer filtering for HTTP requests from Web proxy clients. Figure 7-2 shows the core components used by TMG for this request.

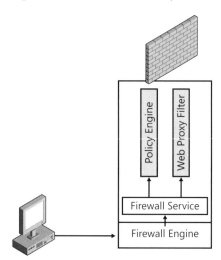

FIGURE 7-2 TMG core components used for processing HTTP requests from Web proxy clients

The following sequence is used when a Web proxy client requests a HTTP resource. However, if the user is trying to use the HTTPS protocol (HTTP over SSL) in a URL, the sequence is slightly different. Any CERN-compliant Web browser starts SSL connection requests by sending an *HTTP CONNECT (CONNECT host_name:port HTTP/1.1)*, followed by these steps:

1. The browser sends an *HTTP CONNECT* request to TMG's Web proxy listener.

2. The Firewall service checks firewall policy to determine whether the request may be sent from the source (client) to the destination (Web server) using the HTTP protocol.

3. Assuming that the request is allowed, the Firewall service forwards the request to the Web proxy filter.

4. The Web proxy filter determines whether the port specified in the *CONNECT* request is included in a tunnel port range defined in TMG. (By default, only TCP port 443 is allowed for SSL connections; if an alternate port is required, TMG's tunnel port range must be extended.) If the port number requested by the client is allowed, the Web proxy filter connects to the destination host on that port.

5. The request is sent to the destination host.

6. When this operation succeeds, TMG responds with an HTTP 200 status code to inform the client that the connection has been established.

TMG then goes into tunnel mode so that the SSL handshake can proceed between the client and destination server. Figure 7-3 illustrates these steps.

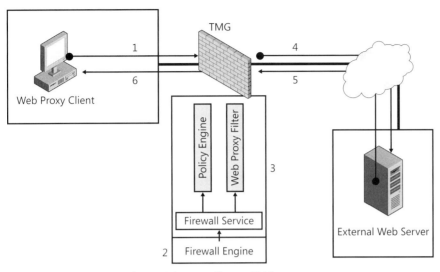

FIGURE 7-3 HTTPS request from Web proxy client to TMG

During this process the client sends encrypted packets to TMG on the Web proxy listener and TMG forwards them to the destination server using the port specified in the *CONNECT* request.

> **IMPORTANT** By default only two ports are allowed by TMG for SSL Tunnels: TCP port 443 and TCP port 593. If you need to add more ports, use the script provided in KB283284 (*http://support.microsoft.com/kb/283284*) or the script at ISATools.org (*http://www.isatools .org/tools/isa_tpr.js*).

Server-Side Configuration

By default, TMG already enables access for Web proxy clients located on the default internal network. The default listening port is TCP port 8080. You can confirm this by following these steps:

1. Open the Forefront TMG Management Console.
2. Expand the Forefront TMG (Server Name) node in the left pane.
3. Click Networking node in the left pane and then click the Networks tab in the middle pane. Click the Internal network.
4. Click Edit Selected Network in the right pane.
5. In the Internal Properties dialog box, click the Web Proxy tab (Figure 7-4).

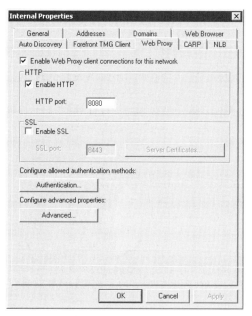

FIGURE 7-4 Web proxy configuration in the Forefront TMG Management console

When to Use the Web Proxy Client

You need to consider some key points when planning what type of TMG client configuration you should use. Table 7-1 lists common network requirements and how the Web proxy client can address them.

TABLE 7-1 Achieving Network Needs with TMG Web Proxy Client

NETWORK REQUIREMENTS	DEPLOYMENT OPTION	GENERAL NOTES
Centralized configuration and deployment	Automatic deployment of Internet Explorer proxy settings through Group Policy.	Not all browsers support GPO deployment.
Automatic configuration	By using Web Proxy Autodiscovery Protocol (WPAD), you can configure automatic deployment of browser settings.	Many browsers support WPAD.
Platform independence	The Web proxy client configuration is platform-independent because the only requirement is that the application be CERN-proxy aware.	Configuration details are dependent on the application.

NETWORK REQUIREMENTS	DEPLOYMENT OPTION	GENERAL NOTES
Authentication	The Web proxy client supports Basic, Digest, Kerberos, and NTLM authentication.	Internet Explorer 7 or higher supports Kerberos authentication.
		Not all applications that support Web proxy configuration will support authentication, or all types of authentication.
Backup route	This is also achieved by using WPAD. You can configure a backup route in case TMG is unavailable.	You can use another TMG Web proxy for a backup route or another device that allows Internet access.
Auditing	Because the Web proxy client supports authentication, the user name will be recorded in TMG's logs, allowing later auditing capabilities.	To achieve this you also need to put policies in place that require users to authenticate before accessing the Internet.

MORE INFO Chapter 15, "Web Proxy Auto Discovery for TMG," will also discuss Group Policy options for Web proxy client configuration with Internet Explorer.

Although using the Web proxy client configuration has many advantages, it also has some significant restrictions. The main restriction is protocol support. The Web proxy client supports the following protocols: Hypertext Transfer Protocol (HTTP), HTTP over SSL (HTTPS), and File Transfer Protocol (FTP) for download requests. (Computers configured as only Web proxy clients do not support uploads.) This means that if you need to access an application that uses Winsock, the Web proxy client won't work for that request.

SecureNET Client

Any computer with a TCP/IP networking stack can be configured as a SecureNET client. No additional software is required. The only requirement is that the default gateway is configured to route all traffic destined to the Internet through TMG. The traffic can be routed through a router if the computer is on a different subnet than TMG.

For TMG to support SecureNET clients, it needs at least two network cards.

SecureNET clients participate in one of two types of networks:

- **Simple Networks** In the configuration shown in Figure 7-5, the client and TMG are on the same subnet, and all that needs to be configured on the client is to point its default gateway to the IP address on the internal interface of the TMG firewall.

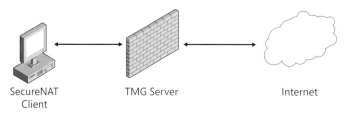

SecureNAT   TMG Server   Internet
Client

FIGURE 7-5 Simple Network configuration

- **Complex Networks** In the configuration shown in Figure 7-6, TMG and SecureNET clients are located on different subnets, with one or more routers separating the SecureNET clients from TMG. In this scenario, the last router in the chain between the clients and the TMG should have its default gateway pointing to the TMG's internal IP address.

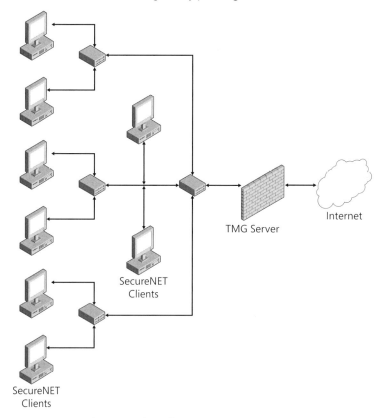

SecureNET
Clients

TMG Server   Internet

SecureNET
Clients

FIGURE 7-6 Complex Network configuration

How the SecureNET Client Works

TMG has no knowledge of the SecureNET client other than in the context of an IP address and the protocol used in the request. The Firewall service handles requests from SecureNET clients. SecureNET traffic is received by the TMG NDIS miniport, passed to the packet filter, and then passed to the Firewall service to determine whether the request is allowed or denied. At this point the Firewall service determines whether the request should be cached or the content should be returned from the cache. It then passes filters and filter extensions to the application layer to be inspected, if appropriate for the connection type. If the TMG policies allow this traffic, it is passed back to the TMG packet filter, where the original SecureNET client IP is replaced with an external IP address as defined by TMG-enhanced NAT and ISP Redundancy configuration.

A SecureNET client does not encrypt traffic other than as performed by the application that creates the traffic. Policies regarding protocol usage, destinations, and content allowed are applied to the request before it is filtered again by the application-layer filters.

A SecureNET client can handle complex protocols (which require multiple primary or secondary connections) only when an application filter is available to modify the protocol stream for the particular protocol. If there is no application filter for the complex protocol, one alternative is to configure the application to be a SOCKS 4 client of TMG's SOCKS 4 application filter. The SOCKS 4 option depends on whether the application supports SOCKS client configuration. Not many applications are designed to support SOCKS 4 proxies.

Name Resolution for SecureNET Clients

Unlike the TMG client (formerly the ISA Server Firewall Client) or the Web proxy client, the SecureNET client does not rely on TMG to perform name resolution on its behalf. The SecureNET client issues name lookup queries according to the client's IP addressing configuration and then connects to the destination server through TMG. Therefore, it is essential that DNS is properly configured on SecureNET clients so that they can perform both local and Internet host name resolution.

The most common DNS deployment scenario is to have a DNS server resolve all internal names and then use forwarders or root hints to resolve names outside the internal namespace. If the DNS server is also behind TMG, it is essential that TMG is properly configured to allow outbound DNS requests so that the internal DNS server can connect to a forwarder, or to all DNS servers on the Internet (if configured to use root hints).

One of the most common DNS issues seen with SecureNET clients is the client's inability to connect to either external or internal servers. If the SecureNET client points to a DNS Server that cannot resolve external host names, it should be obvious that connectivity to external servers will be affected.

On the other hand, many small organizations do not host their own internal DNS, in which case the SecureNET client points to an external DNS Server in its TCP/IP settings. Because the external DNS server does not have any information on any internal name space, it will not resolve any internal domain names and SecureNET clients won't be able to connect to internal resources using host names.

Another important DNS issue to avoid with SecureNET clients is *looping back* through the firewall to access internal resources. This generally happens when the Web server is published by the TMG firewall and the SecureNET client resolves the name of an internal Web server to an external IP address on the firewall. To better understand this scenario, take a look at Figure 7-7.

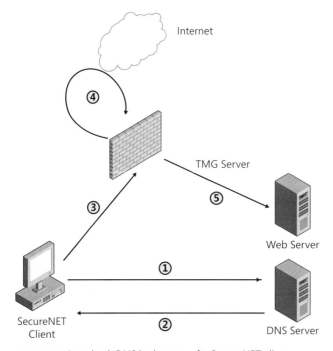

FIGURE 7-7 Loopback DNS in the case of a SecureNET client

In this scenario we have a Web server published by the TMG firewall. The SecureNET client resolves public names using a DNS server on the default internal network.

We can break this scenario into five steps:

1. The SecureNET client sends a DNS query request to the DNS server to resolve the Web server's name.
2. The DNS server replies with the TMG's external IP address.
3. The SecureNET client forwards the request to TMG's internal IP address.
4. The request is looped back from TMG's external IP address to TMG's internal IP address.
5. TMG forwards the request back to the internal Web server.

When the request is passed from TMG to the published Web server, the source IP address seen by the Web server is the client's internal IP address (if the rule is set to Requests Appear To Come From The Original Client). The Web server will recognize this as internal and respond directly to the SecureNET client. Because the client initiated the connection to the external IP address of the TMG firewall, the client won't accept the response traffic from the Web server (since this is seen as an unsolicited response from an IP address that no request was made to) and the traffic is dropped.

If the rule is set to Requests Appear To Come From The Forefront TMG Computer, it would work, but access will be slower and cause extra load on TMG because requests are needlessly looped back from external to internal.

You can avoid the loopback situation by using a split DNS infrastructure or by ensuring that the DNS server that the SecureNET client is configured to use resolves the name of the published Web server to the internal IP address of the Web server itself. Thus requests go directly to the Web server instead of being routed through TMG.

A split DNS infrastructure is helpful in cases where client computers are moved in and out of the network. The solution is to have DNS Servers configured in such a way that all clients on the internal network always resolve the internal IP addresses of the computers in the same network, but any computer on the external network resolves those same names to the external IP address of the TMG firewall, to provide access to published resources.

SecureNET Client Advantages

The SecureNET client is by far the easiest type of client to deploy. If for any reason corporate IT policy prevents you from installing software on networked computers or from changing Web browser settings (such as Web proxy client configuration), the SecureNET client is the solution. All you need to do is set the computer's default gateway to TMG's internal IP address (when the SecureNET clients are on-subnet to TMG). Or, when SecureNET clients are off subnet from TMG, configure the default gateway on the last router in the chain to point to the internal IP address of the TMG firewall, so that any traffic destined for the Internet is routed through TMG.

The SecureNET client is your only option for supporting non-Web protocols for non-Windows clients. This is because if you do not configure the client as a SecureNET client, the only other option to support non-Web protocols is to use the TMG client. The problem is that the TMG client is not supported on non-Windows clients. Thus, the SecureNET client is your only option for non-Web protocol support for non-Windows clients.

The SecureNET client is the only client type that supports non-TCP/UDP protocols. The two most common non-TCP/UDP protocols used by TMG administrators are ICMP and PPTP. PPTP uses a combination of TCP port 1743 and Generic Routing Encapsulation (GRE), which uses IP protocol 47. ICMP and GRE replace UDP or TCP as in the transport protocol part of the network stack and hence cannot be intercepted and evaluated by the TMG client software. To provide outbound support for these protocols the client must be configured as a SecureNET client.

The SecureNET client configuration is preferred for any server published to the Internet. In addition to accepting new inbound connections, published servers may need to initiate new outbound connections. To ensure that traffic is always routed back through TMG from the published server (because TMG sent the connection to the published server), it is simpler to have the published server configured as a SecureNET client to maintain the connection (because both sides of the TCP session must go through TMG).

SecureNET Client Disadvantages

The SecureNET client's biggest disadvantage is its inability to authenticate to TMG. The basic TCP/IP stack up to layer 4 (OSI model) does not provide for user authentication and requires an application component to send user credentials. Unlike the TMG Client or the Web proxy client configurations, which have built-in capability to send user credentials, for SecureNET clients you cannot enforce rules based on users or groups. The only way to provide restricted access for SecureNET clients is to set up rules based on source and destination IP addresses and domains.

SecureNET clients require TMG application filters to support complex protocols (protocols that require multiple primary or secondary connections). If an application filter is not available, you can configure a SOCKS4 proxy–aware application to use the TMG's SOCKS4 application filter. However, you still cannot force or restrict access based on users or groups when using the SOCKS4 proxy filter.

In the case of complex networks, where you have clients spread across multiple subnets, the SecureNET client is completely dependent on the network's routing infrastructure. Connections will fail if for any reason a router on the network isn't configured to route Internet-based traffic through TMG.

For a protocol to be allowed for SecureNET clients, TMG must have a corresponding protocol definition. This potentially increases your administrative overhead because you may need to create additional protocol definitions to support applications if a pre-built protocol definition isn't already configured on TMG.

Because the TMG firewall doesn't know the SecureNET client exists except in the context of a source IP address and protocol, and because you cannot enforce rules based on users and groups, if you want to log user activity you cannot do it by using the user name. The only way you can keep track of the activity is by using the client's source IP address. This doesn't work well in reports or for administrators who wish to keep a track of all Internet activity via reports based on users or user groups.

Table 7-2 summarizes the advantages and disadvantages of the SecureNET client.

TABLE 7-2 SecureNET Client Advantages and Disadvantages

SECURENET CLIENT ADVANTAGES	SECURENET CLIENT DISADVANTAGES
Easy to deploy and configure; does not require client-side software installation.	Dependent on environment's routing infrastructure.
The SecureNET client is the only way to provide support for protocols other than those handled by the Web proxy client configuration for non-Windows operating systems.	Does not authenticate to TMG; therefore, no user- or group-based access rules can be applied to SecureNET clients.

SECURENET CLIENT ADVANTAGES	SECURENET CLIENT DISADVANTAGES
The SecureNET client is the only way to provide support for any non-TCP or UDP protocol.	Support for complex protocols is available only if there is an application filter for that protocol.
The SecureNET client is the most reliable configuration for published servers because it ensures that the session is always maintained via TMG.	Logs will not include user information other than the client's source IP address.

Forefront TMG Client

Like the Web proxy and SecureNET clients, the TMG Client (TMGC) configuration depends as much on how the computer itself is configured as how the application software is written and behaves. Before you dwell too deeply on the concept of the TMGC, let's define its three components:

- **TMGC Winsock plug-in**   The TMGC Winsock plug-in extends the client host's Winsock functionality so that calls to Winsock, such as *gethostbyname*, *bind*, *connect*, and so on may be sent to TMG for handling on behalf of the client application.

- **TMGC Agent service**   The TMGC Agent is responsible for auto-detection, configuring the Winsock plug-in, and reporting status to the management applet.

- **TMGC management applet**   The TMGC management applet is a system tray applet that monitors the state of the TMGC agent service and provides configuration options for the user.

The TMGC Winsock plug-in is made up of two components:

- Winsock Transport Service Provider
- Winsock Namespace Service Provider

Now that we've defined all the pieces, you need to understand a bit about Winsock and how it's used by applications before the mechanisms provided by the TMGC can make sense.

Winsock: A Primer

Winsock is an abbreviation for *Windows Sockets*, which is the Microsoft implementation of Berkeley Sockets, a Unix-based standardized API for creating, managing, and using network connections. Winsock provides mechanisms for name resolution, data transfer between hosts, and other network management processes so that the application itself need not be bothered with the fine details of these processes. In the overall Windows networking model, Winsock operates above TCP/IP. Figure 7-8 provides a simplified diagram of this relationship.

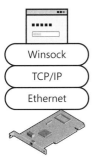

FIGURE 7-8 Winsock functional relationship

It's difficult to understand how an application uses Winsock because an application may never use Winsock directly. One such example is a typical Web browser, such as Internet Explorer. When Internet Explorer communicates on the network, it does so by calling another network abstraction layer called WinInet. WinInet translates HTTP and FTP calls made by Internet Explorer into Winsock calls. Figure 7-9 illustrates this concept.

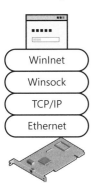

FIGURE 7-9 Browser relationship to Winsock

Applications written to execute as plug-ins to Internet Explorer, such as ActiveX controls or browser helpers, may use Internet Explorer, WinInet, or Winsock, depending on the network functionality they require. For example, WinHTTP is another Windows HTTP-based network library that some applications—such as Outlook 2003, Outlook 2007, and the RDP v6.1 client—employ through their use of RPC over HTTP calls. When the RPC team added HTTP to the transport options for the RPC protocol, they chose WinHTTP as their HTTP library. This relationship is depicted in Figure 7-10.

Complex protocol abstractions such as these make troubleshooting application misbehavior fairly difficult, regardless of the applications that use them, simply because good network troubleshooting techniques should include testing that eliminates the applications themselves whenever possible, rather then including them. RPC over HTTP in particular makes it difficult to abide by this practice simply because so few tools exist that understand the various layers involved and the traffic and error state translations that occur along the way.

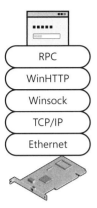

FIGURE 7-10 RPC over HTTP relationship to Winsock

When an application wants to communicate on the network, it has to exercise a series of Winsock API calls; the order and selection of these API calls depend on what the application needs to accomplish. This may be sending a status update or, as in the case of a Web browser, making a request to a Web service, and then receiving the results of that request. Although we will discuss some common Winsock calls and sequences to illustrate TMGC behavior in those cases, we will not delve into the finer details of Winsock programming.

Some of the more commonly used Winsock APIs include the following:

- **gethostbyname()**   This API is one of several that allow a Winsock application to obtain an address that corresponds to the name provided by the application.

- **gethostbyaddr()**   A Winsock application calls this API to obtain a host name from an address.

- **getaddrinfo()**   This API combines all of the functionality of *gethostbyname()* and *gethostbyaddr()* and extends the functionality of both.

- **socket()**   This API creates a socket for sending and receiving data.

- **bind()**   This API gives the application the means to reserve a socket for its exclusive use.

- **listen()**   This API allows the application to accept data received on a previously bound socket.

- **send()**   This function accepts a pointer to a data buffer that is to be sent to a predefined destination.

- **recv()**   This function receives data from a connected or bound and listening socket.

> **NOTE**   These are just a few of the many Winsock APIs. A complete list is available on MSDN at *http://msdn.microsoft.com/en-us/library/ms740673.aspx*.

What is interesting about an application that is handled by the TMGC is that as far as the application itself is concerned, the client host is a SecureNET computer; the application literally doesn't know the difference. This state is equal parts boon and bane, because it eliminates the need for application developers to write Winsock code with LSP in mind, but it also means that the application may find itself with a configuration it didn't expect.

Winsock Service Providers

For the TMGC to function with Winsock, it must have access to the application requests made to Winsock. This is made possible through Winsock extensions called *Layered Service Providers* (LSPs). LSPs extend Winsock functionality by allowing the programmer to write code as a dynamic-linked library (DLL) for specific behaviors such as name resolvers or traffic routers and adding them to Winsock by registering the DLL with Winsock. The Winsock *Service Provider Interface* (SPI) model defines specific APIs that are provided for and required of the custom DLL. The links between various service and namespace providers are maintained in the registry and referenced as the *Winsock catalog*. In the case of the TMGC, two service provider types are added to the Winsock catalog:

- **Transport Service Provider (TSP)**   This provider type extends Winsock functionality for all data-handling mechanisms such as *Open()*, *Bind()*, *Send()*, *Receive()*, and so on. When the TSP registers with Winsock, it tells Winsock which protocols it is able to process. The TMGC registers as a transport handler for TCP and UDP protocols.

- **Name Service Provider (NSP)**   This provider type extends Winsock name resolution mechanisms, such as *gethostbyname()* and *getaddrinfo()*. When the TMGC registers as a Name Service Provider, it informs Winsock that it wishes to be notified of any name- or address-resolution requests made to Winsock.

In all cases, Service Providers are registered with and used by Winsock in a database maintained in the Winsock catalog. You can see which providers are registered with Winsock by opening a command window and typing **netsh winsock show catalog**. The following code shows an example output. You must remember that the order in which service providers are registered in the Winsock catalog *does not* represent the order in which they were installed. It represents the order in which the providers wish to be called by Winsock.

```
C:\Users\jimmyjoebobalooba\Desktop>netsh winsock show catalog


Winsock Catalog Provider Entry
------------------------------------------------------
Entry Type:                        Base Service Provider
Description:                       Forefront TMG Client IPv4 Service Provider
                                   [TCP/IP]
Provider ID:                       {ADACE6A1-3BB1-11D0-A7CA-00A0248E631B}
Provider Path:                     C:\Program Files\Forefront TMG Client\FwcWsp.dll
Catalog Entry ID:                  1058
Version:                           2
```

```
Address Family:                    2
Max Address Length:                16
Min Address Length:                16
Socket Type:                       1
Protocol:                          6
Protocol Chain Length:             1

Winsock Catalog Provider Entry
-------------------------------------------------------
Entry Type:                        Base Service Provider
Description:                       Forefront TMG Client IPv4 Service Provider
                                   [UDP/IP]
Provider ID:                       {9CE7A941-3BB6-11D0-A7CA-00A0248E631B}
Provider Path:                     C:\Program Files\Forefront TMG Client\FwcWsp.dll
Catalog Entry ID:                  1060
Version:                           2
Address Family:                    2
Max Address Length:                16
Min Address Length:                16
Socket Type:                       2
Protocol:                          17
Protocol Chain Length:             1

Winsock Catalog Provider Entry
-------------------------------------------------------
Entry Type:                        Base Service Provider
Description:                       Forefront TMG Client IPv4 Service Provider for
                                   RSVP [UDP/IP]
Provider ID:                       {C057A6EE-181B-44F6-9173-CEADFF360A39}
Provider Path:                     C:\Program Files\Forefront TMG Client\FwcWsp.dll
Catalog Entry ID:                  1061
Version:                           2
Address Family:                    2
Max Address Length:                16
Min Address Length:                16
Socket Type:                       2
Protocol:                          17
Protocol Chain Length:             1

Winsock Catalog Provider Entry
-------------------------------------------------------
Entry Type:                        Base Service Provider
Description:                       Forefront TMG Client IPv4 Service Provider for
                                   RSVP [TCP/IP]
Provider ID:                       {49678D2B-BCEB-46A4-87BB-F3F9E11425B9}
Provider Path:                     C:\Program Files\Forefront TMG Client\FwcWsp.dll
```

```
Catalog Entry ID:              1059
Version:                       2
Address Family:                2
Max Address Length:            16
Min Address Length:            16
Socket Type:                   1
Protocol:                      6
Protocol Chain Length:         1


...
```

Winsock passes calls it receives from applications into each LSP based on their registered order in the catalog. Because an LSP informs Winsock which protocols and services it supports during registration, Winsock can decide during run time if an LSP is appropriate for a particular application request. For instance, if LSP1 in Figure 7-11 has registered as a TCP-only transport provider, Winsock doesn't notify LSP1 of any non-TCP traffic it may be processing.

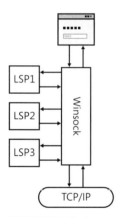

FIGURE 7-11 Block representation of Winsock LSP usage

An LSP can act as the authoritative handler for a service by telling Winsock that it should consider this request completed at this point. In many cases, the TMGC behaves this way because it needs to handle the request in a special way. When this occurs, it has the effect of functionally removing any LSP that may follow in the catalog. This can cause some interesting behaviors and is very difficult to troubleshoot under the best of conditions, because Winsock logging and tracing don't exist prior to Windows Vista. Even with Winsock tracing provided in Windows Vista and later, the data may be difficult to decipher if you don't know how the applications and LSP are designed.

> **NOTE** More information on Winsock Service Providers is available at *http://msdn.microsoft*
> *.com/en-us/library/ms740467(VS.85).aspx.*

LSP Conflicts

Many cases of network communication failures have been caused by various LSPs and their installers. In some cases, these were malware installed by nefarious persons; in other cases, they resulted from another LSP that was not intended to operate in collaboration with any other LSP. In still other cases, a corrupted Winsock catalog resulted from a failed or poorly written installation package. The Winsock programming model is complex enough for normal application usage; LSPs and their installation routines can create a complex interrelationship of dependencies and functionality that even the most seasoned Winsock programmer is hard-pressed to resolve. The good news is that if you find yourself in the unenviable position of having malicious LSP registration or a corrupted Winsock catalog, you can recover from this state by simply executing **netsh winsock reset** in a command shell. This restores the Winsock catalog Transport Service Provider database to its default state. If the TMGC is installed when you execute that command, you simply run a repair action to restore it to an operation state.

The TMGC as a Layered Service Provider

Like the ISA Server Firewall Client (FWC) before it, the TMGC registers as a Transport Service Provider and a Name Service Provider. During registration with Winsock, the TMGC informs Winsock that it supports directed IPv4 traffic for the TCP and UDP transport protocols. As a Name Service Provider, TMGC indicates support for the *gethostbyname*, *gethostbyaddr*, and *getaddrinfo* name service functions. In short, the TMGC supports TCP and UDP transports on IPv4 as well as common name resolution services. This means that the TMGC will not process any traffic that uses any IP protocol other than IPv4 or any transport protocol other than TCP or UDP.

Fun with Layered Service Providers

Things are rarely simple in network programming. In fact, even though an application might use an IP protocol other than IPv4 or a transport protocol other than TCP or UDP, TMGC may still have an impact on this application's ability to communicate because of the TMGC's role as a Name Service Provider combined with the way an application behaves based on its design and how it's used.

ping.exe

Ping.exe is a tool that tests network connectivity according to the client configuration and run-time options provided by the user. In this case, let's assume that your internal name resolution structure does not support resolving names outside of your network. If you were to use ping.exe to discover the IP address of *www.microsoft.com*, your results would appear as follows:

```
C:\Windows\system32>ping www.microsoft.com
Ping request could not find host www.microsoft.com. Please check the
name and try again.
```

If you install the TMGC on the protected client (we assume TMG is installed and configured) and repeat the same test, you'll see the following results:

```
C:\Windows\system32>ping www.microsoft.com

Pinging lb1.www.ms.akadns.net [207.46.193.254] with 32 bytes
of data:

Request timed out.

Request timed out.

Request timed out.

Request timed out.
```

This result tells us two things: The TMGC allowed ping.exe to resolve the name *www.microsoft.com* to an IP address, and even though ping.exe sent ICMP Echo Request packets to IP address 207.46.193.254, it never received a response to those requests. We can conclude from the successful name lookup that the TMGC has a functioning connection with TMG, even though the ICMP traffic was not passed. The reason ping.exe was able to resolve the name *www.microsoft.com* to an external IP address is that when ping.exe issued *gethostbyname* ("www.microsoft.com"), the TMGC recognized this name as being "not internal" and forwarded the request to TMG for resolution. TMG issued then its own *gethostbyname()* to Winsock on the server where TMG operates and returned the result of this request back to the TMGC, which then passed it back to ping.exe.

TMGC Configuration Data

TMGC discovers the TMG server and determines its own operational state and definitions of application behavior from data it obtains from TMG in two ways:

- **wspad.dat**   This is data obtained from TMG that defines various TMGC behaviors specific to individual applications. In Chapter 15, you'll see the details of the wspad.dat file.

- **TMGC Control Channel information request** This data duplicates much of the data provided in wspad.dat because TMGC may be using a static configuration and the data carried by the wspad.dat response is still necessary to TMGC operation.

NOTE By default, TMGC encrypts all control channel communications following initial channel setup and authentication. This makes evaluating TMC control channel behavior impossible with network analysis tools such as Network Monitor.

The configuration data TMGC receives from TMG is built upon several data points that you define during and after installation. Each non-VPN protected network has the capability of servicing Web proxy and TMG clients. Figure 7-12 shows the Forefront TMG Client tab of the default Internal Network Properties dialog box.

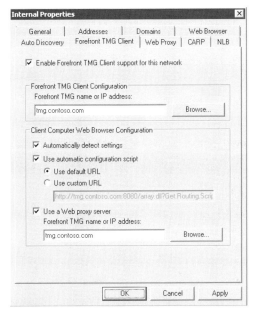

FIGURE 7-12 The Forefront TMG Client tab

The information in this tab is necessary for the proper operation of the TMGC. The name entered in the *Forefront TMG name or IP address* field must resolve to the IP address used by TMG on the network defining these settings. Otherwise, the TMGC will not be able to connect to TMG. Alternatively, you can enter the IP address used by TMG in this network to avoid name resolution issues. The disadvantage of this option is that if the TMG-owned IP address for this network ever changes, your TMGC-enabled hosts will no longer function. When TMGC requests wspad.dat or the configuration data via the control channel, the data it receives is based on the TMG configuration points outlined in Table 7-3.

TABLE 7-3 Network Properties of TMGC Configuration Data Mapping

NETWORK PROPERTIES	WSPAD.DAT	TMGC CONTROL CHANNEL
Forefront TMG Client tab		
Forefront TMG Name or IP Address	[Servers Ip Addresses] Name=tmg.contoso.com	[Servers Ip Addresses] Name=tmg.contoso.com
Automatically Detect Settings	Set Browsers to use Auto Detect=1	Set Browsers to use Auto Detect=1
Use Automatic Configuration Script	Set Browsers to use Auto Config=1	Set Browsers to use Auto Config=1
Use a Web Proxy Server	Set Browsers to use Proxy=1	Set Browsers to use Proxy=1
Configuration URL	Configuration URL=http://tmg .contoso.com:8080/array.dll?Get .Routing.Script	Configuration URL=http://tmg .contoso.com:8080/array .dll?Get.Routing.Script
Web Proxy tab		
HTTP port	WebProxyPort=8080	WebProxyPort=8080
Addresses tab	Not included	[Local Address Table] Range0=10.10.1.0–0.10.1.255 Range1=127.0.0.0–127 .255.255.255 Range2=224.0.0.0–255 .255.255.254
Domains tab	LocalDomains=contoso.com, .contoso.com	LocalDomains=contoso.com, .contoso.com

> **NOTE** Pay particular attention to the places where the TMG name is used in the configuration UI. This name must be resolvable to the IP address used by TMG for this network or else the TMGC and Web Proxy client's behavior will be erratic at best.

The remaining data sent in wspad.dat and the control channel configuration response includes data used by the TMGC to provide application-specific behavior. Figure 7-13 provides an example of the Forefront TMG Client Settings dialog box.

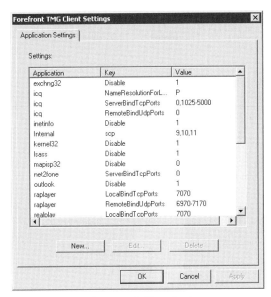

FIGURE 7-13 Forefront TMG Client Settings

All of the data contained in this dialog box provides specific information that tells the TMGC how to handle various Winsock requests from specific applications. The default settings provide tested configurations for such applications as excng32 (Exchange Client), icq (one of many peer-to-peer chat applications), and many others.

Along with the dynamic data acquired from TMG, the TMGC can also use static configuration data in the form of text files. The most common use for this functionality is to inform the TMGC that certain address ranges that are not actually part of the local network should be treated as if they were local addresses. This is most frequently used when the TMGC-enabled host has a VPN connection through or around TMG. Traffic to and from the remote network must not be processed by the TMGC or else it will never reach the remote VPN network. For the TMGC to understand that an address range such as a remote VPN network is "local," you must create a special file on the TMGC host computer called locallat.txt.

> **NOTE** You can find out more about the locallat.txt file and its placement on the TMGC host for various Windows versions at *http://support.microsoft.com/kb/268326*.

Example Winsock Usage without TMGC

Because the browser is our favorite example in the discussions so far, we'll continue to use it. We can simplify the process for accessing a Web page as the following four steps. (The relevant Winsock commands are in parentheses.)

1. Translate the host name into a network address (*gethostbyname*)
2. Connect to the Web server (*socket, bind, connect*)
3. Issue a request (*send*)
4. Receive the response (*recv*)

This process operates in the network as shown in Figure 7-14.

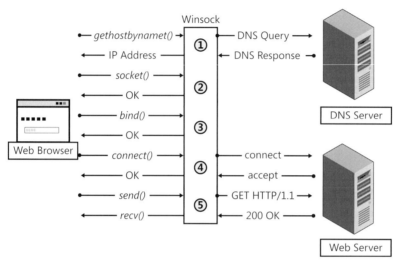

FIGURE 7-14 Simplified Web request

The process shown in Figure 7-14 follows these steps:

1. The Web browser issues a *gethostbyname()* call to translate the host name used in the URL into an IP address. Winsock converts this into a DNS query that is sent to the DNS server as configured in the client's IP addressing settings. The IP address in the DNS response is passed back to the browser.

2. The Web browser issues a call to *socket()*, which instructs Winsock to build a socket and pass a handle (programmatic reference) back to the browser.

3. The Web browser calls to *bind()* so that Winsock will create a mapping to a specific source port for the communication that is to follow on this socket.

4. The Web browser issues a call to *connect()* using the IP address it received in step 1. When Winsock has completed the connection setup process with the Web server, it responds back to the Web browser.

5. The Web browser issues a *send()* call to Winsock and includes a pointer to a data buffer that contains the data it wishes to send to the Web server—in this case, *GET/HTTP/1.1*.

Winsock sends this data. Because the Web server also responds to this request with 200 OK Winsock notifies the Web browser that data is available. The Web browser issues a *recv()* call to obtain the data waiting in the Winsock receive buffer.

We simplified the process described here for clarity. Quite a bit more actually passes between the Web browser and Winsock.

Winsock Usage with the TMGC

The process operates a bit differently when the TMGC is in the picture, but the Web browser is unaware that anything has changed. The process when the TMGC is involved follows these steps:

1. When Winsock passes the *gethostbyname()* call to the TMGC, the host name in the request is evaluated to determine whether it is either an unqualified name or falls within the local domains as provided in the wspad.dat or control channel data. If the host name is an unqualified name or part of the local domains set, the call is passed back to Winsock for further processing. If the host name is determined to be non-local, TMGC passes the call to TMG for handling. The resulting IP address is passed back to the TMGC via the control channel, then back to the Web browser via Winsock.

2. When Winsock passes the *socket()* call to the TMGC, the TMGC creates a socket of its own. If the TMGC *socket()* call is successful, it passes this state back to the Web browser via Winsock.

3. When Winsock passes the *bind()* call to the TMGC, the TMGC also issues a *bind()* call on the socket it created in step 2. If this bind is successful, the TMGC sends a *bind()* command to TMG on the control channel. This command includes the IP address and source port provided to TMG from Winsock in the *bind()* response, so that TMG knows what IP address and port number will be used by the TMGC to send data between TMGC and TMG. If the *bind()* is successful at TMG, it responds with a *bind ack*, which includes the destination IP address and port that the TMGC should use to send the application data to TMG. TMGC then passes the status back to Winsock for forwarding to the Web browser.

4. When the Web browser issues the *connect()* call, the TMGC performs the same action and also issues a *connect()* request to TMG. This connect call also tells TMG that the TMGC will be sending data for this connection on the socket it created in step 2 and includes the IP address and port from which TMG should expect to receive data for this connection from the TMGC host. TMG attempts to create a connection with the destination host at the IP address specified in the *connect()* call and responds to the TMGC with the *connect()* status.

> **NOTE** If any of the Winsock calls or TMGC-to-TMG control channel commands fail, a Winsock or Windows error is sent back to the application. Winsock errors are listed at *http://msdn.microsoft.com/en-us/library/ms740668(VS.85).aspx*.

Web Proxy Client with TMGC

Web proxy clients and the TMGC can coexist on the same host because the Web proxy client will connect to the TMG Web proxy listener (typically on TCP port 8080), and then issue its requests. Because the IP address of the TMG Web proxy listener is included in the local address range set for the network where the TMGC host operates, the IP address in the Winsock *connect()* request from the browser is recognized by TMGC as a local IP address and the *connect()* call is passed back to Winsock for normal processing.

TMG Client Authentication

TMG Client authentication uses one of two authentication mechanisms:

- If TMGC is a non-domain member, NTLM SSPI is used.
- If the TMGC and TMG are in trusted domains, Kerberos SSPI is used.

In either case, TMGC authentication only occurs as part of the initial control channel setup process. Because the control channel setup process occurs before TMG receives any Winsock request, TMG cannot evaluate the rules before deciding whether authentication is required. Thus, if any access rule requires authentication, TMG requires the TMG Client to authenticate *before* accepting *any* Winsock commands.

The TMGC uses credentials associated with the process making the Winsock calls. For applications running in the context of an interactive login session, this is that user account.

Choosing the Right Client for Your Environment

Now that you know the capabilities of each client type, you can choose which one is best for your environment and applications. To choose the right client type, you need to consider the functionality and security requirements of your network and applications. Your main considerations in deciding what TMG client type is best suited for your network are:

- Ease of deployment and restrictions on installing software
- Support for various operating systems (both Windows and others)
- Protocol support (simple versus complex protocols)
- Authentication requirements for user- or group-based access controls
- Security

Ease of Deployment

One of your toughest tasks is to deploy the client configuration. Some companies do not allow any software that makes changes at the network layer on client computers. On the other hand, even if you allow software installation, it is not an easy task to deploy software automatically to client computers when that software installation routine requires local administrative privileges. The same is true for setting up Web proxy settings for Web browsers, which requires either Group Policy configuration or auto-configuration support (both of which are relatively easy to deploy, but still generate administrative overhead). When taking all these factors into account, the easiest type of client to deploy is the SecureNET client. The next-easiest client to deploy is the Web proxy client, followed by the TMG Client.

Support for Heterogeneous Operating Systems

If you have a mixed environment with both Windows and other operating systems, and you need to provide protocol support for them, your options are somewhat limited. If you require support only for Web protocols, the Web proxy client configuration is fine, but if you need to support protocols other than those handled by the Web proxy client, the only option is a SecureNET client. TMGC only installs on Windows operating systems and thus is not an option for other operating systems.

Protocol Support

Applications have different requirements in terms of ports and protocols. Most users only need access to the Internet using Web protocols. The Web proxy client configuration easily supports these users. TMGC can provide support for all TCP and UDP applications and is the most secure of the three client configurations. It can also provide support for complex protocols. However, only SecureNET clients support non-TCP or UDP protocols such as ICMP or GRE. In contrast to TMGC, the SecureNET client can only handle complex protocols when there is an application layer filter to manage the traffic on behalf of the client.

Authentication Requirements and User- or Group-Based Access Control

TMG does not know whether a SecureNET client exists except in the context of the source IP used and protocols used. An OSI application layer component is required to provide user credentials to the firewall. This is why you cannot enforce access policy based on users or groups for SecureNET clients. However, the TMGC sends credentials during the control channel setup process. Web proxy clients provide credentials only when challenged for authenticated access.

Security

Web proxy clients establish connections to a port on TMG that is set to listen for Web proxy client connections. To make the application a Web proxy client, you must configure the application to connect to TMG's Web proxy listener on this port. Web proxy clients establish unencrypted connections to the TMG Web proxy listener.

In contrast, TMGC first sets up a control channel connection with TMG on TCP port 1745. The control channel encrypts connections *after* authentication is complete. A network sniffer can show you the connections, but it cannot tell you the content of those connections.

Encryption for SecureNET clients is application-dependent. For example, if the application uses SSL, the tunnel is encrypted; if the application uses RDP, that tunnel is encrypted. If the application does not use a secure protocol, the only way to encrypt traffic for SecureNET clients (other than any encryption they may use as part of the communication they establish) is by using IPsec, which is a separate and potentially complex configuration.

Tables 7-4, 7-5, and 7-6 can act as a decision matrix to assist you in choosing the TMG client type(s) that best match your requirements.

TABLE 7-4 Considerations and Preferences for Choice of Client

CONSIDERATION	FIRST PREFERENCE	SECOND PREFERENCE	THIRD PREFERENCE
Ease of deployment	SecureNET client	Web proxy client	TMGC
Support for heterogeneous operating systems	SecureNET client	Web proxy client	TMGC
Multiple protocol support	TMGC	SecureNET client	Web proxy client
Authentication requirements	TMGC	Web proxy client	SecureNET client
Security	TMGC	Web proxy client	SecureNET client

TABLE 7-5 Requirements and Best Client Fit

REQUIREMENT	BEST CLIENT FIT
No software installation	Web proxy client or SecureNET client
Anonymous access for Web browsing only (Web protocol support)	Web proxy client or SecureNET client
Authenticated access for Web browsing	Web proxy client or TMGC
Support for operating systems other than Windows	SecureNET client or Web proxy client
Support for OCS or voice and video	TMGC with the help of an application filter
Support for complex protocols	TMGC
Support for non-TCP or UDP Protocols (for example, ICMP or GRE)	SecureNET client

TABLE 7-6 Feature Comparison Among the Three Clients

FEATURE AND CONSIDERATION	SECURENET CLIENT	WEB PROXY CLIENT	TMG CLIENT
Ease of deployment	No configuration is required other than setting up a default gateway.	Need to specify Web proxy settings in the Web browser or use WPAD.	Need to install the TMGC software.
Support for heterogeneous operating systems	Supports all operating systems (Windows and others) that understand TCP/IP networking.	Any application that is Web proxy–aware can use the Web proxy client configuration; access is limited to Web protocols.	Can be installed on only Windows operating systems.
Multiple protocol support	A SecureNET client supports all simple protocols. Application filters enable support of complex protocols. SecureNET provides support for non-TCP and -UDP protocols.	Supports only HTTP, HTTPS, and HTTP proxied FTP protocols.	Supports all TCP and UDP simple and complex protocols.
Authentication	Does not forward user credentials and cannot support authentication-based access rules.	Forwards credentials when challenged for authentication.	Forwards credentials of the logged-in user automatically; supports authentication-based access rules.
Security	Connections are unencrypted; uses the application's protocol default port.	Connections are unencrypted and are sent to the port on TMG that is set to listen for Web proxy connections (TCP port 8080 by default).	The TMGC sets up a control channel on TCP port 1745 and then all information within the control channel may be encrypted if any rule requires authentication.
Name resolution	Done by the client.	TMG resolves names on the client's behalf.	TMG resolves names on the client's behalf.

REAL WORLD Troubleshooting Scenarios for TMG Client Types

Table 7-7 includes real-world troubleshooting scenarios and solutions for TMG client types. You can avoid the most common errors related to client-type selection and configuration by understanding each issue and its solution.

TABLE 7-7 Common TMG Client Type Issues and Solutions

COMMON ISSUES	SOLUTION
No Internet access for SecureNET clients.	Use *nslookup* to test client DNS behavior. If name resolution for external hosts is not working, make sure that a rule on TMG allows DNS protocol access to the external DNS server used by the client. This scenario applies only when no internal DNS server is available.
Slow Internet access for SecureNET clients.	You might have configured deny rules based on destination domain names. If so, reverse lookups could be a problem. TMG performs reverse DNS lookups on the IP address to determine whether the IP address matches any of the blocked domain names. Reverse DNS lookups are expensive and often fail or lead to delays.
User- or groups-based allow rules outbound connections to the Internet.	Confirm that the user is a member of the group assigned to the allow rule. Also ensure that the client is not only a SecureNET client. If it is, make sure you specify Web proxy settings so that it can make use of the Web proxy client configuration to send user credentials when challenged for authentication. If possible, install the TMGC and test the connection again.
Clients cannot access resources on a remote site network through a TMG site-to-site VPN tunnel.	The clients might not have a correct route to reach to the remote site network, and the clients in the remote network might not have a route back to the client from where the request originated. Ensure that routes are set up correctly or test by making sure both the originating client and the destination resources are SecureNET clients.
Application does not work when using TMGC.	Ensure that the application is a Winsock application and uses TCP or UDP protocols. If it does not, use the SecureNET client configuration.

COMMON ISSUES	SOLUTION
TMG drops connections from a published Web server or non–Web Server as spoofed connections.	Make sure the published server is a SecureNET client when configuring the Web Publishing Rule to preserve the original client IP address. If it is not possible to make the published server a SecureNET client, configure the publishing rule to replace the original client IP address with the IP address of TMG.
You see a lot of anonymous requests in reports; IP addresses appear in reports instead of user names.	By default, all Web proxy clients first send an anonymous connection to TMG. Web proxy clients forward credentials only when challenged. Therefore, if you have a large number of computers configured as Web proxy clients, you might see a lot of anonymous connections in reports. SecureNET clients do not authenticate, so if you have a rule allowing All Users, all requests will show up as anonymous. Because SecureNET clients do not send credentials, you will see client IP addresses in the user name section of reports.

Summary

You now should have a basic understanding of each TMG client type and how it behaves under normal circumstances. You should be able to use this basic knowledge to determine when applications act as Web proxy clients, SecureNET clients, or TMGCs (or some combination of the three). Now that you know which clients are available for TMG, it is time to install TMG on your Windows Server 2008. In the next chapter you will learn how to do that for Forefront TMG MBE and Forefront TMG 2010.

PART III

Implementing a TMG Deployment

CHAPTER 8   Installing TMG   **141**

CHAPTER 9   Troubleshooting TMG Setup   **169**

CHAPTER 10   Exploring the TMG Console   **185**

Installing TMG

- Final Considerations Before Installing TMG   **141**

- Installing TMG MBE   **145**

- Installing TMG 2010   **156**

- Summary   **168**

This chapter begins the implementation phase of your Forefront TMG deployment. In this phase you will install TMG. This chapter covers TMG installation for both versions of the product: Forefront TMG Medium Business Edition (MBE) and Forefront TMG 2010.

Final Considerations Before Installing TMG

Before you start to install TMG, it is always important to summarize the key elements you defined during the planning phase. To assist you in summarizing these key elements, use the checklist provided in Table 8-1.

TABLE 8-1 Final Preinstallation Checklist

ITEM	RECOMMENDATION
Internal addresses	Determine what IP address range will define the default internal network.
Authentication methods and requirements	Define internal client authentication methods and requirements.
Network template	Decide which network template to apply during and after installation.
Name resolution	Define the DNS server that will provide name resolution for TMG.

ITEM	RECOMMENDATION
Installation location	Define the physical disk that you will use during TMG installation.
Operating system security update level	Update the operating system by visiting Microsoft Update and installing all important and critical security updates before and after installing TMG.
Drivers	Ensure that all system drivers are up to date by visiting the vendor's Web site. This is especially important for network interface card (NIC) drivers.

Use this checklist before you install TMG. By addressing these items early, you will have a better TMG installation experience.

Additional Recommendations

Consider renaming your network interfaces in the Network Connections window. Give the network interfaces names that help you identify which network they are connected to. For example, the network interface connected to the external network might be renamed **WAN**. This simplifies management as well as TMG installation because you can easily see which NIC is connected to the default internal network.

Note that if you are using TMG for Web proxy only, using the single NIC template, you do not need to rename the interface because there is only one.

You can use the Rename option in Windows Server 2008 Network Connections window, as shown in Figure 8-1.

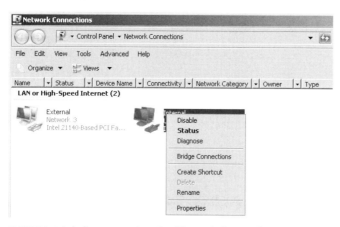

FIGURE 8-1 Labeling networks using Network Connections options

To rename the interface you can use one of the following two methods:

- **Rename command** Right-click the interface and choose the Rename option. Provide the new name when the current name is highlighted.

- **Netsh command** Type the following command in an elevated command prompt: **netsh interface set interface name="Local Area Connection" newname="External".**

> **NOTE** The name of your network interface may differ from Local Area Network depending on how your computer is constructed. You should replace *Local Area Network* with the name of the network as you see it in ipconfig results.

You can verify the network binding order in the Network Connections window. The network interface binding order can greatly affect TMG performance because this order determines how Windows uses name-resolution services. For best performance and reliability, we recommend that you put the internal interface at the top of the binding order.

Follow these steps to change the binding order:

1. In the Network Connections window, select the Advanced Settings option from the Advanced menu. A dialog box similar to Figure 8-2 appears.

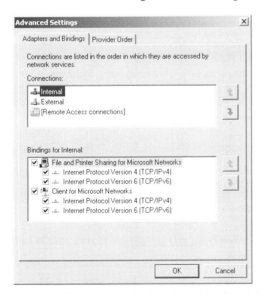

FIGURE 8-2 The Adapters And Bindings tab of the Advanced Settings dialog box

2. In the Advanced Settings dialog box, use the up or down arrow to place the internal interface at the top of the list.

In addition to moving the Internal interface to the top of the interface list, you should also disable all unnecessary services from the External interface to ensure that TMG will not handle external requests to these services. To disable these services, you need to select the External interface and disable both the File And Printer Sharing For Microsoft Networks and Client For Microsoft Networks services. Your external interface configuration should look like Figure 8-3.

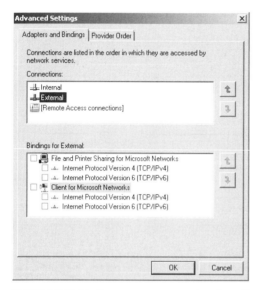

FIGURE 8-3 Unbinding unnecessary services from the External interface

After making these changes, click OK and restart the server before starting TMG installation.

You're almost ready to install TMG. However, before you do, you should verify your data-link layer devices. Consider the following recommendations prior to TMG installation:

- **Set same speed and duplex** To avoid problems with autosense incompatibility between the network interface card and the switch, you should set the same speed and duplex manually on the network interface card and switch. (You can review the steps of how to do this at *http://blogs.technet.com/sbs/archive/2007/04/24/common-networking-issues-after-applying-windows-server-2003-sp2-on-sbs.aspx*.)

- **Explicit Congestion Notification (ECN) for TCP** ECN is implemented in the Windows Server 2008 TCP/IP stack natively. This feature provides a way for routers to inform TCP peers that their buffers are filling because of congestion in the network. Routers that don't implement this feature might drop packets because ECN uses bits in the IP and TCP headers that were previously defined as unused or reserved. If your network has routers that are not compliant with RFC 3168, we recommend that you disable ECN on Windows Server 2008 by typing the command **netsh interface tcp set global ecncapability=disabled** at an elevated command prompt window**.

You should now be ready to install TMG.

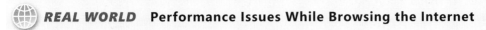

REAL WORLD   Performance Issues While Browsing the Internet

Many things can cause performance issues while browsing the Internet through TMG; in general these issues aren't due to any single TMG configuration option. Name-resolution issues, interface or network misconfiguration, logging problems, and other components can lead to performance degradation, resulting in a bad end user experience.

Consider the following scenario: users experienced slow performance while browsing through TMG, but claimed that when they bypassed TMG, performance for the same Web sites was very fast.

The first step was to get more information about the environment, including the network layout and other devices in use on the network. After determining that the issue was not related to TMG, we examined the networking stack for any operating system components that could cause the performance problems. We determined that the operating system was not causing the problem. We moved further down the stack and looked at the data-link level (NIC and Switch). We were able to determine that auto-negotiation was failing and that the NICs were falling back from full duplex to half duplex mode.

Our solution was to manually set each side (switch port and NIC) to the same speed and duplex mode. It is very important to do this on both sides; otherwise, you are still vulnerable to a duplex mismatch, which will result not only in slow performance, but also in intermittent connectivity issues and data link errors.

> **NOTE**   For more information on how auto-negotiation works, see the IEEE 802.3 Standard at *http://standards.ieee.org/reading/ieee/interp/IEEE802 .3af-2003interp-6.pdf.*

Installing TMG MBE

In this section, we will cover the installation of a stand-alone TMG Medium Business Edition (MBE), which is not the TMG MBE that shipped with Windows Essential Business Server. As the name suggests, TMG Medium Business Edition is targeted for small and medium-sized businesses. TMG MBE has certain limitations that you should be aware of before installation, such as the fact that the computer on which TMG MBE is installed must be a domain member.

TMG MBE does not offer array support, and the CSS can only be on the same computer. You cannot install TMG MBE on a computer that is in a workgroup and then change its domain membership after TMG MBE is installed.

Manual Installation

If your installation is not a part of the Windows Essential Business Server, you will have to use the stand-alone installation of TMG MBE by following these steps:

1. Insert the TMG MBE DVD in your computer's DVD drive. If your computer has autorun enabled, you will see the Welcome page, as shown in Figure 8-4. If you have autorun disabled, open Windows Explorer, navigate to your DVD drive, and double-click isautorun.exe.

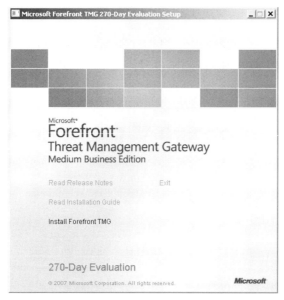

FIGURE 8-4 The TMG Welcome page

2. Read the release notes and the installation guide by clicking the relevant links. These will give you information on any late-breaking issues or caveats that could not be included in documentation prior to RTM.

3. Click Install Forefront TMG. The Microsoft Forefront TMG Installer dialog box and a Windows Installer Preparing To Install dialog box appear, as shown in Figures 8-5 and 8-6.

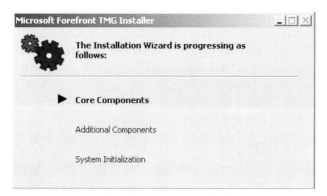

FIGURE 8-5 Microsoft Forefront TMG Installer dialog box

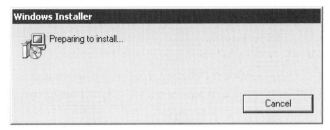

FIGURE 8-6 Installation startup dialog box

4. On the Welcome page of the Microsoft Forefront Threat Management Gateway Installation Wizard, shown in Figure 8-7, click Next.

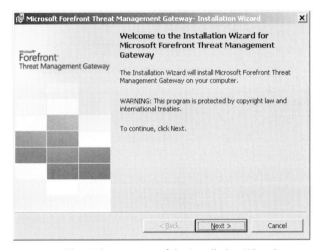

FIGURE 8-7 The Welcome page of the Installation Wizard

5. On the License Agreement page, read the Microsoft Software License Terms and select the I Accept The Terms In The License Agreement option. Click Next.

6. On the Customer Information page, shown in Figure 8-8, you may choose to enter the user and company information, but these can also be left blank. You do need to enter the product serial number. Click Next.

7. On the Setup Scenarios page, shown in Figure 8-9, you can choose to install the complete TMG MBE software or you can choose to only install remote management. Choosing the Install Forefront Threat Management Gateway option installs the TMG MBE services, Active Directory Lightweight Directory Services (LDS)—which holds the TMG MBE configuration—and SQL Express 2005, which is used for reporting, along with the MMC to let you control all of the TMG policies and services. If you choose Install Forefront Threat Management Gateway Management Only you only install the MMC and related components, which will let you connect to a remote TMG MBE installation to monitor and control the TMG MBE policies and services. For our setup, we will install a fresh TMG MBE firewall. Choose Install Forefront Threat Management Gateway Management and click Next.

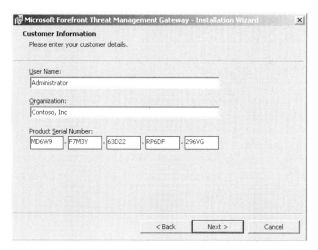

FIGURE 8-8 The Customer Information page of the Installation Wizard

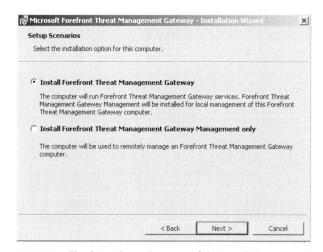

FIGURE 8-9 The Setup Scenarios page of the Installation Wizard

8. On the Component Selection page, shown in Figure 8-10, you can choose which feature will be installed. For TMG MBE, we strongly recommend that you don't change any of these settings—as a stand-alone gateway, TMG MBE needs all three of them. Notice that the default directory to install TMG is also predefined as the C: drive. If you want to change the drive in which TMG MBE is installed, you can change it from here. However, please note that SQL Express 2005 and LDS will still be installed beneath %ProgramFiles%. Click Next.

9. On the Internal Network page, shown in Figure 8-11, you define the IP addresses of your default internal network, which helps TMG distinguish between internal and external IP address ranges. An external IP address range is defined as any address range that is not specified in any other TMG network address range definition. Click Add.

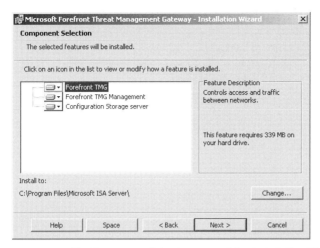

FIGURE 8-10 The Component Selection page of the Installation Wizard

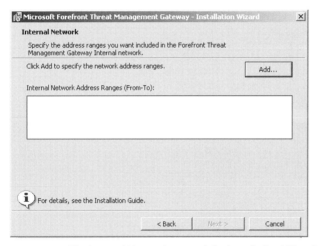

FIGURE 8-11 The Internal Network page of the Installation Wizard

10. In the Addresses dialog box, shown in Figure 8-12, click Add Adapter to set the ranges automatically from the identified network interface and routing table. You could instead click Add Range to define the IP address range manually, but choosing to set the ranges automatically is simpler because TMG identifies the proper address ranges based on the network interface selected and adds appropriate ranges from the routing table built by the operating system.

11. In the Select Network Adapters dialog box, shown in Figure 8-13, you select the internal network interface card that lets you see the NICs IP address and route information it has automatically picked up from the routing table. The route information holds the internal network address range, including the broadcast addresses. In this example, the broadcast IP addresses are 10.1.1.0 and 10.1.1.255, thereby completing the entire subnet range. Select your internal network interface card from the Select Network Adapter dialog box and click OK.

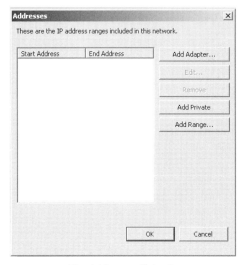

FIGURE 8-12 The Addresses dialog box

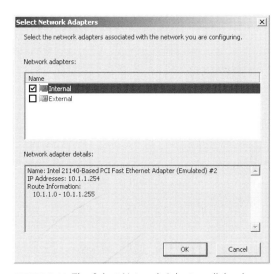

FIGURE 8-13 The Select Network Adapters dialog box

12. The range is now added, as shown in Figure 8-14. You can define off-subnet ranges, but make sure the route for that particular range is added manually to the route table; otherwise, TMG will drop the packet as spoofed and you will see configuration errors in alerts for the default Internal Network address range. Click OK.

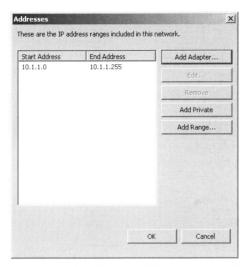

FIGURE 8-14 The Addresses dialog box after the IP range
has been added

13. The range is now added in the Internal Network Address Ranges (From-To) field, as
shown in Figure 8-15. Click Next.

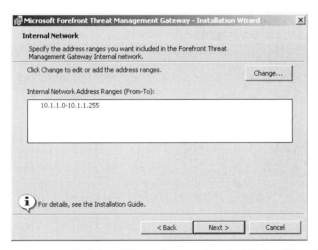

FIGURE 8-15 The Internal Network page of the Installation Wizard
after the IP range has been added

14. On the Services Warning page, shown in Figure 8-16, you can see the services that will
be restarted during installation. Click Next.

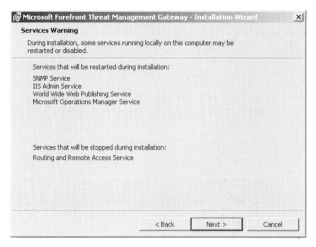

FIGURE 8-16 The Services Warning page of the Installation Wizard

15. If you are installing TMG MBE over a Remote Desktop connection, you would be notified that the IP address of your computer will be added in the system policy to allow you access to TMG MBE after the installation is complete. If you are passing through a NAT device, that IP address will be added to the System Policy setting. Because we are doing a local installation at the console, we do not get that notification. On the Ready To Install The Program page, shown in Figure 8-17, click Install.

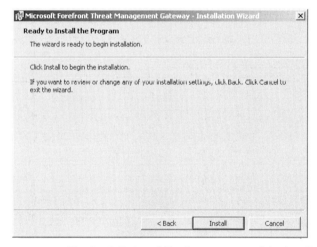

FIGURE 8-17 The Ready To Install The Program page of the Installation Wizard

16. The gears in the Microsoft Forefront TMG installer dialog box (shown earlier in Figure 8-5) start rotating. The installer performs some routine checks such as calculating space requirements, copying new files, installing LDS, creating a TMG instance in LDS, creating TMG services, and performing driver and filter registration. The dialog boxes shown in Figures 8-18 through 8-23 illustrate the progress of the installation.

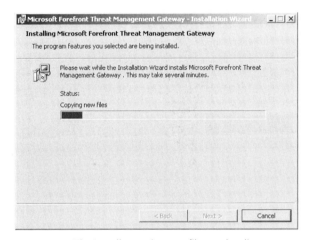

FIGURE 8-18 The Installer computes space requirements to install TMG MBE.

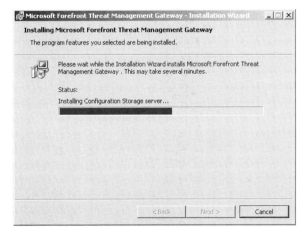

FIGURE 8-19 The Installer copies new files to the directory.

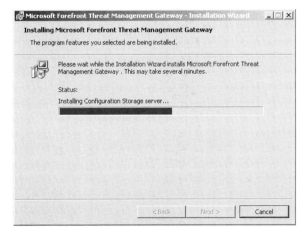

FIGURE 8-20 LDS is installed on the server.

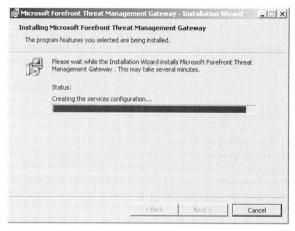

FIGURE 8-21 TMG Service objects are created.

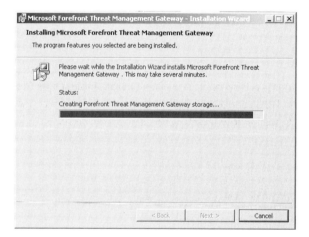

FIGURE 8-22 A TMG instance is created in LDS.

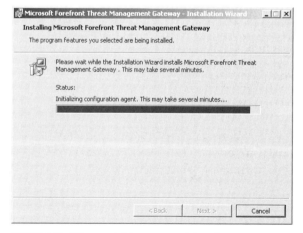

FIGURE 8-23 Filters and drivers are registered.

17. As additional components are installed, the gears keep turning (Figure 8-24). You will not see a status or progress bar other than the rotating gears. During this time, the TMG installer is installing SQL 2005 for logging and reporting purposes and making necessary changes in IIS. This process takes a while and you will see this screen for a long time.

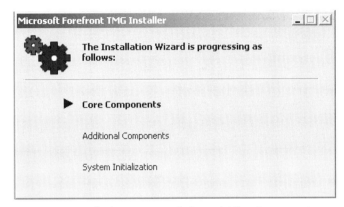

FIGURE 8-24 Installation progress window – Adding Components

18. After the additional components are installed, system initialization begins, as shown in Figure 8-25. At this point the TMG services are being started up. If you are connected to the TMG installation setup via Remote Desktop, the starting of the services will momentarily cause you to lose your connection. It will be reconnected in a few seconds.

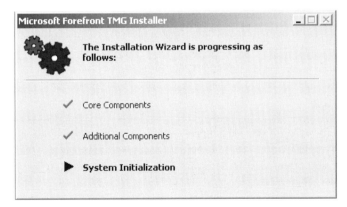

FIGURE 8-25 Installation progress window – System Initialization

19. You should now see the Installation Wizard Completed page of the Installation Wizard, as shown in Figure 8-26. Click Finish to complete and exit the wizard. Internet Explorer will open to %ProgramFiles%\Microsoft ISA Server\Secure.htm.

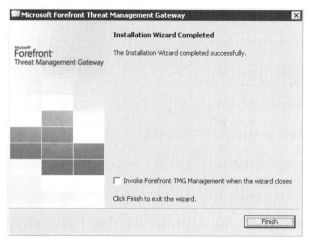

FIGURE 8-26 The Installation Wizard Completed page of the Installation Wizard

NOTE ISA Setup files are located in the %windir%\temp directory and they all will be labeled as ISA*. %windir% resolves to C:\Windows by default.

Installing TMG 2010

Forefront TMG 2010 includes some features not offered in TMG MBE, so you need to make some additional decisions prior to actually beginning the installation process. Additionally, because TMG 2010 does not include the wizards provided in Windows Essential Business Server, automating the installation process requires a bit more effort on your part.

Manual Installation

For environments that will have only a few TMG firewalls or proxies, manual installation may be more efficient than spending the time devising, testing, and rewriting an automated installation routine. Even if you prefer to automate your TMG installations, it is still worthwhile to read through the following manual steps so that you gain an understanding of the mechanisms underlying the automation.

1. Insert the Forefront TMG 2010 DVD in your server's DVD drive. If your computer has autorun enabled, you will see the Welcome page as shown in Figure 8-27. If you have disabled autorun, open Windows Explorer, navigate to your DVD drive, and double-click isaautorun.exe.

2. Read the release notes and the deployment guide. You can access both by clicking the relevant link on the Welcome to Microsoft Forefront TMG screen. These documents include late-breaking issues or caveats that could not be included in the documentation prior to RTM. Remember, forewarned is forearmed.

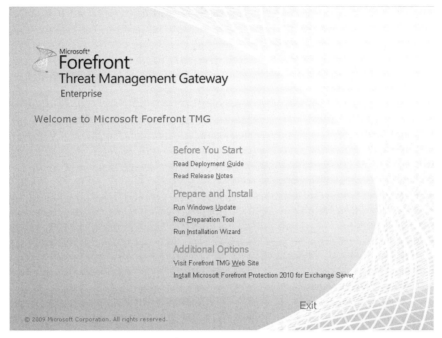

FIGURE 8-27 The Welcome screen of TMG

3. Start the installation by clicking Run Preparation Tool on the Welcome page. On the Welcome To The Preparation Tool for Microsoft Forefront Threat Management Gateway (TMG) page, as shown in Figure 8-28, click Next.

FIGURE 8-28 Forefront TMG Preparation Tool

4. When the License Agreement page appears, as shown in Figure 8-29, read the Microsoft Software License Terms, select I Accept The Terms In The License Agreement, and click Next.

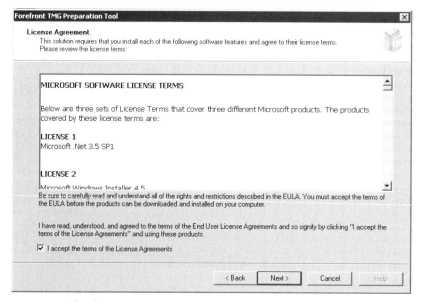

FIGURE 8-29 The License Agreement page of the Installation Wizard

5. On the Setup Scenarios page, shown in Figure 8-30, select the installation option you want to use for this installation of TMG.

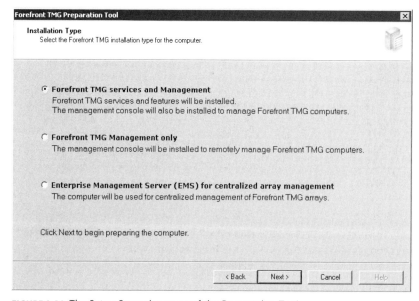

FIGURE 8-30 The Setup Scenarios page of the Preparation Tool

These options enable the following scenarios:

- **Install Forefront TMG Services and Management** This option installs the components necessary to operate as a TMG Firewall or proxy and also the management console.

- **Install Forefront TMG Management Only** This option installs only the components required to remotely manage TMG.

- **Enterprise Management Server (EMS) for centralized array management** This option installs the components necessary to operate as an Enterprise Management Server. You must have at least one server installed with this role to create and join Enterprise arrays. This component is not required for stand-alone arrays.

For now, you should choose Install Forefront TMG Services and Management. Click Next.

6. The Preparation Tool will start running, as shown in Figure 8-31, and verify the current Windows installation to see whether it satisfies the requirements. If it does not, it will take steps to make it capable of installing TMG.

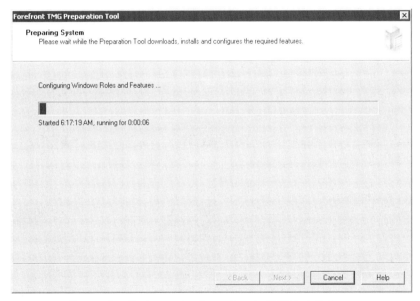

FIGURE 8-31 Preparation Tool preparing the system for TMG installation

7. When Preparation Tool finishes preparing the system it will notify you that the preparation was done successfully and from this window you can launch TMG setup to proceed with the installation. On the Preparation Complete page leave the Launch Forefront TMG Installation Wizard check box selected, as shown in Figure 8-32, and click Finish.

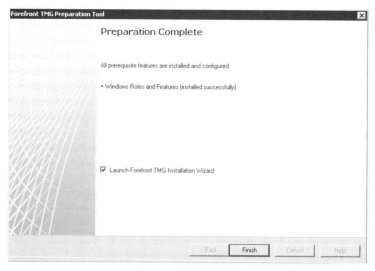

FIGURE 8-32 Preparation Tool completed successfully

8. The Installation Wizard Progress dialog box appears, as shown in Figure 8-33. Next, the Welcome To The Installation Wizard For Forefront TMG Enterprise page appears, as shown in Figure 8-34. Click Next.

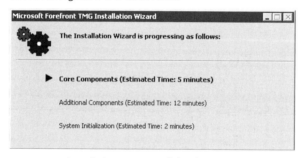

FIGURE 8-33 Installation progress dialog box

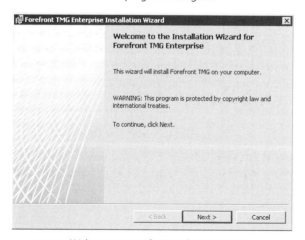

FIGURE 8-34 Welcome screen for Forefront TMG Setup

9. The license agreement for Forefront TMG installation appears. Read through the license page and then select I Accept The Terms In The License Agreement, as shown in Figure 8-35. Click Next.

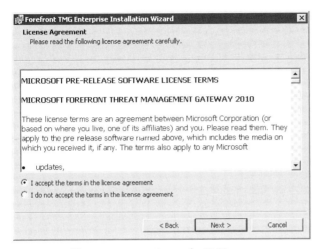

FIGURE 8-35 License agreement page for TMG

10. On the Customer Information page, shown in Figure 8-36, you may choose to leave the User Name and Organization fields blank, but you must enter your product serial number before you can continue.

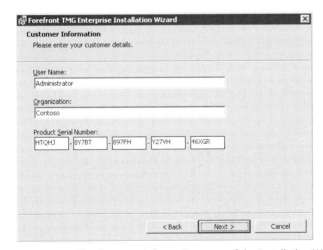

FIGURE 8-36 The Customer Information page of the Installation Wizard

11. On Installation Path page, choose the location where you want to install TMG. For the purpose of this demonstration, leave the default path as shown in Figure 8-37 and click Next.

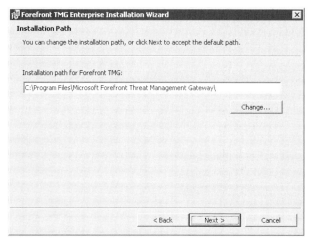

FIGURE 8-37 Choosing the installation path for TMG

12. On the Define Internal Network page, shown in Figure 8-38, click Add.

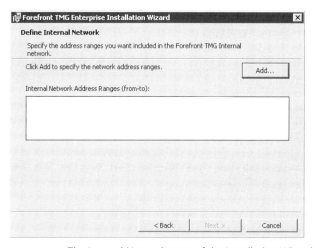

FIGURE 8-38 The Internal Network page of the Installation Wizard

13. In the Addresses dialog box, shown in Figure 8-39, click Add Adapter.

14. In the Select Adapters dialog box, shown in Figure 8-40, select the network adapter that represents the default internal network. If you have more than one protected network, do not add them at this time. You can change the network structure for TMG later. Click OK to close this dialog box.

15. In the Addresses dialog box, shown in Figure 8-41, verify that the IP address ranges listed match those used by hosts on the default internal network, and that they are reachable from TMG. If these addresses are not reachable, the Windows routing table is not properly configured to allow TMG to reach those networks. You should correct this before continuing.

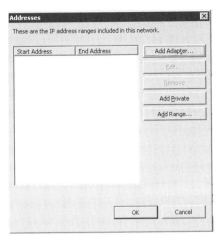

FIGURE 8-39 The Addresses dialog box

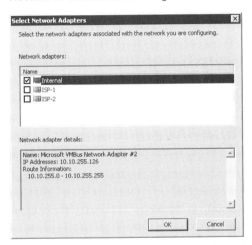

FIGURE 8-40 The Select Network Adapters dialog box

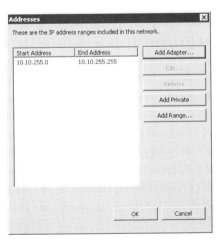

FIGURE 8-41 Addresses that belong to the internal network

NOTE Unlike DHCP scopes, which limit address ranges to unicast IP addresses only, TMG address ranges should include Network ID and the broadcast address. For instance, the preceding example illustrates the proper address range for a network on which TMG is using an IP address of 10.10.255.126 with a subnet mask of 255.255.255.0, or /24. In this case, the network ID is 10.10.255.0 and the subnet broadcast address is 10.10.255.255.

Click OK to close this dialog box.

16. On the Internal Network page, shown in Figure 8-42, click Next.

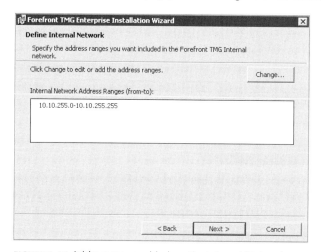

FIGURE 8-42 Address range added on the Internal Network page of the Installation Wizard

17. The Services Warning page appears (Figure 8-43), listing the services that will be stopped or disabled if found running. Click Next to proceed.

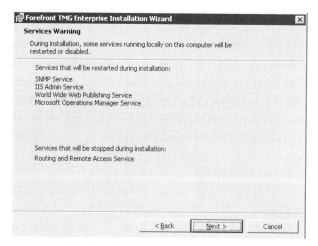

FIGURE 8-43 Services that will be restarted during the installation

NOTE As shown in Figure 8-44, if you are logged onto TMG using Remote Desktop, you will see a notice informing you that the IP address used by your remote computer will be added to the System Policies to allow remote management of TMG. This is necessary to complete the installation after the TMG services have been installed and started.

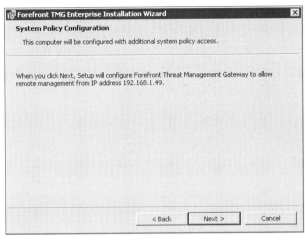

FIGURE 8-44 System Policy changes during installation over an RDP connection

18. On the Ready To Install The Program page, shown in Figure 8-45, click Install.

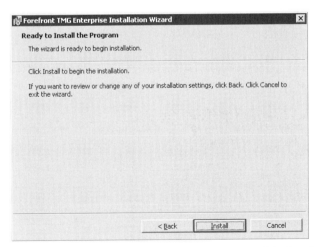

FIGURE 8-45 The Ready To Install The Program page of the Installation Wizard

While installation is in progress you will notice:

■ The Installation Wizard progress dialog box gears start turning and the TMG components are installed.

■ During this time, Lightweight Directory Services (LDS) will be configured to function as the Configuration Storage Service (CSS).

- Forefront TMG management, services, drivers, and registration of various filters will be completed.

- Eventually, the installing progress dialog box disappears and the Progress state indicator checks off Core Components and moves to Additional Components, as shown in Figure 8-46.

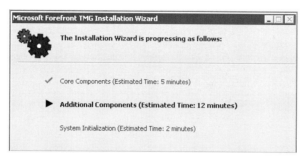

FIGURE 8-46 Installation Wizard progress dialog box - Additional Components

- The progress dialog box moves to System Initialization, as shown in Figure 8-47.

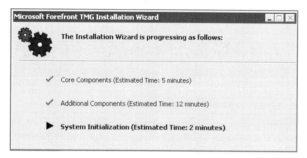

FIGURE 8-47 Installation Wizard progress dialog box - System Initialization

> **NOTE** If you are logged on to TMG using Remote Desktop, the connection will be broken briefly as the firewall service starts, but the connection should be re-established almost immediately.

19. The progress dialog box disappears and it is replaced with the Installation Wizard Completed page, as shown in Figure 8-48. Click Finish.

    Internet Explorer will open to display %ProgramFiles%\Microsoft Forefront Threat Management Gateway\Secure.htm, as shown in Figure 8-49.

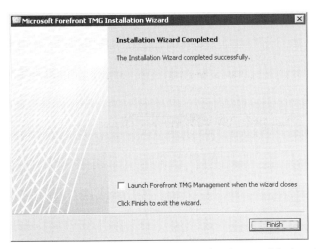

FIGURE 8-48 The Installation Wizard Completed page of the Installation Wizard

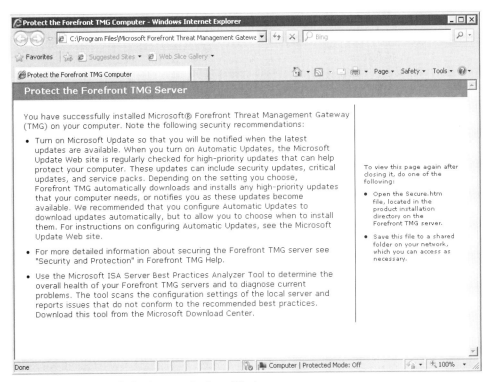

FIGURE 8-49 Post-Installation Internet Explorer Window

NOTE %ProgramFiles% typically resolves to C:\Program Files.

Unattended Installation

TMG may be installed using unattended installation description files. TMG comes with three preconfigured files stored on the installation DVD under \FPC\UNATTENDED_SETUP_SAMPLE\:

- **INSTALLENTERPRISEMANAGEMENTSERVER.INI**   This file includes installation options preconfigured to install TMG as an Enterprise Management server.
- **INSTALLREMOTEMANAGEMENT.INI**   This file includes installation options preconfigured to install TMG as a Remote Management server.
- **INSTALLSTANDALONESERVER.INI**   This file contains installation options preconfigured to install TMG as a stand-alone server.
- **UNINSTALLSERVER.INI**   This file contains installation options preconfigured to uninstall TMG from the computer.

The settings you must change prior to executing an unattended installation are described within each .ini file according to the installation options related to that scenario.

To perform an unattended installation, copy the relevant file to the TMG computer, modify it with the required settings, and run the file from a command window; for example: <DVD>\FPC\setup.exe REBOOT=ReallySuppress /v"/qb FULLPATHANSWERFILE=\"c:\<Selected AnswerFile>.ini\"".

Summary

In this chapter, you learned what you need to do prior to installing TMG in your environment. You also learned how to install Forefront TMG MBE and Forefront TMG 2010, and how to perform an automated installation. In Chapter 9, "Troubleshooting TMG Setup," you will learn how to find and solve problems in the setup.

## CHAPTER 9

Troubleshooting TMG Setup

- Understanding Setup Architecture **169**

- Setup Options **172**

- What to Look for When Setup Fails **174**

- Summary **184**

E ven when you expend the considerable effort necessary to ensure a worry-free installation and initial configuration, failures are bound to happen. When they do, understanding how TMG Setup operates and knowing how to track down the root cause of the problem can mean the difference between a quick retry and hours spent chasing false errors. In this chapter you will gain an understanding of the TMG setup process and the logic behind it, as well as some tips for resolving common installation and initial configuration errors.

Understanding Setup Architecture

The TMG setup mechanism is built to provide the simplest and most stable setup experience possible. All software installation and primary configuration procedures are automated based on choices you make using the Preparation Tool and the Installation Wizard. As discussed in Chapter 8, "Installing TMG," unattended installation is also supported to provide for more efficient installation and initial setup.

Setup Goals

TMG setup has a lot to do to create a functional TMG installation. To support these tasks, the following goals were defined by the Forefront Edge product team:

- **Simplify the process as much as technically possible.** Because TMG includes technology from multiple sources (Forefront Server Security, Active Directory Lightweight Directory Services, SQL Server 2008 Express with Reporting Services), the TMG installer seeks to isolate the user from the complexity of installing and configuring each of these dependencies.

- **Ensure that a successful installation produces a functional TMG deployment.** Few things are more confounding and frustrating than an installation process that completes successfully, but leaves the application (or worse, the computer itself) unusable.

- **If an installation doesn't succeed, the installer should restore the computer to its pre-installation state.** If the installer cannot satisfy this requirement, it should advise the user on which corrective steps to take before attempting another installation.

- **Create detailed logs of all installation actions.** This is primarily to support troubleshooting failed installations, but also serves to provide a record of all changes made to the computer to help support installing TMG and related components.

- **Provide an unattended installation mechanism.** The more complex an installation becomes, the longer it takes to complete. If the user is tasked with creating multiple TMG firewalls, having to work through the wizard for each and every installation is a terrible waste of time.

Setup Architecture

The TMG Installation Wizard is an application written to collect the information needed to install the TMG components required to satisfy the operational needs for a particular host. Whether it is to act as a Configuration Storage Server, Enterprise Management server, or a full-blown TMG firewall, the wizard guides the user through the choices necessary to satisfy those goals. The primary TMG setup components are depicted in Figure 9-1.

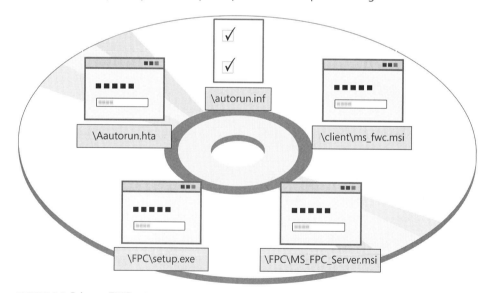

FIGURE 9-1 Primary TMG setup components

- **\autorun.inf**   A standard autorun definition file. When you insert the DVD into the DVD drive, Windows autorun functionality reads this file and starts spash.hta that launches autorun.hta.

- **\autorun.hta**   The initial Welcome Screen (as shown in Chapter 8, Figure 8-27). This provides a starting point from which you can read online or on-disk setup documents or begin the setup process.

- **\FPC\setup.exe**   This component performs two tasks: It acts as the TMG setup wizard and it acts as the unattended setup manager.

- **\client\ms_fwc.msi**   The TMG Client installation package.

To provide the full functionality offered by TMG, the setup process includes components not produced by the TMG team, which are listed here with their relative placement on the DVD, if applicable:

- **PowerShell 2.0**   Used for Exchange Edge Transport.

- **SQL Server 2008 Express with Advanced Features**   Used for logging and report generation and located at \FPC\Program Files\Microsoft ISA Server\SQLE.

- **URL Filtering engine**

The following Windows Server features are also verified during the setup process:

- **.Net Framework 3.5**   Used for Forefront Protection 2010 for Exchange Server.

- **Message Queuing**   Used for eSAS integration.

- **Network Load Balancing (NLB)**   Used for high availability.

> **NOTE**   Prior to the RTM version, you had to install .Net Framework and MSMQ and Windows PowerShell before installing TMG, however with the Preparation Tool those items are verified and installed in case you didn't install.

The following Windows Server roles are also added or verified during the execution of Preparation Tool:

- **Active Directory Lightweight Directory Services (AD LDS)**   Used for Configuration Storage Services (CSS).

- **Internet Authentication Services (IAS)**   Used for NAP and RADIUS.

- **Routing and Remote Access Service (RRAS)**   Used for VPN services.

Because the following components may be required for other purposes or offer improved functionality or performance, they will be left behind after TMG removal or setup failure rollback:

- .NET Framework 3.5

- Windows PowerShell 2.0

Setup Process

Whether you use the setup wizard or an unattended installation, the actual component installation process is essentially the same. Setup.exe uses the options provided by the user either through the wizard or the unattended answer file and command-line options to select and install the appropriate components. To effectively troubleshoot TMG setup problems, it's important to understand the order of operations:

1. Gather the user-definable configuration options.

2. Execute the setup according to the chosen configuration.

3. Create logs containing detailed actions and results.

Setup Options

After you install TMG—depending on whether the administrator installed it locally or remotely—certain changes are made to the system policy. By default when TMG is installed all traffic to or from TMG is blocked because no firewall policy is available. The only traffic allowed is defined in the system policy. The system policy defines necessary traffic such as DNS, Active Directory, Remote Monitoring, and Intra Array Communication to be allowed outbound from TMG even when no firewall policy is available. To make sure that the administrator installing TMG remotely is not disconnected after TMG is installed, the IP address of the remote computer is automatically added to the Remote Management Computers computer set, as shown in Figure 9-2.

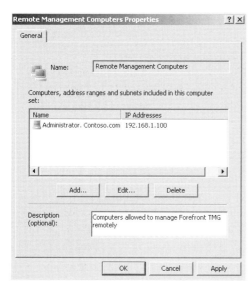

FIGURE 9-2 The Remote Management Computers computer set

You can view the Remote Management Computers computer set by clicking the Toolbox tab in the Task pane, clicking Network Objects, and then clicking Computer Sets. If you need to add additional IP addresses to the computer set to manage TMG from multiple workstations, you can do so by adding the IP addresses to this computer set. To turn off this feature, clear the Enable This Configuration Group check box on the General tab in the System Policy Editor, as shown in Figure 9-3.

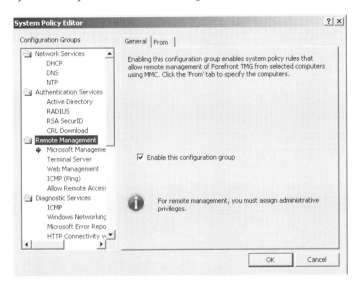

FIGURE 9-3 The System Policy Editor

Applying Security Updates and Service Packs

After you install TMG, it is important that you install any available TMG rollup updates or service packs. There might be known issues needing attention immediately after the installation that are already fixed in the rollup update or service pack. The updates or service packs might also have some new features that weren't included in the RTM, and based on customer requests or known issues, are released in the updates. It is also important to keep the Windows Server 2008 operating system on which TMG is installed up to date with the latest Windows updates and hotfix packages.

You might have to go through change management to approve the update or service pack installations. Make sure the updates are tested first in a test environment before applying them to a production server to minimize any chance of a production down situation. All updates are already tested for a variety of scenarios, but because every deployment is different, unforeseen regressions may occur. Installing the updates immediately after installing TMG makes it easier to catch regressions so that it does not affect your computer when it goes into production. A *regression* is an unwanted problem or issue that wasn't present before applying a hotfix or a security update and makes a feature or a scenario not function as intended after applying a hotfix or a security update.

Installing TMG with Updates

You can also choose to install TMG along with security rollup updates or service packs. No slipstreamed version of TMG is available, but it is fairly simple to combine service packs or rollup updates with the TMG installation by following these steps:

1. Copy all TMG files from the DVD Media onto a folder on the server (such as **C:\TMGInstall**).

2. Download the rollup update or service pack for TMG and copy it to the same folder.

3. Open the command prompt and change the directory to **C:\TMGInstall\FPC.**

4. Run the command **msiexec /a MS_FPC_Server.msi /p** *rollupupdate.msp* where *rollupupdate.msp* is the actual filename of the rollup update.

5. Browse to the C:\TMGInstall folder and double-click ISAAutorun.exe to start the installation.

What to Look for When Setup Fails

During the installation process, TMG Setup stores information about each step that was performed in the %systemroot%\temp folder. The information in TMG Setup log files is based on Microsoft Windows Installer logging. It is the responsibility of Windows Installer to write the log files that contain actions and errors that occur when TMG Setup is running. The Windows Temp folder contains files that are created during the initial setup and during post-setup, when you run the Getting Started Wizard. You can open the files using any text editor.

If you want to use the SMTP Protection feature on TMG, you need to install Microsoft Exchange Edge Transport Role and Forefront Protection 2010 for Exchange Server. TMG will then be capable of using the E-mail Protection feature. The log files for the Exchange component of the installation are stored at %systemdrive%\ExchangeSetupLogs. We will cover the E-mail Protection feature in more detail in Chapter 19, "Enhancing E-Mail Protection."

> **NOTE** For more information about the Exchange Setup Logs, see *http://technet.microsoft.com/en-us/library/bb125254(EXCHG.80).aspx.*

Last but not least, the Forefront Protection 2010 for Exchange Server component adds setup information in the file FssSetupLogYYMMDDTimeStamp.txt, which is located in %sytemdrive%\Users\All Users\Microsoft\Forefront Security for Exchange Server.

If TMG Setup fails for any reason, first read the description of the error message that appears onscreen. The error message is often self-explanatory. However, in some situations you'll need to use the error message to dig in and look for details in the setup logs.

Understanding the Setup Log Files

Although the logs can assist you in solving setup problems, they can also cause frustration if you don't understand how the information flows within the file. You also need to know what type of information you will see on each file. Table 9-1 summarizes the files located in %windir%\temp.

TABLE 9-1 TMG Setup Log files

LOG FILE NAME	DESCRIPTION
ISAWRAP_*XXX*.log	Contains general information about the Forefront TMG installation.
ISAFWSV_*XXX*.log	Contains information about events (informational events as well as errors) related to the firewall configuration. Here you will find the parameters that were passed during the installation and how those parameters are applied in the system.
ISAFWUI_*XXX*.log	Contains information recorded by the MSI UI with events logged during the installation process.
ISAADAM_INSTALL_*XXX*.log	An AD LDS installation log file that has events and errors related to the installation of this component.
ISAADAM_IMPORTSCHEMA_*XXX*.log	An AD LDS import schema log file that has the records for successful schema changes that occurred during the installation.
ISA_GettingStarted_*XXX*.log	Contains the log that records the options chosen during the Getting Started Wizard execution.
ISA_IpsUpdateInstall.log	Contains update information for the IPS feature.
IsaUpdateAgent.log	Contains the logs regarding the TMG update agent; used to get new definitions at the time the agent was set up in the Update Center.
*.etl	Tracing logs that are not available in a readable format for the end user. They can be sent to Microsoft Customer Services and Support Forefront TMG Team for analyzes and troubleshooting purpose.
PrerequisiteInstaller.DATE-TIME.log	File that is created during the execution of the Preparation Tool. This file contains details about the verification process and what components were installed by the Preparation Tool.
Microsoft.Isa.ManagedPerfCounters.dll.log	Contains information related to the registration TMG perfmon counters.
ServerManagerCmdInstallLogDATE-TIME	This file contains the logging output for the interaction that Preparation Tool has with the Windows Server Manager command-line interface.

Reading Log Files

By default, the logs are saved in *verbose* mode, which means they contain detailed information about each step in the installation process. The log information is saved from the top down, so that the end of the file contains the latest information of the most recent setup run on the system. To help you better understand how to read these files, we will use two example files. The first one is the ISAWRAP_*XXX*.log, which has the following structure:

General information about the setup initialization

```
13:02:25 INFO:  Installer activated, command-line='/v"ADDLOCAL=Storage_
                Server,MSFirewall_Services,MSFirewall_Management"'
13:02:26 INFO:  Expanded full extraction path of SQL Express 2008 SP1 Package is
                'C:\Windows\temp\{4E6CF6C6-2805-444D-8775-B5A2245086A4}'.
13:02:26 INFO:  Install scenario
13:02:26 INFO:  CMsiAttendantInstaller::Prepare: Upgrade code is not set
13:02:26 INFO:  CMsiAttendantInstaller::Prepare: There is no any product code for
                upgrade code
13:02:26 INFO:  CMsiAttendantInstaller::Prepare: Upgrade code is not set
13:02:26 INFO:  CMsiAttendantInstaller::Prepare: There is no any product code for
                upgrade code
```

Installation of the core components and registration of the log session

```
13:02:26 INFO:  CSSEInstaller::Prepare: Failed to get the instace id of ISARS
13:02:26 INFO:  CMsiAttendantInstaller::Prepare: Upgrade code is not set
13:02:26 INFO:  CMsiAttendantInstaller::Prepare: There is no any product code for
                upgrade code
13:02:26 INFO:  Installing ISA (Core components)...
13:02:26 INFO:  CFirewallInstaller: Activating installation, command line args = '-I
                "D:\FPC\MS_FPC_Server.msi "ADDLOCAL=Storage_Server,MSFirewall_
                Services,MSFirewall_Management WRAPPER=1 ARPSYSTEMCOMPONENT=1
                REBOOT=ReallySuppress'
```

Error information

```
13:02:54 ERROR: Setup failed. Error returned: 0x643
13:02:54 ERROR: CBasicInstaller: Install failed, hr=0x80070643
13:02:54 ERROR: Installation failed. hr = 0x80070643
13:02:54 ERROR: Installation failed, hr=0x80070643
13:02:54 ERROR: InstallProducts: Install ISA (Core components) failed, hr=0x80070643
13:02:58 ERROR: Wrapper: Install failed, hr = 0x80070643
13:02:58 ERROR: Wrapper: DoSetup failed, hr = 0x80070643
13:02:58 ERROR: Wrapper: DoSetup failed, hr = 80070643
13:02:58 ERROR: Setup of ISA failed. Return value: SETUP_ERROR_ISA
```

The error session contains the error number in HRESULT format and represents the reason why setup failed at that point. For this example the HRESULT (0x80070643) means ERROR_INSTALL_FAILURE.

> **MORE INFO** For more information about HRESULT format see *http://msdn.microsoft.com/en-gb/library/cc231198.aspx*. You can also download the err.exe tool to rapidly translate the HRESULT error into a readable format: *http://www.microsoft.com/downloads/details.aspx?displaylang=en&FamilyID=be596899-7bb8-4208-b7fc-09e02a13696c*.

The other file that you can use for troubleshooting purposes, which contains much more information about TMG installation, is ISAFWSV_*XXX*.log. This file has the following sessions:

MSI package information

```
MSI (c) (14:90) [10:39:27:778]: Machine policy value 'DisableUserInstalls' is 0
MSI (c) (14:90) [10:39:27:793]: Note: 1: 1402 2: HKEY_CURRENT_USER\Software\Microsoft\
                                Windows\CurrentVersion\Policies\Explorer 3: 2
MSI (c) (14:90) [10:39:27:856]: SOFTWARE RESTRICTION POLICY: Verifying package -->
                                'D:\FPC\MS_FPC_Server.msi ' against software
                                restriction policy
MSI (c) (14:90) [10:39:27:856]: SOFTWARE RESTRICTION POLICY: D:\FPC\MS_FPC_Server.msi
                                has a digital signature
MSI (c) (14:90) [10:39:43:215]: SOFTWARE RESTRICTION POLICY: D:\FPC\MS_FPC_Server.msi
                                is permitted to run at the 'unrestricted' authorization
                                level.
MSI (c) (14:90) [10:39:43:387]: Cloaking enabled.
MSI (c) (14:90) [10:39:43:387]: Attempting to enable all disabled privileges before
                                calling Install on Server
MSI (c) (14:90) [10:39:43:387]: End dialog not enabled
MSI (c) (14:90) [10:39:43:387]: Original package ==> D:\FPC\MS_FPC_Server.msi
MSI (c) (14:90) [10:39:43:387]: Package we're running from ==> C:\Users\ADMINI~1.CON\
                                AppData\Local\Temp\6389b0.msi
MSI (c) (14:90) [10:39:43:434]: APPCOMPAT: Compatibility mode property overrides found.
MSI (c) (14:90) [10:39:43:450]: APPCOMPAT: looking for appcompat database entry with
                                ProductCode '{AEBCA466-489C-4E03-B667-C89DCD5EFF24}'.
MSI (c) (14:90) [10:39:43:450]: APPCOMPAT: no matching ProductCode found in database.
MSI (c) (14:90) [10:39:43:684]: MSCOREE not loaded loading copy from system32
MSI (c) (14:90) [10:39:43:762]: Machine policy value 'TransformsSecure' is 1
MSI (c) (14:90) [10:39:43:762]: Machine policy value 'DisablePatch' is 0
MSI (c) (14:90) [10:39:43:762]: Machine policy value 'AllowLockdownPatch' is 0
MSI (c) (14:90) [10:39:43:762]: Machine policy value 'DisableLUAPatching' is 0
MSI (c) (14:90) [10:39:43:762]: Machine policy value 'DisableFlyWeightPatching' is 0
MSI (c) (14:90) [10:39:43:778]: APPCOMPAT: looking for appcompat database entry with
                                ProductCode '{AEBCA466-489C-4E03-B667-C89DCD5EFF24}'.
MSI (c) (14:90) [10:39:43:778]: APPCOMPAT: no matching ProductCode found in database.
MSI (c) (14:90) [10:39:43:778]: Transforms are not secure.
MSI (c) (14:90) [10:39:43:778]: PROPERTY CHANGE: Adding MsiLogFileLocation property.
                                Its value is 'C:\Windows\TEMP\ISAFWSV_156.log'.
```

TMG setup general information

```
10:39:44 ISA setup CA INFO   : ENTRY: EE_ValidatePropertiesSyntax, PID 1996 (0x7CC),
                               Current user is CONTOSO\administrator
10:39:44 ISA setup CA INFO   : Checking the length of properties
10:39:44 ISA setup CA INFO   : VerifyPropertyLength: Property ENTERPRISE_NAME length
                               < 300
10:39:44 ISA setup CA INFO   : VerifyPropertyLength: Property ENTERPRISE_DESCR length
                               < 300
10:39:44 ISA setup CA INFO   : VerifyPropertyLength: Property STORAGESERVICE_ACCOUNT
                               length < 300
10:39:44 ISA setup CA INFO   : VerifyPropertyLength: Property STORAGESERVICE_PWD
                               length < 300
10:39:44 ISA setup CA INFO   : VerifyPropertyLength: Property STORAGESERVER_CONNECT_
                               ACCOUNT length < 300
10:39:44 ISA setup CA INFO   : VerifyPropertyLength: Property STORAGESERVER_CONNECT_
                               PWD length < 300
10:39:44 ISA setup CA INFO   : VerifyPropertyLength: Property ARRAY_NAME length < 300
10:39:44 ISA setup CA INFO   : VerifyPropertyLength: Property ARRAY_DESCR length < 300
10:39:44 ISA setup CA INFO   : VerifyPropertyLength: Property ARRAY_DNS_NAME length
                               < 300
10:39:44 ISA setup CA INFO   : VerifyPropertyLength: Property REPLICATION_SOURCE_PATH
                               length < 260
10:39:44 ISA setup CA INFO   : VerifyPropertyLength: Property ARRAY_ENTERPRISEPOLICY
                               length < 300
10:39:44 ISA setup CA INFO   : VerifyPropertyLength: Property CLIENT_CERTIFICATE_
                               FULLPATH length < 260
10:39:44 ISA setup CA INFO   : VerifyPropertyLength: Property SERVER_CERTIFICATE_
                               FULLPATH length < 260
10:39:44 ISA setup CA INFO   : VerifyPropertyLength: Property SERVER_CERTIFICATE_
                               PASSWORD length < 32
10:39:44 ISA setup CA INFO   : VerifyPropertyLength: Property FULLPATHANSWERFILE
                               length < 260
10:39:44 ISA setup CA INFO   : Length of all properties is correct
10:39:44 ISA setup CA INFO   : Checking the syntax of some properties
10:39:44 ISA setup CA INFO   : Syntax condition of all properties is correct
10:39:44 ISA setup CA INFO   : Checking the syntax of the MSIPROP_ARRAY_INTERNALNET
                               properties
10:39:44 ISA setup CA INFO   : Syntax of the properties internal range property is
                               correct
10:39:44 ISA setup CA INFO   : Checking the syntax of the property ARRAY_INTERNALNET_
                               ENT_NETS
10:39:44 ISA setup CA INFO   : Syntax of the property ARRAY_INTERNALNET_ENT_NETS is
                               correct
10:39:44 ISA setup CA INFO   : Checking the syntax of the property INTRA_ARRAY_
                               ADDRESS_IP
10:39:44 ISA setup CA INFO   : Checking the syntax of the property HOST_ID
```

```
10:39:44 ISA setup CA INFO    : Checking the existance of files in properties
10:39:44 ISA setup CA INFO    : All properties that contain files exist
10:39:44 ISA setup CA INFO    : EXIT: EE_ValidatePropertiesSyntax, Custom Action
                                succeeded
```

TMG parameters set during installation

```
Property(S): DiskPrompt = [1]
Property(S): Registration = No
Property(S): UpgradeCode = {5511D21C-DE76-471F-B405-A59952F00E85}
Property(S): ConfigureFweng = **********
Property(S): ConfigureFwServices = **********
Property(S): CreateStorage_ArrayAndServer = **********
Property(S): CreateStorage_Enterprise = **********
Property(S): CreateStorage_JoinedServer = **********
Property(S): DeleteCache = **********
Property(S): InitConfigurationAgent = **********
Property(S): InstallADAM = **********
Property(S): InstallClientSideCertificate = **********
Property(S): InstallReplicaADAM = **********
Property(S): RegisterFiltersCOM = **********
Property(S): RegisterFiltersDllInstall = **********
Property(S): RegisterPerfmon = **********
Property(S): RegisterManagedPerfmon = **********
Property(S): RegisterVPNPlugin = **********
Property(S): RemoveGeneratedFiles = **********
Property(S): RemoveServerFromArrayMembersComputerSet = **********
Property(S): RemoveServerFromManagedServersComputerSet = **********
Property(S): RestoreServicesConfiguration = **********
Property(S): SetArrayAuthMethodOnRepair = **********
Property(S): SetFileInfo = **********
Property(S): SetISAServerEdition = **********
Property(S): SetMSDEInfo = **********
Property(S): SetNetworkInfo = **********
Property(S): SetPropertyADAMServerToWorkWith = **********
Property(S): SetVPNMaximumClients = **********
Property(S): StartServerServices = **********
Property(S): StopServerServices = **********
Property(S): UnregisterFilters = **********
Property(S): UnregisterPerfmon = **********
Property(S): UnregisterManagedPerfmon = **********
Property(S): UnregisterVPNPlugin = **********
Property(S): UnregisterWspadminCom = **********
Property(S): UpdateArrayMembersComputerSet = **********
Property(S): UpdateEnterpriseConfigurationDomainNameSet = **********
Property(S): UpdateManagedServersComputerSet = **********
```

```
Property(S): AUTHZ_FOUND = C:\Windows\SysWOW64\authz.dll
Property(S): IE6FOUND = C:\Windows\SysWOW64\shdocvw.dll
Property(S): GlobalAssemblyCache = C:\
Property(S): INSTALLDIR = C:\Program Files\Microsoft Forefront Threat Management Gateway\
Property(S): ValidServer = 1
Property(S): ADAM = C:\Program Files\Microsoft Forefront Threat Management Gateway\ADAM\
Property(S): APPLIANCE = C:\Program Files\Microsoft Forefront Threat Management
             Gateway\Appliance\
Property(S): MPENGINE = C:\Program Files\Microsoft Forefront Threat Management
             Gateway\MPEngine\
Property(S): URLFILTERING = C:\Program Files\Microsoft Forefront Threat Management
             Gateway\UrlFiltering\
Property(S): IPS_Directory = C:\Program Files\Microsoft Forefront Threat Management
             Gateway\IPS\
Property(S): UI_HTMLS = C:\Program Files\Microsoft Forefront Threat Management
             Gateway\UI_HTMLs\
Property(S): BASICPANE = C:\Program Files\Microsoft Forefront Threat Management
             Gateway\UI_HTMLs\BasicPane\
Property(S): COMMON = C:\Program Files\Microsoft Forefront Threat Management Gateway\
             UI_HTMLs\_image\common\
Property(S): COMMON_EE = C:\Program Files\Microsoft Forefront Threat Management
             Gateway\UI_HTMLs\_image\common\
Property(S): CONFIG1 = C:\Program Files\Microsoft Forefront Threat Management Gateway\
             UI_HTMLs\_image\config\
Property(S): GENERAL = C:\Program Files\Microsoft Forefront Threat Management Gateway\
             UI_HTMLs\_image\general\
Property(S): GROUPINGBAR = C:\Program Files\Microsoft Forefront Threat Management
             Gateway\UI_HTMLs\_image\GroupingBar\
Property(S): LOGPANE = C:\Program Files\Microsoft Forefront Threat Management Gateway\
             UI_HTMLs\_image\logpane\
Property(S): TASKBAR = C:\Program Files\Microsoft Forefront Threat Management Gateway\
             UI_HTMLs\_image\Taskbar\
Property(S): HELPPANE = C:\Program Files\Microsoft Forefront Threat Management
             Gateway\UI_HTMLs\HelpPane\
Property(S): TABSHANDLER = C:\Program Files\Microsoft Forefront Threat Management
             Gateway\UI_HTMLs\TabsHandler\
Property(S): TASKHANDLER = C:\Program Files\Microsoft Forefront Threat Management
             Gateway\UI_HTMLs\TaskHandler\
Property(S): UI_HTMLS_EE = C:\Program Files\Microsoft Forefront Threat Management
             Gateway\UI_HTMLs\
Property(S): _COMMON = C:\Program Files\Microsoft Forefront Threat Management Gateway\
             UI_HTMLs\_common\
Property(S): CHAINCFG = C:\Program Files\Microsoft Forefront Threat Management
             Gateway\ChainCfg\
Property(S): CHAINCFG_W2K = C:\Program Files\Microsoft Forefront Threat Management
             Gateway\ChainCfg\
```

End of the installation with the final result

```
=== Logging stopped: 9/7/2009  10:42:09 ===
MSI (c) (14:90) [10:42:09:981]: Note: 1: 1708
MSI (c) (14:90) [10:42:09:981]: Product: Microsoft Forefront Threat Management Gateway
EE  -- Installation operation failed.
MSI (c) (14:90) [10:42:09:997]: Windows Installer installed the product. Product Name:
Microsoft Forefront Threat Management Gateway EE . Product Version: 7.0.7700. Product
Language: 1033. Manufacturer: Microsoft Corporation. Installation success or error
status: 1603.
MSI (c) (14:90) [10:42:10:013]: Grabbed execution mutex.
MSI (c) (14:90) [10:42:10:013]: Cleaning up uninstalled install packages, if any exist
MSI (c) (14:90) [10:42:10:013]: MainEngineThread is returning 1603
=== Verbose logging stopped: 9/7/2009  10:42:10 ===
```

Notice that this file contains many more sessions and a lot more information about the setup process. However, the end result is the same code that the previous file showed you, but in a different format. The code 1603 is the same as 0x80070643, but in another format.

Setup Failed—Now What?

Now that you understand how the setup log files are stored and what type of information each one contains, you can troubleshoot a real setup failure. When setup fails, the TMG Installation Graphical User Interface triggers an error as a result of the failure, such as the one shown in Figure 9-4.

FIGURE 9-4 Error message while installing TMG

This error message explains the reason why Forefront TMG can't proceed with the installation process. If you click OK, the TMG Setup rolls back the changes and when finished displays the page shown in Figure 9-5.

To track down this error you can search for this description in the file ISAFWSV_*XXX*.log. Open this file in Notepad, press Ctrl+End (to go to the end of the file), and then press Ctrl+F to open the Find dialog box. Type the first five words of this description (for example **a computer restart is required**). By performing this search and finding this keyword in the log file, the prompt will be in the same location where the error message occurred (the one that appeared in the UI). You need to move up in the log file to find what happened before this event. The following example in the file ISAFWSV_*XXX*.log shows where the real error message is located:

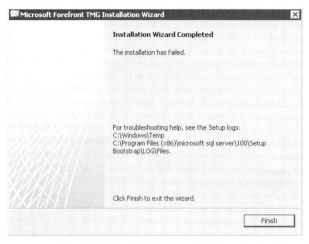

FIGURE 9-5 The Installation Failed page of the Installation Wizard

Starting the installation of the optional components

```
MSI (c) (EC:74) [13:02:45:558]: Invoking remote custom action. DLL:
C:\Users\ADMINI~1.CON\AppData\Local\Temp\MSIBE1D.tmp, Entrypoint:
SetRebootRequiredBeforeInstallationProperty
13:02:45 ISA setup CA INFO    : ENTRY: SetRebootRequiredBeforeInstallationProperty,
                                PID 812 (0x32C), Current user is CONTOSO\administrator
13:02:45 ISA setup CA INFO    : Restart is required. Indicated by the registry value
                                PendingFileRenameOperations.
MSI (c) (EC!48) [13:02:45:589]: PROPERTY CHANGE: Adding REBOOT_REQUIRED_BEFORE_
                                INSTALLATION property. Its value is '1'.
13:02:45 ISA setup CA INFO    : EXIT: SetRebootRequiredBeforeInstallationProperty,
                                Custom Action succeeded
Action ended 13:02:45: SetRebootRequiredBeforeInstallationProperty. Return value 1.
```

Error message right after running the previous command line

```
MSI (c) (EC:C0) [13:02:45:589]: Doing action: LaunchConditions
Action 13:02:45: LaunchConditions. Evaluating launch conditions
Action start 13:02:45: LaunchConditions.
A computer restart is required. You must restart this computer before installing
Forefront TMG.
```

Actual message that appears in the GUI

```
MSI (c) (EC:C0) [13:02:54:527]: Product: Microsoft Forefront Threat Management
Gateway EE  -- A computer restart is required. You must restart this computer before
installing Forefront TMG.
Action ended 13:02:54: LaunchConditions. Return value 3.
MSI (c) (EC:C0) [13:02:54:542]: Skipping action: SetupCompleteError (condition is false)
Action ended 13:02:54: INSTALL. Return value 3.
```

The preceding example is very straightforward, and you might think that this is easy to fix; however, the troubleshooting approach that you will use in most of the installation failures scenario is the same.

In some other scenarios (such as a component failure during TMG installation) you can use other logs besides the setup failure information in the log file. Other details might also be available in the Windows Event Log under the Setup category, as shown in Figure 9-6.

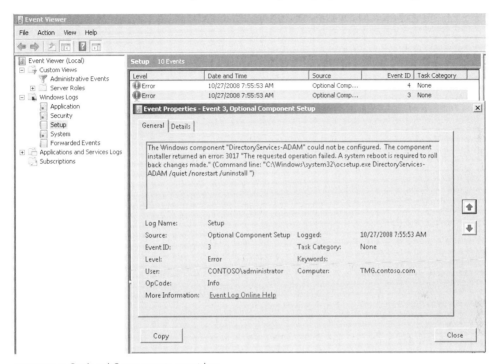

FIGURE 9-6 Optional Components event log

In the previous example the TMG installation failed after the execution of the command *C:\Windows\system32\ServerManagerCmd.exe -inputpath "E:\Program Files\Microsoft ISA Server\OCDATA\OCDataInstall.xml" -logPath "C:\Windows\TEMP\OC_INSTALL_191_0.log*. This command has a parameter that dumps the logging information to a file that is also located in the Windows Temp folder. You can also open this file using Notepad and go to the end of the file and scroll up. For this example, the failure occurred in the following point, indicated by the line in bold type:

```
2020: 2008-10-27 07:44:08.482 [CbsUIHandler]          Initiate:
2020: 2008-10-27 07:47:37.141 [CbsUIHandler]          Error: -2147021879 :
2020: 2008-10-27 07:47:37.172 [CbsUIHandler]          Terminate:
```

After finding the error you can search for it at *technet.microsoft.com* to find out whether any documentation for it is available. Sometimes (such as in the case of our example) the error message has more information only available internally (Microsoft) or by parsing the ETL files located in the %windir%\temp folder. When you can't proceed because no more elements are visible, you should open a service request with Microsoft Customer Service and Support for further assistance. We won't leave this example behind. This scenario was based on a real-world incident, and in the sidebar "Unable to Install TMG" we will tell you how we fixed it.

REAL WORLD   Unable to Install TMG

We received a question regarding this installation problem while TMG was still in beta. The setup log file we presented to you in this chapter was based on a reproduction scenario we did in our lab to simulate the real issue that was happening in the original request.

After parsing the ETL file and using the internal Microsoft trace files to investigate further, we were able to determine that the failure occurred because of a lack of permissions in the destination container. The drive that the administrator was trying to install TMG was hardened in a standard not supported by Microsoft, and some key permissions were removed.

This was a brand-new partition that was hardened even before installing TMG, which is really a bad idea. After reformatting the drive and enabling the default permissions, the installation was done successfully. The lesson learned was to not implement any type of hardening on the TMG computer not officially supported by Microsoft.

Summary

TMG Setup is designed for a successful end-user experience by simplifying the process and ensuring that a successful installation produces a functional TMG service. However, some scenarios and specific situations can cause setup to fail. When this happens, it is important to know exactly which files will be available for troubleshooting purposes and how to review the information logged in these files. In this chapter you learned how to identify the setup log and the setup options, how to install TMG along with updates, and how to troubleshoot a setup failure.

## CHAPTER 10

Exploring the TMG Console

- TMG Medium Business Edition **185**

- Updates for TMG 2010 **192**

- New Wizards **199**

- Summary **206**

The user interface is something that most administrators are concerned about when a new release for software that they are used to working with comes to the market. The good news is that with TMG, the changes in both releases (TMG MBE and TMG 2010) are based on enhancements each version brings to the table. This chapter will go through the new options available for TMG MBE and also for TMG 2010. After viewing the new options, you will see the new wizards that were added in TMG 2010 and which wizards were changed from ISA Server 2006.

TMG Medium Business Edition

The TMG MBE console doesn't look much different from the ISA Server 2006 console. You can immediately see some new nodes in the left pane, and you might also spot a few missing ones. Before we go into the new tabs that expose new features, review the TMG MBE Welcome Screen, as shown in Figure 10-1.

In the left pane you can see the main options available to you in TMG MBE. Notice the following things that were added or removed from the left pane of the console:

- A new node called Update Center is added.

- A new node called Web Access Policy is added.

- A new node called System is added.

- The Configuration node available in ISA Server 2006 has been removed.

- The Networks node available in ISA Server 2006 under Configuration is now available as the Networking node in the main window.

- The Cache node, which was available under Configuration, is no longer exposed in the main window.

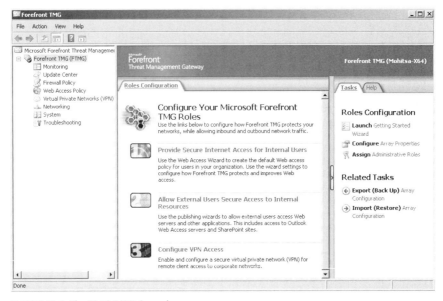

FIGURE 10-1 The TMG MBE Console

- The Add-ins node, which was available under Configuration, is no longer exposed in the main window.

- The Troubleshooting node available in ISA Server 2006 Service Pack 1 and ISA Server 2004 Service Pack 3 is now available in TMG MBE.

Monitoring

The Monitoring node in TMG MBE has almost all the same options as ISA Server 2006 except for the Configuration tab. One of the major changes in TMG MBE was the installation of Active Directory Lightweight Directory Service (AD LDS) where configuration information is now stored. Just like in ISA 2004 or 2006 Enterprise edition, TMG MBE has a tab called Configuration under Monitoring where the administrator can see whether the firewall has synchronized with its Configuration Storage, as shown in Figure 10-2.

FIGURE 10-2 Configuration status in TMG MBE

Another change on the Monitoring node is the list of available services under the Services tab. ISA Server 2006 had Microsoft Data Engine, Microsoft ISA Server Job Scheduler, and Microsoft Firewall as the listed services. TMG MBE now has the SQL Server Express service along with Microsoft Firewall and Microsoft Forefront TMG Job Scheduler service listed under the Services tab, as shown in Figure 10-3.

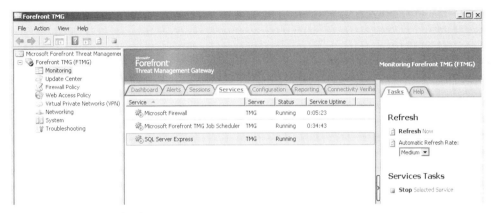

FIGURE 10-3 TMG MBE Services

Update Center

The Update Center node is a new node introduced in TMG MBE. The Update Center lets you control the settings for HTTP Malware Inspection. You can define actions to check and install malware definition updates from the Microsoft Update site manually or you can automate the process. We will cover this topic of HTTP malware inspection and how to configure it in Chapter 17, "Malware Inspection." Figure 10-4 shows the Update Center settings.

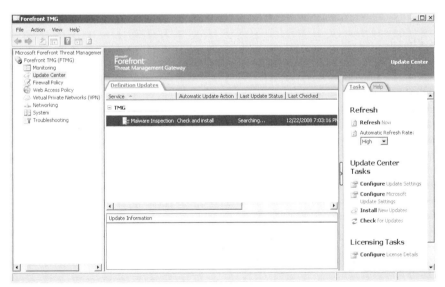

FIGURE 10-4 The TMG MBE Update Center

Firewall Policy

Firewall Policy in TMG MBE controls inbound and outbound policy rules as it did in ISA Server 2006. The Additional Security Policy and Global Link Translation setting in ISA Server 2006, which were available under the General node, are now available on the Tasks tab under Firewall Policy Tasks in the left pane. These settings allow you to control all security access settings from one node. Figure 10-5 shows the new options now available under Firewall Policy Tasks.

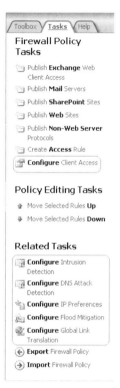

FIGURE 10-5 New tasks available under Firewall Policy Tasks

Another new option available under Firewall Policy Tasks is Configure Client Access, which lets you configure options on the selected network in the same way you would via the Networks node. Figures 10-6 and 10-7 show the options Configure Client Access exposes.

Web Access Policy

You can use Web Access Policy to define access rules that specify whether all sites will be inspected or some sites will be exempt from inspection. You can also configure the Malware Inspection settings to define the default action in the event that malware is detected in a file. We will cover the details of malware inspection in Chapter 17, "Malware Inspection." Figure 10-8 shows the options available under Web Access Policy.

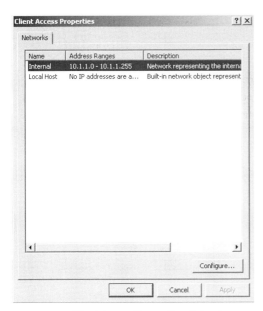

FIGURE 10-6 Client Access Properties dialog box

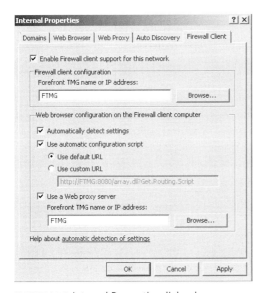

FIGURE 10-7 Internal Properties dialog box

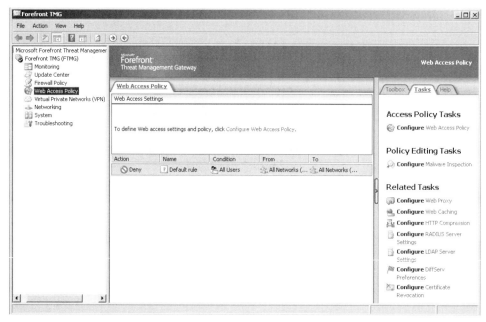

FIGURE 10-8 Web Access Policy

The Global HTTP Policy Settings available under the General node in ISA Server 2006 are now listed under Web Access Policy Tasks in TMG MBE. The only missing setting is Configure Global Link Translation, which is listed under the Firewall Policy tasks in TMG MBE. The other tasks that are now listed here are Configure Radius Server Settings and Configure LDAP Server Settings, which have been moved from the General node in ISA 2006 to Web Access Policy Tasks. Caching, which was available as an option in the main window in ISA Server 2006 and removed in TMG MBE, is now listed as a task under Web Access Policy Tasks. The option to enable or disable Web Proxy settings from the Internal Network is also available as the task Configure Web Proxy, found under Web Access Policy Tasks. Figure 10-9 shows the tasks listed under Web Access Policy Tasks.

Related Tasks

Configure Web Proxy

Configure Web Caching

Configure HTTP Compression

Configure RADIUS Server Settings

Configure LDAP Server Settings

Configure DiffServ Preferences

Configure Certificate Revocation

FIGURE 10-9 Web Access Policy Tasks

Networking

The Networking node in TMG MBE has not changed greatly from ISA Server 2006. The only exception is that the Configure Firewall Client Settings and Configure Firewall Chaining options are now available under Networks Tasks. They were previously available under the General node in ISA Server 2006. Figure 10-10 shows the tasks listed under Network Tasks.

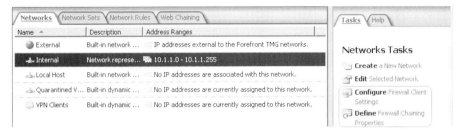

FIGURE 10-10 Networks Tasks

System

The System node provides server details the same way the Servers tab provided the details of available servers in an array in ISA Server 2006 Enterprise edition. A major change here is the Add-ins tab, which was available in the main window in ISA Server 2006 to display the Web Filters and the Application Filters. In TMG MBE, the Add-ins node has been removed from the main window and is now available as an Application Filter tab and a Web Filter tab under the System node. Figure 10-11 shows the list of tabs available under the System node; Figure 10-12 shows the System node display.

FIGURE 10-11 Tabs available under the System tab

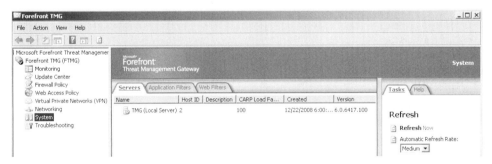

FIGURE 10-12 The System tab in TMG MBE

Updates for TMG 2010

Because of a natural concern about drastic changes in the user interface (UI), Forefront TMG 2010 uses the core interface design used by TMG MBE. TMG 2010 doesn't change the core aspect of those options—the addition of new options are part of the new feature set that is only available for this version of the product. Figure 10-13 shows the main TMG 2010 management console.

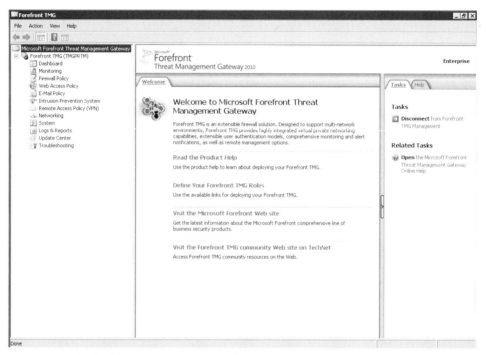

FIGURE 10-13 The TMG 2010 management console

The left pane shows the nodes that were added or modified from TMG MBE to TMG 2010, which are:

- **E-Mail Policy**   This option enables you to configure SMTP protection, which is covered in detail in Chapter 19, "Enhancing E-Mail Protection."

- **Intrusion Prevention System**   Here you can configure network protection, which is covered in Chapter 14, "Network Inspection System."

- **Remote Access Policy (VPN)**   This option was previously called Virtual Private Networks (VPN). It was renamed to provide a better understanding of the final goal, which is to allow remote access through TMG. Chapter 26, "Implementing Dial-in Client VPN," explains VPN in more details.

- **Logs & Reports**   Although this is not a new option, it was moved so that logging and reporting features are located in one place. Those options are covered in detail in Chapter 28, "Logging."

Figure 10-14 compares the left panes in TMG MBE and TMG 2010.

FIGURE 10-14 TMG MBE and TMG 2010 core options

Also notice that the Update Center node has been moved. The management options are now concentrated at the bottom of the console and the configuration options are at the top.

Now that you've seen an overview of the core changes in the main console, let's explore each option and see those changes.

Monitoring

The monitoring node no longer includes the Logging, Reporting, and Dashboard tabs—they have been moved to their own nodes in the left pane of the console. This was a good decision, because the goal of the monitoring option is to enable real-time access to the main TMG components and identify their current status. The new options are shown in Figure 10-15.

FIGURE 10-15 Monitoring options

Within the monitoring option, on the Services tab, the way that TMG presents the running services has also changed. Now the reporting services are separated into their own group. This is beneficial in helping you understand which component needs those services. Figure 10-16 shows the new entries in the Services tab.

FIGURE 10-16 New services categorization

Firewall Policy

This node experienced minor changes in the middle pane; however, the toolbar adds new options that can assist you in rapidly accessing related tasks. Figure 10-17 shows the new toolbar that is available when you click Firewall Policy.

FIGURE 10-17 The Firewall Policy toolbar

The other changes are located in the task pane and also are related to new features of TMG 2010, such as the option to configure Voice over Internet Protocol (VoIP).

Web Access Policy

Web Access Policy did not change that much in TMG 2010—it was already a new feature in TMG MBE. The only additional options are access to URL Filtering and HTTPS Inspection in the task pane, as shown in Figure 10-18.

FIGURE 10-18 Accessing URL Filtering and HTTPS Inspection from Web Access Policy

In addition, the toolbar changes when you select Web Access Policy and provides new shortcuts for other options, as shown in Figure 10-19.

FIGURE 10-19 The Web Access Policy toolbar

E-Mail Policy

E-mail protection is one of the major areas where TMG 2010 introduces a set of new features. This option was designed to provide easy access for configuring e-mail policy, spam filtering, and virus and content filtering. The first tab (E-Mail Policy) has options for creating a new policy and associating it to the internal SMTP server. Figure 10-20 shows the options for the E-Mail Policy tab.

When you click the E-Mail Policy tab, the task pane makes available the options shown in Figure 10-21.

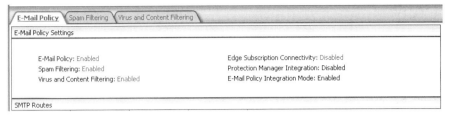

FIGURE 10-20 The E-mail Policy tab

E-Mail Policy Tasks

 Configure **E-Mail Policy**

 **Create** SMTP Route

Edge Subscription Tasks

Enable Connectivity for
EdgeSync Traffic

Related Tasks

Publish **Exchange** Web Client
Access

Publish **Mail** Servers

Export E-Mail Policy
Configuration

Import E-Mail Policy
Configuration

FIGURE 10-21 E-mail protection options

Figures 10-22 and 10-23 show the options available for the other two tabs.

FIGURE 10-22 The Spam Filtering tab

FIGURE 10-23 The Virus And Content Filtering tab

Intrusion Prevention System

Network protection provided by TMG 2010 is configured using the Network Inspection System (NIS). This option allows you to configure signatures and also configure the action (response) when TMG 2010 detects network traffic matching such a signature. Figure 10-24 shows the main screen for IPS, which is divided in two tabs: Network Inspection System (NIS) and Behavioral Intrusion Detection (Figure 10-25). More options are available in the task pane.

FIGURE 10-24 The Network Inspection System tab

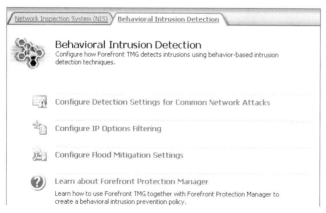

FIGURE 10-25 The Behavioral Intrusion Detection tab

After clicking the Network Inspection System Tab, you have the options shown in Figure 10-26.

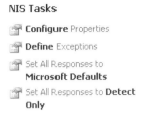

NIS Tasks

Configure Properties

Define Exceptions

Set All Responses to **Microsoft Defaults**

Set All Responses to **Detect Only**

Selected Signature Tasks

Related Tasks

Link to Update Center

Link to Microsoft Malware Protection Center

FIGURE 10-26 The Network Inspection System Task Pane options

The Remote Access Policy (VPN) has the same options that TMG MBE has; nothing has changed in the main interface.

Networking

Although TMG MBE has a Networking node, the options available in TMG 2010 are extended and include new features such as ISP Redundancy. Figure 10-27 shows the tabs that are new in TMB 2010.

FIGURE 10-27 Options added to the Networking node for TMG 2010

The first new tab, Network Adapter, allows you to view the IP configuration of the network adapters installed on the TMG computer. This can save you time if you want to quickly review your TCP/IP configuration because you don't have to open Windows Control Panel and go to the Network and Sharing Center. Figure 10-28 shows this new tab.

FIGURE 10-28 The Network Adapters tab

The other great addition to the Networking node is that now you can see your routing table without having to use the route print command from the command prompt. Figure 10-29 shows the new Routing tab.

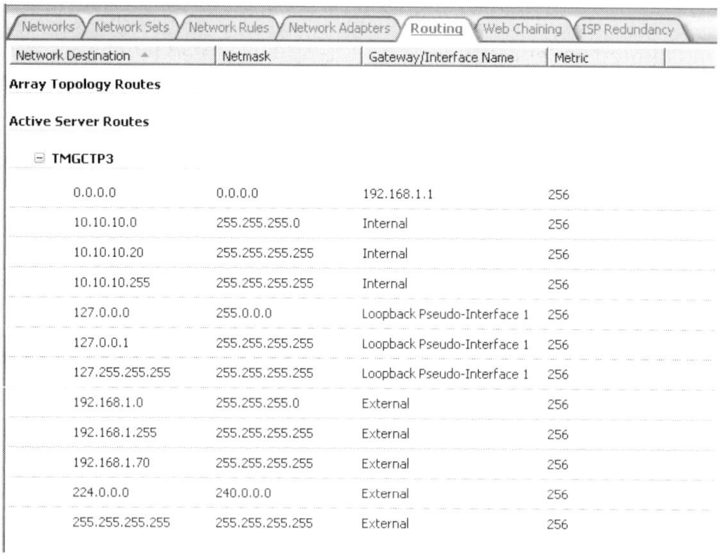

Network Destination ▲	Netmask	Gateway/Interface Name	Metric
Array Topology Routes			
Active Server Routes			
⊟ **TMGCTP3**			
0.0.0.0	0.0.0.0	192.168.1.1	256
10.10.10.0	255.255.255.0	Internal	256
10.10.10.20	255.255.255.255	Internal	256
10.10.10.255	255.255.255.255	Internal	256
127.0.0.0	255.0.0.0	Loopback Pseudo-Interface 1	256
127.0.0.1	255.255.255.255	Loopback Pseudo-Interface 1	256
127.255.255.255	255.255.255.255	Loopback Pseudo-Interface 1	256
192.168.1.0	255.255.255.0	External	256
192.168.1.255	255.255.255.255	External	256
192.168.1.70	255.255.255.255	External	256
224.0.0.0	240.0.0.0	External	256
255.255.255.255	255.255.255.255	External	256

FIGURE 10-29 The Routing tab

The last tab, ISP Redundancy, will be disabled by default, as shown in Figure 10-30.

ISP Redundancy

You can configure ISP redundancy to distribute outbound traffic between two ISP connections using failover between a primary and backup link, or load balancing and failover.

To define the ISP connections and the distribution mode, on the task pane, click Configure ISP Redundancy.

FIGURE 10-30 The ISP Redundancy tab

The options available in the task pane for this feature are shown in Figure 10-31.

ISP Redundancy Tasks

Configure ISP Redundancy

Related Tasks

Monitor ISP Redundancy Connections

Export ISP Redundancy Configuration

Import ISP Redundancy Configuration

FIGURE 10-31 The ISP Redundancy Tasks tab

The System node experienced only minor changes—the addition of the SIP Access Application Filter and the Generic Web Protocol Analyzer Web Filter.

Logs and Reports

The Logging option that was located under Monitoring in TMG MBE migrated to the Logs & Reports node without changes. The same thing happened to the Reporting option.

Update Center

The Update Center was first introduced in TMG MBE and TMG 2010 enhances this option by adding new services, such as Network Inspection System. Figure 10-32 shows the new design of Update Center in TMG 2010.

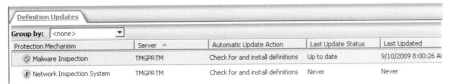

FIGURE 10-32 The new Update Center for TMG 2010

The last node is Troubleshooting. This node still contains the same options from TMG MBE: BPA, Review Alerts, View TMG Logging, and TMG Documentation.

New Wizards

TMG provides many new wizards and improves on many of the old ones offered in ISA Server 2006. As with ISA Server 2006, TMG wizards are targeted at specific tasks or scenarios where the user may wish to be guided through the process, or when specific settings that are unexposed to the user need to be configured.

 REAL WORLD **More About Wizards**

Wizards tend to be a great source of debate. Many feel that they serve users' needs by simplifying complex tasks, thus making those tasks less error-prone. Others insist that wizards merely impede users' product education because they tend to hide the underpinnings of the processes handled by the wizard.

To illustrate this debate, we have to go back in time to the heady days of ISA Server 2000. In this product, the process of creating a Web publishing rule went something like this:

1. Start the Web Publishing Rule Wizard. When you get to the point where the wizard asks for the destination set, you realize that you don't have one built for this purpose and have to close the wizard.

2. Start the new Destination Set Wizard and add the destinations for the new Web publishing rule.

3. Restart the Web Publishing Wizard and reach the point where it asks for the destinations. Now you can add the destination set you just built.

This was a very common occurrence in ISA Server 2000 and represents a good example of both schools of thought on the subject:

- **User education** After failing the Web Publishing Wizard enough times for lack of a predefined destination set, the user eventually learns to create the destination set first and then start the Web Publishing Wizard. The user thus learns the interrelationships between ISA policy elements. (Web publishing rules require preexisting destination sets.)

- **User-friendliness** The current Web Publishing Wizard design includes the opportunity to create the rule's dependent objects as part of the wizard's progression. At the point where you have to select an object, you are also given the opportunity to create one, if necessary.

Thus, the goals of user education and user-friendliness need not always be at odds. Good product design and usability testing can produce a result that serves both goals and provides a good user experience.

The Getting Started Wizard

The Getting Started Wizard is available immediately following initial TMG installation and as a link in the array-context task pane. Figure 10-33 shows this option.

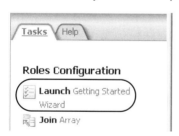

FIGURE 10-33 The Getting Started Wizard link

This wizard allows you to define basic TMG settings by providing easy access to four other wizards:

- The Network Setup Wizard
- The System Configuration Wizard
- The Deployment Wizard
- The Web Access Policy Wizard

Each of these wizards helps simplify the task of configuring TMG to support the needs of a deployment. Although you can execute the Getting Started Wizard anytime you like, it is normally executed only once. The Getting Started Wizard Start page is shown in Figure 10-34.

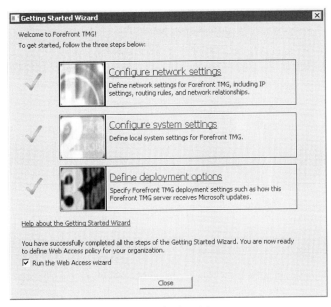

FIGURE 10-34 The Getting Started Wizard Start page

When you see the Getting Started Wizard for the first time, the three primary tasks can only be executed in the order they are presented. When these tasks have been completed, you can use them in any order you like.

The Network Setup Wizard

The Network Setup Wizard is an extension of the ISA Server 2006 Network Template Wizard. Like the ISA Server 2006 Network Template Wizard, you can select from four basic network configurations:

- Edge Firewall
- 3-Leg Perimeter (disabled in EBS)
- Back Firewall
- Single-Network Adapter

Unlike the ISA Server 2006 Network Template Wizard, the TMG Network Setup Wizard also allows you to define the IP settings for each NIC as you associate it with the related TMG network.

Another improvement over the ISA Server 2006 Network Template Wizard is presented when you select the 3-Leg Perimeter or the Back Firewall template. In these cases, the Network Setup Wizard gives you the ability to select the network relationship for the

Perimeter network. This is a great improvement over the ISA Server 2006 Network Template Wizard in that no assumptions are made regarding this relationship; it's your choice to make it a NAT or Route relationship. Figure 10-35 illustrates these additions.

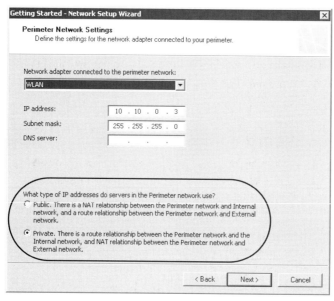

FIGURE 10-35 The Perimeter Network Settings page of the Getting Started Wizard

The System Configuration Wizard

The System Configuration Wizard allows you to define three operational properties for the TMG computer itself:

- Computer name
- Domain or workgroup membership
- Primary DNS suffix

Although these properties are the same as those accessed through Computer Properties in the Windows Server Management console, adding them to the TMG System Configuration Wizard set proved to be very useful in this part of the server configuration process.

The Deployment Wizard

The Deployment Wizard provides access to five configuration pages:

- **Microsoft Update Setup**   Allows you to choose whether to use Microsoft Update or a manual update process to acquire TMG malware definition updates. This does not affect the URL filter subscription-based update process.
- **TMG Protection Features Settings**   Allows you to define the licensing for Intrusion Protection System (IPS), Web access protection, and e-mail protection, in addition to which aspects of Web access and e-mail filtering you want to employ.

- **Customer Feedback**   Allows you to indicate whether you wish to provide automated customer experience feedback regarding TMG usage patterns and configuration.
- **Microsoft Telemetry Service**   Allows you to select whether you wish to join this program using two membership options—Basic or Advanced—or not to join at all. The caveat for this option is that because some raw data is provided to Microsoft Telemetry Services, some personally identifying information (PII) may be included if it is part of the traffic being monitored for malicious behavior. Although Microsoft promises not to use this data for anything other than malicious behavior research, you are offered the ability to opt out of this reporting level.

The Web Access Policy Wizard

The Web Access Policy Wizard is accessible as an optional step in the Getting Started Wizard or from a shortcut menu accessed by right-clicking the Web Access policy element in the left pane, as shown in Figure 10-36.

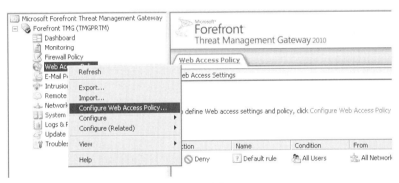

FIGURE 10-36 The Web Access Policy Wizard shortcut menu

The Web Access Policy Wizard provides a guided method through which you can define HTTP-based access rules. It also allows you to configure this policy in the context of malware inspection and user-based versus source-based access controls. You can edit the policy later to suit your specific requirements, but if you chose to rerun the wizard later, the existing Web access policy will be completely replaced in favor of the new configuration.

The Join Array and Disjoin Array Wizards (TMG 2010 only)

The Join Array Wizard is located in the Tasks pane when you select the Forefront TMG (ArrayName) node and represents two new concepts introduced with Forefront TMG:

- Stand-alone, stand-alone array, or enterprise array operation
- Moving a server between array and stand-alone operation without reinstalling the product

Figure 10-37 shows the Join Array link, whereas Figure 10-38 shows the Disjoin Array link.

FIGURE 10-37 The Join Array Wizard link

FIGURE 10-38 The Disjoin Array Wizard link

This wizard provides the means to move between stand-alone or enterprise array operation and back again with relative ease.

The Connect to Forefront Protection Manager 2010 Wizard (TMG 2010 only)

This wizard is located in the Tasks pane when you select Forefront TMG (ArrayName) node, as shown in Figure 10-39. The Link to Forefront Protection Manager (FPM) 2010 Wizard provides the means to join the Forefront TMG array or firewall to the FPM 2010 system. Doing so allows TMG to collaborate with the other sensors and remediation mechanisms provided by FPM 2010, effectively making them both more effective and aware of the network environment. Because FPM 2010 only operates in a domain environment, this wizard cannot function when TMG is installed in a workgroup.

FIGURE 10-39 The Connect to Forefront Protection Manager Integration Page link

The Configure SIP Wizard (TMG 2010 only)

The Configure SIP Wizard is accessed from the Firewall Policy Context Tasks pane. This wizard allows you to configure TMG to support VoIP traffic using Session Initiated Protocol (SIP) signaling. This wizard expects you to define the VoIP destination through which your VoIP traffic will flow. Figure 10-40 shows the link to the Configure SIP Wizard.

FIGURE 10-40 The Configure SIP Wizard link

The Configure E-Mail Policy Wizard (TMG 2010 only)

The E-Mail Policy Wizard is located in the E-mail Protection context tasks pane, as shown in Figure 10-41. This wizard helps you define e-mail SPAM and malware filtering between your organization and the SMTP peers with which you share direct mail transfer policies. Server to Server mail protection is discussed in Chapter 19.

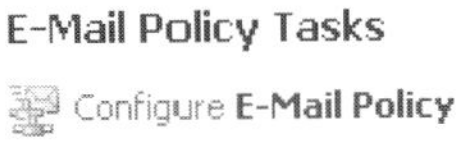

E-Mail Policy Tasks

Configure **E-Mail Policy**

FIGURE 10-41 The Configure Server To Server Mail Protection Wizard link

The Enable ISP Redundancy Wizard (TMG 2010 only)

The Enable ISP Redundancy Wizard is available from the Networking context task pane when the ISP Redundancy tab is selected, as shown in Figure 10-42. This wizard allows you to configure Forefront TMG to use two ISP connections in one of two ways:

- **ISP Redundancy** This mode allows TMG to use both ISP connections simultaneously and thus provide greater bandwidth.

- **ISP Failover** This mode allows TMG to use one ISP connection at a time and shift to the other connection if the primary connection fails.

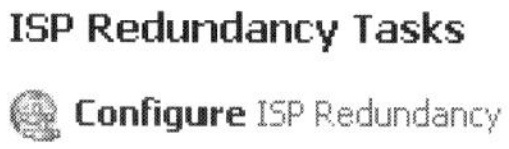

ISP Redundancy Tasks

Configure ISP Redundancy

FIGURE 10-42 The ISP Redundancy Wizard link

ISP Redundancy is discussed in detail in Chapter 13, "Configuring Load Balancing Capabilities."

Summary

The interface evolution from ISA Server 2006 to TMG MBE and TMG 2010 shows strategic changes. Preserving the core interface was a result of the main goal, which was to improve the user experience. It was also necessary to rearrange some options. In addition to the new features—and the changes in the interface that reflect them—TMG also brings a new set of wizards to facilitate the administrator's work. This investment in wizards is important because it reduces human error. For example, instead of manually configuring rules, you have a new wizard to guide you in creating a Web access policy.

Now that you are familiar with the changes in the interface and the new features, it is time to start configuring your TMG. In the next chapter, you will learn how to configure and administer TMG Networks.

PART IV

TMG as Your Firewall

CHAPTER 11 Configuring TMG Networks **209**

CHAPTER 12 Understanding Access Rules **241**

CHAPTER 13 Configuring Load-Balancing Capabilities **263**

CHAPTER 14 Network Inspection System **307**

Configuring TMG Networks

- Understanding Network Relationships **209**

- Creating Networks **222**

- Configuring Your Protected Networks **231**

- Summary **240**

One of the most powerful and misunderstood aspects of ISA Server 2006 deployments was the definition and use of networks. This was made all the more confusing if the person deploying ISA was an experienced network administrator because the term *network* has a much more general meaning than that used by ISA Server 2006. Because Microsoft Forefront Threat Management Gateway (TMG) 2010 uses the term *network* in the same context, you need a clear understanding of how TMG defines these terms.

Understanding Network Relationships

TMG, like ISA Server before it, defines a network as a logical representation of a network connection owned by the computer where TMG operates. These networks can be a physical connection such as network interface card (NIC) or modem, or they can be a logical interface such as a dial-in or site-to-site VPN connection. In each case, TMG must have a clear understanding of how to define and process the traffic that is received from a given network.

The simplest definition for a network relationship is that relationship indicated by the source and destination hosts as defined in the traffic 5-tuple.

> **NOTE** *5-tuple* is an industry-standard standard term describing the criteria used to uniquely identify an IP communication channel. This data includes:
> - Source and destination IP addresses
> - Source and destination ports (if used)
> - Transport Protocol (TCP, UDP, and so on)
>
> Source and destination ports are only valid if the transport is TCP or UDP.

Figure 11-1 illustrates the logical relationship of 5-tuple data in an IP packet.

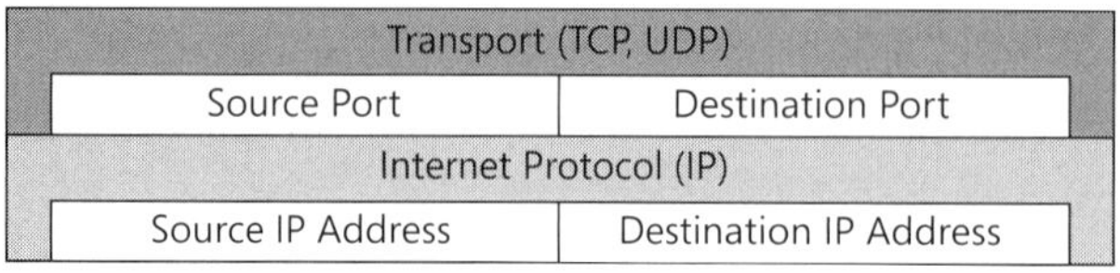

Transport (TCP, UDP)	
Source Port	Destination Port
Internet Protocol (IP)	
Source IP Address	Destination IP Address

FIGURE 11-1 IP packet 5-tuple

A network relationship and the traffic 5-tuple form the primary criteria used by TMG to determine whether traffic should be passed to the policy engine for further processing. It also helps TMG determine which network rule should be applied to the traffic. This section will discuss network relationships as defined by network rules and their effect on TMG traffic processing.

Basic IP Routing

All IP packets contain two address sets: the IP addresses and the link-layer protocol addresses. The protocol below the IP layer is most frequently Ethernet, although other protocols such as Token-Ring are still used, though rarely. For Ethernet, the host physical address is called the Media Access Control (MAC) address. Figure 11-2 illustrates the logical relationship between Ethernet and IP addresses.

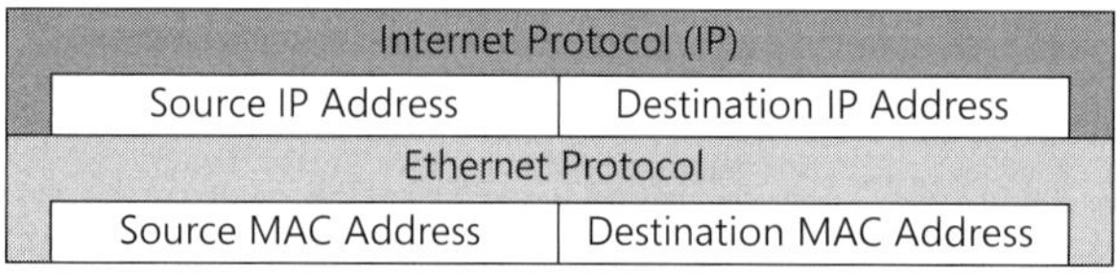

Internet Protocol (IP)	
Source IP Address	Destination IP Address
Ethernet Protocol	
Source MAC Address	Destination MAC Address

FIGURE 11-2 Ethernet and IP address relationships

For one host to send traffic to another host, it must first answer the following questions:

1. Is the destination IP address part of the local subnet, and if not, does the computer IP configuration include a router through which that destination may be reached?

2. Does the local ARP table include a MAC address associated with the destination IP address, or if the destination IP address is not part of the local subnet, does the local ARP table have the MAC address related to the IP address of the nearest router?

If a host cannot answer "yes" to those questions, it cannot send traffic to the destination host.

When a host needs to send IP traffic, it issues an Address Resolution Protocol (ARP) request to obtain the MAC address of the host or router that owns the destination IP address.

> **NOTE** ARP is an Ethernet protocol used by hosts in an IP network to determine the MAC address of the destination host. More information on ARP can be found at *http://www.networksorcery.com/enp/protocol/arp.htm.*

Once the sender has obtained the MAC address of the destination, it can populate the appropriate address fields in the Ethernet frame. The example shown in Figure 11-3 and outlined in the steps that follow illustrates this process using Network Monitor 3.2. In this example, Host1 is assigned IP address 10.10.1.10 and Host2 is assigned IP address 10.10.1.11.

Host1
IP Address   10.10.1.10
MAC Address   00-1C-25-18-99-BB

Host2
IP Address   10.10.1.11
MAC Address   00-18-8B-72-A5-91

FIGURE 11-3 Same-subnet hosts

1. Host1 sends an ARP request:

```
Ethernet: Etype = ARP,DestinationAddress:[FF-FF-FF-FF-FF-FF],SourceAddress:
[00-1C-25-18-99-BB]
Arp: Request, 10.10.1.10 asks for 10.10.1.11
 HardwareType: Ethernet
 ProtocolType: Internet IP (IPv4)
 HardwareAddressLen: 6 (0x6)
 ProtocolAddressLen: 4 (0x4)
 OpCode: Request, 1(0x1)
 SendersMacAddress: 00-1C-25-18-99-BB
 SendersIp4Address: 10.10.1.10
 TargetMacAddress: 00-00-00-00-00-00
 TargetIp4Address: 10.10.1.11
```

ARP Request	
Ethernet Protocol	
00-1C-25-18-99-BB	FF-FF-FF-FF-FF-FF

2. Host2 sends an ARP reply:

```
Ethernet: Etype = ARP,DestinationAddress:[00-1C-25-18-99-BB],SourceAddress:
[00-18-8B-72-A5-91]
Arp: Response, 10.10.1.11 at 00-18-8B-72-A5-91
 HardwareType: Ethernet
 ProtocolType: Internet IP (IPv4)
 HardwareAddressLen: 6 (0x6)
 ProtocolAddressLen: 4 (0x4)
 OpCode: Response, 2(0x2)
```

```
SendersMacAddress: 00-18-8B-72-A5-91
SendersIp4Address: 10.10.1.11
TargetMacAddress: 00-1C-25-18-99-BB
TargetIp4Address: 10.10.1.10
```

ARP Reply for IP=10.10.1.11	
Ethernet Protocol	
00-18-8B-72-A5-91	00-1C-25-18-99-BB

NOTE Because the ARP process provides IP-to-MAC address mapping for both hosts, the process is not repeated in reverse.

In packet 1, Host1 provided its IP and MAC addresses in the SendersMacAddress and SendersIp4Address fields of the ARP request, as well as the IP address to which Host1 wants to send data in the TargetIp4Address field. In packet 2, Host2 responds and populates the SendersMacAddress and SendersIp4Address fields with its MAC and IPv4 address. At the end of this process, both hosts understand the IP-to-MAC relationship they each have.

When a host uses a router to send traffic to a remote subnet, it first determines the appropriate router for the destination IP address from its IP routing table. Host1 uses ARP to discover the MAC address of that router IP address.

The following example illustrates a ping (ICMP Echo) request-response process between Host1 and Host2. Pay particular attention to the IP and MAC address relationships in each packet.

1. Host1 issues an ARP request to discover the MAC address of Host2:

ARP Request for IP=10.10.1.11	
Ethernet Protocol	
00-1C-25-18-99-BB	FF-FF-FF-FF-FF-FF

2. Host2 responds to Host1 with an ARP reply:

ARP Reply for IP=10.10.1.11	
Ethernet Protocol	
00-18-8B-72-A5-91	00-1C-25-18-99-BB

3. Host1 sends an ICMP echo request to Host2:

ICMP Echo Request	
Internet Protocol (IP)	
10.10.1.10	10.10.1.11
Ethernet Protocol	
00-1C-25-18-99-BB	00-18-8B-72-A5-91

4. Host2 responds to Host1 with an Echo Reply:

ICMP Echo Reply	
Internet Protocol (IP)	
10.10.1.11	10.10.1.10
Ethernet Protocol	
00-18-8B-72-A5-91	00-1C-25-18-99-BB

When a host must use a router to reach another host, the preceding process is extended to the router itself and any other routers in the path between the two endpoints. Each router in the path represents one IP "hop." This process is illustrated in Figure 11-4 and the steps that follow for a single-hop traffic path.

Host1
IP Address   10.10.1.10
MAC Address 00-1C-25-18-99-BB

IP Address   10.10.1.1
MAC Address 00-18-8B-12-34-56
Router1
IP Address   192.168.0.1
MAC Address 00-1C-25-78-90-AB

Host3
IP Address   192.168.0.11
MAC Address 00-18-8B-72-A5-92

FIGURE 11-4 Single-hop routing

1. Host1 issues an ARP request to discover the MAC address of Router1:

ARP Request for IP-10.10.1.1	
Ethernet Protocol	
00-1C-25-18-99-BB	FF-FF-FF-FF-FF-FF

2. Router1 sends an ARP reply to Host1:

ARP Reply for IP=10.10.1.1	
Ethernet Protocol	
00-18-8B-12-34-56	00-1C-25-18-99-BB

3. Host1 sends an ICMP Echo Request to Host3 through Router1:

ICMP Echo Request	
Internet Protocol (IP)	
10.10.1.10	192.168.0.11
Ethernet Protocol	
00-1C-25-18-99-BB	00-18-8B-12-34-56

NOTE The destination MAC address in packet 3 includes the MAC address provided by Router1 in the ARP conversation. Because the destination IP address belongs to a host on the opposite side of Router1, Router1 knows that it must forward this packet.

4. Router1 uses ARP to discover the MAC address of Host3:

ARP Request for IP=192.168.0.11	
Ethernet Protocol	
00-1C-25-78-90-AB	FF-FF-FF-FF-FF-FF

5. Host3 sends an ARP reply to Router1:

ARP Reply for IP=192.168.0.11	
Ethernet Protocol	
00-18-8B-71-A5-92	00-1C-25-78-90-AB

6. Router1 forwards the ICMP Echo Request to Host3:

ICMP Echo Request	
Internet Protocol (IP)	
10.10.1.10	192.168.0.11
Ethernet Protocol	
00-1C-25-78-90-AB	00-18-8B-71-A5-92

7. Host3 responds with an ICMP Echo Reply to Host1, using the MAC address for Router1:

NOTE For Host3 to respond to any IP traffic from Host1, Host3 must also use Router1 as the next hop to Host1 or else Host3 will be unable to respond to the ICMP Echo Request from Host1.

ICMP Echo Reply	
Internet Protocol (IP)	
192.168.0.11	10.10.1.10
Ethernet Protocol	
00-18-8B-71-A5-92	00-1C-25-78-90-AB

8. Router1 forwards the ICMP Echo Reply to Host1:

ICMP Echo Reply	
Internet Protocol (IP)	
192.168.0.11	10.10.1.10
Ethernet Protocol	
00-18-8B-12-34-56	00-1C-25-18-99-BB

Although the source and destination IP addresses remain the same as the packet crosses the router, the MAC addresses change to represent the Router1 interface that is adjacent to the sending or receiving host. As more routers are added to the path, the "ARP and forward" process is repeated between each router until the traffic reaches the destination.

Route Relationships

A route relationship informs TMG that no changes are to take place in the source or destination IP address fields as the traffic passes between the source and destination hosts. In this regard, TMG behaves much like a basic network router. Figure 11-5 depicts the basic traffic flow in a route relationship.

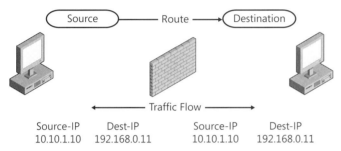

FIGURE 11-5 Route relationship

Route relationships define a bidirectional relationship; that is, the source and destination network are interchangeable in the network rule logic. A network rule that describes a route relationship behaves identically for traffic that originates from the "source" network as it will for traffic that originates from the "destination" network.

For traffic that uses TCP or UDP transport protocols, the source and destination ports are likely to change if an application filter is involved in the traffic processing. This behavior is caused by the application filter terminating the traffic and re-establishing it anew to the destination host.

When non-Web publishing rules are defined across a route relationship, the originating host must send its traffic to the destination host IP address. Because this mimics the same traffic flow as for access rules from the originating host point of view, you might wonder why a non–Web server publishing rule would be used. The reason to choose a non-Web server publishing rule in place of an access rule is to enable proper context for any application filter that would be used to process that traffic. In particular, the VoIP (H.323, SIP) and SMTP filters are context-sensitive and behave differently for access and non–Web publishing rule contexts.

NAT Relationships

A NAT relationship informs TMG that it must apply IP address editing to the traffic as it passes between the hosts.

NOTE NAT refers to Network Address Translation. You can read more about this at *http://en.wikipedia.org/wiki/Network_Address_Translation*.

A NAT relationship defines a unidirectional relationship for traffic crossing TMG; that is, the IP address that represents the host in the source side of the relationship will always be changed. The behavior for the host IP address in the destination side of the relationship depends on the type of firewall rule used to process the traffic. In the case of publishing rules, you can define two NAT forms:

- **Full-NAT** In this case, the destination address is changed to match the IP address of the published host and the source IP address is changed to reflect the default TMG IP address in the relevant network.

- **Half-NAT** In this case, only the destination address is changed to match the IP address of the published host. The source address remains unchanged.

Figure 11-6 and the rule type list that follows illustrate the various traffic behaviors across a NAT relationship.

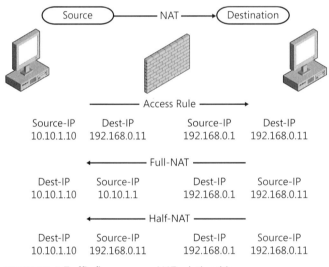

FIGURE 11-6 Traffic flow across a NAT relationship

- **Access Rules** The IP address for the host in the destination network will always remain unchanged for all traffic. The IP address for the host in the source network will be changed according to the network rule relationship configuration.

- **Publishing Rules** The IP address for the host in the destination network will be changed according to the settings illustrated in Figures 11-7 and 11-8.

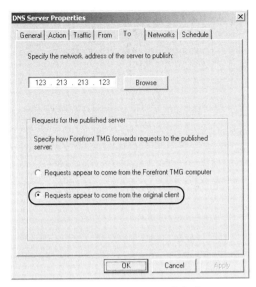

FIGURE 11-7 Half-NAT publishing (default)

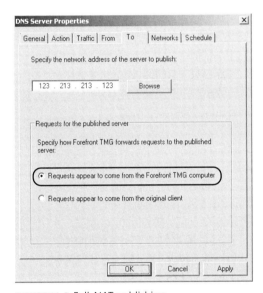

FIGURE 11-8 Full-NAT publishing

The choice of full- or half-NAT is determined primarily by two factors:

- Whether TMG is part of the default route to the Internet
- The requirement to include the original client IP address in the published server logs

If TMG is part of the default route from the published host to the Internet, you can use either full- or half-NAT. If TMG is not part of the default route, only full-NAT is functional, and only if the host has a route to TMG and vice versa. The reason for this is basic IP routing: If a host receives a packet from an IP address that is not in its local subnet, it must use a router to respond to the originating host. If the local routing table does not define a route for the remote subnet, the response cannot be sent.

If your server administrators require that their server logs include the original client IP, you can only use half-NAT. If you choose half-NAT, TMG must be in the default route to the Internet.

Although it's possible to configure a publishing rule for full-NAT across a route relationship, doing so will break the traffic flow, because it would not accurately represent the real relationships between the source and destination networks or their hosts.

Although Web publishing rules default to full-NAT configuration, they can also be configured for full- or half-NAT. Because this traffic is always terminated at a TMG-local Web listener, half-NAT is simulated by changing the source IP for traffic destined to the published Web server. Selecting half-NAT for Web servers is desirable if the Web administrators require the original client IP in their Web logs, but this incurs the additional requirement that the Web servers use TMG as a hop on the path to the Internet.

NAT Address Selection

One of the problems faced by many ISA 2006 administrators was the default behavior for traffic crossing a NAT-based access rule. Regardless of how many IP addresses had been assigned to the network interface in the destination network, only the default (first-bound) IP address was ever used as the source-IP in traffic originating from a host in the source network.

REAL WORLD   Fun with Outbound NAT

Because of the problems caused by SPAM and mail-borne malware, many mail administrators started using Sender Policy framework (SPF) and source-IP to MX record validation in an attempt to stem the flood of SPAM reaching their servers. ISA 2006 default NAT behavior caused problems for many mail administrators if they published their mail server using a non-default IP address. Any mail server that validated the incoming source-IP against the MX and SPF records used by the ISA-source mail host would reject the connection.

MORE INFO   You can read more on Sender Policy Framework at *http://www.openspf.org/* and MX records at *http://en.wikipedia.org/wiki/MX_record.*

TMG includes a new feature that allows the TMG administrator to select which of the TMG server's destination network IP address will be used to represent the host that originates traffic in the source network of a NAT relationship. This functionality allows the TMG administrator to associate one or more hosts in the source network with one TMG-owned

IP address in the destination network, according to the option selected. Figure 11-9 depicts the default option for any NAT-based network rule.

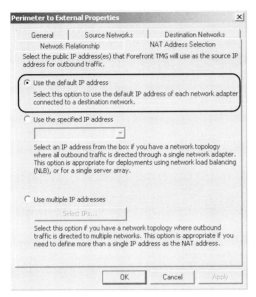

FIGURE 11-9 Default NAT address selection

TMG offers three choices for this behavior:

- **Always Use The Default IP Address**   This option causes TMG to behave exactly the same as ISA 2006. Traffic that originates from the source network used in this rule will be received in the destination network with a source-IP representing TMG's default IP address in the destination network. Figure 11-10 illustrates this behavior using 192.168.0.1 as TMG's default IP address.

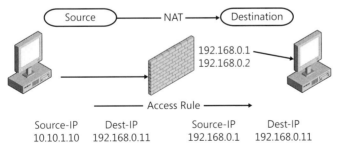

FIGURE 11-10 Default NAT behavior

- **Use The Selected IP Address**   This option configures a single TMG firewall or proxy or an NLB-enabled TMG array to use a single IP address (virtual IP for NLB clusters) to represent traffic originating from the source network. Figure 11-11 illustrates this behavior for an NLB-enabled TMG array using 192.168.0.3 as the virtual IP address.

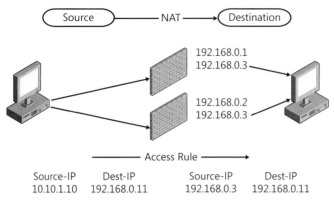

FIGURE 11-11 Single-IP (NLB) outbound NAT

- **Use The Selected IP Address For Each Network**   This option causes TMG to use a unique IP address per TMG firewall or proxy in an array to represent traffic originating from the source network. Figure 11-12 illustrates this behavior.

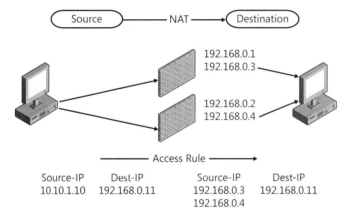

FIGURE 11-12 IP-per-server outbound NAT

> **NOTE**   The source-IP in the traffic received by the host in the destination network will be assigned according to TMG that processed the traffic. Because TMG does not support split routing, response traffic must take the same path as originating traffic.

NAT Address Selection offers a great deal of functionality for the TMG administrator, but take care to ensure that you don't create mismatched traffic routes between the endpoint hosts.

Network Rules

Like firewall policy rules, network rules define how TMG will handle traffic between source and destination hosts. Network rules are also processed in the order in which they are defined. Because network rules form a primary criterion for traffic processing, they have the power to discard traffic before any firewall policy rule has the opportunity to evaluate it. When this happens, the firewall log will not include a name in the rule field because no firewall policy rule processed the traffic. As is the case with firewall policy rules, the order of network rules is critical to correct traffic evaluation by TMG. Figure 11-13 illustrates the default network rules created for an Edge firewall scenario.

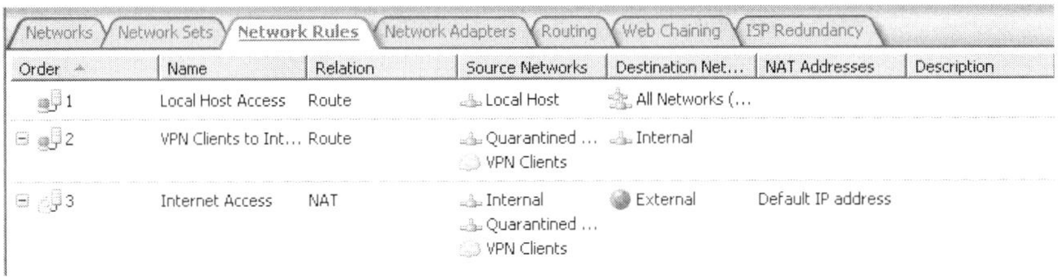

Networks	Network Sets	Network Rules	Network Adapters	Routing	Web Chaining	ISP Redundancy		
Order ▲	Name	Relation	Source Networks	Destination Net...	NAT Addresses	Description		
1	Local Host Access	Route	Local Host	All Networks (...				
2	VPN Clients to Int...	Route	Quarantined ... VPN Clients	Internal				
3	Internet Access	NAT	Internal Quarantined ... VPN Clients	External	Default IP address			

FIGURE 11-13 Default network rules for edge deployment

Regardless of the network template used, all network rule sets will begin with the same rule, Local Host Access, which defines a route relationship for traffic that is sourced or terminated by TMG itself. This rule cannot be modified by the TMG administrator.

For a network rule to function properly, it must have accurate data from which to draw its conclusions. This data is provided by the TMG administrator when the source and destination criteria are selected for each rule.

All network rules operate in the context of network objects. This can include most of the criteria collectively referred to in firewall policy as *network objects*. When you run the Network Rule Wizard, you are given the opportunity to select from a subset of the firewall policy network objects, as shown in Figure 11-14.

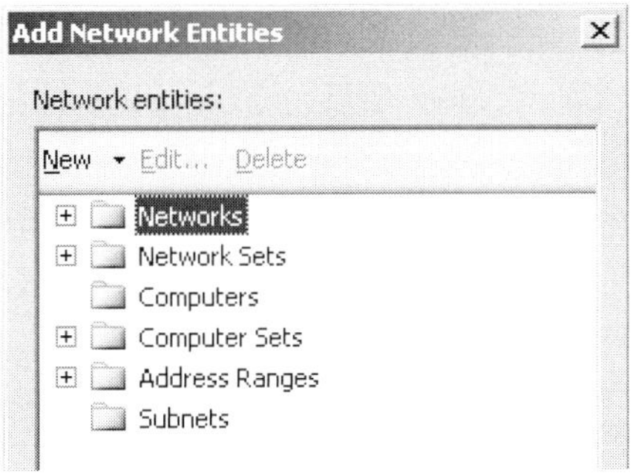

Add Network Entities

Network entities:

New ▼ Edit... Delete

- ⊞ Networks
- ⊞ Network Sets
- Computers
- ⊞ Computer Sets
- ⊞ Address Ranges
- Subnets

FIGURE 11-14 Network Entities selection dialog box

You may have noticed that the options presented for a network rule source and destination criteria are limited to those items that are defined as some variation or grouping of an IP address, IP subnet, IP address range, or combinations of these as in Computer or Network Sets. No firewall policy elements which abstract the source or destination into a name (such as domain or URL sets) can be used for network rules because they cannot represent literal network membership.

Because network rules are processed in the order defined, and because they now include NAT Address Selection as part of any NAT relationship, you should plan to spend a significant amount of time planning, simulating, and testing your deployment. Failure to do so could result in a TMG deployment that is barely functional, or simply doesn't function at all.

Creating Networks

TMG provides a multinetworking model that helps you exert more granular control over the traffic between networks. Although TMG has built-in networks that are created at the time of installation and when a network template is used, you might need to create a new network if you change the physical network structure on the TMG computer itself, such as if you add another NIC connected to a new network. This section discusses the built-in networks in TMG, how you can create a network, and what steps to follow after creating a network.

Built-In Networks

When you install TMG, you are asked to define your Internal Network. After installing TMG you will notice that certain networks are already built in on the Networks tab. These networks vary depending on the applied network template. Before we discuss the networks created during installation, let's look at what each built-in network represents.

- **Local Host**   The Local Host network includes any IP address used by the computer on which TMG is installed. This includes any other IP address assigned to the TMG computer. Using the Local Host network allows TMG to make use of a "Local host" context that extends beyond the standard "localhost" definition that is more commonly associated with the 127/8 subnet.

- **Internal Network**   This network is created during installation and defines a network that includes addresses used by a set of clients protected and controlled by TMG policies. This includes the network on which TMG has IP configurations that match the address range associated with this network as well as any network accessed through nearby routers in this subnet that should be considered an extension of this local network based on the Windows routing table.

- **VPN Clients Network**   This network includes all IP addresses assigned to VPN clients connected to the TMG computer. This provides you with granular traffic control by creating policies to only specify certain protocols or destinations for clients that connect into the network through a Virtual Private Network (VPN). If the Routing and Remote Access service on TMG is set to allocate addresses to client from a DHCP server, this network is dynamic and addresses are dynamically added and removed as VPN clients connect and disconnect. If the VPN service on TMG is set to allocate addresses from a manual pool of IP address range, this network will hold the defined address range that the TMG administrator provides.

- **Quarantined VPN Clients Network** This network includes all IP addresses assigned to VPN clients that are quarantined and have limited access. This is a dynamic network based on computers that are quarantined and addresses are added and removed as VPN clients are added or removed from the quarantine list.

- **Perimeter** This network includes IP addresses of your Perimeter network. You can create multiple Perimeter networks as long as you have a physical interface on TMG in the same address range.

- **External** This network includes all IP addresses that are not defined in any of the other networks.

As mentioned earlier, the built-in networks that are visible after installed depend on the network template used. Table 11-1 summarizes the networks associated with different templates.

TABLE 11-1 Network Templates

NETWORK TEMPLATE	BUILT-IN NETWORKS
Edge Firewall	External Internal Local Host Quarantined VPN Clients VPN Clients
3-Leg Perimeter	External Internal Local Host Perimeter Quarantined VPN Clients VPN Clients
Front Firewall	External Local Host Perimeter Quarantined VPN Clients VPN Clients
Back Firewall	External Internal Local Host Quarantined VPN Clients VPN Clients
Single Network Adapter	External Internal Local Host Quarantined VPN Clients VPN Clients

NOTE When a Single Network Adapter template is used, even though there is an External Network object by default, from the TMG perspective everything is considered internal because the default gateway lies on the same network interface as the internal network.

Creating a New Network

In the firewall policy, you can control access based on source and destination. This is particularly beneficial for remote offices or networks. Note that before creating a network, you need to ensure that a physical network interface is present on TMG with an IP address on the same network range. For example, if you are creating a network for the range 10.0.0.0–10.0.0.255, TMG should have a separate physical network interface with an IP address in that range. If you create a network without having a separate physical network interface on that range, TMG will drop the packet as spoofed.

NOTE Only one NIC should have a default gateway configured on it. Multiple default gateways will result in connectivity issues.

To create a new network, navigate to Networking in the TMG console, click the Networks tab, and then click Create A New Network under Network Tasks, as shown in Figure 11-15.

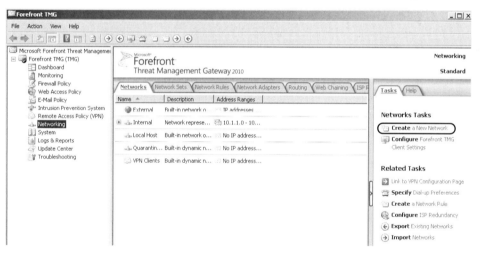

FIGURE 11-15 The Networking tab in the TMG console

This launches the New Network Wizard, shown in Figure 11-16.

In our example we will create a new network called Perimeter that will define a Perimeter network. The IP address range of our Perimeter network will be 192.168.1.X.

On the Welcome page of the New Network Wizard, type **Perimeter** in the Network Name box and click Next. On the next page, choose the type of network you are defining, as shown in Figure 11-17. Because our example network lies in the Perimeter network, choose Perimeter Network and click Next.

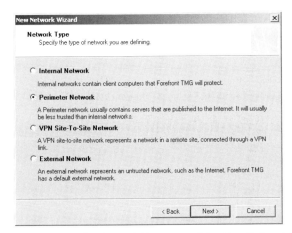

FIGURE 11-16 The New Network Wizard

FIGURE 11-17 The Network Type page of the New Network Wizard

On the Network Address page, click Add Adapter as shown in Figure 11-18.

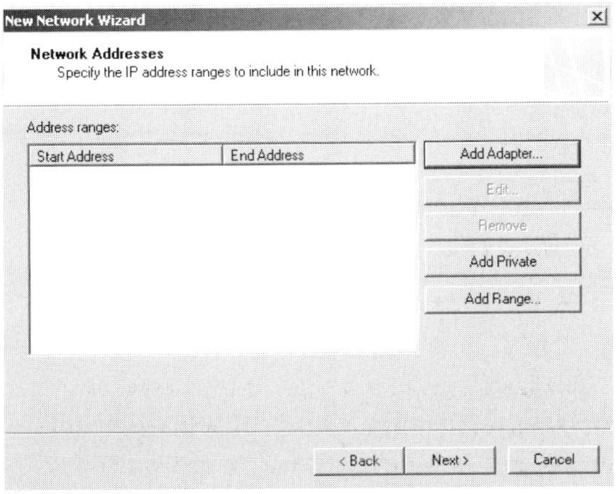

FIGURE 11-18 The Network Addresses page of the New Network Wizard

On the Select Network Adapters page, select the network interface that corresponds to the perimeter network, as shown in Figure 11-19. It is always a good idea to give your network interfaces friendly names so that you can easily recognize them.

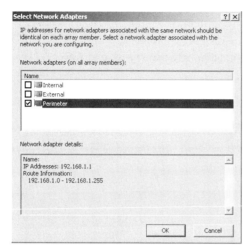

FIGURE 11-19 The Select Network Adapter page of the New Network Wizard

Click OK. On the next page of the wizard, click Next. The Completing The New Network Wizard page opens, giving you a brief summary of the new network you have created, as shown in Figure 11-20. Click Finish to create the new network.

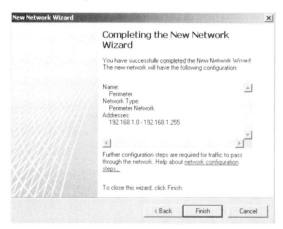

FIGURE 11-20 The Completing The New Network Wizard page of the New Network Wizard

Creating a Network Rule

After you create a network it is required that you create a network rule to define the network relationship between the new network and any others. Network relationships, as discussed previously, can either be route relationships or NAT relationships. A route network rule defines a bidirectional relationship, whereas a NAT network rule defines a unidirectional relationship. This means that if two networks have a route relationship, you can allow traffic in either direction between the networks using access rules. If two networks have a NAT relationship, you can use access rules to allow traffic from the source to the destination network but inbound traffic can only pass from the destination to the source network through the use of publishing rules. Keeping all these considerations in mind will help you choose the type of network relationship to use between the new network you created and the other networks available to TMG.

Typically, you create network rules from your internal network to the new network you created and from the new network to the external network. If you have other defined networks and you want access between those networks and the new network, you have to create network rules for those as well. In our example we will create a route relationship between the default internal network and the new perimeter network we just created.

To create a new network rule, navigate to Networking in the TMG console, click the Network Rules tab, and then click Create A Network Rule under Network Rule Tasks, as shown in Figure 11-21.

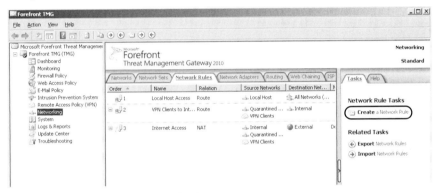

FIGURE 11-21 Creating a new network rule

This opens the New Network Rule Wizard, as shown in Figure 11-22. Give the network rule a name and then click Next. We'll give our example the name **Perimeter Access**.

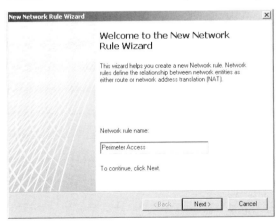

FIGURE 11-22 The New Network Rule Wizard

The next page of the wizard lets you specify the source network, as shown in Figure 11-23. In either relationship, the source network should be the network from where the traffic will be sourced. In other words, the source network contains the host that originates the traffic. Click Add to specify the source network.

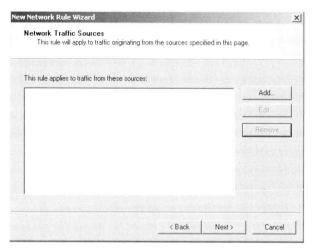

FIGURE 11-23 The Network Traffic Sources page of the New Network Rule Wizard

The Add Network Entities dialog box opens, where you can select the source network, as shown in Figure 11-24. You can specify one or more network entities in the same network rule. For our example we will select Internal as the source network. Click Internal and then click Add. You are then redirected to the Network Traffic Sources page with the Internal network selected. Click Next to continue.

FIGURE 11-24 The Add Network Entities dialog box

On the next page, specify the network traffic destination, as shown in Figure 11-25.

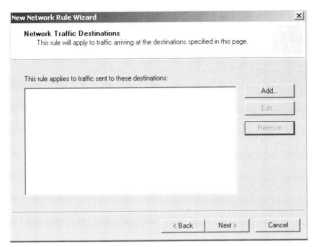

FIGURE 11-25 The Network Traffic Destinations page of the
New Network Rule Wizard

Click Add. The Add Network Entities dialog box opens again, as shown in Figure 11-26. Select Perimeter from the list and then click Add. You are then returned to the Network Traffic Destinations page with the Perimeter network selected. Click Next.

FIGURE 11-26 The Add Network Entities
dialog box with Perimeter selected

On the next page, shown in Figure 11-27, you choose the network relationship between the source and the destination networks that we selected. As mentioned before, choose Route for this example and then click Next.

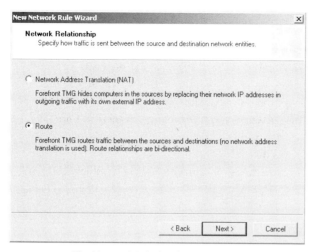

FIGURE 11-27 The Network Relationship page of the New Network Rule Wizard

The Completing The New Network Rule Wizard page opens, as shown in Figure 11-28. This page gives you a brief summary of the name of the network rule, the source and the destination network, and the network's route relationship. Click Finish to create the network rule.

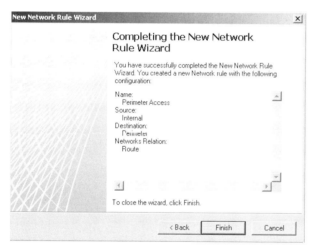

FIGURE 11-28 The Completing the New Network Rule Wizard page of the New Network Rule Wizard

With the network and the network rule both created, you can now create rules to allow traffic between the networks.

> **NOTE** Network rules are ordered and processed in defined order. Rules are first matched based on source and destination addresses and then the matching rule defines the network relationship. If any of the default rules need to be overridden, a custom network rule needs to be placed higher in the order.

REAL WORLD   TMG Drops Packets as Spoofed

A customer reported that he could not access any resources between two networks he had defined in TMG. When we checked TMG Alerts we found that TMG was dropping the packets from his custom network as spoofed. When we verified the configuration of the custom network, we found that there was no physical network interface on TMG that was available for that particular network range. The issue was resolved after we deleted the custom network and removed the custom network from network rules, and added a physical network interface with an IP address on the custom network range and re-created the custom network and rules.

Configuring Your Protected Networks

All networks behind TMG are known as protected networks. These networks are protected from the default external network (which is usually the Internet), which is considered an unprotected network. You can't think of the Internet as a network where you can transmit your data in plain text and believe that you are safe. This is just like going to a war zone inside a bulletproof tank thinking that you are safe just because you are inside the tank. Figure 11-29 shows an example of the network layers and categorization.

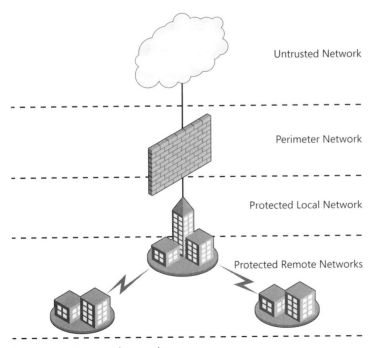

FIGURE 11-29 Protected networks

As shown in Figure 11-29, the protected networks can be located in the local LAN right behind TMG, or they can be located in remote offices where you have a private WAN link connection. In this case the only path to the unprotected network (Internet) is by sending the traffic through TMG Firewall. In other words, the only device that should have direct access to the protected and unprotected networks is TMG Firewall.

When you first install TMG and select the networks using the Getting Started Wizard, you define the core parameters so that TMG can identify what is considered a protected network and what it is not. To determine this, TMG relies on the template that you choose in the wizard and also the networks that you associated with each network interface.

After running the Getting Started Wizard and the Web Access Wizard, you are ready to use TMG. However, you can configure some additional options afterward. To access the options for the internal protected network, follow these steps:

1. On the TMG computer, open the Forefront TMG Management Console.

2. Click Forefront TMG (Server Name) in the left pane.

3. Click the Networking node in the left pane of the console and then click the Internal tab in the middle pane.

4. Click Edit Selected Network in the right pane and you should see a dialog box similar to the one shown in Figure 11-30.

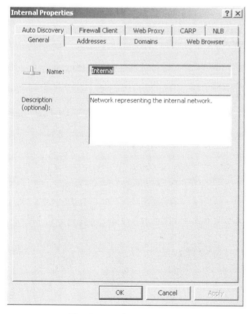

FIGURE 11-30 The Internal Properties dialog box

On an Enterprise edition, the Internal Network properties have the following configuration options:

- **Addresses** Allows you to configure the IP addresses that define the network. Chapter 4, "Analyzing Network Requirements," covered this in detail.

- **Domains** Allows you to specify what domains are considered internal. This is used for the TMG Client to know that the traffic for domains specified in this tab should be sent directly to them.

- **Web Browser** This tab has the parameters that determine how TMG handles traffic coming from Web Proxy Clients. This will be covered in more detail in Chapter 15, "Web Proxy Auto Discovery for TMG."

- **Automatic Discovery** On this tab you can enable automatic discovery for TMG Clients and Web Proxy Clients. Chapter 15 will explain in more detail how to use that.

- **TMG Client** This tab allows you to configure parameters that will be used by Firewall Clients. Chapter 4 covered this in detail.

- **Web Proxy** Here you configure which port TMG will listen on for Web Proxy requests and also how it will handle authentication. We will cover authentication options in this chapter.

- **CARP** This tab allows you to enable the cache array routing protocol to balance Web requests and cache content across members of the array. Chapter 16, "Caching Concepts and Configuration," will cover this in more detail.

- **NLB** This tab allows you to enable Network Load Balance capability in TMG. Chapter 13, "Configuring Load Balancing Capabilities," will cover this in more details.

When TMG receives traffic coming from this network you also have a chance to authenticate the user that is sending the connection request.

Authenticating Traffic from Protected Networks

In an enterprise environment one common requirement is to authenticate users before they have access to the Internet. This requirement is part of access control requirements established by company security policy. As the TMG administrator, you have to make the system compliant with policy. TMG provides two methods of authenticating user requests for Web access:

- Globally at a network listener
- Per firewall policy rule

At the network listener you can specify the authentication method, whereas at the firewall policy level you specify the user or group that needs to authenticate. When TMG receives the user's request, if authentication is required from the network where the user sent the request, TMG evaluates the rules to find a rule that matches with the request. At that point, if the user's credentials are denied by the authenticator (Active Directory, for example) the request is denied and no other rules are evaluated.

NOTE Chapter 32, "Exploring the HTTP Protocol," explains how authentication works for HTTP requests.

To access the authentication options for the default internal network in the Web proxy traffic scenario, follow these steps:

1. On the TMG computer, open the Forefront TMG Management Console.
2. Click Forefront TMG (Server Name) in the left pane.
3. Click the Networking node in the left pane of the console and then click the Internal tab in the middle pane.
4. Click Edit Selected Network in the right pane.
5. Click the Web Proxy tab and then click the Authentication button. You should see a dialog box similar to that shown in Figure 11-31.

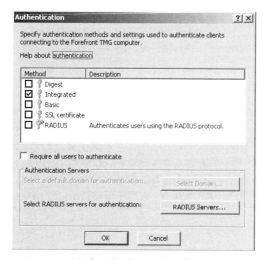

FIGURE 11-31 Authentication options for the internal network

Multiple authentication methods are available; however, the default method is integrated. The method in use dictates the way TMG validates users requesting access to the resource.

Digest

Digest authentication relies on the HTTP 1.1 protocol to work properly. This means that the Web browser needs to support HTTP 1.1. Requests sent by non-HTTP 1.1–compliant browsers will be rejected. This authentication method works only with Microsoft Windows Server 2000 and later domains.

The restriction imposed by this authentication method will be brought to your attention when you enable this method, as shown in Figure 11-32.

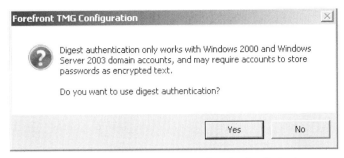

FIGURE 11-32 Information about digest authentication limitation

WDigest

WDigest was first introduced in Windows XP (Wdigest.dll) and inherited in Windows Server 2003. WDigest has some unique characteristics, such as:

- The user name and domain name are case-sensitive, which differs from Digest, Basic, and Integrated authentication. This means that the user name needs to be typed exactly the way it was registered when administrator created the user account in Active Directory.

- It requires that the value in the resource part of the URL path is explicitly specified. For instance, let's say the user sends a HTTP GET for *http://host.contoso.com.* This request will fail because the URL resource (*/index.htm* in this example) is missing.

When TMG is a member of a Windows Server 2003 or later domain and the authentication method is set to Digest, TMG will use WDigest by default. The primary advantage of WDigest over Digest is that WDigest does not require that reversibly encrypted copy of user's password to be stored in Active Directory. For more information on how Digest and WDigest authentication work on the Windows operating system level, review the article at *http://technet.microsoft.com/en-us/library/cc780170.aspx.*

Integrated Authentication

Integrated authentication allows TMG to use Windows Security Support provider (SSP) to validate user credentials. This authentication method supports the use of Negotiate, NTLM, or Kerberos authentication. The advantage of these authentication methods is that user passwords are never sent across the network in readable form, if at all.

Basic

When you use basic authentication, user names and passwords are sent through the network in encoded format, but no encryption is used. This means that this authentication method is the weakest of all those available. Some people think that because basic authentication uses Base64 encoding, the information is secure. It is not—encoding is not encryption. If a Base64-encoded password is intercepted over the network by a network sniffer, that password can be decoded and accessed.

By enabling basic authentication, you can be vulnerable because credentials traverse the network in a weakly encoded format. You might wonder why people use this method. People use basic authentication because it is compatible with the majority of browsers and applications in use today. It is possible to overcome this weakness by adding SSL on top of HTTP to encrypt the traffic and protect the credentials.

When you select this authentication method in the authentication window, the message shown in Figure 11-33 appears.

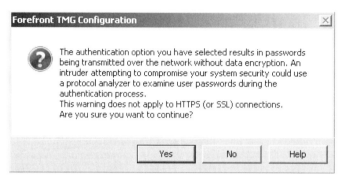

FIGURE 11-33 Message when enabling basic authentication

This informational dialog box alerts you to the dangers of enabling this authentication method on a protected network. If you confirm that you want to use this method by clicking Yes, you will notice that in the Authentication Servers section in the Authentication dialog box as shown in Figure 11-34, the Select Domain button now is enabled. This is because when the user sends credentials, TMG uses the default domain for Basic authentication.

For example, when a user (Bob) sends a request to access a resource, TMG appends its own domain (contoso) to the request and forwards the authentication request as CONTOSO\BOB. If the Select Domain button is now available, you can click it and add the domain you want TMG to use for authentication purposes, as shown in Figure 11-34.

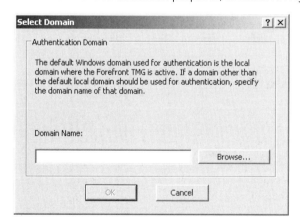

FIGURE 11-34 Choosing the default domain that will be used

SSL Certificate

Also known as client certificate authentication, this method uses a certificate provided by the client. TMG uses this certificate to validate the client's credentials and capability of accessing the resource. This certificate could be embedded in a smart card or it could be used by a mobile device to access Microsoft Exchange using ActiveSync.

If you enable this option without an SSL certificate installed on TMG, the message shown in Figure 11-35 appears.

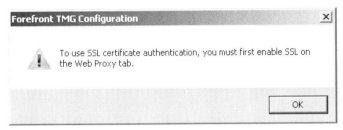

FIGURE 11-35 Message when enabling SSL authentication without having the certificate

RADIUS

Remote Authentication Dial-In User Service (RADIUS) is a network protocol specified in RFC 2865 to be used as a centralized authentication repository. TMG can act as a RADIUS client and send user credentials and connection parameter information to a RADIUS server. The RADIUS server evaluates the request and authenticates the RADIUS client (TMG) request, and sends back a RADIUS response message.

When RADIUS is used as the authentication provider, the traffic between client application (Internet Explorer, for example) and TMG will be authenticated using HTTP-Basic. This is an important point to understand because HTTP-Basic passes the user name and password without encryption. When you use RADIUS as an authentication provider for a Web publishing scenario, you can enhance security by using HTTPs. This way all traffic from TMG to the client will be encrypted.

When you enable this option, you must specify the RADIUS Server that will be used by TMG. To do so, click the RADIUS Servers button. Figure 11-36 shows the RADIUS Servers dialog box.

Because no RADIUS Server is yet configured, you need to click Add to create a new definition for the server. Figure 11-37 shows the Add RADIUS Server dialog box.

This dialog box allows you to specify the RADIUS Server's information, such as server name (or IP address), a shared secret that will be used between RADIUS Server and RADIUS Client (TMG), the authentication port (1812 by default), and what the timeout will be (five seconds by default).

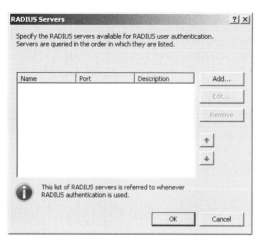

FIGURE 11-36 The RADIUS Servers dialog box

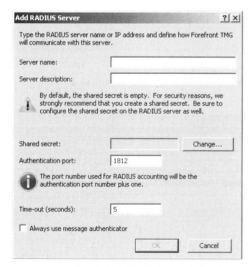

FIGURE 11-37 The Add RADIUS Server dialog box

You can create multiple RADIUS Servers and TMG will use them in order, checking the list from the top down, to authenticate the request.

Require All Users To Authenticate

The Require All Users To Authenticate option was misinterpreted for many years by ISA firewall administrators. The myth was that if you disabled this setting, users wouldn't be able to authenticate, which is not true. User requests will still be evaluated according to the authentication method used by the network and the firewall rule that applies to the user's request.

Enabling the Require All Users To Authenticate option simply means that you cannot have anonymous access coming from this network. This means that if you need to allow one group of computers to have anonymous access to a particular Web site and you create a rule to allow this, the rule will be superseded by this setting. This option has priority over any authentication setting that you specify in the firewall policy level.

In addition to this scenario, some other issues might arise when you use this option, such as:

- Users are randomly prompted for authentication. When a connection request matches a firewall policy rule that allows anonymous access and this option is enabled, TMG will send an authentication request to the client because this setting indicates that no anonymous requests are allowed.

- SecureNET Clients cannot access resources. Because SecureNET doesn't provide credentials to TMG, the requests originated by those clients will be denied.

 REAL WORLD **Web Page Doesn't Display Correctly**

This scenario is based on a situation where the user calls the help desk and says, "I'm trying to access a Web site and it prompts for authentication after the page being partially rendered." The TMG administrator collects basic troubleshooting information and identifies that the user's requests match a rule that allows all traffic for the target Web site and that the user is a member of the group that has access to the Web site. In other words, TMG received the user's credentials, it authenticates the user, the user sees parts of the page but some other parts that appear, and the authentication prompt appears.

When using Network Monitor 3.2 to capture the traffic while reproducing the problem, we saw that the problematic object was a Java application. After some research, we identified that this Java application did not support authentication with TMG. To solve the problem, the TMG administrator created an anonymous rule allowing access to the problematic Web site. An anonymous access rule was created because the administrator didn't know whether more applications on the site could cause similar problems, and this issue was causing too many problems for his users.

To the administrator's surprise, after changing the rule to allow anonymous access, none of the Web site content would load and the authentication prompt window appeared immediately. This occurred because the Require All Users To Authenticate option was enabled for the default internal network and therefore no anonymous request was supposed to be allowed. The solution was to disable this option.

Summary

In this chapter you learned how network relationships work with TMG and the difference between route and NAT network rules. This chapter also covered aspects of TMG Networks configuration and how physically separated networks communicate through TMG. The concept of protected networks and how those networks can securely pass traffic through TMG was also an important concept covered here. With those elements in place you can build a secure network configuration on TMG and allow communication between hosts located in different segments. In the next chapter you will learn how to configure access rules on TMG and how these rules are processed to enable you to secure outbound connections through the TMG Firewall.

## CHAPTER 12

Understanding Access Rules

- Traffic Policy Behavior   **241**

- Understanding Policy Re-Evaluation   **249**

- Troubleshooting Access Rules   **253**

- Summary   **262**

The single most flexible part of TMG—and thus most difficult for most administrators to understand—is the traffic policy engine. This is a deeply complex mechanism, so we decided to cover it in multiple chapters. In this chapter, you'll learn about access rules and how they're processed in the context of traffic flow through TMG. Publishing rules will be covered in Chapters 21 through 24.

Traffic Policy Behavior

TMG offers the same top-down policy engine that ISA Server 2006 administrators have become accustomed to. This means that with very few exceptions, policy rules processed by TMG will be evaluated in the order in which they are defined.

Policy Engine Rule Basics

TMG manages traffic flow through the creation and use of connection objects. For every traffic path allowed by a firewall rule, TMG builds a connection object that maintains an internal map of the relationships between the source and destination networks as well as the protocols used. TMG application and Web filters help with traffic flow evaluation and management because they can dynamically modify TMG policies in support of protocols that negotiate connection points as their communication progresses. RPC, MMS, RTSP, and FTP are a few examples of such protocols. The policy engine operates at several levels for all traffic handled by policy rules:

- **Network rules**   These rules evaluate the packet in the context of the 5-tuple and determine the basic context of the traffic flow. Enhanced NAT definitions are also processed here.

- **Firewall policy rules**   These rules determine whether traffic is to be allowed or denied and whether any protocol-specific action must be taken (such as HTTP-based authentication).
- **Web chaining rules (HTTP and HTTPS only)**   These rules define custom behavior determined by the destination associated with the traffic.
- **ISP redundancy**   This configuration determines the ISP connection through which TMG will forward the traffic.

> **NOTE**   ISP redundancy and failover settings supersede Web chaining rule decisions.

The access rule examples described in the following sections are created in the context of Figure 12-1.

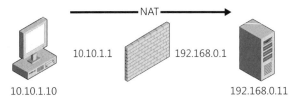

FIGURE 12-1 Access rule scenario

TMG evaluates the traffic against the rules in the order in which they are defined.

Ping Access Rule Example

ICMP packets are defined by the ICMP code and type fields, as shown in Figure 12-2. In particular, PING traffic (ICMP Echo Request and ICMP Echo Response) uses the combination of code 0, type 8 and code 0, type 0 for Echo Request and Echo Response, respectively.

> **MORE INFO**   More information on ICMP messages can be found at *http://www.iana.org/assignments/icmp-parameters.*

ICMP	
Code	Type
Internet Protocol (IP)	
Source IP Address	Destination IP Address

FIGURE 12-2 ICMP packet construction

TMG is configured with two networks: the default internal network and the default external network. The address range of the internal network is defined as 10.10.1.0–10.10.1.255. The default network rule for traffic sourced from internal and destined for external is defined as NAT. An access rule allows ICMP from internal to external. NAT address selection has not been configured for this traffic.

1. TMG receives a packet from the Internal Network, constructed as shown in Figure 12-3.

ICMP Echo Request	
0	8
Internet Protocol (IP)	
10.10.1.10	192.168.0.11

FIGURE 12-3 ICMP Echo Request

2. The source IP address is 10.10.1.10, which matches the internal network address range. The destination IP address fails to match any other network and thus is associated with the External Network by default. TMG matches this packet to the default network rule (named Internet Access), which defines a NAT relationship between the internal and external networks.

> **NOTE** If the source address had not matched the address range defined for the internal network, TMG would have dropped the packet, logged it as spoofed, and triggered an IP spoofing alert. Likewise, if the destination IP address has not been owned by TMG for the internal network but was within the internal network address range, TMG would also have dropped it as spoofed.

3. TMG then examines the firewall rules to determine whether this traffic should be allowed or denied. To make this process more efficient, TMG first collects all the rules that match the 5-tuple data—in this case source- and destination-IP, ICMP, and the ICMP type and code. TMG then traverses the rule set in the order in which the rules are defined to determine how to handle the traffic. In this case, the Allow Ping rule is determined to match the packet and the packet is allowed to pass.

4. TMG creates a connection object and populates it with the information known up to this point: source- and destination-addresses, highest-level protocol (ICMP), the transport-specific information (ICMP Echo Request), and the relevant network rule. Return traffic can thus be processed in the context of the originating traffic.

5. TMG now prepares to send the ICMP packet to the destination host. Because the network rule specifies a NAT relationship, TMG examines the NAT Address Selection setting to determine which TMG-owned IP address is to be used to replace the original IP address in this packet. Because NAT Address Selection is configured for the default, TMG populates the source-IP address field with the default IP address from the destination network interface, building a packet as illustrated in Figure 12-4.

ICMP Echo Request	
0	8
Internet Protocol (IP)	
192.168.0.1	192.168.0.11

FIGURE 12-4 ICMP sent from TMG

6. The host at 192.168.0.11 receives the ICMP Echo Request. Because the request appears to have come from TMG, the host sends a response packet as shown in Figure 12-5.

ICMP Echo Response	
0	0
Internet Protocol (IP)	
192.168.0.11	192.168.0.1

FIGURE 12-5 ICMP response from the external host

7. When TMG receives this packet on its external interface, it validates that the source-IP address in this packet is appropriate for the external network. As with the ICMP Echo request in Step 3, if the source-IP is not what TMG expects on this network, the packet will be dropped and a spoof alert logged.

8. TMG then repeats the rule association process, as discussed in Step 4. If TMG locates a rule that denies this traffic, TMG will drop it and log the rule that triggered this action.

> **NOTE** ICMP is an interesting protocol in that although the TMG PING protocol is defined in accordance with the construction of an ICMP Echo Request packet, and Echo Request packets use code 0, type 8, Echo Response packets do not behave as you see with TCP and UDP traffic, where the response uses a mirror aspect of the origination traffic (the source and destination ports are reversed with the IP addresses). The correct response to an ICMP code 0, type 8 message is ICMP code 0, type 0. TMG understands this requirement and thus understands what to expect from the responding host.

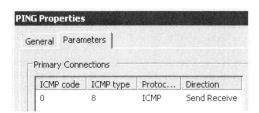

9. If no deny action is found, TMG then examines the destination-IP address of the incoming ICMP packet. If it is owned by TMG in that network, it scans the existing connection objects to determine whether this traffic is expected. TMG will locate the connection object created in Step 5.

10. When TMG examines the connection object, the state map indicates that TMG has sent an ICMP Echo Request to the IP address, which is now sending an ICMP Echo Response. Because this packet is an expected response to an ICMP Echo Request, the traffic is allowed.

11. TMG examines the network rule associated with this conversation. Because it specified a NAT relationship, TMG retrieves the original source-IP from the connection object and uses that to replace the destination-IP and then forwards the packet as shown in Figure 12-6.

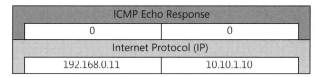

ICMP Echo Response	
0	0
Internet Protocol (IP)	
192.168.0.11	10.10.1.10

FIGURE 12-6 ICMP response to the internal host

12. TMG updates the connection object to reflect the fact that no specific traffic is expected from either host. If no traffic is received that can be matched to this connection object after two minutes, TMG will destroy the connection object. We will explore connection objects through the use of netsh in the section "Troubleshooting Access Rules" later in the chapter.

CERN Proxy HTTP Example

HTTP is one of many protocols where an application filter and several Web filters are required for TMG to process the traffic flow effectively and to evaluate the traffic flow against defined behavior. This example will provide some insight into how application filters bear on TMG traffic policies. To support this example, a new access rule was created to allow the default HTTP protocol definition from internal to external, as shown in the following steps.

> **NOTE** The HTTP protocol is defined by RFC 2616, which you can read at *http://www.ietf.org/rfc/rfc2616.txt*.

1. The user working at the host using IP address 10.10.1.10 opens the browser and types **http://www.contoso.com.**

2. Because the browser is configured to use a proxy at 10.10.1.1 at TCP port 8080 for all requests, the browser opens a connection to 10.10.1.1, port 8080.

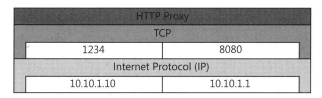

HTTP Proxy	
TCP	
1234	8080
Internet Protocol (IP)	
10.10.1.10	10.10.1.1

3. TMG examines the network definition for the network interface where this traffic is received and validates the source-IP against the address ranges found in the network definition.

4. TMG tests the firewall rules to see whether any rules match the traffic 5-tuple. Because we have configured the TMG internal network to allow Web Proxy clients, TMG accepts the Web Proxy client connection, builds the connection object, and populates it with the connection state at this point.

NOTE Because the connection terminates at TMG, the Local Host Access network rule is the one that applies to this connection. Thus, the network relationship for this connection is route.

5. Because the Web Proxy filter owns the listener operating at TCP port 8080, it has the primary responsibility for processing the traffic sent from and to the client.
6. Because the browser is configured to use a Web Proxy, it sends the request as GET *http://www.contoso.com/HTTP/1.1*. This request includes additional information in the form of HTTP headers. The request sent by the Web Proxy client will appear similar to the following:

```
- Http: Request, GET http://www.contoso.com/
    Command: GET
  + URI: /
    ProtocolVersion: HTTP/1.1
    Accept-Language:  en-us
    UA-CPU:  x86
    Accept-Encoding:  gzip, deflate
    UserAgent:  Mozilla/4.0 (compatible; MSIE 7.0; Windows NT 6.0; WOW64; SLCC1;
.NET CLR 2.0.50727; InfoPath.2; .NET CLR 3.5.21022; MS-RTC LM 8; .NET CLR
3.5.30729; .NET CLR 3.0.30618; MS-RTC EA 2)
    Host:  www.contoso.com
    Proxy-Connection:  Keep-Alive
```

7. The Web Proxy filter separates this request into its component parts, as shown in Figure 12-7.

Method	Scheme	Host	Path	Version
GET	http://	www.contoso.com	/	HTTP/1.1

FIGURE 12-7 HTTP GET

8. Because access rule destinations can include anything in the rule destination from computer objects to URL sets, the Web Proxy filter needs to resolve the host to an IP address.

NOTE TMG maintains a local DNS cache to make repeated successful and failed name lookups return faster in order to improve performance. If the name query for *www.contoso.com* is unsuccessful, TMG will not be able to make the reverse query for this site and will be unable to evaluate access rules defined using IP- or network-based destinations. This can cause unwanted behavior for these rules.

9. The Web Proxy filter passes requests to the Web filters in the order they are registered.

> **NOTE**   Web filters are ordered so as to preserve proper encoding, compression, and special handling in the contest of the TMG Web cache. Traffic that would be stored in the cache is processed by Web filters in the order they are listed. Web requests that are served from the cache are processed by the Web filters in reverse order. This preserves the encoding, compression, and DiffServ state that was applied to cached content.

10. The HTTP filter is responsible for evaluating the request according to RFC-2616 (Hypertext Transfer Protocol—HTTP/1.1) and applying any additional restrictions on the traffic processed by the access rule that allows this traffic. An example of some of the settings available in this filter is shown in Figure 12-8.

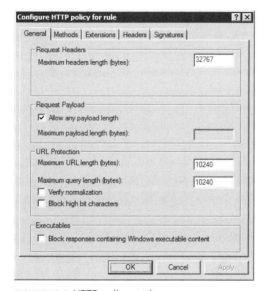

FIGURE 12-8 HTTP policy settings

11. If the HTTP filter allows the traffic, the Web Proxy filter evaluates the Web chaining rules to determine how this request should be directed. Because no custom Web chaining rules exist, the Web Proxy filter creates a connection from TMG to the Web server as shown in Figure 12-9. The term *HTTP Direct* refers to the fact that the connection is direct from TMG to the destination Web server.

HTTP Direct	
TCP	
2345	80
Internet Protocol (IP)	
192.168.0.1	192.168.0.11

FIGURE 12-9 Non–Web Proxy HTTP

NOTE Because the connection is created by the Web Proxy filter and exists between TMG and the server, TMG allows the connection. Because the Local Host Access network rule applies, a route relationship is used.

12. The Web server at 192.168.0.11 accepts the connection and the Web Proxy filter forwards a modified form of the original request as GET / HTTP/1.1, including headers, as shown in the following example. (Note the addition of the VIA header; this indicates to the upstream host that this request was processed by an intermediate entity.)

```
- Http: Request, GET http://www.contoso.com/
    Command: GET
  + URI: /
    ProtocolVersion: HTTP/1.1
    VIA: 1.1 TMGProxy01
    Accept-Language:  en-us
    UA-CPU:  x86
    Accept-Encoding:  gzip, deflate
    User-Agent:  Mozilla/4.0 (compatible; MSIE 7.0; Windows NT 6.0; WOW64;
SLCC1; .NET CLR 2.0.50727; InfoPath.2; .NET CLR 3.5.21022; MS-RTC LM 8; .NET CLR
3.5.30729; .NET CLR 3.0.30618; MS-RTC EA 2)
    Host:  www.contoso.com
    Proxy-Connection:  Keep-Alive
```

13. The Web server processes the request and responds with 200 OK and whatever content is associated with this request:

```
- Http: Response, HTTP/1.1, Status Code = 200, URL: /
    ProtocolVersion: HTTP/1.1
    StatusCode: 200, Ok
    Reason: OK
    Connection:  Keep-Alive
    Content-Length:  2266
    Expires:  Fri, 01 Jan 1990 00:00:00 GMT
    Date:  Mon, 22 Dec 2008 03:58:12 GMT
    Content-Type:  text/html; Charset=utf-8
    Server:  Microsoft-IIS/6.0
    Cache-Control:  no-cache, must-revalidate
    Pragma:  no-cache
    X-RADID:  P5384519-T8362238-C1501580
    HeaderEnd: CRLF
  + payload: HttpContentType =  text/html; Charset=utf-8
```

NOTE This response included the Cache-control: no-cache; must-revalidate; and Pragma: no-cache headers. The no-cache directives instruct the client and all intermediate entities that they should not cache this content. The server also included a must-revalidate directive in the cache-control header. This directive instructs the client and all intermediate entities that if they hold this content in their local cache, they should verify that they have the current version as indicated by the Date and Expires headers. The result of this combination is such that the client and intermediate entities will clear this content from their cache if it exists and the no-cache directives will prevent future caching of this response. Additionally, the Expires header includes a date that is in the past. This Expires header data is intended to immediately delete this content if it is already cached by the client or proxy.

14. The Web Proxy filter receives the response and content from the Web server and passes it through the Web filters in their defined order. If the request and response headers allow caching of the Web server response and TMG is configured to cache Web requests, TMG will store the response in the cache.

15. The Web proxy then forwards a modified form of the Web server response to the client (again, note the addition of the VIA header to the forwarded content):

```
- Http: Response, HTTP/1.1, Status Code = 200, URL: /
    ProtocolVersion: HTTP/1.1
    StatusCode: 200, Ok
    Reason: OK
    ProxyConnection:  Keep-Alive
    Connection:  Keep-Alive
    ContentLength:  2266
    Via:  1.1 TmgServer01
    Expires:  Fri, 01 Jan 1990 00:00:00 GMT
    Date:  Mon, 22 Dec 2008 03:58:12 GMT
    ContentType:  text/html; Charset=utf-8
    Server:  Microsoft-IIS/6.0
    Cache-Control:  no-cache, must-revalidate
    Pragma:  no-cache
    X-RADID:  P5384519-T8362238-C1501580
    HeaderEnd: CRLF
+ payload: HttpContentType =  text/html; Charset=utf-8
```

Understanding Policy Re-Evaluation

One major improvement included with TMG over ISA 2000, ISA 2004, and ISA 2006 is the way a policy is implemented. In ISA 2000 a restart of ISA services was required for new policies to take effect instantaneously. In ISA 2004 and ISA 2006 restart of the services wasn't required for new policies to take effect. However, a common question was why a new policy affected some connections and not others. The reason was that in ISA 2004 and ISA 2006, the new policy did not affect established connections; it only applied new policies to new connections.

Applications with established connections had to disconnect and reconnect before a new policy was applied to their connections. This behavior changes with TMG. When a policy change is made in TMG and the administrator clicks Apply, TMG will apply the policy on all anonymous connections as well as any new ones. Any anonymous client application connection that does not comply with the new policy will be terminated and further connections from the client application will not be allowed until they match the new policy. This feature in TMG is known as *Policy Reevaluation*, or *Policy Enforcement*.

Policy Enforcement

The Policy Enforcement feature in TMG enforces new policies on all new and anonymous established connections. This is useful in the event of a change in company security policy that needs to be deployed immediately. Applying the new policy on TMG will force the change as soon as TMG loads and applies the policy from the storage server.

Policy Enforcement takes place for all existing connections when the following rule elements change:

- Source addresses and port
- Destination addresses, names, and URLs
- Schedules
- User sets and content types

Policy Enforcement of existing connections uses information obtained during the establishment of the connection rather than renegotiating the establishment of the connection with the server. If the new policy is more restrictive, that might result in termination of the connection, even if the new policy does not allow it. If a firewall policy includes schedules that are changed, TMG will monitor every connection request that matches the rule to ensure that the connection hasn't expired. If the connection has expired based on the schedule aspect of the rule, TMG will terminate the client connection. It is important to note that if you modify any rule elements that are not re-evaluated, it is critical to ensure that after the new policy is in place, no existing connections violate the new policy. The best way to make sure all existing connections are disconnected is by either disconnecting the existing sessions from the Monitoring, Sessions page or by restarting the Firewall service if downtime is permitted.

The new policy is enforced for all new HTTP connections, mainly because HTTP requests are short in duration and mostly finish before the newer policy version is loaded from the storage server. As long as the HTTP connection is not passing any traffic, the newer policy will not apply to it, as illustrated in Figure 12-10. If an HTTP connection takes two seconds to complete where as the time between the policy is changed and finally loaded by TMG is five seconds, that HTTP connection isn't subjected to policy re-evaluation; however, any new HTTP connection to that site or from that client will be subjected to the new policy.

After you click Apply in the details pane, the policy is updated and the policy enforcement starts in the background. In Figure 12-11 you can see that TMG notifies you the policies are being re-evaluated.

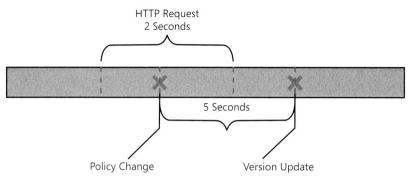

FIGURE 12-10 An exception in Policy Enforcement

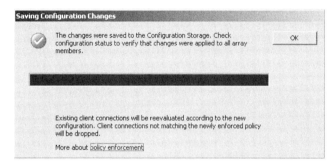

FIGURE 12-11 Policy Enforcement for existing client connections

When the re-evaluation is complete, an alert is generated notifying the TMG administrator that all non-HTTP connections were re-evaluated, as shown in Figure 12-12.

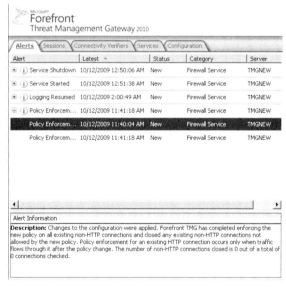

FIGURE 12-12 Policy Enforcement alert

The alert also mentions that Policy Enforcement on HTTP connections only happens if traffic is flowing through the HTTP connection after the policy change.

Any existing connection or new connection violating the new security policy will be denied and can be seen in logging with a new logging result code, FWX_E_POLICY_CONNECTION_CLOSED, for firewall connections. For Web requests they will simply be denied with an HTTP Status code 12202 The Forefront TMG Denied The Specified Uniform Resource Locator (URL). Figures 12-13 and 12-14 show the logging errors for firewall connections and Web Proxy connections.

Client IP	Destination IP	Protocol	Rule	Action	Result Code
157.58.197.148	10.0.0.2	FTP	Allow FTP to Internet	Initiated Connection	0x0 ERROR_SUCCESS
157.58.197.148	10.0.0.2	FTP	Specific Deny FTP	Closed Connection	0xc0040039 FWX_E_POLICY_CONNECTION_CLOSED

FIGURE 12-13 New logging result code for firewall connections

Protocol	Action	HTTP Status Code	Result Code
HTTP	Initiated Connection		0x0 ERROR_SUCCESS
http	Denied Connection	12202 The Forefront TMG denied the specified Uniform Resource Locator (URL).	
HTTP	Closed Connection		0x80074e20 FWX_E_GRACEFUL_SHUTDOWN

FIGURE 12-14 Error code for Web Proxy connections

Exemptions in Policy Enforcement

Policy Enforcement does not evaluate the following scenarios or elements:

- No custom policy element associated with an application filter is considered in policy re-evaluation. For example, if you add an interface to an RPC definition used in a deny firewall policy rule, existing connections to that interface will not be terminated. Similarly, if you disable an SMTP command in the SMTP filter, existing connections that use that command will not be terminated. The proper way to terminate these existing connections is to disconnect them using the Session tab within Monitoring.

- Modifications in protocol definitions, such as changes in protocol properties or addition of new protocols, do not affect existing connections. This is because a connection is associated with a specific protocol only during connection establishment, and this association remains unchanged throughout the lifetime of the connection. For example, if a connection is associated with FTP protocol, which uses TCP port 21, and later another protocol element with the same TCP port 21 is added, the connection will still match policy rules containing the FTP protocol and will not match policy rules that do not contain FTP protocol, even if they contain the newly defined protocol.

- Re-evaluation of existing HTTP sessions takes place only when there is a traffic exchange along the corresponding connection. Thus it is possible that some HTTP sessions may exist in the Session Monitoring view even if they are not allowed by the new policy, as long as they do not pass any traffic.

Policy Enforcement in Certain Scenarios

To understand how Policy Enforcement is applied when a firewall policy is changed, consider the following examples.

Forcing Authentication

Firewall Client authentication takes place when the control channel is set up, whereas Web Proxy client authentication takes place when the first HTTP request is made. What if an older rule allowed anonymous connections and a new firewall policy only allows authenticated users? Because authentication cannot be applied to existing connections, the connection will remain anonymous and will be terminated if no other rule matches the request or allows it.

Changing Authentication Type

If the authentication type for a publishing rule is changed, TMG will use the previous authentication information provided by the client and the session will continue even if the client is not using the new authentication scheme.

Changing Allowed Content Type

If initially there was no restriction on the content type allowed in a Firewall Policy access rule allowing HTTP, and a new rule allows access only for specific content types, the request for the previously allowed content type will be denied, and the session that uses the previously allowed content type will be terminated. However, in certain scenarios, the content type can be derived from the requested URL path, and then this information will be used to match the policy. No renegotiation will be performed with the Web server.

Troubleshooting Access Rules

The first step in troubleshooting outbound access is to have a good understanding of how the access rules are evaluated, which was the first thing covered in this chapter. In summary, when you are troubleshooting access rules, you need to consider the following questions:

- Where did the traffic originate?
- Where is the traffic destined?
- Is authentication required?
- Is the access rule placed in the most optimized order?

These core questions are part of an initial approach to understanding whether your access rules will achieve their desired results. It is easy to make mistakes while configuring access rules because errors in simple configuration details can lead to unexpected results.

The best way to start troubleshooting TMG access rules is by using the Logging feature. This feature allows you to see what traffic is arriving to the TMG and which rule is being used to allow or deny this traffic.

Basic Internet Access

For this example, Figure 12-15 shows the basic diagram in use on this network.

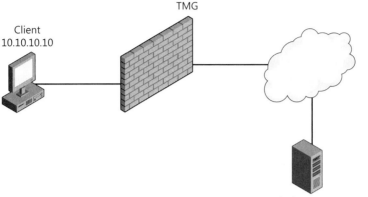

FIGURE 12-15 Diagram for basic Web access through TMG

The goal of the client (10.10.10.10) located behind TMG is to have access to the Web site *http://www.fabrikam.com*. However, when the user tries to access it, she receives the following error: 502 Proxy Error. The Forefront TMG denied the specified URL.

To gather more data to understand what is happening, follow these steps to access the TMG Logging feature and create a filter:

1. On the TMG computer, open the Forefront TMG Management Console.

2. Click Forefront TMG (Server Name) in the left pane.

3. Click Logs & Reports. You will see something similar Figure 12-16.

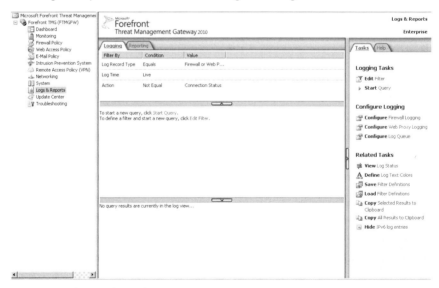

FIGURE 12-16 Logs and reports

4. In the Task pane, click Edit Filter.

5. In the Filter By drop-down box, choose Client IP. In the Condition drop-down box, choose the Equals option. In the Value text box type, the IP address of the workstation that you are using for testing purposes. Figure 12-17 shows how the filter should be set. Click Add To List.

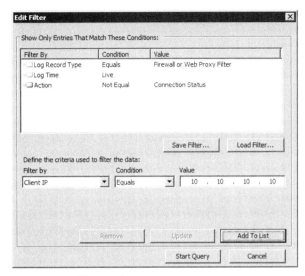

FIGURE 12-17 Filtering the query

6. Click Start Query. TMG will start monitoring traffic originated from the host specified in the Edit Filter dialog box.

After preparing TMG to monitor traffic originating from this client, you need go to the client and reproduce the problem. For this example, after accessing the Web site you can see that the request is triggering the default rule, as shown in Figure 12-18.

The question that is asked most often after seeing the default rule trigger is "Why is the connection triggering the default rule?" As explained earlier in this chapter, when TMG evaluate the rules, it checks whether the traffic matches each rule. If there is no match, the default rule (Deny All) is applied.

In this example, the problem was that the access rule was configured incorrectly. The rule was allowing traffic only from localhost (TMG) to the external network, as shown in Figure 12-19.

To fix the preceding rule you need to change the source from localhost to Internal. This way, internal clients can correctly browse the Internet.

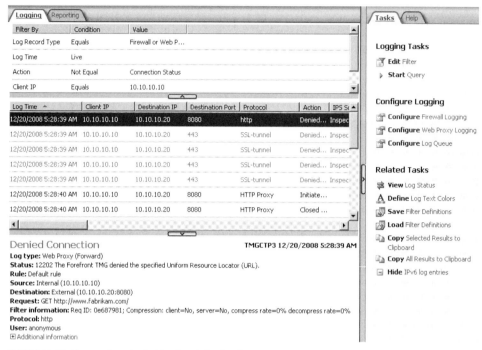

FIGURE 12-18 Connection denied by the default rule

FIGURE 12-19 Internet access rule

Authentication

You have an additional element to troubleshoot when access rules require authentication. The Web browser you use to access a resource—and how it is configured—play a major role when authentication is required for outbound access. A classic example is the difference in authentication mechanisms when you use Internet Explorer 6.0—which doesn't support Kerberos—versus when using Internet Explorer 7 or higher, which does support Kerberos. Chapter 32, "Exploring HTTP Protocol," will cover in more detail how HTTP authentication works. For now, let's focus on some common scenarios where access rules that require authentication cause problems.

When you monitor outbound access for a rule that requires authentication, you will see two requests to the same destination—the first is denied (as shown in Figure 12-20) and the second is allowed (as shown in Figure 12-21). An exception is for NTLM Authentication with which you will see two denials and one success in ISA logging.

FIGURE 12-20 The first access request is denied.

FIGURE 12-21 The second attempt is allowed.

Notice the message in Figure 12-20: "12209 The Forefront TMG requires authorization to fulfill the request." This happens because the first HTTP request is anonymous (which is expected). In Figure 12-21, notice that in the Client Username column the credentials were successfully passed to TMG and the traffic was allowed.

> **NOTE**   Notice that in Figure 12-21 there are two protocols, http (lowercase) and HTTP Proxy. The difference is that the http (lowercase) protocol indicates that request was handled by the Web Proxy filter in TMG.

Table 12-1 shows you some of the core issues when dealing with authenticated traffic through TMG.

TABLE 12-1 Common Authentication Problems

MAIN PROBLEM	SCENARIO DETAILS	TROUBLESHOOTING STEPS
Some users have problems accessing the Internet.	Users having problems are SecureNET users and some guest computers that are not part of the domain.	■ Verify whether the access rule requires authentication. If it does, this behavior is expected because SecureNET clients cannot forward credentials to TMG. ■ Verify whether the option Require All Users To Authenticate is selected on the Web Proxy listener. If it is, this behavior is expected for those types of clients. As a work-around, disable this option.
Users are prompted multiple times for authentication.	Users browsing the Internet as Web Proxy clients are prompted for credentials.	■ Verify whether the option Require All Users To Authenticate is selected. If it is, disable this option. ■ Review the Event Viewer System Log in TMG to see whether you have events 5783 or 5719. If you do, check possible connectivity or performance issues while TMG is authenticating with the DC described in this event.
Users are always prompted for authentication while browsing the Internet.	For each new HTTP connection, users are prompted for authentication. Clients are domain-joined and are using Web Proxy client.	■ Review your internal network configuration and determine whether you have any other authentication method besides Integrated Windows Authentication. If you have Basic Authentication, this behavior may be expected depending on the Web Proxy application in use.

Most issues involving authenticated traffic are related to the same root cause, as described in the troubleshooting steps column. There may be some variations, but the options that you usually review during troubleshooting are those specified in this table.

> **NOTE** RFC 2617 dictates that the client is responsible for selecting the single strongest authentication method from those offered by the proxy or server. Falling back to weaker authentication methods is called a downgrade attack and is not supported by any well-written proxy client. For more information see RFC 2617 at *http://www.ietf.org/rfc/rfc2617.txt*.

Name Resolution

In Chapter 4, "Analyzing Network Requirements," you learned how important it is to plan an optimized name resolution infrastructure prior to deploying TMG. Name resolution has a direct impact on how well access rules are performed—even more so when you create access rules containing URL and Domain Name Sets.

The TMG Firewall Service includes its own DNS cache that improves name resolution performance. If the rule that is evaluating the connection request contains an IP address or a host name that exists in the DNS cache, the request is processed without issuing a DNS request. If the name or IP address is not in the cache, a DNS request is sent for name or IP address resolution.

It is also important to note that access rules that require name resolution are evaluated and enforced in accordance with DNS information configured in the Windows operating system. If DNS settings are incorrectly configured, access rules may not be applied as expected.

> **NOTE** DNS is a key component for TMG. If DNS is unavailable, this can eventually cause downtime on TMG. For more information on such behavior, see *http://blogs.technet.com/isablog/archive/2009/01/12/isa-server-2006-stops-answering-requests.aspx*.

Using the Traffic Simulator

The traffic simulator helps troubleshoot access rules and publishing rules by simulating traffic as defined in the simulator and comparing them against the existing rule set on TMG. This is helpful specifically when there is no client to test with. The traffic simulator is found under the Troubleshooting tab, as shown in Figure 12-22.

The traffic simulator has four scenarios that the TMG administrator can use to simulate:

- **Web Access**   Internal users accessing the Internet using a Web protocol such as http or https, which are intercepted by the Web Proxy filter in TMG
- **Non-Web Access**   Internal users or VPN users accessing the Internet or another network using a non-Web protocol such as DNS, which isn't intercepted by the Web Proxy filter
- **Web Publishing**   External users accessing a Web server published through TMG
- **Server Publishing**   External users accessing a non–Web service published through TMG

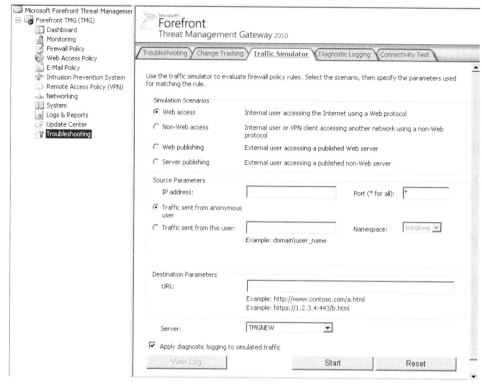

FIGURE 12-22 Traffic Simulator in TMG

The administrator can specify the client's IP and source port that the client might use (if applicable) and choose whether the request should be simulated as an anonymous request or from an authenticated user. Then she can specify the destination URL or target Web server depending on the type of scenario selected and simulate the traffic to see which rule might be matched to allow or deny the traffic. Depending upon whether the request is allowed or denied, TMG will show an entry log that specifies the rule that allowed or denied the traffic, along with the network relationship that applied to that traffic, as shown in Figures 12-23 and 12-24.

Allowed Traffic

Rule Name: DC to Outside
Rule Order: 1
⊟ Additional information

- **From:** Internal
- **To:** External
- **Network Rule Name:** None - NAT implied (Web Proxy traffic)
- **Network Relationship:** NAT
- **Protocol:** HTTP
- **Rule Application Filter:** Web Proxy Filter

Traffic allowed by firewall policy rules may be blocked by Web or Application filters.

FIGURE 12-23 Allowed log from Traffic Simulator

Denied Traffic

Rule Name: Allow Web Access for All Users
Rule Order: 4

⊟ Additional information

- **From:** Internal
- **To:** External
- **Network Rule Name:** Internet Access
- **Network Relationship:** NAT
- **Protocol:** HTTP
- **Rule Application Filter:**

FIGURE 12-24 Denied log from Traffic Simulator

The administrator also has access to view the diagnostic log associated with the traffic simulation. When the simulation is complete, the view diagnostic log option is available for viewing, as shown in Figure 12-25.

FIGURE 12-25 View diagnostic logging

The diagnostic logging is fairly similar to the logging that Microsoft engineers use to troubleshoot customer issues, except that the diagnostic logging available in TMG relies only on public symbols. When you click View Log, TMG displays the log information, which will show how and why TMG made the decision to allow or deny the traffic. Figure 12-26 shows what diagnostic logging looks like.

1368	10/12/2009 9:42:41 PM	fff4b074	Firewall service	destination does not match the packet.
1369	10/12/2009 9:42:41 PM	fff4b074	Firewall service	Forefront TMG is evaluating the rule Allow Web Access for All Users.
1370	10/12/2009 9:42:41 PM	fff4b074	Firewall service	The rule Allow Web Access for All Users matches the packet and may deny it. However, a rule that precedes this rule in the list of policy rules and matches the packet will take precedence and may allow the packet.
1371	10/12/2009 9:42:41 PM	fff4b074	Firewall service	The rule Allow Web Access for All Users blocked the packet.
1372	10/12/2009 9:42:41 PM	fff4b074	Firewall service	The Firewall service is performing rule evaluation.
1373	10/12/2009 9:42:41 PM	fff4b074	Firewall service	Packet properties: Source IP address: 10.1.1.121 Source array network: Internal Destination IP address: 149.7.40.13 Destination array network: External
1374	10/12/2009 9:42:41 PM	fff4b074	Firewall service	Forefront TMG is looking for an applicable network rule.
1375	10/12/2009 9:42:41 PM	fff4b074	Firewall service	Forefront TMG is evaluating the network rule Local Host Access.
1376	10/12/2009 9:42:41 PM	fff4b074	Firewall service	The source IP address in the packet does not match the source specified in the network rule.
1377	10/12/2009 9:42:41 PM	fff4b074	Firewall service	Forefront TMG is checking the reverse direction of the network rule Local Host Access.
1378	10/12/2009 9:42:41 PM	fff4b074	Firewall service	The destination IP address in the packet does not match the source specified in the network rule.
1379	10/12/2009 9:42:41 PM	fff4b074	Firewall service	Forefront TMG is evaluating the network rule VPN Clients to Internal Network.
1380	10/12/2009 9:42:41 PM	fff4b074	Firewall service	The source IP address in the packet does not match the source specified in the network rule.
1381	10/12/2009 9:42:41 PM	fff4b074	Firewall service	Forefront TMG is checking the reverse direction of the network rule VPN Clients to Internal Network.
1382	10/12/2009 9:42:41 PM	fff4b074	Firewall service	The destination IP address in the packet does not match the source specified in the network rule.
1383	10/12/2009 9:42:41 PM	fff4b074	Firewall service	Forefront TMG is evaluating the network rule Internet Access.
1384	10/12/2009 9:42:41 PM	fff4b074	Firewall service	The source and destination in the packet match the source and destination specified in the network rule, which specifies a NAT relationship.
1385	10/12/2009 9:42:41 PM	fff4b074	Firewall service	The network rule Internet Access matches the source and destination. A NAT relationship is specified.

FIGURE 12-26 Diagnostic Logging Log

As shown in Figure 12-26, the diagnostic logging log shows how TMG made the decision to match the traffic against an access rule and a network rule. Diagnostic logging can be enabled separately as well from the Diagnostic Logging tab; however, it should only be enabled for troubleshooting scenarios and turned off after data has been collected—keeping diagnostic logging on can create performance issues.

Summary

In this chapter you learned how firewall rules are evaluated and the importance of organizing access in a logical order that provides the desired result. After understanding how access rules are evaluated, you also learned about scenarios in which access rules are used and how the HTTP filter has an important role in access rule processing. You also learned about a new feature added to TMG called Policy Enforcement and how this feature provides faster updates based on changes made to firewall policy. Last but not least, you learned how to troubleshoot access rules using real-time logging and the traffic simulator. In the next chapter you will learn how to implement TMG's load-balancing capabilities.

## CHAPTER 13

Configuring Load-Balancing Capabilities

- Multiple Paths to the Internet **263**

- Implementing ISP Redundancy **267**

- Understanding and Implementing NLB **284**

- Summary **306**

Service availability is easily one of the most critical aspects of any deployment. In this chapter, you will become familiar with two TMG features designed to ensure the availability and reliability of your service offering—whether it is deployed for access to the Internet, from the Internet, or both.

Multiple Paths to the Internet

Today, all enterprises require around-the-clock connectivity to the Internet. Although it is possible to configure ISP multi-homing on routers, it introduces a significant amount of administrative overhead and isn't cost-effective. TMG introduces a new feature called ISP Redundancy (ISP-R). ISP-R helps administrators configure two ISP links to provide failover or load balancing between two separate ISP links.

What Is ISP Redundancy?

ISP Redundancy is a feature in TMG that provides high availability or load sharing of Internet connections by making use of two ISP links. This feature ensures that if the primary ISP link goes down, TMG will move all client connections to the secondary ISP link. Once the primary ISP link is back up, TMG moves all connections back to the primary ISP link, as shown in Figure 13-1. There are two different scenarios in ISP-R:

- **ISP Failover** In this scenario you configure failover from a primary ISP link to a secondary ISP link. The secondary or backup ISP link is only used when the primary is unavailable. This is especially useful when you have a pay-by-traffic connection as a backup, which is used only when the primary ISP link is down. ISP Failover does not provide load-balancing capabilities.

- **ISP Load Balancing** In this scenario you can configure load balancing between two ISP links so that traffic can be balanced between them; the aggregated links can also back each other up in case of failure. This is specifically useful when you have fixed-price ISP links. ISP Load Balancing enables you to utilize all available ISP bandwidth as well as provide ISP Failover capabilities. With ISP Load Balancing, you can provide per-ISP traffic usage controls by specifying a relative weight ratio to each ISP connection.

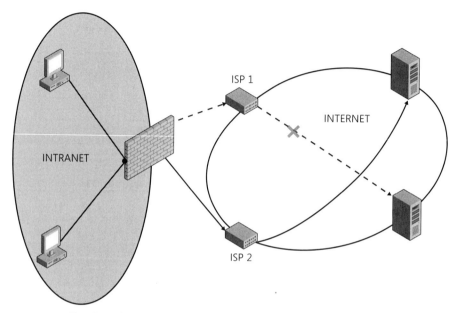

FIGURE 13-1 The ISP Redundancy feature in TMG

> *NOTE* Where ISP-R and Enhanced NAT (E-NAT) both apply, E-NAT takes priority over ISP-R.

In general, a high-availability solution is one that provides connection failover from one link to another without any end-user downtime. This also includes all connections from a failing link being moved over to the active link without the user having to retry the connection. This is also known as *stateful failover*. Windows Network Load Balancing does not provide stateful failover, hence it does not classify as high availability. It is also important to note that ISP-R is mainly focused on outbound connections, such as Access Rule traffic. However, it also helps for inbound connections. If the primary link goes down, the client accessing a Web server or a non–Web server published through TMG would have to make a new DNS request to get the IP address of the working ISP link and then can access the Web or non–Web server again. The client has to resolve the new IP for the published URL; hence, DNS changes are needed on the public name to resolve to the IP address of the working ISP link.

How ISP Redundancy Works

TMG uses ISP subnet information to direct traffic to each of the ISPs. An ISP link is identified by an ISP gateway and the gateway subnet. This enables TMG to support an array configuration without the need to require a per-server configuration. However, the servers in the array need to have an external local IP address on each of the gateway subnets. Whenever a new connection is established, TMG chooses which link will be used for the new connection. This decision is made based on link availability and stickiness. (Client-server traffic prefers reuse of same link.) This is also dependent on Enhanced NAT (E-NAT), where an administrator can specify a specific NAT address for a particular rule. E-NAT overrides ISP-R configuration. Once the decision is made, the new connection uses the NAT address associated with the ISP link. TMG then overrides the TCP/IP routing decision and enforces routing at NDIS (Layer 2) to the associated link. We will discuss E-NAT further in Chapter 29, "Enhanced NAT."

ISP-R only works for a NAT network relationship. This means that any testing should be performed from a client operating in the source network of a NAT relationship. This also means you cannot test ISP-R from TMG itself. Web traffic (like HTTP) will be intercepted by the Web proxy filter, thereby enforcing NAT. Any traffic not intercepted by the Web proxy filter doesn't benefit from ISP-R if testing is done from TMG itself.

When you use ISP-R, keep the following in mind:

- ISP Redundancy only works for the default external network.
- You need two separate ISP subnets.
- You need unique IP addresses on the external network card associated with each ISP.
- A default route to each ISP must exist.
- ISP-R is only functional for a NAT relationship.

For a detailed list of ISP-R constraints, see the section "Implementing ISP Redundancy" later in the chapter.

Link Availability Testing

Link availability is one of the factors TMG uses when choosing which ISP link to use for a new outbound connection. TMG determines availability by polling the Root DNS servers on the default DNS port, UDP port 53. TMG polls these DNS servers every 60 seconds to check whether the link connectivity is up.

The DNS root servers are 13 DNS server clusters that are responsible for delegating DNS requests to the top-level domain (TLD) name-servers. For more information about the Root DNS servers, see *http://www.root-servers.org/.*

Multiple servers are polled sequentially (at each attempt only one server is polled) to determine whether there are any connectivity problems to a particular Root DNS server. If multiple Root DNS servers fail to respond, TMG retries the connection to check the link state two more times (for three total attempts including the first one) at an interval of 60 seconds each before switching over to the secondary ISP link for subsequent connection and requests from the clients. Once the switch from primary link to the secondary link is made, TMG will test the primary link every 300 seconds and whenever the primary link responds for the first time, two more subsequent consecutive requests at an interval of 60 seconds each must be successful before the primary link is marked as working again. Once the primary link is considered operational, TMG creates new connections using the primary ISP link.

As shown in Figure 13-2, connectivity to the Root DNS servers should fail three times before TMG switches from the primary ISP link to the secondary ISP link. Similarly, connectivity to the Root DNS servers should succeed three times before TMG switches back from the secondary ISP link to the primary ISP link. As soon as you see the connection back up on the primary ISP link, it will take about two more minutes before TMG will move client connections back to the primary ISP link.

In Figure 13-2 you can see that the testing interval between successful polling is 60 seconds. At time 00:03:02, TMG marks the link as down for the first time. It makes two more attempts to connect to the Root DNS at an interval of 60 seconds each—00:04:02 and 00:05:02—before marking the link as permanently down. It then waits for 300 seconds before it retries the connection at 00:10:02. It keeps retrying the connection at an interval of 60 seconds to check whether the link is up, as seen at 00:11:02 and 00:12:02. At 00:12:02 the connection succeeds for the first time, and then it retries the connection at an interval of 60 seconds each to see whether the connection succeeds twice more—at 00:13:02 and 00:14:02—before finally marking the link as working again.

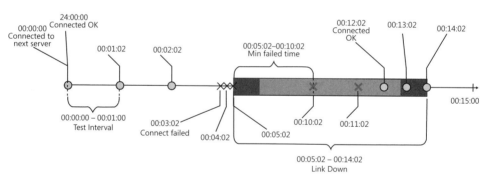

FIGURE 13-2 Polling intervals to mark a link as up or down

The default values between polling intervals or number of times a connection is attempted is not configurable through the TMG User Interface, but can be changed by a COM setting. The COM object that controls these settings is *ISPredundancyConfig*. The default settings for this object are shown in Table 13-1.

TABLE 13-1 *ISPredundancyConfig* COM property default values

NAME	POSSIBLE VALUES		
IspRedundancyPolicy	*fpcIspRedundancyDisabled*		
	fpcIspRedundancyLoadBalancing		
	fpcIspRedundancyFailover		

NAME	TYPE	DEFAULT VALUE	DESCRIPTION
MinimalResumeTime	Long	300	Time period TMG waits and doesn't check specific ISP link after its state changes to Down
TestIntervalLinkAvailable	Long	60	Time between consequent link poll actions when the link state is Up
TestIntervalLinkUnavailable	Long	60	Time between consequent link poll actions when the link state is Down
SuccessesToAvailable	Long	3	Number of consequent successes to switch link from Down state to Up state
FailuresToUnavailable	Long	3	Number of consequent successes to switch link from Up state to Down state
ConnectivityRemoteVerificationPort	Long	53	Port to poll (one for all servers)

You can call the COM value by writing a simple script. We will learn more about how to script a COM object in Chapter 30, "Scripting TMG."

Implementing ISP Redundancy

As noted in Chapter 1, "What's New in TMG," and in the previous section, ISP-R is a new feature provided with TMG that can be used to provide better service availability.

Planning for ISP-R

ISP-R is made up of two operational modes: ISP Load Balancing and ISP Failover. Although ISP Load Balancing provides failover and fail-back, ISP Failover does not provide ISP Load Balancing functionality.

ISP Load Balancing is primarily targeted at those deployments where you want to provide per-ISP traffic usage controls by applying a relative weight to each ISP connection. This feature provides failover/failback functionality as well.

ISP Failover is primarily targeted at those deployments where you want to provide single-ISP connectivity with automatic failover/failback functionality. In this case, the bandwidth provided by the secondary ISP connection is not considered sufficient for normal business needs, or is designated purely as a backup path.

ISP-R Constraints

Because ISP-R was designed for a specific purpose, you need to consider several issues before deciding whether you can enable this feature and if so, which options you can use:

- Network connections associated with ISP-R must exist only in the default external network.
- Each ISP connection must represent a unique IP subnet and use a unique default gateway.

> **NOTE** Windows does not allow multiple default gateways for DHCP-assigned links. If your ISP connections provide only DHCP-assigned addressing, Windows will only add one of the default gateways to the routing table. In this case, you must manually add both default gateways to using the ISP-R wizard. Alternately, you can add them to the routing table before you can enable ISP-R. For instance, if ISP-1 uses a subnet of 10.10.0.0/24 and ISP-2 uses a subnet of 10.10.1.0/24, you would enter the following commands:
>
> ```
> route -p add 0.0.0.0 mask 0.0.0.0 10.10.0.1
> route -p add 0.0.0.0 mask 0.0.0.0 10.10.1.1
> ```

- All TMG array members must use an identical ISP-facing network configuration.
- All NICs on all array members must have the same network offload processing configuration, which means that all NICs on all array members should have identical checksum offloading settings. These settings are typically part of the NIC configuration Advanced settings. The options provided are unique to each NIC and its drivers. To minimize the chance of NIC configuration incompatibilities, you should ensure that all array members are built identically.
- Only traffic processed in NAT relationships and Web proxy traffic are supported.
- ISP-R functionality is secondary to E-NAT. This means that when you configure E-NAT, you must select an IP address in each ISP for each array member or the outbound traffic may fail.
- ISP-R does not support traffic originating from TMG itself, because this represents a route relationship. The exception to this is traffic originating from TMG that is handled by the Web proxy filter.
- ISP-R is limited to two ISP connections

Enabling ISP-R

You enable ISP-R through the link available on the Tasks tab when the Networks node is selected in the left pane, as shown in Figure 13-3.

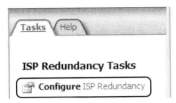

FIGURE 13-3 ISP-R Task link

When you click this link, the ISP Redundancy Configuration Wizard starts, as shown in Figure 13-4.

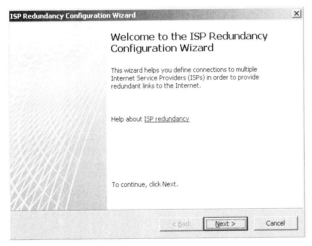

FIGURE 13-4 ISP Redundancy Configuration Wizard Welcome page

When you click Next, you have the option of choosing ISP Redundancy for load balancing or failover. Each option is outlined in separate wizard pages, beginning with Failover mode.

Failover Mode

To configure ISP-R in Failover mode, follow these steps:

1. Select Failover using a primary and backup link, as shown in Figure 13-5.

2. Click Next on the ISP Redundancy Method page. You have the option to choose which ISP link will be designated ISP Link 1, as shown in Figure 13-6.

3. Give this link a name reflecting its purpose in your environment, such as **ISP-1**. Choose the ISP connection by selecting the adapter name, which will display the ISP default gateway and mask bit length, as shown in Figure 13-7.

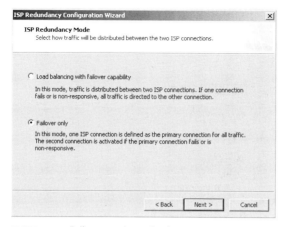

FIGURE 13-5 Failover option selection

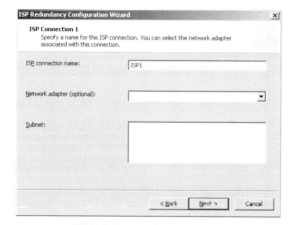

FIGURE 13-6 ISP Link 1 properties page

4. Click Next to access the Connection Properties page, as shown in Figure 13-7.

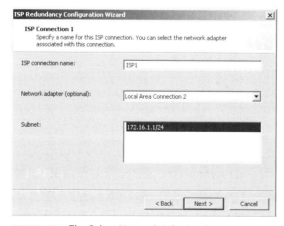

FIGURE 13-7 The Select Network Adapter Page

NOTE If your TMG computer is configured to use multiple ISP subnets on a single NIC, this page will appear as shown in Figure 13-8.

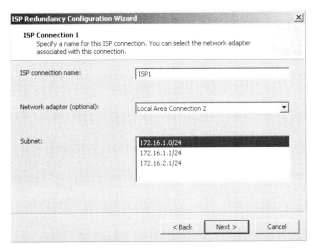

FIGURE 13-8 The Single-NIC Select Network Adapter page

5. Click Next to access the ISP Link 1 Connection Properties page, as shown in Figure 13-9. Any changes you make here will be reflected in the IP configuration for this NIC.

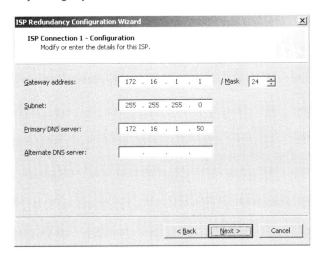

FIGURE 13-9 ISP Link 1 Connection Properties page

6. Click Next on the ISP 1 Connection Properties page. The ISP Link 2 Properties page opens, as shown in Figure 13-10. You *must* select a network adapter or subnet and mask that represents a different logical subnet than you selected for ISP Link 1.

7. Give this link a name reflecting its purpose in your environment, such as **ISP-1**, as shown in Figure 13-11.

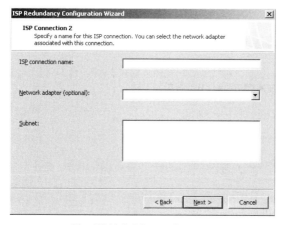

FIGURE 13-10 The ISP Link 2 Properties page

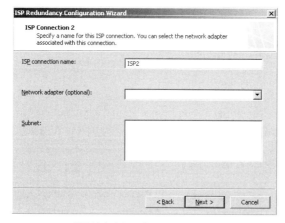

FIGURE 13-11 ISP Link 2 Naming

8. To select the adapter associated with ISP Link 2, select the NIC name. The default gateway and mask bit length will appear, as shown in Figure 13-12.

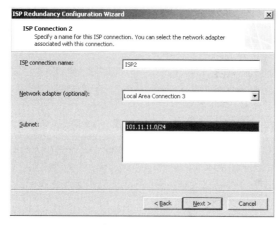

FIGURE 13-12 ISP Link 2 NIC selection

NOTE **NOTE** If your TMG computer is configured to use multiple ISP subnets on a single NIC, this page will appear as shown in Figure 13-13.

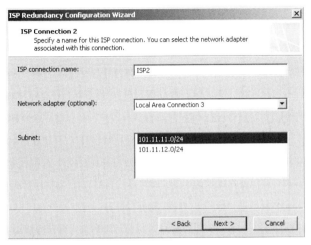

FIGURE 13-13 The Single-NIC Select Network Adapter page

9. Click Next to access the ISP Link 2 Connection Properties page, as shown in Figure 13-14. Any changes you make here will be reflected in the IP configuration for this NIC.

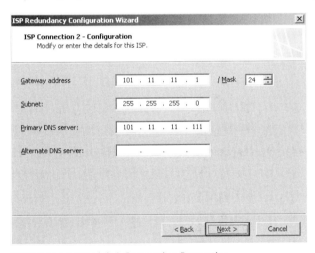

FIGURE 13-14 ISP Link 2 Connection Properties

10. Click Next on the ISP Link 2 Connection properties page. The Primary ISP Selection page opens, as shown in Figure 13-15. This is where you designate which ISP link is considered primary and which is secondary. By selecting the primary link, you automatically assign the remaining link as secondary.

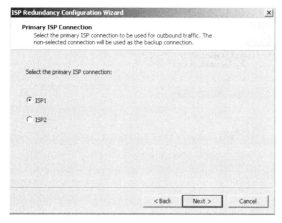

FIGURE 13-15 The Primary ISP Link page

11. Click Next on the Primary ISP Link page. The Completing The ISP Redundancy Configuration Wizard summary page opens, as shown in Figure 13-16.

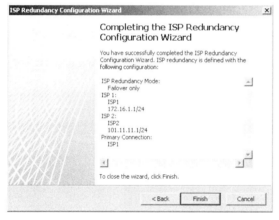

FIGURE 13-16 The ISP Wizard Completion page

12. Click Next. The TMG management center pane changes, as shown in Figure 13-17. If the configuration shown agrees with your planned configuration, click Apply to save the changes to storage.

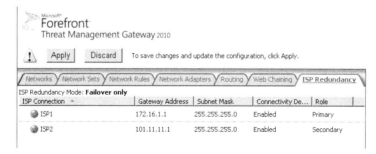

FIGURE 13-17 Completed configuration

Note that if you choose the same logical network for both ISP Links, you will see an error message at the end of the wizard, as shown in Figure 13-18.

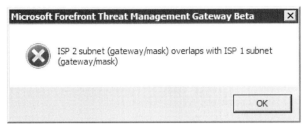

FIGURE 13-18 Same-subnet error message

13. To configure the additional ISP link connection test and connection role, select the desired ISP link and click Edit ISP Properties in the right pane, as shown in Figure 13-19.

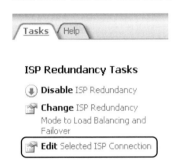

FIGURE 13-19 Edit ISP Properties control

Figure 13-20 shows the options available for the Connection Test mechanism.

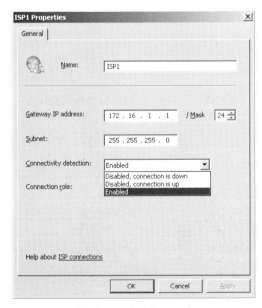

FIGURE 13-20 ISP Connection Test options

14. To determine ISP availability using the process defined earlier, choose Enabled. Select Disabled, Connection Is Up or Disabled, or Connection Is Down to manually configure the ISP link to assume the Available or Failed state, respectively. These settings are useful when the automatic detection fails because of circumstances beyond your control, such as ISP traffic flow problems.

Figure 13-21 shows the Connection Role option.

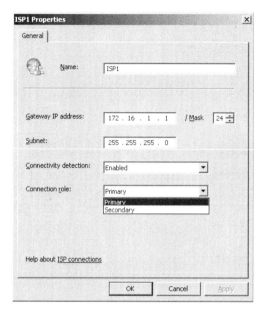

FIGURE 13-21 ISP Link Connection Role

This option also controls the other ISP link. When you select Primary in ISP Link 1, ISP Link 2 is automatically set to Secondary for you.

Load-Balancing Mode

To configure ISP-R for load-balancing mode, follow these steps:

1. Select Load Balancing Between Two ISP Links and click Next on the ISP Redundancy Method page, as shown in Figure 13-22.

2. When you see the ISP Link 1 Properties page shown in Figure 13-23, enter a name in the ISP link name field, such as **ISP1**.

3. Select the Adapter name to choose the NIC for this ISP connection. The Select Network Adapter Properties dialog box will change, as shown in Figure 13-24.

> **NOTE** If your TMG computer is configured to use multiple ISP subnets on a single NIC, this page will appear as shown in Figure 13-25.

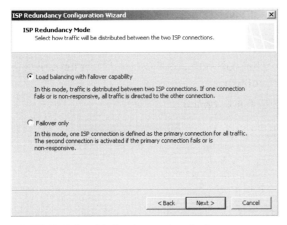

FIGURE 13-22 Load-balancing mode selection

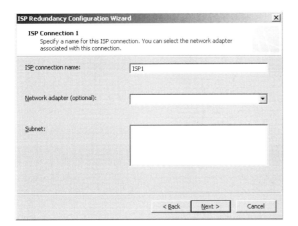

FIGURE 13-23 The ISP Link 1 Properties page

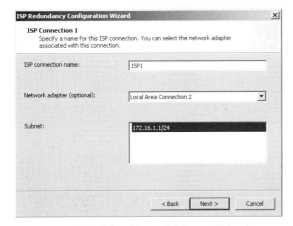

FIGURE 13-24 The Select Network Adapter dialog box

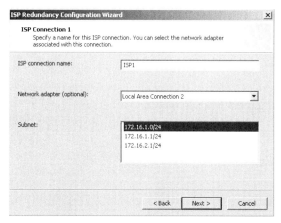

FIGURE 13-25 Single-NIC Select Network Adapter page

4. Click Next to access the ISP Link 1 Connection Properties page, as shown in Figure 13-26.

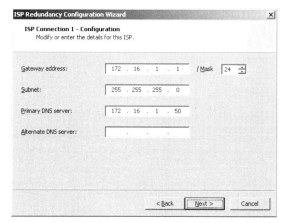

FIGURE 13-26 The ISP Link 1 Connection Properties page

5. Click Next to access the ISP 1 Dedicated Servers list, as shown in Figure 13-27.

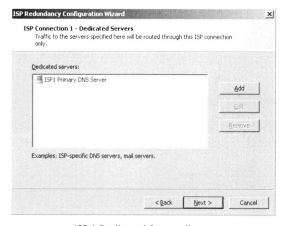

FIGURE 13-27 ISP 1 Dedicated Servers list

NOTE Because the IP configuration for ISP 1 includes a DNS server in the same subnet as the TMG computer, this IP address is added automatically to a computer object that is then included in this list.

6. If you need to define other computers that can only be reached through this ISP connection, click Add to access the Add Network Entities page. Click New and then click Computer, as shown in Figure 13-28.

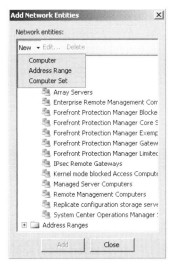

FIGURE 13-28 The Add New Computer dialog box

7. When the New Computer Rule Element page appears, type **ISP1 Time** in the name field and type **172.16.1.200** in the Computer IP Address field as shown in Figure 13-29.

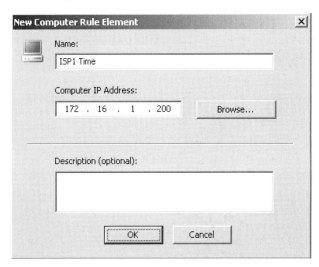

FIGURE 13-29 The New Computer Rule Element page

8. Click OK to return to the updated Add Network Entities page, as shown in Figure 13-30.

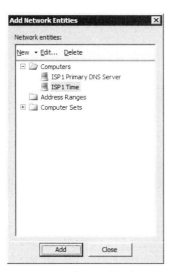

FIGURE 13-30 The Modified Add Network Entities page

9. Select ISP1 Time, click Add, and then click Close to return to the ISP1 Dedicated Servers list, as shown in Figure 13-31.

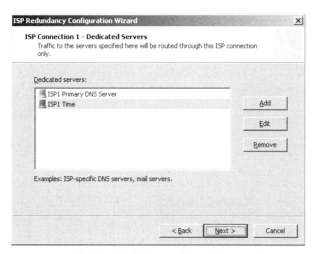

FIGURE 13-31 The Modified ISP 1 Dedicated Servers List page

10. Click Next to access the Select Network Adapter – ISP 2 page, as shown in Figure 13-32.

> **NOTE** If your TMG computer is configured to use multiple ISP subnets on a single NIC, this page will appear as shown in Figure 13-33.

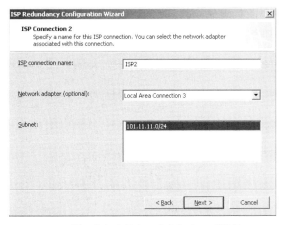

FIGURE 13-32 The Select Network Adapter – ISP 2 page

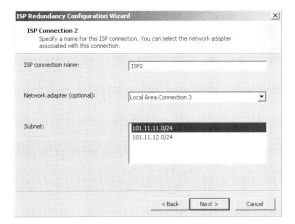

FIGURE 13-33 The Single-NIC Select Network Adapter page

11. Click Next to access the Connection Properties – ISP 2 page, as shown in Figure 13-34.

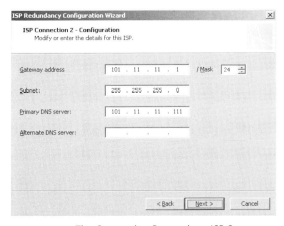

FIGURE 13-34 The Connection Properties – ISP 2 page

12. Click Next to access the ISP 2 Dedicated Servers list. If you need to add computers or address ranges for ISP 2, follow the same steps as outlined in steps 6 through 9. Click Next to access the Load Balancing Factor page, as shown in Figure 13-35.

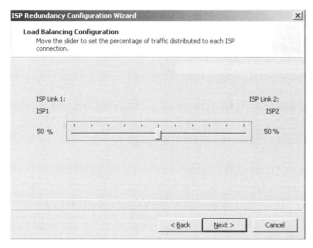

FIGURE 13-35 The Load Balancing Factor properties page

13. On the Load Balancing Factor page, you assign a relative weighting factor to each ISP link. Generally, you would use the bandwidth difference between the two ISP links to assign the relative weight. For instance, if ISP 1 provides 15 MbpS and ISP 2 provides 30 MbpS, you would slide the arrow toward ISP 2 until the ISP 2 value reads 66%. Click Next to access the Completing The ISP Redundancy Configuration Wizard page, as shown in Figure 13-36.

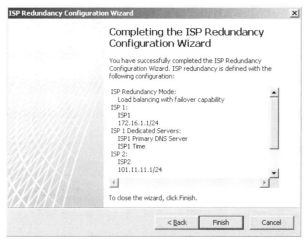

FIGURE 13-36 The Completing The ISP Redundancy Configuration Wizard page

14. Click Finish. The TMG management console changes to display the new ISP Redundancy configuration, as shown in Figure 13-37. If the configuration displayed matches your requirements, click Apply to save the changes to storage.

FIGURE 13-37 Load Balancing Configuration summary

15. To change the ISP properties, select the desired ISP and click Edit ISP Properties in the right pane. The selected ISP1 Properties dialog box appears, as shown in Figure 13-38.

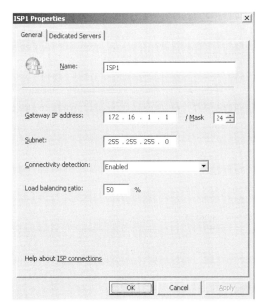

FIGURE 13-38 The General tab

16. On the General tab, you configure the connection test and define the relative traffic percentage directed through this ISP connection. Figure 13-39 shows the ISP1 Properties Dedicated Server List tab.

17. On the Dedicated Server List tab, you manage the server list relative to this ISP connection. When you're satisfied that the TMG settings match your desired configuration, click Apply in the center pane.

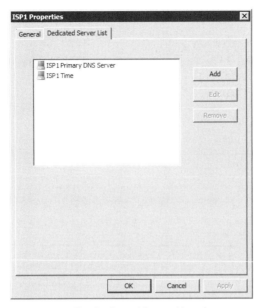

FIGURE 13-39 The Dedicated Server List tab

18. Select Monitoring in the left pane and click the Configuration tab in the center pane to verify successful application of the changes you've made. If the changes are successful, you will see results shown in Figure 13-40.

FIGURE 13-40 The updated configuration

Understanding and Implementing NLB

ISP-R allows you to have high availability by providing multiple paths to Internet. But it is also important to have multiple firewalls to allow high availability and load balancing. TMG uses the Network Load Balancing to provide for high availability of the firewalls themselves. It was first called Windows NLB in Windows NT and later changed to NLB in Windows 2000.

Because TMG uses NLB, most of the boundaries, recommendations, and limitations are due to the Windows operating system, with a few exceptions. For example, Network Load Balancing is designed to scale up to 32 hosts as a Windows operating system limitation, but for TMG the limit is eight nodes. For this reason, you should understand how this feature works before you implement NLB on TMG.

NLB Architecture

NLB operates as an NDIS driver so that it can process traffic before the TCP/IP stack sees it. Each node that is part of an NLB cluster has a unique IP address, known as the Dedicated IP (DIP) address. All nodes in an NLB array share a set of common IP addresses, known as Virtual IP (VIP) addresses. Figure 13-41 shows the basic architecture diagram for NLB.

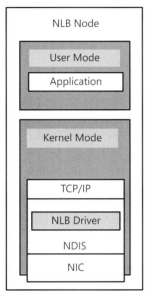

FIGURE 13-41 Basic NLB architecture

NLB has three modes of operation, which are used to determine how NLB will communicate with clients and among the nodes in the NLB array. These three modes are unicast, multicast, and multicast with IGMP. Regardless of the mode, the MAC address in the traffic leaving a host in the NLB array is set to the same value on all nodes. NLB on TMG can operate in integrated and non-integrated mode. When you enable Integrated NLB the default operation mode is unicast. In unicast mode, packets are delivered in parallel to all nodes and then the NLB driver filters out the packets not intended to be processed by a particular node. NLB also supports multicast mode, which adds a multicast MAC access to the node's adapters on all servers that are part of the NLB cluster. Although all nodes will share a common multicast MAC address, the nodes also retain their original MAC addresses.

ISA Server 2006 was the first version to support NLB multicast mode as well as multicast with IGMP support. This feature was added in *http://support.microsoft.com/kb/938550*. TMG 2010 inherited this capability; TMG MBE did not.

> **MORE INFO** For more information on how NLB works, go to *http://technet.microsoft.com/en-us/library/cc756878.aspx*.

Table 13-2 shows the difference between unicast and multicast MAC addresses.

TABLE 13-2 Differences Between Unicast and Multicast Addresses

NLB MODE	MAC ADDRESS	DESCRIPTION
Unicast	02:BF:c0:a8:00:91	c0:a8:00:91 corresponds to the primary virtual IP address of the node.
Multicast	03:BF:c0:a8:00:91	

Because MAC addresses are represented in colon-separated hexadecimal notation and IP addresses are represented in dotted-decimal notation, the association between the virtual IP address and the MAC address may not be obvious. If we take each IP address octet and convert it to its hexadecimal value, the relationship becomes clearer, as shown in the following list:

- 192 decimal equals c0 hexadecimal
- 168 decimal equals a8 hexadecimal
- 0 decimal equals 0 hexadecimal (not a huge surprise, is it?)
- 145 decimal equals 91 hexadecimal

Thus, the IP address 192.168.0.145 becomes c0:a8:00:91 when converted for use in a MAC address.

Network Considerations When Using NLB

If you use the default operation mode (unicast), you may notice an increase in traffic on the network where NLB is enabled. This is expected because unicast sometimes induces switch flooding. Figure 13-42 illustrates this behavior, which follows these steps:

1. The source computer sends the packet to the destination VIP—in this case, 192.168.0.145 (02:bf:c0:a8:00:91).

2. The switch receives the packet and checks whether the destination MAC address is recorded in the MAC address table.

3. Because more than one port has this MAC address on it, the switch floods to all ports.

Switch flooding in unicast mode is an expected behavior. One way to work around that is by separating the NLB nodes into their own VLAN. This way you limit the broadcast to nodes that are on that broadcast domain.

> **MORE INFO** For more information about VLAN and how it works, visit *http://en.wikipedia.org/wiki/VLAN*.

For troubleshooting purposes, when two nodes are not converging and you aren't sure whether the switch has functionalities that could potentially block the NLB convergence, it is recommended that you use a hub and see whether the convergence between nodes takes place. If it does, you must seek assistance from the switch's vendor.

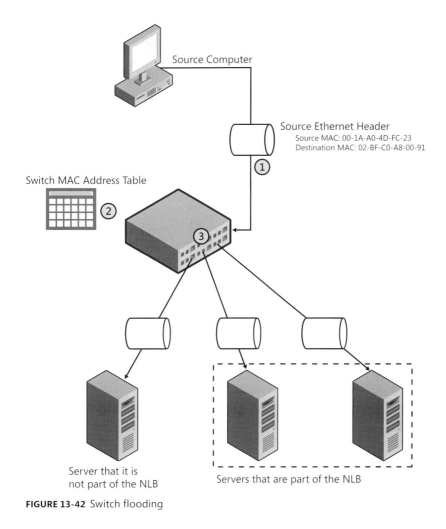

Source Computer

Source Ethernet Header
Source MAC: 00-1A-A0-4D-FC-23
Destination MAC: 02-BF-C0-A8-00-91

Switch MAC Address Table

Server that it is
not part of the NLB

Servers that are part of the NLB

FIGURE 13-42 Switch flooding

NOTE *Broadcast domain* and *collision domain* are terms used to define boundaries of the packet flow. Read more about broadcast domain at *http://en.wikipedia.org/wiki/Broadcast_domain* and about collision domain at *http://en.wikipedia.org/wiki/Collision_domain*.

Multicast mode includes a feature called *IGMP support*, which was introduced in Windows Server 2003. IGMP allows you to limit the effect of switch flooding behavior because only the NLB nodes on the same multicast group will be used.

MORE INFO For more information about the NLB features added in Windows Server 2003, see *http://download.microsoft.com/download/4/d/e/4de815ef-2904-420a-b726-e57de31ae63a/ClusteringOverview.doc*.

REAL WORLD   **All Traffic Is Going to a Single ISA Server 2006**

n this case, one ISA Server 2006 computer of a two-node NLB cluster was extremely busy with traffic coming from the internal clients, whereas the other server was idle. Both nodes of the NLB cluster were converged and there were no other indicators of problems within NLB itself.

To narrow down this issue we had to first understand how the lower-level communication (layer 2) was happening by looking to the ARP resolution process. (See Chapter 12, "Understanding Access Rules," for more information about the ARP resolution process.) The network administrator was asked to review the switch configuration—specifically, the switch's ARP Table—and discovered that the problem was that the switch was mapping a virtual MAC address in the NLB cluster to the MAC address of one ISA Server 2006 node. The switch was temporarily replaced with a hub for troubleshooting purposes and the issue was resolved.

NOTE   Another consideration when using NLB is NIC teaming (802.1ad) or VLAN tagging (802.1q) in combination with NLB, when both are configured on the same NIC. Please refer to KB *http://support.microsoft.com/kb/278431* for more information about known issues with this type of scenario. You can read more on link aggregation at *http://en.wikipedia.org/ wiki/Link_aggregation* and VLAN tagging at *http://www.ieee802.org/1/pages/802.1Q.html*.

Considerations When Enabling NLB on TMG

In TMG you can use NLB in two modes: integrated or non-integrated NLB. When using integrated mode, you will use the TMG Management Console to configure NLB. By using this mode you have the benefits of integrated management, configuration, maintenance, multi-networking support, virtual private network (VPN) support, and troubleshooting through management console. When using integrated mode, TMG also uses bidirectional affinity (BDA). BDA guarantees that the response traffic takes the same path as origination traffic.

With non-integrated NLB you use Windows-based NLB tools to configure and manage NLB on TMG. Because non-integrated NLB disconnects TMG from NLB, this mode does not automatically provide the benefits of TMG integrated network load balancing.

MORE INFO   For more information on bidirectional affinity, see *http://blogs.technet.com/ isablog/archive/2008/03/12/bi-directional-affinity-in-isa-server.aspx*.

Before you enable NLB on TMG you should identify the following components in your network:

- The location of the TMG Configuration Storage Server (CSS)
- The location of the TMG Firewall nodes that will be part of the NLB cluster
- Which TMG networks will be balanced
- Which Virtual IP addresses will be used in the NLB configuration
- Which types of clients will use the VIP to access TMG (SecureNET, Web proxy, or Firewall Client)
- Any additional network management or high-availability mechanisms that may be in use on the network or NLB hosts, such as 802.1q (VLAN tagging) or 802.1ad (Link Aggregation)

It is important to identify those elements first because you need to understand their impact on the NLB configuration. The TMG CSS placement is a key factor when using NLB. As a matter of fact, when you enable NLB an informational window pops up, as shown in Figure 13-43.

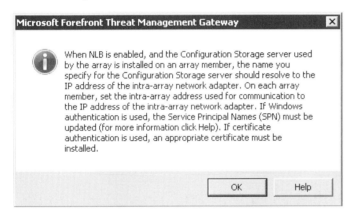

FIGURE 13-43 Informational window when enabling NLB on TMG

The general recommendation is that you do not install the Configuration Storage Server on one of the array members that has NLB enabled on it. If this cannot be avoided, you need to configure the name of the CSS in DNS or WINS to resolve to the dedicated IP address of the array member that holds the CSS role. Figures 13-44 and 13-45 show the two common scenarios for TMG CSS placement on an NLB environment.

DNS Configuration

The next step is name resolution for NLB array members. Because both nodes are using only the internal DNS Server for name resolution, it is expected that when each node tries to resolve the other's name, it will resolve using the network defined for use by Intra-Array communication. The recommendation here is to disable DNS auto registration in all TMG NICs to avoid name-resolution issues because TMG will have multiple addresses. Figure 13-46 shows this setting in the Advanced TCP/IP Settings dialog box.

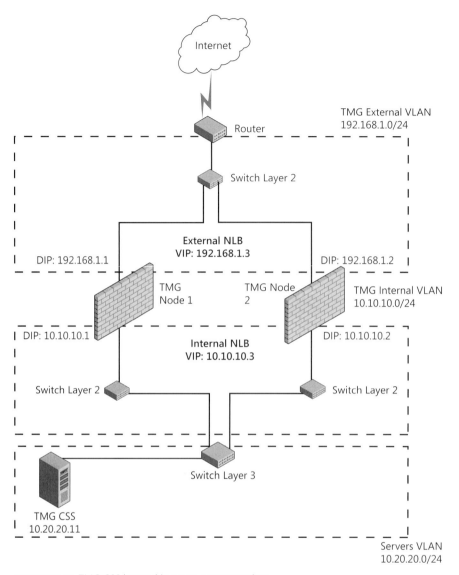

FIGURE 13-44 TMG CSS located in a non-array member

You will need to manually separate host (A) records for your DIPs and VIPs associated with members of the TMG firewall array. After creating these DNS resource records, your DNS entries (in the case of this scenario contoso.com) may resemble those in Figure 13-47.

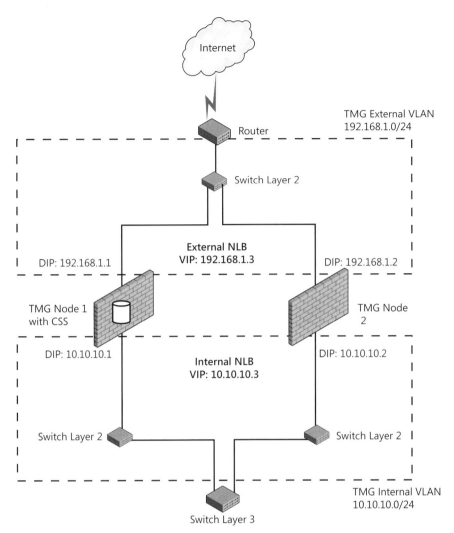

FIGURE 13-45 TMG CSS located in the array member

> **MORE INFO** For more information on how to create an A record on Windows Server 2008 DNS, follow the instructions at *http://technet.microsoft.com/en-us/library/cc816775.aspx*.

Client Consideration

When you use NLB, you need to understand how different TMG client types interact with NLB-enabled TMG firewalls. Table 13-3 summarizes the general considerations.

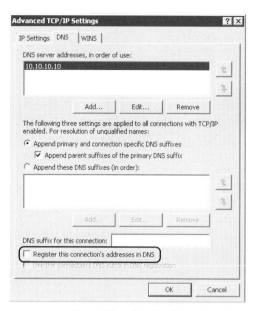

FIGURE 13-46 The DNS setting check box that should be unchecked

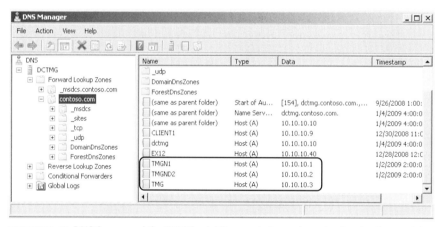

FIGURE 13-47 DNS Server and the TMG host (A) records for each node plus the A record for a VIP

> **NOTE** When you configure Web proxy and Firewall clients to use the CNAME as proxy
> server, the authentication method falls back to NTLM. This is an expected behavior. For more
> information on this and to learn how to work around this behavior, see *http://blogs.technet*
> *.com/isablog/archive/2008/06/26/understanding-by-design-behavior-of-isa-server-2006-*
> *using-kerberos-authentication-for-web-proxy-requests-on-isa-server-2006-with-nlb.aspx.*

TABLE 13-3 Client Considerations When Using NLB

CLIENT	CONSIDERATIONS
SecureNET	■ The default gateway should be set to a VIP on the array. ■ If DHCP is in use in the network, you need to change the router record to point to a VIP on the array. ■ Note that if other routers within the network use TMG as their default gateway, you need to change those routers to point to a VIP as a default gateway.
Web proxy	■ Web proxy clients will point to the CNAME (created in DNS) as proxy. CNAME should point to a host (A) record that points to virtual IP of the NLB. ■ If you use a browser that supports Active Directory Group Policy and you deploy Proxy Configuration through Group Policy, you need to point to this CNAME as proxy. ■ Web proxy clients also rely on the DHCP setting for WPAD. Therefore, the name that you use for the virtual IP needs to reflect the WPAD record in the DHCP scope option 252.
Firewall	■ Firewall clients may also rely on DNS depending on the TMG client configuration options chosen for the TMG network. Therefore, the same approach used for Web proxy clients also applies to Firewall clients. ■ Firewall clients also rely on DHCP setting for WPAD. Therefore, the name that you use for the virtual IP needs to reflect the WPAD record in the DHCP scope option 252.

Configuring NLB on TMG

After addressing all the prerequisites and general recommendations for using NLB on TMG, you can enable this feature by following these steps:

1. On the TMG computer, open the Forefront TMG Management Console.
2. Click Forefront TMG (Server Name) in the left pane.
3. Click Networking.
4. Click Enable Network Load Balancing Integration in the task pane, as shown in Figure 13-48.
5. Click Next on the Network Load Balancing Integration Wizard welcome page, as shown in Figure 13-49.

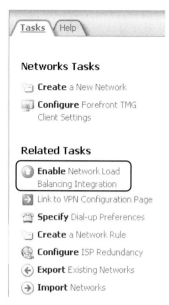

FIGURE 13-48 Enable NLB selection

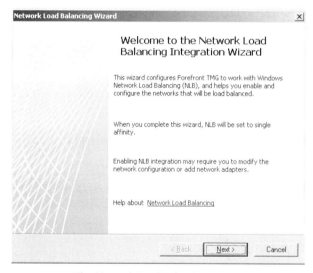

FIGURE 13-49 The Network Load Balancing Integration Wizard welcome page

6. The Select Load Balanced Networks page appears, as shown in Figure 13-50.

7. Select the network that you want to balance and then click Configure NLB Settings. Type in the IP, as shown in Figure 13-51.

8. If you have more than one virtual IP to add, add the first one in the Primary VIP field and then click Add VIP to add additional VIPs. The dialog box shown in Figure 13-52 appears.

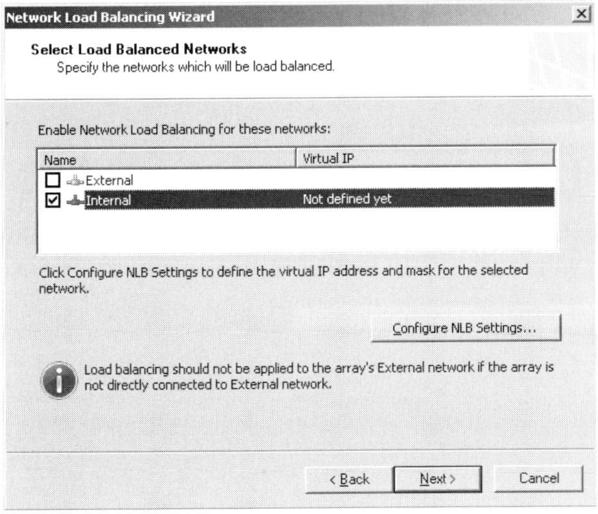

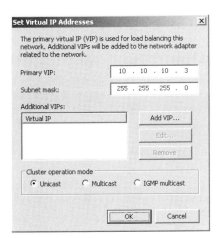

FIGURE 13-50 Selecting networks

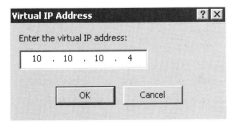

FIGURE 13-51 Adding the VIP

FIGURE 13-52 Additional VIPs dialog box

9. Click OK to close the current window. Choose the type of NLB (Unicast, Multicast, or IGMP Multicast) depending on your needs, and then click OK again to confirm. You should see something similar to what appears in Figure 13-53.

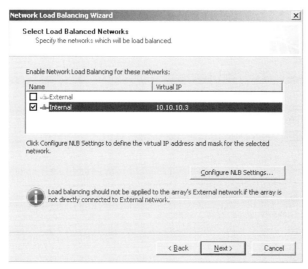

FIGURE 13-53 Internal VIP added

10. Repeat steps 6 to 8 for the external network, and then click Next. Figure 13-54 shows the wizard's summary page. Click Finish, click OK to confirm the message that pops up (similar to Figure 13-43), then click Apply to commit the changes.

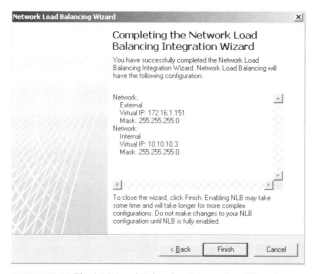

FIGURE 13-54 The NLB Load Balancing Integration Wizard summary page

After you complete the preceding steps, go to the Monitoring node in the left pane, click the Configuration tab, and confirm that the servers are synchronized with the CSS. Figures 13-55 through 13-57 show the different phases of synchronization until the array becomes fully synchronized.

FIGURE 13-55 Servers out of sync

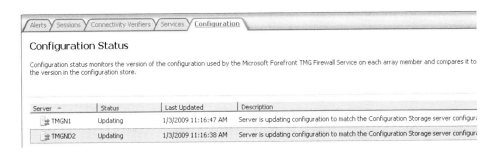

FIGURE 13-56 Servers updating

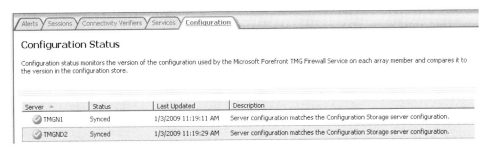

FIGURE 13-57 Servers fully synchronized

Now you can also click the Services tab to check the status of the NLB configuration on each node. This process requires some downtime because TMG will restart the services; therefore, it is important to perform this task when it will least impact your services. While TMG is configuring NLB, you might notice that the services appear unavailable, as shown in Figure 13-58.

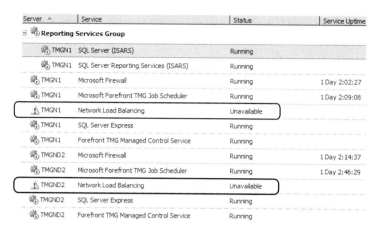

FIGURE 13-58 NLB services unavailable while TMG configures them

After finishing the configuration, the NLB, service is running on both TMG nodes, as shown in Figure 13-59.

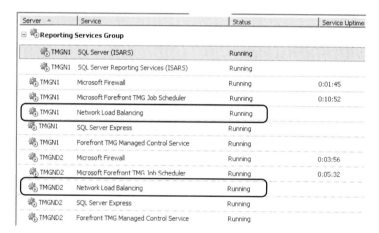

FIGURE 13-59 NLB services up and running

Post-Installation Best Practices

After enabling NLB, you can follow these best practices to properly adjust intra-array communication to occur on one specific network. The following steps are based on the scenario displayed in Figure 13-45, in which there is a third network in addition to internal and external:

1. On the TMG computer, open the Forefront TMG Management Console.

2. Click Forefront TMG (Server Name) node in the left pane.

3. Click the System node.

4. In the middle pane, right-click the first TMG firewall and then choose Properties.

5. Click the Communication tab and choose the IP address (it should not be part of the external network) that will be used for the intra-array communication, as shown in Figure 13-60.

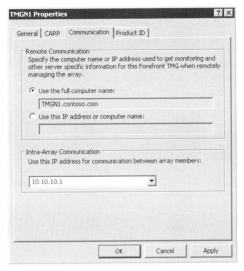

FIGURE 13-60 Choosing the intra-array communication IP

NOTE On the Communication tab you can specify the TMG server's FQDN or the server's IP address as selected in the Intra-Array Communication section for remote management. When you select FQDN, the remote management host will rely on DNS to resolve this name. The advantage to using FQDN is that if the intra-array IP changes, you don't have to update the Remote Communication section for each array member.

6. After selecting the IP that corresponds to the network that will be used for intra-array communication, click OK.

7. Repeat the same procedure for the remaining nodes. After you finish them all, click Apply.

When this process is done, TMG will update the Array Servers computer set with the IP address that was chosen in the previous procedure. This computer set belongs to the Intra-array Communication and Local Configuration Storage Server Access system policies. Figure 13-61 shows the array member communication system policy and Figure 13-62 shows the Array Member Computer Set in the Array Server properties.

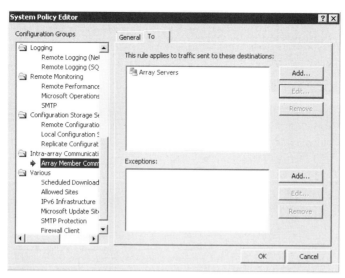

FIGURE 13-61 Array communication system policy

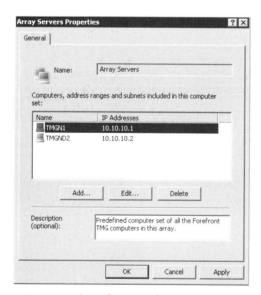

FIGURE 13-62 Array Computer Set

Considerations When Using TMG NLB in Virtual Environments

Virtualization is a technology that is growing substantially and we expect that administrators will want to implement NLB in a virtualized TMG environment. This is possible, but it is important to understand the boundaries and functional limitations of this deployment.

If you install TMG in a virtualized environment that is using Windows Server 2008 Hyper-V RTM, you need to install the hotfix available from *http://support.microsoft.com/kb/953828* in the guest operating system to allow the nodes to converge. This hotfix updates the nlb. sys driver in Windows. If you do not install this hotfix, the nodes will not converge. You will also need to perform the manual steps listed in that article before unicast NLB will be functional.

VMWare also offers a virtualization platform that can be used with TMG. By using this virtualization solution you may have issues that need to be addressed when enabling NLB, such as the one outlined in VMWare KB 1002847, which you can find at *http://kb.vmware.com/ selfservice/search.do?cmd=displayKC&docType=kc&externalId=1002847&sliceId=1&docTypeID =DT_KB_1_1&dialogID=12220269&stateId=1%200%2012216494* and KB 1006778, which you can find at *http://kb.vmware.com/selfservice/search.do?cmd=displayKC&docType=kc&externalId =1006778&sliceId=1&docTypeID=DT_KB_1_1&dialogID=12220269&stateId=1%200%2012216494*.

Although virtualization is already officially supported by TMG, when you choose to use a third-party virtualization platform you will need to understand the official Microsoft support policy for that platform. You can read more about this at *http://support.microsoft .com/kb/897615*.

Troubleshooting NLB on TMG

To troubleshoot NLB on TMG, you must first have a working knowledge of NLB functionality. This is important because most of the issues with NLB are caused by layer 2 or layer 3 devices. Problems that cause NLB to malfunction while installed on the operating system also affect NLB only while using with TMG.

You can use two methods to monitor NLB operation on your TMG computer. The first is the TMG Console Services tab in the Monitoring node (shown earlier in Figure 13-59). This allows you to see the status of NLB in all nodes. The other approach is to use the command-line tool WLBS.exe. The following sections offer some examples for using wlbs.exe.

Using the TMG Management Console

You can see the status of the NLB service in the local array or also in another member of the array on the Services tab on the Monitoring node in the left pane of the console. You can manage the following options related to NLB from there:

- **Stop Selected Service**   This option allows you to remotely stop NLB service in any array node.
- **Drain And Stop Selected Service**   When you use this option, only active connections will be served by the array member where you choose this option. No new connections to the array will use this server. Clients that close connections to this server will have new connections sent to NLB cluster nodes that are not in a draining state.
- **Suspend Selected Service**   When you use this option, existing connections to the NLB node are disconnected. Although users can reconnect using the virtual IP address, they will reconnect in another array member NLB service because the service on this array is suspended.

In the TMG Console, in Monitoring under the Services tab, you can see the options shown in Figure 13-63. You can use the options in some troubleshooting scenarios, such as the ones shown in Table 13-4.

FIGURE 13-63 NLB control options

TABLE 13-4 Possible Scenarios in Which to Use the NLB Service Tasks

OPTION	POSSIBLE SCENARIOS
Stop Selected Service	Nodes are not converging and you want to stop one node to isolate issues on the node where you stop the service.
Drain And Stop Selected Service	You want to leave the NLB node running but don't want to accept any new connection so that you can make other tests in the drained node.
Suspend Selected Service	You want to keep the NLB service running but want to force a disconnection from all current session so that clients can reconnect on another node.

You can use these options when you want to isolate the NLB node that is having problems or you want to force users to connect to a different NLB member. When TMG detects configuration errors in NLB or inconsistency among the NLB members it triggers an alert on the Monitoring/Alerts tab. You can use those alerts to identify possible issues and start troubleshooting them. Figure 13-64 shows an example of many entries on the Alerts tab for NLB service.

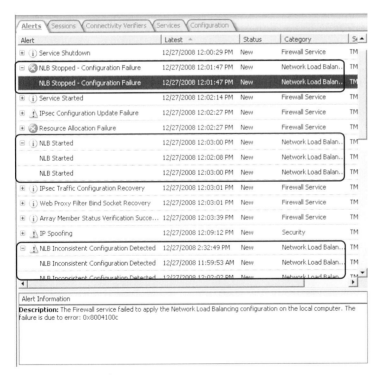

FIGURE 13-64 NLB alerts

The first alert selected in Figure 13-64 shows a configuration failure that caused NLB to stop working. At the bottom of the window you can see alert information with more details about the issue.

Using wlbs.exe

Wlbs.exe is a Windows command-line utility that you can use for troubleshooting NLB and to query the current status of the NLB node. This command has many parameters; this section addresses the most common of them.

WLBS QUERY

The first WLBS parameter that will assist you in understanding the basic configuration and state of the NLB cluster is *wlbs query*, which has an output similar to the following:

```
C:\>wlbs query
WLBS Cluster Control Utility V2.5 (c) 1997-2007 Microsoft Corporation.
Cluster 192.168.1.3
Host 2 is a slave to cluster 10.10.10.3.
Cluster 10.10.10.3
Host 2 has entered a converging state 1 time(s) since joining the cluster
  and the last convergence completed at approximately: 12/27/2008 12:03:04 PM
Host 2 converged as DEFAULT with the following host(s) as part of the cluster:
2, 3
```

This output shows the NLB VIP for both interfaces that are balanced—in this case 192.168.1.3 for the network 192.168.1.0/24 and 10.10.10.3 for the network 10.10.10.0/24. It also shows that this node is converged with the other node in this NLB cluster.

If the output for this command shows that the nodes could not converge, you can use the following checklist to narrow down the issue:

- Are both nodes in the same VLAN?
  - Refer to your switch vendor's user guide to answer this question. Don't assume that because both nodes are on the same subnet IP that they belong to the same VLAN. VLAN is a layer 2 configuration and you need to verify your switch configuration to precisely confirm this.
- Are both nodes connected to the same switch?
  - Determine whether both nodes are physically connected to the same switch.
- Can you reset the switch and see whether the nodes are still having a problem converging?
  - Refer to your switch vendor's user guide to determine how to accomplish this task.
- If the problem continues, can you connect the nodes to a hub and uplink the hub to the switch?
  - A hub is a device that acts as a network bridge, sending all traffic to all connected ports.

WLBS IP2MAC

The *wlbs ip2mac* command provides the MAC addresses that NLB uses relative to the IP address you provide:

```
C:\>wlbs ip2mac 10.10.10.3
WLBS Cluster Control Utility V2.5 (c) 1997-2007 Microsoft Corporation.
Cluster:            10.10.10.3
Unicast MAC:        02-bf-0a-0a-0a-03
Multicast MAC:      03-bf-0a-0a-0a-03
IGMP Multicast MAC: 01-00-5e-7f-0a-03
With these MAC address in hand you can make the necessary associations with the packet
that you are reading using Network Monitor (netmon).
```

> **MORE INFO**   For more information on how to use Network Monitor and read captures, see Chapter 33, "Using Network Monitor 3 for Troubleshooting TMG."

WLBS DISPLAY

The most complete parameter in WLBS used to review the whole NLB configuration is the display parameter. Because of the amount of information provided by this parameter, the following sample only summarizes the items of each section of the command output:

```
WLBS Cluster Control Utility V2.5 (c) 1997-2007 Microsoft Corporation.
Cluster 192.168.1.73
=== Configuration: ===
```

The configuration part includes parameters shared among all the nodes that are part of the NLB cluster. Notice that this is done for each interface that has NLB enabled:

```
=== Event messages: ===
#5576 ID: 0x0000001d Type: 4 Category: 0 Time: 12/27/2008 12:03:04 PM
NLB cluster [10.10.10.3]: Host 2 converged with host(s): 2,3. It is now an active
member of the NLB cluster and will start load balancing traffic as the default
host. The default host is the host with the lowest host priority. It handles all
traffic that isn't covered by any of the defined port rules.
```

In the Event message session you will see a detailed explanation of all the events that were triggered across the NLB cluster. For instance, this section will include the time when each node entered in converging state and when the convergence completed:

```
=== IP configuration: ===
Windows IP Configuration
```

This session shows the IP configuration of the node, similar to the output of the *ipconfig /all* command:

```
=== Current state: ===
Host 2 is a slave to cluster 10.10.10.35
```

The current state section shows the current state of this node in the NLB cluster. The next session is also called configuration and it will have the same output that it had for the initial configuration session—but now for the other interface that has NLB enabled. The other session repeats the same sequence but with information related to the interface that was shown in the configuration session.

Summary

In this chapter you learned about a new TMG feature called ISP Redundancy (ISP-R) and how you can use this feature for load balancing and failover. This chapter explained how this feature works and how to implement it in scenarios with multiple- and single-NIC scenarios. You also learned how NLB works, general considerations when implementing NLB on TMG, and client considerations for this type of configuration. You learned how to implement NLB on TMG and troubleshooting tools that can assist you in identifying whether NLB is working properly on TMG. In the next chapter you will learn more about the TMG Network Protection System.

## CHAPTER 14

Network Inspection System

- Understanding Network Inspection System **307**

- Implementing Network Inspection System **309**

- Implementing Intrusion Detection **323**

- Summary **341**

One of the primary reasons network administrators deploy a firewall or proxy is to reduce the threat of malware by filtering traffic crossing their network borders. Although ISA Server was quite good at evaluating traffic based on application-awareness, it was very limited in its ability to detect malware. In this chapter, you will become familiar with the malware detection functionality provided by Microsoft Forefront Threat Management Gateway (TMG).

Understanding Network Inspection System

Network Inspection System (NIS) is a new traffic analysis mechanism included in TMG. NIS is built on network protocol analysis work done by Microsoft Research on the Generic Application-Level Protocol Analyzer (GAPA). GAPA was completed and expanded by the TMG development team and is used by all Forefront Security products to protect against network-level misbehavior for servers, clients, and TMG for network edge traffic protection.

> **MORE INFO** You can read more about GAPA at *http://research.microsoft.com/apps/ dp/search.aspx?q=gapa.*

NIS differs from many protocol analysis technologies. Although NIS is able to discover invalid traffic based on static signatures (conceptually similar to the HTTP Filter), NIS expands on basic signature matching by evaluating three aspects of the network traffic:

- **Protocol state** The expected condition of the protocol at any point in time
- **Message structure** The validation of a message according to the protocol definition
- **Message context** The validation of a message in the context of the protocol state

This design allows NIS to identify specific protocol abuses that operate beyond simple byte-stream signature recognition, which is more difficult to identify when using static application filters. As each packet is received by TMG, it is filtered through the policy engine and protocol filters before being processed by NIS. When an NIS signature is triggered, NIS has the ability to close a connection if the NIS detection for that signature is set to Block. Configuring this is discussed in the next section.

NIS functional operation is shown in Figure 14-1.

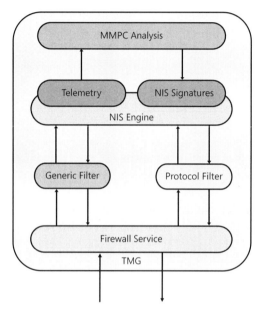

FIGURE 14-1 NIS functional operation

NIS operations are driven by signature definitions. These signatures are created by Microsoft Malware Protection Center (MMPC) malware analysts using a combination of telemetry data from TMG and other sources and a protocol definition language not unlike the Network Monitor 3 parser language. However, the NIS protocol definition language is far more complex than the Network Monitor parser language. NIS signatures are developed and tested as attack methodologies are encountered and these signatures are delivered through Microsoft Updates. Because of the complexity of the protocol definition language and the lack of readily available tools for signature creation and testing, NIS signatures are not user-definable in this release.

Because TMG frequently operates in the context of higher-layer protocols such as HTTP, SMTP, and others, the concept of deep packet inspection is a poor description for what happens while traffic is being processed through TMG. A more accurate term would be *application-layer inspection*. The NIS engine receives traffic from protocol filters that are themselves evaluating the protocols at a functional level. Although this may seem like duplication of effort, great care was taken by the product team to avoid this state as much as possible. Conversely, because NIS may be disabled by the TMG administrator, the loss of NIS should not impair the application filter's normal operation.

Although NIS is driven primarily by existing protocol definitions, you can connect NIS to a protocol simply by selecting NIS inspection for the protocol. This operation will be discussed in the next section.

Implementing Network Inspection System

The Network Inspection System (NIS) configuration in TMG is divided in three main options: general configuration, exceptions, and updates. First you should define the general behavior from NIS, then you add exceptions to the general rule, and last you can configure how NIS will check for signature updates.

To configure Network Inspection System, open the TMG Console and go to Intrusion Prevention System node in the left pane of the console. Figure 14-2 shows the Network Inspection System tab in the middle pane of the console.

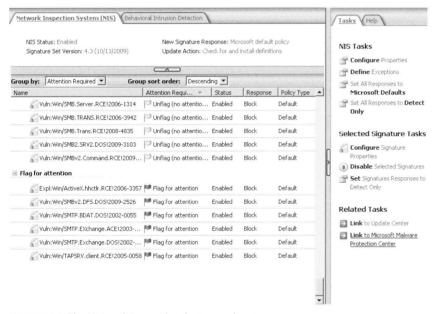

FIGURE 14-2 The Network Inspection System main pane

This window shows the following fields in the middle pane:

- **Name** Displays the name of the filter as defined by Microsoft Security.
- **Attention** Displays a red flag when the signature is marked for attention and a gray flag otherwise.
- **Status** Shows the current status for the signature, which can be Enabled or Disabled.
- **Response** Shows the current type of response that will be taken if this signature is trigged. It can be set to Detect Only or Block.
- **Policy Type** Shows the type of policy that was selected. This setting is initially defined by the Getting Started Wizard.

- **Date Published** Shows the date that the vulnerability covered by this signature was published.
- **Related Bulletins** Shows the Microsoft Security Bulletin number associated with this vulnerability.
- **CVE Number** Shows the Common Vulnerabilities and Exposures (CVE) number associated with this vulnerability.

NOTE For more information about CVE and how it works, see *http://cve.mitre.org*.

The task pane options available change according to the selection on the middle pane, as shown in Figures 14-3 and 14-4.

FIGURE 14-3 Task pane options with no signature selected

FIGURE 14-4 Task pane options when a signature is selected

Configuring NIS

To configure NIS for a specific scenario, you will use the topology shown in Figure 14-5.

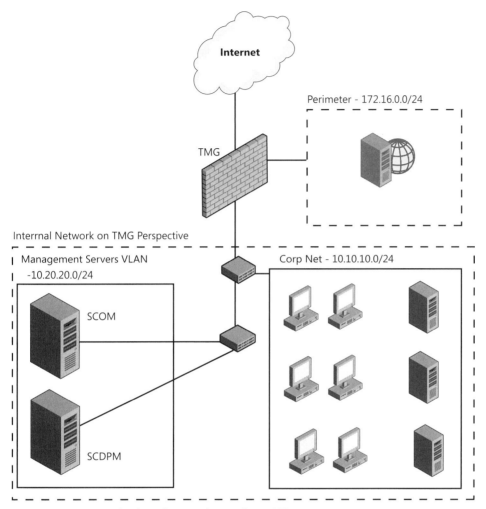

FIGURE 14-5 An example of topology used to configure NIS

In this example the goal is to enable NIS to all networks except for servers located in the network range 10.20.20.0 to 10.20.20.255. Those servers are considered management servers, and are not interesting for NIS traffic evaluation. Based on this scenario, you use the following steps to configure the general NIS settings, exceptions, and updates:

1. Open the Forefront TMG Management Console.

2. Click Forefront TMG (Server Name) in the left pane.

3. Click Intrusion Prevention System in the left pane of the console.

4. In the task pane, click Configure Properties. A dialog box similar to Figure 14-6 will appear.

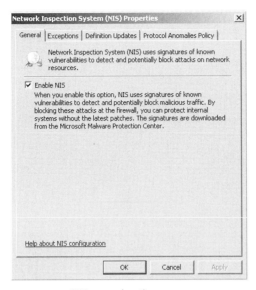

FIGURE 14-6 NIS general options

5. The General tab allows you to enable or disable NIS. Leave this option selected and click the Exceptions tab. Figure 14-7 shows the options for that tab.

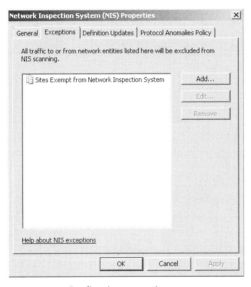

FIGURE 14-7 Configuring exceptions

6. On the Exceptions tab, you will already find a predefined set for sites to be exempt from NIS. For our example, we will add a management server to this exception. To add a management server, click Add to add the exception range required for this example. In the Add Network Entities dialog box, click New and then click Address Range, as shown in Figure 14-8.

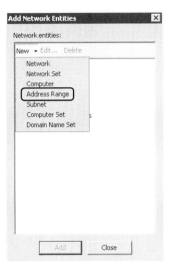

FIGURE 14-8 Adding an address range

7. In the New Address Range Rule Element dialog box, type a name for this new network element and then type the start address and end address accordingly. Figure 14-9 shows the how the addresses should be entered.

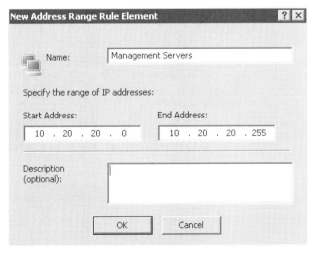

FIGURE 14-9 Creating a rule element

8. Click OK to close the New Address Range dialog box. In the Add Network Entities dialog box, select the Management Servers object, click Add, and then click Close to close the Add Network Entities dialog box as shown in Figure 14-10.

FIGURE 14-10 Selecting the new network object

9. At this point the Exceptions tab should look similar to Figure 14-11.

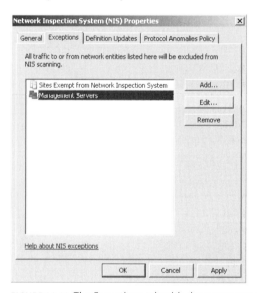

FIGURE 14-11 The Exceptions tab with the new network object

10. To configure the signature update properties, click the Update Configuration tab, as shown in Figure 14-12.

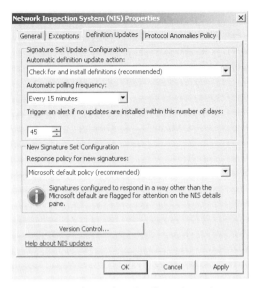

FIGURE 14-12 The Update Configuration tab

11. The Update Configuration tab has the following options for NIS update customization:

- **Automatic Update Action**   This field allows you to configure how TMG will handle updates for NIS. The default option is Check For And Install Definitions (Recommended), but you can change that to Only Check For Definitions or No Automatic Action.

- **Automatic Polling Frequency**   Here you can determine how frequently TMG will check for updates when Microsoft Update is used to obtain new signatures. By default TMG is configured to check for new updates every 15 minutes.

- **Response Policy For New Signatures**   This permits you to define how NIS will react when network traffic matches one of the active signatures. The options available are Detect Only Response, Microsoft Default Policy (which blocks all traffic that doesn't match any other rule), and No Response (NIS signature updates will be disabled).

- **Version Control**   Version Control lets you select the version of NIS update that will be activated for TMG. By default the latest update that is downloaded and installed for NIS is activated; however, if an administrator wishes to use a previously working update, the same can be selected by clicking Version Control, choosing the desired version, and activating the configuration.

12. Click the Protocol Anomalies Policy tab, as shown in Figure 14-13.

13. Because NIS checks whether the network traffic is in compliance with protocol standards, it might block certain anomalies that exist by design, whereas other anomalies might represent an actual threat. To provide flexibility to administrators, an administrator can decide whether to allow or block traffic detected by NIS as a protocol anomaly. For our example we will keep this at its default setting.

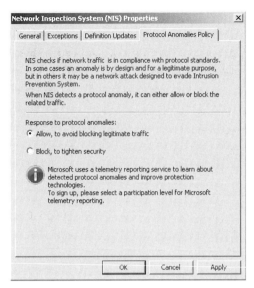

FIGURE 14-13 Protocol Anomalies Policy tab

14. Click OK to close the NIS properties dialog box.

Customizing Individual Signatures

As new threats arrive, new actions may be required to minimize the effect of these threats and sometimes emergency situations drive security administrators to configure specific rules besides the default rule. This means that in many situations companies need to create dynamic responses for more severe threats while keeping the default policy for moderate and lower threats.

REAL WORLD   **Urgent Response to New Threats**

A t the time we wrote this book, a severe threat was spreading through the Internet, causing downtime and impacting many companies. The malware was using a vulnerability associated with MS08-067 and many actions were taken to mitigate this threat and control the spread of this malware. Some companies kept the default security policy on their network at the same level but raised awareness and controls to mitigate the threat, whereas others updated their traffic policies and malware detection mechanisms as quickly as they could.

The Microsoft Malware Protection Center published details on how to protect against this threat. They are listed at *http://www.microsoft.com/security/portal/ Entry.aspx?Name=Worm%3aWin32%2fConficker.B*. Additionally, the Forefront Edge Team created a HTTP signature script to run on ISA Server and TMG to block attempts to exploit vulnerability associated with MS08-067 by sending traffic to the Internet. This script is available at *http://www.isatools.org/tools/block_conficker.vbs*.

This is an example of reactive action appropriate to the level of the threat. With NIS you have a proactive action because signature updates will have information about new threats and dynamic responses will be added to your TMG NIS configuration.

To customize signature actions, follow these steps:

1. Open the Forefront TMG Management Console.
2. Click Forefront TMG (Server Name) option in the left pane.
3. Click Intrusion Prevention System in the left pane.
4. For this example, look for the signature Test:Win/NIS.HTTP.Signature.!0000–0000 (which is used for testing purposes), right-click in the signature, and select Configure Signature Properties as shown in Figure 14-14.

FIGURE 14-14 Accessing signatures properties

5. In the Signature Information Properties dialog box (shown in Figure 14-15) you can change the effective configuration for this signature by changing the way that TMG will react if network traffic matches this signature.

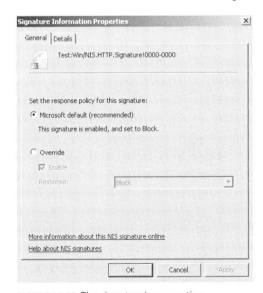

FIGURE 14-15 The signature's properties

6. Change the effective configuration to Microsoft Default (Recommended). You can also click the Details tab to see more information about this signature, as shown in Figure 14-16.

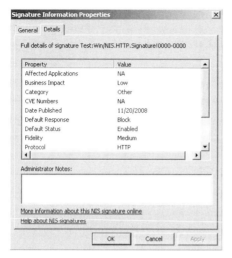

FIGURE 14-16 The signature's details

7. Click OK. Notice that NIS tab now shows this signature as No Attention Required and the response is Block, as shown in Figure 14-17.

FIGURE 14-17 NIS signature with unflag signature

8. Click Apply.

Additional Options

During signature configuration you can also change the signature display order based on business impact or other characteristics, as shown in Figure 14-18.

FIGURE 14-18 Options available for organizing signatures

When you organize for business impact, you will see Low, Medium, and High groups (as shown in Figure 14-19) that can assist you in viewing high priorities and addressing those accordingly.

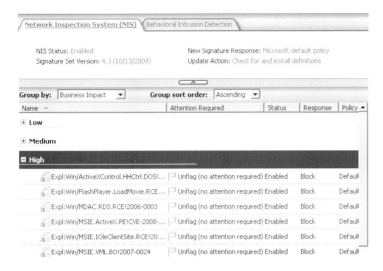

FIGURE 14-19 Signatures organized by business impact

You can also unflag the signature by right-clicking it and choosing the option Unflag (No Attention Required), as shown in Figure 14-20.

FIGURE 14-20 Unflagging a signature

Monitoring NIS

You can test and monitor NIS behavior to better understand how TMG reacts when a threat is detected. You can also see what the user's experience will be when a threat is blocked by NIS. For this example we will use the same scenario shown in Figure 14-5. The goal is to monitor the workstation 10.10.10.9 to determine whether this workstation is trying to perform an unwanted operation. Follow these steps to perform this test:

1. Click Forefront TMG (Server Name) option in the left pane.

2. Click the Logs & Reports node in the left pane and click Edit Filter in the task pane, as shown in Figure 14-21.

3. Click Filter By and then select Client IP. Select the condition Equals and the value will be 10.10.10.9, as shown in Figure 14-22.

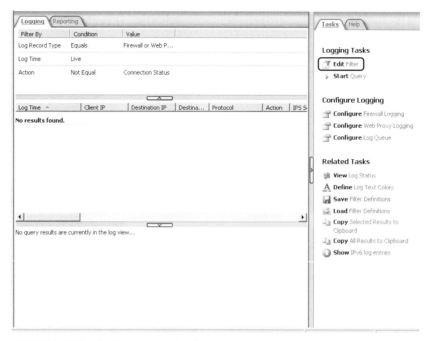

FIGURE 14-21 The Configuring Logging feature

FIGURE 14-22 Configuring a filter for the client IP address

4. Click Add To List and then click Start Query.

5. At a test client workstation, try to access the URL that is detected by the signature that we configured previously. We will use a test URL (*http://www.contoso.com/ testNIS.aspx?testValue=1!2@34$5%6^[{NIS-Test-URL}]1!2@34$5%6^*) for which this

signature has been already preconfigured by the NIS dev team. TMG Logging indicates NIS detection and action, as shown in Figure 14-23.

FIGURE 14-23 Traffic blocked because of NIS signature match

6. The user sees the page shown in Figure 14-24. Notice the URL that the user typed and the error code (502) triggered by TMG.

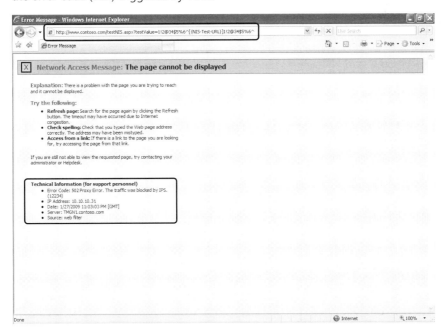

FIGURE 14-24 Error message that the client receives when the traffic matches the signature that IPS is blocking

NIS Update

NIS Updates rely on the TMG update agent, which relies on the Microsoft Update service. Communication with the Microsoft Update servers is performed using the Windows Update Agent (WUA) API. This API defines COM interfaces for searching, downloading, and installing updates. The TMG Windows Update Agent executable uses this API to install updates. Besides those components there is a slight addition on NIS because it uses the GAPA signature client (GapaClient.dll).

> **MORE INFO** You can read more on the WUA COM API at *http://msdn.microsoft.com/en-us/ library/aa387099(VS.85).aspx.*

The Update Center has the status of all the update mechanisms; NIS status also appears there. To access the Update Center, follow these steps:

1. Open the Forefront TMG Management Console.

2. Click Forefront TMG (Server Name) option in the left pane.

3. Click the Update Center node in the left pane and the middle pane should appear, as shown in Figure 14-25.

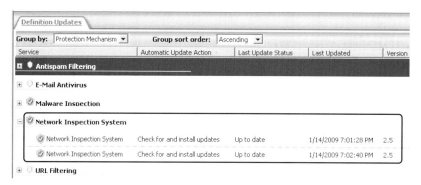

FIGURE 14-25 Definition updates for NIS

> **NOTE** Update Center will be covered in more detail in Chapter 18, "URL Filtering."

IPS Compared to IDS

The features configured with NIS are considered part of the Intrusion Prevention System (IPS) on TMG. The goal of IPS is to be proactive and prevent threats based on known vulnerabilities. Whereas IPS has a more proactive approach, the Intrusion Detection System (IDS) has more a reactive approach. In the next section we will discuss the IDS features on TMG.

Implementing Intrusion Detection

Every company needs to ensure that malware and attacks have no damaging effects on their network. To satisfy this requirement, TMG provides Intrusion Detection, spoof detection, flood mitigation, and other attack detection features.

To understand how TMG offers protection against different malware or attacks, let's first look at the different types of attacks. Table 14-1 summarizes the common attacks a network is susceptible to.

TABLE 14-1 Different Types of Attacks

ATTACK	DESCRIPTION
Internal worm propagation attack over TCP	Client computers will first be infected by a worm and then will attempt to infect other client computers by connecting to random TCP ports on other client computers in the network.
Connection table exploit	An attacker will use many IP addresses or create many zombie hosts to open excessive connections and thereby exhaust all server resources to the point where a server can neither be managed nor administered.
Sequential TCP connections during flood attack	An attacker uses an internal host to launch a Denial of Service (DoS) attack against any server or a protected server by sequentially opening and immediately closing many TCP connections, thereby bypassing the quota limit mechanism and consuming a large amount of server resources.
Hypertext Transfer Protocol (HTTP) Distributed Denial of Service (DDoS) using existing connections	An attacker sends HTTP requests at a high rate over a persistent (keep-alive) TCP connection. TMG needs to authorize every request. This consumes a large amount of resources from TMG. TMG includes this mitigation specifically for HTTP sessions, which are kept alive for a set period with numerous connections as part of a single session.

If your network is infected by a worm, the infected computers might produce a high number of TCP connections to random addresses on specific ports to find other computers to infect. In this case, TMG compares the actual connect rate to the allowed connect rate for each source IP. TMG then raises alerts for specific IP addresses that exceed the preconfigured threshold of allowed or denied connections per minute. If the IP address belongs to a user who is not intentionally launching a malicious attack, the user can contact the TMG administrator who can then ensure that the computer hosting the IP address isn't infected by running a manual scan on that computer locally and removing the worm. After this the computer no longer floods the network and traffic from that host is no longer denied.

Configuring Intrusion Detection

An administrator can set up Intrusion Detection to determine when an attack is triggered against TMG and to perform actions and log alerts in case of an attack. TMG does so by comparing the network traffic and logging entries against well-known attack methods. Traffic that looks suspicious causes TMG to respond according to the action specified by the administrator. These actions include connection termination, service termination, e-mail alerts, and logging.

To set up Intrusion Detection, open the TMG console and click Intrusion Prevention System. Then click the Behavioral Intrusion Detection tab in the middle pane, as shown in Figure 14-26.

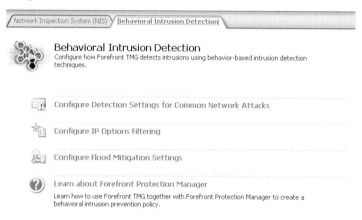

FIGURE 14-26 Related tasks in IPS

Click Configure Detection Settings For Common Network Attacks. This will open the Intrusion Detection settings dialog box, where the administrator can enable Intrusion Detection for common attacks, as shown in Figure 14-27.

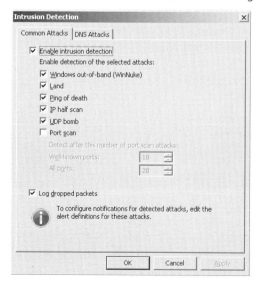

FIGURE 14-27 The Intrusion Detection settings dialog box

Enabling Intrusion Detection configures TMG to trigger alerts based on the type of attack selected. Table 14-2 summarizes the list of alerts that TMG will trigger based on an attack when Intrusion Detection is enabled.

TABLE 14-2 Attacks and the TMG Alerts They Generate

ATTACK	DESCRIPTION OF ALERT
Windows Out-of-Band (WinNuke)	This alert notifies you that an out-of-band DoS attack was attempted against a computer protected by TMG. A TCP/IP connection is established with the target IP address using port 139. The attacker then sends data using a flag called MSG_OOB in the packet header. This flag instructs the computer's Winsock to send data called out-of-band (OOB) data. When the target computer receives this packet, it expects a pointer to the position in the packet where the OOB data ends with the normal data following, but the OOB pointer in the packet created by the attacker points to the end of the frame with no following data. Because the target computer does not know how to handle this situation, if this attack is mounted successfully it causes the computer to fail or causes a loss of network connectivity on vulnerable computers until the system is restarted.
Land	This alert notifies you that a TCP SYN packet was sent with a spoofed source IP address and port number that matches that of the destination IP address and port. If the attack is successfully mounted, it can cause some TCP implementations to go into a loop because it causes the computer to reply to itself continuously, eventually leading the computer to crash.
Ping of Death	This alert notifies you that an IP fragment was received with more data than the maximum IP packet size. If the attack is successfully mounted, a kernel buffer overflow occurs, which causes the computer to fail.
IP half scan	This alert notifies you that repeated attempts to send TCP packets with invalid flags were made. During a normal TCP connection, the source initiates the connection by sending a SYN packet to a port on the destination system. If a service is listening on that port, the service responds with a SYN ACK packet. The client initiating the connection then responds with an ACK packet, and the connection is established. If the destination host is not waiting for a connection on the specified port, it responds with an RST packet. Most system logs do not log completed connections until the final ACK packet is received from the source. Sending other types of packets that do not follow this sequence can elicit useful responses from the target host without causing a connection to be logged. This is known as a TCP half scan, or a stealth scan, because it does not generate a log entry on the scanned host.

ATTACK	DESCRIPTION OF ALERT
UDP bomb	This alert notifies you that an attempt was made to send an illegal UDP packet. A UDP packet that is constructed with illegal values in certain fields causes some older operating systems to fail when the packet is received. When the target computer fails, it is often difficult to determine the cause.
All port scan attack	This alert notifies you that an attempt was made to access more than the preconfigured number of ports. When multiple or a range of ports are being scanned, it causes the target machine to run out of resources and if a port does respond the attacker can then use another attack like IP half scan to elicit useful responses from the target computer.
Enumerated port scan attack	This alert notifies you that an attempt was made to count the services running on a computer by probing each port for a response.

MORE INFO For more information about these attacks, please refer to *http://technet.microsoft .com/en-us/library/cc722757.aspx.*

Configuring DNS Attack Detection

TMG also includes Intrusion Detection filters for Domain Name System (DNS) and Post Office Protocol (POP). The DNS Intrusion Detection filter applies to DNS Server Publishing rules and intercepts and analyzes all inbound DNS traffic destined to the published server or network. The POP Intrusion Detection filter checks for POP3 buffer overflow attacks in collaboration with the POP3 application filter. The only setting for POP3 Intrusion Detection is enabling the POP3 Intrusion Detection filter under application filters.

Additionally, you can configure DNS Intrusion Detection alerts by clicking Configure Detection Settings For Common Network Attacks and then clicking DNS Attacks tab in the Intrusion Detection dialog box. This opens the DNS Attacks settings in the Intrusion Detection dialog box, as shown in Figure 14-28. The administrator can select the alerts she wants to receive for the DNS attacks shown in the figure. Table 14-3 summarizes the DNS attacks for which the administrator can set up detection and filtering.

Enabling DNS Zone Transfer blocking will block DNS zone transfers that occur between DNS servers in networks that are separated by TMG. If you require DNS zone transfers to pass through TMG, do not enable this filter.

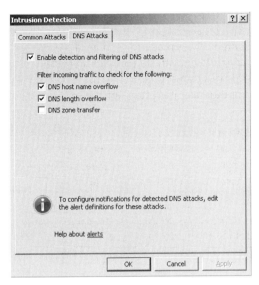

FIGURE 14-28 DNS Attacks settings

TABLE 14-3 Summary of DNS Attacks

ATTACK	DESCRIPTION
DNS host name overflow	A DNS host name overflow occurs when a DNS response for a host name exceeds a certain fixed length (255 bytes). Applications that do not check the length of the host names may return internal buffer overflow when copying this host name, allowing a remote attacker to execute arbitrary commands on a targeted computer.
DNS length overflow	DNS responses for IP addresses contain a length field, which should be four bytes. By formatting a DNS response with a larger value, some applications executing DNS lookups will cause internal buffer overflow, allowing a remote attacker to execute arbitrary commands on a targeted computer.
DNS zone transfer	A DNS zone transfer occurs when a client system uses a DNS client application to transfer zones from an internal DNS server.

Configuring IP Preferences

TMG includes a collection of options that lets an administrator customize support for IP-level communication. Configuring IP preferences lets you choose whether to deny any packet with any IP option or those with some specific options. To configure this setting, click Configure IP Options Filtering in the Behavioral Intrusion Detection tab, as shown earlier in Figure 14-26. This opens the IP Preferences dialog box, where an administrator can enable IP options filtering as shown in Figure 14-29.

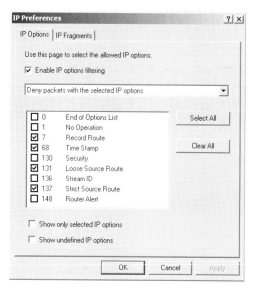

FIGURE 14-29 The IP Options tab in the IP Preferences dialog box

You can choose the following IP options:

- Deny Packets With The Selected IP Options (Default)
- Deny Packets With Any IP Options
- Deny Packets With All Except Selected IP options

These options appear in the drop-down menu shown in Figure 14-30.

When you select Show Only Selected IP Options, you will only see the options you have already configured. When you select Show Undefined IP Options, you will only see the options you haven't configured.

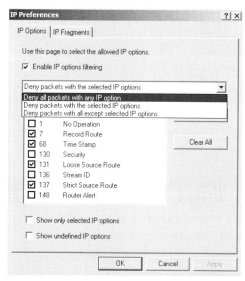

FIGURE 14-30 Allowed actions for IP Options filtering

In general, the IP option most often exploited is the source routing option. TCP/IP supports source routing, which allows a sender of network data to route packets through a specific point on the network. The source route option in the IP header allows the sender to override the routing decisions generally made by the router to route packets between the source and the destination computer. Source routing is generally used to map the network or to troubleshoot routing issues. It is also used by administrators to force traffic through a specific route to achieve best network performance. There are two types of source routing:

- **Strict Source Routing (option 137)**   The sender of the data can specify the exact route for a packet to be routed but it is rarely used.

- **Loose Source Routing (option 131)**   The sender of the data can specify certain hops or routers through which a packet must pass.

Even though source routing is useful in a lot of scenarios, an attacker can, if required, use source routing to reach an address on a protected network that normally isn't reachable through other networks by routing traffic through a computer that is reachable from both the protected and the other network. This results in flooding of connections, causing network performance issues. Hence TMG provides an option to block these options.

TMG also provides an option to filter IP fragments. A single IP datagram can be broken down into multiple datagrams of smaller size also known as IP fragments. IP fragments may need to be filtered because they are sometimes used in various attacks, such as a teardrop attack. The teardrop attack and its variants send IP fragments to a computer on the network to exploit the overlapping IP fragments in such a way that the TCP/IP fragment reassembly code improperly handles the overlapping IP fragment reassembly, causing the computer to shut down. The user experience in this case would most probably be a blue screen with a STOP error or reboot of the computer.

The IP fragment code is exploited by using overlapping offset field in an IP packet when fragmented. The offset field indicates the portion (in bytes) of the original packet contained in the fragment. For example, when an IP datagram is fragmented, the normal offset fields in the fragmented packet appear as follows:

```
Fragment 1:  (offset) 100 - 200
Fragment 2:  (offset) 201 - 400
```

This indicates that the first fragment contains bytes from 100 to 200, whereas the second fragment contains bytes from 201 to 400 of the original packet. An overlapping offset field appears as follows:

```
Fragment 1:  (offset) 100 - 300
Fragment 2:  (offset) 200 - 400
```

When the destination computer tries to reassemble the packet, it fails because it does not know how to handle this request, causing it to either crash with a blue screen with a STOP error or stop responding to all requests until the computer is restarted.

To block IP fragments, click the IP Fragments tab in the IP Preferences dialog box, as shown in Figure 14-31, and select the Block IP Fragments check box.

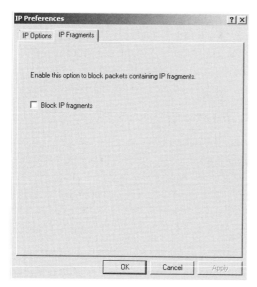

FIGURE 14-31 IP fragments blocking option

It is important to note that if you block IP fragments you will have issues with streaming audio and video as well as Layer 2 Tunneling Protocol (L2TP) over IPsec because streaming requires IP fragmentation and L2TP over IPsec requires IP fragmentation during certificate exchange. When you select Block IP Fragment, TMG will warn you about this issue as well, as shown in Figure 14-32.

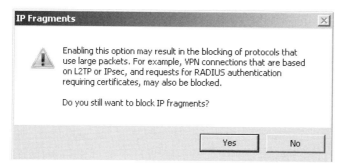

FIGURE 14-32 The warning that appears when you enable Block IP Fragments

Configuring Flood Mitigation

Flood attacks are the most common type of attack. Flood attacks represent a type of DoS attack where an infected computer or an attacker floods the network or a service with a large amount of traffic. A flood attack can be initiated using a variety of different transport mechanisms.

For example, an attacker can target the network by using a specific IP address to flood the network or by using a specific host as a target to open multiple TCP connections by flooding it with a lot of SYN packets. Such types of flooding would cause the following issues:

- High CPU load on the target computer
- High memory consumption on the target computer
- Heavy disk load and resource consumption on the target computer
- High network bandwidth consumption

TMG allows you to set specific connection limits to protect it and the network from various forms of flood attacks and worm propagation, thereby limiting the ability of the attacker to infiltrate the network. Using TMG flood mitigation settings, you can specify the maximum number of concurrent connections from a specific client in one minute. When the maximum number of concurrent connection limit is reached, any more traffic from that client is denied for the remainder of that minute.

By default, flood mitigation already has a defined connection limit and time set for clients. These settings are based on tests performed by the product stress team and reflect typical numbers that allow TMG to function when under attack. This behavior occurs because TMG can classify traffic and allow or deny service based on traffic classification. Malicious traffic (traffic classified as a flood attack) is so classified and denied, whereas other traffic is be allowed.

To configure flood mitigation settings, click Configure Flood Mitigation on the Behavioral Intrusion Detection tab, as shown earlier in Figure 14-26. This opens a dialog box where you can select the Mitigate Flood Attacks And Worm Propagation check box, as shown in Figure 14-33. You can also set the connection limits for some of the different types of traffic, except for the maximum half-open TCP connection, which is automatically calculated and set based on maximum concurrent TCP connections per IP address, as shown in Figure 14-34.

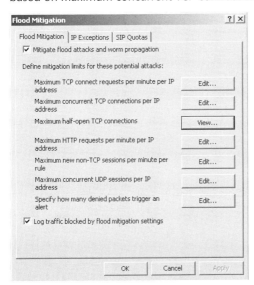

FIGURE 14-33 Flood Mitigation settings

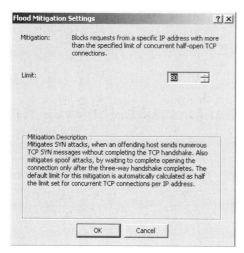

FIGURE 14-34 Concurrent half-open TCP connections limit

While setting any of the connection limits, you will also see a Custom Limit option (shown in Figure 14-35) that applies to IP exceptions. We will discuss IP exceptions later in this section; however, the importance of IP exception is that certain computers often require a lot of open connections, such as a DNS server being used by TMG. If TMG has DNS-based access rules it will query the DNS server a lot and might hit the maximum number of allowed connections within a certain time. However, you can choose certain computers or IP addresses and define higher connection limits for those computers by placing them in the IP exceptions.

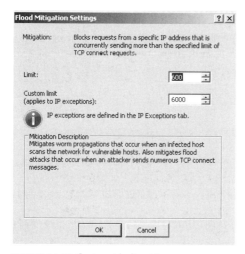

FIGURE 14-35 Custom Limit settings

To help you understand how TMG protects the network using its flood mitigation settings, Table 14-4 summarizes potential flood attacks and worm propagations and how TMG protects a network against them.

TABLE 14-4 Flood Attacks, Worm Propagations, and TMG Mitigations

ATTACK	TMG MITIGATION	DEFAULT VALUES
Flood Attack A specific IP address attempts to connect to various IP addresses, causing a flood of connection attempts and disconnections.	**TCP connect requests per minute, per IP address** TMG will only allow certain number of TCP requests from a specific IP in a minute, after which it will be blocked for the remainder of that minute.	By default TMG limits the number of TCP requests per client to 600 per minute. By default the custom limit applying to the IP exception list is set to 6,000 connection requests per minute.
Flood Attack A specific IP address attempts to flood either TMG or a server protected by TMG by opening multiple TCP connections concurrently.	**TCP concurrent connections per IP Address** TMG will limit concurrent connections per IP address to prevent a host from opening multiple TCP connections concurrently.	By default TMG limits the number of concurrent TCP connections per client to 160. By default the custom limit applying to IP exceptions is 400 concurrent connections per client.
Half Open Attack An attacker attempts to flood either TMG or a server protected by TMG by sending numerous SYN packets in succession, accepting the TMG SYN_ACK response but not providing an ACK to the TMG SYN_ACK response, hence not completing the TCP 3-way handshake.	**TCP half-open connections** TMG limits the number of half-open connections by monitoring the state of the connection and closing any half-open connections that exceed this limit.	By default TMG limits this to half the TCP concurrent connections per IP address. You cannot modify this default setting without changing the TCP concurrent connection per IP address limit.
Denial of Service (DoS) Attack Using HTTP An attacker attempts to launch a DoS attack by sending numerous HTTP connection requests in succession.	**HTTP requests per minute, per IP address** TMG mitigates this attack by only allowing a certain number of HTTP requests per minute from a specific IP address.	By default TMG limits the number of HTTP requests per client to 600 requests per minute. By default the custom limit applying to IP exceptions is 6,000 HTTP requests per client per minute.

ATTACK	TMG MITIGATION	DEFAULT VALUES
Denial of Service (DoS) non-TCP Attack An attacker uses an infected computer to send numerous non-TCP packets, such as ICMP in succession, to flood the network or a server.	**Non-TCP new sessions per minute, per rule** If a non-TCP session is allowed by a rule, TMG limits the number of new sessions per rule in a minute.	By default TMG limits the number of non-TCP new session to 1,000 per minute for specific rules.
User Datagram Protocol (UDP) Flood Attack An attacker sends numerous UDP packets to the target or victim computer, causing flooding.	**UDP concurrent sessions per IP address** TMG limits the concurrent UDP connections per IP address. In case of a UDP flood attack, TMG discards all older sessions so that no more than the specified numbers of connections are allowed concurrently.	By default TMG limits the number of concurrent UDP sessions per IP address to 160. By default the custom limit applying to IP exceptions is 400 concurrent UDP sessions per IP address.

When a packet is blocked by TMG after it exceeds its connection limit, it remains blocked for the remainder of the minute. For example, if the connection limit for concurrent TCP connections is 100 and the client reaches 100 concurrent TCP connections in 30 seconds, it is then blocked for the remaining 30 seconds. Similarly, if the client reaches 100 concurrent TCP connections in 59 seconds, it is then blocked for the remaining 1 second.

Note that for TCP connections, no new connections are accepted from the source IP of the attack after flood mitigation limit is exceeded. For other connections, such as raw IP and UDP, older connections are terminated when the flood mitigation limit is exceeded to allow newer connections to be created.

IP Exceptions and Custom Limits

In general, the default settings in flood mitigation should be sufficient to protect your network resources from a flood attack. However, in certain scenarios the default settings can generate false alerts. In many cases where Network Address Translation (NAT) is involved, TMG can generate false alerts mainly because it does not know the end user's computer IP address and will treat all connections coming from the NAT device as a single client connection. To ensure that connectivity is not broken from these known devices, you can set the IP address of the NAT device or server acting as a NAT server in the IP Exceptions and then define custom limits for them, as shown earlier in Figure 14-35.

To set IP exceptions, click the IP Exception tab in the Flood Mitigation dialog box, as shown in Figure 14-36.

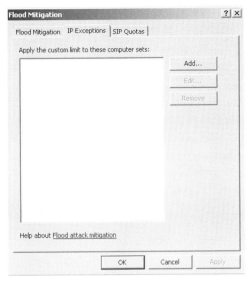

FIGURE 14-36 IP Exceptions settings

The following scenarios require IP Exceptions:

- **Back to Back Firewall Scenario**   An internal TMG applies NAT to all outgoing requests that are forwarded to an edge TMG firewall. The edge TMG sees the IP address of the back-end TMG for all requests. When a number of clients try to access the Internet, the number of connections sent from the back-end TMG to the edge TMG firewall increase, and the default connection limit of 600 concurrent TCP connections per IP address per minute could be exhausted very easily. Similarly, any connections from the edge TMG to the back-end TMG firewall will see the traffic coming from a single IP address and the same connection limit on the back-end TMG will be exhausted very quickly. In this scenario it is essential to set an IP exception on both the edge TMG and back-end TMG for each other's IP address and set custom limits to connections.

  This is similar to a scenario in which users connecting from a hotel, public Wi-Fi, or any other proxy source that applies NAT to the connection try to access a server published by your edge TMG. In this case, TMG will see the connection coming in from a single IP and thus treat it as a single client, thereby exhausting the connection limit for that IP very quickly.

- **Firewall Chaining or Web Chaining Scenario**   When Web chaining is used, all Web proxy requests are routed to the upstream proxy server. In case of firewall chaining, the downstream TMG is configured as a SecureNET client or a Firewall Client of the upstream TMG. In both cases requests are sent after NAT is applied, causing the upstream TMG to treat all requests coming from the downstream TMG as requests coming from a single client's IP address. This will lead the default connection limit for the IP address to exhaust quickly. In this scenario the IP address of the downstream TMG is added to the IP exception of the upstream TMG and custom limits are applied to the connections to ensure uninterrupted service.

- **Site to Site VPN Scenario**   Connection limits are enforced for site-to-site virtual private network (VPN) connections. Although NAT can be applied to traffic between the remote networks, the IP address that replaces the internal addresses is automatically assigned a custom limit. An exceeded limit error does not generally occur in this scenario.

- **Non-TMG Firewall or Load Balancer**   If a non-TMG firewall or a load balancer is in front of or behind the TMG and is applying NAT to all connections that are passed through it, TMG effectively sees only the IP address of the NAT device and treats it as a single client connection. This leads to the default connection limit for that IP address to be exhausted quickly. In this scenario the IP address of the NAT device needs to be added to the IP Exceptions list so that custom limits can be set and applied to that IP address.

Session Initiation Protocol (SIP) Quotas

In TMG we introduced the SIP Access filter, which enables SIP communications to be handled and allowed through TMG. To ensure that no client floods the network with SIP traffic or causes TMG to become overloaded with SIP traffic, TMG allows you to set SIP quota settings for SIP calls that can be registered on the filter and made by the client.

To configure SIP quotas, click the SIP Quotas tab in the Flood Mitigation dialog box as shown in Figure 14-37.

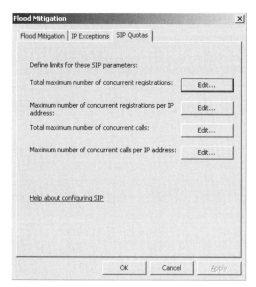

FIGURE 14-37 SIP Quotas settings

To help you understand these parameters, Table 14-5 summarizes the SIP Quota parameter definitions and its default settings.

TABLE 14-5 SIP Quotas Parameters and Default Settings

PARAMETER	DESCRIPTION	DEFAULT
Global Max Number Of Registrations On The Filter	Specifies the total number of registrations that are allowed to register with the SIP Access filter by all clients.	By default, the total number of registrations allowed on the SIP filter is 5,000.
Max Number Of Registrations For Specific IP Address	Specifies the number of registrations that are allowed to register with the SIP access filter from a specific IP address or client.	By default, 10 registrations are allowed per IP address.
Global Max Number Of Calls On The Filter	Specifies the total number of calls that will be allowed by the SIP access filter for all clients.	By default, the total number of calls allowed is 5,000.
Max Number Of Calls For Specific IP Address	Specifies the total number of calls that will be allowed by the SIP access filter from a specific IP address.	By default, 10 calls are allowed per IP address.

TMG Preconfigured Attack Protection

Apart from all the attack detection features that we have discussed so far, TMG is already preconfigured for protection against specific attacks. These preconfigured detection features are:

- Spoof detection
- Broadcast protection
- Syn attack protection
- TCP sequence protection

Spoof Detection

Anytime a packet is received by TMG, it determines whether the packet's source-IP address is a valid address for the specific network interface on TMG, which received the packet. TMG also makes sure that all packets sent through an interface have a valid destination-IP address. This prevents packets from being routed through the wrong interface in the event of routing table configuration issues. An IP address is considered valid for a specific network interface only if:

- The IP address resides in the network of the interface on which it was received.
- The routing table indicates that the traffic destined for that address may be routed through one of the interfaces belonging to that network.

The following example will help you understand this better: A network includes IP addresses in the range 192.168.X.X. The routing table would be as follows:

```
Network          Netmask          Destination      Gateway interface
192.168.0.0      255.255.0.0      192.168.10.1     192.168.1.1
30.0.0.0         255.0.0.0        30.0.0.1         192.168.1.1
0.0.0.0          0.0.0.0          100.0.0.1        100.1.1.1
```

Packets received on interface 192.168.1.1 with source-IP addresses in the range from 192.168.0.1 through 192.168.255.255 will not be discarded as spoofed because those addresses can be routed back through this interface and they belong to the address range of the network. However, packets with source-IP addresses that are outside this range (including the range from 30.0.0.1 through 30.255.255.255, which can be routed through the interface 192.168.1.1) will be dropped as spoofed, because they do not belong to the network.

It is important to note that if a network in TMG isn't defined properly with its specific address ranges, and some extra address ranges are added without proper configuration, spoofing errors will be generated. Hence it is important to ensure that whenever a network is defined in TMG it is properly configured with its valid address ranges.

Broadcast Protection

TMG does not allow any broadcast messages to be sent between network interfaces on the TMG firewall. TMG will allow the broadcast and attempt to match a rule to broadcast addresses only in the following situations:

- If the destination address is not a subnet broadcast address, TMG considers the address as the subnet broadcast address of the network interface on TMG on which the packet was received.

- If the packets are an incoming broadcast (to the Local Host network), TMG considers the destination as the network interface on the TMG firewall (Local Host).

- If this is an outgoing broadcast (from the Local Host network), TMG considers the source as the network interface on the TMG firewall (Local Host).

By blocking broadcasts, TMG ensures that the traffic generated from broadcasts has no performance impact because it is blocked from reaching to any network protected by the TMG.

TCP Syn Attack Protection

TMG monitors the TCP SYN packet rate from each source-IP address. If the remote host exceeds the predefined SYN packet rate, TMG triggers a SYN attack alert and ignores any further SYN packets from that host until the attack ceases. Once the attack stops, TMG will trigger a "SYN attack ended" alert and resume accepting packets from that host. This is controlled using the Max Half open TCP connection limit.

TCP Sequence Protection

The TCP protocol defines a clear process for client/server communications, especially where the initial connection process is concerned. If a remote host violates this process, TMG triggers an alert and rejects any packets that appear to be related to this failed connection attempt. TMG validates the sequence number in RST and SYN packets and drops packets that are out of sequence. This limits the ability of the attacker to terminate existing connections from other clients.

Logging and Alerts

Anytime an attack is detected and the flood mitigation settings in TMG block the traffic, TMG can log the attack attempt if the Log Traffic Blocked By Flood Mitigation Settings check box is selected, as shown earlier in Figure 14-32.

Table 14-6 shows the result codes returned by the TMG firewall service if logging is enabled for flood mitigation.

TABLE 14-6 Result Codes in Logging When Flood Mitigation Is Enabled

RESULT CODE	HEX ID	DETAILS
WSA_RWS_QUOTA	0x80074E23	A connection was refused because a quota was exceeded.
FWX_E_RULE_QUOTA_EXCEEDED_DROPPED	0xC0040033	A connection was rejected because the maximum number of connections created per second for this rule was exceeded.
FWX_E_TCP_RATE_QUOTA_EXCEEDED_DROPPED	0xC0040037	A connection was rejected because the maximum connections rate for a single client host was exceeded.
FWX_E_DNS_QUOTA_EXCEEDED	0xC0040035	A DNS query could not be performed because the query limit was reached.

TMG will also generate events during the time flood mitigation blocks any attack. These events can be viewed in the event viewer on the TMG computer. Table 14-7 shows a list of some common event IDs generated by flood mitigation.

TABLE 14-7 Event IDs Generated by TMG When Flood Mitigation Is Enabled

EVENT ID	MESSAGE
15112	The client *%clientname%* exceeded its connection limit. The new connection was rejected.
15113	ISA Server disconnected the following client, *%clientname%,* because its connection limit was exhausted.
15114	ISA Server disconnected a connection because its connection limit was exceeded.
15116	The request was denied because the number of connections per second allowed for a rule was exceeded.
15117	The request was denied because the number of connections per second allowed for the *%rulename%* rule was exceeded.

TMG can also be configured to display alerts when flood mitigation blocks any attack. You can view these alerts on the Alerts tab in Monitoring in the TMG Management Console and acknowledge them or reset them after taking an action on the threat. Table 14-8 shows some common alerts generated in case of a flood attack.

TABLE 14-8 Alerts Generated During a Flood Attack

ALERT	DESCRIPTION
Low Non-Paged Pool	The size of the free non-paged pool is below the system-defined minimum.
Low Non-Paged Pool Recovered	The size of the free non-paged pool no longer exceeds the system-defined minimum.
Pending DNS Requests Resource Usage Limit Exceeded	The percentage of threads used for pending DNS requests out of the total number of available threads exceeds the system-defined maximum.
Pending DNS Requests Resource Usage Within Limits	The percentage of threads used for pending DNS requests out of the total number of available threads is below the system-defined maximum, and connections that require DNS name resolution can be accepted.
TCP Connections Per Minute From One IP Address Limit Exceeded	The number of TCP connections per minute allowed from one IP address is exceeded.
Concurrent TCP Connections From One IP Address Limit Exceeded	The number of concurrent TCP connections allowed from one IP address is exceeded.

ALERT	DESCRIPTION
Non-TCP Sessions From One IP Address Limit Exceeded	The number of non-TCP sessions allowed from one IP address is exceeded.
Connection Limit For A Rule Was Exceeded	The number of non-TCP sessions per second allowed by one rule exceeds the configured limit.
Denied Connections per Minute from One IP Address Limit Exceeded	The number of connections per minute from one IP address blocked by the firewall policy exceeds the configured limit.
Global Denied Sessions Per Minute Limit Exceeded	The total number of blocked TCP and non-TCP sessions per minute exceeds the configured limit.
HTTP Requests From One IP Address Limit Exceeded	The number of HTTP requests per minute from one IP address exceeds the configured limit.

Summary

In this chapter you learned that Network Inspection System (NIS) is built on network protocol analysis that uses Generic Application-Level Protocol Analyzer (GAPA). With this technology in place NIS can proactively minimize threats for which TMG has signatures. The signatures are updated using Microsoft Update and TMG controls using Update Center. You also learned how TMG implements Intrusion Detection system and how flood mitigation can prevent unwanted traffic through TMG as well as how to explicitly exempt computers from the default flood mitigation settings. In the next chapter you will learn the fine points of Web proxy configuration and automation.

## PART V

TMG as Your Caching Proxy

CHAPTER 15 Web Proxy Auto Discovery for TMG **345**

CHAPTER 16 Caching Concepts and Configuration **387**

Web Proxy Auto Discovery for TMG

- WPAD as Protocol and Script **345**

- Configuring Automatic Discovery in the Network **364**

- Configuring Client Applications **374**

- Summary **385**

Web Proxy Automatic Discovery (WPAD) is the mechanism through which a CERN proxy client can discover a Web proxy and request and use a script that helps the application behave according to the wishes of the network administrator. In this chapter you will learn how the WPAD protocol and the TMG script behave and the various configuration choices you can use to further enhance this functionality.

WPAD as Protocol and Script

Many people refer to the configuration script provided by ISA Server and TMG as the WPAD script, but this is actually incorrect. WPAD actually refers to the wire protocol used to discover the location of the script. The correct term used in reference to the script itself is *CFILE*, which means *configuration file*.

> **MORE INFO**   You can learn the details of the WPAD protocol definition at *http://www.ietf.org/proceedings/99nov/I-D/draft-ietf-wrec-wpad-01.txt.*

WPAD Protocol

The WPAD protocol is the process by which a CERN proxy client discovers the location of a Web proxy on the network and requests the configuration file (CFILE). The client can make use of one or more detection mechanisms defined for the WPAD protocol, but only two methods are required of the application: DNS and DHCP. Many clients support both methods, but all of them process the CFILE in the same way. This behavior is dependent on the client application developer's knowledge of WPAD and how much support he or she wants to include.

Dynamic Host Configuration Protocol (DHCP)

Although most network administrators think of DHCP simply as an IP-assignment process, it is actually a very flexible protocol that provides a wide array of host configuration capabilities.

> **MORE INFO** You can read more about DHCP at *http://www.networksorcery.com/enp/ protocol/dhcp.htm.*

The Windows DHCP Client API allows an application to obtain DHCP-provided data without having to write DHCP client code into the application. Specifically, the Windows API *DhcpRequestParams()* provides the client application the means by which to request specific data from the DHCP server. If the DHCP client service on the user's computer does not have the information requested by the application, it will issue a DHCP INFORM broadcast message on the network. This mechanism will work even if the user's computer is configured with static IP settings. When the DHCP server receives this message, it checks the scope and server configuration. If the requested INFORM option has been defined, it will populate the DHCP response with the data defined by the DHCP administrator. Figure 15-1 illustrates the DHCP-based automatic discovery process.

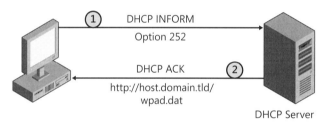

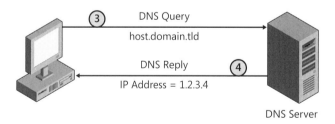

FIGURE 15-1 DHCP-based WPAD

Using Network Monitor 3 at the client, we can see how this progresses:

1. The Web proxy client issues a DHCP INFORM message, including option 252 in the parameter list:

```
- Dhcp: Request, MsgType = INFORM, TransactionID = 0xF1561CFE
  OpCode: Request, 1(0x01)
  Hardwaretype: Ethernet
  HardwareAddressLength: 6 (0x6)
  HopCount: 0 (0x0)
  TransactionID: 4048952574 (0xF1561CFE)
  Seconds: 1024 (0x400)
  + Flags: 0 (0x0)
  ClientIP: 10.10.255.130
  YourIP: 0.0.0.0
  ServerIP: 0.0.0.0
  RelayAgentIP: 0.0.0.0
  + ClientHardwareAddress: 00-03-FF-7D-A7-49
  ServerHostName:
  BootFileName:
  MagicCookie: 99.130.83.99
  + MessageType: INFORM - Type 53
  + clientID: (Type 1) - Type 61
  + HostName: WINXP-PRO-1 - Type 12
  + VendorClassIdentifier: MSFT 5.0 - Type 60
  - ParameterRequestList: - Type 55
   Code: Parameter Request List, 55(0x37)
   Length: 12 UINT8(s)
   Parameter: Subnet Mask, 1(0x01)
   Parameter: Domain Name, 15(0x0F)
   Parameter: Router, 3(0x03)
   Parameter: Domain Name Server, 6(0x06)
   Parameter: NetBIOS over TCP/IP Name Server, 44(0x2C)
   Parameter: NetBIOS over TCP/IP Node Type, 46(0x2E)
   Parameter: NetBIOS over TCP/IP Scope, 47(0x2F)
   Parameter: Perform Router Discovery, 31(0x1F)
   Parameter: Static Route, 33(0x21)
   Parameter: Classless Static Route, 249(0xF9)
   Parameter: Vendor specific information, 43(0x2B)
   Parameter: Web Proxy Auto Detection (WPAD), 252(0xFC)
  + End:
```

2. The DHCP server examines the relevant DHCP scope and server configuration to determine what answer to provide and populates the DHCP ACK message with the data it finds:

```
- Dhcp: Reply, MsgType = ACK, TransactionID = 0xF1561CFE
 OpCode: Reply, 2(0x02)
  Hardwaretype: Ethernet
  HardwareAddressLength: 6 (0x6)
  HopCount: 0 (0x0)
  TransactionID: 4048952574 (0xF1561CFE)
  Seconds: 0 (0x0)
  + Flags: 0 (0x0)
  ClientIP: 10.10.255.130
  YourIP: 0.0.0.0
  ServerIP: 0.0.0.0
  RelayAgentIP: 0.0.0.0
  + ClientHardwareAddress: 00-03-FF-7D-A7-49
  ServerHostName:
  BootFileName:
  MagicCookie: 99.130.83.99
  + MessageType: ACK - Type 53
  + ServerIdentifier: 10.10.255.127 - Type 54
  + SubnetMask: 255.255.255.0 - Type 1
  + DomainName: contoso.com - Type 15
  + DomainNameServer: 10.10.255.127 - Type 6
  + NodeType: P-node (2) - Type 46
  + WPAD: http://host.contoso.com/wpad.dat - Type 252
  + End:
```

> **NOTE** The primary advantage to DHCP-based WPAD is that you must specify the entire URL. This allows you to specify a custom port or a completely different file path. For instance, if you decide to host a custom CFILE on port 666 at a Web server, your DHCP options 252 record might appear as *http://webserver.contoso.com:666/myscript.js*.

3. The client extracts the host portion of the URL and issues a *GetAddrInfo()* call to Winsock to determine the IP address for host.contoso.com. If the client computer does not have this record cached locally or in the hosts file, it will query DNS:

```
- Dns: QueryId = 0x514F, QUERY (Standard query), Query for host.contoso.com of
 type Host Addr on class Internet
  QueryIdentifier: 20815 (0x514F)
  + Flags: Query, Opcode - QUERY (Standard query), RD, Rcode - Success
  QuestionCount: 1 (0x1)
  AnswerCount: 0 (0x0)
  NameServerCount: 0 (0x0)
  AdditionalCount: 0 (0x0)
  - QRecord: host.contoso.com of type Host Addr on class Internet
```

```
QuestionName: host.contoso.com
QuestionType: A, IPv4 address, 1(0x1)
QuestionClass: Internet, 1(0x1)
```

4. The DNS server examines its cache and database to discover the IPv4 address for host.contoso.com and responds to the client with the IP address:

```
- Dns: QueryId = 0x514F, QUERY (Standard query), Response - Success,
10.10.255.126, 10.10.255.125 ...
QueryIdentifier: 20815 (0x514F)
 + Flags: Response, Opcode - QUERY (Standard query), AA, RD, RA, Rcode - Success
QuestionCount: 1 (0x1)
AnswerCount: 3 (0x3)
NameServerCount: 0 (0x0)
AdditionalCount: 0 (0x0)
 + QRecord: host.contoso.com of type Host Addr on class Internet
 + ARecord: host.contoso.com of type CNAME on class Internet:
domainarray.contoso.com
 + ARecord: domainarray.contoso.com of type Host Addr on class Internet:
10.10.255.126
 + ARecord: domainarray.contoso.com of type Host Addr on class Internet:
10.10.255.125
```

> **NOTE** Note that in this example the DNS server located a CNAME record for the host named host.contoso.com. The DNS server followed the CNAME reference and located two host names that match, but use different IP addresses. The technique of creating multiple A records for a single host name is known as *DNS Round-Robin load-balancing* because the client application can choose from the entire list of IP addresses. If the DNS server is configured for netmask ordering, it can order the response according to the requesting client IP address.
>
> You can read more about DNS Round-Robin at *http://support.microsoft.com/kb/842197* and netmask ordering at *http://technet.microsoft.com/en-us/library/cc787373.aspx*.

5. The client connects to one of the IP addresses provided in the DNS response and issues a GET /wpad.dat request:

```
- Http: Request, GET /wpad.dat
 Command: GET
 + URI: /wpad.dat
 ProtocolVersion: HTTP/1.1
 Accept: */*
 Accept-Language: en-us
 UA-CPU: x86
 Accept-Encoding: gzip, deflate
 UserAgent: Mozilla/4.0 (compatible; MSIE 7.0; Windows NT 6.0)
 Host: host.contoso.com
 Connection: Keep-Alive
```

6. TMG processes the request and responds to the client with data relevant to the context of the network where TMG received the request:

```
- Http: Response, HTTP/1.1, Status Code = 200, URL: /wpad.dat
ProtocolVersion: HTTP/1.1
StatusCode: 200, Ok
Reason: OK
Date: Sun, 25 Jan 2009 23:09:12 GMT
Connection: close
ContentType: application/x-ns-proxy-autoconfig
Cache-Control: max-age=3000
```

The client application caches and processes the CFILE according to its needs and capabilities. You will read more about the script action in the section "WPAD Script" later in the chapter.

Domain Name Service (DNS)

When DHCP WPAD is not available, the client may choose to use DNS WPAD. In this case, the process operates much the same as in the DHCP example, except that because the client cannot discover the name of the host that hosts the CFILE, it must issue a *GetAddrInfo()* call for wpad.domain.tld. If the client can obtain a reachable IP address for this query, it will connect to that IP address on port 80 and issue an HTTP request as GET /wpad.dat. Figure 15-2 illustrates this process.

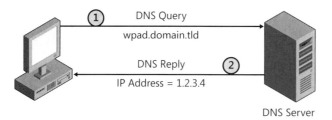

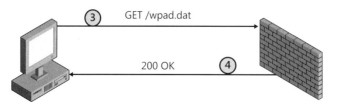

FIGURE 15-2 DNS-based WPAD

1. The client issues a *GetAddrInfo()* call to Winsock to determine the IP address for *wpad.contoso.com*. If the client computer does not have this record cached locally or in the hosts file, it will query DNS:

```
 - Dns: QueryId = 0x514F, QUERY (Standard query), Query for wpad.contoso.com of
type Host Addr on class Internet
  QueryIdentifier: 20815 (0x514F)
  + Flags: Query, Opcode - QUERY (Standard query), RD, Rcode - Success
  QuestionCount: 1 (0x1)
  AnswerCount: 0 (0x0)
  NameServerCount: 0 (0x0)
  AdditionalCount: 0 (0x0)
  - QRecord: .contoso.com of type Host Addr on class Internet
    QuestionName: wpad.contoso.com
    QuestionType: A, IPv4 address, 1(0x1)
    QuestionClass: Internet, 1(0x1)
```

2. The DNS server examines its cache and database to discover the IPv4 address for *wpad.contoso.com* and responds to the client with the records it finds:

```
 - Dns: QueryId = 0x514F, QUERY (Standard query), Response - Success,
10.10.255.126, 10.10.255.125 ...
  QueryIdentifier: 20815 (0x514F)
  + Flags: Response, Opcode - QUERY (Standard query), AA, RD, RA, Rcode - Success
  QuestionCount: 1 (0x1)
  AnswerCount: 3 (0x3)
  NameServerCount: 0 (0x0)
  AdditionalCount: 0 (0x0)
  + QRecord: wpad.contoso.com of type Host Addr on class Internet
  + ARecord: wpad.contoso.com of type CNAME on class Internet: domainarray.
contoso.com
  + ARecord: domainarray.contoso.com of type Host Addr on class Internet:
10.10.255.126
  + ARecord: domainarray.contoso.com of type Host Addr on class Internet:
10.10.255.125
```

3. The client connects to port 80 one of the IP addresses provided in the DNS response and issues a GET /wpad.dat request:

```
 - Http: Request, GET /wpad.dat
  Command: GET
  + URI: /wpad.dat
  ProtocolVersion: HTTP/1.1
  Accept: */*
  Accept-Language: en-us
  UA-CPU: x86
  Accept-Encoding: gzip, deflate
```

```
UserAgent: Mozilla/4.0 (compatible; MSIE 7.0; Windows NT 6.0)
Host: wpad.contoso.com
Connection: Keep-Alive
```

NOTE Because DNS A and CNAME records cannot contain a URL, the client must use port 80. The WPAD specification provides for the use of TXT or SRV records that can contain a URL, but few if any WPAD-aware clients use them.

4. TMG processes the request and responds to the client with data relevant to the context of the network where TMG received the request:

```
- Http: Response, HTTP/1.1, Status Code = 200, URL: /wpad.dat
ProtocolVersion: HTTP/1.1
StatusCode: 200, Ok
Reason: OK
Date: Sun, 25 Jan 2009 23:09:12 GMT
Connection: close
ContentType: application/x-ns-proxy-autoconfig
Cache-Control: max-age=3000
```

The client application caches and processes the CFILE according to its needs and capabilities.

WPAD Script

The primary reason for supporting WPAD in your network environment is to ensure that all WPAD-aware clients can obtain their CFILE from the preferred location: the TMG server. This script is built upon the original specification devised by Netscape in 1996.

MORE INFO You can read more about the Netscape specification at *http://web.archive .org/web/20080208114016/http://wp.netscape.com/eng/mozilla/2.0/relnotes/demo/ proxy-live.html.*

In accordance with the original Netscape specification, and because all Web browsers support Jscript as the default scripting language, the CFILE is written using Jscript. Successful script execution produces one of two results as text strings; "DIRECT" or a semicolon-separated list of proxies, terminated with the value of "BackupRoute" as provided in the script.

 **REAL WORLD** **Applications and WPAD Support**

Although the WPAD protocol is fairly well defined, the WPAD specification never progressed beyond the initial draft stage. This fact allows a great deal of implementation flexibility for developers and can create some interesting behaviors between them.

Windows provides two HTTP libraries that give developers the flexibility to choose an HTTP library that best suits their application. These libraries are WinHTTP and WinInet, with WinInet being the older of the two.

Although both HTTP libraries provide support for WPAD, the level of support provided in each does not exactly match the support provided by the other. WinHTTP has a limitation in the way it processes the script and thus presents different behavior than WinInet does when faced with the same script content.

The key phrase in the article that discusses WinHTTP WPAD script limitations is "WinHTTP does not currently support proxy configurations that specify more than one proxy server." What this means to you is that regardless of how many servers you have in your TMG array, if an application calls the WinHTTP *WinHTTPGetProxyForURL()* method, the application will only receive the first server in the list provided by the script.

If the first server in the list provided by the script action is unresponsive, the application making this request to WinHTTP will fail to connect the proxy and will thus not be able to make any requests to the upstream server. If the application includes retry logic (as most do), it will continue making the same request to WinHTTP until the application's retry logic calls an end to the effort.

Three applications that make use of WinHTTP are Microsoft Office Outlook 2003 and Microsoft Office Outlook 2007, the RDP client version 6 and later, and Windows Media Player. There will likely be many more because WinHTTP is much easier to use than WinInet.

> **MORE INFO** You can read more about WinInet at *http://msdn.microsoft.com/ en-us/library/aa383630.aspx,* WinHTTP at *http://msdn.microsoft.com/en-us/ library/aa384273(VS.85).aspx,* and the WinHTTP script limitation at *http://msdn .microsoft.com/en-us/library/aa383157(VS.85).aspx.*

A full description of this behavior using Network Monitor and WinHTTP tracing is available in Appendix C.

The CFILE provided by TMG includes the same functionality as that provided by ISA Server 2006, although the contents of the CFILE have changed quite a bit. The majority of changes were made in preparation for IPv6 in the protected networks and to take advantage of and offer support for new interfaces provided and expected by the Web proxy client applications.

> **MORE INFO** You can read more about the extensions to the CFILE Web proxy client applications mechanisms at *http://blogs.msdn.com/wndp/archive/2006/07/18/IPV6-WPAD-for-WinHttp-and-WinInet.aspx* and *http://blogs.msdn.com/wndp/articles/IPV6_PAC_Extensions_v0_9.aspx*.

The purpose of the CFILE is to provide code and data that allows the Web proxy client application to make informed decisions regarding how to handle the request made by the user. These decisions to be made by the CFILE script are:

1. Determine whether the request uses a protocol that is unsupported by the TMG Web proxy.
2. Determine whether the requested destination is is to be accessed by the client host with or without using the proxy.
3. Determine whether CARP is to be considered for the requested destination.
4. Determine how the client should act if TMG is not available.

> **NOTE** In the interest of brevity, the following discussions are limited to select portions of the CFILE. A complete copy of the example CFILE used in this discussion is included in Appendix D.

Figure 15-3 illustrates the network environment used to define the TMG configuration that produces the CFILE in the following discussion. The CFILE under discussion was requested by a host on the wireless network.

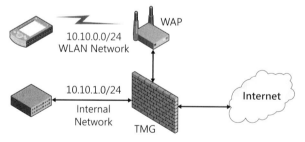

FIGURE 15-3 Environment for CFILE discussion

Script Initialization

Immediately after receiving the CFILE from TMG, the application executes the code as illustrated in Figure 15-4.

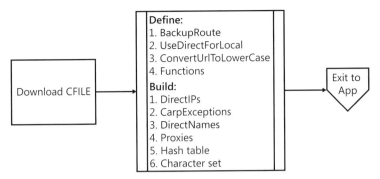

FIGURE 15-4 CFILE Initialization

The following functions perform the "Define" actions described in Figure 15-4:

```
//Copyright (c) 1997-2006 Microsoft Corporation
BackupRoute="DIRECT";
UseDirectForLocal=true;
ConvertUrlToLowerCase=false;
```

> **NOTE** The *ConvertUrlToLowerCase* value is new to the CFILE in TMG and is configurable using TMG COM, as described in *http://msdn.microsoft.com/en-us/library/dd421206.aspx*.

The statement *BackupRoute="DIRECT"* specifies that the script should encourage the Web proxy client application to attempt a direct connection to the destination if the proxy connection attempt fails. You will learn more about how this mechanism works when we discuss the proxy ordering mechanism in Appendix D. *"DIRECT"* is the default if no option has been chosen. This setting is defined by the option If Forefront TMG Is Unavailable, Use This Backup Route To Connect To The Internet shown in Figure 15-5.

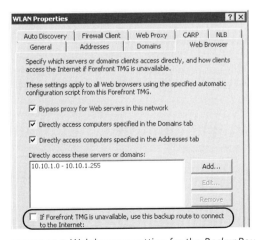

FIGURE 15-5 Web browser setting for the *BackupRoute* property

The statement *UseDirectForLocal=true* specifies that the script should encourage the Web proxy client application to use a direct connection to any host that is determined to be directly accessible by the client application. This mechanism will be discussed in the section "Determine Local Destinations" in Appendix D. The option that controls this value is shown in Figure 15-6.

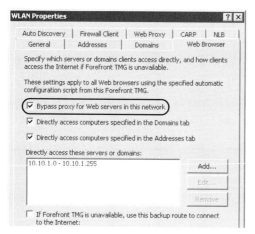

FIGURE 15-6 Web browser setting for the *UseDirectForLocal* property

The statement *ConvertUrlToLowerCase=false* specifies that the URL should not be converted to lowercase. RFC 2616 requires all clients to process URLs in a case-insensitive fashion, but the CFILE provided by ISA Server did not provide the means to do this. If the Web client application failed to translate the URL or host to lowercase before calling *FindProxyForUrl()* or *FindProxyForUrlEx()* in the CFILE, you might find yourself chasing a failure in your local names, addresses, or CARP exceptions. The option to define the *ConvertUrlToLowerCase* property is only available in Forefront TMG COM. You can find an example of this script in Chapter 30, "Scripting TMG."

The Major Functions

The functions in the script are defined by the function statement and include all of the statements between the opening bracket ({) and the closing bracket (}). The functions that serve as data are treated as Jscript arrays.

MAKEIPS()

```
function MakeIPs(){
this[0]= new IpSubnet("127.0.0.0", "255.0.0.0", "127.0.0.0/8");
this[1]= new IpSubnet("10.10.1.0", "255.255.255.0", "10.10.1.0/24");
this[2]= new IpSubnet("10.10.0.0", "255.255.255.0", "10.10.0.0/24");
}
```

The *MakeIPs* function operates as a custom Jscript object that includes the set of IP subnet definitions that are defined in the network object where the CFILE request was received. In this case, the subnet sets in *MakeIPs* are actually more custom Jscript objects that represent a combination of settings derived from the choices made in Figures 15-7 and 15-8.

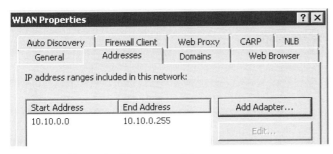

FIGURE 15-7 Network address range list

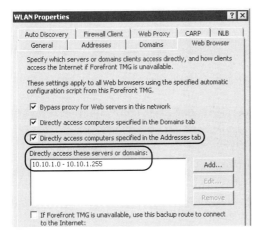

FIGURE 15-8 Web browser settings for *MakeIPs()*

You may have noticed that although TMG includes the local host network (127.0.0.0/8) definition in the CFILE, it has not been specified in the configuration. This functionality first appeared when the WPAD changes were made in ISA 2004 Service Pack 2 to avoid the errors that would result if the TMG administrator removed it from the list.

MAKECARPEXCEPTIONS()

```
function MakeCARPExceptions(){
this[0]="*.windowsupdate.com";
this[1]="windowsupdate.microsoft.com";
this[2]="*.windowsupdate.microsoft.com";
this[3]="*.update.microsoft.com";
this[4]="download.windowsupdate.com";
```

```
this[5]="download.microsoft.com";
this[6]="*.download.windowsupdate.com";
this[7]="wustat.windows.com";
this[8]="ntservicepack.microsoft.com";
this[9]="forefrontdl.microsoft.com";
}
```

The *MakeCARPExceptions* function is another custom Jscript object that is used as an array of domain names for which client-side CARP should not be used. This helps avoid those situations where remote servers use the IP address of the connecting client as a means to determine whether a connection is being spoofed. This information is derived from the settings shown in Figure 15-9.

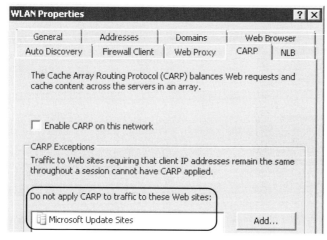

FIGURE 15-9 Domains tab setting for *MakeCARPExceptions*

NOTE The selection Enable CARP on this network does not affect client-side CARP.

MAKENAMES()

```
function MakeNames(){
this[0]="*.contoso.com";
}
```

The *MakeNames* function also operates as a custom Jscript object and contains an array of names that should be accessed directly by the WPAD client. The contents of this function are built from the data specified in Figures 15-10 and 15-11.

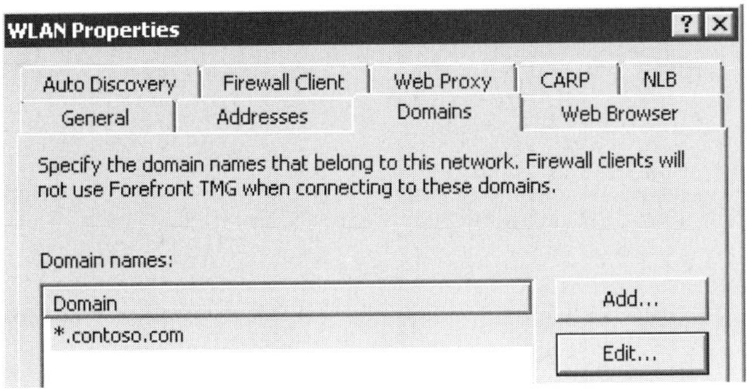

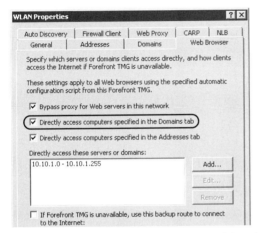

FIGURE 15-10 Network-local domains

FIGURE 15-11 Option to Include network-local domains

MAKEPROXIES()

```
function MakeProxies(){
this[0]=new Node("tmg.contoso.com",84461486,1.000000);
}
```

This function is another custom Jscript container that contains a list of the TMG array members defined by another custom Jscript object, *Node*.

> **IMPORTANT** If you have more than one server in the array, but the *MakeProxies()* function does not list all of the array members, you should verify that all of the array members use the same network for intra-array communication and that all of them are responsive.

Each TMG array member entry is accompanied by two numbers that the script uses to properly sort the proxy list: the server identity hash and the CARP load factor. Table 15-1 defines these associations.

TABLE 15-1 Node Value Relationships

SERVER NAME	SERVER HASH	TMG PROXY CARP LOAD FACTOR
tmg.contoso.com	84461486	1.000000

Figure 15-12 illustrates the location where the CARP load factor is defined. This value seen in the script is an integer representation of the percentage defined in the CARP load factor option.

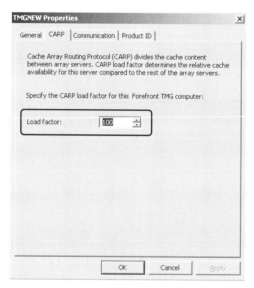

FIGURE 15-12 CARP load factor

Each proxy definition is built based on a combination of the CARP settings of each server on the CARP configuration tab and the value specified for the TMG COM *WebProxy* .*CARPNameSystem* property. Table 15-2 defines the results of the valid values used in the *CARPNameSystem* property.

TABLE 15-2 *CarpNameSystem* Effects

CARPNAMESYSTEM VALUE	TMG REPRESENTATION
fpcNameSystem_DNS (0)	Node("tmg.contoso.com",84461486,1.000000)
fpcNameSystem__WINS (1)	Node("tmg",84461486,1.000000)
fpcNameSystem_IP (2)	Node("10.10.0.2",84461486,1.000000)

The *CARPNameSystem* property derives the domain suffix from the array FQDN property as defined in the Array properties, as shown in Figure 15-13.

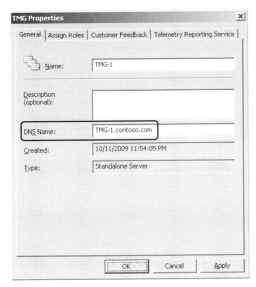

FIGURE 15-13 Array FQDN definition

MORE INFO   You can read more about the CarpNameSystem property at *http://msdn .microsoft.com/en-us/library/dd447608.aspx*.

NODE()

```
function Node(name, hash, load){
 this.name = name;
 this.hash = hash;
 this.load = load;
 this.score = 0;
 return this;
}
```

The *Node* function is a Jscript custom object and defines the properties used for sorting the TMG server list. You may have noticed that it contains one property not provided when this function is used to populate the *MakeProxies* list: the *score* property. This property is used during the proxy sorting process so it is predefined as 0 when the script is first loaded by the application.

IPSUBNET()

```
function IpSubnet(ip, mask, prefix){
 this.ip = ip;
 this.mask = mask;
 this.prefix = prefix;
 var isIpV4Addr = /^(\d+.){3}\d+$/;
 this.isIpv6 = !isIpV4Addr.test(ip);
 return this;
}
```

The *IpSubnet* function defines the properties used to describe each entry in the *MakeIPs* set. As with the *Node* function, the *IpSubnet* function defines a property that is not provided by the calling statement: the *isIpv6* property. Unlike the *Node* function, the *isIpv6* property is defined by testing the *ip* argument to see whether it matches a regular expression that describes an IPv4 address. If the *ip* argument matches the regular expression, the *isIpv6* property is defined as false.

> **MORE INFO** You can read more about Jscript Regular Expressions at *http://msdn.microsoft .com/en-us/library/ae5bf541.aspx.*

FINDPROXYFORURL(), FINDPROXYFORURLEX(), IMPLEMENTFINDPROXYFORURL()

The first two of these three functions serve as primary entry points for the Web client application—specifically, to support Internet Explorer PAC extensions. To understand what to expect from the CFILE script, you need to have a logic diagram of it. As a reminder, the script performs two primary tasks when called by the Web client application:

1. Determines whether the request should be handled as direct or proxy

2. Determines whether CARP, No-CARP, or Client-CARP should be applied to the request

When the application receives a URL, it passes it to the CFILE script at one of two functions (*FindProxyForURL*, *FindProxyForURLEx*), depending on whether the application supports PAC extensions. Both of these entry functions defer to the same primary function, *ImplementFindProxyForURL*, to perform the two primary tasks. Figure 15-14 illustrates the logic applied for the direct or proxy decision.

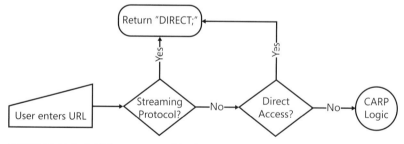

FIGURE 15-14 Script "direct or proxy" logic

If the destination is determined to be a common streaming protocol or the destination is found in the *MakeIps()* or *MakeNames()* sets, the script returns the word "DIRECT" to the Web application.

> **NOTE** The point where the "direct" decision is made is where the Web application ceases to act as a Web proxy client and potentially becomes a TMG client if the client host has the TMG Client installed and enabled for this application or it may behave as a SecureNET client. Because the TMG Web browser settings can use a larger address set than the Firewall Client can, a destination that is determined to be "DIRECT" by the CFILE

script can actually be considered remote by the TMG Client. If the script and the TMG client configurations match, or if the TMG client is not installed or is disabled, the Web application will behave as a SecureNET client.

When the script determines that the destination is one that must be served by a proxy, it evaluates the destination host and URL to determine what sort of CARP processing should be applied. There are three possible CARP states in the script:

- **Normal-CARP**   This is the behavior that has been in effect since Proxy Server 2.0. This state is where the script processes the destination the same way the proxy does to determine the location of the content being requested. Because of some problems encountered with some Web sites, ISA Server administrators needed a way to disable this CARP on a per-destination basis. No-CARP was the answer.

- **No-CARP**   This feature was added in ISA Server 2004 SP2 to alleviate problems caused when a Web proxy client accessed the same site via different FQDN and was directed through different proxies because of CARP behavior. Because many banking sites consider a change in source-IP to be a form of attack, this behavior caused the remote site to reject the connection or request. By allowing the ISA Server administrator to define sites that should not be "CARPed", these problems were alleviated. This change brought about another issue that was solved with the third CARP state: client-CARP.

- **Client-CARP**   This feature was added to alleviate a side effect of No-CARP that occurs when a common destination such as Microsoft Updates was heavily used by many clients concurrently. The net effect of this behavior was that the No-CARP choice caused all clients to use the same array member because they all calculate the same hash for the destination. This behavior would cause one proxy server to work much harder than the rest for these requests. Figure 15-15 illustrates the simplified CARP logic.

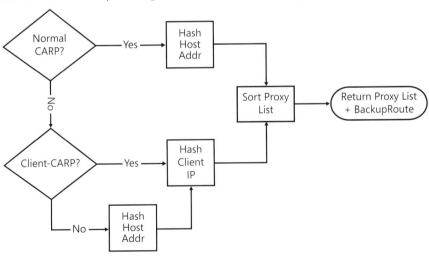

FIGURE 15-15 Script CARP logic

If the script determines that Client-CARP is disabled, it calculates a hash from the destination host and passes it to the No-CARP decision point. If No-CARP is enabled, the No-CARP decision point incorporates the current hash value into the Client IP hash calculation. The script logic is designed so that if the Client-CARP state is set, the No-CARP state will also be set. The net result of all this is that the hash used in the proxy sorting routine represents the following:

- **Normal-CARP** only the destination host
- **No-CARP** an amalgam of the destination host hash and the client IP address
- **Client-CARP** only the client IP address

The net result of these actions is that the script will loop through the *MakeProxies* set and create an array of proxy names ordered according to the relative numerical position of their hash and their CARP load factor.

Configuring Automatic Discovery in the Network

When configuring a Web proxy client to automatically detect the proxy server that is available in the network, the only action that you need to do on the client side is to select an option on the Web browser to enable this. This is a true statement assuming that your client workstation has the correct DNS configuration and name resolution is working properly. However, there are more actions to be performed for the server side. It is important to bring the brief definition because many system administrators have a wrong conception that by enabling automatic discover on the client side no other setting on the server side needs to be done.

As explained in the beginning of this chapter, the Web Proxy Automatic Discovery (WPAD) protocol is used in background to enable this communication. WPAD was created by Microsoft and has been used since Internet Explorer 5. Microsoft submitted WPAD for IETF standardization, but the draft expired in 1999 without an official agreement for a standard. Internet Explorer and other browsers (such as Mozilla Firefox) are capable of using WPAD and taking advantage of the automatic configuration setting. For the purpose of the following discussions, we will refer to the diagram from Figure 15-16.

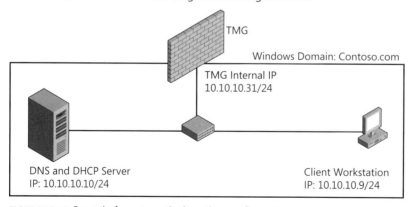

FIGURE 15-16 Scenario for automatic detection configuration

Preparing for Automatic Discovery

Now that you know how the automatic discovery process works, you need to assemble the pieces and define the configuration on each computer that has a role in this process.

Configuring TMG

TMG configuration allows automatic discovery on a per-network basis. This means that if you have multiple networks on TMG and want to allow automatic discovery in some of them, you can enable it only on the networks you want. For purposes of the scenario presented in Figure 15-16, the only network that will have automatic discovery enabled is the internal network. Follow these steps to configure TMG's internal network for automatic discovery:

1. On the TMG computer, open the Forefront TMG Management Console.

2. Click Forefront TMG (Server Name) in the left pane.

3. Click Networking.

4. Right-click Internal and then click Properties.

5. Click the Auto Discovery tab and select Publish automatic discovery information for this network. Figure 15-17 illustrates this completed task.

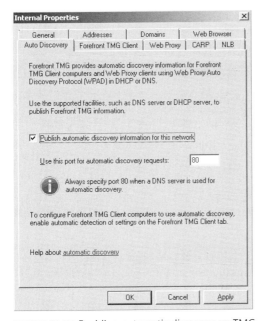

FIGURE 15-17 Enabling automatic discovery on TMG

6. By default TMG uses port 80 for automatic discovery requests. Leave this port enabled and click OK.

7. Click Apply.

After applying the changes, TMG will provide access to the CFILE for properly formed requests received on port 80. The next step is to configure DHCP WPAD to support automatic discovery.

Configuring DHCP

The DHCP WPAD option configuration can be configured on a per-scope or per-server basis. If you want all clients to use the same proxy server regardless of the subnet where they operate, you should configure the WPAD option as a server-level option. For purposes of this scenario this is the option that we will use. Assuming that your DCHP Server already has a scope created you will need to follow these steps to configure the WPAD option:

> **NOTE** The examples in the following process are shown using Windows Server 2008.

1. Click Start, point to Administrative Tools, and click DHCP.
2. Expand the DHCP Server computer, right-click IPv4, and click Set Predefined Options, as shown in Figure 15-18.

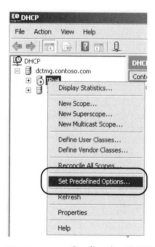

FIGURE 15-18 Configuring WPAD record

3. The Predefined Options And Values dialog box opens. Click Add, as shown in Figure 15-19.
4. In the Option Type dialog box, fill the values as shown in Figure 15-20.
5. The values that you filled represent the following:
   - **Name** A friendly name for this record.
   - **Data Type** This value is expected to be a string of printable characters that represent the complete WPAD URL, therefore you select the String option.
   - **Code** For a WPAD option, the code should be set to 252.

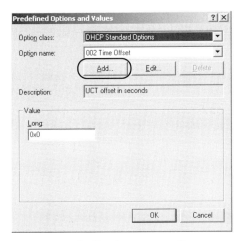

FIGURE 15-19 Configuring a new option

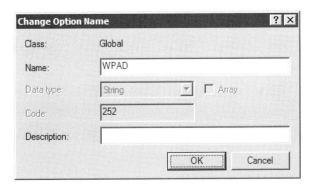

FIGURE 15-20 Creating a WPAD option type

6. Click OK and type the URL that clients will use to access the CFILE in the String text box, as shown in Figure 15-21. Make sure that all values are typed in lowercase. Click OK when you are finished.

FIGURE 15-21 The URL for the CFILE

MORE INFO   See the Knowledge Base article at *http://support.microsoft.com/kb/307502* for an explanation of the lowercase requirement.

7. In the DHCP console, right-click Server Options and then click Configure Options, as shown in Figure 15-22.

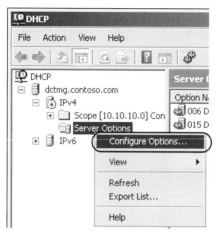

FIGURE 15-22 Configure Options

8. In the Server Options window, scroll down until you find the 252 option. Select it, as shown in Figure 15-23.

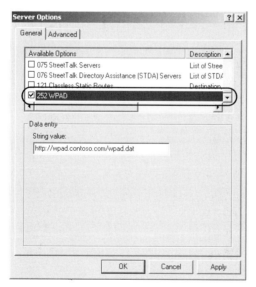

FIGURE 15-23 Adding server options

9. Click OK. The WPAD option will appear in the DHCP console right pane, as shown in Figure 15-24.

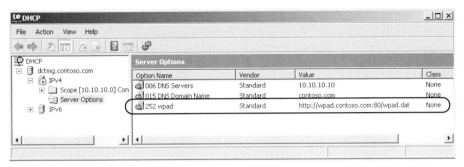

FIGURE 15-24 Adding wpad entry (252) in Server Options

After this procedure the DHCP Server is ready to provide WPAD option information when the client requests it.

Configuring DNS

Many system administrators think that if they configure DHCP to provide WPAD information they don't need to configure DNS. This is a misconception; you must still define a DNS record for a host named wpad.contoso.com because of the name resolution process that will follow the DHCP NFORM request. When the client receives the URL from the DHCP server, the client will start a name resolution process to resolve the host name wpad.contoso.com. If you don't have an entry on your DNS for this name, the client may try to contact WINS Server or send a NetBIOS broadcast for name resolution. Again, this will depend on the client's NetBIOS node type. You may wish to review the options available for node type in Chapter 4, "Analyzing Network Requirements."

If your environment includes multiple TMG computers using NLB to provide high availability, you may wish to create a CNAME record for wpad.contoso.com pointing to the A record that corresponds to the virtual IP address used by the TMG NLB array. In this scenario we just have a single TMG server in the array and therefore the wpad.contoso.com record should point to the A record of this TMG computer. Follow these steps to configure a CNAME record for wpad.contoso.com:

1. Click Start, point to Administrative Tools, and click DNS.

2. Expand your forward lookup zone and right-click the zone that you want to create the record (in this case, contoso.com). Click New Alias (CNAME), as shown in Figure 15-25.

3. In the New Resource Record dialog box, type **wpad** in the Alias name text box and type the FQDN that resolves to the TMG NLB VIP in the FQDN record, as shown in Figure 15-26. Click OK.

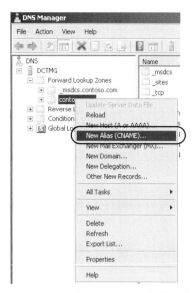

FIGURE 15-25 Creating a new CNAME for wpad.contoso.com

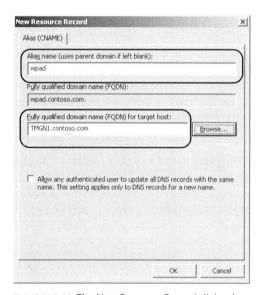

FIGURE 15-26 The New Resource Record dialog box

Securing DNS on Windows Server 2008

Since Windows Server 2000, the DNS service has included a feature called dynamic update that makes it possible for DNS client computers to dynamically update their records with a DNS server. The goal of this feature is to reduce the need for manual updates and therefore reduce administrative overhead involved with maintaining zone records. Although this feature was created with good intentions and indeed helps system administrators maintain their zone data, it may also open a path for malicious users. In some cases, malicious users may be able to modify a special host name and redirect certain types of network traffic to another user's computer.

> **MORE INFO** You can read more about this specific vulnerability in the WPAD protocol and how to mitigate it at *http://www.microsoft.com/technet/security/advisory/945713.mspx.*

If you think about the WPAD process, you may realize that a malicious user can take advantage of the DNS automatic update feature and register itself as wpad.contoso.com, by simply renaming his computer *wpad*. What this will do is direct all clients that are using automatic discovery to the computer named WPAD to obtain the CFILE. The DNS service on Windows Server 2008 brings a new security feature called Global Query Block List that is designed to mitigate the WPAD vulnerability. By default this feature is enabled for all zones and all resource records. What this feature does is ignore queries for *wpad* and *isatap*. You can view the records that are enabled in the global query block list by using the *dnscmd* command in a command window with two other parameters. The default output will be similar to the one shown here:

```
C:\>dnscmd dctmg /info /globalqueryblocklist
Query result:
String:
String:  isatap
Command completed successfully.
Query result:
String:  wpad
String:  isatap
Command completed successfully.
```

> **NOTE** In the preceding command, *dctmg* is the DNS server name.

This means that at this point if you try to resolve wpad.contonso.com, the DNS server will return an error to the client. An example of this process is illustrated in the following network monitor trace from the client that is sending a query for this name using *nslookup*:

1. Client sends the DNS Query (see DNS header) to wpad.contoso.com:

```
10.10.10.12     10.10.10.10     DNS       DNS:QueryId = 0x3, QUERY (Standard
query), Query  for wpad.contoso.com of type ALL on class Internet
- Dns: QueryId = 0x3, QUERY (Standard query), Query  for wpad.contoso.com of
type ALL on class Internet
    QueryIdentifier: 3 (0x3)
  + Flags:  Query, Opcode - QUERY (Standard query), RD, Rcode - Success
```

```
      QuestionCount: 1 (0x1)
      AnswerCount: 0 (0x0)
      NameServerCount: 0 (0x0)
      AdditionalCount: 0 (0x0)
    - QRecord: wpad.contoso.com of type ALL on class Internet
        QuestionName: wpad.contoso.com
        QuestionType: A request for all records, 255(0xff)
        QuestionClass: Internet, 1(0x1)
```

2. DNS server replies with a name error:

```
10.10.10.10    10.10.10.12    DNS    DNS:QueryId = 0x3, QUERY (Standard
query), Response - Name Error
 - Dns: QueryId = 0x3, QUERY (Standard query), Response - Name Error
     QueryIdentifier: 3 (0x3)
   + Flags:  Response, Opcode - QUERY (Standard query), AA, RD, RA, Rcode - Name
Error
     QuestionCount: 1 (0x1)
     AnswerCount: 0 (0x0)
     NameServerCount: 1 (0x1)
     AdditionalCount: 0 (0x0)
   - QRecord: wpad.contoso.com of type ALL on class Internet
       QuestionName: wpad.contoso.com
       QuestionType: A request for all records, 255(0xff)
       QuestionClass: Internet, 1(0x1)
   + AuthorityRecord: contoso.com of type SOA on class Internet:
PrimaryNameServer: dctmg.contoso.com, AuthorativeMailbox: hostmaster.contoso.com
```

When the DNS server sends this answer to the client it also logs an event in the DNS
System Log, as shown in Figure 15-27.

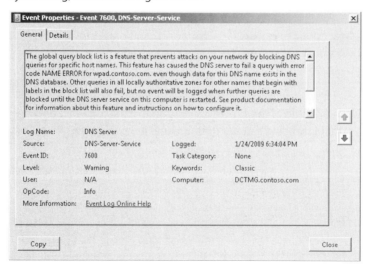

FIGURE 15-27 Event 7600 logged when a query to a name contained in the block list is seen

This is an important event for auditing purposes, mainly if your network doesn't have automatic discovery feature in use and you see entries like that in the DNS system log. This means that someone is searching for the WPAD name.

To complete the necessary steps to configure WPAD to work correctly, you need to remove the wpad name from the block list. Follow these steps to accomplish this:

1. Click Start, click Programs, click Accessories, right-click Command Prompt, and click Run As Administrator, as shown in Figure 15-28.

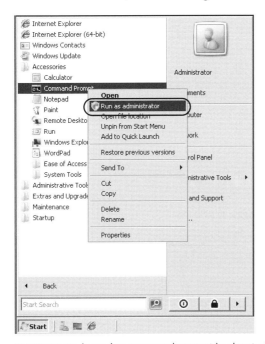

FIGURE 15-28 Accessing command prompt in elevated mode

2. Type the command **dnscmd [<ServerName>] /config /globalqueryblocklist isatap**. This will preserve just the special name *isatap* in the block list and will remove everything else that it is there, in this case *wpad*. The results would be similar to the one shown here:

```
C:\Users\Administrator>dnscmd dctmg /config /globalqueryblocklist isatap
Registry property globalqueryblocklist successfully reset.
Command completed successfully.
```

3. To confirm that the *wpad* name is not in the block list, type the command **dnscmd dctmg /info /globalqueryblocklist**. The result should be similar to the one shown here:

```
C:\Users\Administrator>dnscmd dctmg /info /globalqueryblocklist
Query result:
String:  isatap
Command completed successfully.
```

4. You can test the DNS server to confirm that now it is answering queries for wpad.contoso .com. To do that, type **nslookup wpad.contoso.com**. The result should be similar to the one shown here:

```
C:\Users\Administrator>nslookup wpad.contoso.com
Server:  localhost
Address:  ::1
Name:    tmgn1.contoso.com
Address:  10.10.10.31
Aliases:  wpad.contoso.com
```

5. Type **exit** to close command prompt.

> **MORE INFO** For more information on DNS Server Global Query Block List feature, review *http://technet.microsoft.com/en-us/library/cc794902.aspx.*

Configuring Client Applications

The TMG clients—Web proxy clients and TMG Client (TMGC)—can both be set up for manual proxy as well as automatic discovery. The advantage of using automatic discovery is that users who are mobile do not have to manually change their Internet Explorer or TMG client proxy settings every time they go to a new location. In this section you will see how to configure different types of applications for Auto Discovery. Before we proceed with configuring clients for Auto Discovery, it is essential to understand that based on the operating system and type of client, there is a difference between which mechanism (DNS or DHCP or both) is used if the user is a local administrator on the computer or if she is not an administrator on the local computer. Table 15-3 summarizes the behavior for Auto Discovery between administrators and non-administrators.

TABLE 15-3 Client Behavior for Auto Discovery Based on Permissions

CLIENT OPERATING SYSTEM	INTERNET EXPLORER 5 OR LATER	FIREWALL CLIENT 2004 OR LATER
Windows 2000	All Users (DNS) Admin users only (DHCP)	All Users (DNS + DHCP)
Windows 2000 SP4	All Users (DNS) Admin users only (DHCP)	All Users (DNS + DHCP)
Windows XP	All Users (DNS) Admin users only (DHCP)	All Users (DNS + DHCP)
Windows XP SP1	All Users (DNS) Admin users only (DHCP)	All Users (DNS + DHCP)

CLIENT OPERATING SYSTEM	INTERNET EXPLORER 5 OR LATER	FIREWALL CLIENT 2004 OR LATER
Windows XP SP2 or later	All Users (DNS + DHCP)	All Users (DNS + DHCP)
Windows 2003	All Users (DNS) Admin users only (DHCP)	All Users (DNS + DHCP)
Windows 2003 SP1 or later	All Users (DNS + DHCP)	All Users (DNS + DHCP)

Configuring Internet Explorer for Automatic Discovery

The Web proxy client automatic configuration feature is available in Internet Explorer 5.0 and later versions. You can set up Internet Explorer for Auto Discovery in two ways. The first uses WPAD and the second uses automatic configuration script. Both options are shown in Figure 15-29.

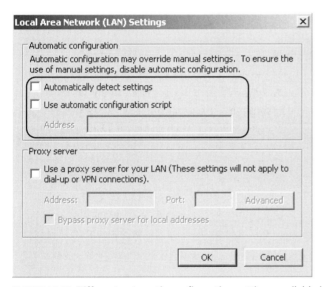

FIGURE 15-29 Different automatic configuration settings available in Internet Explorer

Automatically Detect Settings

When you select Automatically Detect Settings in Internet Explorer, it first tries to locate the server where automatic discovery information is stored. This is done via the WPAD protocol to locate a WPAD entry in DHCP (option 252) or DNS (Alias or CNAME record). When the location of the automatic discovery information is determined, the client then connects to the server, downloads the configuration script, and configures itself according to the information provided in the CFILE. All this is done over HTTP protocol. For Internet Explorer this script has a predefined name: wpad.dat.

The client can use either DNS or DHCP to provide the same results. The client requests the appropriate configuration script file with the URL *http://<HOSTSERVER>:<PORT><PATH>*. The component *HOSTSERVER* should match the fully qualified domain name of the server publishing the automatic discovery information. Normally this will be the fully qualified domain name resolving to TMG's internal interface. The component PORT should match the TCP port number on which you have enabled publishing of the automatic discovery information. If the discovery mechanism does not provide a port component, the client must assume port 80. For this reason it is recommended that you use port 80 when using DNS because when making the WPAD entry in DNS you cannot specify a port number in a DNS Alias or CNAME record. The component *PATH* is /wpad.dat for Internet Explorer and is case-sensitive. Hence it is important to make sure that lowercase letters are used for the path.

To configure Internet Explorer to automatically detect settings perform the following steps:

1. Start Internet Explorer 5.0 or later.

2. On the Tools menu, click Internet Options.

3. Click the Connections tab.

4. Click LAN Settings.

5. Select the Automatically Detect Settings check box, click OK, and then click OK again.

Automatic Configuration Script

When the option Use Automatic Configuration Script is selected in Internet Explorer, Internet Explorer knows the exact location of the configuration script file. Therefore, the main difference between the options Automatically Detect Settings and Use Automatic Configuration Script is that the discovery mechanism based on the WPAD protocol is completely bypassed when using the automatic configuration script. This means that no specific DHCP (Option 252) or DNS (Alias or CNAME record for wpad) configuration is needed. The default configuration URL is *http://Server:Port/array.dll?Get.Routing.Script,* where *Server* can be the name or IP address of the TMG computer and *Port* is the Web proxy port the internal interface on TMG is listening on.

To configure Internet Explorer for automatic configuration script, perform the following steps:

1. Start Internet Explorer 5.0 or later.

2. On the Tools menu, click Internet Options.

3. Click the Connections tab.

4. Click LAN Settings.

5. Select the Use Automatic Configuration Script check box.

6. Enter the configuration script **URL http://Server:8080/array.dll?Get.Routing.Script** and click OK, and then click OK again.

Using Group Policy to Configure Automatic Discovery Settings in Internet Explorer

If you have a large number of clients, you can use Group Policy to configure all clients that use Internet Explorer to use Auto Discovery to connect to TMG. To set up Group Policy for Internet Explorer, follow these steps on the Domain Controller.

> **WARNING** It is important to note that for the sake of example we are using the Default Domain Policy. However, as per best practices of Active Directory management mentioned in *http://technet.microsoft.com/en-us/library/cc779159.aspx*, we should create a new Group Policy and link it to the domain and set it to override the default settings in the default policy.

1. Click Start, click Run, and type **gpmc.msc**. Click OK.

2. The Group Policy Management console opens.

3. Under your domain name, right-click Default Domain Policy and choose Edit.

4. The Default Domain Policy opens, as shown in Figure 15-30.

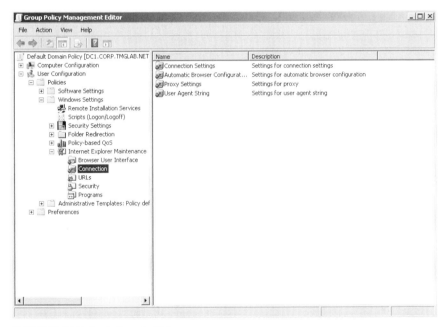

FIGURE 15-30 Default Domain Policy

5. Expand User Configuration, expand Windows Settings, expand Internet Explorer Maintenance, and click Connections.

6. Double-click Automatic Browser Configuration in the right pane. The Automatic Browser Configuration dialog box opens, as shown in Figure 15-31.

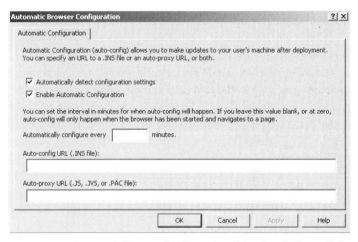

FIGURE 15-31 Automatic Browser Configuration dialog box in Group Policy

7. To enable automatically detect settings only, select the Automatically Detect Configuration Settings check box. With this setting selected, the client browser will look for a wpad.dat file to service the browser.

8. To enable automatic configuration via the script provided in TMG, select the Enable Automatic Configuration check box and then specify the automatic configuration script URL in the Auto-proxy URL (.JS, .JVS, or .PAC file) text box. The Auto-config URL is for INS files commonly known as IEAK profiles. To set up the automatic configuration script for TMG, use Auto-proxy URL because the Auto-config URL is only for INS files. If you specify URLs for both Auto-config and Auto-proxy URL, the Auto-proxy URL will be incorporated in the INS file mentioned in the Auto-config URL.

9. To push the automatic configuration script at a certain time interval, enter a value in the Automatically Configure Every _ Minutes text box. By default, Internet Explorer will look for the configuration script in its cache. The default period for the automatic configuration script to stay in Internet Explorer's cache is 1800 seconds and for the wpad.dat file is 3000 seconds, after which it will download a new configuration script or wpad.dat file the next time it tries to connect to the Internet. If you want to override this setting by pushing out a configuration script more frequently, this setting is helpful. If you specify 0 or do not specify a value, automatic configuration occurs only when the user's computer is restarted.

10. Click OK.

At this time you can either wait 90 minutes, which is the default time for clients to refresh their Group Policy, or you can run a *gpupdate /force* command on a client from the command prompt to enforce the Group Policy on the client.

Proxy settings are usually per user and thus are stored under the user-specific registry hive (HKEY_CURRENT_USER). If you look under the registry key HKEY_CURRENT_USER\Software\ Microsoft\Windows\CurrentVersion\Internet Settings\Connections, you will find one or more values of type REG_BINARY. The value name indicates the connection name and the binary value contains the proxy settings to be used for that connection. Although proxy settings are usually set per user, you can set them per computer by setting a policy. This makes the settings the same for all users on that computer. The registry key that controls this behavior is HKEY_LOCAL_MACHINE\SOFTWARE\Policies\Microsoft\Windows\CurrentVersion\Internet Settings\ProxySettingsPerUser. The type is REG_DWORD and the value is 0. By setting the value to 0 you can then force the proxy settings to be applied per machine. In this case, the proxy settings come from HKEY_LOCAL_MACHINE\Software\Microsoft\Windows\CurrentVersion\Internet Settings\Connections.

The relevant group policy that changes this behavior is located under:

Computer Configuration\Policies\Administrative Templates\Windows Components\Internet Explorer\ make proxy settings per-computer (rather than per-user).

Automatic Proxy Cache

The Automatic Proxy Result Cache is a performance enhancement that was added to Internet Explorer 5.5 and later. The purpose of the cache is to reduce the client-side processing of the automatic proxy configuration script. When you connect to an Internet site, the *FindProxyForURL* function is used to determine whether a proxy should be used and which proxy to use. Internet Explorer 5.5 and later first checks the Automatic Proxy Result Cache to determine whether a proxy was used to connect to the host on previous attempts. If this checks fails, it indicates that this is the first attempt to connect to the host during the current session and the normal proxy detection logic applies. The following list illustrates the logic Internet Explorer 5.5 and later uses to determine whether a proxy should be used and which proxy to use:

- If Automatically Detect Settings is turned on in Internet Explorer, an attempt is made to download the wpad.dat file from the internal network and process it as an automatic proxy configuration script. If a proxy is returned from the script and Internet Explorer has established a connection through the proxy, the Automatic Proxy Result Cache is updated with the host and the proxy server name that was returned.

- If Use Automatic Configuration Script is turned on in Internet Explorer, the automatic proxy configuration script is downloaded and processed. If a proxy is returned from the script and Internet Explorer has established a connection through the proxy, the Automatic Proxy Result Cache is updated with the host and the proxy server name that was returned.

- If Internet Explorer is configured for a static proxy server, the proxy server name is retrieved from the registry.

When Internet Explorer uses an automatic proxy configuration script, a connection is opened with the proxy server if the processing of the script indicates that a proxy is to be used. If the proxy server cannot establish a connection, the proxy server name is added to a link list of bad proxy servers so that it is not used for 30 minutes. If the automatic proxy configuration script contains a *PROXY* return that lists multiple proxy servers, the next proxy in the list is attempted until the list is traversed or a connection is established. If the list is traversed and no connection has been established, you receive a "Page Cannot Be Displayed" error message in Internet Explorer.

When a connection is established through a proxy server, the host name of the site and the proxy server name are cached. On future attempts to access the host name in the same session, Internet Explorer has cached information about which proxy to use. Therefore, all subsequent connections to the host are tried through the proxy that was used previously. This means that if the proxy server name that is cached is unavailable during the same session, the automatic proxy configuration script is not reprocessed, and you receive a "Page Cannot Be Displayed" error message in Internet Explorer.

To provide proxy redundancy, some administrators might like to disable the automatic proxy result cache. This results in client-side processing of every GET request that is issued by Internet Explorer. As a result, Internet Explorer performance may be impacted depending on the logic of the Automatic Proxy Configuration Script and its size.

You can disable Automatic Proxy Result cache via the registry or via the group policy. To disable the Automatic Proxy Result Cache by using the following registry key:

```
HKEY_CURRENT_USER\Software\Policies\Microsoft\Windows\CurrentVersion\Internet Settings
Value: EnableAutoproxyResultCache
Type: REG_DWORD
Data value: 0 = disable caching; 1 (or key not present) = enable automatic proxy caching
(this is the default behavior)
```

To disable Automatic Proxy Result Cache via the Group Policy, perform the following steps on the domain controller:

> **WARNING** It is important to note that for the sake of example we are using the Default Domain Policy. However, as per best practices of Active Directory management mentioned in *http://technet.microsoft.com/en-us/library/cc779159.aspx*, we should create a new Group Policy, link it to the domain, and set it to override the default settings in the default policy.

1. Click Start, click Run, and type **gpmc.msc**. Click OK.
2. The Group Policy Management console opens.
3. Under your domain name, right-click Default Domain Policy and click Edit.
4. In the Group Policy Object Editor, double-click User Configuration\Administrative Templates\Windows Components\Internet Explorer.
5. Double-click Disable Caching Of Auto-Proxy Scripts.
6. Click Disabled and then click OK.

> **MORE INFO** For more information about Automatic Proxy Result Cache please read *http://support.microsoft.com/kb/271361*.

Troubleshooting Issues with Auto Discovery and IE

Many times after setting everything up correctly, you will still find that Auto Discovery isn't working correctly. In some cases you'll also find that after bringing in a new TMG in the domain and setting it up for Auto Discovery, pointing clients from an older proxy server to TMG doesn't work. To that effect you can keep in mind these points to ensure that you haven't missed any needed configuration settings:

- If there is an Authenticated Users Only rule from Internal to Local host or if Require All Users To Authenticate is selected, Auto Discovery will fail. Because the client doesn't expect authentication, it will not supply its credentials to get the Auto Discovery configuration file. To resolve this issue, set the value of *SkipAuthenticationForRoutingInformation* to *True* by running the script mentioned in *http://msdn.microsoft.com/en-us/library/dd447621.aspx*.

- Verify connectivity from the client to TMG. The simplest way to test whether a client can get the Auto-configuration file is by typing **http://<TMG server name** or **IP address>/wpad.dat** and see whether you can pull the wpad.dat file and open it in the notepad.

- In case your latest wpad.dat file is not being applied, make sure you have no other wpad.dat file in the cache. To delete all previous instances of wpad.dat you can run the following command from the command prompt to delete all instances of wpad.dat and then the client can try and download a new one for its next connection: C:\>del \wpad*.dat /s.

- In Internet Explorer, clear the Automatically Detect Settings check box and save the changes. Then restart Internet Explorer, select the Automatically Detect Settings check box, and restart Internet Explorer again. This forces a refresh of the wpad.dat file.

- You can also delete the following HKEY_CURRENT_USER\Software\Microsoft\Windows\CurrentVersion\Internet Settings\Connections registry key entries to force Internet Explorer to use a fresh wpad.dat file:

  - **DefaultConnectionSettings**   This entry specifies the configuration of the default connection used by Internet Explorer.

  - **SavedLegacySettings**   This entry is a copy of DefaultconnectionSettings, and specifies the configuration used by network connections other than the default connection.

> **MORE INFO**   For more information about troubleshooting automatic detection, please visit *http://technet.microsoft.com/en-us/library/cc302643.aspx*.

Configuring TMG Client for Automatic Discovery

The Forefront TMG Client (TMGC) performs Auto Discovery using the WPAD protocol. This means that it, too, relies on DHCP or DNS to provide it with the information on who is hosting the configuration script. When the Firewall Client finds the name of the server hosting the configuration script, it connects to that server over HTTP and downloads the configuration script with a predefined name called wspad.dat.

To configure the TMG client for Automatic Discovery, perform the following steps:

1. Double-click the firewall client icon in the system tray.

2. Select Automatically Detected Forefront TMG, as shown in Figure 15-32.

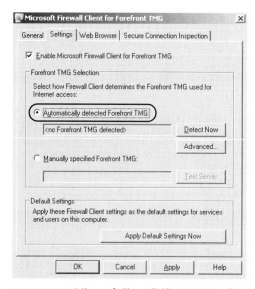

FIGURE 15-32 Microsoft Firewall Client For Forefront TMG dialog box

You can click Detect Now to test whether Automatic Discovery worked for the Firewall Client. The Firewall Client will refresh its configuration by default every six hours unless the Firewall Client program is restarted or manual refresh is applied by clicking Detect Now.

Configuring Windows Media Player

One of the most commonly used media players to stream online videos and music is the Windows Media Player. The Windows Media Player (WMP) can use manual proxy settings or can be set to automatically detect settings. In this case it will behave like an Internet Explorer client. WMP allows you to specify different proxy settings for each streaming media protocol it supports. By default, WMP is configured so that RTSP-based requests do not use a proxy. This is important because the browser defers to the application that is registered in Windows as the RTSP or MMS protocol handler. The default MMS and RTSP protocol handler on a Windows operating system is Windows Media Player, although this may have changed if you've selected another media player as the default.

To set WMP for automatic discovery, follow these steps:

1. Click Tools.

2. Click Options.

3. Click Network and then click Configure, as shown in Figure 15-33.

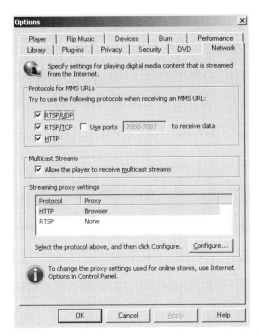

FIGURE 15-33 The Network Tab for Windows Media Player

The Configure Protocol dialog box opens, where you can select Autodetect Proxy Settings, as shown in Figure 15-34.

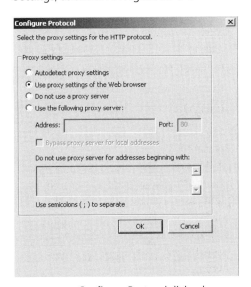

FIGURE 15-34 Configure Protocol dialog box

An administrator can face some issues while setting up Windows Media Player to work through a proxy. When WMP is acting as a Web (CERN) proxy client, and the proxy requires Windows Integrated authentication, WMP will not auto-authenticate to the proxy if the proxy is specified as either Fully Qualified Domain Name or IP address. If the proxy is specified as NetBIOS (unqualified) name, WMP will auto-authenticate using the interactive account credentials. If the proxy requires Basic or Digest authentication, an authentication prompt is expected, regardless of how the proxy is specified. This behavior is the same if the proxy is obtained via an auto-configuration (wpad.dat) script.

By default, ISA 2004, ISA 2006, and TMG list the proxies using their IP addresses in the wpad.dat file. This default was chosen to prevent name resolution errors from impeding normal client-to-Web proxy communications. Although this works well enough for browsers, WMP has issues when the proxy is specified using anything other than NetBIOS name.

To ensure that you do not face errors while connecting via a proxy, you can disable the way HTTP uses proxy in WMP. The easiest way to handle this is to pass everything to the Firewall Client. The Firewall Client will handle all the HTTP traffic for WMP, and in case of any authentication needed the Firewall Client will satisfy the requirements through its Firewall Control channel.

To change the way HTTP connects to a proxy for WMP, follow these steps:

1. Disable proxy settings either by setting HTTP protocol to Do Not Use A Proxy Server, as shown in Figure 15-34, or by changing the following registry key:
    Hkey_Current_User\Software\Microsoft\MediaPlayer\Preferences\ProxySettings\HTTP
    Name: ProxyStyle
    Type: DWORD
    Value: 0

2. If you cannot perform step 1, you can choose to disable this setting via a Group Policy located under "User Configuration\Administrative Templates\Windows Components\ Windows Media Player\Networking". Set the Configure HTTP Proxy option to Disabled.

3. Install the Firewall Client and set it for either Automatically Detect TMG Server or as a manual proxy.

Using AutoProxy in Managed Code

Often developers create custom applications that fail to work through proxy or cannot bypass proxy simply because the application doesn't understand how to use Auto Discovery. The Microsoft .NET Framework does not provide support for AutoProxy. You must use the WinHTTP AutoProxy functions, such as the *WinHttpGetProxyForUrl* function, to obtain the proxy settings in managed code. You can use an auto-configuration script to automatically configure the proxy settings.

WinHTTP implements the WPAD protocol using the *WinHttpGetProxyForUrl* function along with two supporting utility functions, *WinHttpDetectAutoProxyConfigUrl* and *WinHttpGetIEProxyConfigForCurrentUser*. AutoProxy support is not fully integrated into the HTTP stack in WinHTTP. Before sending a request, the application must call *WinHttpGetProxyForUrl* to obtain the name of a proxy server and then call *WinHttpSetOption* using *WINHTTP_OPTION_PROXY* to set the proxy configuration on the WinHTTP request handle created by *WinHttpOpenRequest*.

The *WinHttpGetProxyForUrl* function can execute all three steps of the WPAD protocol described in the previous section:

1. Discover the Automatic Configuration Script URL.

2. Download the Automatic Configuration Script.

3. Execute the script code and return the proxy configuration in a WINHTTP_PROXY_INFO structure.

Optionally, if the application knows in advance the Automatic Configuration Script URL it can specify this to *WinHttpGetProxyForUrl*.

> **MORE INFO**   To learn more about how to use AutoProxy in a managed code and how to use WinHTTP functions, please read *http://msdn.microsoft.com/en-us/library/aa384122.aspx* and *http://support.microsoft.com/kb/873199*.

Summary

In this chapter you explored in great detail how the WPAD protocol works, how to set up TMG for Automatic Discovery, and how the Web proxy and Firewall Client Automatic Configuration really work from a client point of view. You learned some tips to help you troubleshoot Auto Discovery for different types of clients. With that knowledge you should be able to decide which method is the most appropriate for your specific environment. In the next chapter we will explore how caching works in TMG and how to troubleshoot issues related to caching.

## CHAPTER 16

Caching Concepts and Configuration

- Understanding Proxy Cache   **387**

- Configuring the Forefront TMG 2010 Cache   **397**

- Troubleshooting Cache   **417**

- Summary   **424**

One of the primary reasons for deploying a Web proxy server is to reduce bandwidth utilization to the Internet. Microsoft Forefront Threat Management Gateway (TMG) 2010 provides very granular control over cache file management as well as cache content. This chapter will help you understand how to make Forefront TMG 2010 caching much more useful and help you analyze the cache behavior of Web services to help you configure the Forefront TMG 2010 cache and monitor its relative effectiveness.

Understanding Proxy Cache

Forefront TMG 2010 offers Web caching features to provide better performance and response times for Web requests. You can configure Forefront TMG 2010 to cache Web objects that are frequently requested by end users. When an end user makes a Web request to the Internet, Forefront TMG 2010 can serve the request from its cache instead of making a request to the Internet. Web caching can provide two main benefits:

- **Faster Internet access**   Because Web requests are served from the local cache instead of being sent to a remote Web server on the Internet, Web caching provides faster access to Web content for the end user. In a reverse proxy scenario, reverse caching provides faster access for Internet users to the published content by returning the content from the cache instead of requesting it from the published Web server thereby decreasing the load on the Web server.

- **Reduced traffic to Internet**   Because frequently requested content can be served from the cache, bandwidth is saved by reducing the amount of traffic sent to the Internet.

How Caching Works

Forefront TMG 2010 can be configured to maintain a cache of Web objects and fulfill Web requests from its cache. If a request cannot be fulfilled from the cache, Forefront TMG 2010 initiates a new request to the Web server on behalf of the client. After the Web server responds to the request, Forefront TMG 2010 caches the response and forwards the response to the end user.

By default, caching is not enabled on Forefront TMG 2010 because no disk space is allocated for caching. When caching is enabled, an administrator can define cache rules that determine how content from specified sites is stored and retrieved from Forefront TMG 2010's cache. Cache rules apply to destinations and do not factor in the source of the request. A destination can be specified as a network entity, domain name sets, and URL sets. For any network, if the TMG Client support is enabled or if Forefront TMG 2010 is configured as the default gateway for internal computers (SecureNET clients), Forefront TMG 2010 may cache requests for them as well.

If a request is allowed by an access or publishing rule, Forefront TMG 2010 analyzes its cache configuration and cached objects to determine whether a request should be served from the cache or retrieved from the Web server. If the object is not present in the cache, Forefront TMG 2010 checks the Web Chaining rules to determine whether the request needs to be forwarded directly to the requested Web server, to another upstream proxy server, or to an alternate destination.

If the request is present in the cache, Forefront TMG 2010 performs the following steps:

1. Forefront TMG 2010 checks whether the object is valid. If the object is valid, Forefront TMG 2010 retrieves the object from the cache and returns it to the user. Forefront TMG 2010 determines whether the object is valid by performing the following checks:

   - The Time to Live (TTL) specified in the source has not expired.

   - The TTL configured in the content download job has not expired.

   - The TTL configured for the object has not expired.

2. If the object is invalid, Forefront TMG 2010 checks the Web Chaining rules.

3. If a Web Chaining rule matches the request, Forefront TMG 2010 performs the action specified by the Web Chaining rule; for example, route the requested directly to a specified Web server, an upstream proxy, an alternate specified server.

4. If the Web Chaining rule is configured to route the request to a Web server, Forefront TMG 2010 determines whether the Web server is accessible.

5. If the Web server is not accessible, Forefront TMG 2010 determines whether the cache was configured to return expired objects. If the cache was configured to allow Forefront TMG 2010 to return an expired object as long as a specific maximum expiration time hasn't passed, the object is returned from the cache to the end user.

6. If the Web server is available, Forefront TMG 2010 determines whether the object may be cached depending on whether the cache rule is set to cache the response. If it is, Forefront TMG 2010 caches the object and returns the object to the end user.

Cache Storage

Forefront TMG 2010 can store objects on the local hard disk, and for faster access can store most of the frequently requested objects on both the disk and the RAM. Cached pages can be stored immediately in memory (RAM) to be accessed by end users requesting the Web content. A lazy-writer or buffered-writer approach is used to write pages to the disk. By default, 10 percent of physical memory is allocated for RAM caching. This approach results in faster availability of content. All additional data is stored on the disk. As objects are cached, Forefront TMG 2010 adds them to the cache content file on the disk. If the cache content file is too full to hold new objects, Forefront TMG 2010 removes older objects from the cache based on age of the object, size of the object, and how frequently the object is accessed. The recommendation and properties of the cache file are as follows:

- A formatted NTFS partition must be used and the cache drive must be local. When the cache drive is configured, a cache-content file, Dir1.cdat, is created in the location *<drive>*:\urlcache according to your selections while enabling caching.

- The maximum size for a cache file on a single partition is 64 GB.

- To avoid write conflicts with other Windows activity, you should place the cache file on a physical disk separate from the operating system, Forefront TMG 2010 installation, and page files.

- The size and the location of the cache can be configured on a per-TMG-computer basis.

- Having a large cache is recommended because objects are dropped from the cache when the maximum size if exceeded. However, if the cache is too large (greater than 60 GB), file read-write delays may impact service shutdown and startup.

An administrator can take the following actions for the content to be stored in the cache:

- Specify the type of objects that can be cached.

- Specify how long the objects should remain in cache for objects that do not have a timestamp.

- Specify objects that do not return an OK response (HTTP 200 status code) to be cached.

- Specify URLs larger than the maximum size limit of the RAM cache not to be stored in the RAM. Because objects cached in memory are retrieved faster than those on the disk, it is important to decide what needs to be cached in the RAM versus what needs to be cached on the disk to prevent excessively large objects from filling the RAM cache. The default maximum size limit is 12,800 bytes.

Caching Scenarios

Forefront TMG 2010 provides caching in two different scenarios. Forefront TMG 2010 caches objects when an internal user makes a Web request to the Internet. This type of caching is known as *forward caching*. In a Web publishing scenario, Forefront TMG 2010 provides cached content from the internal Web server published by Forefront TMG 2010 to the external users. This type of caching is known as *reverse caching*.

Forward Caching

Forward caching happens when a user located on a network protected by Forefront TMG 2010 requests Web content through Forefront TMG 2010. Forefront TMG 2010 makes a decision on how to serve that content depending on its availability in the cache.

If the content is available in cache, the process is as follows:

1. The user requests a Web page on the Internet.

2. Forefront TMG 2010 intercepts this request and determines whether the content is available in cache (RAM cache or disk-based cache).

3. If the content it available, it is returned to the user in accordance with the cache settings. The settings determine whether only valid objects can be returned to the client.

4. The content is then moved to the in-memory cache (RAM cache) as per the cache settings. After a period of time, if the content is no longer being requested regularly (is no longer "popular"), Forefront TMG 2010 copies this content from RAM to disk-based cache and flushes it from memory. If another user requests the content stored in disk-based cache, Forefront TMG 2010 returns it to the RAM cache.

If the content is not available in cache, the process is as follows:

1. The user requests a Web page through Forefront TMG 2010.

2. Forefront TMG 2010 intercepts this request and determines whether the content is available in cache (RAM cache or disk-based cache).

3. If the request is not present in cache or has expired, Forefront TMG 2010 forwards the request to the Web server.

4. The Web server returns the requested information and, based on the cache settings, Forefront TMG 2010 caches the object in its RAM cache where frequently requested content can be stored for fast retrieval.

5. The content is returned to the end user.

6. After a period of time, or if the content is no longer frequently requested, Forefront TMG 2010 copies the content from RAM to disk cache and flushes it from the memory, leaving the only available copy on disk. It is only returned to RAM cache if another user requests the content.

Reverse Caching

Reverse caching happens when Internet users request content from a Web server published by Forefront TMG 2010. The process is as follows:

1. The Internet user requests a Web server published by Forefront TMG 2010.

2. Forefront TMG 2010 intercepts the request and determines whether the content is present in cache. If the content is not available in cache or has expired, Forefront TMG 2010 forwards the request to the published Web server.

3. After the published Web server responds, Forefront TMG 2010, as per its cache settings, stores the content in RAM cache where frequently requested content is stored for fast retrieval.

4. Forefront TMG 2010 returns the content to the Internet user who requested it.

5. After a period of time, if the content is no longer frequently requested, Forefront TMG 2010 copies this content from RAM to disk-based cache and flushes it from the memory.

> **NOTE** The user doesn't need to be an Internet user. The user can be located in the perimeter network. As long as the user is requesting information from a Web server published by Forefront TMG 2010, if caching is enabled, the request will be processed as described in the preceding section.

Cache Rules

Caching behavior in Forefront TMG 2010 can be made granular and more configurable by creating specific cache rules. Each cache rule allows for specific types of content to be processed in different ways, depending on your needs.

By default, when caching is enabled, a default cache rule is created that caches objects based on its default settings. You can create additional caching rules based on your specific caching needs and requirements. Each rule created can contain the following customizations:

- Specify how content retrieved by the rule is returned to the end user. Objects that are valid or expired can be returned and requests can be routed to the Web server if no cached object is found, or they can be dropped entirely.

- Specify type of content to be cached. By default, objects are only stored in the cache when source or request headers in the HTTP request indicate caching. You can define content that should not be cached or content that should be cached even if the source or request headers do not indicate caching.

- Specify a maximum size for the objects that the rule caches.

- Specify whether SSL responses should be cached. This does not apply to forward caching for sites exempted from HTTPS inspection.

- Enable caching of HTTP objects.

- Specify how long objects should remain in cache. Unless the source specifies an expiration time, HTTP objects remain in cache according to the TTL setting in the rule. The TTL is based on a percentage of time that has passed since the object was created or modified.

- Enable caching of FTP objects and specify a TTL to indicate how long FTP objects should remain in the cache.

You can see some of these settings on the Advanced tab when creating a cache rule, as shown in Figure 16-1.

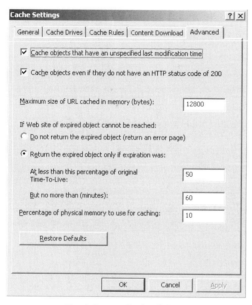

FIGURE 16-1 The Advanced tab of the Cache Settings dialog box

Caching Web Objects

Even though you can configure Forefront TMG 2010 to cache Web content that does not indicate caching, certain Internet content cannot be cached. Per RFC 2616, Forefront TMG 2010 does not cache Web pages with specific information in the response or the request header, as described in Table 16-1.

> **MORE INFO** For more information on HTTP headers that control caching behavior please read *http://www.w3.org/Protocols/rfc2616/rfc2616-sec13.html*.

TABLE 16-1 Header Types Not Cached by Forefront TMG 2010

HEADER TYPE	DETAILS
Cache-control: no-cache response or request header	The HTTP 1.1 cache-control header prevents all caching.
Cache-control: private response header	The HTTP 1.1 cache-control: private response header indicates that the object must not be stored in a shared cache and is intended only for the specific client.
Pragma: no-cache response header	HTTP 1.0 servers cannot use the cache-control header. The pragma: no-cache header ensures that if the client communicates with the server over a secure HTTPS connection and the server returns a pragma: no-cache header with the response, the response is not cached.
WWW-authenticate response header	Indicates that authentication is required.
Set-cookie response header	Indicates a page that uses a browser cookie to identify the user.
Authorization response or request header	This is not cached unless the origin server explicitly allowed this by including the cache-control: public header in the response.
Cache-control: no-store request or response header	Indicates that the cache must not store any part of the request or any response to it.

Caching Compressed Content

HTTP compression reduces file size by using algorithms to eliminate redundant data. Most common Web-related file types can safely be compressed. HTTP compression uses the industry standard GZIP and Deflate algorithms. These algorithms compress static files, and optionally perform on-demand compression of dynamically generated responses before sending them over the network. These same algorithms are again used to decompress the static files and dynamic responses on an HTTP 1.1–supported client. A client that is configured to use HTTP 1.1 may request compressed content from a Web server. Web servers indicate in their responses whether they support compression.

HTTP compression in Forefront TMG 2010 is a global HTTP policy setting. It applies to all HTTP traffic that passes through Forefront TMG 2010 to or from a specified network or network object, rather than to traffic handled by a specific rule. HTTP compression is provided by two Web filters:

- **Compression Filter**   This filter is responsible for compression and decompression of HTTP requests and responses. This filter has a high priority, and is high in the ordered list of Web filters. This is because the filter is responsible for decompression. If you choose to enable inspection of compressed content, decompression must take place before any other Web filters inspect the content.

- **Caching Compressed Content Filter**   This filter is responsible for caching of compressed content and serving a request from the compressed content in the cache. This filter has the lowest priority, and is low in the ordered list of Web filters, because caching can take place after all other filters have handled the content.

Caching and compression together provide a more efficient way to serve compressed requests. Content is cached on Forefront TMG 2010 in one of the following ways:

- **Compressed**   Content is requested in compressed format and cached in compressed format.

- **Uncompressed**   Content is requested in uncompressed format and cached in uncompressed format.

- **Uncompressed and incompressible**   If an end user requests compressed content and it arrives at the cache uncompressed, it is stored in the cache as incompressible. The next time the request for the same compressed content is received, Forefront TMG 2010 will recognize that the content is incompressible and serves it from the cache uncompressed rather than from the Internet. Content that is inspected is also stored as uncompressed.

Compression settings applied to cache content are persistent. Therefore, if you want compression configuration changes to be reflected in the cached content, the cache on Forefront TMG 2010 needs to be cleared (this is discussed later in this chapter). Another important thing to remember is that when inspecting incoming compressed content, Forefront TMG 2010 Web filters must have access to the decompressed content. When compression is enabled, content is cached in compressed form. The Caching Compressed Content Web filter is responsible for decompressing the content so that the other Web filters can inspect the decompressed version of the cache content. When Forefront TMG 2010 receives a request for the cached content, the Compression Web filter recompresses the content before sending it to the end user. This in turn increases the amount of time it takes to transfer the content from Forefront TMG 2010 to the user.

Monitoring Cache

Monitoring the Forefront TMG 2010 cache behavior involves data gathering and analysis. When monitoring cache behavior, you need to first determine your scenario: forward cache or reverse cache. The main difference between these scenarios is that in reverse caching the number of clients involved can be unlimited; however, the servers involved in publishing contain only several Web sites (the ones that you are publishing) and thus a relatively small number of objects need to be cached. On the other hand, in a forward caching scenario the Web servers are almost unlimited (because you don't know what sites the clients are going to access). To handle this large working set, a large disk cache should be defined.

The best tool to use for monitoring Forefront TMG 2010 cache behavior is Windows Performance Monitor. Forefront TMG 2010 includes a set of counters that allow you to observe very granular details about Forefront TMG 2010 caching behavior.

> **MORE INFO**   For a complete list and descriptions of the cache counters review the article at *http://technet.microsoft.com/en-us/library/cc995280.aspx*.

General Recommendations

To improve your caching experience, here are some best practices for cache utilization on Forefront TMG 2010:

- General sizing calculation for cache is: Cache size (chosen during the configuration) plus 0.5 MB for each Web proxy client. For example, let's say you have a 4-GB cache size and need to expand this for 100 more users. The total size of the new cache file will be 4.050 GB.

- In a forward caching scenario the object's hit ratio and peak HTTP request rate are used to determine the number of necessary disks. To calculate, use this formula:

  Number of Physical Disks = (Peak request rate X Object hit ratio) / 100

  In a scenario where the peak request rate is 1,500 requests per second and the object hit ratio is 40 percent, you will need six disks.

- For best performance, use a separate disk and dedicated controller for caching. This will increase read and write performance.

- Exclude the cache folder from file scan antivirus and backup jobs.

- If you need to have a cache bigger than 64 GB, you need to create multiple cache files because the per-partition size limit for a cache file is 64 GB.

Cache Array Routing Protocol (CARP)

Forefront TMG 2010 uses Cache Array Routing Protocol (CARP) to optimize scaling and efficiency when using multiple Forefront TMG 2010 proxies in an array. Using CARP, the array with multiple Forefront TMG 2010 proxies can act as a single logical cache. CARP allows an array to distribute Web proxy client requests and distribute cached content among the array members. CARP provides client computers with the information and algorithm required to identify the best proxy in the array to serve the request and thereby eliminate the need for array members to forward the request among themselves. The request resolution path, which is based upon a hash of array member identities and Uniform Resource Locators (URLs), which implies that for any given URL request, the browser or downstream proxy will know exactly where in the array the information will be accessed whether it is already cached from a previous request or found on the Internet for delivery and cached for the first time.

CARP provides the following benefits:

- Because CARP determines the best request resolution path, there is no query messaging between proxy array members, as is found with conventional Internet Cache Protocol (ICP) networks. By doing this, CARP avoids the heavier query congestion that normally occurs with a greater number of proxy array members.

- CARP eliminates the duplication of contents that otherwise occurs on a proxy array. The result is a faster response to queries and a far more efficient use of server resources.

- CARP has positive scalability. Because of its hash-based routing and its resultant independence from peer-to-peer pinging, CARP becomes faster and more efficient than other caching protocols as more members are added to the array.

- CARP automatically adjusts to additions or deletions to array membership. The hash-based routing means that when an array member is either taken offline or added, only minimal reassignment of URL caches is required.

- CARP ensures that the cache objects are distributed according to the load factor that is configured for each member of the array.

How CARP Works

CARP provides efficient routing for requests on client sides and server sides. A script generated by Forefront TMG 2010 implements the client-side CARP algorithm. The script includes information about the configuration and current status of the array.

The result is a specific location for each cached object, meaning that the Web browser or downstream proxy can know exactly where a requested URL is either already stored locally or will be located after caching. The hashing functions used helps to ensure that the load is distributed across the array.

Client-Side CARP

Clients can either be Web browsers or downstream proxies. The client selects an array member to serve each individual URL. On the client side, Forefront TMG 2010 web proxy clients use CARP as follows:

1. The Web browser retrieves a proxy selection script from an array. This script is generated by Forefront TMG 2010 in response to an automatic discovery request and specific queries sent to an array member using its name, its IP address, or the DNS name of the array for *Wpad.dat* and *Array.dll?Get.Routing.Script* requests and is specific to the network where the client resides. A downstream proxy sends an *array.dll?Get.Info.v2* request to an upstream proxy for a script containing a table that lists the fully qualified domain name (FQDN), NetBIOS name, and default IP address of the upstream array members on the network where the downstream proxy resides.

2. The host name in the URL entered for the Web request is passed to the script, which computes a prioritized list of array members that will serve Web content from any URL containing that host name. Each array member in the list is identified by its FQDN, NetBIOS names, or default IP address in the client's network.

3. The Web browser connects to the first array member in the list and requests that it retrieve the page. If the first array member does not respond, the next array member in the list is contacted, and so on until the object can be retrieved.

4. The script always returns the same array member list for a given host name, ensuring that content from all URLs containing the same host name is cached on one member of the array.

Server-Side CARP

With server-side CARP, clients send the request to an array member. If the array member receiving the request cannot serve the requested object from its cache, it uses the CARP algorithm to create a prioritized list of array members for the host name in the URL and forwards the request to the IP address for intra-array communication of the first array member in the list. If that array member cannot serve the requested object, the next array member in the list is contacted until all the array members in the list have been contacted.

Configuring the Forefront TMG 2010 Cache

When you first run the Configure Web Access Policy Wizard, you have the opportunity to configure Forefront TMG 2010 caching. Unless you've already performed the required traffic analysis for your organization, you probably decided to leave that for later. This section will walk you through the cache and CARP settings.

Enable Web Caching

If you elect to leave caching disabled when you run the configure Web Access Policy Wizard, the management console will appear as shown in Figure 16-2. If you have already enabled caching and defined the cache drives, you can skip these steps and go to the "Add A Cache Rule" section.

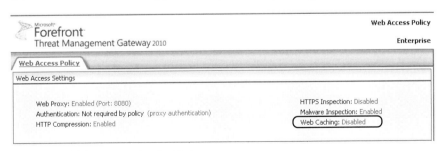

FIGURE 16-2 Web proxy cache disabled

To enable Web caching, click Disabled next to Web Caching. You may also click Configure Web Caching in the right pane under the Tasks tab, as shown in Figure 16-3.

FIGURE 16-3 Configuring Web Caching on the Tasks tab

You'll see the Cache Settings dialog box, as shown in Figure 16-4.

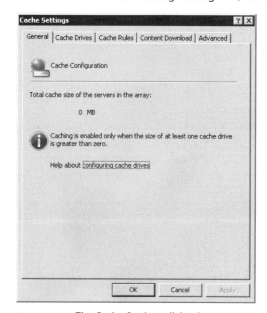

FIGURE 16-4 The Cache Settings dialog box

1. Click the Cache Drives tab to access the Forefront TMG 2010 cache storage configuration.

2. Select the array member to enable the Configure button, as shown in Figure 16-5.

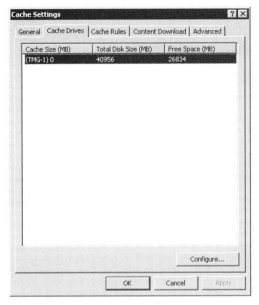

FIGURE 16-5 Cache Drives tab

3. Click Configure to define the cache size and location.

4. Figure 16-6 shows the Define Cache Drives dialog box. To define the cache location and size, select the drive where you want to store the cache file and enter the desired size of the cache file in the Maximum Cache Size (MB) text box. Click Set and then click OK.

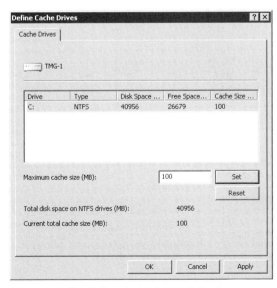

FIGURE 16-6 The Define Cache Drives dialog box

5. If you have previously defined a cache file and then disabled it, the old cache file was not deleted by Forefront TMG 2010. This state will result in the warning dialog shown in Figure 16-7. If you want to delete the old file, click Yes. If you click No, you will be returned to the Cache Settings dialog box shown earlier in Figure 16-5.

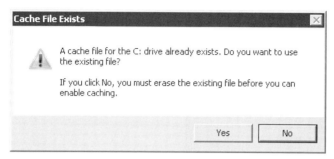

FIGURE 16-7 The Cache File Exists warning

6. If you are finished making changes to the Forefront TMG 2010 cache settings, click OK to close the Cache Settings window. If you wish to make additional changes, continue with the next section of this chapter that describes steps you wish to take, such as "Add a Cache Rule."

7. When the Apply and Discard buttons appear in the center pane as shown in Figure 16-8, click Apply to apply your changes.

FIGURE 16-8 The TMG Apply Or Discard Changes dialog box

8. When the Configuration Change Description window appears, type the appropriate text that reflects the changes that were made and click Apply.

9. Click OK to close the Saving Configuration Changes window.

Add a Cache Rule

If you have closed the Cache Settings dialog box, select Web Access Policy in the left pane and click Enabled next to Web Caching in the middle pane or click Configure Web Caching in the Tasks pane on the right.

In this example, you will configure a cache rule so that no content from a Web site will ever be cached. This task is frequently performed when the freshness of the content is more important than the ability to obtain the content when the destination site is unavailable.

1. Click the Cache Rules tab to access the Web Cache rules set. Figure 16-9 illustrates the default Web Cache rules configuration.

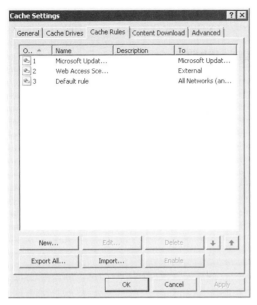

FIGURE 16-9 The default Cache Rules settings

This page allows you to create, edit, delete, import, export, and enable or disable the Forefront TMG 2010 cache rules. To examine or modify the configuration of each rule, select the rule and click Edit. To change the rule order, select the rule you want to relocate and click the up or down arrows on the right until the selected rule is placed where you want.

> **MORE INFO** For details on an easy way to move items multiple positions with a single arrow click, see *http://blogs.technet.com/isablog/archive/2008/11/18/isa-ui-trick-move-rule-several-places.aspx.*

2. Click New to add a new cache rule. The New Cache Rule Wizards begins, as shown in Figure 16-10. Type **ISATools.org** in the Cache Rule Name text box and click Next.

3. On the Cache Rule Destination page, shown in Figure 16-11, click Add to create a new destination set.

4. In the Add Network Entities dialog box, click New and then click Domain Name Set, as shown in Figure 16-12.

5. In the New Domain Name Set dialog box, type **isatools.org** in the Name text box.

FIGURE 16-10 The New Cache Rule Wizard Welcome page

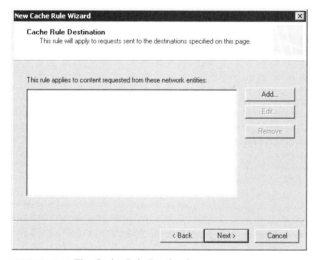

FIGURE 16-11 The Cache Rule Destination page

FIGURE 16-12 New Network Entities selection

6. Click Add and type **isatools.org**. Repeat this action and type the following:

jim.isatools.org

steve.isatools.org

isatools.org

When you finish, the isatools.org destination set should appear as in Figure 16-13. Click OK to close this page.

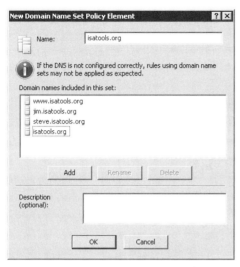

FIGURE 16-13 The ISATools.org Domain Name Set

7. On the Add Network Entities page, expand Domain Name Sets and select isatools.org as shown in Figure 16-14. Click Add and then click Close.

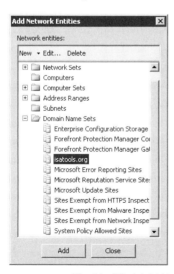

FIGURE 16-14 The Modified Add Network Entities dialog box

8. The New Cache Rule Wizard should now appear, as shown in Figure 16-15. Click Next.

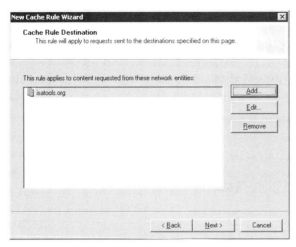

FIGURE 16-15 Updated Cache Rule Destination page

9. On the Content Retrieval page, leave the default option selected as shown in Figure 16-16 and click Next.

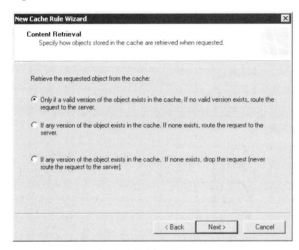

FIGURE 16-16 The Content Retrieval page

NOTE   The options available in Figure 16-16 change Forefront TMG 2010 caching behavior to the following:

- **Only If A Valid Version Of The Object Exists In The Cache**   If no valid version exists, route the request to the server. A *valid version* is a cache object that has not expired according to the original TTL and the Forefront TMG 2010 cache retention settings. If the local freshness information is current, Forefront TMG 2010 queries the server regarding the validity of the cache contents and if the content is valid, Forefront TMG 2010 answers the request using the cached contents.

- **If Any Version Of The Object Exists**   If none exists, route the request to the server. In this case, Forefront TMG 2010 does not check the validity of the cache contents before delivering it to the user. If the requested content exists in the cache, Forefront TMG 2010 delivers it as it exists in the Forefront TMG 2010 cache.

- **If Any Version Of The Object Exists In The Cache**   If none exists, drop the request. This case is similar to the second option except that if the object does not exist in the cache, Forefront TMG 2010 rejects the request.

10. On the Cache Content page, select Never, No Content Will Ever Be Cached as shown in Figure 16-17 and click Next.

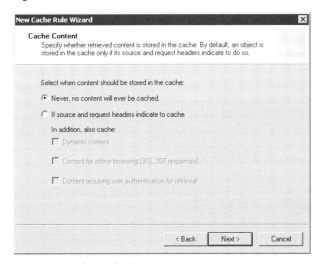

FIGURE 16-17 The Cache Content page

NOTE   The options available in Figure 16-17 change ISA caching behavior to the following:

- **Never, No Content Will Ever Be Cached**   Forefront TMG 2010 will always deliver the request the content only from the server—never from the cache.

- **If Source And Request Headers Indicate To Cache**   Forefront TMG 2010 caches the response in accordance with the header restrictions noted in Table 16-1.

- **In Addition, Also Cache**

   1. **Dynamic Content**   Forefront TMG 2010 caches content where the request URL includes qualifying data, collectively referred to as the *querystring*. This data is defined as any URL data that follows the first question mark (?).

   2. **Content For Offline Browsing (302, 307 Response)**   RFC 2616 includes these responses to allow the server the means to indicate a temporary alternate location for the requested content. When this option is selected, Forefront TMG 2010 caches the actual 302 or 307 response.

3. **Content Requiring User Authentication For Retrieval**   As noted in Table 16-1, Forefront TMG 2010 does not normally cache user-specific content. Selecting this option instructs Forefront TMG 2010 to cache authenticated content for the destinations related to this rule.

11. On the Completing The New Cache Rule Wizard page, review the settings summarized. If they match the settings shown in Figure 16-18, click Finish.

FIGURE 16-18 Completing The New Cache Rule Wizard page

12. The Cache Rules list will change to reflect the addition of the ISATools.org rule, as shown in Figure 16-19. At this point you can either click OK to close this page or leave it open if you want to add a content download job, as in the following section.

FIGURE 16-19 The adjusted Cache Rules list

> **NOTE** You may need to change the order of cache rules if you have created multiple rules for the same site, differentiated only by the virtual directory.
>
> For instance, let's say you create two rules:
>
> - Rule1: destination = *http://host.domain.tld/**, action = always cache
> - Rule2: destination = *http://host.domain.tld/nocache/**, action = never cache
>
> Because Rule1 precedes Rule2, content delivered from the */nocache vdir* will be cached because Rule1 is configured to cache content from all *vdirs* on site *host.domain.tld*. If you reorder the rules so that Rule2 precedes Rule1, the net effect of that change will be that all content *except* content delivered from the */nocache vdir* will be cached. Of course, if you have already cached content from the */nocache vdir*, you will have to remove it using the cachedir tool.

13. If you're finished making changes, click Apply in the center pane. Otherwise, continue with the next section that describes the changes you wish to make.

Add a Content Download Job

If you have closed the Cache Settings control, select Web Access Policy in the left pane and click Enabled next to Web Caching in the middle pane or click Configure Web Caching in the Tasks pane on the right.

In this example, you will create a content download job to retrieve content from *www.msn .com* on a daily basis.

1. Click the Content Download tab, as shown in Figure 16-20, and then click New.

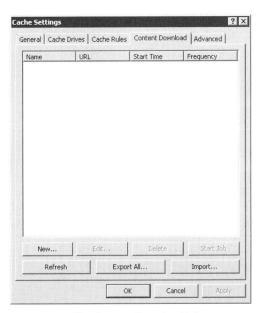

FIGURE 16-20 The Content Download tab

NOTE If the policy changes necessary to support content download jobs have not been configured, you will receive the warning shown in Figure 16-21.

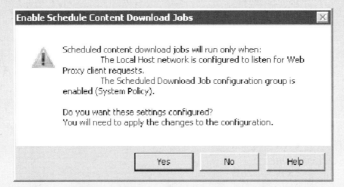

FIGURE 16-21 Cache Settings Enable Scheduled Content Download Jobs warning

1. Click Yes to close the warning dialog box.

2. Click OK to close the Cache Settings dialog box, and when prompted as shown in Figure 16-22, click Apply in the Management Console center pane.

FIGURE 16-22 TMG Apply or Discard Changes dialog box

3. When the Configuration Change Description window appears, type the appropriate text that reflects the changes that were made and click Apply. When the changes have been applied, as shown in Figure 16-23, click OK.

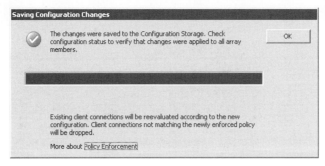

FIGURE 16-23 Saving Configuration Changes dialog box

4. In the right pane, click Configure Web Caching.

5. When the Cache Settings dialog box appears, click the Content Download tab.

2. In the Cache Settings dialog box, on the Content Download tab, click New.

3. On the Welcome To The content Download Job Wizard page, type **www.msn.com** as shown in Figure 16-24 and click Next.

FIGURE 16-24 The Welcome to the Content Download Job Wizard page

4. On the Download Frequency page, select Daily as shown in Figure 16-25 and click Next.

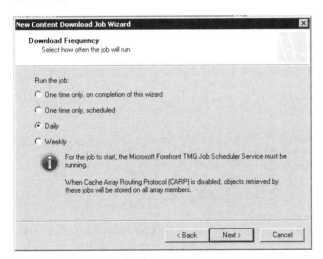

FIGURE 16-25 The Download Frequency page

5. On the Daily Frequency page, as shown in Figure 16-26, do the following:

   a. Enter a date and time that is within your TMG least active period.

   b. Select Run The Job One Time Every Day.

   c. Click Next.

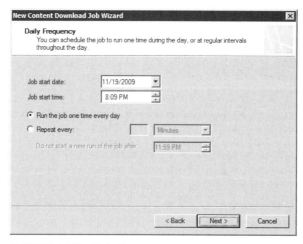

FIGURE 16-26 The Daily Frequency page

6. On the Content Download page, as shown in Figure 16-27, do the following:

   a. Type **http://www.msn.com/**.

   b. Select Do Not Follow Link Outside The Specified URL Domain Name.

   c. Select Maximum Depth Of Links Per Page.

   d. Type **100** in the Associated field.

   e. Click Next.

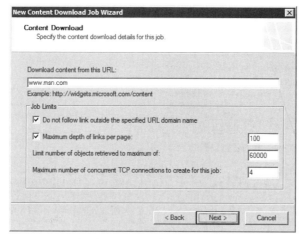

FIGURE 16-27 The Content Download page

> **NOTE** The options available in Figure 16-27 modify Forefront TMG 2010 content download job behavior as follows:
>
> ■ Do Not Follow Link Outside The Specified URL Domain Name   Forefront TMG 2010 limits the content search only to links that are either relative (contain no scheme (http://) and host (www.msn.com)) or those that only use the same host as specified in the URL; *www.msn.com* in this instance.

- Maximum Depth Of Links Per Page   Because one page can link to another, which can link to another, and so on, it's possible for these links to create a circular chain of links. Forefront TMG 2010 will use the value specified for this option to prevent such a loop from taking place.

- Limit Number Of Objects Retrieved To A Maximum Of   Forefront TMG 2010 will maintain a count of all objects retrieved during this download job and stop the job if the total number of objects (pages, pictures, and so on) exceeds this number.

- Maximum Number Of Concurrent TCP Connections To Create For This Job   Forefront TMG 2010 will not use more than the specified number of TCP connections to obtain the content specified in this job. For sites that reference a large number of offsite content, this may cause the job to run longer if all of the allowed TCP connections are busy retrieving content from one site.

7. On the Content Caching page, leave the defaults selected as shown in Figure 16-28. Click Next.

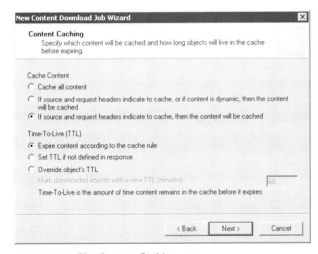

FIGURE 16-28 The Content Caching page

NOTE   **The options available in Figure 16-28 modify Forefront TMG 2010 download job caching behavior as follows:**

- Cache All Content   Forefront TMG 2010 will store all retrieved content in the cache, regardless of the response headers cache directives.

- If Source And Request Headers Indicate To Cache, Or If Content Is Dynamic, Then The Content Will Be Cached   Forefront TMG 2010 will cache the content in accordance with Table 16-1 and RFC-2616 (default behavior) and when the response used 302 and 307 status codes.

- **Limit Number Of Objects Retrieved To A Maximum Of** Forefront TMG 2010 will maintain a count of all objects retrieved during this download job and stop the job if the total number of objects (pages, pictures, and so on) exceeds this number.

- **Expire Content According To The Cache Rule** Forefront TMG 2010 will retain the content retrieved during this content download job according to the TTL specified by the server and the cache settings specified by the cache rules that apply to the sites included in this job.

- **Set TTL If Not Defined In Response** If the server does not specify a TTL in the response, Forefront TMG 2010 will apply a TTL as defined in the cache configuration or the cache rule that governs content from this site.

- **Override Object's TTL** Forefront TMG 2010 will ignore any TTL specified by the server and replace it with one as determined by the general cache configuration or as defined in the cache rule that governs content from this site.

8. On the Completing The Scheduled Content Download Job Wizard page, review the job configuration summary as shown in Figure 16-29. If the settings are correct, click Finish.

FIGURE 16-29 The Completing The Scheduled Content Download Job Wizard page

9. In the Cache Settings dialog box, on the Content Download tab, the list should appear as in Figure 16-30. Click OK to close this dialog box.

10. When the Apply and Discard buttons appear in the middle pane, click Apply to save your changes to storage.

11. When the Configuration Change Description window appears, type the appropriate text that reflects the changes that were made and click Apply.

12. Click OK to close the Saving Configuration Changes window.

FIGURE 16-30 The modified Content Download Job list

CARP Configuration

When multiple Forefront TMG 2010 proxies are configured to form an array, CARP settings become critical to proper array membership behavior.

> **NOTE** Although it is possible to configure the intra-array network and CARP load factor in single-server deployments (except in Medium Business edition), doing so has no effect on proxy functionality.

Configuring CARP correctly requires you to properly define two Forefront TMG 2010 settings:

- The network where intra-array communication will occur. Each array member *must* use the same network for intra-array communication or CARP, which depends on intra-array communication, may fail.

- The relative load factor for each cache location. This setting defines each array member's relative cache capacity. Because very few Forefront TMG 2010 deployments will build an array using servers of greatly different capability, the load factor is rarely used.

If all array members can communicate freely using the same network, CARP and other intra-array mechanisms will work quickly and reliably. You access this configuration dialog box by selecting the System node in the left pane, selecting the server to manage in the center pane, and choose one of the servers:

1. Double-click the server you want to manage.

2. Right-click the server you want to manage and select Properties, as shown in Figure 16-31.

FIGURE 16-31 Server Properties shortcut menu

3. In the right pane, under the Tasks tab, click Configure Selected Server as shown in Figure 16-32.

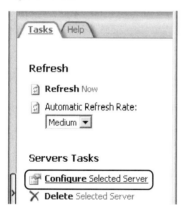

FIGURE 16-32 Configure Selected Server selection

The Server Properties dialog box opens to the General tab, as shown in Figure 16-33.

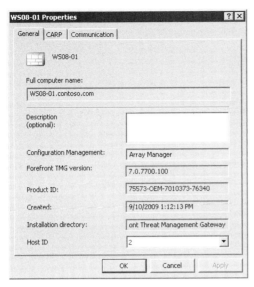

FIGURE 16-33 The Server Properties dialog box

Configuring the Intra-Array Address

In the following example, you will configure the intra-array IP address for your Forefront TMG 2010 array members.

1. Click the Communication tab, as shown in Figure 16-34.

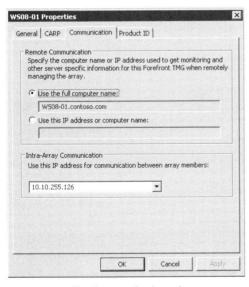

FIGURE 16-34 The Communication tab

2. From the Intra-Array Communication drop-down list, select the IP address that is part of a protected network, as shown in Figure 16-35.

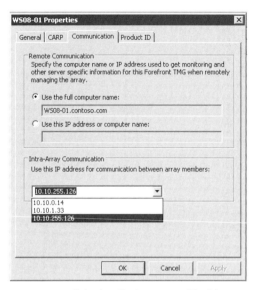

FIGURE 16-35 Selecting the intra-array IP address

NOTE The IP address selected for each Forefront TMG 2010 array member *must* be part of the same protected network.

3. If you are finished changing server properties, click OK to close the Server Properties dialog box. Otherwise, continue to the next section, "Configuring the CARP Load Factor."

4. When the Apply and Discard buttons appear in the center pane, click Apply to save the changes.

Configuring the CARP Load Factor

In the following example, you will examine the CARP load factor for your Forefront TMG 2010 array members.

NOTE Unless an array member is significantly underpowered compared to any other array member, the Load Factor value should not change. If the array members are composed of computers that vary greatly in CPU, RAM, or available network bandwidth, you'll have to perform load testing on the array members to determine their relative request capacity. Go to *http://www.microsoft.com/downloads/details.aspx?FamilyID=e2c0585a-062a-439e-a67d-75a89aa36495* to access a tool that provides the means to perform load testing for HTTP traffic.

1. In the Server Properties dialog box, click the CARP tab, as shown in Figure 16-36.

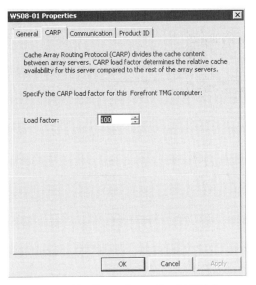

FIGURE 16-36 The Server Properties CARP tab

2. In the Load Factor box, enter a number that represents the relative percentage of CARP requests this server should process.

3. Click OK to close the Server Properties dialog box.

4. When the Apply and Discard buttons appear in the center pane, click Apply to save the changes.

Troubleshooting Cache

The first step in troubleshooting cache issues is determining whether the issue is related to cache. Many times you might tend to believe that cache is causing problems because the Web site doesn't appear as it should.

Analyzing Cache Behavior

You can use TMG Logging to see whether the page that you are trying to access is cacheable. To do so, use the following steps:

1. On the TMG computer (or using the Remote Management console), open the Forefront TMG Management Console.

2. Click Forefront TMG (Server Name) in the left pane.

3. Click Logs & Reports.

4. In the Task Pane, click Start Query.

5. Access the Web site *www.msn.com* from the client workstation behind Forefront TMG 2010. The result should appear similar to that shown in Figure 16-37.

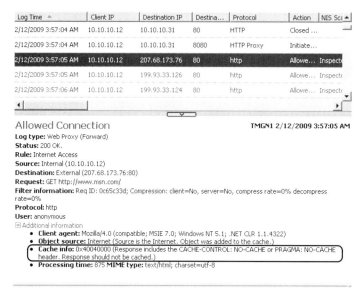

FIGURE 16-37 Logging showing that page is not supposed to be cached

In Figure 16-37, you can read details about the Forefront TMG 2010 cache behavior for this page. You can see, for example, that this page should not be cached.

6. Although this particular page should not be cached, some objects (such as images) on this site may be cached. Scroll through the log query results to find objects similar to those shown in Figure 16-38.

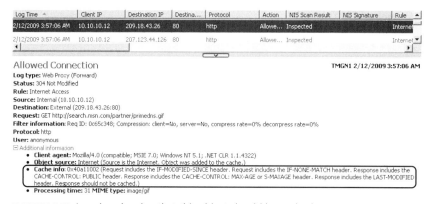

FIGURE 16-38 Logging showing that this object should be cached

Logging information is very useful when troubleshooting cache issues because it can tell you the details about the cache in a user-friendly way. Another way to look at cache information is by using Network Monitor trace. In the HTTP header you can see the information that TMG Logging shows you, but not in such a friendly view.

Using the same destination (*www.msn.com*) as an example, you can see the HTTP GET request sent by the client:

```
10.10.10.12    10.10.10.31    HTTP    HTTP:Request, GET http://www.msn.com/
- Http: Request, GET http://www.msn.com/
    Command: GET
  + URL: http://www.msn.com/
    ProtocolVersion: HTTP/1.1
    Accept:  */*
    Accept-Language:  en-us
    UA-CPU:  x86
    Accept-Encoding:  gzip, deflate
    UserAgent:  Mozilla/4.0 (compatible; MSIE 7.0; Windows NT 5.1; .NET CLR 1.1.4322)
    Host:  www.msn.com
    ProxyConnection:  Keep-Alive
    Cookie:  MC1=V=3&GUID=63cffd38fc6d4281a85fc4f874665d68; MUID=554A8F6B828F4861A0AE338
36B3E6C52; mh=MSFT; CULTURE=EN-US; zip=z:75201|la:32.8|lo:-96.787|c:us|hr:1; hpsvr=M:5|
F:5|T:5|E:5|D:blu|W:F; hpcli=W.H|L.|S.|R.|U.L|C.|H.; ushpwea=wc:USTX0327; FlightGroupId=
    HeaderEnd: CRLF
```

After Forefront TMG 2010 determines that traffic policy allows this request, Forefront TMG 2010 determines whether any cache rule is defined for this site. If there is no cache rule for this site, Forefront TMG 2010 sends the request to the destination server and will cache the response according to the request and response headers. You can see in the following Network Trace that the response headers indicate that the recipient should not cache the content. Forefront TMG 2010 forwards the response to the client based on Web server's response:

```
10.10.10.31    10.10.10.12    HTTP    HTTP:Response, HTTP/1.1, Status Code = 200,
URL: http://www.msn.com/
- Http: Response, HTTP/1.1, Status Code = 200, URL: http://www.msn.com/
    ProtocolVersion: HTTP/1.1
    StatusCode: 200, Ok
    Reason: OK
    Via:  1.1 TMGN1
    Connection:  Keep-Alive
    ProxyConnection:  Keep-Alive
    ContentLength:  52044
    Date:  Fri, 13 Feb 2009 12:26:52 GMT
    ContentType:  text/html; charset=utf-8
    Server:  Microsoft-IIS/6.0
    P3P: CP="BUS CUR CONo FIN IVDo ONL OUR PHY SAMo TELo"
    S:  TK2CHNRENC09
    XPoweredBy:  ASP.NET
    XAspNetVersion:  2.0.50727
    Pragma:  no-cache
    Cache-Control:  no-cache
    HeaderEnd: CRLF
```

When the Web server allows the content to be cached, the result for the response *Cache-Control* field is different. Here is an example of an HTTP header that allows the content to be cached:

```
- Http: Response, HTTP/1.1, Status Code = 200, URL: http://a.ads1.msn.com/ads/11749/0000
011749_000000000000000667488.swf
    ProtocolVersion: HTTP/1.1
    StatusCode: 200, Ok
    Reason: OK
    Via:  1.1 TMGN1
    Connection:  Keep-Alive
    ProxyConnection:  Keep-Alive
    ContentLength:  33678
    Expires:  Sat, 13 Feb 2010 05:00:03 GMT
    Date:  Fri, 13 Feb 2009 12:26:53 GMT
    ContentType:  application/x-shockwave-flash
    Server:  Microsoft-IIS/6.0
    Accept-Ranges:  bytes
    Cache-Control:  max-age=31536000
    Last-Modified:  Fri, 06 Feb 2009 18:11:46 GMT
    PICS-Label:  (PICS-1.1 "http://www.rsac.org/ratingsv01.html" l comment "RSACi North
America Server" by "inet@microsoft.com" r (n 0 s 0 v 0 l 0))
    XPoweredBy:  ASP.NET
    P3P:  CP="BUS CUR CONo FIN IVDo ONL OUR PHY SAMo TELo"
    HeaderEnd: CRLF
```

Notice that the *Cache-Control* field defines the maximum age for this object, this field determines how long the recipient should store this content. Later in this chapter, you will see that it is possible to store an object in cache even if the age of this object is already expired.

> **MORE INFO** For more information on the *Cache-Control* field, review RFC 2616 at *http://tools.ietf.org/html/rfc2616*.

As explained in the beginning of this chapter, not all objects should be cached. In some scenarios you will also want to exclude a whole Web site from being cached by Forefront TMG 2010. In this case you will need to create a cache rule, as shown previously in this chapter.

Using CacheDir

CacheDir is a tool that allows you to observe the contents of the disk cache. You can download this tool from the Microsoft Download Center at *http://www.microsoft.com/downloads/details.aspx?displaylang=en&FamilyID=dff77975-84bf-484f-a3bd-9d8dd800e220*. Most of the time this tool is used for troubleshooting purposes. However, it can also be used for reviewing cache content when you want to see the pages that are currently stored in Forefront TMG 2010 cache.

To ensure that the disk cache contains all of the cacheable content, you must exit CacheDir, restart the Microsoft Firewall Service, and launch CacheDir again. Because this creates a service outage, it is recommended that you schedule an appropriate time to use this tool, according to your environment.

> **MORE INFO**   To better understand the cache file usage, review the article *http://blogs .technet.com/isablog/archive/2008/07/30/files-larger-than-512mb-are-not-served-from-cache-after-isa-server-firewall-service-is-restarted.aspx.*

Using FetchURL

You can also create a script using VBScript or C++ to delete content from the cache using the method *FetchURL()*. For C++ you use *IFPCCacheContents::FetchUrl* and for VBScript you use *FPCCacheContents.FetchUrl*. You can use the following sample script to delete the cache—in this case, for the page *http://analytics.live.com/Sync.html*:

```
Const fpcTtlIfNone = 0
customTTL = 0
Flags = 0
Set root = CreateObject("FPC.Root")
Set tmgArray = root.GetContainingArray()
Set myCache = tmgArray.Cache.CacheContents
myCache.FetchURL "http://analytics.live.com/Sync.html", "",  customTTL,  fpcTtlIfNone,
flags
```

> **MORE INFO**   For a complete description of this method, review TMG SDK at *http://msdn .microsoft.com/en-us/library/dd421135.aspx.*

Rebuilding the Cache

During some troubleshooting scenarios it may be necessary to rebuild the cache file. One example of when this action is necessary is when the cache file is corrupted as the result of a drive error. A corrupted cache can cause Forefront TMG 2010 performance issues and affect the end-user experience. The best approach for such cases is to simply re-create the cache file. This procedure imposes service downtime because you will need to restart the Microsoft Firewall Service.

Follow these steps to re-create the Forefront TMG 2010 cache file:

1. In Forefront TMG Management Console, click Forefront TMG (Server Name) in the left pane.

2. Click Monitoring and then click the Services tab.

3. Select Microsoft Firewall Service. In the task pane, click Stop Selected Service, as shown in Figure 16-39.

FIGURE 16-39 Stopping the Microsoft Firewall Service

4. Minimize Forefront TMG Console and open Windows Explorer.

5. Select the folder where the cache resides (by default is called URLCache), click File, and select Delete as shown in Figure 16-40.

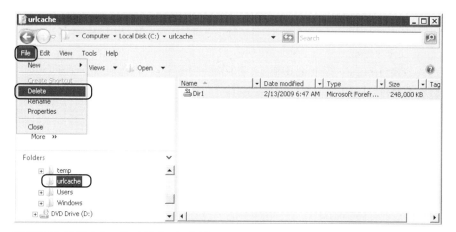

FIGURE 16-40 Deleting the URL Cache folder

6. Confirm that you want to delete the folder. Notice that if the cache file is too big you will see a prompt telling you that the file will not go to the recycle bin and will be permanently deleted.

7. Minimize Windows Explorer and maximize Forefront TMG Management.

8. Select Microsoft Firewall Service and click Start Selected Service in the Task pane, as shown Figure 16-41.

9. After the service starts, go to Windows Explorer and verify that the URLFolder and a new cache file were created.

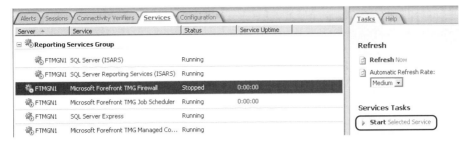

FIGURE 16-41 Starting the Firewall Service

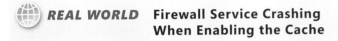 **REAL WORLD** **Firewall Service Crashing When Enabling the Cache**

An ISA administrator called in to Microsoft Support saying that the Microsoft ISA Server 2006 Firewall Service was crashing each night and he noticed that this started to happen after he enabled caching. My first thought was: Why would enabling the cache cause a firewall service to crash, and why only during the night?

During the symptom isolation, the key question posed to the customer was "What process usually runs during the night in this box?" Sometimes the Firewall administrator does not administer the Windows system and may not know the answer. For this particular scenario, the Firewall administrator wasn't aware of anything that was running on that server during the night.

After reviewing the Windows Application event logs, the following event was found:

```
Event Type:      Error
Event Source:    Microsoft ISA Server Web Proxy
Event Category: None
Event ID:        14197
Date:            01/10/2009
Time:            2:58:03 AM
User:            N/A
Computer:        ISASRV
Description:
ISA Server was unable to write content to the cache file.
```

We also noticed that the same event occurred every day at nearly the same time. After discussing the problem with the Windows administrator, we determined that the nightly backup process was locking the cache file and causing the cache write error.

To resolve this issue we excluded the cache drive from the nightly backup job. This resolution is documented in the KB Article *http://support.microsoft.com/kb/887311*.

Summary

In this chapter you learned how a proxy cache works regardless of Forefront TMG 2010 products. The design goals for the CARP Protocol were also explained, as were the general recommendations for proxy configuration on Forefront TMG 2010. You also learned how to configure the Forefront TMG 2010 cache, and how to configure CARP, and how to perform Forefront TMG 2010 cache troubleshooting. In the next chapter we will discuss how to use the Forefront TMG 2010 malware detection feature.

## PART VI

TMG Client Protection

CHAPTER 17 Malware Inspection **427**

CHAPTER 18 URL Filtering **465**

CHAPTER 19 Enhancing E-Mail Protection **487**

CHAPTER 20 HTTP and HTTPS Inspection **529**

Malware Inspection

- Understanding Malware Inspection in TMG   **427**

- Configuring Malware Inspection   **431**

- Creating Reports with Malware Statistics   **446**

- Summary   **463**

Chapter 1, "What's New in TMG," gave you a detailed breakdown of the traffic flow through the Malware and the Web Proxy filters. What you'll gain in this chapter is a functional understanding of the malware inspection options and their impact on TMG behavior as well as the user experience created by those selections.

Understanding Malware Inspection in TMG

As more ne'er-do-wells and miscreants try to gain access to our wallets, medical histories, and financial resources through attacks on Web sites; and as the malware they create in support of their nefarious deeds grows ever more prevalent; and as more users are drawn to compromised or just-plain-evil Web sites delivering these tools of social destruction, we find ourselves in need of a better tool to defend against this sort of user-empowered attack methodology.

Although it's true that much of the malware found in networks today is carried through the door on user's laptops, it's equally true that all manner of malware is downloaded by unsuspecting users from Web sites. The question of whether these sites deliver the malware intentionally or through remote compromise isn't really relevant during the time when your users are downloading it.

TMG Malware Inspection was designed to detect and stop the evil bits in the HTTP stream that is sent to clients in protected networks before the evil bits can gain access to the unsuspecting user's computer and produce irreparable damage.

As shown in Figure 17-1, Malware Inspection operates as one of the TMG Web filters.

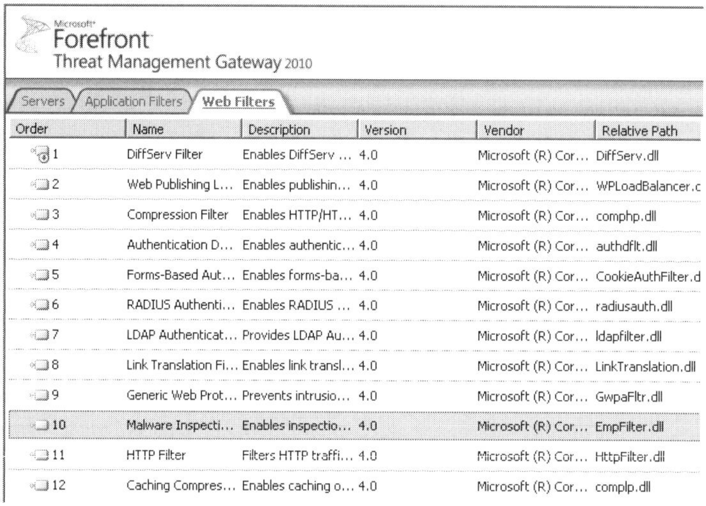

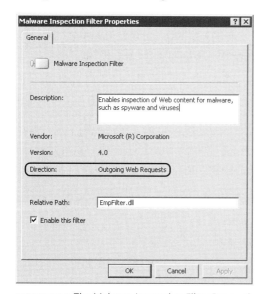

FIGURE 17-1 Malware Inspection Filter placement

> **NOTE** The position of the filters in the Web filters set is critical to their proper interoperation. You must not change the order of the filters without specific instructions from Microsoft.

If you double-click the Malware Inspection Filter entry, you will see the basic filter configuration as shown in Figure 17-2.

FIGURE 17-2 The Malware Inspection Filter Properties dialog box

The Malware Inspection filter is designed to inspect traffic that is processed by the Web Proxy filter in the context of access rules. Thus, any access rule that explicitly or implicitly includes the HTTP or HTTPS protocols that are associated with the Web Proxy filter can take advantage of malware inspection.

The primary goals of TMG Malware Inspection are:

- Minimize the threat imposed by Web-sourced malware
- Provide malware defense for hosts in TMG-protected networks
- Minimize the impact on TMG performance
- Provide a mechanism that is reliable and flexible

TMG includes a single malware inspection engine that is tuned specifically for HTTP traffic and allows you to control how and when the engine is used. By default, TMG installs with a basic malware detection signature database. If you have chosen to use Microsoft Updates, TMG will attempt to acquire an updated database using Windows Automatic Update mechanisms, or if you have chosen not to use Microsoft Update, TMG will wait for you to manually update the database.

> **NOTE** The manual URL Filtering, EMP, and Network Inspection System (NIS) update processes were not finalized at the time this chapter was written.

In recognition of the fact that TMG may be required to scan large files, TMG Malware Inspection uses a temporary disk cache located by default at %SystemRoot%\Temp\. As with the Firewall and Web Proxy logs, this disk cache should be relocated to a separate spindle to prevent disk contention with other system disk usage *before* you place TMG into full production. Ideally, the location you choose will also be on a separate spindle from the logging location.

> **NOTE** The term *spindle* refers to the center shaft of a physical disk drive to which the disk drive platters are attached. It is used here to emphasize the physical aspect of the terms *disk* and *drive*, which are frequently used interchangeably (albeit incorrectly) in reference to the logical and physical forms of the terms *disk* and *drive*.

To provide maximum flexibility, malware inspection can either be enabled globally or on a rule, source, or destination basis. By combining these aspects with user and anonymous rules in the Web Access Policy rules, you can even decide which users may benefit or be exempted from malware inspection.

Additionally, you can exercise even more granular control by specifying the type, size, archive depth, and so on of the files to be scanned as well as the disposition of any files that the Malware Inspection filter determines cannot be scanned or cleaned.

TMG provides logging and, of course, reports specificly to malware inspection so that you can quickly and easily determine what threats your users may have been subjected to as well as the impact of these threats or their mitigation to TMG performance. Figures 17-3 and 17-4 provide examples of log and report data specific to malware inspection.

FIGURE 17-3 Malware inspection log entry example

Inspection Times

The following report shows the Web sites for which client downloads required the longest average inspection time. Sites with longest average inspection duration are listed first.

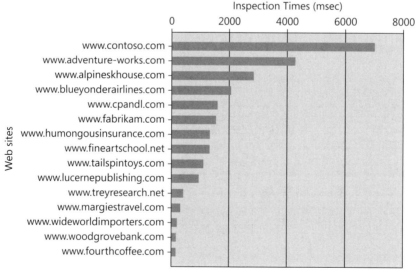

FIGURE 17-4 Malware inspection times report example

> **NOTE** Logging and report for malware inspection will be covered in more detail later in this chapter.

To improve the user's experience, TMG provides content inspection status notification. When this is not possible because of the client application's behavior or state, TMG provides a mechanism called *trickling* to make sure the client application doesn't time out while TMG is scanning the downloaded content.

Configuring Malware Inspection

When you run the Web Access Policy Wizard, you have an option to enable malware inspection. When you enable or disable malware inspection at this point, you control malware inspection for TMG as a whole.

Configuring Malware Inspection for Your Environment

The first step is to review the default settings for malware inspection and determine whether they meet your organization's requirements. For purposes of this example we will use the topology shown in Figure 17-5.

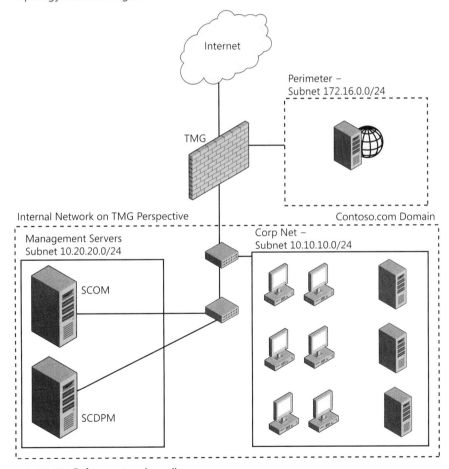

FIGURE 17-5 Reference topology diagram

This scenario has the following requirements for malware inspection:

- Do not inspect traffic where the destination domain is contoso.com.
- Traffic originating from subnet 10.20.20.0/24 must not be inspected.

To access malware inspection global settings, follow these steps:

1. On the TMG computer (or using remote management console), open the Forefront TMG Management Console.

2. Click Forefront TMG (Array Name) in the left pane.

3. Click Web Access Policy.

4. Click Tasks in the Tasks pane in the right side of the management console.

5. Click Enable Malware Inspection. A dialog box similar to Figure 17-6 will open.

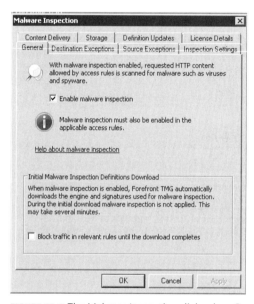

FIGURE 17-6 The Malware Inspection dialog box General tab

6. From the General tab you can decide whether malware inspection will be enabled and what action TMG should take if the malware engine is not updated. The default action is to block all traffic for the Access rules that have malware inspection enabled.

7. Your environment may require that some destination Web sites should not be inspected. To configure malware inspection destination exceptions, click Destination Exceptions. Figure 17-7 shows this tab.

8. You can add an existing object (URL Set, for example) or edit the current Domain Name Set to add your Web site. For this example, select Sites Exempt From Malware Inspection and click Edit. Figure 17-8 illustrates this dialog box.

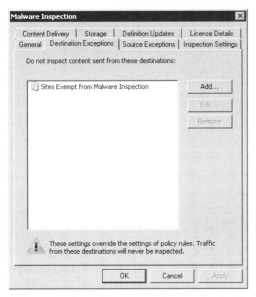

FIGURE 17-7 The Malware Inspection Destination Exceptions tab

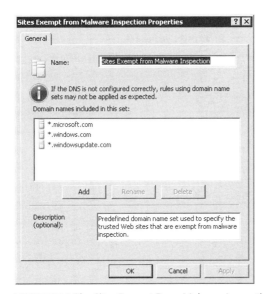

FIGURE 17-8 The Sites Exempt From Malware Inspection Properties dialog box

9. Click Add, type ***.contoso.com,** and click OK. Figure 17-9 shows how this new domain will appear in your configuration.

10. Click OK to close the Sites Exempt From Malware Inspection Properties dialog box.

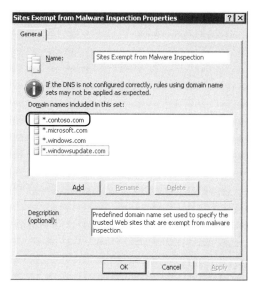

FIGURE 17-9 A new domain added to sites exempt from malware inspection

11. Another requirement for this scenario is that traffic originating from subnet 10.20.20.0/24 must not be inspected. To accomplish that, click the Source Exceptions tab. Figure 17-10 shows that this option is empty by default.

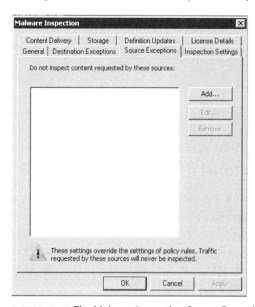

FIGURE 17-10 The Malware Inspection Source Exceptions tab

12. Click Add, click New, and then click Address Range as shown in Figure 17-11.

FIGURE 17-11 Add Network Entities New Address Range selection

13. In New Address Range Rule Element dialog box, you will use the address according to the diagram shown in Figure 17-5. Enter the first IP address in the range in the Start Address text box, and then enter the last IP address in the range in the End Address text box. Be sure to enter a name for this address range in the Name text box. You can also enter an optional description in the Description (Optional) text box. Figure 17-12 demonstrates how this should appear.

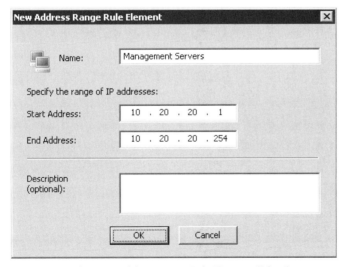

FIGURE 17-12 The New Address Range Rule Element dialog box

14. Click OK in the New Address Range Rule Element dialog box, click Address Ranges, select Management Servers, and click Add as shown in Figure 17-13.

FIGURE 17-13 Adding a new address range

15. Click Close in the Add Network Entities dialog box. Your Source Exceptions list appears, as shown in Figure 17-14.

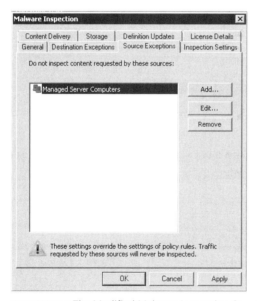

FIGURE 17-14 The Modified Malware Inspection Source Exceptions dialog box

16. Click OK in the Malware Inspection dialog box. After the Malware Inspection window closes, click Apply to commit the changes.

These settings satisfy the environmental requirements presented in Figure 17-5.

Inspection Settings

TMG allows you to configure malware inspection in a granular manner through many options. To access this option, open the Malware Inspection window using steps 3 through 5 in the previous procedure and click Inspection Settings. Figure 17-15 shows the options provided.

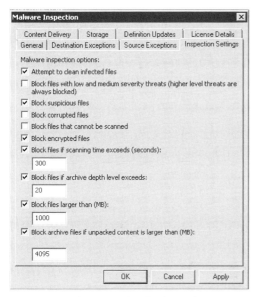

FIGURE 17-15 The Inspection Settings tab

The following options are available in this window:

- **Attempt To Clean Infected Files**   TMG will try to clean an infected file and if this action fails, TMG will present a HTML page to the end user saying that the file was blocked because it was infected.

- **Block Files With Low And Medium Severity Threats (Higher Level Threats Are Blocked Automatically)**   By default TMG blocks high-level threats when inspecting for malware. By selecting this option you also are mitigating threats that are considered low or medium impact.

- **Block Suspicious Files**   Files that are scanned and are suspected of being infected are blocked when this option is selected. TMG will categorize a file as suspicious when it does not find specific malware but the inspection results strongly indicate that this file may be infected.

- **Block Corrupted Files**   If TMG determines that a file under scan is corrupted, TMG will block it.

- **Block Files That Cannot Be Scanned**   Enable this option if you want TMG to block files that cannot be scanned. One example of a file that TMG cannot scan is a password-protected archive. Because the file contents cannot be accessed without the password, TMG cannot scan the file for malware. Selecting this option may generate some false blocking action for otherwise legitimate content. This option is disabled by default for this reason.

- **Block Encrypted Files** As with password-protected archives, TMG is unable to scan files it cannot decrypt.

- **Block Files If Scanning Time Exceeds (Seconds)** To optimize the end-user experience, TMG allows you to configure a timeout for file scanning. The default value is 300 seconds (5 minutes).

- **Block Files If Archive Depth Level Exceeds** This option is one way for advanced users or malicious Web sites to evade or cause overflow conditions for scanning mechanisms. An archive file is fed to the archive application repeatedly to produce an archive that contains an archive, which contains an archive, and so on. This option allows you to mitigate such attempts by setting a maximum archive depth level that TMG will seek before blocking the file.

- **Block Files Larger Than (MB)** By default TMG blocks files larger than 1,000 MB (1 GB). This default setting helps reduce the performance and time impact of large file scanning.

- **Block Archive Files If Unpacked Content Is Larger Than (MB)** TMG will decompress archive files so that the contents may be scanned. To limit the performance impact to TMG you should keep this value low. By default this limit is 4,095 MB (4 GB).

Content Delivery

You can configure malware inspection content delivery options by clicking the Content Delivery tab, as shown in Figure 17-16.

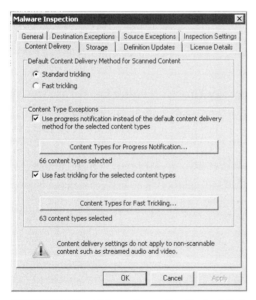

FIGURE 17-16 The Malware inspection Content Delivery tab

The default content delivery option uses standard trickling. This method uses slow packet delivery to the user to keep the connection alive and thus avoid application failure. The other available method for content delivery is called *fast trickling*. If you select this method TMG sends the data to the user as fast as possible, but in the last part of the transfer the data is held until TMG completes the scan. The caveat is that it uses more resources from the TMG; however, the user experience is enhanced.

You can also specify which types of content will be excepted from Malware Inspection. The option Use Download Progress Notification Instead Of The Default Method For The Selected Content Types includes 66 content types by default. You can specify more by clicking Content Types For Progress Notification. If you click the Content Types tab, the window shown in Figure 17-17 will appear.

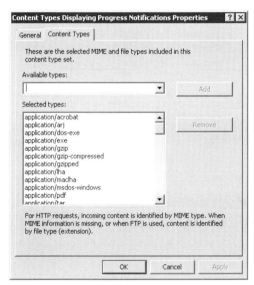

FIGURE 17-17 The Content Types Displaying Progress Notifications Properties dialog box

In the Available Types drop-down, click the drop-down button to select the content type that you want to add, and then click Add. If you want to remove a specific content type from the list, select it in the Selected Types combo box and click Remove. The same approach applies to the Content Types For Fast Trickling button shown in Figure 17-16. As explained earlier, fast trickling enhances the user's experience; therefore, some content will use this method by default. The content types for fast trickling primarily target the media type file by default, which makes sense because these types of files are those for which latency imposed by scanning mechanisms could greatly impact the user experience.

Storage

When TMG is inspecting a file it temporarily stores this file in the %systemroot%\temp\ScanStorage folder by default. You can change that setting using the Storage tab, as shown in Figure 17-18.

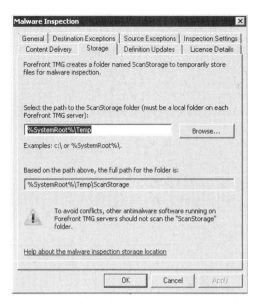

FIGURE 17-18 The Malware Inspection Storage tab

> **NOTE** Do not change the default settings for this folder (NTFS permissions and compression); if you have file-based antivirus running on TMG it is recommended that you exclude this folder from real-time scanning. For more information about antivirus recommendations on TMG (and ISA), review the article *http://technet.microsoft.com/en-us/library/cc707727.aspx*.

Update Configuration

TMG uses the settings under the Definition Updates tab to control the automatic update of malware definitions and the polling frequency, as shown in Figure 17-19.

By default TMG will check for and install new updates automatically, which is the recommended option. You can use the drop-down menus to change these settings. In addition to the default, the available options are:

- **Only Check For Updates** This option will not install new updates—it only verifies and notifies that new updates are available.
- **Do Nothing Automatically** This forces the administrator to manually check for new updates.

The automatic polling options are 15 minutes, 30 minutes, 45 minutes, 1 hour, or 4 hours. The recommendation is to leave the default (15 minutes) to ensure that TMG has the most current signatures.

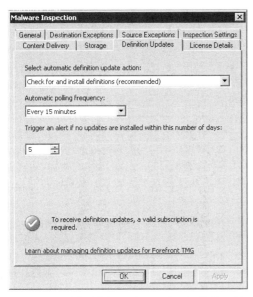

FIGURE 17-19 The Malware Inspection Definition Updates tab

License

To receive new definitions through the update service you need to have a valid subscription with Microsoft. By clicking the License Details tab you can verify which license agreement you have and its expiration date, as shown in Figure 17-20.

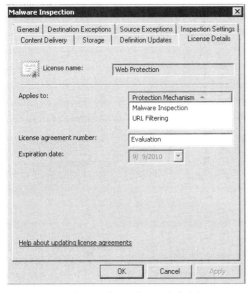

FIGURE 17-20 License for malware definitions

Defining Per-Rule Malware Inspection

Now that the global settings are configured according to your environment's needs, you can define malware inspection settings for each access rule. The following steps illustrate this process:

> **NOTE** For more information about access rules, review Chapter 12, "Understanding Access Rules."

1. On the Forefront TMG Management Console, click Web Access Policy.
2. Select the access rule that you want to change, right-click it, and choose Properties as shown in Figure 17-21.

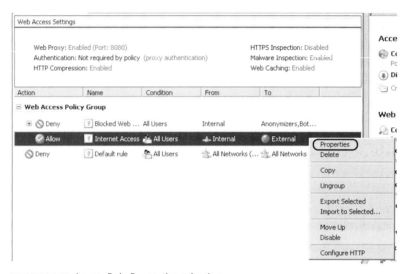

FIGURE 17-21 Access Rule Properties selection

3. Click the Malware Inspection tab, as shown in Figure 17-22.

> **MORE INFO** On the Malware Inspection tab shown in Figure 17-22, Malware Inspection is selected because the check box Inspect Content Downloaded From Web Servers To Clients is selected. You can disable this option if you don't want to inspect for malware in this rule. You can customize malware settings just for this rule by enabling the option Use Rule Specific Settings For Malware Inspection. When you enable this option, the Rule Settings button becomes available. If you click it you will see the same options shown in Figure 17-16.

For purposes of this example, leave the default options and click OK.

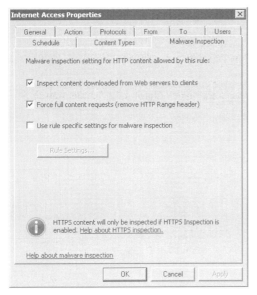

FIGURE 17-22 The Access Rule properties Malware Inspection tab

Testing Internet Access with Malware Inspection

The scenario in this section will be the same as the one used in Figure 17-5. The target Web site will be the European Institute for Computer Antivirus Research (EICAR), *http://www.eicar.org*. EICAR provides standard virus test files that can be used to validate your antivirus solution; those files are located at *http://www.eicar.org/anti_virus_test_file.htm*.

> **NOTE**   Please read the important note in this page and the EICAR code of conduct at *http://www.eicar.org/about_us/code_of_conduct.htm* before downloading these test files in your environment.

Follow these steps to perform this validation:

1. Click Forefront TMG (Array Name) in the left pane.
2. Click the Logs & Reports node in the left pane and then click Edit Filter in the Task pane, as shown in Figure 17-23.
3. In the Filter By drop-down list, select Client IP.
4. In the Condition drop-down list, select Equals.
5. In the Value field, enter the IP address of the test client, such as **10.10.10.9**. Figure 17-24 shows the resulting display.

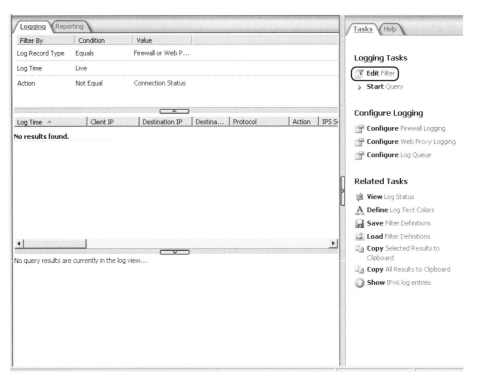

FIGURE 17-23 The Configuring Logging feature

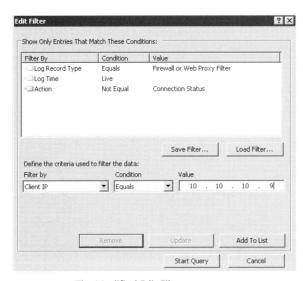

FIGURE 17-24 The Modified Edit Filter page

6. Click Add To List and then click Start Query.

7. At a test client workstation, launch Internet Explorer and open the Web site *http://www.eicar.org/anti_virus_test_file.htm*.

8. Click the file called eicar.com in the download area for HTTP Protocol. The user will receive the notification from TMG, as shown in Figure 17-25.

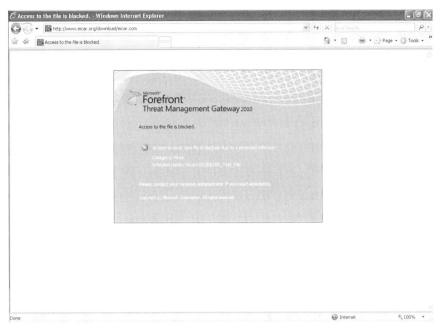

FIGURE 17-25 The TMG Blocked File error page

9. In TMG Logging you can see that the file was blocked, along with details about the reason why was blocked. Because there are more fields than will fit in the screen, Figures 17-26 and 17-27 show the main fields for this type of access.

FIGURE 17-26 TMG Blocked File log example

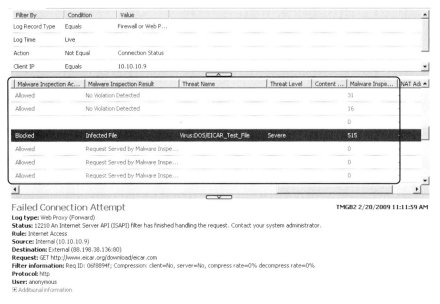

Filter By	Condition	Value
Log Record Type	Equals	Firewall or Web P…
Log Time	Live	
Action	Not Equal	Connection Status
Client IP	Equals	10.10.10.9

Malware Inspection Ac…	Malware Inspection Result	Threat Name	Threat Level	Content …	Malware Inspe…	NAT Ad
Allowed	No Violation Detected				31	
Allowed	No Violation Detected				16	
					0	
Blocked	Infected File	Virus:DOS/EICAR_Test_File	Severe		515	
Allowed	Request Served by Malware Inspe…				0	
Allowed	Request Served by Malware Inspe…				0	
Allowed	Request Served by Malware Inspe…				0	

Failed Connection Attempt   TMGB2 2/20/2009 11:11:59 AM

Log type: Web Proxy (Forward)
Status: 12210 An Internet Server API (ISAPI) filter has finished handling the request. Contact your system administrator.
Rule: Internet Access
Source: Internal (10.10.10.9)
Destination: External (88.198.38.136:80)
Request: GET http://www.eicar.org/download/eicar.com
Filter information: Req ID: 06f8894f; Compression: client=No, server=No, compress rate=0% decompress rate=0%
Protocol: http
User: anonymous
⊞ Additional information

FIGURE 17-27 TMG Malware Inspection details

Creating Reports with Malware Statistics

With the introduction of new features such as malware inspection, TMG provides reporting to create permanent records of common usage patterns to summarize and analyze log information for malware activity. A malware inspection content report shows the names of current threats, the users and Web sites that generate the largest number of malware incidents, and statistics regarding the Malware filter and a daily summary of malware activity. The report will collect activity from the previous day or earlier. Two types of reports can be generated to view this information:

- **One-time reports** These are one-time ad-hoc reports that can provide the TMG administrator with an immediate picture of the activity recorded by TMG over a specified period.

- **Recurring reports** These are scheduled automated reports on a daily, weekly, or monthly basis. The time periods available for this report are more structured than those for a one-time report. The reports generated will show daily activity, weekly activity, or monthly activity depending on how it is set.

TMG reports are based on log summaries derived from the Web Proxy and Firewall logs. Using SQL Server reporting services, TMG generates two types of log summaries, daily and monthly, which all reports are based on. Log summaries are generated at night (by default at 12:30 A.M.); however, this time is configurable.

Configuring a One-Time Report

To configure a one-time report, follow these steps:

1. Click Logs & Reports in the TMG console, click the Reporting tab, and then click Create One-Time Report under Tasks in the right pane as shown in Figure 17-28.

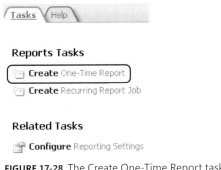

FIGURE 17-28 The Create One-Time Report task

2. The One-Time Report Wizard launches, as shown in Figure 17-29. Enter a name for the report and click Next.

FIGURE 17-29 The Welcome To The One-Time Report Wizard page

3. On the Report Period page, shown in Figure 17-30, you can specify the start time and end time for data collection to be shown in the report. The start and end times can be based on a day or a month. Because reports are based on the previous day, the date needs to be prior to the current date. After selecting the start and end dates, click Next.

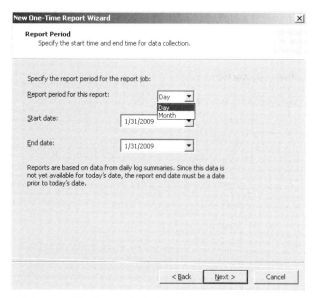

FIGURE 17-30 The Report Period page

4. On the Report Content page, shown in Figure 17-31, you can select the content to be included in the report. If you want only malware statistics, clear all other check boxes except Malware Protection and click Next.

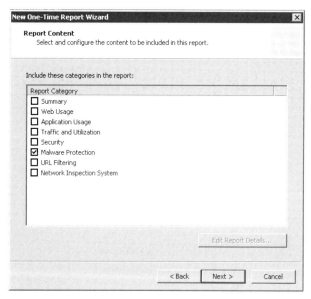

FIGURE 17-31 The Report Content page

5. On the Send E-Mail Notification page, shown in Figure 17-32, you can configure TMG to send e-mail notification for completed reports. After filling in the relevant fields, click Next.

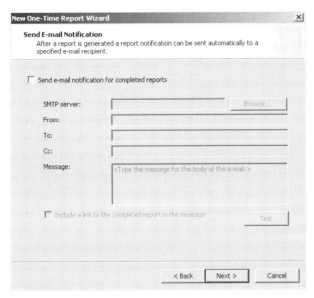

FIGURE 17-32 The Send E-Mail Notification page

6. On the Report Publishing page, shown in Figure 17-33, the administrator can choose to publish the report to a central directory either on the same TMG server or a remote different server. After filling in the relevant fields, click Next.

> **NOTE** The destination path must exist because TMG report generator will not create it. When publishing a report, TMG requires write permissions to the folder where you publish the report. By default, the Local System account is used to publish the report. However, if you publish the report to a folder that resides on a different computer, the Local System account credentials are passed as the account of the TMG firewall. Therefore, the TMG account must have sufficient permissions to write to the destination folder. If you specify a user account to publish the report, you must make sure that this user account is granted write permissions to the destination folder. If TMG is installed in a workgroup, TMG uses anonymous credentials. In this case, we recommend that you specify user credentials when publishing reports to another computer.

7. On the Completing the One-Time Report Wizard page, shown in Figure 17-34, you are notified that you have successfully completed the One-Time Report Wizard. You can also view a brief summary of the report's configuration. Click Finish.

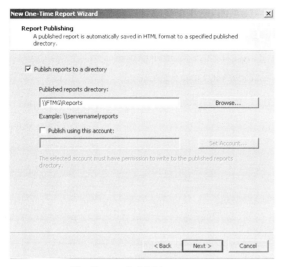

FIGURE 17-33 The Report Publishing page

FIGURE 17-34 The Completing The One-Time Report Wizard page

8. The report now appears under the Reporting tab with the information that you just configured, as shown in Figure 17-35. Click Apply to process the report.

FIGURE 17-35 One-Time Report summary

Configuring a Recurring Report

To configure a Recurring Report job, follow these steps:

1. Click Logs & Reports in the TMG console and then click Create Recurring Report Job under Tasks in the right pane, as shown in Figure 17-36.

FIGURE 17-36 Create Recurring Report Job

2. The One-Time Report Wizard launches, as shown in Figure 17-37. Enter a name for the report job and click Next.

FIGURE 17-37 The Welcome To The One-Time Report Wizard page

3. On the Recurring Report Job Scheduling page, shown in Figure 17-38, you can specify how often the reporting job will run. You can choose to create a recurring report on a daily, weekly, or monthly basis. After making the selection, click Next.

4. On the Report Content page, shown in Figure 17-39, you can select the content to be included in the report. If you want only malware statistics, clear all other check boxes except Malware Protection and click Next.

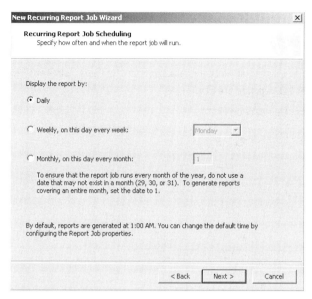

FIGURE 17-38 The Recurring Report Job Scheduling page

FIGURE 17-39 The Report Content page

5. On the Send E-Mail Notification page, shown in Figure 17-40, you can configure TMG to send e-mail notification for completed reports. The following fields need to be filled by the administrator:

- **SMTP Server** This field is used to specify the SMTP server from which TMG will send the e-mail.

- **From**   This field is used to specify whether the e-mail needs to be delivered from a specific name or e-mail address.
- **To**   This field is used to specify one or more recipients for the e-mail notification.
- **Message**   This field is used to specify a message that the administrator would like to be delivered whenever reports are complete.

6. After filling in the relevant fields, click Next.

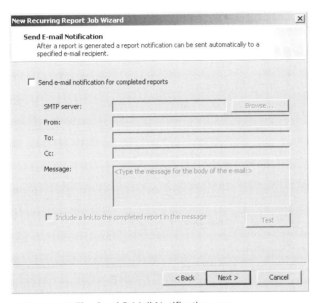

FIGURE 17-40 The Send E-Mail Notification page

7. On the Report Publishing page, shown in Figure 17-41, the administrator can choose to publish the report to a central directory either on the same TMG computer or on a remote computer. For a recurring report job, you are required to publish the reports to a central server or a local share; otherwise, the wizard will fail with an error. After filling in the relevant fields, click Next.

> **NOTE**   The destination path must exist because TMG report generator will not create it. When publishing a report, TMG requires write permissions to the folder where you publish the report. By default, the Local System account is used to publish the report. However, if you publish the report to a folder that resides on a different computer, the Local System account credentials are passed as the account of the TMG firewall. Therefore, the TMG account must have sufficient permissions to write to the destination folder. If you specify a user account to publish the report, you must make sure that this user account is granted write permissions to the destination folder. If TMG is installed in a workgroup, TMG uses anonymous credentials. In this case, we recommend that you specify user credentials when publishing reports to another computer.

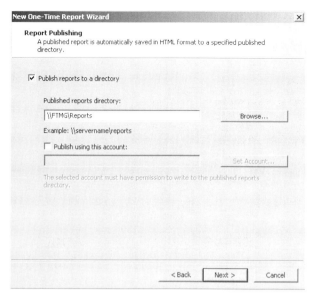

FIGURE 17-41 The Report Publishing page

8. On the Completing The Recurring Report Job Wizard page, shown in Figure 17-42, you are notified that you have successfully completed the Recurring Report Job Wizard. You can also view a brief summary of the report's configuration. Click Finish.

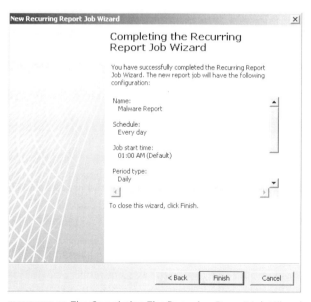

FIGURE 17-42 The Completing The Recurring Report Job Wizard page

9. The report now appears under the Reporting tab with the information that you just configured, as shown in Figure 17-43. Click Apply to process the report.

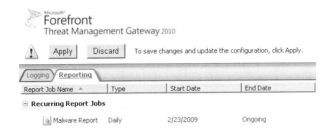

FIGURE 17-43 Recurring Report summary

Generating and Viewing Malware Inspection Reports

Publishing reports allows you to share the report data with others who do not have access to TMG physically or to the TMG console remotely. In the case of one-time reports, publishing also allows you to save a snapshot of the data for the time period specified in the report. Note that recurring report jobs are always published; publishing one-time reports is optional.

Published reports are stored in a subfolder of the directory you specify named *<Report_Job_Name>_* (*Start date—End date*). For example, if you publish a report job named DailyReports, scheduled to run from January 1, 2009 through January 15, 2009, the published reports folder will be named DailyReports_(1.1.2009—1.15.2009).

To generate and view the report, right-click the report and choose Generate And View Report, as shown in Figure 17-44, or click View Published Report under Tasks in the right pane under Logs & Reporting, as shown in Figure 17-45.

FIGURE 17-44 Generate And View Report

Reports Tasks

Create One-Time Report

Create Recurring Report Job

Generate and View Selected
Report

View Published Report

Edit Selected

Delete Selected

FIGURE 17-45 View Published Report

A dialog box with turning gears and the message Generating The Report, Please Wait... appears, as shown in Figure 17-46.

FIGURE 17-46 Generating The Report

The report.htm opens in a browser window with the summary view and a statistical report view of the top threats, top Web sites, top users, inspection times, and a summary of the inspection statistics, as shown in Figures 17-47 through 17-56.

Malware Protection
- Top Threats
- Top Web Sites
- Top Users
- Inspection Times
- Inspection Statistics

FIGURE 17-47 Malware protection report quick links

Top Threats

The following threats were most frequently encountered by the HTTP Malware Protection filter during the report period. Most frequent threats are listed first.

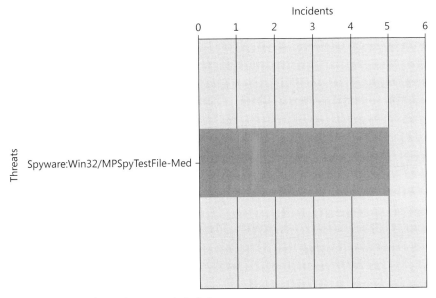

FIGURE 17-48 Top malware threats statistical view

No	Threat	Threat Level	Incidents	% of Total Incidents
1	Spyware:Win32/MPSpyTestFile-Med	Medium	5	100.00 %
	Total		**5**	**100.00 %**

FIGURE 17-49 Top malware threats summary view

Top Web Sites

Client downloads from the following Web sites generated the largest number of malware incidents during the report period. Web sites which generated the most incidents are listed first.

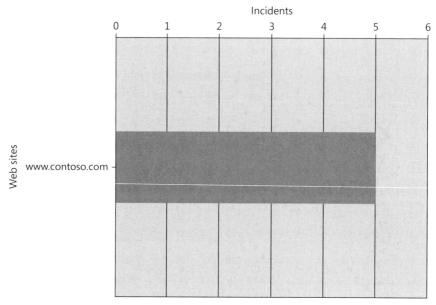

FIGURE 17-50 Top Web sites generating malware statistical view

No	Site	Incidents	% of Total Incidents
1	www.contoso.com	5	100.00 %
	Total	**5**	**100.00 %**

FIGURE 17-51 Top Web sites generating malware summary view

Top Users

The following users generated the largest number of incidents in which malware was detected during the report period. Users who generated the most incidents are listed first. Network addresses are presented when user names are unknown to Forefront TMG (unauthenticated Web Proxy clients).

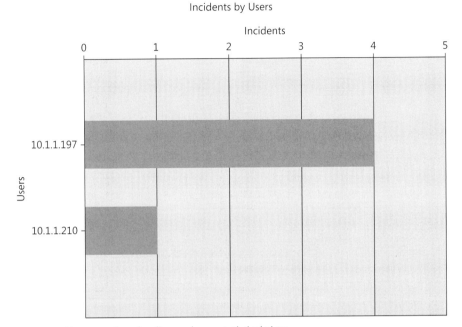

FIGURE 17-52 Top users downloading malware statistical view

No	User	Incidents	% of Total Incidents	Total files blocked	Total files cleaned
1	10.1.1.197	4	80.00 %	4	0
2	10.1.1.210	1	20.00 %	1	0
	Total	**5**	**100.00 %**	**5**	**0**

FIGURE 17-53 Top users downloading malware summary view

Inspection Times

The following report shows the Web sites for which client downloads required the longest average inspection time. Sites with longest average inspection duration are listed first.

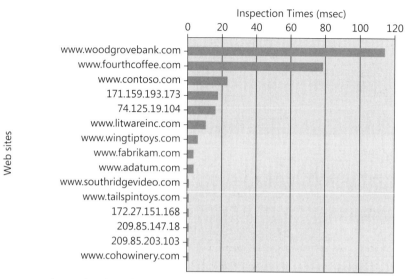

FIGURE 17-54 Inspection times for Web sites statistical view

No.	Site	Average Inspection Times (msec)	Requests	% of Total Requests
1	www.woodgrovebank.com	114.20	179	37.68 %
2	www.fourthcoffee.com	79.00	1	0.21 %
3	www.contoso.com	23.16	37	7.79 %
4	171.159.193.173	17.54	41	8.63 %
5	74.125.19.104	16.40	5	1.05 %
6	www.litwareinc.com	10.38	21	4.42 %
7	www.wingtiptoys.com	5.96	154	32.42 %
8	www.fabrikam.com	3.33	6	1.26 %
9	www.adatum.com	3.33	6	1.26 %
10	www.southridgevideo.com	1.00	1	0.21 %
11	www.tailspintoys.com	1.00	2	0.42 %
12	172.27.151.168	1.00	8	1.68 %
13	209.85.147.18	1.00	10	2.11 %
14	209.85.203.103	1.00	2	0.42 %
15	www.cohowinery.com	1.00	2	0.42 %
	Total	**49.22**	**475**	**100.00 %**

FIGURE 17-55 Average inspection time for Web sites summary view

Inspection Statistics

The following report shows general statistics summarizing the HTTP malware protection during the report period.

Total number of files scanned	475
Total number of files blocked due to malware	5
Total number of files cleaned from malware	0
Total number of files containing malware	5
Average file inspection duration (msec)	49

FIGURE 17-56 Total inspection statistics summary

This is an example of what a report that has been just set for malware inspection content looks like. A one-time report and a recurring report job would both present the same output. The only difference is the generation mechanism. A one-time report needs to be generated before it is published, whereas a recurring report job gets published automatically at 12:30 A.M. or whatever time the TMG administrator defines. By using this report the TMG administrator can get a quick snapshot of the network or use the data over a period of time to summarize and analyze usage patterns and monitor network security.

 REAL WORLD **Reports Failure Scenarios**

In the real world we often hear questions about reports not being generated or some general questions about a report or its data. We have collected some general scenarios we have heard a lot of questions about in Table 17-1.

TABLE 17-1 Real-World Scenarios Questions and Resolution

SCENARIO	RESOLUTION
Reports for current day cannot be viewed.	TMG creates reports from log summaries. By default, the daily summary log process runs at 12:30 A.M. regardless of whether you have scheduled reports. This time is configurable, however. Reports are created from those logs. Therefore, even if you request the report immediately, the current day's report data will not be available for viewing until the next day.
Reports are only displaying IP addresses instead of user names.	By default all Web Proxy clients send anonymous authentication to TMG. If the Access rule is allowing traffic for a computer set and not by domain user groups, the IP address will be logged instead of user names.

SCENARIO	RESOLUTION
Unknown protocols appear in reports.	Any protocol that isn't a part of the predefined protocol list in TMG will appear as unknown in the TMG report.
Report job was configured as Generate Once A Month; however, reports are not being generated monthly.	When selecting Generate Once A Month, you may have selected the date as 29th, 30th, or 31st. Reports are only generated after the previous day and not all months have a 29th, 30th, or 31st. Changing the date to the 1st will generate a report for every month, and the report will be generated the day after the month completes.

Customizing Malware Inspection Content in Reports

An administrator can customize the malware report that is to be generated based on the number of elements that need to be seen in the report. To customize malware reports, click Logs & Reports in the TMG console and follow these steps:

1. Select the report that was created previously and then click Edit Selected.

2. Click Content tab, highlight Malware Protection, and click Edit Report Details.

3. In the Report Details window, click the Subcategory drop-down box and select Top Threats as shown in Figure 17-57.

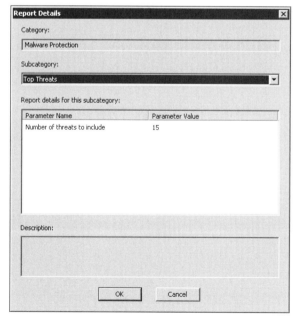

FIGURE 17-57 Customizing the number of top threats

4. In this window you can change the parameter value for the number of top threats by highlighting the default value (15) and typing the new value. When you are finished, click OK twice and then click Apply to apply the changes.

You can also customize the following subcategories:

- **Inspection Times**   Allows you to determine the number of sites to be included in the report
- **Top Users**   Allows you to specify the number of users that will appear in the report
- **Top Web Sites**   The rank of the first X Web sites, where X is the parameter that you can customize (15 is the default)

Summary

In this chapter you learned how TMG malware inspection works and how this feature can assist you in mitigating threats for Internet access in an environment where TMG is used as an Internet gateway. TMG malware inspection includes a single malware inspection engine that is tuned specifically for HTTP traffic and allows you to control how and when the engine is used. You also learned how to configure global settings for malware inspection and also per-rule-based configuration. You learned how to configure TMG reports and how they can assist you in understanding malware inspection statistics on traffic from your protected networks, such as what top threats were detected by TMG. In the next chapter you will learn about another layer of protection for outbound access using URL filtering.

## CHAPTER 18

URL Filtering

- How URL Filtering Works   **465**

- Configuring URL Filtering   **470**

- Update Center   **478**

- Summary   **485**

One of the biggest challenges for a firewall administrator is to keep internal users away from sites that are not allowed by company policy. Company policy usually determines which sites internal users can't access by categorizing the subject—not the site itself. To accomplish this you will need a feature that dynamically obtains updates about sites that are considered part of a category that should be blocked. URL Filtering brings this capability to Forefront TMG. By using the Microsoft Reputation Service (MRS) you have the dynamism and accuracy that you need to meet your company's requirements.

How URL Filtering Works

URL filtering enhances TMG firewall policies by controlling access to Web sites based on their URL category membership. Unlike policies based on domain name sets or URL sets, this feature works dynamically. Web sites categorized by the MRS are posted to Microsoft Update (MU) and downloaded from MU by TMG. MRS aggregates reputation data from multiple vendors and uses telemetry to improve data accuracy. Figure 18-1 shows the relationship between URL Filtering action and updates.

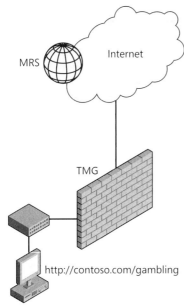

MRS

Internet

TMG

http://contoso.com/gambling

Client Workstation

FIGURE 18-1 URL Filtering decision flow

The following steps offer a very high-level overview of how URL Filtering works:

1. User sends a request for a Web site.

2. TMG intercepts the request and determines whether URL categorization is needed. TMG needs to determine the category to which this URL belongs to allow or deny this traffic based on the rules available.

3. If URL categorization is needed, name resolution is done for the URL and the URL is matched to a category.

4. When URL categorization is not needed, TMG marks the request as not categorized and logs the category to be used in case it needs to send a denial to the user.

5. The rule allowing the request is then matched and TMG determines whether the rule allows or denies the category.

6. If categorization is needed at the rule, a request marked as not categorized is blocked and a denial is sent to the user; otherwise, the rule verifies the category matched and then TMG allows or denies the action based on whether the rule allows that category.

The diagram shown in Figure 18-2 also describes the same decision flow for TMG, as discussed in the preceding steps when it when receives a request from the client to access a Web site.

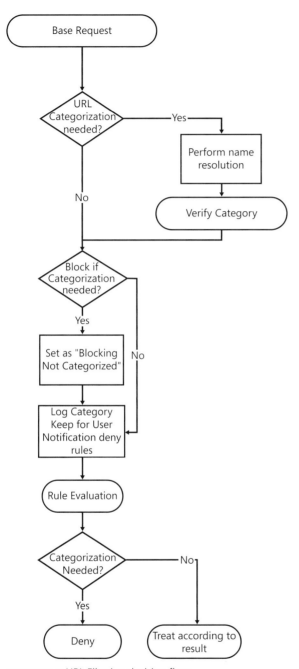

FIGURE 18-2 URL Filtering decision flow

To understand how URL Filtering works under the hood, let's take a look to the following sample scenario:

A client in the internal network sends a request for a Web site with the URL *http://www .fabrikam.com/patha/pathb* to TMG. When receiving this URL, TMG needs to determine the category this URL belongs to in order to allow or deny this traffic according to the access policy rules. To do so, TMG cuts this URL into parts called *variants* in the terminology of MRS. The variants for this URL will be:

- Com
- fabrikam.com
- www.fabrikam.com
- www.fabrikam.com/patha
- www.fabrikam.com/patha/pathb

TMG sends the list of these variants to MRS to determine their reputation. MRS replies to the TMG with the following response:

- **Com**   unknown
- **fabrikam.com**   "general business"
- **www.fabrikam.com**   unknown
- **www.fabrikam.com/patha**   "phishing" (Not inherited)
- **www.fabrikam.com/somepath/pathb**   "anonymizer"

In the preceding response, *Not inherited* means that the category determined for *http://www.fabrikam.com/patha* is not inherited down to subpaths like *http://www.fabrikam .com/patha/pathb*.

> **NOTE**   In some cases, MRS might return a response to a variant as Inherited. For instance, in the preceding example, if the response to *http://www.fabrikam.com/patha* was flagged as "inherited", it would mean that *http://www.fabrikam.com/patha/pathb* would be categorized as Phishing because it inherits the categorization from the parent (*http://www.fabrikam.com/patha*).

Based on the response, TMG knows that two categories might apply to this URL:

- General business
- Anonymizer

To identify the category that will apply, TMG does some sorting of the possible categories
based on their importance by evaluating parameters such as the category with the highest
hierarchy from the returned categories. In this example, we can consider that the Anonymizer
category might be the most important category, meaning the category that an administrator
might want to block access to. The URL category information obtained from MRS is then used
at different places in TMG as follows:

- **Firewall rules**   Allow or deny according to the category
- **Web Proxy Log**   The category is written in the log for each request (will be used for
  reporting)
- **Enterprise Malware Protection (EMP) exclusion list**
- **HTTPS exclusion list (For instance, we don't want to inspect sites that
  belong to the Financial category.)**

Components Involved in URL Filtering

URL categorization is only called if both of the following conditions are met:

- URL Filtering is enabled
- Categories are required by either policy rules or log

URL Filtering operates as part of the Microsoft Firewall Service (wspsrv.exe). The categorizer
component has an important role in the whole URL Filtering process because it is responsible
for interacting with the core TMG components involved in this process (rules engine, malware
protection exception, HTTPS exception, category query, and deny page). The other component
that plays an important role during the categorization is the MRS categorizer, which gathers
information from the MRS Service provided by Microsoft using Windows Web Services API
(WWSAPI) via calls to WinHTTP.

Figure 18-3 shows a diagram with these components.

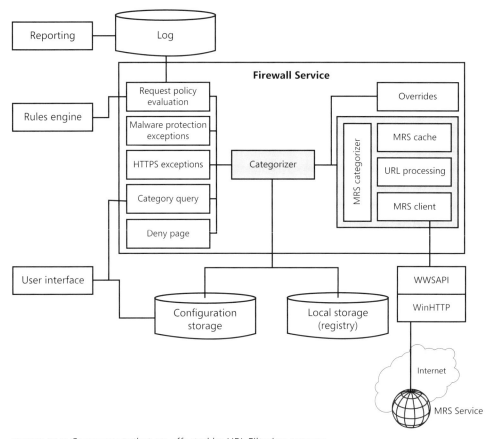

FIGURE 18-3 Components that are affected by URL Filtering process

The changes to URL categorization made through the user interface are controlled by the categorizer.

Configuring URL Filtering

For URL Filtering to satisfy your organization's Internet security and compliance goals, you will have to translate the legal and corporate phrasing into terms that describe content delivered from the Internet. For instance, if your company policy states "no one may access malicious content from within the company network," you must be able to transform that generic statement into something your Internet gateway is able to act on.

REAL WORLD **URL Categories, Bing Safe Search, and Microsoft Reputation Services**

At about the same time that TMG beta 3 was released, the Bing search team released Bing on an unsuspecting public (and an unsuspecting competition). One thing Bing offers is a feature called safe search, which provides the means to help the gateway administrator block requests for pornographic content by configuring the Web Proxy component to append a query string as *adlt=strict* to the original request; the intent of this is to trigger the Bing service to filter out any content that might be considered offensive.

Unfortunately, the requirement to add information to the client's original request could not be implemented with ISA or TMG, so many administrators were less than pleased with this solution. Fortunately, the Forefront Edge community is known for its verbosity and the Bing team was quickly overrun with requests to provide a more Microsoft-friendly method.

To answer this need, the Bing Safe Search team created a new domain namespace for use by Web Proxy administrators who cannot take advantage of Microsoft Reputation Services (MRS) or who cannot use the query string method. The new domain namespace they used is *explicit.bing.net,* which makes it possible for ISA administrators to take advantage of Bing Safe Search.

During testing of these domains, we discovered that MRS had categorized this domain namespace as "mature content" instead of "pornography," as the Bing team wanted. After a short exchange of e-mail between the MRS and Bing teams, this domain namespace was re-categorized as "pornography" as shown in Figure 18-4. Now there are three methods for blocking Bing searches that produce potentially offensive content: adding "adlt=strict" to the request, blocking domain names, and URL categories.

You can read more about this at *http://www.bing.com/community/blogs/search/ archive/2009/06/04/smart-motion-preview-and-safesearch.aspx* and at *http://blogs.technet.com/isablog/archive/2009/06/19/bing-safe-search-isa- server-and-forefront-tmg.aspx.*

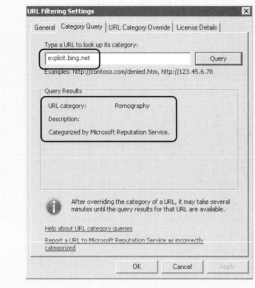

FIGURE 18-4 Bing safe search categorization

After you install TMG and complete the Getting Started Wizard, you are offered the opportunity to run the Web Access Wizard, during which you can choose whether TMG will use the recommended URL Filtering configuration or one of your own devising. For this process, we assume that you have chosen to let the wizard build the default rules for you.

Global URL Filtering Configuration

URL Filtering requires that you make choices for TMG globally and on a per-rule basis. The following steps describe the process for configuring URL Filtering separate from the Web Access Wizard. Figure 18-5 shows the location of the global URL configuration options.

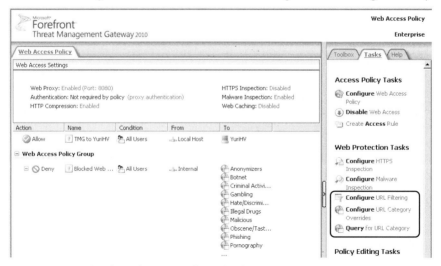

FIGURE 18-5 Starting the Web Access Policy Wizard

In this scenario, the Contoso Security team has reviewed the default blocked URL categories defined by TMG and has decided that they want you to augment the Web policy created by the Web Access Wizard default action with the following sites:

- Name: Contoso Blocked Categories
- URL categories:
  - Dating/Personals
  - Media Sharing
  - Web Phone

Additionally, they want the user to know what URL category was matched for any denied requests so that categories can be adjusted as needed.

To configure global URL Filtering, use the following steps:

1. In the left pane of the TMG management console, select Web Access Policy.
2. In the right pane, click Configure URL Filtering.
3. To enable URL Filtering globally, on the General tab of the URL Filtering Settings dialog box, select Enable URL Filtering as shown in Figure 18-6.

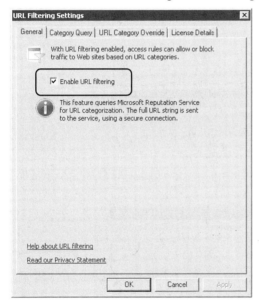

FIGURE 18-6 URL Filtering control setting

IMPORTANT **If any rule depends on URL categories or URL sets and you disable URL Filtering globally, the TMG firewall policy engine cannot match the client requests to URL categories or sets and will not process those rules in the context of the current request.**

4. In the URL Filtering Settings dialog box, click the URL Category Override tab. Note that by default this list is empty.

NOTE You can add the sites provided by the Contoso Security team to this list, but you cannot create a new category from this page. Because you need to create a new category set, you need to do this in the Toolbox.

5. Click OK to close the URL Filtering Settings dialog box.

6. In the right pane of the TMG management console, click the Toolbox tab.

7. In the Toolbox, click New and then click URL Category Set as shown in Figure 18-7.

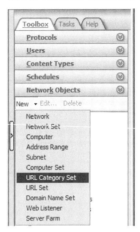

FIGURE 18-7 Creating a new URL category set

8. On the Welcome To The New URL Category Set Wizard page, type **Contoso Blocked Categories** and click Next.

9. On the URL Category Selection page, do the following:

   a. Select Includes All Selected URL Categories.

   b. In the URL Category list, select Dating / Personals, Media Sharing, and Web Phone as shown in Figure 18-8. Click Next.

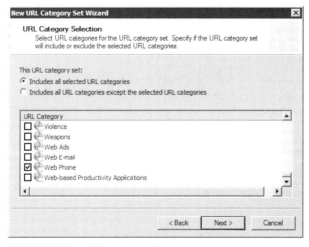

FIGURE 18-8 New URL category items

10. On the Completing The New URL Category Set Wizard summary page, verify that the configuration agrees with that described by the Contoso Security team and click Finish.

Rule-Based URL Filtering Configuration

Now that you have the primary URL Filtering configuration defined, you need to update the default rule built by the Web Access Wizard so that it behaves as directed by Contoso Security. To do so, follow these steps:

1. In the TMG management console center pane, double-click the Blocked Web Destinations deny rule.

2. In the Blocked Web Destinations Properties dialog box, click the To tab, and then click Add.

3. In the Add Network Entities dialog box, expand URL Category Sets, select Contoso Blocked Categories, click Add, and then click Close.

4. In the Blocked Web Destination properties dialog box, verify that the destinations list appears as shown in Figure 18-9.

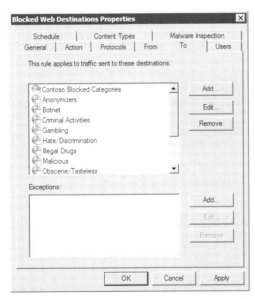

FIGURE 18-9 Modified Blocked Web Destination rule

5. Click the Action tab.

6. In the Denied URL Request Action section, do the following:

   a. Select Display Denial Notification To User.

   b. Type **Access to this site is blocked by Contoso Security** in the Add Custom Text Or HTML To Notification Text field.

   c. Select Add Denied Request Category To Notification.

The rule Action tab should appear, as shown in Figure 18-10.

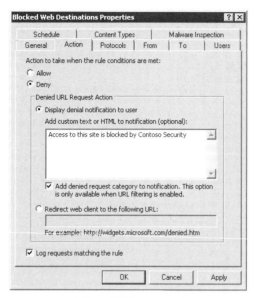

FIGURE 18-10 Adjusted Web access rule

> **NOTE** You may customize the appearance of the message text in this text box by using HTML properties. You can only include HTML that may be contained in a <body> element. You can read more about the <body> element at *http://msdn.microsoft.com/library/ms535205(VS.85).aspx.*

7. Click OK to close the Blocked Web Destinations Properties dialog box.
8. In the TMG management console center pane, click Apply to enforce the rule changes. When prompted by Change Control, enter a description of your actions and click Apply.

Testing URL Filtering

You've created a configuration that should satisfy the Contoso Security team's desires, but unless you know of a URL that will trigger the Blocked Destinations rule, you can't verify this state. Luckily, the Bing Safe Search team has seen fit to provide just such a mechanism.

At any client served by TMG, open a browser and type **explicit.bing.net** in the address bar. You should receive a response, as shown in Figure 18-11.

Notice that the request denial page includes the messaging you specified in step 6 of Rule-Based URL Filtering Configuration. When you examine the TMG logs for requests where the URL contains *bing*, you'll see an entry similar to that shown in Figure 18-12.

FIGURE 18-11 URL Filtering block message

FIGURE 18-12 Log entry for URL category action

URL Category Overrides

Now that you have the URL categories configured per the Contoso Security team's direction, the Contoso Security team is satisfied that their Web access policies will be enforced—that is, until the CEO discovers that a site she needs to reach (*http://www.margiestravel.com*) is categorized as "Malicious" according to the TMG error she just received. Because she's trying to demonstrate this site during a board meeting, she's not happy and she wants this fixed—*now*.

Use the following steps to provide an exception for this site:

1. In the right pane of the TMG management console, click the Tasks tab.
2. In the Tasks pane, click URL Category Overrides.
3. In the URL Filtering Settings dialog box, click Add.
4. In the URL Categories Override dialog box, in the Override The Default URL Category For This URL Pattern text box, type **www.margiestravel.com/*** as shown in Figure 18-13.
5. In the Move URL Pattern To This URL Category drop-down list, select General Business, and then click OK.

FIGURE 18-13 New URL category override

6. In the URL Filtering Settings dialog box, click OK.
7. In the TMG management console center pane, click Apply. When prompted for a change comment, click Apply again.

Update Center

Forefront TMG maintains the definitions of known viruses, worms, and other malware. To keep these important definitions up to date, Forefront TMG has built in a centralized mechanism called the Update Center that allows the administrator to configure the update frequency as well as the automatic update action. The Update Center can be accessed from the Forefront TMG console.

The following features in TMG rely on signature updates:

- **Network Inspection System (NIS)**   Microsoft Update delivers signatures and protocols that help protect the network.
- **Malware Inspection**   Microsoft Update delivers Microsoft Antivirus definitions to filter virus-infected files that can be downloaded by the users from the Internet.

- **Exchange (Anti Spam)** Microsoft Update delivers Anti Spam signatures to the Exchange Anti Spam agent.
- **Forefront Security for Exchange (FSE)** Recipient Update Services deliver definitions to multiple antivirus engines used in FSE.
- **URL Filtering Updates** Microsoft Updates delivers new URL Filtering categories to filter out unwanted sites.

How Update Center Works

By default, Forefront TMG uses the Windows Automatic Updates agent to pull updates from the Microsoft Update service to refresh definitions. The update agent uses the computer's default update server selection; therefore, if the computer uses updates from Windows Server Update Services (WSUS), the agent will also get updates from WSUS—otherwise it will get them directly from Microsoft Update. These transactions are recorded in the %systemroot%\windowsupdate.log file (as are the regular Windows Updates). The frequency settings in the Forefront TMG Update Center do not override the Windows Update settings. These settings are completely separate; therefore, Windows downloads software updates whereas Forefront TMG only downloads signatures.

The following sequence of actions (shown in Figure 18-14) is executed in the update process:

1. The TMG scheduler reads the schedule from the local policy store.
2. The scheduler then invokes Updateagent.exe.
3. The Updateagent.exe then calls the Windows Update API.
4. The Windows Update service communicates with Microsoft Update and downloads the update package. The service may be configured to check and retrieve the signatures in one of the following ways (provided that the server updates are managed by WSUS):
   - **Use WSUS server (Option 1)** TMG will request updates from the local WSUS server.
   - **Use Microsoft Update Live Servers (Option 2)** TMG will request updates from the live MU servers through the Internet.
   - **Use WSUS servers and if not working use Microsoft Update live servers (Default Option 1, then fall back to Option 2)** TMG will request updates from the local WSUS server and if the update does not exist, it will request it from the live Microsoft Updates servers.
5. The Windows Update service executes the package, which in turn unpacks and executes the stubs.

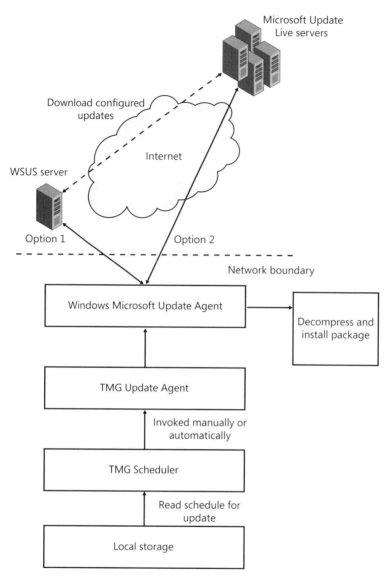

FIGURE 18-14 Basic flow of the TMG Update Center

After the Windows Update service unpacks and executes the stubs, each feature and package has its own procedure to get updated and stores information that is relevant to the feature itself. The following components are involved in the update process:

- **Update Agent (UpdateAgent.exe)** After it is invoked, the component is responsible for detecting an available update in Microsoft Update. If an update is available the agent downloads and installs it. After the update is installed, the firewall service is notified to load the definition.

- **TMG Scheduler (ISASCHED Service)** This service is responsible for invoking the update agent either automatically according to the polling frequency defined by the Administrator, or on manual request from the Administrator.
- **Local Storage (Registry)** This component stores the following update configuration–related information:
  - Update polling frequency (Minutes, Hours)
  - Update action (Check And Install, Check Only, No Automatic Action)
  - Number of days to trigger an alert after if an update was not received during this period
  - License expiration date (for the relevant services)

Configuring Update Center

To configure Update Center, follow these steps:

1. In the left pane of the TMG management console, click Update Center.
2. In the right pane, under Tasks, click Configure Settings as shown in Figure 18-15.

FIGURE 18-15 Configuring settings for Update Center

3. The Update Center Properties setting appears, with the Definition Updates tab selected as shown in Figure 18-16.

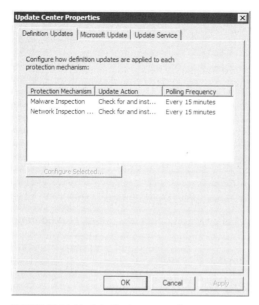

FIGURE 18-16 Update Center properties

4. Highlight Malware Inspection and click Configure Selected.

5. The Definition Update Configuration settings appear, as shown in Figure 18-17.

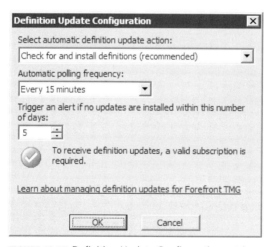

FIGURE 18-17 Definition Update Configuration settings

6. The default automatic update action is Check For And Install Updates. The other two options available are Only Check For Updates and No Automatic Action. For this example we will leave this at its default and recommended setting.

7. The Automatic polling frequency is set to 15 minutes by default. This is the time interval in which TMG will poll for new definition updates. This can be increased up to 4 hours. Again for this example we will leave it at 15 minutes.

8. You can also set an alert to be triggered in case no new updates are installed within a certain number of days. The default value for that is set to 5 days.

9. Click OK to return to the Definition Updates tab under Update Center Properties settings.

10. Highlight Network Inspection Service (NIS) and click Configure Selected. Again the Definition Update Configuration settings for NIS appears, which is the same as what we saw for Malware Inspection except for the number of days to trigger an alert (45 days for NIS).

11. Click OK to return to the Definition Updates tab under Update Center Properties settings.

12. Click the Microsoft Update tab, as shown in Figure 18-18.

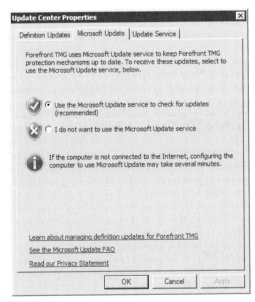

FIGURE 18-18 Microsoft Update settings in the Update Center Properties dialog box

13. TMG uses Microsoft Update services to deliver malware updates to TMG. For TMG to receive these updates make sure that the option Use The Microsoft Update Service To Check For Updates is selected.

14. Click Microsoft Update Service to configure the policy configuration for protection mechanism definition updates, as shown in Figure 18-19.

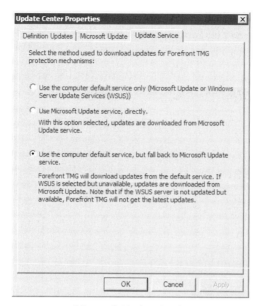

FIGURE 18-19 Microsoft Update Service settings

15. The option selected by default is Use Machine Default Service But Fallback To Microsoft Update. This option is particularly useful if the machine default service is set to use Windows Server Update Services (WSUS). However, if the WSUS is not available TMG can use Microsoft Updates directly to download definitions.

16. Click OK to return to the TMG console.

If an administrator needs to determine when updates were installed, the Definition Updates panel also shows the status of the last update and the time when the last check for new updates was performed along with the version number for the definitions and their license status as shown in Figure 18-20.

FIGURE 18-20 Definition Updates panel

You can force Forefront TMG to look for updates by clicking Check For Definitions in the Task pane, as shown earlier in Figure 18-15. If new updates are detected and installed, an informational alert will appear on the Alerts tab, as shown in Figure 18-21. As you can see, the bottom part of the window shows details about the update as well as the versions of the files that were updated.

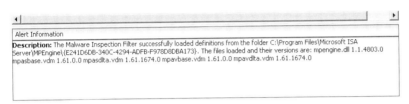

Alert Information

Description: The Malware Inspection Filter successfully loaded definitions from the folder C:\Program Files\Microsoft ISA Server\MPEngine\{E241D6DB-340C-4294-ADFB-F978D8DBA173}. The files loaded and their versions are: mpengine.dll 1.1.4803.0 mpasbase.vdm 1.61.0.0 mpasdlta.vdm 1.61.1674.0 mpavbase.vdm 1.61.0.0 mpavdlta.vdm 1.61.1674.0

FIGURE 18-21 Alerts for definition updates

If for any reason TMG is unable to load the definitions, a corresponding alert will be issued alerting the administrator that definition updates failed. The administrator then should check the connection to Windows Server Update Services (WSUS) is available if WSUS is being used for updates or if TMG can get to Microsoft Updates site and install any update. If getting to Microsoft Update fails and no WSUS is present, definition updates through Update Center will fail as well.

Summary

In this chapter, you learned about the functionality provided by Forefront TMG URL Filtering and MRS, how to configure it to satisfy specific requirements dictated by the Contoso security team, and how to define exceptions to the MRS-provided URL classifications. You also learned how to manage the Update Center configuration behavior and licensing. In Chapter 19, "Enhancing E-Mail Protection," you will learn about how TMG and Exchange Edge can be combined to further improve your e-mail service security and availability.

## CHAPTER 19

Enhancing E-Mail Protection

- Understanding E-Mail Threats   **487**

- How SMTP Protection Works in TMG   **490**

- Configuring SMTP Protection on TMG   **493**

- Summary   **527**

I n this chapter, you will learn about the e-mail protection provided when Microsoft Forefront Threat Management Gateway 2010 (TMG) is installed on a computer that has Microsoft Exchange Server 2007 installed in an edge role with Forefront Protection 2010 for Exchange Server. The discussions in this chapter include general e-mail threats, SMTP protection functionality provided in Exchange Server and Forefront Protection 2010 for Exchange Server, and SMTP protection management offered in TMG.

Understanding E-Mail Threats

Throughout the years the widespread use of e-mail has been associated with the deployment of malicious code. E-mail has been used by hackers to distribute malicious content to users. Networks have been breached by attacks using malicious code and worms that bypass the protection offered by a common firewall because they effectively tunnel the malicious code through the e-mail protocol because most firewalls do not inspect e-mail content.

Because e-mail can include file attachments, hackers can send malicious code in files with the hope that users receiving these messages will open them and run the malicious code on their local computers. One example of this was the Melissa virus in 1999 and the ILOVEYOU e-mail virus in 2000. These e-mail viruses took advantage of the user's habits or the e-mail application's tendency to automatically take an action that was harmful to the user's system. More advanced methods were soon developed by hackers to inject code through e-mail to run custom applications automatically while the end users were reading their e-mail. These attacks were made possible because of the prevalence of the HTML e-mail format; worms and viruses such as the KaK worm, BubbleBoy virus, and Nimda virus have used HTML-rendered e-mail to spread.

Although antivirus solutions on the end user's computer can detect many viruses and worms, a hacker may circumvent such protection by creating and running new code, which can result in malicious code penetrating the network through lesser known or new attack methods.

E-Mail Attack Methods

Over the years the risks of—and methods for—breaching e-mail security have increased. Viruses, worms, spyware, spam, and phishing make e-mail communications and use of e-mail management infrastructure extremely risky. Hackers around the world already use a lot of e-mail attack methods to exploit and run malicious code in a protected network, but new attacks are still being developed.

E-Mail Attachments with Malicious Code

The simplest and the most common form of e-mail attack is the use of malicious code in an e-mail attachment. The Melissa, AnnaKournikova, SirCam, and ILOVEYOU viruses were examples of e-mail malware that exploited user habits and mail reader weaknesses through malicious e-mail attachments. These attacks made use of the trust that exists between familiar users such as friends, family, and colleagues. Upon being executed, these worms sent themselves to e-mail addresses found in the victim's address book, recently sent e-mails, Web pages cached on the local computer, and other locations. When a user received an e-mail from a known sender that contained an attachment, the general tendency for the recipient was to open and view the attachment, activating the malicious code on the user's computer and allowing the malware to spread again in a similar fashion. Virus writers often use attractive or familiar names to entice the victim to open the attachment. An administrator may be able to block files with extensions such as .exe at the firewall, but a hacker can use files with extensions such as .cmd, .bat, and others to run the malicious code and infect the end user's computer, making the firewall administrator's job that much more difficult.

At one point, it was thought that users might avoid getting infected by only clicking known extension types such as .jpg or .mpg. The default configuration for Microsoft Windows is to hide the file extension, and one well-known worm that took advantage of this behavior was AnnaKournikova. This worm persuaded the user to click a file that had more than one extension—AnnaKournikova.gif.vbs. Because of the Windows default behavior of hiding the actual file extension .vbs, the user executed the file thinking it was a picture. The malicious VBScript executed in the background, with the user completely unaware. In fact, because the user didn't see the picture he was expecting, he might have clicked it repeatedly, further ensuring the computer's infection.

Hackers also try to steal passwords by sending attachments that look like flash movies. While displaying animations, the attachment can run commands in the background to steal passwords and gain network access to the protected network. A hacker may also use common vulnerabilities such as the Class ID (CLSID) extension of the application to be run. This allows the hacker to hide the actual extension of the file, thereby hiding the fact that, for example, virusfreefile.jpg could be an HTML Application (HTA) file running malicious code.

Malformed MIME Headers

The Multipurpose Internet Mail Extension (MIME) is an Internet standard specified in six RFCs (2045, 2046, 2047, 4288, 4289, and 2049). MIME headers specify fields such as date, filename, or subject line. In Outlook Express the date and filename fields were previously found to be susceptible to some common coding vulnerabilities such as buffer overflow attacks. By utilizing a specially crafted header string, a hacker could execute arbitrary code on the victim's computer. The Nimda worm was the first to use such an exploit because it effectively bypassed most of the security tools that didn't anticipate this type of an attack. The worm used a vulnerability in Outlook Express and Internet Explorer to spread through e-mail. Nimda could run automatically on computers with a vulnerable version of Internet Explorer or Outlook Express. Because Internet Explorer and Outlook Express were installed on all computers hosting the Windows operating system when these exploits were released, users who received this worm through e-mails were easily infected. Nimda used a crafted MIME header to make Outlook Express think that the attached infected file was a Waveform audio format (.wav) file. After using the specially crafted MIME header, the worm could be automatically executed.

> **MORE INFO** For more information on Nimda worm, read the following security alert: *http://www.microsoft.com/technet/security/alerts/info/nimda.mspx.*

> **MORE INFO** For more information on Outlook buffer overflow attacks, read the following security alert: *http://www.microsoft.com/technet/security/Bulletin/MS03-044.mspx.*

Embedded Scripts and ActiveX Content

With the progress in technology, all e-mail clients can now send and receive HTML e-mail that may include scripts and ActiveX content, which in turn can allow programs or code to be executed on the target computer. Outlook and other products use Internet Explorer components to display HTML e-mails. Because an Internet Explorer component (mshtml.dll) is used to render the HTML in e-mail, the security vulnerabilities found in Internet Explorer, Outlook, or other programs using Internet Explorer inherit security vulnerabilities that can be exploited by hackers through e-mails to launch various worms and enable execution of system functions such as reading, writing, or deleting files on the target computer. The KaK worm and the BubbleBoy virus are examples of malicious code used to exploit vulnerabilities and spread the attack in protected networks.

Other viruses based on HTML scripts can run automatically when the malicious e-mail is opened and therefore do not rely on attachments. E-mail anti-malware tools that only examine attachments may not detect these worms if they do not understand HTML script viruses. A common example of this kind of exploit is the BadTrans.B virus, which exploited vulnerabilities in Internet Explorer 5.01 SP1, 5.5 SP1, and Outlook Express.

MORE INFO   For more information about BadTrans Worm, read the following security alert: *http://www.microsoft.com/technet/Security/alerts/badtrans.mspx*.

Spam and Phishing

Spam and phishing are the most common form of advertising or attack e-mails. Spam is defined as the use of electronic media such as e-mail to send unsolicited bulk e-mail to a list of undisclosed recipients. Spamming relies on a simple technique of sending bulk e-mail to a large number of recipients through a single or multiple e-mail address list. Although spamming might not have any adverse effects on a particular computer, spam accounts for a large amount of wasted network bandwidth and irritates the users who receive such messages.

MORE INFO   In June 2003, Bill Gates wrote to *The Wall Street Journal* formally saying why he hated spam and the big impact that this type of unwanted message has from a business perspective. To read this complete article visit *http://www.microsoft.com/presspass/ofnote/06-23wsjspam.mspx*.

Phishing, on the other hand, relies on redirecting users to a malicious Web site while giving the impression to the user that the site she is visiting represents a Web site she might normally intend to visit. When the end user enters personal information in the phishing site, that information is used by the hacker to steal the end user's personal information. Spam and phishing are frequently used in tandem because it is through spam e-mails that the hacker generally sends out phishing links.

MORE INFO   For more information on spam please visit *http://en.wikipedia.org/wiki/E-mail_spam*.

MORE INFO   For more information on phishing please visit *http://en.wikipedia.org/wiki/Phishing*.

How SMTP Protection Works in TMG

If you were involved in managing e-mail through ISA Server 2000 or ISA Server 2004, you might recall a mechanism called the SMTP Message Screener. This mechanism operated as an SMTP service plug-in that provided basic protection against threats and spam, where the unwanted data was detectable in the mail header, and to a lesser extent, in the body of the e-mail itself. Although the Message Screener worked reasonably well, any updates to the signature data required the ISA administrator to define and enter these manually and restart the SMTP service where the filter was operating. Needless to say, as e-mail threats proliferated, this process became terribly unwieldy.

The Message Screener was removed from ISA Server 2006 because the Exchange Intelligent Message Filter offered much better spam and malware detection.

> **MORE INFO** You can read more about the ISA Server Message Screener at *http://technet .microsoft.com/en-us/library/cc713320.aspx* and the Exchange Intelligent Message Filter at *http://technet.microsoft.com/en-us/library/aa996624.aspx*.

TMG SMTP Protection relies on three mechanisms:

- **Exchange 2007 SPAM protection** Exchange 2007 offers strong message filtering capabilities, such as connection filtering, sender and recipient filtering, and sender ID and reputation. Although these features are quite effective, they fall short in malware detection.

> **MORE INFO** You can read more about Exchange Server 2007 mail filtering at *http://technet.microsoft.com/en-us/library/aa996604.aspx*.

- **Forefront Protection 2010 for Exchange Server** Forefront Protection 2010 for Exchange Server extends Exchange Server 2007 e-mail filtering capabilities by adding enhanced malware protection through the use of multiple anti-malware engines.

> **MORE INFO** You can read more about Forefront Protection 2010 for Exchange Server at *http://blogs.technet.com/forefront/archive/2009/09/04/forefront-protection-2010-for- exchange-server-rc.aspx*.

- **TMG SMTP filter and centralized management** The SMTP application filter verifies the SMTP conversation by validating the SMTP verbs against a predefined list and the current SMTP protocol state. TMG also provides a single place from which to manage the e-mail protection features in Exchange 2007 anti-spam and anti-virus and Forefront Protection 2010 for Exchange Server.

Figure 19-1 and the following steps outline the basic mail flow through TMG SMTP Protection for a "clean" action.

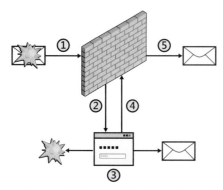

FIGURE 19-1 Basic e-mail flow for a clean action

1. E-mail carrying malware is received at TMG; SMTP state is validated.

2. E-mail is forwarded to Exchange Server 2007 on the local computer.

3. The malware is isolated from the e-mail.

4. The cleaned e-mail is sent back to TMG.

5. The cleaned e-mail is forwarded to the receiving SMTP server, where SMTP state is once again validated.

Within Exchange Server itself, the mail flow operates as shown in Figure 19-2 and described in the following steps.

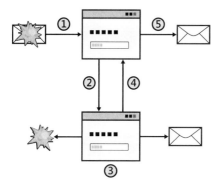

FIGURE 19-2 Detailed mail flow for a clean action

1. E-mail carrying malware is received by Exchange 2007.

2. E-mail is sent to Forefront Protection 2010 for Exchange Server.

3. Forefront Protection 2010 for Exchange Server isolates the malware from the e-mail.

4. The cleaned e-mail is sent back to Exchange 2007 Server.

5. The cleaned e-mail is forwarded to the receiving SMTP server.

When deployed with the Exchange 2007 edge role, TMG combines Exchange 2007 and Forefront Protection 2010 for Exchange Server to provide a far more secure e-mail transport than ISA Server 2006.

Configuring SMTP Protection on TMG

Before you begin configuring TMG SMTP protection, it is important to collect all the necessary information related to your Exchange topology. Ideally, you should have a diagram describing the network topology including all of the Exchange Servers that are involved and the corresponding IP address of each one. For the purpose of this scenario, we'll use the topology shown in Figure 19-3.

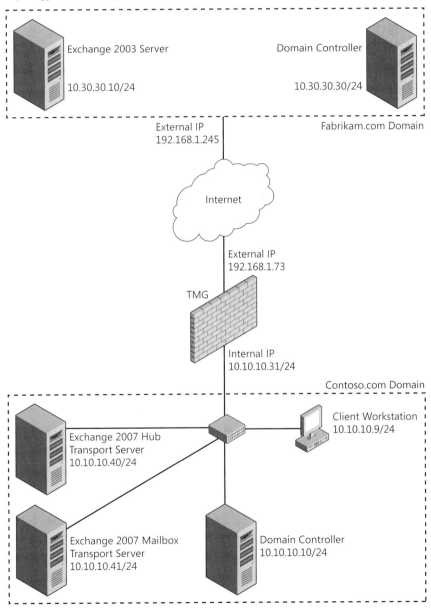

FIGURE 19-3 Topology used to assist during the configuration

In this scenario we will use an external domain (fabrikam.com) to communicate with the internal domain (contoso.com) to validate mail flow. In this case the external DNS Server (located in the Internet cloud) will point to TMG's external IP for the Mail Exchange (MX) record. In this topology the internal Exchange Servers are using TMG's internal IP address as default gateway. Let's start configuring SMTP Protection.

> **MORE INFO** To better understand Exchange Server 2007 nomenclature, acronyms, and server roles download the Exchange Server 2007 Component Architecture from *http://www.microsoft.com/downloads/details.aspx?FamilyID=FDCDF6E5-DE47-4B58-8086-282101BCDDE9&displaylang=en.*

Running the E-Mail Protection Wizard

The first step in configuring SMTP Protection on TMG is to run the E-Mail Protection Wizard to establish the internal and external listener for SMTP. To do so, follow these steps:

1. On the TMG computer (or using the remote management console), open the Forefront TMG Management Console.

2. Click Forefront TMG (Array Name) in the left pane.

3. Click E-Mail Policy and in the task pane click Configure E-Mail Policy, as shown in Figure 19-4.

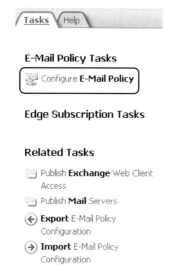

FIGURE 19-4 Server to server mail protection configuration

4. When you access this option, the E-mail Protection Wizard launches as shown in Figure 19-5. Click Next to continue.

FIGURE 19-5 The E-Mail Protection Wizard welcome page

5. The next step allows you to define two options: the internal mail server that TMG will send e-mail to and the domain from which TMG will accept messages. The internal mail server for this scenario will be the Exchange 2007 Hub Transport Server (10.10.10.40/24) and TMG will accept messages only when the destination is contoso.com. If you have multiple domains within your organization you also can add multiple entries in this option. Figure 19-6 shows the page of the wizard that allows you to perform this configuration.

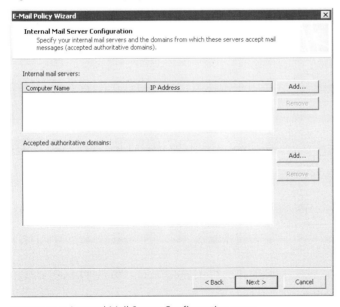

FIGURE 19-6 Internal Mail Server Configuration page

6. To add Exchange 2007 Hub Transport Server's IP Address, click Add. Add the Exchange 2007 Hub Transport Server's computer name and IP address, as shown in Figure 19-7.

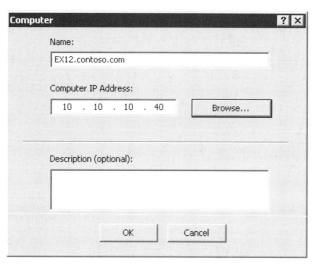

FIGURE 19-7 Adding the IP address for the internal SMTP Server

7. Click OK. The Internal Mail Server Configuration page now has the Exchange server's name and IP address, as shown in Figure 19-8.

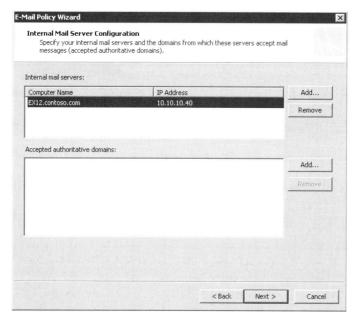

FIGURE 19-8 Internal mail configuration with Exchange server's name and IP address

8. Click Add to add contoso.com, as shown in Figure 19-9.

FIGURE 19-9 Adding the domain that TMG will accept message as destination

9. Click OK. The Internal Mail Server Configuration page now shows the accepted domains, as shown in Figure 19-10. Click Next to continue.

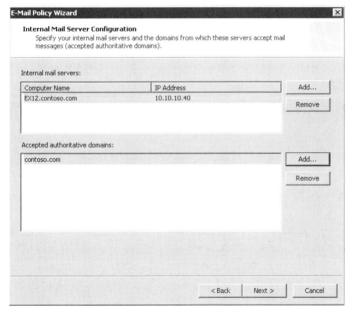

FIGURE 19-10 Internal Mail Server page with all fields configured

10. On the next page of the wizard, you define which network interface TMG uses to communicate with the Exchange Server that you specified in step 6 (10.10.10.40). For this example select Internal Interface where TMG has connectivity to the Exchange Hub Transport Server, as shown in Figure 19-11.

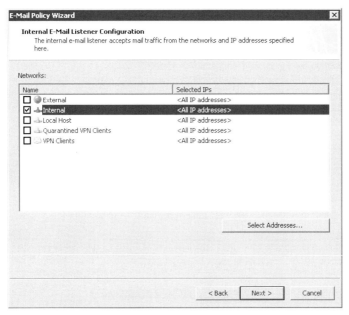

FIGURE 19-11 Selecting the interface that will be used to communicate with the internal Exchange Server.

NOTE If you have multiple addresses in your internal network you also can click Select Addresses and specify one or more IPs that will be used to communicate with the internal Exchange Server. If you are using NLB on TMG you can also specify the Virtual IP address in this option. If you have only one IP it doesn't really make any difference whether you select the interface directly or click Select Address, as in this example where TMG's external interface is 192.168.1.73.

11. Click Next. The External Mail Routing Configuration page appears, as shown in Figure 19-12.

12. Enter the fully qualified domain name (FQDN) that will appear in the response to a HELO or EHLO SMTP command. This name should be the one that resolves to the reverse DNS lookup of the external TMG's IP address. Select the TMG interface that will be used to communicate to the Internet. For this example the FQDN is **mail.contoso.com** and the interface will be External, as shown in Figure 19-13.

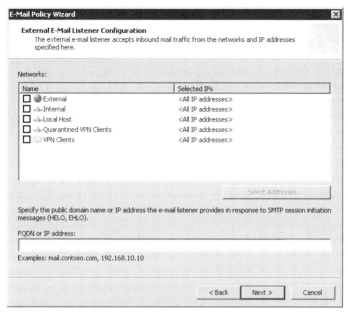

FIGURE 19-12 External configuration for SMTP Protection

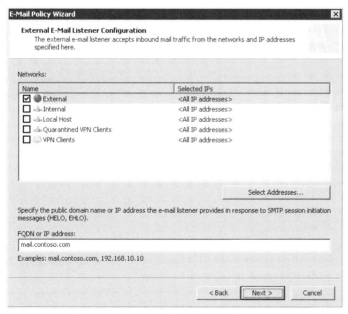

FIGURE 19-13 Customizing external SMTP Protection configuration

13. Click Next and the Mail Protection Configuration page appears. Select both options (Enable Spam Filtering and Enable Virus And Content Filtering), as shown in Figure 19-14.

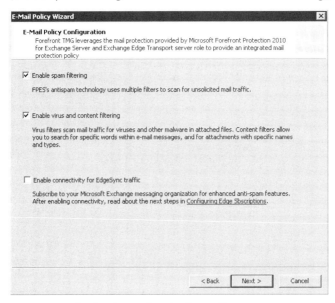

FIGURE 19-14 Configuring mail protection options

> **NOTE**   To read more about the option to enable connectivity for EdgeSync traffic go to *http://technet.microsoft.com/en-us/library/dd897094.aspx*.

14. Click Next. A summary page with all selections appears, as shown in Figure 19-15.

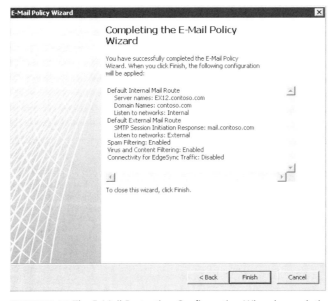

FIGURE 19-15 The E Mail Protection Configuration Wizard completion page

15. Click Finish. The dialog box shown in Figure 19-16 appears, asking whether you want to enable the system policy for SMTP Protection. Click Yes.

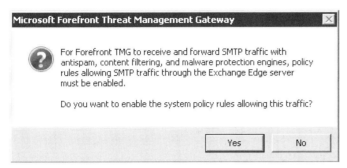

FIGURE 19-16 Enabling the SMTP Protection system policy

16. The E-Mail Policy tab changes according to the settings that you selected in the wizard, as shown in Figure 19-17.

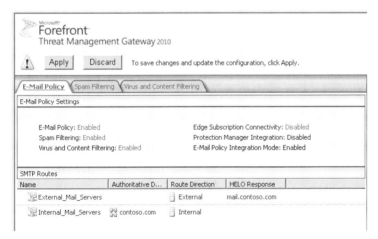

FIGURE 19-17 E-Mail Policy tab

17. Click Apply to save the changes and then click OK.

Your SMTP Protection Configuration is ready to allow mail flow. Using the default options for spam, virus, and content filtering, you already have a reasonable level of protection.

> **NOTE** What happens after you apply this configuration on TMG is that a set of Windows PowerShell commands are executed against the Exchange Edge Transport located on the TMG computer to configure the Receive and Send Connectors. If you use the Exchange Management Console you see those settings configured there. You can also use Exchange Management Shell to retrieve Receive (*Get-ReceiveConnector*) and Send (*Get-ReceiveConnector*) Connector's information.

Configuring Spam Filtering

The spam filtering options available in TMG form a part of the Exchange Edge Transport Server Anti-Spam capabilities. When you click the Spam Filtering tab in TMG, the corresponding options from Exchange Edge Transport are now available through the TMG Console as shown in Figure 19-18.

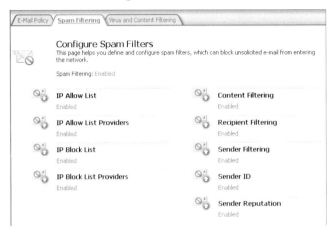

FIGURE 19-18 Spam Filtering options on TMG

IP Allow List

The IP Allow List allows you to add one or more IP addresses that are considered trusted and should always be allowed to send e-mail. You can use this option for example in a scenario where you have partners that you want to categorize them as source trust of e-mails and therefore allow them to send e-mail without passing through the normal SMTP filters. This feature is enabled by default on the Spam Filtering tab as shown in Figure 19-18. When you click IP Allow List, the dialog box shown in Figure 19-19 appears with a drop-down list where you can change the status.

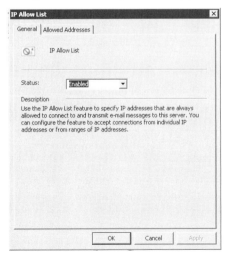

FIGURE 19-19 IP Allow List option is enabled by default.

By clicking the Allowed Addresses tab you can add the IPs that you want to always allow, as shown in Figure 19-20.

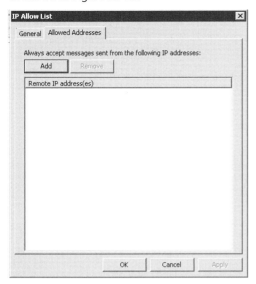

FIGURE 19-20 The Allowed IP list is empty by default.

IP Allow List Providers

You can use the IP Allow List Providers dialog box to maintain a list of IP addresses that are known to not be associated with any type of spam activity. The IP Allow List Providers feature is also referred to as *safe list services*. This feature is enabled by default on the Spam Filtering tab, as shown in Figure 19-18. When you click IP Allow List, the dialog box shown in Figure 19-21 appears with a drop-down list where you can change the status.

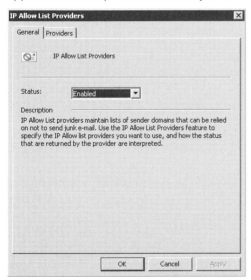

FIGURE 19-21 The IP Allow List Providers dialog box, where you can manipulate the status of this feature

By clicking the Providers tab you can add the IPs of the providers that you trust, as shown in Figure 19-22.

FIGURE 19-22 The IP Allow List Providers tab, where you can add trusted IPs

To specify the parameters for the provider, click Add and type the details related to the provider that you want to add on this list. Figure 19-23 shows an example of those parameters.

FIGURE 19-23 The IP List Provider tab where you can add trusted providers

This dialog box provides the following options:

- **Provider Name**   The name that identifies the provider for your own reference—in other words it doesn't have to be the full real name of the provider.

- **Lookup Domain**   This field should have the domain name that the Exchange Connection Filter agent will use to query for updates related to IP Block list information.

- **Match To Any Return Code**   This option makes the Exchange Connection Filter agent treat any IP Address status code that is returned by the IP Block List provider option as a match.

- **Match To The Following Mask**   This option makes the Exchange Connection Filter agent act only on messages that match the return status code of 127.0.0.x, where x can be:

  - 1 The IP address is on an IP Block list.
  - 2 The SMTP server is open for relay.
  - 4 The IP address supports a dial-up IP address.

- **Match To Any Of The Following Responses**   This option makes the Exchange Connection Filter agent act only on messages that match the same IP address status code that is returned from the IP Block List provider service.

IP Block List

In contrast with the IP Allow List, the IP Block List allows you to add one or more IP that should never be allowed to establish an SMTP connection with TMG. For example, let's say you identify a particular IP address that is sending a massive amount of spam to your organization. You want to block this IP during the connect phase (the initial attempt to establish the SMTP connection). Figure 19-24 shows the General tab where you can enable or disable this filter.

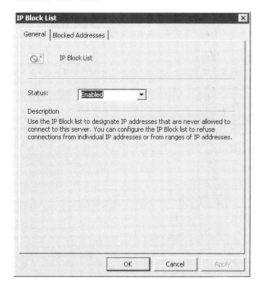

FIGURE 19-24 IP Block List General tab

Figure 19-25 shows the Blocked Addresses tab, where you can add the IPs that are supposed to be blocked.

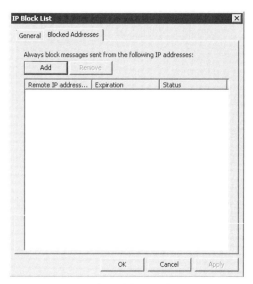

FIGURE 19-25 List of IP addresses that are supposed to be blocked

> **NOTE** When you enable this option and add an IP to this list, that IP is blocked immediately after the source SMTP Server (that owns this IP) sends the HELO (or EHLO) to TMG and Exchange Connection Filter Agent sends a SMTP 550 error message to the sender.

IP Block List Provider

The IP Block List Provider option is the opposite of the Allow List Provider. In this case, you have the capability to add the providers that are known (or suspected) to send spam. This option is enabled by default and you can change the status in the Status drop-down box, as shown in Figure 19-26.

The Providers tab has the same options that was presented earlier in Figure 19-22, with the same options and meaning. The only difference is that in this case those options are used to categorize the provider in the block list rather than on the allow list. Like all block lists, this one also has an option to allow you to add an exception to it. On the Exceptions tab (Figure 19-27) you can enter one or more e-mail addresses that you wish to exclude from the block list providers.

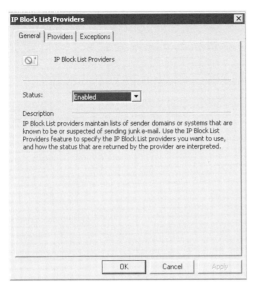

FIGURE 19-26 IP Block List Providers status dialog box

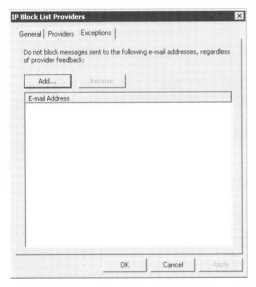

FIGURE 19-27 Exception list for the block list providers

Content Filtering

The Content Filtering feature filters e-mails based on settings that you define. To do that it uses an algorithm that learns what is and what is not spam. The following scenario will use the following settings:

- Allowed words: contoso
- Blocked words: nudity
- Recipient exception: monitor@contoso.com

MORE INFO For more information about the how Content Filtering works, review the following article: *http://technet.microsoft.com/en-us/library/aa997242.aspx*.

Click the Content Filtering option and follow these steps to configure these settings:

1. The first dialog box that appears (see Figure 19-28) is the General tab. You can leave the option enabled (as we want for this scenario) or you can disable it later if necessary.

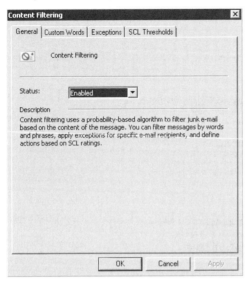

FIGURE 19-28 Content filtering option

2. Click the Custom Words tab, as shown in Figure 19-29, to add allowed and blocked words or phrases.

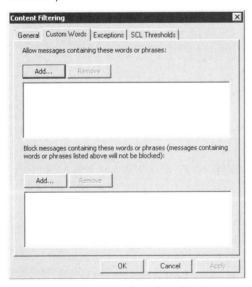

FIGURE 19-29 Custom words option with allowed and blocked words

3. Click Add in the first field to specify the allowed word and type **contoso,** as shown in Figure 19-30.

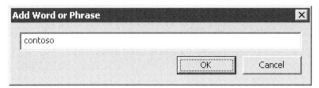

FIGURE 19-30 Allowed word

4. Click OK and click Add in the second field to specify the blocked word. Type **nudity,** as shown in Figure 19-31.

FIGURE 19-31 Blocked word

5. Click OK and confirm that your custom words appear, as shown in Figure 19-32.

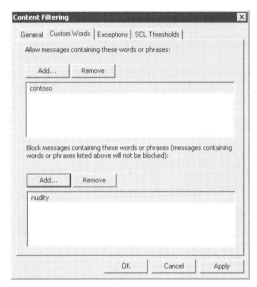

FIGURE 19-32 Custom words added

6. Click the Exception tab. A dialog box should appear as shown in Figure 19-33. Here you will add an exception to the current rule to not filter messages to monitor@contoso.com.

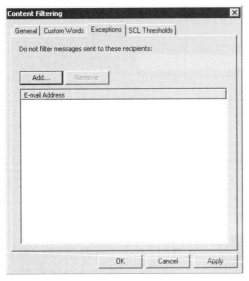

FIGURE 19-33 List of exceptions to the general content filtering rule

7. Click Add and type **monitor@contoso.com,** as shown in Figure 19-34.

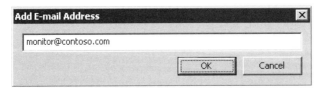

FIGURE 19-34 E-mail address that will be an exception to the rule

8. Click OK and confirm that your Exceptions dialog box looks like Figure 19-35.

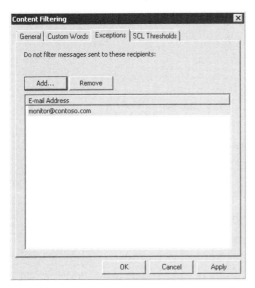

FIGURE 19-35 Exceptions tab with the e-mail address added

9. Click OK and then click Apply in the TMG management console center pane to commit your changes.

We are intentionally skipping the Action tab settings because it is important to have a better understanding of how this option works before you configure it.

Spam Confidence Level

The Spam Confidence level (SCL) threshold defines what action the content filter agent should take on a specific message, such as rejecting or deleting the message. The Content Filter agent uses Microsoft SmartScreen technology to inspect the contents of a message and to assign a SCL rating to each message.

Click Content Filtering and then click the SCL Thresholds tab to see the SCL settings. The dialog box shown in Figure 19-36 appears.

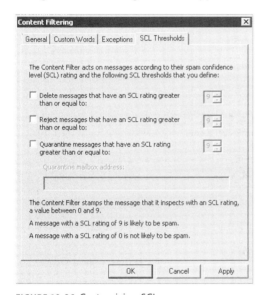

FIGURE 19-36 Customizing SCL

The following options are available in this dialog box:

- **Delete Messages That Have A SCL Rating Greater Than Or Equal To** The message is deleted and the sending server is not notified of the message deletion. Exchange Edge Transport Server (installed on the TMG computer) accepts and then deletes the message. Because the sending server understands that the message was accepted, the sending server doesn't retry sending the message in the same session.

- **Reject Messages That Have A SCL Rating Greater Than Or Equal To** This option rejects the message by sending one of several SMTP negative responses to the sending server.

MORE INFO SMTP command and response sequences are defined in RFC 2821: *http://www.ietf.org/rfc/rfc2821*.

- **Quarantine Messages That Have A SCL Rating Greater Than Or Equal To** When using this option you need to specify a mailbox to hold the quarantined e-mail. You must have the mailbox account already created prior to configuring this option. In other words, this option does not create a mailbox for quarantine—it can only use an existing mailbox.

The numbers that are configured besides each of those option have a range from 0 to 9, where 9 indicates that the e-mail is very likely to be spam and 0 indicates that the e-mail is least likely to be spam. Notice that by default all options are dimmed, but if you select any of those check boxes the option will be enabled. For this example leave all these settings at their default values and click OK to close the dialog box.

Recipient Filtering

In the Recipient Filtering dialog box, you can specify a list of e-mail addresses or a distribution list that would like to receive e-mails from outside your organization. It is very common within an organization to have some distribution lists that are used regularly and those you might want to prevent receiving e-mail from Internet. Click the Recipient Filtering option and then click the Blocked Recipients tab to see the available options, as shown in Figure 19-37.

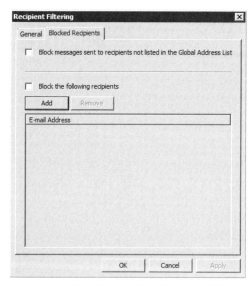

FIGURE 19-37 Blocking recipients from receiving messages from Internet

The first option is Block Messages Sent To Recipients That Are Not In The Global Address List (GAL). This a good technique for blocking spam sent to addresses that do not appear in the GAL. This is important because you can have recipients that are hidden from the GAL for security purposes and you don't want those recipients to receive messages from outside your organization. The second option available is Block The Following Recipients. Here you can add one or more recipients that are not supposed to receive messages from the Internet at all. Click OK to close this dialog box.

Sender Filtering

If you learn of a specific e-mail address that is sending lots of spam to your organization and you want to block that source e-mail address from sending messages, you can use the Sender Filtering feature. For our example we'll use the following parameters:

- Block the e-mail address administrator@fabrikam.com.
- Block the domain fourthcoffee.com.
- Block messages from senders that did not identify themselves (blank).
- Reject all messages that are categorized with the above parameters.

Click Sender Filtering and follow these steps to configure those options:

1. Click the Block Senders tab and notice that by default there is already a filter to block blank senders, as shown in Figure 19-38.

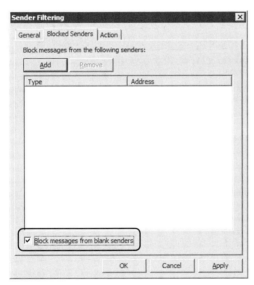

FIGURE 19-38 Sender Filtering dialog box with the default blank sender option selected

2. Click Add, and then add the e-mail address (**administrator@fabrikam.com**) that you want to block, as shown in Figure 19-39.

FIGURE 19-39 Adding the sender that will be blocked

3. Click OK. Click Add again and then specify the domain (**fourthcoffee.com**) that you want to block. Select Including Subdomains, as shown in Figure 19-40.

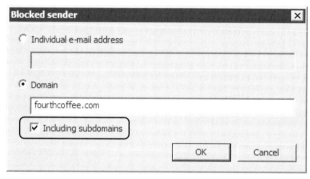

FIGURE 19-40 Adding the domain that will be blocked

4. Click OK. Your Blocked Senders tab should appear as shown in Figure 19-41.

FIGURE 19-41 Blocked Senders listed by e-mail and domain

5. Click the Action tab to specify the action to be taken when a message contains one of the senders specified in the Block Senders list. Select the Reject Message option, as shown in Figure 19-42.

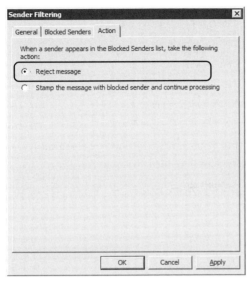

FIGURE 19-42 Selecting an action to take when blocked senders are detected

6. Click OK and then click Apply to commit those changes.

Sender ID

The Sender ID feature works by verifying that the source of the message is the organization it claims to be. Sender ID checks the IP address of the sending server against a registered list of servers that the domain owner has authorized to send e-mail.

In the Sender ID window, click Action to see the available options shown in Figure 19-43.

> **MORE INFO** *Sender ID* is another term for Sender Policy Framework (SPF), which is a process used to validate the origin of SMTP mail. You can read more about SPF at *http://en.wikipedia.org/wiki/Sender_Policy_Framework*.

The following actions are available if the Sender ID check fails:

- **Reject Message** This option rejects a message and sends an SMTP negative action message to the sending server.
- **Stamp The Message With Sender ID And Continue Processing** When you select this option the Sender ID status is included in the headers of all inbound messages to your organization. Later this metadata is evaluated by the Content Filter agent for the purpose of SCL calculation. The Sender Reputation feature also uses this metadata while calculating the Sender Reputation Level (SRL) for the message sender.

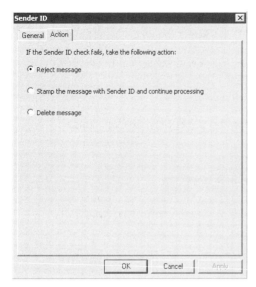

FIGURE 19-43 Sender ID options

- **Delete Message**   The message is deleted and no negative response is sent to the SMTP server that originated the message.

Leave the Reject Message option selected and click OK.

> **MORE INFO**   For more information about the Content Filter Agent, review Exchange 2007 documentation at *http://technet.microsoft.com/en-us/library/bb124739.aspx*.

Sender Reputation

The Sender Reputation feature relies on persisted data about the sender to determine what action, if any, to take on when an inbound message arrives. This feature calculates the Sender Reputation Level (SRL) by using the following statistics:

- **HELO/EHLO analysis**   This analysis is done on a per-sender basis to determine whether the sender is likely to be a spammer. For example, a single sender that provides many different HELO (or EHLO) statements in a specific period of time is more likely to be a spammer.

> **MORE INFO**   For more information about HELO/EHLO, review RFC 1869 (*http://www.ietf.org/rfc/rfc1869.txt*).

- **Reverse DNS lookup**   This analysis verifies whether the originating IP address from which the sender transmitted the message matches the registered domain name that the sender submits in the HELO (or EHLO) SMTP command.

NOTE Many small or medium-sized organizations do not own a whole netblock; thus they may not control the reverse lookup records relevant to their assigned IP space. Because this state can cause valid SMTP servers to appear invalid, you should use this option with great care.

- **Analysis of SCL ratings on messages from a particular sender**   This analysis is based on the rating number that has been defined according to the sender's reputation.
- **Sender open proxy test**   This is a verification to determine whether there is an open proxy in the sender. The open proxy server is an SMTP server that accepts and forwards e-mail that is destined for any e-mail address. Open proxies are often referred to as *open relays*.

These parameters are weighed and an SRL is calculated for each sender. The SRL is represented as a number between 0 and 9 that predicts the probability that a specific sender is a spammer or a malicious user. To configure Sender Reputation, click the Sender Reputation option and then click Sender Confidence as shown in Figure 19-44.

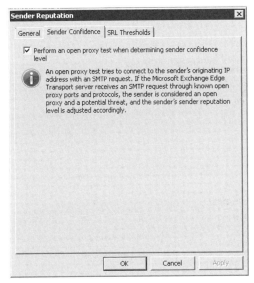

FIGURE 19-44 The perform open proxy test is enabled by default

The first option, Perform An Open Proxy Test When Determining Sender Confidence Level, is selected by default. Click the SRL Thresholds tab to configure the sender repudiation threshold, as shown in Figure 19-45.

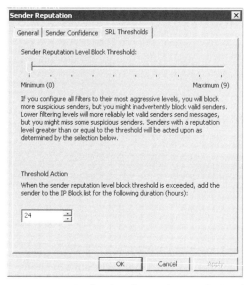

FIGURE 19-45 Configuring the sender repudiation threshold

Using the threshold control you can scroll to the right to be more aggressive in the analysis level (which can cause false positives) or you can leave it in the middle if you want to be more balanced in the analysis and avoid a high false positive rate. At the bottom of the dialog box you can set Threshold Action, which by default is 24 hours. This action determines the amount of time that the source IP will be in the block list.

Configuring Virus and Content Filtering

The next part of the E-Mail Protection configuration is configuring Virus and Content Filtering. During this process, TMG configures Forefront Protection 2010 for Exchange Server in the background. When you click the Virus And Content Filtering tab your dialog box appears, as shown in Figure 19-46.

FIGURE 19-46 Virus And Content Filtering tab

File Filtering

This filtering option allows you to restrict attachment files by file extension or by filename. For our scenario we'll use the following restrictions:

- Delete files where the extension is equal to MP3, WAV, and AVI
- Delete files that match the pattern *eicar*

To perform this configuration, click File Filtering on the Virus And Content Filtering tab and follow these steps:

1. In the File Filtering dialog box, click the File Filters tab as shown in Figure 19-47.

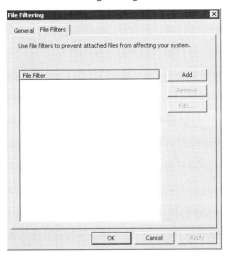

FIGURE 19-47 File Filters tab without any filters added

2. Click Add to create a new filter policy. The File Filter dialog box appears. Type **Media Filter** in the Filter Name field, as shown in Figure 19-48.

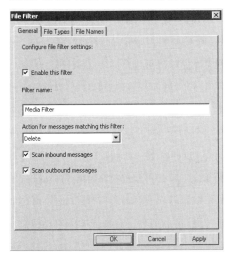

FIGURE 19-48 Creating a new File Filtering policy

3. Leave the options scan Inbound Messages and Scan Outbound Messages enabled. In the Action For Messages Matching This Filter drop-down list, leave the default, which is Delete. Notice the following additional actions for the Action For Messages Matching This Filter drop-down list:

- **Identity**   Using this option the message is tagged in the subject line or message header. This is done so that later the message can be identified by the Forefront Server Security Administrator and to alert the user that this message is possibly spam.

- **Purge**   Deletes the message from the e-mail system. The message is purged and will be unrecoverable.

- **Skip**   When you select this option the message is recorded (if it meets the filter criteria), but it is still routed normally.

4. Click the File Type tab and select the options that were described in the beginning (MP3, WAV, and AVI), as shown in Figure 19-49.

FIGURE 19-49 Selecting the file type for this filter

> **NOTE**   Although the goal was to filter MP3, WAV, and AVI files, it doesn't mean that only those extensions will be blocked. The filter is configured to block by file type, which is more robust than blocking by extension.

5. Click the File Names tab and the dialog box appears, as shown in Figure 19-50.

FIGURE 19-50 File Names tab

6. Click Add and type ***car.***, as shown in Figure 19-51.

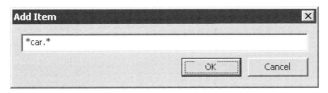

FIGURE 19-51 Filter by pattern of characters

> **NOTE** When you use *car.* as a filter you are saying that you want this filter to trigger on any filename that ends in *car,* using any extension. For more information on matching patterns in the filename see *http://technet.microsoft.com/en-us/library/ bb795068.aspx.*

7. Click OK and your File Filter dialog box appears, as shown in Figure 19-52.

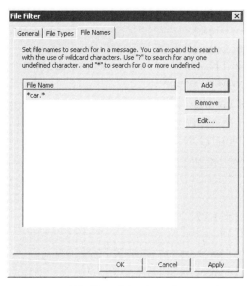

FIGURE 19-52 File Filter dialog box after creating a new filter

8. Click OK to finish this filter's configuration.

Virus Filtering

The Virus Filtering option available in TMG uses Forefront Protection 2010 for Exchange Server for transport scanning. The mailbox store server that is protected by TMG can have Forefront Protection 2010 for Exchange Server installed as well. Click Virus Filtering on the Virus And Content Filtering tab and follow these steps:

1. In the Antivirus Configuration dialog box click the Engines tab, as shown in Figure 19-53.

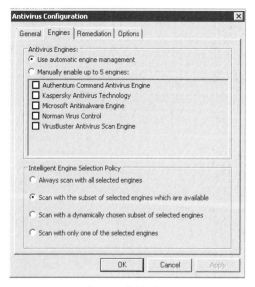

FIGURE 19-53 Engines available for transport scanning

2. On the Engines tab you can select up to five engines that will be used for transport scanning (inbound and outbound messages) by selecting the option Manually Enable Up To 5 Engines, or you can leave the option Use Automatic Engine Management selected by default. You can also select how the engines will be used to scan the messages by selecting one of the following options:

- **Always Scan With All Selected Engines**   Using this option Forefront Protection 2010 for Exchange Server queues messages for scanning if any of the selected engines becomes busy, such as during signature updates or heavy e-mail traffic times.

- **Scan With The Subset Of Selected Engines Which Are Available**   This option scans using all selected engines. Scans alternate between engines when one of the selected engines is busy.

- **Scan With A Dynamically Chosen Subset Of Selected Engines**   Using this option Forefront Protection 2010 for Exchange Server heuristically chooses from the selected engines, based on recent results and statistical projections.

- **Scan With Only One Of The Selected Engines**   Using this option only one of the selected engines listed in this dialog box is used to scan any single object.

NOTE   When selecting multiple engines it is important to consider performance and sizing of the server. CPU utilization can increase 20 to 40 percent depending on bias and engines. For more information on Forefront Server Security for Exchange sizing, refer to Forefront Security for Exchange Server SP1 Capacity Planning Tool at *http://www.microsoft.com/downloads/details.aspx?FamilyID=522da65d-5263-4f5d-b929-8428a394b9af&displaylang=en.*

3. Select Microsoft Antimalware Engine, leave the intelligent engine selection as default, and click the Remediation Tab, shown in Figure 19-54.

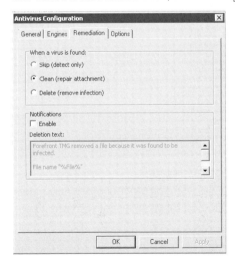

FIGURE 19-54 Remediation action when a virus is found

4. For the purpose of this example you can leave the default option, Clean (Repair Attachment) under When A Virus Is Found. Select the Send Notifications check box and leave the default text. This notification is sent to the recipient indicated by the SMTP commands and e-mail headers. Click the Options tab to continue and a dialog box appears, as shown in Figure 19-55.

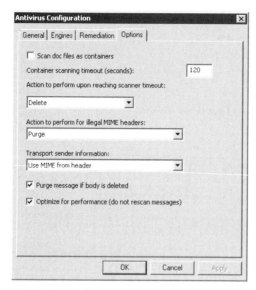

FIGURE 19-55 Additional options for antivirus protection

5. The following options are available on the Options tab:

- **Scan Doc Files As Containers**   When you select this option the antivirus engines scan .doc files and any other types of files that use structured storage standard and OLE embedded data format, such as .xls, .ppt, or .shs, as container files. The advantage of selecting this option is that any embedded files are scanned as potential virus holders.

- **Container Scanning Timeout (Seconds)**   This option defines the timeout for container file scanning. This is similar to the Scanning Timeout option but is used only for container files.

- **Action To Perform Upon Reaching A Scanner Timeout**   By default this option is configured as Delete because if the scan fails to complete within the timeout period, it is better from a security perspective that the file is deleted.

- **Action To Perform For All Illegal MIME Headers**   An illegal header is one that is not in accordance with RFCs that govern the SMTP protocol or MIME. This option allows you to define which action will be taken by the scan when it detects such headers in a message.

- **Transport Sender Information**   This option allows you to configure which sender information is used for evaluating the sender. The available options are:
  - **Use MIME From Header**   The MIME from header data is used for the transport antivirus scan.
  - **Use Transport Protocol MAIL FROM**   The sender address MAIL FROM within the SMTP protocol is used for the transport antivirus scan.
- **Purge Message If Body Is Deleted**   This option deletes a message if the body of the message was deleted by the transport scanner. An example of this is when part of the message body is deleted to remove a virus and the message body that is deleted is replaced with deletion text.
- **Optimize For Performance (Do Not Rescan Messages)**   This option skips scanning for messages that were previously scanned by any instance of Forefront Protection 2010 for Exchange Server.

6. Leave all options as default and click OK.

Message Body Filtering

The last option available is Message Body Filtering, which operates based on keywords that you can customize. To configure this option click Message Body Filtering on the Virus And Content Filtering tab and follow these steps:

1. In the Message Body Filtering dialog box click the Message Body Filters tab, as shown in Figure 19-56.

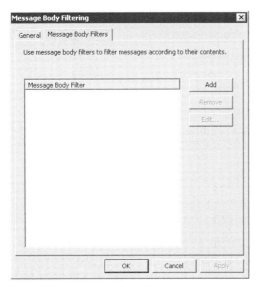

FIGURE 19-56 Message Body Filters dialog box

2. Click Add to configure a new filter for keywords and type **Unwanted Words** in the Filter Name field, as shown in Figure 19-57.

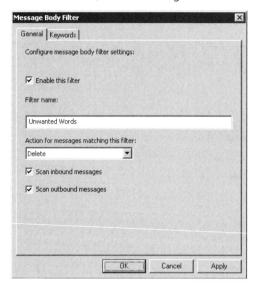

FIGURE 19-57 Creating a new filter for keywords

NOTE All options available on the General tab were covered in step 3 of the section "File Filtering."

3. Click the Keywords tab, as shown in Figure 19-58.

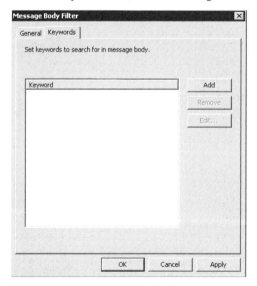

FIGURE 19-58 Keywords in the message body

4. Click Add to configure a new set of keywords and type **war,** as shown in Figure 19-59.

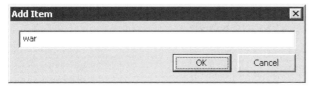

FIGURE 19-59 Adding a new keyword

5. Click OK and your Keyword tab should appear, as shown in Figure 19-60.

FIGURE 19-60 A new keyword added to the keyword list

> **NOTE** Forefront Server Security for Exchange uses keyword list syntax where you can use operators such as AND, OR, NOT, and so on. For more information on how to set up your keyword list using those operators refer to the Forefront Server Security for Exchange Operations Guide at *http://technet.microsoft.com/en-us/library/cc483075.aspx.*

Summary

In this chapter you learned about different types of e-mail threats, how they work, and what impact those threats have from a business perspective. You learned how TMG SMTP Protection works and the integration between the products involved: TMG, Exchange 2007 Edge Transport Server, and Forefront Protection 2010 for Exchange Server. You also learned how to configure the E-Mail Protection feature in TMG by using the E-Mail Protection Wizard and configuring spam filtering and virus and content filtering. In the next chapter you will learn more about HTTPS inspection.

## CHAPTER 20

HTTP and HTTPS Inspection

- The Web Proxy Application Filter **529**

- Configuring HTTPS Inspection **534**

- Configuring the HTTP Filter **550**

- Summary **570**

The main protocol used in the World Wide Web is HTTP. However, when this protocol was created, security was not a big concern. The traffic that transits the Web using HTTP is generally open and the content can be accessible to any user using a network sniffer. The Internet changed through the years from a research network (ARPANET) to a commercial network, which created the need to add a secure protocol to allow private information over HTTP; this is known as Secure Sockets Layer (SSL), and when used with HTTP, is known as HTTPS. Microsoft Forefront TMG is able to inspect traffic that uses HTTP and identify malformed or malicious content within the data stream. TMG also includes a new feature that allows you to inspect HTTPS by decrypting the traffic, and analyzing and re-encrypting it before forwarding it to the destination. This chapter will cover the conceptual design of the Web Proxy filter and HTTP Application filters with regard to HTTPS and HTTP inspection.

The Web Proxy Application Filter

The main purpose of the Web Proxy application filter is to process HTTP traffic. In TMG, it adds additional functionality in the form of HTTPS inspection. The Web Proxy filter provides compression, authentication, and caching features through the use of Web filters, which operate as plug-ins to the Web Proxy filter.

   The Web Proxy filter is an application filter that acts as an entry point to the Web Proxy engine. Web Proxy client requests are intercepted by the Web Proxy listener, which is defined on a TMG-protected network by the administrator. The Web Proxy listener is owned and created by the Web Proxy engine and not by the Web Proxy filter. The Web Proxy engine views the Web Proxy application filter as just a request generator for transparently handling Firewall clients and SecureNET clients requesting for HTTP and HTTPS content. Figure 20-1 shows a high-level architecture of TMG and where exactly the Web Proxy engine and Web Proxy application filter are placed.

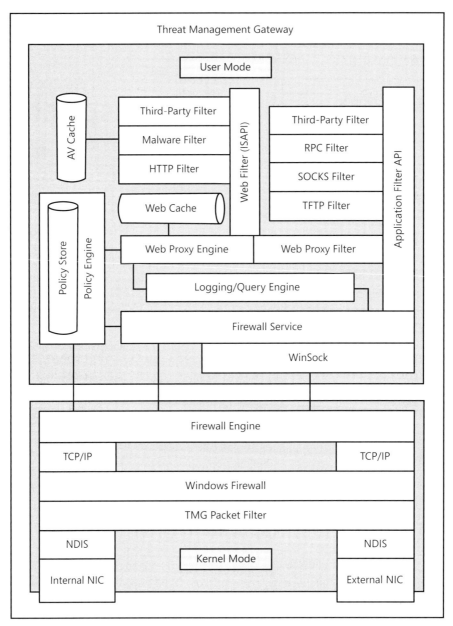

FIGURE 20-1 TMG Architecture

The three entry points to the Web Proxy engine are through the Web Proxy application filter, the Web Proxy listener on a TMG-protected network, and a Web listener defined in a publishing rule. After the request is passed to the Web Proxy engine, the request is processed according to the Web filter ordering and state and handed back to the Firewall service to return the response to the client. Figure 20-2 shows entry points to the Web Proxy engine.

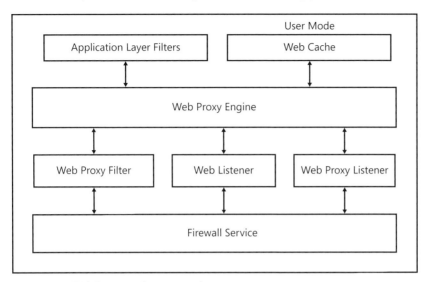

FIGURE 20-2 Web Proxy engine entry points

A client's communication packets are intercepted by the Firewall Engine in kernel mode and handed over to the Firewall service in user mode. These packets are treated as requests when they reach the Web filter, which accumulates enough packets to gain an application-level understanding. If an access rule has the Web Proxy application filter associated with the HTTP protocol, the request will be processed by the Web Proxy application filter and handed over to the Web Proxy engine for application-layer inspection and further processing by the Web filters. The response is passed back to the client through the Firewall service and the Firewall Engine.

If the access rule does not have the Web Proxy application filter associated with the HTTP protocol, all Web Proxy functionality is bypassed for that traffic but the Firewall Client or SecureNET client may still be able to access the resource because the traffic will be allowed— just not inspected.

For a Web Proxy client in a protected network, the request is always passed from the Firewall service to the Web Proxy engine through the Web Proxy listener. Thus, all requests will be subjected to application-layer inspection and can benefit from the functionality provided by the Web filters.

In the case of a client trying to access a Web resource that is published through TMG, the request is sent from the Firewall service to the Web Listener, which forwards it to the Web Proxy engine where application-layer inspection is performed and Web filters are called for additional processing.

Troubleshooting Web Proxy Traffic in TMG

One role of the Web Proxy application filter is to intercept HTTP and HTTPS requests from Firewall Clients and SecureNET clients for transparent handling. Because in these cases all Web Proxy client traffic is seen as coming from the TMG computer itself rather than the original client, the traffic appears to have been processed by a NAT filter. This behavior may cause some unexpected problems described in Table 20-1.

TABLE 20-1 Common Issues and Solutions When Using NAT with Web Proxy Filter

ISSUE	CAUSE	SOLUTION
A Site to Site VPN is established between two TMG firewalls. A client attempts to make an HTTP request to the remote site through TMG. The client is not configured as a Web Proxy client. The access attempt fails, even though there is an access rule allowing outbound HTTP requests between the local site and remote site. The related network rule is configured to apply a route relationship between the two networks.	TMG intercepts the client's request and redirects it to the Web Proxy filter. It is handled as a transparent Web Proxy request, and the resulting source IP address is translated (NAT) as the request is forwarded to the destination. If the remote site does not include TMG's external IP as an allowed IP, the request will fail.	Create a custom protocol for port 80 and make sure that the Web Proxy filter is not bound to this custom protocol. Use this custom protocol to allow HTTP traffic from local clients to the remote site to prevent TMG from processing the traffic through any other HTTP-based rules, create an identical deny rule, and position it immediately below this custom rule.
A Web request from TMG itself to a resource on the internal network fails with Error 12209: Threat Management Gateway denied the specified Uniform Resources Locator. Require All Users To Authenticate is enabled on the Internal network, and Web Proxy settings are not specified in the browser.	TMG sets the source IP address of the request to the default IP address of the internal network (the destination network). TMG applies the policy for the Internal network, which requires client authentication. The transparent Web Proxy request cannot be authenticated, and the connection fails.	Enable the Web Proxy listener on the TMG Local Host network and configure the browser on TMG to use the Local Host Web Proxy listener.

ISSUE	CAUSE	SOLUTION
A client request (authenticated with a client certificate) for a published Web resource fails, even though the client certificate is valid. This may occur when you publish a Web server over Secure Sockets Layer (SSL) allowing access to authenticated users only. When a client presents a client certificate for authentication, the certificate cannot be validated.	During the client authentication process, TMG tries to retrieve the CRL. This request is a transparent Web Proxy request from the Local Host network to the network in which the Certification Authority that issued the client certificate resides, which fails because authentication may be required on the network on which the CA is located. Without a valid CRL, the client certificate is assumed to be revoked.	Enable the CRL Download rule in TMG System Policies.

HTTP Filter

The HTTP Filter is an application-layer filter, as shown in Figure 20-1, and is utilized by the Web Proxy engine for HTTP protocol application-layer filtering. The HTTP Filter provides granular control over HTTP communication by examining HTTP commands and data. HTTP traffic is generally allowed through all firewalls because it is the default protocol used to access Web resources on the Internet.

You can block ports on the firewall to deny unwanted applications access to the Internet, but many applications can still use the HTTP protocol to pass other kinds of traffic, such as RPC over HTTP, Kazaa, Messenger, WebDav, and so on. This makes it harder for you to block specific application traffic. The TMG HTTP Filter helps you restrict traffic by blocking requests according to several HTTP features such as HTTP headers, length and URL patterns, HTTP method, HTTP body content and content-types, and file extensions. By filtering and blocking unwanted HTTP traffic we can limit the amount of unwanted traffic through TMG.

HTTP filtering can be applied in two general scenarios:

- Clients on one network access HTTP objects (HTML pages and graphics and other data that can be transferred using the HTTP protocol) on another network through TMG. This access is controlled by TMG access rules, to which an HTTP policy can be applied using the HTTP Filter.

- Clients on a source network access HTTP objects on a Web server that is published through TMG. This traffic is generally controlled by TMG Web publishing rules, to which an HTTP policy can be applied using the HTTP Filter.

TMG HTTP filtering configuration is rule specific, so that you can apply different levels and types of filtering depending on the specific requirements of your firewall policy. For example, you can use HTTP filtering to block a particular peer-to-peer file sharing service for one set of users, but allow it for another set.

Configuring HTTPS Inspection

One of the biggest problems facing any proxy administrator is the existence and popularity of anonymous public proxy servers. If you've been hiding under a rock for the last several years, these are servers placed on the Internet that will accept clear- or SSL-encrypted connections and operate as a "public proxy" for the purposes of circumventing the local proxy traffic policies. The owners of these public proxies don't care who uses them and offer no forensic assistance to anyone trying to track down malicious activity.

When HTTP proxies were first conceived, the need to allow direct connectivity between SSL-negotiating hosts was acknowledged. Unfortunately, this need also created a conflict with the concurrent requirement of controlling the requests issued by the local proxy users. We dig deeper into the details of this mechanism in Chapter 32, "Exploring HTTP Protocol."

The point is this: when a Web Proxy client creates an SSL session to a remote server, the proxy is required to "go transparent" and thus ceases to evaluate the traffic. (It has to; it's encrypted between the client and remote server.) Thus, it's a simple matter to bypass local proxy policies by connecting to an anonymizer proxy and reaching any illegal, amoral, irreverent, unfriendly Web site you want, because the proxy can't see what you're doing.

The answer is HTTPS inspection. TMG provides the ability to spoof the remote server's certificate to the client, but *not* until TMG is satisfied that the remote server is presenting an acceptable certificate. Thus, TMG can separate the SSL session between the client and remote server into two distinct SSL session, and gains the ability to evaluate the unencrypted traffic sent between the client and remote server.

If this isn't cool, I don't know what is!

Before you configure HTTPS inspection, it's important to understand the implications of the choices you make. The primary thing to understand is that in many places, a "my network, my rules" policy is not validated by legislation and, in fact, laws may exist that specifically prohibit just this sort of mechanism. You should seek legal and organizational guidance before enabling this feature. The following list is a good starting point for your thoughts on this subject. You will likely find a few not listed here that apply to your particular requirements and limitations.

1. TMG creates cloned server certificates using the information gleaned from the certificate offered by the remote server. The organizations that own the service or certificates may not take kindly to this behavior.

2. HTTPS inspection allows TMG to include the entire URL in the Web Proxy logs. Many Web administrators believe that because they're using SSL to protect the data

exchanged between the user and server, they can include the user's logon credentials in the URL. The resulting log contents may impose serious privacy or legal concerns for your organization.

3. HTTPS inspection may allow TMG to cache the content retrieved from the server. In these cases, TMG caching will behave as described in Table 16-1 of Chapter 16, "Caching Concepts and Configuration."

4. Because TMG issues cloned certificates, all TMG array members must be recognized by the clients in the protected networks as trusted Certificate Authorities (CAs). This requirement may be satisfied in two ways:

   ■ The self-signed certificate created by TMG must be included in the client's Trusted Root certificate store. This is the simplest option for Windows domain deployments because Group Policy may be employed to satisfy this requirement.

   ■ Each array member must use a CA certificate that is already included in the client's Trusted Root certificate store. Using this option imposes greater management overhead, because it requires that you provide a unique CA certificate to each array member and register each in Active Directory as part of the PKI structure.

5. To prevent man-in-the-middle attacks, TMG is very strict about validating the server certificate it receives from the Web server. TMG validates certificates through Windows Crypto API (CAPI) as follows:

   a. The host name requested by the client match the Subject or Subject Alternative Names (SAN) certificate fields.

   b. The certificate must be issued for server authentication.

   c. The certificate's date of issue and date of expiration must be valid.

   d. The issuing CA certificate must be valid and trusted by the TMG computer.

   e. The issuing CA Certificate Revocation List must be available and must not include the server certificate.

 REAL WORLD **Fun with Certificate Validation**

As soon as it was possible, I took the opportunity to deploy TMG at home. At the time, my wife was taking an online class from a local community college and was preparing for her final examination in that course. (Yes, my timing was extremely questionable.)

Because HTTPS inspection is a new feature, I decided to test it in a real environment and enabled it on our TMG firewall. Shortly after I finished configuring HTTPS inspection, my wife complained that I had "broken the Internet again." Excited at the prospect of finding an obscure bug in TMG, I set about investigating the problem.

While I watched over her shoulder, I asked her to retry her connection to the site. She opened her browser, typed in the URL, hit the Enter key, and was immediately rewarded with a TMG error page stating "Error Code: 502 Proxy Error. The name on the SSL server certificate supplied by a destination server does not match the name of the host requested. (12227)." Assuming that she had not encountered certificate errors for this site prior to my having enabled HTTPS inspection, I decided to test this site using a computer connected directly to the Internet. When I typed the URL into the browser and hit the Enter key, I received a warning from the browser stating that the certificate was invalid. When I examined the certificate, I discovered that the subject name included *site2.domain.tld*, and the host name in the URL we had been using was *site1.domain.tld*. Rats—no obscure TMG bug for me that day, but at least I knew TMG certificate validation was working as advertised.

Momentarily avoiding the fact that my wife had been ignoring certificate errors for an indeterminate amount of time, I decided to investigate a little deeper. I changed the URL in my browser to *https://site1.domain.tld*, hit Enter, and was rewarded with a logon page that did *not* raise a certificate error. I thought it a bit odd that an established organization such as this community college would make such a rookie error, so I decided to determine the IP address for each site using nslookup. As it turned out, both host names resolved to the same IP address. I contacted the community college to let them know that their Web site or DNS management was in error. I collected a copy of the certificate, the URLs I used to test the connection and the nslookup results, and sent it all off to the site administrators.

A few days later, I received a response from the site administrators thanking me for the information and informing me that the actual host name in the URL for the online courses should have been *site2.domain.tld*. They went on to explain that this problem was the result of an effort to rename the Web site. Essentially, a combination of Web site and DNS management errors had failed to redirect *site1.domain.tld* to *site2.domain.tld* so that students using the old URL would be redirected to the new URL and thus avoid certificate validation errors. Now to address the question of my wife ignoring browser certificate errors. . .

> **NOTE**   My wife is also the proud (?) owner of eight Forefront Edge product bugs: five for ISA Server and three for TMG (maybe more by the time this book goes to print!).

You can configure HTTPS inspection through the Web Access Policy Wizard, as shown in Figure 20-3, or by clicking Configure HTTPS Inspection in the TMG management console right pane, as shown in Figure 20-4.

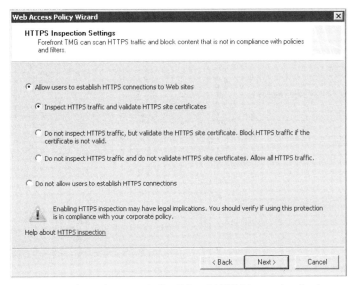

FIGURE 20-3 The Web Access Policy Wizard HTTPS Inspection Settings page

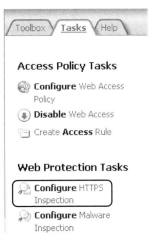

FIGURE 20-4 The Configure HTTPS Inspection task

For the exercise in the following section, you will start by using the Configure HTTPS Inspection link on the Tasks tab. The process described in the following steps will satisfy the following requirements dictated by the Contoso network security team:

- Enable HTTPS Inspection for all sites except *www.contoso.com* and *www.fabrikam.com*.
- Enforce certificate validation for *www.contoso.com* and *www.fabrikam.com*.
- Use a self-signed certificate identified as Contoso Edge Firewall.
- Automatically publish the HTTPS inspection certificate to Active Directory.
- Block sites that use certificates with an expiration date older than one week.
- Users must be notified that HTTPS inspection is in effect for sites that are not excluded.

Configuring HTTPS Inspection

To enable and configure HTTPS Inspection as defined by the security team, follow these steps:

1. Click Configure HTTPS Inspection, as shown in Figure 20-4.

2. In the HTTPS Outbound Inspection dialog box, select Enable HTTPS Inspection, as shown in Figure 20-5.

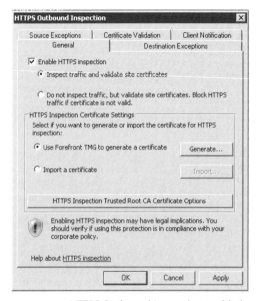

FIGURE 20-5 HTTPS Outbound Inspection enabled

- **Import A Certificate**   This option allows you to import an existing CA certificate *that was exported with the private key*. TMG cannot sign the simulated server certificate without the private key used to create the CA certificate.

3. Click the Generate button and the Generate Certificate dialog box will appear, as shown in Figure 20-6.

FIGURE 20-6 Initial Generate Certificate dialog box

NOTE   Because there is no such thing as a certificate that cannot expire, selecting the Never option creates a certificate with an expiration date 39 years in the future.

4. Select the Trusted Certificate Authority (CA) name text field and replace the existing text with **Contoso Edge Firewall,** as shown in Figure 20-7.

FIGURE 20-7 Modified Generate Certificate dialog box

5. Leave the Issuer Statement field blank and click Generate Certificate Now. You will see a certificate display similar to that shown in Figure 20-8. Click OK to close the Certificate display and click Close to close the Generate Certificate window.

FIGURE 20-8 Initial Certificate display

6. On the HTTPS Outbound Inspection page, click HTTPS Inspection Trusted Root CA Certificate Options. You will see the Certificate Deployment Options dialog box, as shown in Figure 20-9.

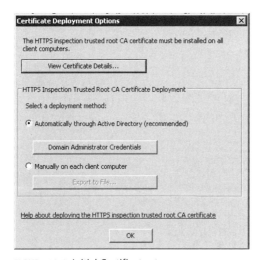

FIGURE 20-9 Initial Certificate store page

> **NOTE** The buttons shown in Figure 20-9 operate as follows:
>
> - **View Certificate Details** This button allows you to view the details of the HTTPS inspection certificate, similar to that shown earlier in Figure 20-8.
> - **Domain Administrator Credentials** This button allows the TMG administrator the means to deploy the TMG HTTPS inspection CA certificate to the domain enterprise trusted root store. The contents of this location are propagated to all domain members whenever those machines or users refresh group policies (normally every 15 minutes).
> - **Export To File** This button allows the TMG administrator the means to share the HTTPS inspection certificate with the PKI management team so that the PKI team can manage the certificate propagation to the users.

7. Click Automatic Deployment. You will see an authentication dialog box, as shown in Figure 20-10.

FIGURE 20-10 Authentication dialog box

8. In the authentication dialog box, enter the credentials for an account that has write access to the domain Enterprise Trusted Root certificate store. Click OK. A command window will appear briefly and if the procedure succeeds, the dialog box shown in Figure 20-11 will appear.

FIGURE 20-11 Confirmation that the certificate was deployed correctly

9. Click OK to close this dialog box.

> **NOTE** To verify successful publication of the TMG HTTPS inspection CA certificate to Active Directory, perform the following steps on any computer in the domain:
>
> **1.** Click Start and select Run. When the Run dialog box appears, type **cmd** and click OK as shown in Figure 20-12.

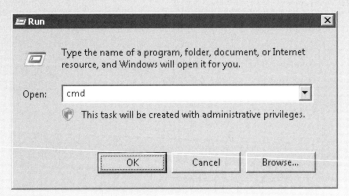

FIGURE 20-12 Run dialog box

2. In the command window, type **gpupdate /force** and press Enter. If you are prompted to log off, type **n** and press Enter again.

3. When the update completes, type **certutil –store –enterprise root** and press Enter. You should see output similar to the following:

```
C:\Users\administrator>certutil -store -enterprise root
================ Certificate 0 ================
Serial Number: e23be5293037cf22
Issuer: CN=Contoso Edge Firewall
NotBefore: 3/7/2009 6:08 PM
NotAfter: 12/31/2048 4:00 PM
Subject: CN=Contoso Edge Firewall
Signature matches Public Key
Root Certificate: Subject matches Issuer
Cert Hash(sha1): f4 17 5c 7e 6e d7 74 31 ba 9b 67 c5 56 dd f6 2c
                4c 5a 92 51
No key provider information
Cannot find the certificate and private key for decryption.
CertUtil: -store command completed successfully.
```

Note that the Issuer and Subject fields should agree with the text you entered in step 4.

10. Click OK to close the Certificate Deployment options dialog box.

11. In the HTTPS Outbound Inspection dialog box, click the Destination Exceptions tab to display the HTTPS inspection exceptions list as shown in Figure 20-13.

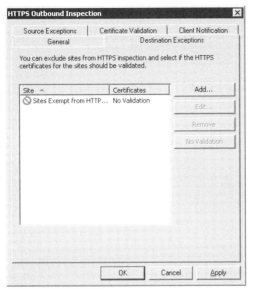

FIGURE 20-13 HTTPS Inspection Exceptions tab default contents

12. Click Add to open the Add Network Entities dialog box, as shown in Figure 20-14.

FIGURE 20-14 Add Network Entities dialog box

13. In the Add Network Entities dialog box, click New and then click Domain Name Set. You will see the New Domain Name Set Policy Element dialog box, as shown in Figure 20-15.

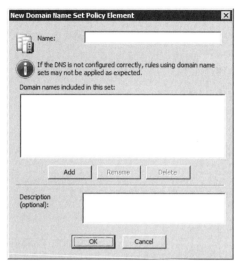

FIGURE 20-15 New Domain Name Set Policy
Element dialog box

14. In the Name field, type **Contoso Corp Excluded Sites**. Click Add. When "new Domain"
    appears in the Domain names included in this list, change it to display **www.contoso
    .com**. Click Add again and change New Domain to display **www.fabrikam.com**. In the
    Description field, type **Sites approved by NetSec for HTTPS inspection exclusion**.
    The page should now appear as shown in Figure 20-16.

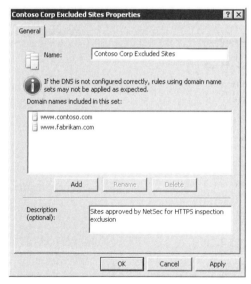

FIGURE 20-16 Modified New Domain Name Set Policy
Element dialog box

15. Click OK to close the window. In the Add Network Entities window expand Domain Name Sets, highlight Contoso Corp Excluded Sites, click Add, and then click Close. The HTTPS Outbound Inspection dialog box will appear, as shown in Figure 20-17.

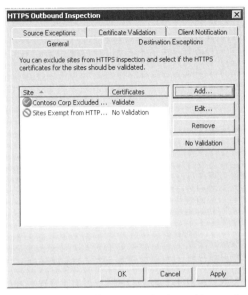

FIGURE 20-17 Modified HTTPS Outbound Inspection Excluded Sites list

16. In the HTTPS Outbound Inspection dialog box, click the Certificate Validation tab.

17. In the Block Expired Certificate After (Days) text box, type **7** as shown in Figure 20-18.

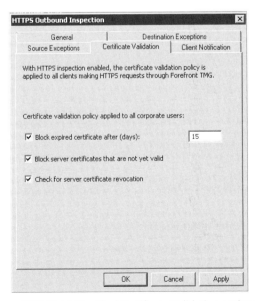

FIGURE 20-18 Modified Certificate Validation options

NOTE The options shown in Figure 20-17 have the following effect on HTTPS inspection:

- **Block Certificates After (Days)**   TMG will reject the connection if the server certificate's expiration date exceeds the value specified in this option (15 days by default).
- **Block Server Certificates That Are Not Yet Valid**   If the server certificate specifies an issued date that is in the future, TMG will reject the connection.
- **Check For Server Certificate Revocation**   TMG will extract the URL specified in the CA certificate referenced in the server certificate. If the Certificate Revocation List (CRL) indicates that the server certificate is revoked, or if TMG is unable to acquire the CRL, the connection will be rejected.

18. In the HTTPS Outbound Inspection dialog box, click the Client notification tab.
19. Select Notify Users That Their HTTPS Traffic Is Being Inspected, as shown in Figure 20-19.

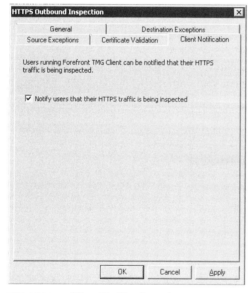

FIGURE 20-19 Client Notification tab

20. Click the Source Exceptions tab to add the computers that you want to exempt from HTTPS inspection. By default this list is empty, as shown in Figure 20-20. For the purpose of this example we will leave this option empty.
21. Click OK to close the HTTPS Outbound Inspection dialog box.

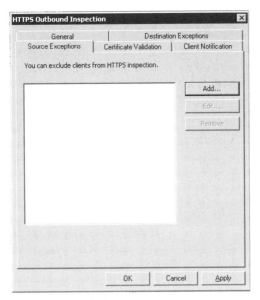

FIGURE 20-20 Default source exemption list

22. Click Apply in the TMG management center pane, type the appropriate notes in the Configuration Change Description window and click Apply to save your changes. The center pane feature display will change, as shown in Figure 20-21.

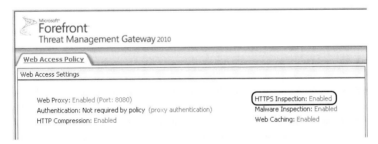

FIGURE 20-21 Updated HTTPS Inspection

23. Click the Monitoring tab in the left pane, and then click the Alerts tab in the center pane. You should find an informational alert indicating successful CA certificate import, as shown in Figure 20-22.

You have now satisfied the HTTPS inspection requirements of the Contoso network security team.

FIGURE 20-22 CA Certificate import informational alert

Common HTTPS Inspection Errors

In general, your users may encounter two error types, depending on the options you have selected for HTTPS inspection:

- **HTTPS Inspection CA certificate errors**   These are generally seen by the user as an "invalid certificate" message when the user attempts to reach a site that uses HTTPS, as shown in Figure 20-23.

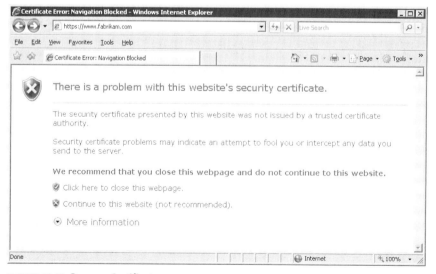

FIGURE 20-23 Browser Certificate error page

The specific error seen by the user depends on the state of the CA certificate used by TMG, but in each case, one of the alerts highlighted in Figure 20-24 will accompany it.

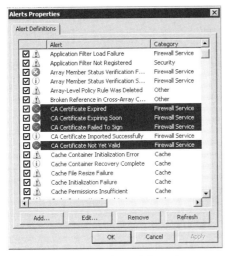

FIGURE 20-24 CA certificate failure alerts

■ **Server Certificate errors** These errors will be seen as error pages generated by TMG due to specific server certificate validation failures. The user application will receive an HTTP 502 Bad Gateway response, with the error text providing the details of the failure, such as:

● "The name on the SSL server certificate supplied by a destination server does not match the name of the host requested."

● "The SSL server certificate supplied by a destination server has expired."

● "The SSL server certificate supplied by a destination server has been revoked."

Figure 20-25 provides an example of one of the TMG certificate error pages.

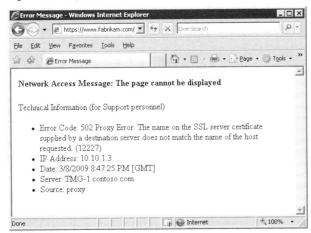

FIGURE 20-25 TMG Certificate Validation Failure

In all cases, the specific error (12227 in this case) will be recorded in the TMG Web Proxy log.

Configuring the HTTP Filter

The HTTP Filter is a Web filter that inspects HTTP headers and data that pass through the TMG Web Proxy filter and allows the user to specify more stringent filtering than TMG provides by default. The HTTP Filter is enabled by default and validates HTTP headers. Although the HTTP Filter provides a certain level of protection, you can customize it to provide stricter HTTP header and content validation. The HTTP Filter can also be used to secure inbound requests when configured in a Web Publishing rule.

For the purpose of this example, we will satisfy the following requirements from the Contoso Network Security Team. For HTTP traffic the following requirements will be covered for the main Internet access rule and a Web Publishing rule for Contoso's Web site:

- Allow HTTP request Header no larger than 32,768 bytes.
- Allow any payload length.
- Allow a maximum URL length of 10,240 bytes.
- Allow a maximum query length of 10,240 bytes.
- Block the HTTP PUT method.
- Block the MP3 file extension (TMG does not detect the actual file type).
- For the rule that publishes *www.contoso.com*, hide the fact that the internal Web server is hosted on IIS 7.
- Block Microsoft MSN Messenger.
- Block outbound requests from the CONFICKER worm.

General Options

To configure the first four requirements from the Contoso Network Security Team, follow these steps:

1. On the TMG Server computer (or using remote management console), open the TMG Management Console.
2. Click TMG (Array Name) in the left pane.
3. Click Web Access Policy, right-click your main Internet Access policy, and choose Configure HTTP as shown in Figure 20-26.
4. When you choose Configure HTTP, the Configure HTTP Policy For Rule dialog box will appear as shown in Figure 20-27.

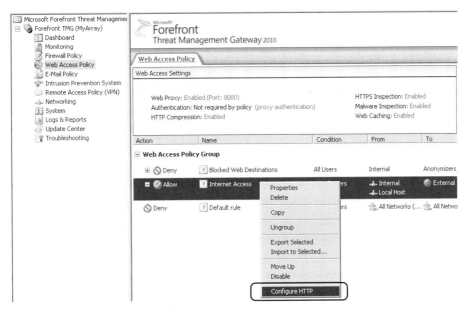

FIGURE 20-26 Configuring HTTP Filter

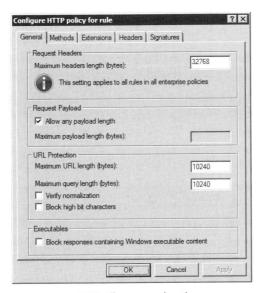

FIGURE 20-27 HTTP Filter general options

The first set of options dictated by the Contoso network security team are available on this first tab (General). Here the definitions of each one of those options:

- **Maximum Headers Length (Bytes)**   This option allows you to specify the maximum size (in bytes) of the URL and HTTP header for HTTP requests processed by this rule. The main goal of this option is to mitigate the risk of attacks that use long headers to exploit buffer overflows.

- **Allow Any Payload Length**   This option allows you to limit the amount of data that a user can POST to a Web site. Although this can mitigate possible attacks, it also can have a negative impact if you do not know what the maximum realistic value should be. For Web Publishing rules, this may be easier to define because your organization operates the Web servers, but will require coordination with your Web developers or administrators.

- **Maximum URL Length (Bytes)**   This option allows you to limit the size of the URL sent by the client. Generally, the default value is sufficient.

- **Maximum Query Length (Bytes)**   This option allows you to control the maximum acceptable query length, which is the portion of the URL that follows the question mark (?). This option can help you mitigate attacks based on long query strings.

- **Verify Normalization**   This option allows you to block URLs that contain escaped characters after having been normalized. Normalization is a process that reverses the process used by many Web applications (and some malcontents) to encode URL content. The use of the percent (%) character is one example of an encoding scheme. For instance, the combination of % plus 20 (%20) represents a space character. Therefore, a request for *http://www.contoso.com/My%20Documents/MS%20Tmg%20 book.htm* is equivalent to *http://www.contoso.com/My Documents/MS Tmg book.htm*. To mitigate attacks, this filter normalizes the URL twice. So in a case where the URL after the first normalization pass is different from the second normalization pass, the HTTP Filter rejects the request.

- **Block High Bit Characters**   When enabled, this option will block URLs that contain a double-byte character set (DBCS) or Latin 1 characters. It is important to mention that when you select this option you can impact scenarios such as Outlook Web Access publishing, Microsoft SharePoint publishing, and any scenario in which an HTTP GET request has a parameter that includes a character from a DBCS.

NOTE   An example of an issue that can happen when this option is enabled is documented at *http://support.microsoft.com/kb/837865*.

- **Block Responses Containing Windows Executable Content**   This option will analyze the response from the Web server and determine whether it contains Windows executable content and will block the response if this option is selected.

NOTE   The Verify Normalization option helps to mitigate double encoding attacks. For more information about double encoding, read Chapter 12 of *Writing Secure Code* from Microsoft Press at *http://www.microsoft.com/mspress/books/sampchap/5612b.aspx*.

The default options on the General tab are now compliant with the requirements from the Contoso network security team. Click the Methods tab to continue.

HTTP Methods

This part of the HTTP configuration deals with controlling HTTP methods. By default, the HTTP Filter allows all HTTP methods. You can see this by clicking the Methods tab, as shown in Figure 20-28.

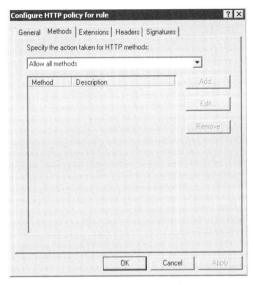

FIGURE 20-28 HTTP methods available

NOTE   For more information on how HTTP Protocol works and available HTTP methods, read Chapter 32.

The options available in this dialog box are:

- **Allow Only Specified Methods**   If you select this option, only the methods that are manually specified will be allowed.
- **Block Specified Method (Allow All Others)**   Use this option if you want to block certain HTTP methods.
- **Block Requests Containing Ambiguous Extensions**   This option will block any file extension or content-type where TMG is unable to determine the content-type.

Follow these steps to configure this option according to the requirements:

1. Open the drop-down list in the option Specify The Action Taken For HTTP Methods and select Block Specified Methods (Allow All Others), as shown in Figure 20-29.
2. The Add button will became available. Click Add and type **PUT,** as shown in Figure 20-30.

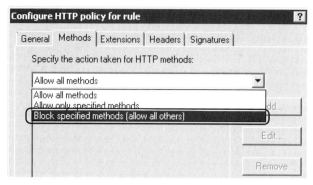

FIGURE 20-29 Configuring HTTP methods

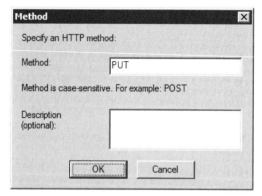

FIGURE 20-30 Adding HTTP PUT method

3. Click OK and your Methods tab will appear, as shown in Figure 20-31.

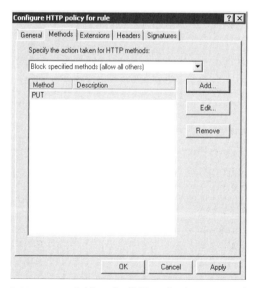

FIGURE 20-31 Adding the PUT method as an unauthorized HTTP method

4. Type the appropriate notes in the Configuration Change Description window and click Apply to commit this change.

With this option selected all methods except the PUT method will be allowed. This is an example of an approach where you know exactly what needs to be blocked. Another technique is to specify that all requests should be blocked except for a specified set.

Extensions

The Extensions tab allows you to control what file extensions are allowed. By default all extensions are allowed, as shown in Figure 20-32.

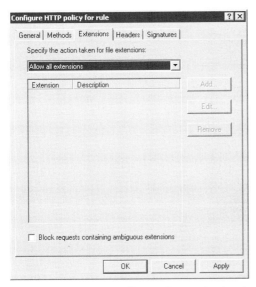

FIGURE 20-32 The Allow all extensions option is selected by default.

The options available in this window are:

- **Allow Only Specified Extensions**   When you select this option, only the specified extensions are allowed.
- **Block Specified Extensions (Allow All Others)**   Use this option if you want to block only certain file extensions and allow all others.
- **Block Requests Containing Ambiguous Extensions**   This option will block any file extension where TMG cannot determine the type.

For this scenario use the following steps to block files using an MP3 extension:

1. Open the drop-down list in the option Specify The Action Taken For File Extensions and select Block Specified Methods (Allow All Others), as shown in Figure 20-33.

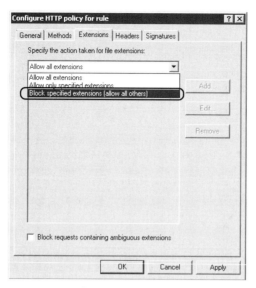

FIGURE 20-33 Selecting the option to block the extension that better fits with the environment's need

2. The Add button will become available. Click Add and type **MP3** as shown in Figure 20-34.

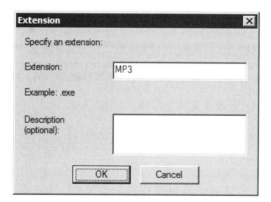

FIGURE 20-34 Adding the file extension that will be blocked

3. Click OK. The Methods tab will appear, as shown in Figure 20-35.

4. Click OK and then, in the main TMG console, click Apply to commit this change.

FIGURE 20-35 The Extensions tab after adding the MP3 file type

Headers

To comply with one of the requirements from the Contoso network security team, it is necessary to hide the fact that the internal Web server uses IIS 7 from external users that are accessing *www.contoso.com*. This information is located in the HTTP header under the Server field. To illustrate that, let's look at an example of a Network Monitor trace from an external client (192.168.1.245) sending an HTTP GET request to *www.contoso.com* for a server that is published by TMG (192.168.1.99):

1. The external client sends the HTTP GET Request for *www.contoso.com*:

```
192.168.1.245  192.168.1.99  HTTP  HTTP:Request, GET /
- Http: Request, GET /
  Command: GET
+ URI: /
  ProtocolVersion: HTTP/1.1
  Accept: image/gif, image/x-xbitmap, image/jpeg, image/pjpeg, */*
  Accept-Language: en-us
  UA-CPU: x86
  Accept-Encoding: gzip, deflate
  UserAgent: Mozilla/4.0 (compatible; MSIE 6.0; Windows NT 5.2; SV1; .NET CLR
1.1.4322)
  Host: www.contoso.com
  Connection: Keep-Alive
  HeaderEnd: CRLF
```

2. TMG sends the HTTP Response and notices the Server field that has the information about the published server:

```
192.168.1.99  192.168.1.245  HTTP  HTTP:Response, HTTP/1.1, Status Code = 200,
URL: /
- Http: Response, HTTP/1.1, Status Code = 200, URL: /
  ProtocolVersion: HTTP/1.1
  StatusCode: 200, Ok
  Reason: OK
  Connection: Keep-Alive
  ContentLength: 458
  Date: Mon, 09 Mar 2009 22:37:10 GMT
  ContentType: text/html
  ETag: "1a1d73cab962c91:0"
  Server: Microsoft-IIS/7.0
  Accept-Ranges: bytes
  Last-Modified: Sat, 20 Dec 2008 15:44:06 GMT
  XPoweredBy: ASP.NET
  Content-Encoding: gzip
  Vary: Accept-Encoding
  HeaderEnd: CRLF
+ payload: HttpContentType = text/html
```

The goal here is to hide this (server) field from external clients so that they don't know what type of Web server is hosting this Web site; this is known as *security by obscurity*, because it relies on providing security through digital sleight-of-hand. Simply changing the data provided in the header does not mitigate any vulnerabilities the server might have. Some companies use this concept while publishing a Web site to fool the attacker into thinking the server is something other than what it actually is.

> **MORE INFO** Read *http://technet.microsoft.com/en-us/magazine/2008.06.obscurity.aspx* to learn more about security by obscurity.

To configure the HTTP Filter to meet this requirement you will need to configure TMG so that it will change the HTTP server Header in the Web Publishing rule for *www.contoso.com*. To do so, follow these steps:

> **MORE INFO** For more information on how to create a Web site publishing rule, review Chapter 22, "Publishing Servers."

1. Click Firewall Policy, right-click the *www.contoso.com* Web Publishing rule and choose Configure HTTP.
2. Click the Headers tab and the window will appear, as shown in Figure 20-36.

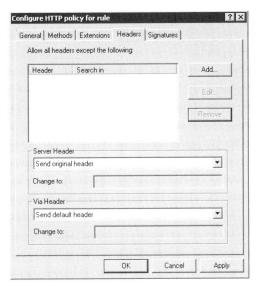

FIGURE 20-36 The Default Headers option in the HTTP Filter

3. In the Server Header drop-down list, choose Modify Header In Response as shown in Figure 20-37.

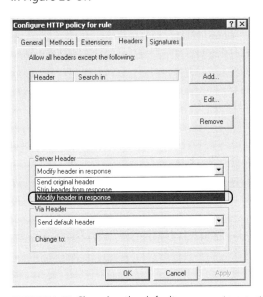

FIGURE 20-37 Changing the default response to a custom one

4. Type the name with which you want to substitute the Server's name (currently shown as Microsoft-IIS/7.0), as shown in Figure 20-38.

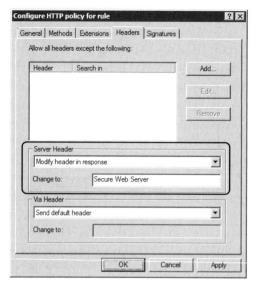

FIGURE 20-38 A new value for the Server Header field

5. Click OK and then click Apply in the main TMG console to commit the changes.

Validating Inbound Access

Now that the configuration indicated by the network security team has been completed, another network monitor capture will reveal what the traffic will look like:

1. The external client sends the HTTP GET Request for *www.contoso.com*:

```
192.168.1.245  192.168.1.99  HTTP  HTTP:Request, GET /
- Http: Request, GET /
  Command: GET
+ URI: /
  ProtocolVersion: HTTP/1.1
  Accept: image/gif, image/x-xbitmap, image/jpeg, image/pjpeg, */*
  Accept-Language: en-us
  UA-CPU: x86
  Accept-Encoding: gzip, deflate
  UserAgent: Mozilla/4.0 (compatible; MSIE 6.0; Windows NT 5.2; SV1; .NET CLR
1.1.4322)
  Host: www.contoso.com
  Connection: Keep-Alive
  HeaderEnd: CRLF
```

2. TMG sends the HTTP Response and notices that the Server field has the value that was inserted by HTTP Filter:

```
192.168.1.99  192.168.1.245  HTTP  HTTP:Response, HTTP/1.1, Status Code = 200,
URL: /
- Http: Response, HTTP/1.1, Status Code = 200, URL: /
  ProtocolVersion: HTTP/1.1
  StatusCode: 200, Ok
  Reason: OK
  Connection: Keep-Alive
  ContentLength: 458
  Date: Mon, 09 Mar 2009 22:37:10 GMT
  ContentType: text/html
  ETag: "1a1d73cab962c91:0"
  Accept-Ranges: bytes
  Last-Modified: Sat, 20 Dec 2008 15:44:06 GMT
  XPoweredBy: ASP.NET
  Server: Secure Web Server
  Content-Encoding: gzip
  Vary: Accept-Encoding
```

Signatures

The HTTP Filter uses the concept of the signature to inspect content in the HTTP headers or body. This is a very powerful option; however, you may block more than you want if you are not careful with how you select the match data for the signature. An application signature is a data point in the HTTP conversation that identifies the application.

For example, the User-agent field in the HTTP header may be used to identify the client application to the Web server. When you see MSN Messenger in the User-Agent header, you may generally assume that this application is MSN Messenger. This is not a guaranteed fact, because malicious applications or users can change this data field relatively easily.

> **MORE INFO** For a list of some common application signatures, go to *http://technet.microsoft .com/en-us/library/cc302520.aspx.*

One way to block certain types of applications or even certain features used by the application is to observe the communication and determine how the application behaves and possibly identify what data can be considered an identifier for that type of traffic. Just to recap, the relevant requirements from Contoso network security team are:

- Block Microsoft MSN Messenger.
- Block outbound requests from CONFICKER worm.

Blocking MSN Messenger

To satisfy the first requirement, follow these steps:

1. Click Web Access Policy, right-click your main Internet Access policy, and choose Configure HTTP as shown in Figure 20-39.

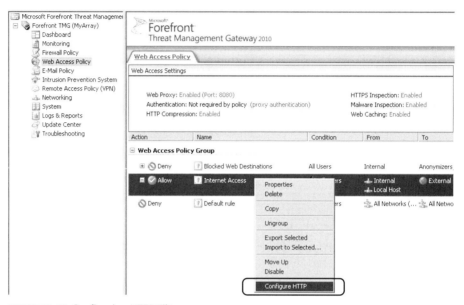

FIGURE 20-39 Configuring HTTP Filter

2. When you click Configure HTTP the Configure HTTP Policy For Rule dialog box will appear. Click the Signatures tab and the window will appear, as shown in Figure 20-40.

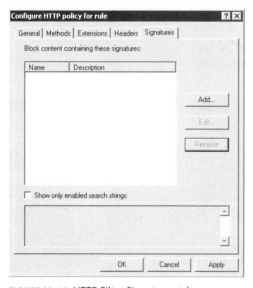

FIGURE 20-40 HTTP Filter Signatures tab

3. Click Add and the do the following in the Signature window:

   a. Type **Block MSN Messenger** in the Name field.

   b. Select Request Headers from the Search In drop-down list.

   c. Type **User-agent** in the HTTP Header field.

   d. Type **Windows Live Messenger** in the Signature field.

   e. The results should appear as shown in Figure 20-41.

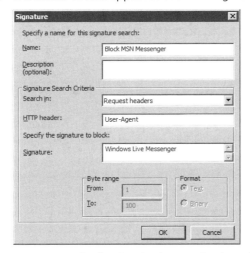

FIGURE 20-41 Configuring the signature for the traffic that you want to block

NOTE HTTP Filter signatures are case-insensitive. If you type **windows live messenger** in the Signature field, it will have the same results as if you typed **Windows Live Messenger**.

4. Click OK and your Signature tab will appear, as shown in Figure 20-42.

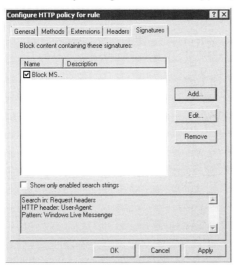

FIGURE 20-42 The Signatures tab after parameters to block MSN have been added

5. Click OK to close this window and then click Apply in the main TMG console to apply the changes.

> **MORE INFO** MSN Live Messenger will use HTTP if the negotiation to use the other ports fails. To learn more about the ports used by MSN Messenger system see *http://support.microsoft.com/kb/960820*.

Validating Outbound Traffic

To verify TMG HTTP Filter action, follow these steps:

1. Click the Logs & Reports node in the left pane and then click Edit Filter in the task pane, as shown in Figure 20-43.

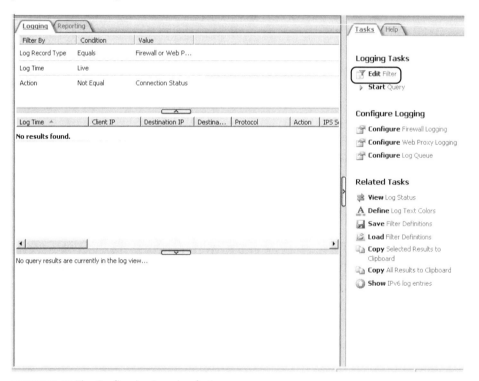

FIGURE 20-43 The Configuring Logging feature

2. In the Filter By drop-down list, select Client IP.
3. In the Condition drop-down list, select Equals.

4. In the Value field, enter the IP address of your test client. In this example, it is **10.10.10.9**. The results will appear, as shown in Figure 20-44.

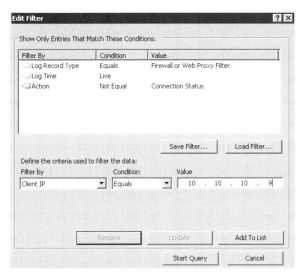

FIGURE 20-44 Modified Edit Filter page

NOTE You should use the IP address assigned to your test client.

5. Click Add To List and then click Start Query.

6. At a test client workstation, launch MSN Messenger and try to log on. An error message similar to Figure 20-45 should appear in the client workstation.

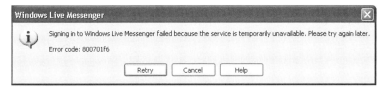

FIGURE 20-45 Generic MSN Messenger error message when MSN Messenger is unable to log on

7. Go to TMG and look at the Logging; the error message should appear as shown in Figure 20-46.

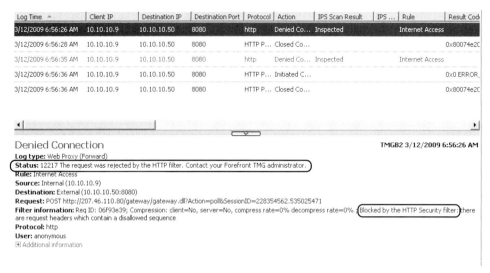

FIGURE 20-46 Log showing that the HTTP Filter blocked the request

As you can see, TMG Logging allows you to demonstrate that the HTTP Filter blocked the user's access to this external resource. If you capture a Network Monitor trace during the logon attempt you will see the following behavior:

1. The internal client attempts to log on to MSN Messenger by sending the request to TMG:

```
10.10.10.9  10.10.10.50  XMLParser  XMLParser:
- Http: Request, POST http://gateway.messenger.hotmail.com/gateway/gateway.dll
   Command: POST
  + URI: http://gateway.messenger.hotmail.com/gateway/gateway.dll?Action=open&Ser
ver=NS&IP=messenger.hotmail.com
   ProtocolVersion: HTTP/1.1
   Accept: */*
   ContentType: text/xml; charset=utf-8
   ContentLength: 35
   UserAgent: Mozilla/4.0 (compatible; MSIE 7.0; Windows NT 5.1; .NET CLR
1.1.4322; Windows Live Messenger 8.1.0178)
   Host: gateway.messenger.hotmail.com
   ProxyConnection: Keep-Alive
   Pragma: no-cache
```

2. TMG sends back the following HTTP response to the client:

```
10.10.10.50  10.10.10.9  HTTP  HTTP:Response, HTTP/1.1, Status Code = 502,
URL: http://gateway.messenger.hotmail.com/gateway/gateway.dll
- Http: Response, HTTP/1.1, Status Code = 502, URL: http://gateway.messenger
.hotmail.com/gateway/gateway.dll
   ProtocolVersion: HTTP/1.1
```

```
StatusCode: 502, Bad gateway
Reason: Proxy Error ( The request was rejected by the HTTP filter. Contact
your TMG administrator. )
Via: 1.1 TMGB2
Connection: close
ProxyConnection: close
Pragma: no-cache
Cache-Control: no-cache
ContentType: text/html
ContentLength: 4094
HeaderEnd: CRLF
```

The HTTP response contains the reason why the traffic is being blocked by TMG ("rejected by the HTTP Filter"). Notice also that TMG closes the connection with the client workstation for that request when it sends the HTTP 502 ("proxy-connection: close").

> **NOTE** For the preceding example we used Windows Live Messenger version 8.1. For this version the User-Agent string was the one shown in Figure 20-39. It is important to remember that in future versions of Windows Live Messenger this can be changed without advance notice. If the preceding steps to block MSN fail in your environment, we recommend that you obtain a Network Monitor trace and confirm that the User-Agent field is correct.

Blocking the Conficker Worm

In 2008 a new worm called Conficker was created. Conficker was responsible for a lot of damage on many networks. Conficker infects computers across a network by exploiting a vulnerability in the Windows Server service (SVCHOST.EXE). Depending on the specific Conficker variant (there are many), it can also spread via removable drives and by exploiting weak passwords. Research conducted by Microsoft Malware Protection Center confirmed that if the date of the system is higher than November 25, 2008, this worm will build a URL to send an HTTP request trying to download files from random places. The URL was identified to be: *http://<randomIP>/search?q=%d&aq=7*.

> **MORE INFO** For a complete description of Conficker worm visit Microsoft Malware Protection Center at *http://www.microsoft.com/security/portal/Entry.aspx?Name=Win32/Conficker*.

Using the TMG HTTP Filter you can block Conficker-based requests from an infected machine on a TMG-protected network. Contoso network security has asked you to implement such a filter in TMG. Use the following steps to satisfy the network security team's request:

1. Click Web Access Policy, right-click your main Internet Access policy, and choose Configure HTTP as shown in Figure 20-47.

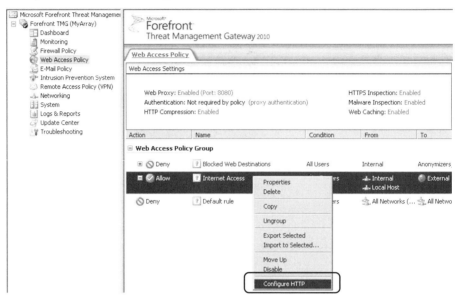

FIGURE 20-47 Configuring HTTP Filter for one specific rule

2. When you click Configure HTTP, the Configure HTTP Policy For Rule dialog box will appear. Click the Signatures tab and the dialog box will appear, as shown in Figure 20-48.

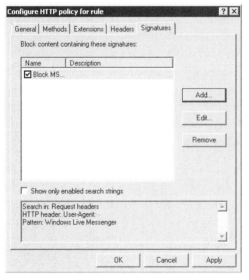

FIGURE 20-48 The Signatures tab with Block MSN already created

3. Click Add and do the following in the Signature window:

  a. Type **Block Conficker** in the Name field.

  b. Select Request URL in the Search In drop-down list.

  c. Type **search?q=%d&aq=7** in the Signature field, as shown in Figure 20-49.

FIGURE 20-49 Adding a new signature to block Conficker

4. Click OK and your Signatures tab will appear, as shown in Figure 20-50.

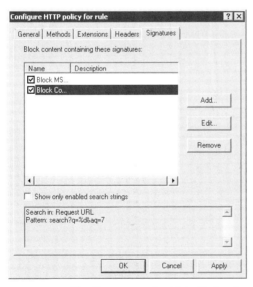

FIGURE 20-50 The Signatures tab with both signatures added

5. Click OK to close this window and then click Apply in the main TMG console to apply the changes.

NOTE You can automate this process by downloading the script that adds those signatures in HTTP Filter. Download the script from *http://www.isatools.org/tools/ block_conficker.vbs*.

Summary

In this chapter you learned about the TMG architecture with an emphasis on the Web Proxy filter and how this filter handles HTTP and HTTPS traffic originating from clients. The TMG component responsible for receiving the request, processing it, and evaluating it if that is a legitimate request is the Firewall Engine that runs in Kernel Mode. After processing this request, the Firewall Engine hands it over to Firewall Service, which runs in User Mode. The first protocol inspection that you learned in this chapter was HTTPS inspection. This is an area where you will need careful planning because some legal concerns are involved when you inspect private information such as online banking or health records. You also learned the steps to configure HTTPS inspection and the requirements to make it work properly. You also learned how to configure HTTP Filter to allow a deep HTTP inspection. You learned that it is possible to make restrictions regard the HTTP header and also block content by signatures that you can customize. In the next chapter you will learn about publishing resources through TMG.

## PART VII

TMG Publishing Scenarios

CHAPTER 21   Understanding Publishing Concepts   **573**

CHAPTER 22   Publishing Servers   **599**

CHAPTER 23   Publishing Microsoft Office SharePoint Server   **661**

CHAPTER 24   Publishing Exchange Server   **697**

Understanding Publishing Concepts

- Core Publishing Scenarios **573**

- Publishing Rule Elements **580**

- Planning Publishing Rules **591**

- Summary **598**

One of the most common reasons for deploying Microsoft Forefront Threat Management Gateway (TMG) 2010 is to publish applications to the Internet or to an isolated network. TMG makes use of two different types of publishing rules, Web Publishing and Server Publishing, to securely publish Web or non-Web servers and services. Both publishing rules have their own requirements. In this chapter we will discuss the core publishing scenarios, how the publishing rules work, what the core elements are, and how to plan publishing rules.

Core Publishing Scenarios

Like ISA Server 2006, TMG provides two types of publishing scenarios: Web Publishing and Server Publishing. The primary distinctions between the two are simple. Web Publishing is dependent on the Web Proxy filter; Server Publishing may use one of any of the remaining application filters. One thing that distinguishes Server Publishing rules from all others is the use of an *incoming* context for the protocol definition—access and Web Publishing rules use *outbound* protocols.

> **NOTE** The concept of *inbound* for server publishing rules originated with ISA Server 2000, which maintained a single-relationship view for three networks: VPN Clients, Internal, and External. In this context, traffic originating in the External network was processed as inbound, whereas traffic originating in any other network was processed as outbound.

Server Publishing

Server Publishing is distinguished by the use of a listener and an associated Server Publishing rule that describes a one-to-one mapping between the listener and published server. Server publishing rules are the only policy rules where the use of "server" protocols is a functional choice. For instance, the difference between the protocols SMTP and SMTP Server are defined in the primary protocol direction. Protocols for access rules define an outbound context for the primary connection, as shown in Figure 21-1.

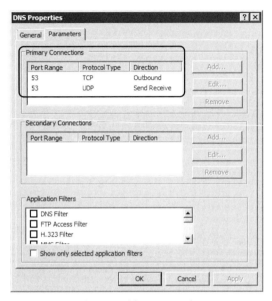

FIGURE 21-1 DNS protocol for access rules

Protocols used for Server Publishing rules define an inbound context for the primary connection, as shown in Figure 21-2.

> **NOTE** DNS is an example of a protocol that is defined by an application filter. Because the DNS application filter works only in the context of Server Publishing, only the DNS Server protocol is associated with the DNS application filter.

Definitions for bidirectional UDP protocols use an explicit bidirectional definition because the UDP protocol does not define a connection as TCP does. UDP was designed as a "fire and forget" transport protocol. For TMG policies to allow UDP responses related to an origination message, TMG must define such UDP usage as *send-receive* for access rules or *receive-send* for Server Publishing rules.

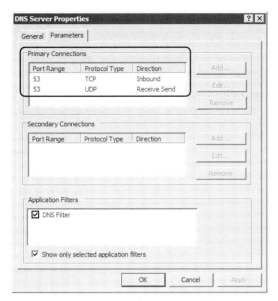

FIGURE 21-2 DNS protocol for Server Publishing rules

Server Publishing operates in the context of a single application filter and some of these filters (such as the DNS filter) are limited to Server Publishing scenarios, whereas others (such as the SMTP and SIP filters) adjust their behavior according to the type of rule that is processing the traffic. Figure 21-3 and the following list describe the basic data flow for Server Publishing.

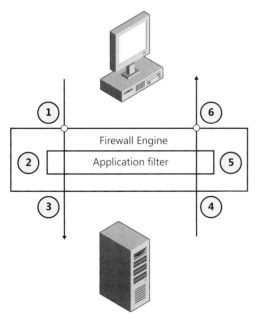

FIGURE 21-3 Server Publishing conceptual diagram

1. Client connects to the listener created by the Firewall Engine. The Firewall Engine recognizes the connection as appropriate to a Server Publishing listener and allows the connection.

2. The application filter processes the request in the context of the protocol definition.

3. The application filter forwards the traffic to the published server.

4. The server processes the request and sends the response to TMG or the original client, depending on the publishing rule settings.

5. The application filter processes the response in the context of the same publishing rule.

6. The application filter forwards the response to the client.

> **NOTE** The Firewall Engine allows application filters to decide whether the request or response should be allowed. Because this decision is made in the context of the selected application layer, the Firewall Engine blocking mechanisms are not involved. In general, when this action occurs, the TMG firewall Result-Code field will contain 0x80074e24, which means *connection closed by filter action*.

Server Publishing and Network Relationships

As discussed in Chapter 11, "Configuring TMG Networks," understanding the network relationship is critical to the proper definition and thus the operation of a Server Publishing rule.

For a Server Publishing rule that operates in the context of a NAT relationship, the Server Publishing rule instructs the packet and firewall filters to allow traffic that matches the source as defined in the publishing rule and is destined for a TMG IP address in the same network. Figure 21-4 illustrates the appropriate originating packet construction for a NAT-based Server Publishing rule listener.

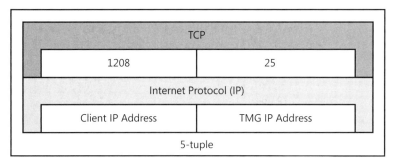

FIGURE 21-4 Packet destined to a NAT-based Server Publishing rule

For a Server Publishing rule that operates in the context of a route relationship, the Server Publishing rule instructs the packet and firewall filters to allow traffic that is destined for a specific IP address owned by a host in the destination network. Figure 21-5 illustrates the appropriate originating packet construction for a route-based Server Publishing listener.

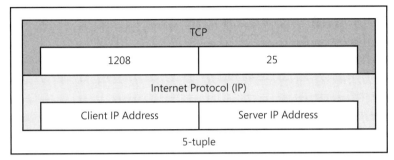

FIGURE 21-5 Packet destined to a route-based Server Publishing rule

Server Publishing vs. Access Rules

Because the packet construction for Server Publishing in route relationship and access rule scenarios is the same, the question of whether a Server Publishing rule or an access rule is more appropriate for a particular scenario. The simple answer to this question is "it depends on whether the related protocol is defined by an application filter and whether the application filter operates unidirectionally or bidirectionally."

Another example of a protocol that is defined by an application filter is the SMTP server protocol. If you separate an SMTP client and server using a route relationship across TMG and you want to apply the SMTP application filter's SMTP conversation intelligence to traffic passing through this path, you must define a server publishing rule between the two networks.

> **NOTE** Because the packets constructed by the client for access rules and route-related server publishing rules are identical, you should not define access and Server Publishing rules for the same traffic path. If you do, the first rule encountered by the Firewall Engine will be the one used to process this traffic. In other words, if an access rule allowing SMTP precedes an SMTP server publishing rule for the same source and destination, the access rule will process the traffic and the SMTP application filter will not be used. The frustration created by attempting to sort out this behavior is likely to result in unwanted cranial follicle freedom.

Web Publishing

Web Publishing is distinguished by the use of a network listener owned by the Web proxy, associated with one or more Web Publishing rules (a one-to-many relationship). Because the Web proxy owns the listener, multiple Web Publishing rules can share a single listener—this is similar to how IIS allows multiple Web sites to share a single listener. The HTTP protocol itself is what makes this functionality possible. We discuss the HTTP protocol and related mechanisms in Chapter 32, "Exploring the HTTP Protocol."

Because Web Publishing depends on the Web Proxy filter and its associated Web filters, Web Publishing scenarios are limited to two protocols used by the originating client: HTTP and HTTPS.

NOTE **Unlike Server Publishing, Web Publishing does not use an inbound protocol context.**

At the server end of the conversation, the Web proxy supports HTTP, HTTPS, and FTP. The details of these cases will be discussed in detail in the section "Publishing Rule Elements" later in the chapter. Web Publishing rules also take advantage of the Web filters hosted in the Web proxy that are registered for Incoming Web Requests or Both (meaning, incoming and outgoing), as shown in Figure 21-6.

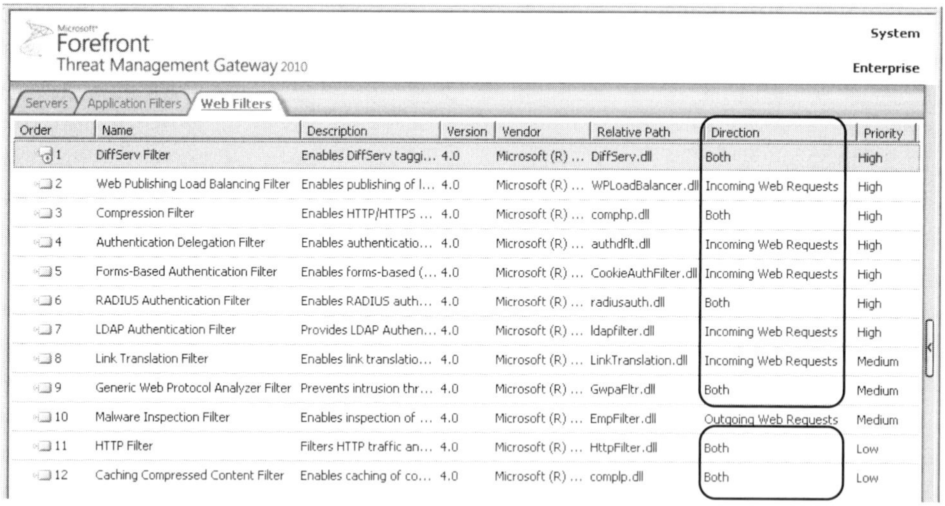

Order	Name	Description	Version	Vendor	Relative Path	Direction	Priority
1	DiffServ Filter	Enables DiffServ taggi...	4.0	Microsoft (R) ...	DiffServ.dll	Both	High
2	Web Publishing Load Balancing Filter	Enables publishing of l...	4.0	Microsoft (R) ...	WPLoadBalancer.dll	Incoming Web Requests	High
3	Compression Filter	Enables HTTP/HTTPS ...	4.0	Microsoft (R) ...	comphp.dll	Both	High
4	Authentication Delegation Filter	Enables authenticatio...	4.0	Microsoft (R) ...	authdflt.dll	Incoming Web Requests	High
5	Forms-Based Authentication Filter	Enables forms-based (...	4.0	Microsoft (R) ...	CookieAuthFilter.dll	Incoming Web Requests	High
6	RADIUS Authentication Filter	Enables RADIUS auth...	4.0	Microsoft (R) ...	radiusauth.dll	Both	High
7	LDAP Authentication Filter	Provides LDAP Authen...	4.0	Microsoft (R) ...	ldapfilter.dll	Incoming Web Requests	High
8	Link Translation Filter	Enables link translatio...	4.0	Microsoft (R) ...	LinkTranslation.dll	Incoming Web Requests	Medium
9	Generic Web Protocol Analyzer Filter	Prevents intrusion thr...	4.0	Microsoft (R) ...	GwpaFltr.dll	Both	Medium
10	Malware Inspection Filter	Enables inspection of ...	4.0	Microsoft (R) ...	EmpFilter.dll	Outgoing Web Requests	Medium
11	HTTP Filter	Filters HTTP traffic an...	4.0	Microsoft (R) ...	HttpFilter.dll	Both	Low
12	Caching Compressed Content Filter	Enables caching of co...	4.0	Microsoft (R) ...	complp.dll	Both	Low

FIGURE 21-6 Web Filter Direction registration

Thus, Web Publishing potentially makes use of all Web filters except the Malware Inspection filter, which is registered only for outgoing Web requests. As a result, Web Publishing also allows TMG to provide additional features such as content caching, compression, Web Publishing Load Balancing, and DiffServ.

Conceptually, Web Publishing operates as shown in Figure 21-7 and described in the following list.

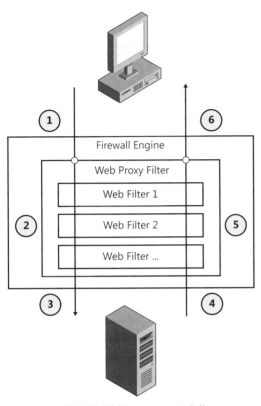

FIGURE 21-7 Web Publishing conceptual diagram

1. The client connects to the listener created by the Web Proxy filter and issues an HTTP request. The Firewall Engine recognizes the connection as appropriate to a Web Proxy listener and allows the connection and request.

2. The Web Proxy filter processes the request in the context of the appropriate Web Publishing rule and passes the request data to the Web filters according to their registered purpose and order.

3. The Web Proxy filter forwards the request to the published Web server including any modifications created by the Web proxy or Web filters.

4. The Web server processes the request and sends the response to the TMG or the original client, depending on the Web Publishing rule settings.

5. The Web proxy processes the response in the context of the same publishing rule and passes the response through the Web filters according to their registered purpose and order.

6. The Web proxy forwards the response to the Web Publishing client including any modifications created by the Web proxy or Web filters.

NOTE The Web proxy allows Web filters to determine the validity of the request or response and decide whether the request or response should be accepted or rejected. Because this decision is made in the context of the HTTP application layer, the Firewall Engine blocking mechanisms are not involved.

Publishing Rule Elements

Web Publishing and Server Publishing rules allow you to publish services through TMG for both users on protected networks and remote users on the Internet. In the previous section we discussed how Web Publishing and Server Publishing rules process traffic. In this section we will cover the core elements that are involved in a Web Publishing rule and in a Server Publishing rule.

Elements in a Web Publishing Rule

Web Publishing rules are used to publish Web services. Web Publishing is often called Reverse Proxy because it provides by-proxy access to Web sites protected by TMG. To ensure that the Web Publishing rule is set up correctly we need to understand the elements involved in the rule type and make sure they are configured accordingly.

Web Listener

The Web listener is owned and created by the Web Proxy filter. The Web listener listens for HTTP and HTTPS requests on the IP addresses or network(s) that you define. The ports that the IP address or all IP addresses on a network listen on are 80 for HTTP and 443 for HTTPS by default; however, you can change the listening port. If TMG is to pre-authenticate the request before it is forwarded to the published Web server, the initial authentication type is also defined on the Web listener. You can also specify Single-Sign-On (SSO) for multiple domains on a single Web listener. You must keep specific considerations in mind for SSO:

- The primary authentication on the listener must be Forms-Based Authentication.
- All domains that should benefit from SSO must be defined on the same Web listener.
- The sites for which we need SSO should be published using the same Web listener with the SSO domains specified on the listener.

Figure 21-8 shows an example of a Web listener.

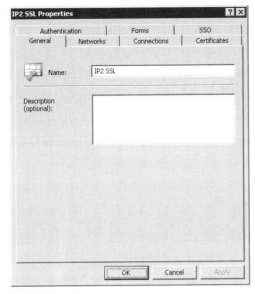

FIGURE 21-8 Web listener properties page

HTTP Policy

One major advantage of Web Publishing over Server Publishing is that the traffic forwarded to the published Web server or service will be subjected to application-layer inspection. This helps minimize the effects from an attack on the published Web server. The HTTP filter improves the security of the published Web application by enforcing specific HTTP filtering on various components involved in a HTTP communication. The HTTP policy enforced on a Web Publishing rule allows you to:

- Set the maximum payload length
- Block high-bit characters
- Verify normalization
- Block responses containing Windows executable content
- Set the exact HTTP methods that you want to allow or block to the published Web site
- Allow only a specific list of file extensions
- Allow only a specific list of Request or Response headers
- Create fine-tuned signatures that can block connections based on Request URLs, Request headers, Request body, Response headers, or Response body

Figure 21-9 shows what the HTTP policy for a rule looks like.

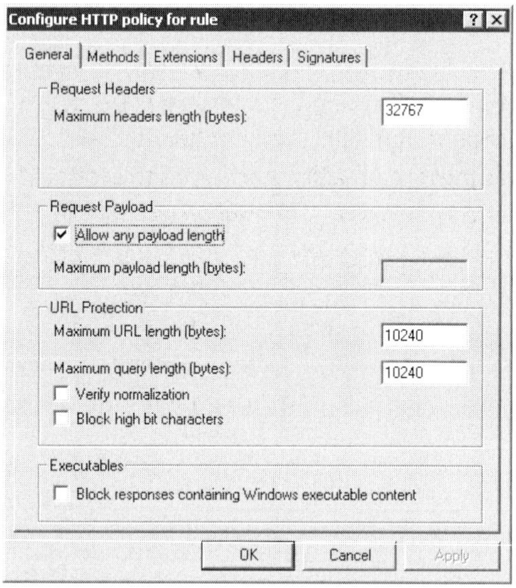

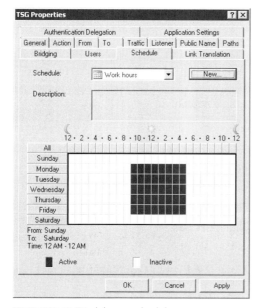

FIGURE 21-9 HTTP Policy properties page

Schedules

TMG can allow or deny access on a Web Publishing rule based on specific schedules. You might want to restrict access to certain Web sites to be accessed only during work hours. On the other hand, be some other Web sites might have a high bandwidth requirement and should only be accessed during off-hours. This can be controlled by using either a built-in or a custom schedule in the Web Publishing rule. Figure 21-10 illustrates a work hours schedule using a Web Publishing rule.

FIGURE 21-10 Work hours schedule

Link Translation

Content returned from published Web servers may contain links that refer to internal computer names or unrelated Web sites. Because the clients using the publishing rule cannot resolve these internal names, their connection to these links will not be successful. TMG includes a link translation filter that translates these internal links or names to external resolvable links by maintaining a mapping table also known as *link translation dictionaries*. In addition to translating links, the link translation filter also translates protocols in the links. For example, if the client is accessing a site published by TMG as HTTPS but the connection from TMG to the published Web server is HTTP, TMG will rewrite the HTTP URLs returned from the Web server to HTTPS before sending the response back to the client. Figure 21-11 shows the Link Translation tab within a Web Publishing rule properties dialog box.

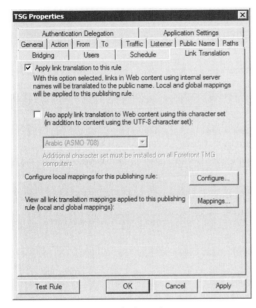

FIGURE 21-11 Link Translation tab

Bridging

TMG allows port and protocol redirection. Port redirection allows TMG to accept requests from external clients on a specific port and then redirect those requests to any other port that the published Web server is set to listen on. For instance, if the client is making an HTTP request to a Web site and connects to TMG on port 80, TMG can forward the request to the published Web server on a different port, such as 8888. Of course, the Web server has to be listening on that port if the connection is to be successful. TMG also allows protocol redirection. The simplest example of this is a client that can connect to a published FTP server over HTTP. The client uses HTTP to connect to TMG, and TMG connects to the FTP server on the port designated by the TMG administrator and translates HTTP methods to FTP methods. Note that when using protocol translation with FTP, that only FTP downloading is available. Figure 21-12 shows the Bridging tab.

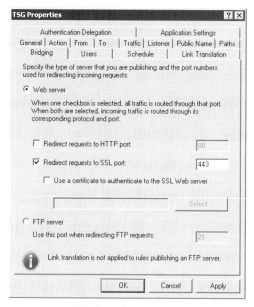

FIGURE 21-12 Bridging tab property page

Web Publishing provides two basic types of bridging:

- **Symmetric**   Symmetric bridging occurs when the same protocols are used between the client and TMG and between TMG and the published server; for instance, HTTP-to-HTTP or HTTPS-to-HTTPS.

- **Asymmetric**   Asymmetric bridging occurs when different protocols are used between the client and TMG and between TMG and the published server; for instance HTTP-to-HTTPS, HTTPS-to-HTTP, HTTP-to-FTP, or HTTPS-to-FTP.

Pre-Authentication

You can configure TMG to allow only authenticated requests to be forwarded to the published Web server. The client connection needs to be authenticated at TMG first, and only after successful authentication is the request allowed to reach the published Web server. TMG defines the type of authentication to be used for connections accepted by the Web listener, and if the authentication succeeds, defers to the authentication provider—the Domain Controller, Radius server, or a LDAP server to authenticate the request and only allow the users specified in the publishing rule. Figure 21-13 shows the Authentication tab of a Web listener property page.

FIGURE 21-13 Web listener Authentication property page

Authentication Delegation

The Authentication Delegation option in a rule allows TMG to forward user credentials to the published Web server upon successful pre-authentication at TMG. This allows the user to sign on to the Web server without being prompted to enter credentials again and at the same time ensures that the Web server is only serving authenticated requests. The authentication delegation method varies depending on the initial authentication at TMG. Table 21-1 summarizes the valid combinations. Figure 21-14 shows the Delegation tab of a Web Publishing rule.

TABLE 21-1 Valid combinations of Client credentials and Delegation methods

RECEIPT OF CLIENT CREDENTIALS	AUTHENTICATION PROVIDER	DELEGATION METHOD
Forms-Based Authentication (password only) Basic	Active Directory (Windows) Active Directory (LDAP) Radius	No delegation, but client may authenticate directly No delegation, and client cannot authenticate directly Basic NTLM Negotiate Kerberos-constrained delegation

RECEIPT OF CLIENT CREDENTIALS	AUTHENTICATION PROVIDER	DELEGATION METHOD
Digest Integrated	Active Directory (Windows)	No delegation, but client may authenticate directly
		No delegation, and client cannot authenticate directly
		Kerberos-constrained delegation
Forms-based authentication with passcode	SecurID RADIUS one-time password	No delegation, but client may authenticate directly
		No delegation, and client cannot authenticate directly
		SecurID
		Kerberos-constrained delegation
Forms-based authentication (passcode and password)	SecurID RADIUS one-time password	No delegation, but client may authenticate directly
		No delegation, and client cannot authenticate directly
		Basic
		NTLM
		Negotiate
		SecurID
Client certificate	Active Directory (Windows)	No delegation, but client may authenticate directly
		No delegation, and client cannot authenticate directly
		Kerberos-constrained delegation

MORE INFO For complete list of authentication mechanisms and delegations, please visit *http://technet.microsoft.com/en-us/library/bb794722.aspx.*

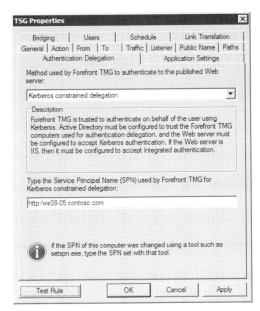

FIGURE 21-14 Authentication Delegation tab

Web Server Farm

TMG allows publishing a farm of Web servers performing the same role or hosting the same content apart from publishing a single Web server. This allows TMG to load-balance and evenly distribute requests among available servers. When creating a Web Publishing rule for a Web server farm, TMG creates HTTP connectivity verifiers to each server in the Web farm, which allows TMG to detect whether the servers in the farm are available or are offline. This helps TMG to keep a track of the offline servers and remove them from load balancing until the server is available again. Another advantage of publishing a Web farm is that the TMG administrator can add or remove the servers in the Web farm without disrupting the existing client connections.

TMG load-balances the connections in a Web server farm using two different mechanisms:

- **Session Affinity (cookie-based load-balancing)**   A session is defined as the number of consecutive Web requests that are shared by the same client application. This is mainly applicable to clients that understand cookies such as browser-based clients. Session affinity uses a round-robin mechanism to ensure that browser sessions with a Web application serviced by a Web farm are distributed evening among farm members that are online. The most common implementation of session affinity is while load-balancing Outlook Web Access servers or Sharepoint services farms.

- **IP Affinity**   IP affinity load-balances requests across the Web server farm based on IP addresses. Thus a client with a specific IP is routed to the same server in the farm for the duration of its connection, unlike in session affinity where it only goes to the same server in the farm for a specific session. The most common implementation of IP affinity is while publishing RPC over HTTP because Outlook clients do not understand cookies. Figure 21-15 shows an example of a Web server farm.

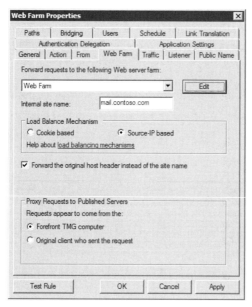

FIGURE 21-15 Web Farm Properties page

NOTE IP affinity is not helpful if all incoming connections to TMG are from across a NAT device or proxy. In that case TMG will treat incoming connections as a single client connection and send that request to the same Web server in the farm and no load-balancing will occur.

Elements in a Server Publishing Rule

A Server Publishing rule is used to publish non-Web services or to provide tunnel-based publishing for Web services. Non-Web services such as SQL or SMTP can only be published using a Server Publishing rule. Server Publishing provides a one-to-one mapping between a TMG listener and a server or service published by TMG. As mentioned in the previous section, a Server Publishing rule only processes protocols that are using primary connections that are inbound. A Server Publishing rule provides application-layer inspection according to the application filters associated with the protocol used in publishing. If you are publishing a Web server, you should use a Web Publishing rule to provide the best possible application-layer awareness. Server Publishing provides no authentication capabilities at TMG.

Network Listener

The Network Listener for a server publishing rule operates on one or more IP addresses in one or more networks that have been selected in the Server Publishing rule. When the Server Publishing rule listener operates in conjunction with a route network rule, no listener is actually created. Instead, TMG recognizes traffic that matches the 5-tuple defined respective to this rule and processes it as an application layer–filtering router. When the Server Publishing rule listener operates in conjunction with a NAT network rule, no listener is created in TCP/IP until the packet filter and Firewall Engine have accepted the incoming connection. Thus you cannot actually observe a Server Publishing listener using Windows networking tools until it has accepted a connection. Figure 21-16 shows an example of a Server Publishing listener.

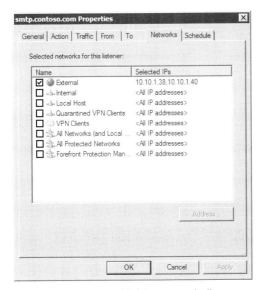

FIGURE 21-16 Server Publishing networks listener page

Protocol

The protocol specified in the Server Publishing rule represents the default port the IP address on the Network Listener listens on. By default, the protocol uses its default port that the service uses, but the rule can be configured to listen on a different port if needed. If the rule is configured to listen on a port other than its original default port, the client has to use the newer port number in the connection to TMG. Similarly, if the published server is using a different port to listen on for this protocol, TMG can forward the request to the custom port instead of the default port. This kind of implementation is commonly seen when the security teams want to avoid port scanners that target default ports. Figure 21-17 illustrates the Traffic tab of a Server Publishing rule.

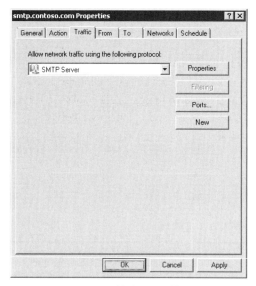

FIGURE 21-17 Server Publishing Traffic tab

Application Filters

TMG application filters provide an extra layer of security in the Server Publishing rule. Application filters can access the data stream or datagram associated with a session when the request is serviced by a server publishing rule. Application filters are registered with the firewall service and work with some or all of the application-level protocol streams or datagram. An application filter can perform protocol-specific or system-specific tasks, such as authentication and virus checking. The following application filters are provided in TMG for Server Publishing:

- DNS filter
- FTP access filter
- H.323 filter
- POP3 Intrusion Detection filter
- RPC filter
- SIP access filter
- SMTP filter
- Streaming media application filters

Ports

TMG can allow or deny access based on the source port the client uses while connecting to the Network Listener. By default, all source ports are allowed because the default for most client applications is to use a dynamic source port when making a connection to a server.

There are some exceptions, such as Network Time Protocol (NTP), but such protocols are not the norm. The TMG administrator can restrict access to a published service to connections coming from a specific source port or a range of source ports. This implementation is useful when a NAT device or another firewall ahead of TMG is only set to send requests from a range of ports. This, however, does not guarantee that access will only be restricted to the firewall or the NAT device because other clients will still be able to access the published server if they can restrict their source ports to the same range as specified in the Server Publishing rule on TMG. Figure 21-18 shows the source- and destination-port options provided in a Server Publishing rule.

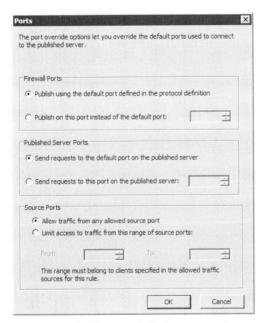

FIGURE 21-18 Publishing rule Ports configuration page

Planning Publishing Rules

In this book we discuss publishing rules for Web and non-Web Servers (Chapter 22), Microsoft Office SharePoint Server (Chapter 23), and Exchange Server (Chapter 24). Each of these chapters covers the planning and execution phases for each type of service. Generally speaking, when you are planning TMG publishing you need to analyze the scenario in the context of the type of service that you want to publish and the requirements TMG places on these scenarios. You need to consider some core elements regardless of the service that you intend to publish.

Evaluating System Capacity

Even if you install TMG on powerful hardware, if the network was not correctly designed for the traffic load, the end-user experience will not be good. You have to consider the network bandwidth and network devices where TMG is connected.

Because the goal is to build a solid foundation for a publishing scenario, you need to consider the following points:

- **WAN Link**   The nature of the typical publishing scenario is a user accessing internal services from the Internet. Therefore, the WAN Link where TMG is connected is a crucial point. The link capacity needs to be provisioned according to the amount of connections and the expected traffic load that it will handle. When you are planning the link capacity you may need to consider the outbound traffic load if Forefront TMG will also be used for outbound access to the Internet from protected networks.

- **LAN Link**   The typical goal of a publishing scenario is to allow access to an internal server. To communicate with the internal server efficiently TMG needs a good connection with the internal network. By having a good connection with the internal server the external user experience can be improved because performance while accessing the published server will be improved.

Some core elements in the hardware subsystem need to be considered during the planning phase of publishing scenario. Review Chapter 4, "Analyzing Network Requirements," for more details on how to trace your network profile and plan your TMG.

Ultimately what you can do to better size your TMG for the expected traffic load is to use the online TMG Capacity Planner. This tool can be accessed from *http://www.microsoft.com/ isaserver/capacityplanner.swf,* and there you can describe your expected traffic profile and load. The tool will calculate what type of hardware you will need for your deployment.

> **NOTE**   When we were writing this chapter, the TMG capacity planner was not yet available. The preceding link takes you to the ISA Server capacity planner, which will provide a basic starting point.

One last element that you need to consider is the performance of the server that you are publishing through TMG. If all the considerations that have been covered in this chapter so far are successfully achieved but the published server was not planned to have internal and external users accessing it at the same time, your publishing scenario is compromised from a performance standpoint. Let's use an SMTP server as an example. If you are performing Server Publishing for SMTP, the internal server needs to be sized for the amount of SMTP connections that will pass through TMG and reach the server in addition to the connections that are already established internally.

The sizing of the published server is outside the scope of TMG administrators, because in almost all scenarios they don't own the server that is going to be published. In any case, size needs to be considered; otherwise, during the deployment phase this could be noticed and easily pointed out as a TMG issue because internally the server that you want to publish works well.

Protocol Considerations

The type of service that you are going to publish dictates which protocol you will use for the publishing rule. As described earlier in this chapter, Web Publishing rules are typically used for Web traffic (HTTP or HTTPs) and Server Publishing rules are used for non-Web traffic, such as SMTP or POP3.

During the planning phase, you need to collect this type of information and decide what type of publishing rule you will use on TMG. In some situations, the server that you want to publish will use a protocol in a custom port. A typical example of this is a scenario in which you have an IIS Server that uses HTTP on port 8081 instead of HTTP on port 80.

The ultimate goal in most of the scenarios is that the external client has a smooth experience when accessing a Web site published by TMG. This means that in a scenario like the one explained previously, you probably want transparency for the external user and therefore you need to publish this server to the Internet using the default HTTP port 80. You need to collect those details from the internal environment before you start configuring the publishing rule. To assist you in remembering the core details you can refer to Table 21-2 during this phase.

TABLE 21-2 Protocol consideration table

QUESTION	INTERNAL SERVER	TMG
What service will be published?	Web Server	Web Server
What protocol will be used?	HTTP	HTTPS
What port will the server be listening for this request?	444	443

One question that might arise when you read this table is: Why use HTTP internally and HTTPS externally? There are many scenarios where you might face a situation like that, but one reason this happens is that the company doesn't have an internal Public Key Infrastructure (PKI) and still needs to securely publish a Web server. For this example the cost of acquiring a certificate to use on TMG was more cost-effective than implementing a whole new PKI internally.

As you can see in Table 21-2, not all the parameters in use in the internal server will match the standard configuration for the service that you are offering. Because TMG can bridge those requests, it can easily transition an incoming request on port 443 to port 444 in the internal Web server. Figure 21-19 illustrates that.

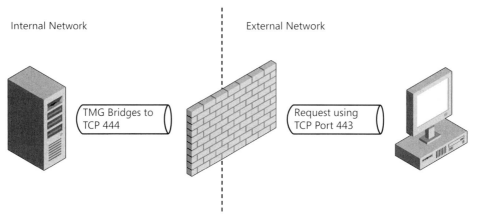

Internal Network

External Network

TMG Bridges to
TCP 444

Request using
TCP Port 443

FIGURE 21-19 TMG bridges requests from the default HTTPS port (443) to a custom port
in the internal server.

The example in Figure 21-19 uses a Web Publishing rule scenario; however, TMG can
perform a similar operation for Server Publishing rules, although Server Publishing cannot
provide bridging. An example of that is when you are publishing a remote desktop service
through TMG. It is common for system administrators to change the default RDP port when
publishing this type of service to avoid a port-scanner attack, but when internal clients are
coming from inside you want to keep the default port (3389). TMG can receive requests in
a custom port and bridge to the default port (3389) in the internal server.

TMG comes with a set of protocols built in that can be used during a Server Publishing
rule, as shown in Figure 21-20.

FIGURE 21-20 Built-in server protocols

You can create new protocols if you are publishing a proprietary application that requires a custom port.

Certificate Considerations

You might find that the publishing scenario requires an extra resource to make the publishing rule work. In the example illustrated in Table 21-2 TMG was publishing a resource using HTTPS. This means that TMG needs a certificate installed in the local computer's "personal" store with the private key to be able to offer this service.

Certificate usage needs to be carefully planned because it involves extra time and cost factors in building an internal PKI infrastructure or acquiring a certificate from an external entity. During this phase, refer to Table 21-3.

TABLE 21-3 Certificate consideration

QUESTION	CONSIDERATION
Does the internal server use a certificate or only TMG?	If the internal server uses a certificate, consider implementing an internal PKI to issue certificates to your internal server.
Do you need to provide access to the same resource using different names, such as mail.contoso.com and autodiscover.contoso.com/?	If you need to provide multiple names for the same resource, you can choose to use a Subject Alternative Name (SAN) certificate or a wildcard certificate (for example, *.contoso.com).
Are you planning to use this certificate for a Web Publishing or Server Publishing rule?	Before acquiring your certificate, evaluate which type of publishing rule you are going to use.
Do you want to prevent external clients from receiving a warning that the certificate was issued by a certificate authority that is not trusted?	Usually this happens when the certificate was issued by an internal root CA and the external client doesn't trust this CA. Consider the following options: ■ Publish the resource by acquiring the certificate that will be used by TMG from a commercial CA. ■ Export the internal root CA certificate and import it to the external client computer.

Load Balancing

One element that is commonly used these days to provide high availability is load balancing. TMG uses the Windows Network Load Balancing feature, as we explained in Chapter 13, "Configuring Load Balancing Capabilities." When you choose an external load-balancing solution, the load balancing is offloaded from TMG and all the processing and traffic mapping is handled by the hardware device.

While planning the publishing rule, you need to determine which IP address will be used by the listener. As explained earlier in this chapter, a Web listener needs to exist to allow a Web Publishing rule to be created. The IP address that will be bound to the Web listener can be the TMG dedicated IP (DIP) or, if NLB is used, it can be the virtual IP (VIP). The IP allocation for the publishing rule should be planned before implementing the publishing rule.

REAL WORLD   Understanding Your Environment

I t is very common to see scenarios in which a publishing rule fails as a result of a misunderstanding of the network architecture. This can cause the publishing rule to be incorrectly created, resulting in a broken traffic path. In one case, a firewall administrator was publishing an IIS Server through ISA Server to the Internet. The end user received a timeout error when attempting to use the Web application. The ISA Server logging also indicated a 10060 result code, which means that the connection attempt failed because the connected party did not respond after a period of time.

We used Network Monitor to capture the traffic at the ISA Server internal interface and at the Web Server network interface. The results indicated that the ISA Server sent the TCP SYN packet on port 80 to the Web server, as shown in Figure 21-21.

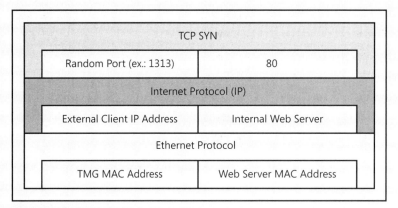

FIGURE 21-21 TCP SYN sent from TMG

The Web server received the TCP SYN packet from ISA Server and responded with a TCP ACK packet, as shown in Figure 21-22.

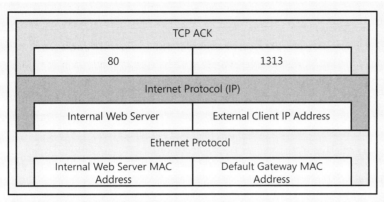

TCP ACK	
80	1313
Internet Protocol (IP)	
Internal Web Server	External Client IP Address
Ethernet Protocol	
Internal Web Server MAC Address	Default Gateway MAC Address

FIGURE 21-22 TCP ACK sent from Web server

ISA Server never received the TCP ACK because the Web server sent the TCP ACK packets to the Web server's default gateway. The ISA computer kept resending the TCP SYN to the Web server until the TCP timeout expired (about 20 seconds). The reason the TCP Handshake was failing in first place was that the source IP in the header (see Figure 21-21) was the external client's IP address. Because this Web server was not using ISA Server as a default gateway, the TCP ACK was going through the router (see Figure 21-22). The router's default route did not direct the traffic through the ISA Server, so the TCP ACK from the Web server never arrived at the ISA Server. We had three options to resolve this:

1. Change the publishing rule and choose the Request Appears To Come From The ISA Server Computer option in the To tab.

2. Change the Web server computer IP configuration to include the ISA Server in the default route.

3. Change the routing path in the router itself.

For this particular case, we chose to change the Web server IP configuration to use the ISA Server internal IP address as default gateway.

MORE INFO For an illustration of this real-world scenario read *http://blogs.technet.com/ isablog/archive/2008/07/10/isa-server-2006-sp1-problems-that-goes-beyond-the-test- button.aspx.*

Summary

In this chapter you learned the core concepts of publishing on TMG. You learned that there are different types of publishing scenarios, such as Server Publishing and Web Publishing. A Server Publishing scenario has a listener and an associated Server Publishing rule that describes a one-to-one mapping between the listener and the published server. It operates in the context of a single application filter and some of these filters are limited to Server Publishing scenarios. You learned that a Web Publishing scenario uses a network listener owned by the Web proxy, which can be associated with one or more Web Publishing rules. To use each one of these scenarios you need to use different parameters that are part of the different publishing elements, such as authentication, authentication delegation, and a Web listener. After understanding those core concepts you also learned what needs to be covered during the publishing planning phase.

This foundation will allow you to better understand the upcoming chapters that will discuss in more specific scenarios. In the next chapter you will learn how to publish Web servers and non-Web servers and also how to troubleshoot publishing rules.

## CHAPTER 22

Publishing Servers

■ How to Publish a Web Server   **599**

■ Publishing a Non-Web Server   **637**

■ Troubleshooting Publishing Rules   **647**

■ Summary   **660**

As explained in Chapter 21, "Understanding Publishing Concepts," application publishing tends to present more problems for more edge administrators primarily because of the additional complexity involved in publishing versus access rule–based traffic policies. In this chapter, you will learn about the process involved with publishing Web and non-Web services and some techniques for troubleshooting them.

How to Publish a Web Server

Before you can publish a protected resource, you need to have a plan in place that covers not only the goal of making this resource accessible across TMG, but also takes into account all the items explained in the previous chapter.

In the following example, Contoso administration wants to publish two Web sites using two different URLs:

■ A corporate information portal. There are no user limitations to access the portal and no encryption is required. To access this page, users will browse to *http://www.contoso.com*.

■ A payroll system. Only authenticated users are allowed to access this page. All traffic must be encrypted. To access this page, users will browse to *https://payroll.contoso.com*.

The Contoso network diagram is shown in Figure 22-1.

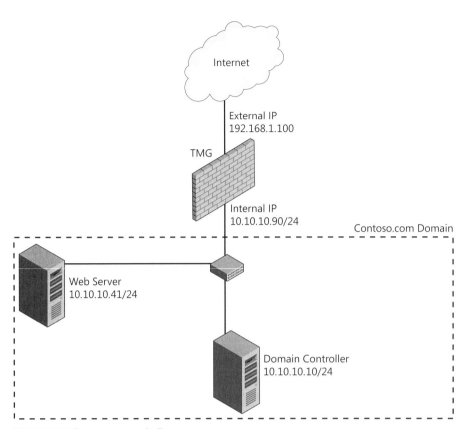

FIGURE 22-1 Contoso network diagram

One important thing to notice in this diagram is that we have one Web server for both services that the company wants to publish. Although it may be preferable from a security standpoint to have one Web server for each application, sometimes budget constraints dictate a combined deployment. Table 22-1 describes the technical details of this Web server.

TABLE 22-1 Web Server Configuration

WEB SITE	AUTHENTICATION TYPE	TCP PORT	CERTIFICATE
Institutional Web Site	Anonymous	80	No
Payroll System	Basic	443	Yes

Publishing a Web Server Using HTTP Protocol

According to Contoso's administration requirements, the first Web site to be published is the institutional page using the HTTP protocol. To allow TMG to accept HTTP traffic, we need to create a Web listener. Depending on your own preferences, you may wish to build the Web listener prior to building the Web Publishing rules. Because Web Publishing wizards offer you the chance to perform this process, it doesn't matter whether you do it during the Web Publishing wizard process or separately. Follow these steps to create a separate Web listener:

1. On the TMG computer (or using remote management console on a management station), open the Forefront TMG Management Console.

2. Click Forefront TMG (Array Name) in the left pane and click Firewall Policy.

3. In the right pane click the Toolbox tab, right-click Web Listener under Network Objects, and then click New Web Listener, as shown in Figure 22-2.

FIGURE 22-2 Creating a new Web listener

4. The New Web Listener Wizard welcome page appears, as shown in Figure 22-3. Type a name for this Web listener and click Next.

FIGURE 22-3 Adding a name for the Web listener

5. The next page allows you to define whether this listener will require SSL (HTTPS) or not (HTTP). For this particular case choose the option Do Not Require SSL Secured Connections With Clients, as shown in Figure 22-4 and click Next.

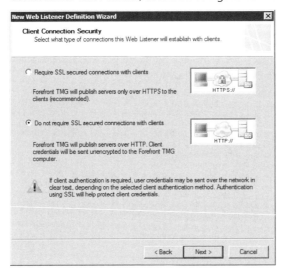

FIGURE 22-4 Specifying the connection type (HTTPS or HTTP) for this Web listener

6. On the Web Listener IP Addresses page you have the option to select which network TMG uses to listen for connection attempts for the protocol selected on the previous page. You can select multiple interfaces and for each interface you can select one or more IPs. For this particular example select External, as shown in Figure 22-5. Click Next.

FIGURE 22-5 Choosing the interface that will be used for this listener

7. The authentication settings available on the Authentication Settings page allow you to configure the authentication type that this listener will use. Because this listener will

be used for a publishing rule that does not require authentication, you should change the default authentication type. Click the drop-down list next to the option Select How Clients Will Provide Credentials To Forefront TMG and choose No Authentication, as shown in Figure 22-6. Click Next.

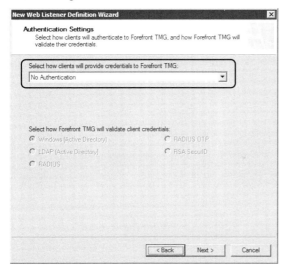

FIGURE 22-6 Selecting No Authentication for this listener

8. Because this listener is not using forms-based authentication, the Single Sign On (SSO) settings are disabled as shown in Figure 22-7. Click Next.

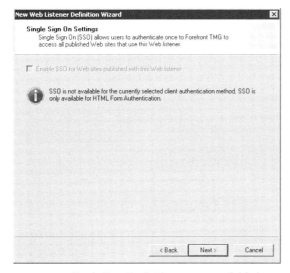

FIGURE 22-7 Single Sign On Settings are unavailable because of the selected authentication method

9. Review the option summary on the Completing The New Web Listener Wizard page, as shown in Figure 22-8. Click Finish to close this page and create the Web listener. Click Apply to commit the changes.

FIGURE 22-8 Reviewing the selections before committing the changes

Now that the Web listener is properly created, the next part is to create the publishing rule that will use this Web listener to allow access to the internal Web server. Follow these steps to create a Web Publishing rule:

1. Click Forefront TMG (Array Name) in the left pane.

2. Right-click Firewall Policy, point to New, and click Web Site Publishing Rule as shown in Figure 22-9.

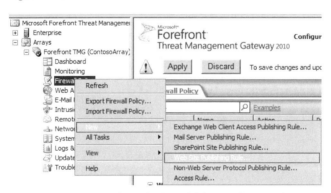

FIGURE 22-9 Accessing the Web Site Publishing Rule Wizard

3. The Welcome To The New Web Publishing Rule Wizard page appears, as shown in Figure 22-10. Type a name for this publishing rule and click Next.

FIGURE 22-10 Adding a name for the Web publishing rule

4. On the Select Rule Action page, you can specify the publishing rule action, whether it is to allow or deny requests matching this rule. Leave the default selection (Allow), as shown in Figure 22-11 and click Next.

> **NOTE** A typical scenario where you use Deny in a publishing rule is when you want to redirect the traffic to another page. See an example of this at *http://blogs.technet.com/ isablog/archive/2009/03/04/how-to-allow-http-301-through-isa-server-2006.aspx*.

FIGURE 22-11 Configuring the publishing rule to allow the traffic

5. On the Publishing Type page, you can specify what type of resource TMG will publish, as shown in Figure 22-12. This page has the following options.

- **Publish A Single Web Server Or Load Balancer** Use this option when you are publishing a server that is using a virtual IP address assigned by the load-balancing solution (Windows NLB or hardware load-balancer) or when there is only one server with a dedicated IP address to it.

- **Publish A Server Farm Or Balanced Web Servers** Use this option if you want Forefront TMG to control the load balancing among multiple Web servers. Forefront TMG will use a Server Farm object with all Web servers that are part of the farm on it.

- **Publish Multiple Web Sites** Use this option if you need to publish more than a single Web site.

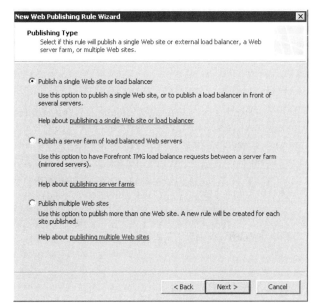

FIGURE 22-12 Choosing the publishing type

Leave the default option selected and click Next.

6. On the Server Connection Security page, you can specify what type of connection TMG creates to the published Web server. For this part we need to refer back to the planning phase because at this point in the implementation we will know whether the internal Web server requires SSL connections. For this particular case choose the option as shown in Figure 22-13 (Use Non-Secured Connections To Connect To Published Web Server Or Server Farm) and click Next.

> **NOTE** This page assumes that your internal Web server uses either port 443 for HTTPs or 80 for HTTP. If your internal Web server uses a custom port, you need to edit the Bridging tab in the publishing rule after completing the wizard.

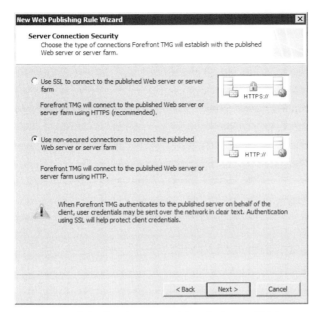

FIGURE 22-13 Selecting the protocol that the internal Web server will use

7. On the Internal Publishing Details page, you can specify the internal Web site name. This can be the alias for the internal Web site or (if this were an HTTPs rule) the subject name, or one of the SAN names of the certificate installed in the internal server. Type the internal site name and optionally you can also select the check box on the bottom of the page to specify the internal server's IP address or fully qualified domain name for the internal server. For the purpose of this example, type the options specified in Figure 22-14.

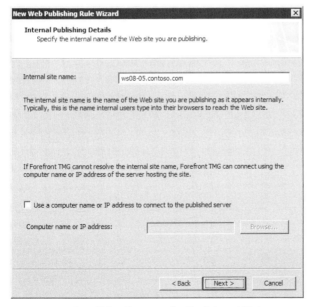

FIGURE 22-14 Specifying the name for the internal Web server

NOTE If you don't specify the IP address in the window that appears in Figure 22-14 you need to rely on the DNS and ensure that it resolves to the internal name of your published server, otherwise it will fail.

8. For this particular Web site the goal is to allow access to all of the content for the Web site *www.contoso.com* without any restriction to any specific folders in the site. Therefore the path should be **/***, as shown in Figure 22-15. Click Next.

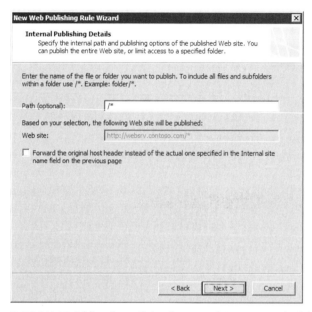

FIGURE 22-15 Adding the path to allow complete access to the folders located within the published site

NOTE By selecting the option Forward The Original Host Header Instead Of The Actual One Specified In The Internal Site Name Field On The Previous Page, TMG will use the original host header for this rule. The choice to use this depends on the application that you are publishing. Some Web applications require that TMG use the original host header instead of the value specified in Figure 22-14.

9. On the Public Name Details page you need to specify the name that the external clients will use to access this server. For this particular case the name will be **www.contoso.com**. Leave the remaining options at the default selection, as shown in Figure 22-16, and click Next.

10. On the Select Web Listener page, choose HTTP Listener (Web listener that was created previously) from the Web Listener drop-down list, as shown in Figure 22-17.

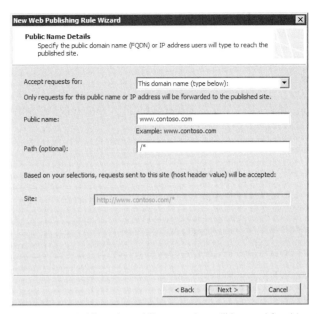

FIGURE 22-16 Adding the public name that will be used for this publishing rule

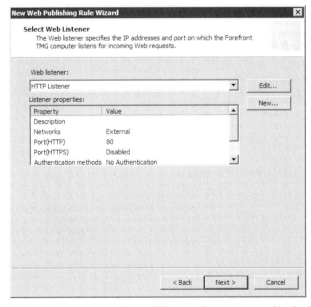

FIGURE 22-17 Choosing the Web listener that was created in the initial phase

11. On the Authentication Delegation page you need to choose an authentication option that matches the internal server authentication requirements. In this case no authentication is required because the requirement is that the site can be accessed by anyone, so leave the default option as shown in Figure 22-18. Click Next.

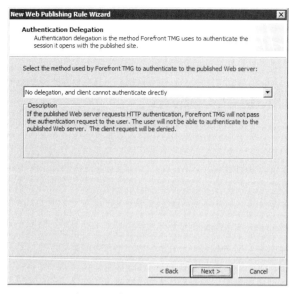

FIGURE 22-18 Choosing the authentication delegation method

> **NOTE** Read Chapter 21 to review the valid authentication delegation options that are available in TMG.

12. The User Sets page allows you to specify which users should have access to this publishing rule. Because this is a public Web site and the goal is that everyone should be able to access it without authentication, leave the default option as shown in Figure 22-19 and click Next.

FIGURE 22-19 Allowing all users to have access to this publishing rule

13. The Completing The New Web Publishing Rule Wizard page (Figure 22-20) provides a summary of the selections that were chosen for this rule. You can also confirm that the publishing rule is working properly by clicking Test Rule. If everything is configured properly, the result will be similar to that shown in Figure 22-21. Click Finish to complete this task and click Apply to commit the changes.

FIGURE 22-20 Summary of the options selected during the publishing rule creation

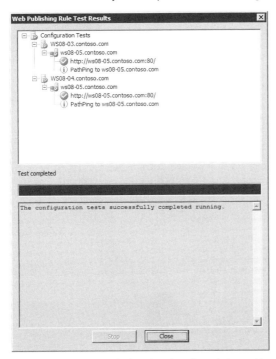

FIGURE 22-21 Test result showing that the rule is working successfully

Using the Test Rule button, you can validate that the TCP/IP connection can be established by a resolvable host name and verify whether the host is accessible on ports defined on the rule's Bridging tab. This test also verifies server certificate information by checking whether the certificate is expired or revoked, checking whether the certificate was issued by a trusted CA, and checking whether the certificate has the correct name. The Test Rule button validates that the HTTP GET request can pass through TMG authentication delegation by checking its compatibility with server authentication requirements, verifies that the published paths exist, and last but not least verifies that the published server accepts the names forwarded in host header as configured on the rule's To tab.

Reviewing the Web Server Publishing Rule

In some cases, you might need to edit settings that are not available through the wizard. For example, if the internal Web server is using a port other than 80 or 443 for HTTPS, the wizard doesn't have the flexibility to allow port changes.

To review the publishing rule, follow these steps:

1. Right-click the Contoso Web Site publishing rule and click Properties. The General tab appears, as shown in Figure 22-22.

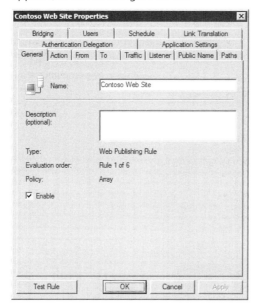

FIGURE 22-22 The General tab contains the rule name and a field to add a brief description.

2. Click the Action tab and notice that this publishing rule is allowing the traffic, as shown in Figure 22-23.

> **NOTE** When using the Deny option in Figure 22-23 and specifying a different path to redirect, TMG sends an HTTP 302 response to the Web application that issued the request that matched the rule.

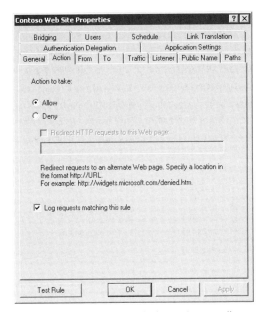

FIGURE 22-23 Action tab with the options to allow or deny the traffic

3. Click the From tab to see which networks are allowed to originate traffic to this rule. After completing the Web Publishing Wizard, the source network is automatically specified as Anywhere, as shown in Figure 22-24. You can also add exceptions to the rule's Exceptions list, which has the effect of allowing traffic from anywhere except the locations you add to the Exceptions list.

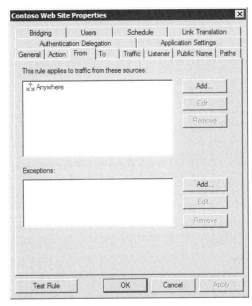

FIGURE 22-24 Networks where the traffic can be originated from

4. Click the To tab to see more details about the target for this publishing rule, as shown in Figure 22-25. Notice in this dialog box that you have the options to specify whether the traffic appears to come from TMG or from the original client. Some companies might have a policy that requires that you change this option to appear to come from the client. When you select Requests Appear To Come From Original Client, the TMG computer's default internal IP address must represent a hop between the published Web servers and the Internet. That is to say, the TMG firewall needs to be in the request/response path between the published client and server.

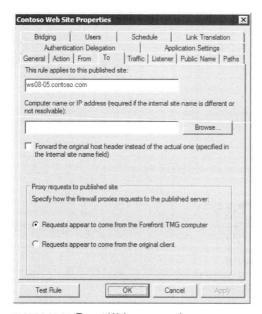

FIGURE 22-25 Target Web server options

NOTE In an environment where the published server doesn't use TMG as a gateway hop to the Internet, changing this can also have a negative impact if the routes are not correctly configured on the device located between the Web server and TMG. For an example of such a scenario, read *http://blogs.technet.com/isablog/archive/2008/07/10/ isa-server-2006-sp1-problems-that-goes-beyond-the-test-button.aspx*.

5. Click the Traffic tab. You can see that the only protocol that appears is HTTP, as shown in Figure 22-26. As explained in Chapter 20, "HTTP and HTTPS Inspection," you can configure HTTP filtering options on this tab.

6. Click the Listener tab to view the listener associated with this publishing rule. Notice that here you can edit this listener by clicking Properties; you can change the listener by choosing a different listener (if one exists) from the drop-down list; and you can create a new listener by clicking New. Figure 22-27 illustrates this page.

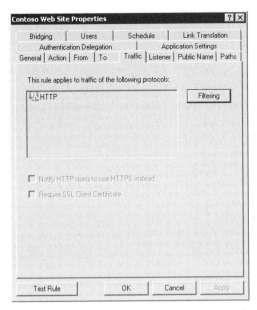

FIGURE 22-26 Traffic covered by this publishing rule

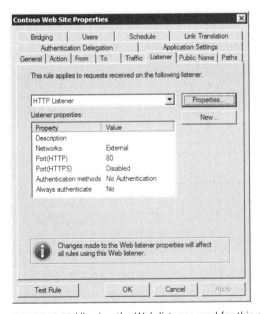

FIGURE 22-27 Viewing the Web listener used for this publishing rule

7. Click the Public Name tab to view the list of names that external users will use to connect to the published server. This set includes the name that you chose in the wizard shown in Figure 22-28. You can click Add to add other names that will be used to access the same internal server. By default the option this rule applies to requests

for the following Web site is enabled, however in some rare scenarios you might want to change this for all requests by changing the option in the drop-down list.

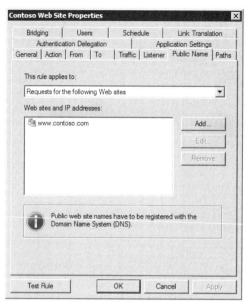

FIGURE 22-28 Public name used by this publishing rule

8. Click the Path tab to review the allowed paths within the Web site that you are publishing. Figure 22-29 shows **/***, which represents all folders, subfolders, and files within the target server site. This can be changed by highlighting the external path and clicking Edit.

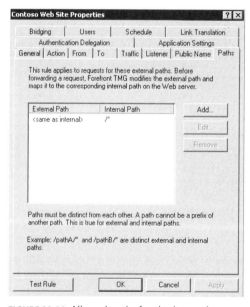

FIGURE 22-29 Allowed paths for the internal server

9. Click the Authentication Delegation tab. The dialog box should appear as shown in Figure 22-30.

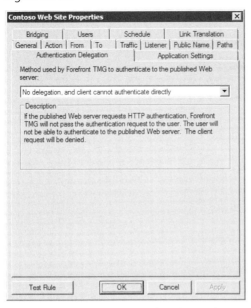

FIGURE 22-30 Authentication Delegation options vary according to the listener authentication.

10. Click the Bridging tab. The page should appear as shown in Figure 22-31. Here you can change the port in the event that your internal Web server is using a port other than port 80.

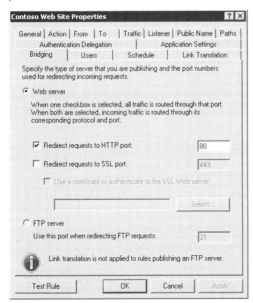

FIGURE 22-31 The Bridging tab allows you to change the communication port with the internal server.

11. Click the Users tab to review which users are allowed to have access to this Web Publishing rule. Because the goal for this rule is to allow anonymous access, you should leave this field with the All Users option as appears in Figure 22-32.

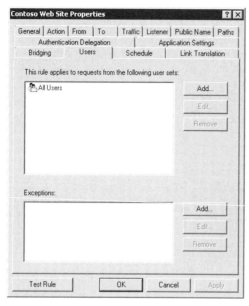

FIGURE 22-32 Users authorized to access the Web Publishing rule

12. Click OK to close this dialog box.

Publishing a Web Server Using HTTPS

The second part of Contoso's requirement for publishing Web servers is to make the payroll system available to external users through TMG using encryption. To satisfy this requirement you need to acquire a certificate and install it on TMG so that you can associate this certificate with the Web listener that will be used for the Web server publishing rule. The certificate can be issued by an internal Certificate Authority (CA) or by an external commercial CA. Regardless of the certificate source, TMG needs to trust the entity that issued that certificate.

Before we start configuring the HTTPS publishing rule, you need to:

- Obtain a certificate from an internal or external CA.
- Install the certificate that TMG's Web listener will use in the TMG Local computer certificate store. You need to make sure that you have the certificate with a private key.
- If the TMG computer does not trust the root (and intermediate if exists) CA, you need to install the certificate chain for this root CA in TMG computer's local machine Trusted Roots store.

For this particular scenario both certificates are physically located in the C:\certs folder on TMG—the certificate that will be used in the TMG's Web listener (payroll.pfx) that contains the private key and the root CA certificate (rootca.cer).

NOTE For more information on certificate file format read the article at *http://technet .microsoft.com/en-us/library/cc770735.aspx.*

Installing Certificates on TMG

Follow these steps to install the PFX certificate in the local computer store:

IMPORTANT TMG cannot use a server authentication certificate that was created using a Windows 2008 version template. Certificates made based on this template profile are created using properties available only in Cryptography Next Generation (CNG). You can read more about CNG at *http://technet.microsoft.com/en-us/library/cc730763(WS.10).aspx.*

1. On the TMG Server computer, click Start, type **mmc,** and then press Enter or click OK. An MMC dialog box similar to Figure 22-33 appears.

FIGURE 22-33 Empty MMC dialog box

2. Click the File menu and then click Add/Remove Snap-in or press Ctrl+M.

3. Under Available Snap-ins, click Certificates and then click Add as shown in Figure 22-34.

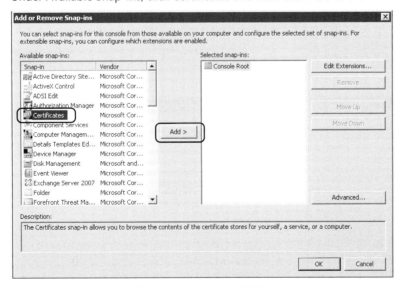

FIGURE 22-34 Adding a certificate snap-in to the MMC

4. Select Computer Account and then click Next, as shown in Figure 22-35.

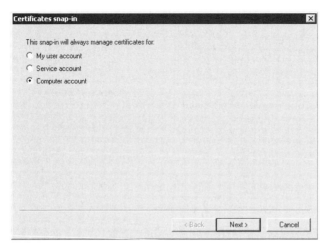

FIGURE 22-35 Managing certificates in the computer account

5. Click Local Computer and then click Finish, as shown in Figure 22-36.

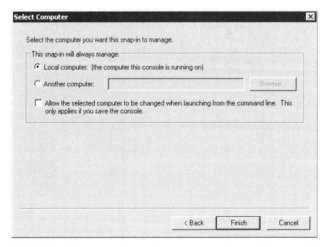

FIGURE 22-36 Choosing the option to manage the certificate on the local computer

6. Click OK in the Add Or Remove Snap-ins dialog box, as shown in Figure 22-37.

7. Expand Certificates (Local Computer), then expand Personal, and then expand Certificates. Right-click the Certificates node, select All Tasks, and then select Request New Certificate as shown in Figure 22-38.

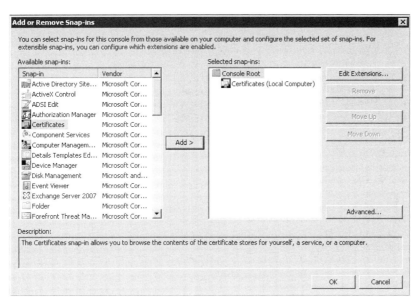

FIGURE 22-37 Confirm that the certificates snap-in is in the right panel before clicking OK.

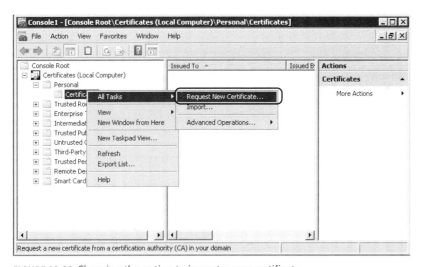

FIGURE 22-38 Choosing the option to import a new certificate

8. As shown in Figure 22-39, the Welcome To The Certificate Import Wizard page appears. Click Next.

FIGURE 22-39 The Welcome page with a brief description of the wizard's goal

9. On the File To Import page, type the location where the certificate is located as shown in Figure 22-40 and click Next.

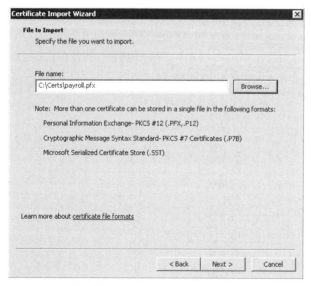

FIGURE 22-40 The File To Import page with the options to type in the certificate location or browse to find it

10. On the Password page, type the password provided by the entity that issued this certificate as shown in Figure 22-41 and click Next.

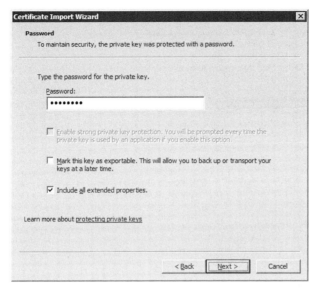

FIGURE 22-41 The Password page also allows you to mark the keys as exportable.

11. On the Certificate Store page confirm that the location is Personal, as shown in Figure 22-42. Click Next.

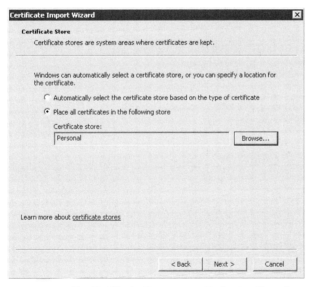

FIGURE 22-42 The Certificate Store page with the location where the certificate will be installed

12. The Completing The Certificate Import Wizard page should appear with a summary of your selections, as shown in Figure 22-43. Review the page and click Finish.

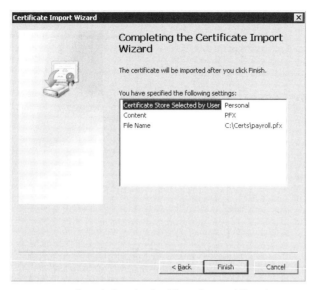

FIGURE 22-43 Completing the Certificate Import Wizard

At this point the certificate is installed in TMG's local computer store and your snap-in should show the new certificate in the right pane. To confirm that this certificate is valid, right-click it and choose Open. If this certificate was issued based on a CNG template, the error TMG will indicate an incorrect key type, as shown in Figure 22-44.

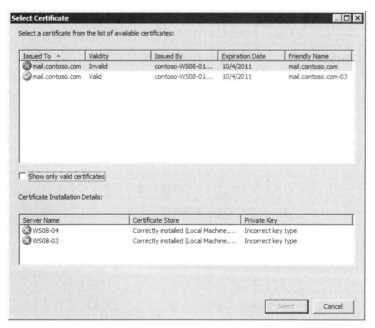

FIGURE 22-44 Error message when the certificate is issued from a CNG template

To resolve this problem, you need to obtain a server authentication certificate issued from a Windows 2000 or Windows 2003 template and install it on all TMG computers as described previously. When this is accomplished, and the valid certificates are selected, the certificate selection page will appear as in Figure 22-45.

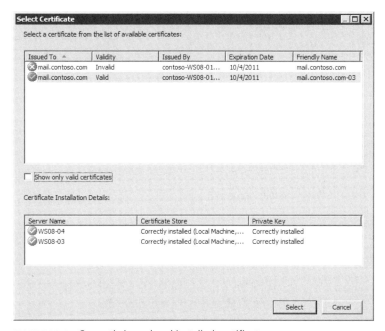

FIGURE 22-45 Correctly issued and installed certificates

Your TMG configuration should be ready for the next step, which is to create a Web listener for HTTPS using the certificate (PFX) that was imported. However, before we move on, it is important to mention a couple of recommendations about certificates:

- If you have an array with multiple nodes, you need to perform these procedures on all nodes. Otherwise, you won't be able to create the listener for HTTPS unless you have only one external IP address on all nodes and you have selected All IP Addresses on the listener.
- If you have any traffic filtering device between TMG and the Root CA CRL URL, you need to make sure that this device is allowing connectivity on port 80 to that destination so that TMG can validate the CRL (Certificate Revocation List).

Creating an HTTPS Web Listener

Follow these steps to create a new Web listener on TMG to use HTTPS:

1. On the TMG computer, open the Forefront TMG Management Console.
2. Click Forefront TMG (Array Name) in the left pane and click Firewall Policy.

3. In the right pane click the Toolbox tab, right-click Web Listener under Network Objects, and then click New Web Listener as shown in Figure 22-46.

FIGURE 22-46 Creating a new Web listener

4. The Welcome To The New Web Listener Wizard page appears, as shown in Figure 22-47. Type a name for this Web listener and click Next.

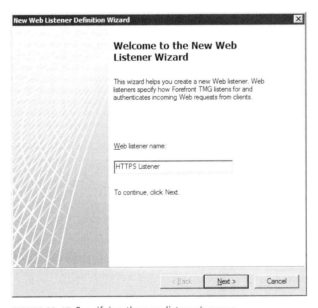

FIGURE 22-47 Specifying the new listener's name

5. Leave the default option selected (SSL), as shown in Figure 22-48, and click Next.

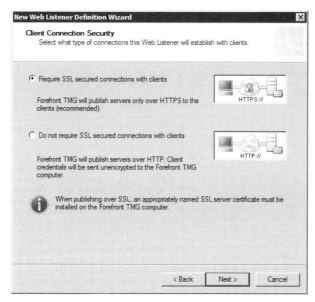

FIGURE 22-48 Choosing SSL for this Web listener

6. On the Web Listener IP Addresses page, select External as shown in Figure 22-49 and click Next.

FIGURE 22-49 Choosing the interface that will be used for this listener

7. On the Listener SSL Certificate page, click Select Certificate, choose the certificate for this listener, and then click Select as shown in Figure 22-50.

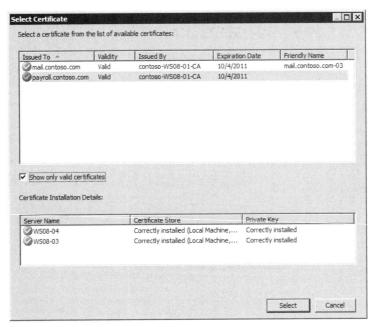

FIGURE 22-50 Choosing the certificate that will be used for this Web listener

8. On the Listener SSL Certificates page, confirm that the selected certificate appears as shown in Figure 22-51 and click Next.

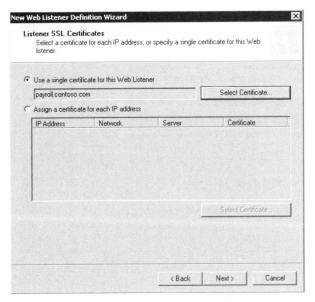

FIGURE 22-51 Binding the certificate to the Web listener

9. On the Authentication Settings page, choose HTML Form Authentication from the drop-down box. Leave the other options at the default selection, as shown Figure 22-52, and click Next.

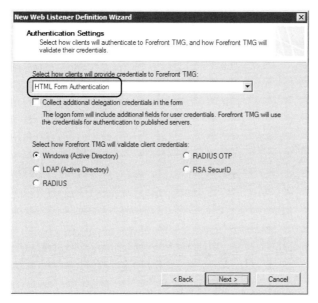

FIGURE 22-52 Changing the Web listener authentication method

10. For the purpose of this example disable SSO settings, as shown in Figure 22-53. Click Next.

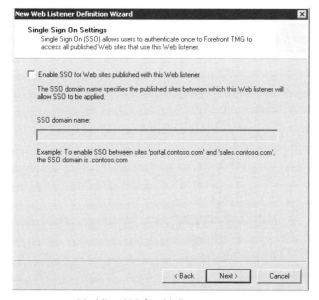

FIGURE 22-53 Disabling SSO for this listener

11. On the Completing The New Web Listener Wizard page, review the selections as shown in Figure 22-54. Click Finish and then click Apply to commit the changes.

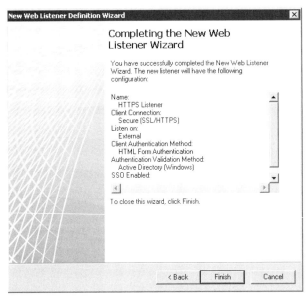

FIGURE 22-54 The wizard's summary page with the selections for this listener

Creating a Secure Web Publishing Rule

Follow these steps to create a secure Web Publishing rule on TMG using the listener that you previously created:

1. Expand Forefront TMG (Array Name) in the left pane.

2. Right-click Firewall Policy, point to New, and click Web Site Publishing Rule as shown in Figure 22-55.

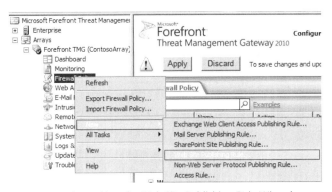

FIGURE 22-55 Launching the Web Site Publishing Rule Wizard

3. The Welcome To The New Web Publishing Rule Wizard page appears, as shown in Figure 22-56. Type a name for this publishing rule and click Next.

FIGURE 22-56 Specifying a name for the new Web Publishing rule

4. On the Select Rule Action page, leave the default selection (Allow) as shown in Figure 22-57 and click Next.

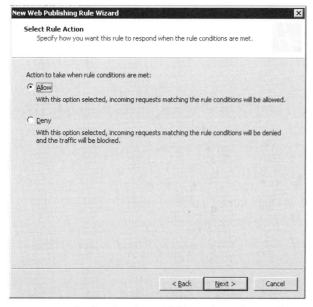

FIGURE 22-57 Configuring the publishing rule to allow traffic

5. On the Publishing Type page, leave the default option as shown in Figure 22-58 and click Next.

FIGURE 22-58 Choosing the publishing type according to the resource that will publish it

6. On the Server Connection Security page, you specify whether TMG will use SSL to connect to the published Web server. For this rule, leave the default option as shown in Figure 22-59 and click Next.

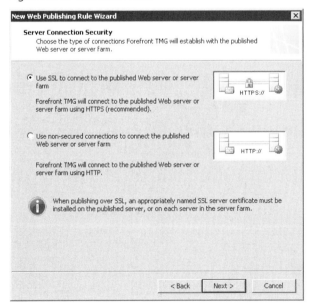

FIGURE 22-59 Selecting the protocol that will be used by the internal Web server

7. On the Internal Publishing Details page, type the internal site name as shown in Figure 22-60 and click Next.

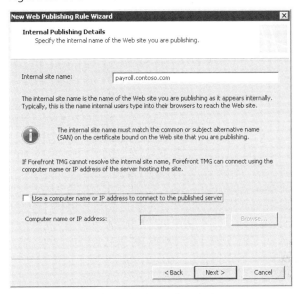

FIGURE 22-60 Specifying the internal Web site name

> **NOTE** The name that you specify on this page must match the subject name or one of the SAN entries in the certificate installed in the target Web server.

8. For the Web site that we are publishing, our goal is to allow access to all the content within the Web server. Therefore, the path should be **/*** as shown in Figure 22-61. Click Next.

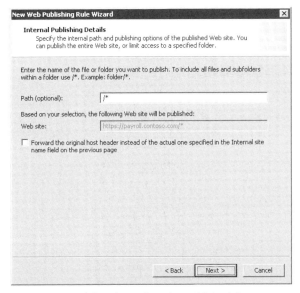

FIGURE 22-61 Adding the path to the published site

9. On the Public Name Details page you need to specify the name that the remote clients will use to reach the published server. Type in **payroll.contoso.com,** leave the other options as default as shown in Figure 22-62, and click Next.

FIGURE 22-62 Adding the public name that will be used for this publishing rule

10. On the Select Web Listener page, choose HTTPS Listener (Web Listener That Was Created Previously) from the Web Listener drop-down list, as shown in Figure 22-63. Click Next.

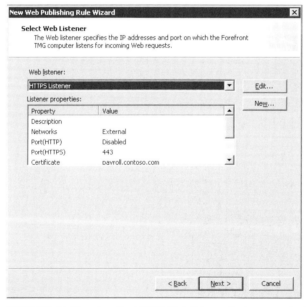

FIGURE 22-63 Choosing the HTTPS Web listener that was created

11. On the Authentication Delegation page, click the drop-down list and choose Basic Authentication, as shown in Figure 22-64. Click Next.

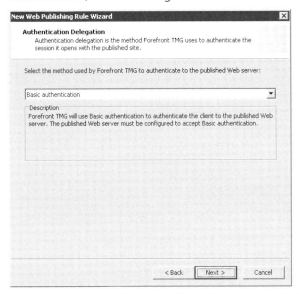

FIGURE 22-64 Choosing the authentication delegation method

> **NOTE** The method that you choose on the Authentication Delegation page, shown in Figure 22-64, must match the authentication used by the Web server that you are publishing. This is information that you need to gather during the planning phase.

12. On the User Sets page, leave the default option to enforce all users to authenticate before accessing the internal Web server as shown in Figure 22-65. Click Next to continue.

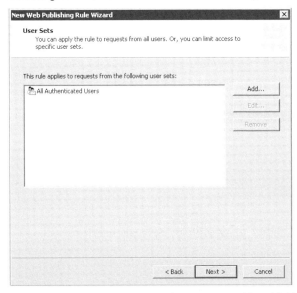

FIGURE 22-65 Allowing all users to have access to this publishing rule

13. On the Completing The New Web Publishing Rule Wizard, shown in Figure 22-66, review the summary of the selections for this rule. To confirm that the publishing rule is working properly, click Test Rule. If everything is configured properly, the result will be similar to that shown in Figure 22-67. Click Finish and then click Apply to commit the changes.

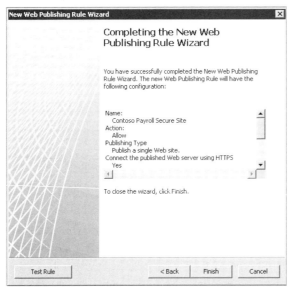

FIGURE 22-66 Summary of the options selected during the publishing rule creation

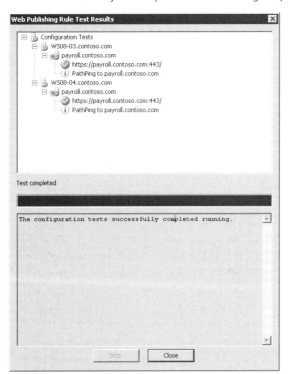

FIGURE 22-67 Test result indicating that the rule is working successfully

Publishing a Non-Web Server

Publishing a non-Web server is referred to as Server Publishing. Unlike Web Publishing rules, a Server Publishing rule only works if you have two or more network interfaces on TMG. As mentioned in Chapter 21, a Server Publishing rule works only for protocols that are defined as using a primary connection using an inbound direction. A Server Publishing rule is commonly used to publish servers using protocols other than HTTP or HTTPS.

A Server Publishing rule is fairly simple to configure; however, it is less flexible than a Web Publishing rule. Although a Server Publishing rule can be used to publish applications or services over TCP, UDP, or PPTP, you cannot apply pre-authentication at TMG to restrict access to the applications. Access can only be restricted based on source IP address. Another disadvantage of Server Publishing is, unlike Web Publishing in which we can publish a farm of identical Web servers, a Server Publishing rule can only publish a single server or a service and a single protocol in one rule.

You can either have a NAT network relationship or a Route relationship between any two networks. When creating a Server Publishing rules, it is essential to consider the relationship between the network where the clients accessing the published server resides and the network where the actual published server resides. Likewise, it's critical to understand the direction of the network rule if the relationship is NAT, because the listener for a Server Publishing rule can only be created in the destination network of a NAT relationship. If the networks where the clients reside and the actual published server resides have a NAT relationship between them, the IP address on which the Server Publishing rule listens will belong to TMG and the clients will connect to the published server by connecting to the IP address the TMG is listening on. If the networks where the clients reside and the actual published server resides have a Route relationship between them, the clients will connect to the published server by making a connection to the actual IP address of the published server because TMG will be expecting connections on the IP address of the actual published server.

A Server Publishing rule offers the application-layer inspection capabilities offered by the related application filter and the GAPA (NIS) filter.

Creating a Non-Web Server Publishing Rule

Before we create a Non-Web Server Publishing rule (Server Publishing rule), consider the following example, which we will use while creating a rule.

An administrator wants to publish two servers over the Internet via Terminal Services. So we will create a Server Publishing rule for RDP protocol and publish the two servers. If you have two IP addresses on the interface on which you are publishing the RDP protocol, you can create two Server Publishing rules—one for each IP address—bind the RDP protocol to that IP address in the Server Publishing rule, and publish both the servers. If you do not have two IP address, you need to do some customization to listen on a different port for RDP requests and then forward the connections to the published server. In our example we only have one IP address and we'll be publishing the internal servers by listening on port 3389 for Server 1 and 3390 for Server 2. Table 22-2 shows the technical details of the setup.

TABLE 22-2 Terminal Services Configuration

SERVER NAME	SERVER IP ADDRESS	SERVER LISTENING PORT LOCALLY	SERVER LISTENING PORT ON TMG
Server 1	10.1.1.120	3389	3389
Server 2	10.1.1.121	3389	3390

To create a Non-Web Server Publishing rule, follow these steps:

1. Open the TMG management console and click Firewall Policy in the left pane. Click the Tasks tab and then click Publish Non-Web Server Protocols, as shown in Figure 22-68.

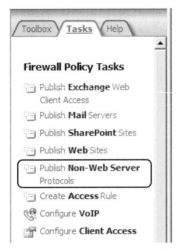

FIGURE 22-68 Creating a Non-Web Server Protocols task

2. The New Server Publishing Rule Wizard launches, as shown in Figure 22-69. Type in the name of the rule you want to create. For our example we will use a friendly name to help us identify this rule: **RDP to Server 1**. Click Next.

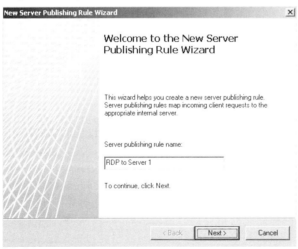

FIGURE 22-69 The New Server Publishing Rule Wizard welcome page

3. On the Select Server page, enter the IP address of the server that you are publishing. For our example, enter **10.1.1.120** in the Server IP Address field as shown in Figure 22-70. Click Next.

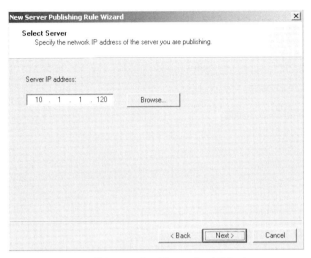

FIGURE 22-70 Specifying an IP address of published server screen

4. On the Select Protocol page, shown in Figure 22-71, you choose the protocol that you are publishing. Choose RDP (Terminal Services) Server from the Selected Protocol drop-down list, as shown in Figure 22-72. The Select Protocol page is now modified, as shown in Figure 22-73. Click Next.

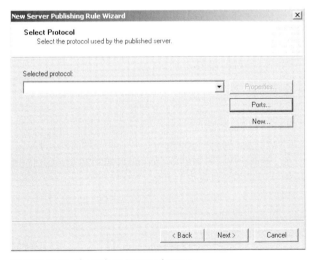

FIGURE 22-71 The Select Protocol page

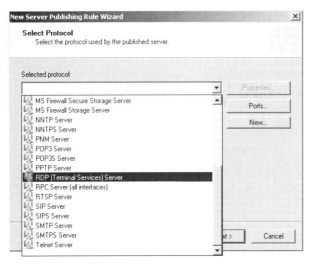

FIGURE 22-72 Selecting RDP (Terminal Services) Server protocol

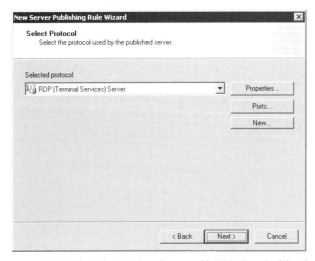

FIGURE 22-73 The Select Protocol page with RDP (Terminal Services) Server protocol selected

5. On the Network Listener IP Addresses page, you specify the IP address or all IP addresses on a network on which TMG will listen for requests for the published Non-Web server. If you have more than one IP address on the network interface that will listen for requests and you want to specify TMG to only listen on a particular IP address, click Address as shown in Figure 22-74.

6. This opens a dialog box where you can select the IP address you want TMG to use to listen for requests for the published Non-Web server, as shown in Figure 22-75. Because our example has only one IP address, select External Network as shown in Figure 22-74 and click Next.

7. The New Server Publishing Rule Wizard completes, displaying a brief summary of the rule as shown in Figure 22-76. Click Finish and then click Apply.

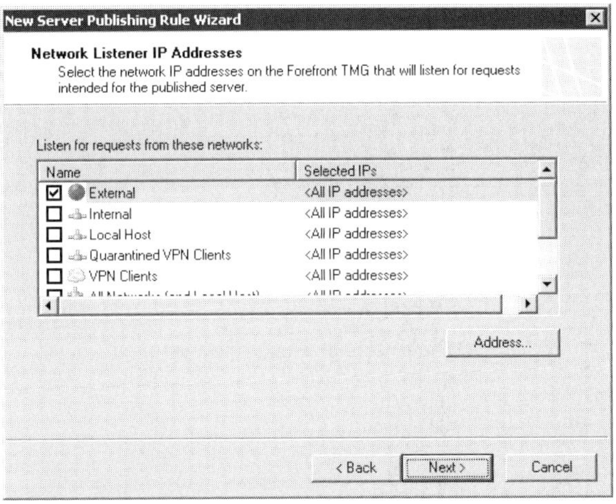

FIGURE 22-74 Selecting Network IP addresses

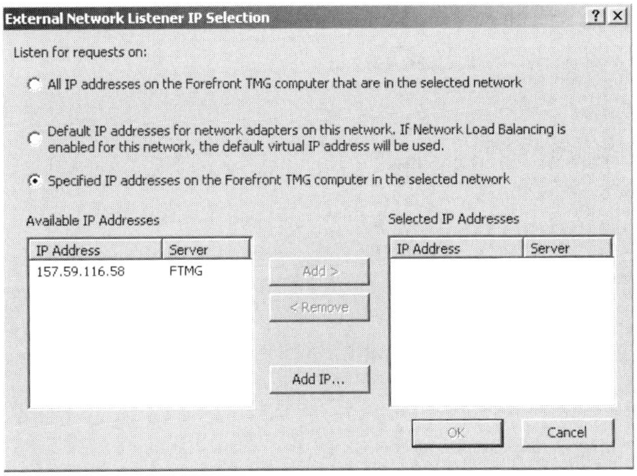

FIGURE 22-75 Selecting a specific IP address on the network

FIGURE 22-76 Completing the New Server Publishing Rule Wizard

You've now completed the publishing of Server 1 for RDP access from the external network. Because we only have one IP address on the external interface, we will configure TMG to listen on port 3390 for RDP requests for Server 2. The clients will have to connect to Server 2 for RDP on port 3390. The simplest command to connect via the RDP client on a non-standard port is the following:

```
mstsc /v:<Server>:<Port>
```

To publish Server 2 on port 3390, follow these steps:

1. Open the TMG management console and click Firewall Policy in the left pane. On the Tasks tab, click Publish Non-Web Server Protocols as shown in Figure 22-77.

FIGURE 22-77 Creating a Non-Web Server Protocols task

2. The New Server Publishing Rule Wizard welcome page opens, as shown in Figure 22-78. Type in the name of the rule you want to create. For our example we'll use a friendly name to help us identify this rule. Type **RDP to Server 2** and click Next.

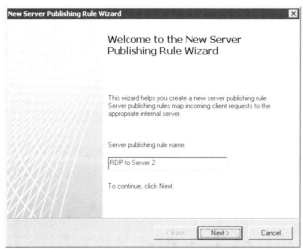

FIGURE 22-78 The Welcome To The New Server Publishing Rule Wizard page

3. On the Select Server page, type in the IP address of the server that you are publishing. For this example, type **10.1.1.121** in the Server IP Address field as shown in Figure 22-79. Click Next.

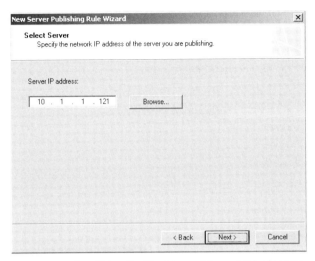

FIGURE 22-79 Specifying the IP address of the published server

4. On the Select Protocol page, shown in Figure 22-80, choose the protocol that you are publishing. Select RDP (Terminal Services) Server from the Selected Protocol drop-down list, as shown in Figure 22-81. Figure 22-82 shows the modified Select Protocol page.

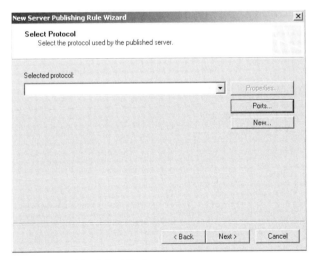

FIGURE 22-80 The Select Protocol page

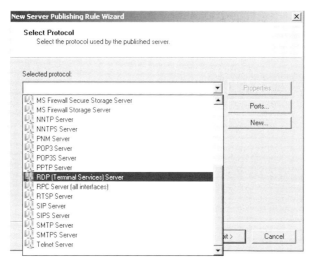

FIGURE 22-81 Selecting RDP (Terminal Services) Server protocol

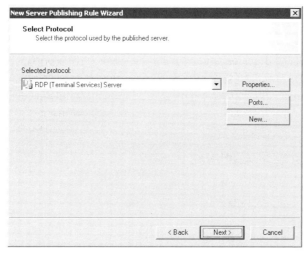

FIGURE 22-82 The Select Protocol page with RDP (Terminal Services) Server protocol selected

5. Click Ports, as shown in Figure 22-82. The dialog box where you can override the default ports opens, as shown in Figure 22-83. Select the option Publish On This Port Instead Of The Default Port and type **3390** as the port number. The RDP (Terminal Services) Server protocol will now listen on port 3390 instead of the default port 3389 just for this rule. Click OK and then click Next.

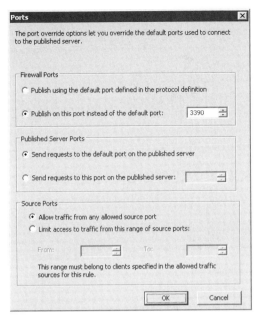

FIGURE 22-83 The Ports dialog box

6. On the Network Listener IP Addresses page, you specify the IP address or all IP addresses on a network that TMG will listen on for requests for the published Non-Web server. If you have more than one IP address on the network interface that will listen on for requests and you want to specify that TMG only listens on a particular IP address instead of all IP addresses, click Address as shown in Figure 22-84.

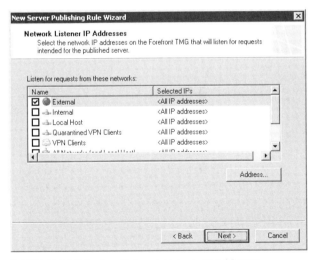

FIGURE 22-84 Selecting Network Listener IP Addresses

7. This opens the dialog box shown in Figure 22-85, where you can select the IP address TMG will use to listen on for requests for the published Non-Web server. Because we have only one IP address, select the External Network as shown in Figure 22-84. Click Next.

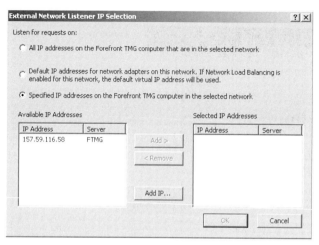

FIGURE 22-85 Selecting specific IP address on the network

8. On the Completing The New Server Publishing Rule Wizard page, you can see a brief summary of the new rule you just created, as shown in Figure 22-86. Click Finish and then click Apply to commit and apply the new settings.

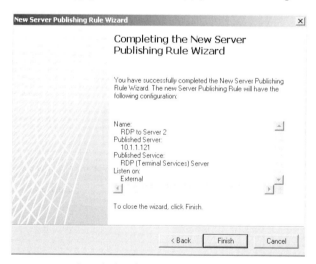

FIGURE 22-86 Completing the New Server Publishing Rule Wizard

Using the following command, open the command prompt to see the ports TMG is listening on:

```
netstat –an
```

You can see that after you created the two Server Publishing rules, TMG is listening on both ports 3389 and 3390, as shown in Figure 22-87. A more reliable way to see the ports listening for a service when published through TMG would be to use fwengmon, which is a part of the netsh command set.

FIGURE 22-87 Ports TMG is listening on

Troubleshooting Publishing Rules

Regardless of how well you may have researched, planned, and executed your publishing scenarios and policies, a time will come when something goes awry. When this happens, you need to have a good understanding of the application behavior at the client and server, but you can usually use some standard troubleshooting methodology.

If you remember nothing else, remember this: The combination of the policy rule and network rule criteria combine to define TMG behavior with regard to all traffic flow. Keep in mind the following guidelines regarding troubleshooting publishing rules:

- Learn to use the TMG log query mechanism. Regardless of whether you're troubleshooting publishing rules or access rules, the TMG logs should be the first place you go.

- Use the troubleshooting tools TMG includes: the traffic simulator and Web Publishing rule Test Rule button were created specifically to simplify your troubleshooting tasks.

- Learn to use a network capture tool, such as Network Monitor or Wireshark. You can learn things from a network capture that you can't find in the logs.

- Learn to enable and interpret the logging mechanisms provided by the client and server applications.

Web Publishing Rules

Although Web Publishing is "just HTTP," the very complexity of this protocol and its blatant abuse by server and client applications are what make it more difficult to troubleshoot than many other protocols.

In general, if more than one Web Publishing rule is associated with the Web listener where the request was received, TMG processes those Web Publishing rules until the request is explicitly allowed or denied. If no rule matches the request, TMG uses the default policy rule to deny the request.

Web Publishing rules that are not associated with the listener where the request was received will not be processed.

The diagram shown in Figure 22-88 illustrates the network used for the following discussion.

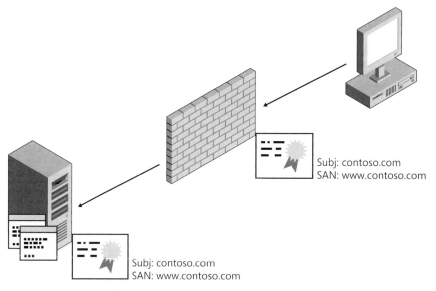

FIGURE 22-88 Example Web Publishing scenario

In this example, there is only one Web listener serving one publishing rule. The Web listener has the following configuration:

- **Network**   External, listening on 80 and 443
- **Certificate**   subject name = contoso.com, Subject Alternate Name = www.contoso.com
- **Authentication**   HTTP-Basic

The Web Publishing rule has the following configuration:

- **Public names**   contoso.com
- **Paths**   /path1
- **Authentication delegation**   HTTP-NTLM

Remember that when an HTTP client application sends a request, it starts with a URL provided by the user or as part of the content received from a server. The majority of what a Web Publishing rule uses to allow or reject the request is contained in the URL itself. Table 22-3 illustrates the breakdown of a URL.

TABLE 22-3 URL Component Breakdown

METHOD	SCHEME	HOST	PORT	PATH	QUERY
GET	http://	www.contoso.com	:666	/path/file.ext	?a=whatever

When a Web client issues an HTTP request, it breaks down the URL into multiple data points that are used to populate various portions of the request data:

```
- Http: Request, GET /path/file.ext
Command: GET
+ URI: /path/file.ext?a=whatever
ProtocolVersion: HTTP/1.1
Accept: image/gif, image/x-xbitmap, image/jpeg, image/pjpeg, */*
Accept-Language: en-us
Accept-Encoding: gzip, deflate
UserAgent: Mozilla/4.0 (compatible; MSIE 6.0; Windows NT 5.2; .NET CLR 1.1.4322)
Host: www.contoso.com:666
Connection: Keep-Alive
HeaderEnd: CRLF
```

The port may not be included in the host header. This data is not required by RFC 2616 and is implemented inconsistently across Web applications. Likewise, the scheme is only included when the client is issuing a CERN proxy request:

```
- Http: Request, GET http://www.contoso.com:666/path/file.ext
Command: GET
+ URI: http://www.contoso.com:666/path/file.ext?a=whatever
ProtocolVersion: HTTP/1.1
Accept: image/gif, image/x-xbitmap, image/jpeg, image/pjpeg, */*
Accept-Language: en-us
Accept-Encoding: gzip, deflate
UserAgent: Mozilla/4.0 (compatible; MSIE 6.0; Windows NT 5.2; .NET CLR 1.1.4322)
Host: www.contoso.com:666
Connection: Keep-Alive
HeaderEnd: CRLF
```

Web Publishing scenario failures fall into a several categories:

Contextually Inappropriate Request

There are two Web request contexts for TMG:

- **Web Proxy**   Operates within a TMG-protected network and makes Web requests in one of two forms:

  - **CERN proxy**   This client is aware that it must communicate to the Web server through a Web proxy. The CERN proxy client connects to a TMG Web Proxy listener and issues requests as:

    ```
    GET http://www.contoso.com:666/path/file.ext
    ```

  - **Transparent proxy**   This client also operates in a TMG-protected network but is unaware that a proxy exists. The transparent proxy client connects directly to the Web server and issues its requests as:

    ```
    GET /path/file.ext
    ```

- **Web Client**   This client operates in any network, connects to a TMG Web Publishing listener, and issues requests in the same format as the transparent proxy client.

Thus, a client can issue a contextually inappropriate request in two ways:

1. The Web client issues a CERN proxy request. If the client connects to a Web Publishing listener and issues a request that would normally be appropriate to a Web Proxy listener, TMG will correctly interpret this as an out-of-context request, reject the request with an HTTP-400 response, and enter 13 (invalid data) in the Web Proxy HTTP Status code log field.

2. The CERN proxy client issues a Web client request. If the client connects to a Web Proxy listener and issues a request that would be appropriate to a Web Publishing listener, TMG responds with an HTTP-502 Proxy Error response and enters 12006 in the Web Proxy HTTP Status code log field.

In these cases, TMG rejects the request based on the default rule because no aspect of any Web Publishing or access rule can contextually match the request.

Host Mismatch

If the client issues a request for "www.contoso.com", but the Web Publishing rule "public names" list only includes "contoso.com" as shown in Figure 22-89, TMG will reject the request with an HTTP-403 response and log 12202 in the HTTP Status Code Web Proxy log field.

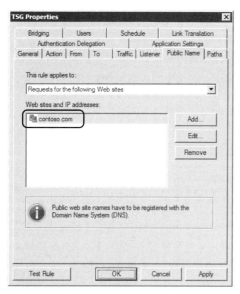

FIGURE 22-89 Web Publishing rule public names

When TMG receives the request, it compares the Public Names list to the data provided in the client request "host" header as shown in the following network capture example:

```
- Http: Request, GET /
Command: GET
+ URI: /
ProtocolVersion: HTTP/1.1
Accept: image/gif, image/x-xbitmap, image/jpeg, image/pjpeg, */*
Accept-Language: en-us
Accept-Encoding: gzip, deflate
UserAgent: Mozilla/4.0 (compatible; MSIE 6.0; Windows NT 5.2; .NET CLR 1.1.4322)
Host: www.contoso.com
Connection: Keep-Alive
HeaderEnd: CRLF
```

Path Mismatch

Let's say the client issues a request for /path2, but the Web Publishing rule Paths list includes only /path1, as shown in Figure 22-90.

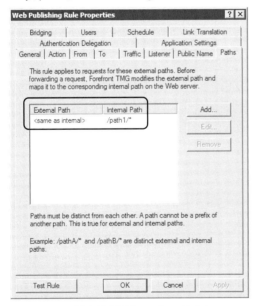

FIGURE 22-90 Web Publishing rule path list

In this case, TMG rejects the request with an HTTP-403 response and logs 12202 in the Web Proxy log HTTP Response Code field:

```
- Http: Request, GET /path2
Command: GET
+ URI: /path2
```

```
ProtocolVersion: HTTP/1.1
Accept: image/gif, image/x-xbitmap, image/jpeg, image/pjpeg, */*
Accept-Language: en-us
Accept-Encoding: gzip, deflate
UserAgent: Mozilla/4.0 (compatible; MSIE 6.0; Windows NT 5.2; .NET CLR 1.1.4322)
Host: www.contoso.com
Connection: Keep-Alive
HeaderEnd: CRLF
```

Authentication Failure

If the Web Publishing rule Users tab is configured for anything other than All Users, TMG must determine the user's identity. If the user fails to satisfy the authentication requirements of the Web Publishing rule, TMG will fail the request and return an HTTP-401 response. The HTTP Response code field will contain one of several codes, depending on the specific authentication failure (12209 or 12309 is typical for HTTP-based authenticating listeners). In this case, the client application might be trying to authenticate using HTTP-NTLM, but the Web listener is configured to accept only HTTP-Basic credentials as shown in Figure 22-91.

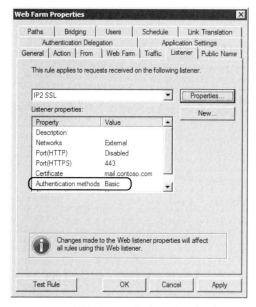

FIGURE 22-91 Web listener Basic authentication

Authentication Delegation Failure

In this example, the Web Publishing rule is configured to employ authentication delegation using HTTP-NTLM as shown in Figure 22-92, but the published service requires an HTTP-Basic authentication.

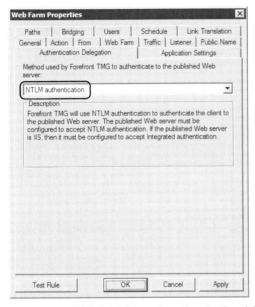

FIGURE 22-92 Web Publishing rule authentication delegation

TMG rejects the request with an HTTP-401 and logs 12202 in the Web Proxy log HTTP-Status field.

Web Listener Certificate Errors

The five most common certificate errors that can occur at a Web listener are:

- The certificate "purpose" does not include Server Authentication.
- The certificate private key was not imported.
- The certificate is issued by a Certificate Authority that is not trusted by the computer where TMG operates.
- The certificate is nearing its expiration date.
- The certificate Subject or Subject Alternative Names list does not agree with the Web Publishing rule's public names.

In all except the last error, TMG will be unable to associate the certificate with the Web listener. In all cases, TMG will trigger one of three alerts as shown in Figure 22-93.

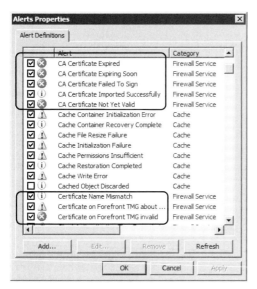

FIGURE 22-93 Alerts related to Web listener certificates

When the certificate subject or SAN fails to match the Web Publishing rule's public names, TMG triggers the Certificate Name mismatch alert, but the Web listener and associated rules will still function. The error state created by this case is that the client application will likely issue an alert to the effect that the certificate name fails to match the server name.

Client Certificate Errors

When the Web listener is configured for client certificate authentication, TMG offers you many choices through which you can completely destroy any chance of successful authentication by the client. These are shown in Figures 22-94 and 22-95.

The options provided in Figure 22-94 allow you to limit the acceptable client certificates to those issued by any or a specific certificate authority. If you choose to limit the acceptable client certificates according to issuing CA and the client does not possess a user authentication certificate that was issued by that CA, the client will be unable to select a certificate and authentication to TMG will fail.

The options provided in Figure 22-95 allow you to limit acceptable certificates to those that include the properties defined in that list. If the client presents an authentication certificate that fails to match *all* of the criteria defined here, TMG will reject the connection and log "connection aborted" in the Web Proxy log.

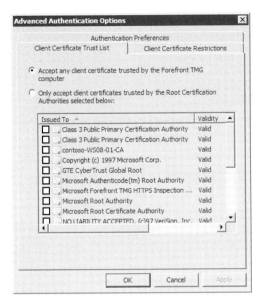

FIGURE 22-94 Client certificate CA trust list

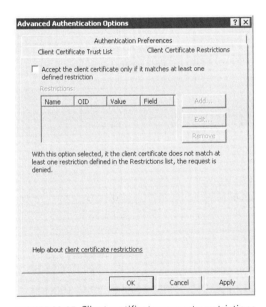

FIGURE 22-95 Client certificate property restrictions

Published Server Certificate Errors

The five most common certificate errors that can occur at a published server are the same as those for the certificate associated with a Web listener because they serve exactly the same purpose:

- The certificate "purpose" does not include Server Authentication.

- The certificate private key was not imported.

- The certificate is issued by a CA that is not trusted by the computer where TMG operates.

- The certificate is nearing its expiration date.

- The certificate Subject or Subject Alternative Names list does not agree with the Web Publishing rule's To tab name.

The problems seen at TMG will be seen at the published server, but unless the published server is also a TMG server, the resulting errors will be somewhat different. You may see resource errors as the service listener cannot bind to the defined IP address and port, or SSL errors resulting from certificate expiration, for example. In particular, if the certificate subject or SAN fails to match the name used in the Web Publishing rule "To" tab, TMG will reject the request with "500 Internet Server Error – The target principal name is incorrect".

> **MORE INFO**   You can read more about troubleshooting certificate errors at *http://technet .microsoft.com/en-us/library/cc302619.aspx.*

Web Publishing Test Button

One of the great additions in the ISA Server 2006 Supportability Pack was a tool called the Web Publishing Test Button. This feature has been carried forward to TMG. With this tool, the TMG administrator can quickly and easily determine whether the Web Publishing rule is defined in accordance with the primary Web application requirements. The rule test button does the following:

1. Verify that the name used in the Web Publishing rule To tab can be resolved to an IP address

2. Verify that the IP resolved from the name in the Web Publishing rule To tab can be accepts connections at that IP address

3. Verify that the redirect port in the Web Publishing rule agrees with the port used in the Web application listener

4. Verify that the listener that accepts the connection obeys basic HTTP communication

5. Verify that the Web Publishing rule authentication delegation configuration matches the application authentication requirements

Figure 22-96 provides an example of a Web Publishing test event where the published server name provided in the rule's To tab fails to resolve in DNS.

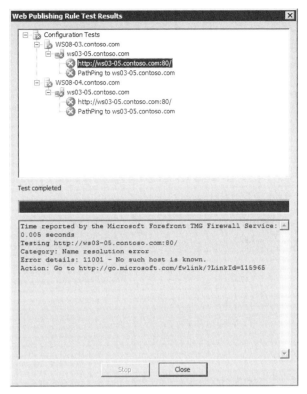

FIGURE 22-96 Web Publishing rule test button results

Figure 22-97 shows the entry you might find for the same results in Diagnostic logging.

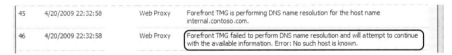

| 45 | 4/20/2009 22:32:58 | Web Proxy | Forefront TMG is performing DNS name resolution for the host name internal.contoso.com. |
| 46 | 4/20/2009 22:32:58 | Web Proxy | Forefront TMG failed to perform DNS name resolution and will attempt to continue with the available information. Error: No such host is known. |

FIGURE 22-97 Diagnostic logging results for the test button action

Non-Web Publishing Rules

Non-Web Publishing rules offer their own set of problems distinct from Web Publishing rules. On one hand, non-Web Publishing rules offer the flexibility of more protocols and a lack of authentication-based problems. On the other hand, they offer the additional complexity of being governed by application filters and network rules. As a result, they are both easier and harder to troubleshoot.

The most common problems stem from a misunderstanding of how network rules affect TMG policy behavior and how listeners are created by TMG in support of publishing rules. If this is still unclear to you, now might be a good time to review Chapter 11, "Configuring Forefront TMG 2010 Networks," but the short form of the relationship is this:

1. Non-Web Publishing always uses a server protocol definition, which is distinguished by an inbound primary connection. This point is due less to how the traffic flows through TMG than how the application filters process the traffic.

2. Network rules determine how the client must create the connection. If the traffic flow is governed by a NAT rule, the client must connect to a listener owned by TMG. If the rule is governed by a route rule, the client must connect to a listener at the published server. Another complication of defining a route relationship between the client and published server is that the route must make sense to the client, TMG, and published server at the IP layer. If the published server operates on a private (RFC-1819 or APIPA) address and the client operates on a publicly routable address, no amount of route table manglement will resolve the traffic flow failure.

3. Non-Web Publishing rules cannot be associated with Web listeners. A very common mistake when troubleshooting Web Publishing is to create a non-Web Publishing rule preceding the Web Publishing rule and using the same IP/port combination as the associated Web listener. This is typically performed in the mistaken belief that the non-Web Publishing rule will supersede the Web Publishing rule and thus help isolate whatever issues are caused by the Web Publishing rule. Because the non-Web Publishing listener definition conflicts with the Web listener created for the Web Publishing rule, TMG cannot create a functioning listener and thus cannot process traffic using either publishing rule.

Although any number of IP- or transport-based status codes may be listed when TMG rejects traffic that is processed by a non-Web Publishing rule, the result-code that is frequently the most useful is 0x80074e24, or "Connection closed by application filter action". This result-code tells you that the application filter governing this traffic determined that the traffic violated the traffic rules relevant to this protocol and the TMG application filter instructed the TMG Firewall Engine to close the connection. The following example demonstrates this behavior for SMTP traffic through a publishing rule.

One of the features offered by the SMTP application filter is the ability to validate the length of the SMTP command and associated data. In Figure 22-98, the maximum length of the NOOP command is six characters.

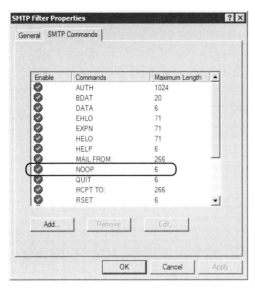

FIGURE 22-98 SMTP filter NOOP length default

In the following text block, we provide the series of commands that lead to the point where the SMTP application filter instructs TMG to close the connection with the remote SMTP client:

```
C:\> telnet mailcontoso.com 25
220 remote.contoso.com Microsoft ESMTP MAIL Service ready at Mon, 20 Apr 2009 22:45:37
-0700
noop: wertewtewtewtetewtewrtertret
421 5.5.2 Syntax error (command line too long)

Connection to host lost.

C:\>
```

In our test client, we simulate an SMTP mail client:

1. We start by instructing the telnet client application to connect to our mail server on port 25.

2. To trigger the SMTP application filter, we issue a NOOP command that exceeds the maximum allowable length.

3. TMG sends the 421 5.5.2 Syntax error (command too long) response and closes the connection from the client.

When we examine the TMG log query window using a log filter that limits results to firewall log entries that include a destination port equal to 25, we see the results shown in Figure 22-99.

FIGURE 22-99 Log results for application filter action 0x80074e24

Summary

In this chapter we discussed how to create Web Publishing rules for HTTP and HTTPS traffic, how to import a certificate and use it on a Web listener, how to create a Server Publishing rule for default and nonstandard ports, and how to troubleshoot issues related to publishing in TMG. In the next chapter we will discuss how to securely publish Microsoft Windows SharePoint Services.

## CHAPTER 23

Publishing Microsoft Office SharePoint Server

■ Planning to Publish SharePoint **661**

■ Configuring SharePoint Publishing **665**

■ Troubleshooting **689**

■ Summary **696**

This chapter discusses how to plan and configure a Microsoft Office SharePoint Services deployment. With Office SharePoint Services, organizations can take file sharing and collaboration to a new level by helping to improve process efficiency and information worker productivity, increase business agility, and reduce operating costs. When you publish Office SharePoint Services to the Internet, TMG can help make these sites available to external users without compromising the security of your organization's network. This chapter explains what you need to consider while planning SharePoint and how to configure a Web Publishing rule in TMG to publish SharePoint services to the Internet. We'll conclude the chapter with a discussion of some common issues related to publishing SharePoint services and how to troubleshoot them.

Planning to Publish SharePoint

To have a stable and successful setup, it is essential to plan every deployment. Before publishing SharePoint, you need to take into account various aspects of the deployment. In this section we will discuss the security aspects, authentication, and Alternate Access Mapping (AAM) considerations before we publish SharePoint. One of the key aspects of every deployment is the security considerations that need to be in place before you publish any Web services. Some of the security considerations also depend on the type of authentication being used to either pre-authenticate the request at TMG or when delegating credentials to the published SharePoint using authentication delegation in TMG. You must consider your authentication requirements carefully because any authentication mismatch will cause failure in users' ability to access the published server.

Security Considerations

Administrators prefer to allow only the most restrictive access to their published servers to reduce the chance that the security of the network can be compromised. Some of the key areas that need to be planned around security are:

- Access based on source networks
- Access for only encrypted traffic (HTTPS) or for both encrypted and unencrypted traffic
- Allowing caching
- Access based on time
- Access based on user groups

Even though most of these considerations are very generic, they are important. Each area affects how the rule is configured.

Access Based on Source Networks

The whole idea of publishing a Web service is to allow external users to access the server for the published service. The most common deployment is to allow access to users on the Internet. When you create a SharePoint Web publishing rule, the default option is to allow access from the Anywhere computer set to the listener that is listening for the requests. An administrator can, however, set up address ranges or specific IP addresses to allow access only from that address range or IP address.

Access for Encrypted or Unencrypted Traffic

One of the most important security considerations when publishing any Web service to the Internet or to a non-trusted network is the encryption of traffic. Most administrators encrypt all incoming traffic from the Internet using certificates. You can set up a listener with a certificate to restrict access to only HTTPS traffic. TMG can then forward the traffic using HTTP to the published SharePoint server or over HTTPS depending on how the SharePoint is configured locally. SSL bridging protects against attacks that are hidden in SSL-encrypted connections. For SSL-enabled Web applications such as SharePoint, after receiving the client's request, TMG decrypts the request, inspects it, and terminates the SSL connection with the client computer. The Web publishing rules determine how TMG communicates the request for the object to the published SharePoint server. If the secure Web publishing rule is configured to forward the request using SSL (HTTPS), TMG initiates a new SSL connection with the published server. Because TMG is now an SSL client, it requires that the published Web server respond with a server-side certificate.

Remember that when you choose a certificate, that certificate needs to have a private key and its Common Name (CN) or one of its Subject Alternate Names (SANs) needs to be the same as the public URL. The certificate should also be trusted up to the Root Certification Authority.

MORE INFO For more information about certificate requirements please read *http://technet.microsoft.com/en-ca/library/dd547090.aspx*.

Allowing Caching

Content caching allows TMG to cache Web content and to respond to user requests from the cache, rather than contacting the Web server. This increases the performance of requests that are being serviced for the clients over the Internet. Caching also helps reduce the traffic from TMG to the published SharePoint server because the requests that are found in TMG's cache will be delivered to the client from TMG itself and will save the round trip to the published server.

Allowing Access Based on Time

Some administrators like to restrict access based on time. This helps prevent wasting bandwidth by allowing access only during business hours and restricting access during off hours. This can be done using either the built-in schedules or creating a custom schedule and allowing and denying access in the SharePoint publishing rule based on that schedule.

Allowing Access Based on User Groups

TMG can pre-authenticate a request before even forwarding it to the SharePoint server. This prevents any unauthenticated requests from even getting to the SharePoint server. You can configure TMG to allow all authenticated requests for any user in Active Directory or restrict access based on a select user group so that only the users belonging to that specific user group are allowed access to the published SharePoint server.

Authentication

TMG provides a variety of authentication mechanisms that can be used to pre-authenticate a request at TMG. Then the client is either allowed to authenticate against the SharePoint server directly or use the credentials collected in the pre-authentication process and delegate them to the SharePoint server, providing a seamless, single sign-on experience to the client. The different types of client authentication methods on TMG are:

- No Authentication
- Forms-Based Authentication
- HTTP Authentication (received in HTTP header)
- Client Certificate Authentication

TMG can validate the client credentials passed on one of these formats using the following providers and protocols:

- No Authentication (allows the internal published server to handle authentication)
- Windows Active Directory

- Active Directory over LDAP protocol
- RADIUS
- RADIUS one-time password
- SecurID

The most commonly used authentication at TMG is Forms-Based Authentication (FBA). When configured with FBA, TMG presents an HTML Form in which the user enters a user name and password, which TMG can then authenticate against Active Directory (in case TMG is a domain member) or Active Directory over LDAP protocol (in case TMG is a non-domain member). Once authenticated, TMG can provide the credentials to the SharePoint Server so that the user is not prompted again for a user name and password.

Remember that when you choose what type of authentication to use for external users, if TMG is set to delegate the user's credentials to the published SharePoint server, the authentication delegation method must be the same as the authentication type set on SharePoint. The delegation method can vary depending on the client authentication method set on TMG and in certain cases only certain combinations can be used. Hence it is important to plan what the client authentication method should be on TMG so that a matching delegation method to the authentication type of SharePoint is available.

> **MORE INFO** For different authentication methods available in TMG and what their valid authentication delegation combinations are, please read *http://technet.microsoft.com/ en-us/library/bb794722.aspx.*

Alternate Access Mapping

Office SharePoint Services relies on absolute hyperlinks. A URL correction approach, such as TMG's link translation, does not provide a complete solution. This is where Alternate Access Mapping (AAM) comes into play. The main purpose of AAM is to create dynamic links for requests forwarded by the reverse proxy to serve to the end user while maintaining a proper mapping of what link should be returned to an internal user versus an external user.

Administrators often make the mistake of confusing link translation with AAM and don't deem AAM to be important. Link translation and AAM must never be used together in TMG. While configuring the SharePoint publishing rule (discussed in the next section), the TMG administrator is prompted to choose whether AAM is configured on the SharePoint server. If the administrator chooses to not configure AAM, TMG sets up link translation mappings for that rule. If the administrator decides that AAM is set up correctly, no link translation mapping is applied to that rule. SharePoint embeds its URLs in many places and in a variety of encodings that cannot be fixed by the reverse proxy server's link translation feature. SharePoint also has features that use or send URLs that do not go through reverse proxy Web publishing rules. E-mail alerts are a good example of this. Only AAM can ensure that the links in the e-mail alerts contain the correct URL, which can then be accessed publicly. Hence it is important to configure AAM on the Office SharePoint server before you publish it.

MORE INFO To learn more about configuring AAM, read *http://technet.microsoft.com/en-us/library/cc261814.aspx.*

Configuring SharePoint Publishing

As explained in the section on planning, publishing a SharePoint site to the Web is similar to publishing any other Web application, with the notable exception that you must use the SharePoint Web Publishing Wizard if you want TMG to process the requests properly. This section will guide you through the process of publishing single-server and Web-farm publishing scenarios.

Regardless of which type of publishing scenario you intend to use, you always begin in the same place. Figure 23-1 illustrates the scenario from which we will derive our publishing configuration.

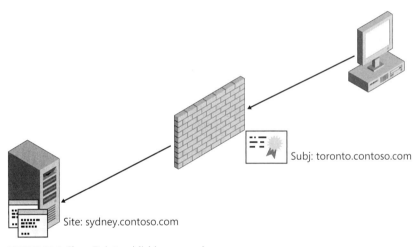

Subj: toronto.contoso.com

Site: sydney.contoso.com

FIGURE 23-1 SharePoint publishing scenario

In this scenario, the SharePoint site administrators have already configured AAM and are using unencrypted connections between TMG and the SharePoint server by directing the Contoso network security team to support their third-party IDS system. The SharePoint administrators want TMG to use Kerberos constrained Delegation (KCD).

The following instructions only provide steps for asymmetric SSL bridging; that is, HTTPS between the client and Forefront TMG and HTTP between Forefront TMG and the SharePoint server.

> **NOTE** The procedures that follow are condensed into four subsections: Common Starting Point (the point from which the remaining steps flow), Single Server (publishing a single computer), Multi-Server (publishing multiple sites in a single action), and Server Farm (publishing a SharePoint Web farm).

Common Starting Point

1. In the Forefront TMG management console, right-click Firewall Policy, select New, and then select SharePoint Site Publishing Rule, as shown in Figure 23-2.

FIGURE 23-2 Creating a new SharePoint publishing rule

2. On the Welcome To The SharePoint Publishing Rule Wizard page, type in the name of the publishing rule, such as **toronto.contoso.com,** as shown in Figure 23-3. Click Next.

FIGURE 23-3 Publishing Wizard Welcome page

3. On the Publishing Type page, select the type of publishing scenario you wish to use, as shown in Figure 23-4. Click Next to proceed to the desired publishing scenario, which is illustrated in the following procedure.

FIGURE 23-4 Single-site publishing selection

Single-Server

The following steps continue from the Common Starting point and will guide you through the process for publishing a single SharePoint server.

1. On the Server Connection Security page, select the connection type for the SharePoint site as shown in Figure 23-5 and click Next.

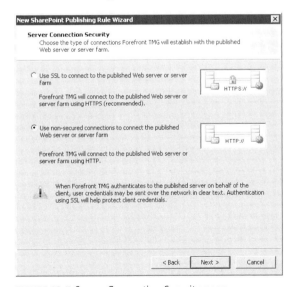

FIGURE 23-5 Server Connection Security page

2. On the Internal Publishing Details page, type in the fully qualified name of the SharePoint site as configured by the SharePoint administrator, shown in Figure 23-6. Select Use A Computer Name Or IP Address and enter the fully qualified host name or IP address in the Computer Name Or IP Address field. Click Next.

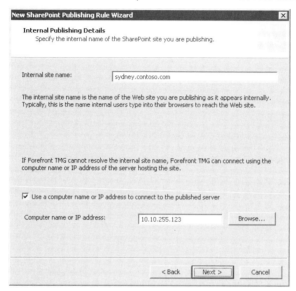

FIGURE 23-6 Internal Publishing Details page

3. On the Public Name Details page, select This Domain Name (Type Below) and enter the FQDN as used by clients in the network where the Web listener will operate. For our scenario, external clients will use **toronto.contoso.com** as shown in Figure 23-7. Click Next.

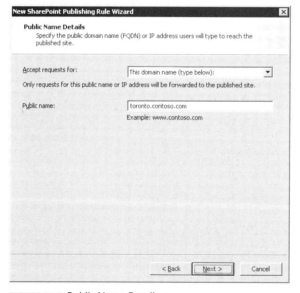

FIGURE 23-7 Public Name Details page

4. On the Select Web Listener Page, select the Web listener that is to accept connections for this publishing rule as shown in Figure 23-8. Click Next.

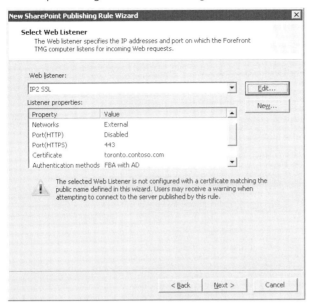

FIGURE 23-8 Web Listener selection page

5. On the Authentication Delegation page, select the authentication method used at the SharePoint site. In this case, we have selected Kerberos Constrained Delegation (KCD). Note that the value provided in the Service Principal Name (SPN) is determined from the value we provided in the Internal site name as shown in Figure 23-9. Click Next.

FIGURE 23-9 Authentication Delegation page

MORE INFO   Selecting the correct Kerberos Constrained Delegation configuration
is a critical point for proper authentication from TMG to the published server.
The considerations related to service accounts and multiple SPN are discussed
in *http://blogs.technet.com/isablog/archive/2009/02/05/another-blog-about-kcd-tips-
and-tricks-on-kerberos-and-delegation-isa2006.aspx.*

6. On the Alternate Access Mappings Configuration page shown in Figure 23-10, select
    the choice that best describes your current SharePoint configuration. Because we
    know that the Contoso SharePoint site has AAM configured, select SharePoint AAM Is
    Already Configured On The SharePoint Server. Click Next.

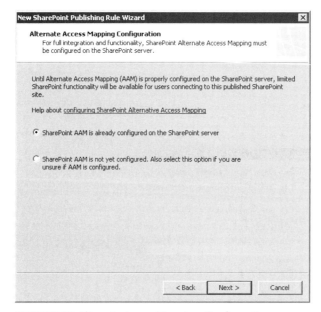

FIGURE 23-10 Alternate Access Mappings Configuration page

7. On the User Sets page, leave the default selection in place as shown in Figure 23-11
    and click Next.

8. On the Completing The New SharePoint Publishing Rule Wizard page, verify the
    summary data as shown in Figure 23-12 and click Finish.

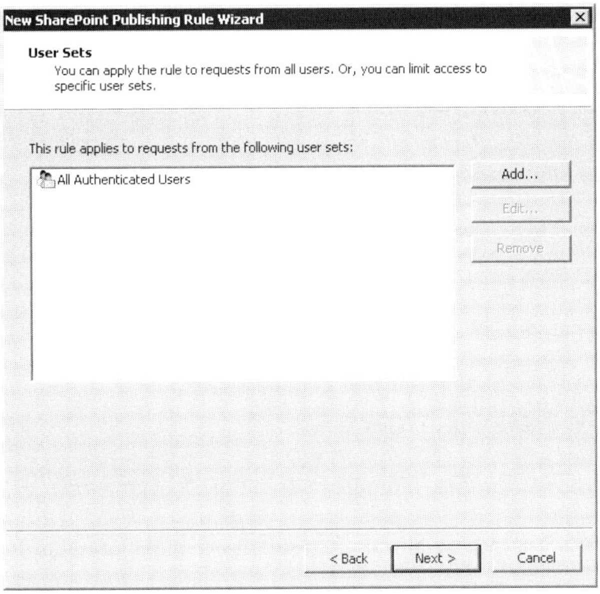

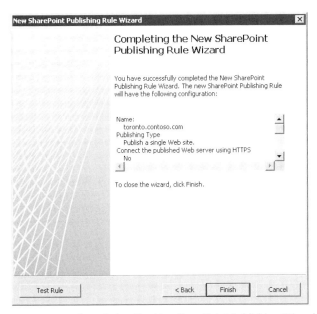

New SharePoint Publishing Rule Wizard
User Sets
You can apply the rule to requests from all users. Or, you can limit access to specific user sets.
This rule applies to requests from the following user sets:
All Authenticated Users
Add...
Edit...
Remove
< Back
Next >
Cancel

FIGURE 23-11 User Sets page

New SharePoint Publishing Rule Wizard
Completing the New SharePoint Publishing Rule Wizard
You have successfully completed the New SharePoint Publishing Rule Wizard. The new SharePoint Publishing Rule will have the following configuration:
Name:
toronto.contoso.com
Publishing Type
Publish a single Web site.
Connect the published Web server using HTTPS
No
To close the wizard, click Finish.
Test Rule
< Back
Finish
Cancel

FIGURE 23-12 Completing The New SharePoint Publishing Wizard page

NOTE Because we selected KCD, the publishing wizard produces the warning shown in Figure 23-13 to remind you that you should verify the necessary domain and server configuration for KCD to operate properly.

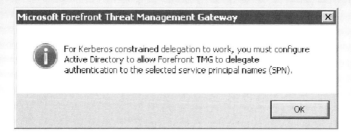

FIGURE 23-13 KCD informational warning

Figure 23-14 illustrates the summary information provided by the TMG rules list.

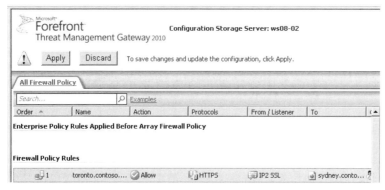

FIGURE 23-14 New SharePoint single-server publishing rule summary

This completes the process required to meet the Contoso SharePoint administrator's requirements for publishing the Contoso SharePoint portal. The remaining steps are included to illustrate the differences in the Web publishing wizards.

Multi-Server

The following steps illustrate the process involved in publishing multiple, individual SharePoint sites as shown in Figure 23-15. You must begin this process with the Common Starting Point Steps. The servers that you are publishing are Sydney and Denver.

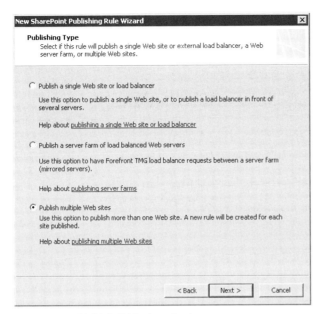

FIGURE 23-15 Multiple Web site selection

1. On the Specify Web Sites To Publish page, shown in Figure 23-16, click Add to add the Sydney server.

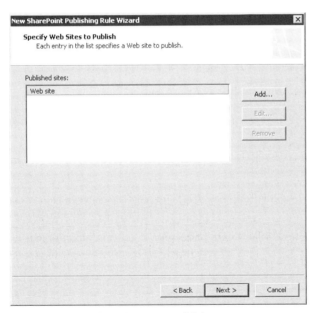

FIGURE 23-16 Specify Web Sites To Publish page

2. In the Internal Site Details dialog box, type **sydney** in the Internal Site Name field as shown in Figure 23-17. Click OK to close the Internal Site Details dialog box.

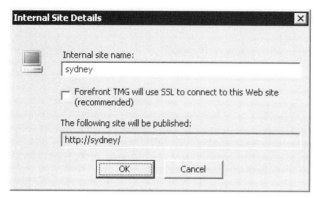

FIGURE 23-17 Adding the Sydney server to the list

3. On the Specify Web Sites To Publish page, click Add to add the Denver server.

4. In the Internal Site Details dialog box, type **denver** in the Internal Site Name field as shown in Figure 23-18. Click OK to close the Internal Site Details dialog box.

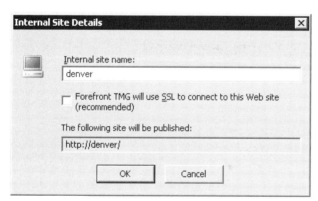

FIGURE 23-18 Adding the Denver server

5. Verify that the Specify Web Sites To Publish page appears as shown in Figure 23-19 and click Next.

6. On the Published Web Sites Public Names page, type in the common domain suffix used by these publishing rules—in this case, **contoso.com** as shown in Figure 23-20. Click Next.

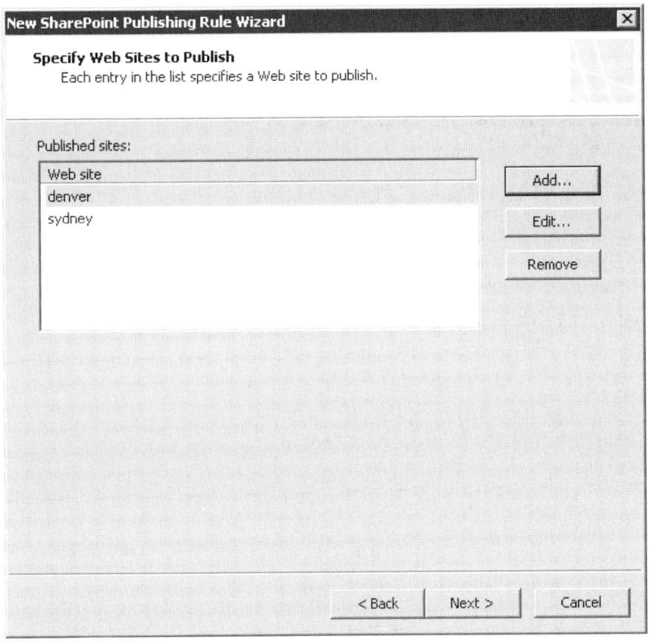

FIGURE 23-19 Completed server additions

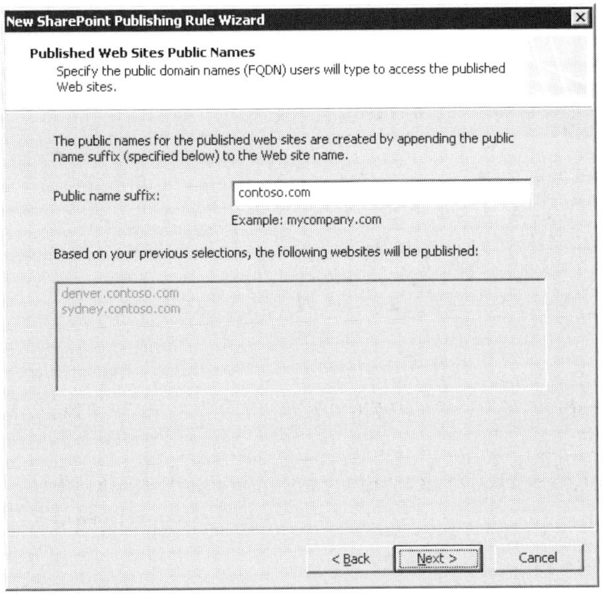

FIGURE 23-20 Published Web Sites Public Names page

7. On the Select Web Listener Page, select the Web listener that is to accept connections for this publishing rule, as shown in Figure 23-21. Click Next.

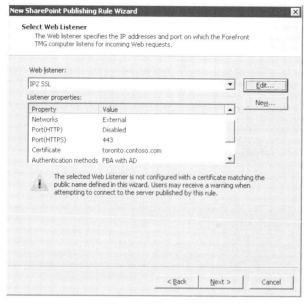

FIGURE 23-21 Multi-server Web listener selection

8. On the Authentication Delegation page, select the authentication method used at the SharePoint site. In this case, we have selected Kerberos Constrained Delegation (KCD) as shown in Figure 23-22. Click Next.

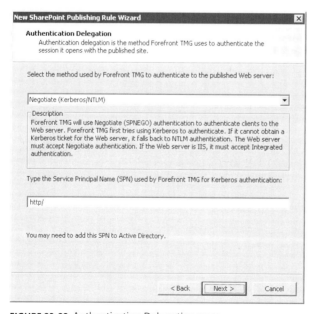

FIGURE 23-22 Authentication Delegation page

NOTE   Notice that the value provided in the Service Principal Name (SPN) field is empty. This is because we are publishing multiple servers with different names. You will have to edit each of the new rules to provide the appropriate SPN for each SharePoint server.

9. On the Alternate Access Mappings Configuration page, select the choice that best describes your current SharePoint configuration. We know that the Contoso SharePoint site has AAM configured, so select SharePoint AAM Is Already Configured On The SharePoint server, as shown in Figure 23-23. Click Next.

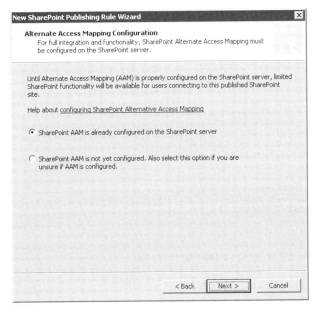

FIGURE 23-23 Alternate Access Mappings Configuration page

10. On the User Sets page, leave the default selection in place as shown in Figure 23-24 and click Next.

11. On the Completing The New SharePoint Publishing Rule Wizard page, verify the summary data as shown in Figure 23-25 and click Finish.

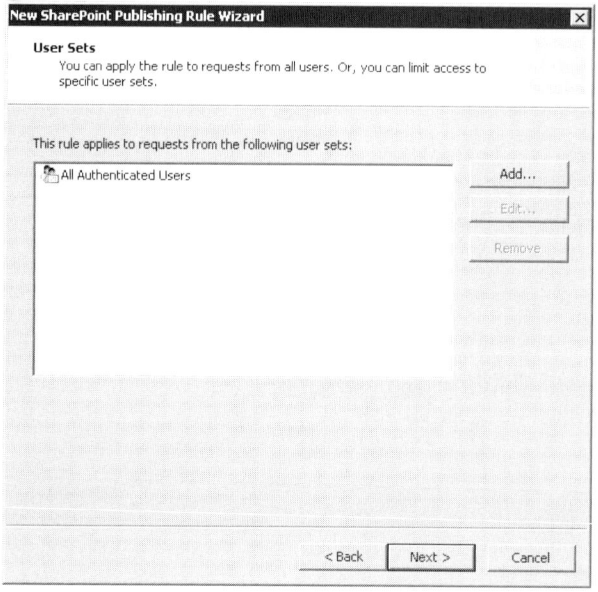

FIGURE 23-24 User Sets page

FIGURE 23-25 Multi-server publishing summary page

NOTE You must now edit each new rule individually to specify the SPN for each server being published or the rules will not work.

Figure 23-26 illustrates the rule summaries for the multi-server publishing rules.

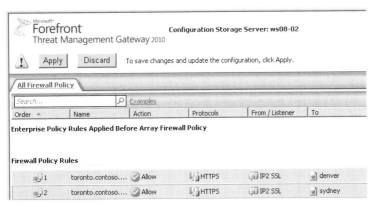

FIGURE 23-26 Multi-server rules list

Server Farm

The following steps illustrate the differences between publishing a single SharePoint site and publishing a server farm of SharePoint sites, as shown in Figure 23-27. You must begin this process with the steps from Common Starting Point. The servers that you are publishing are Sydney and Denver.

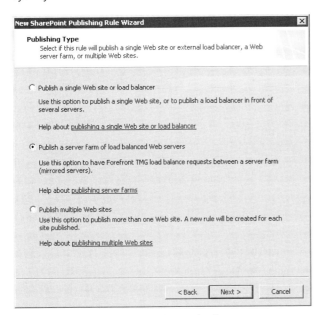

FIGURE 23-27 Server farm publishing selection

1. On the Server Connection Security page, select the connection type expected by the SharePoint site as shown in Figure 23-28 and click Next.

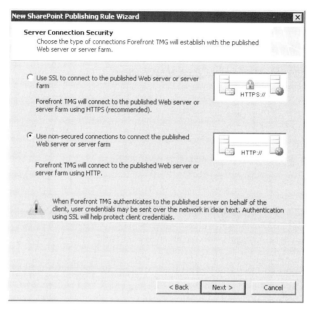

FIGURE 23-28 Server Connection Security page

2. On the Internal Publishing Details page, type in the fully qualified name of the SharePoint site as configured by the SharePoint administrator, shown in Figure 23-29. Click Next.

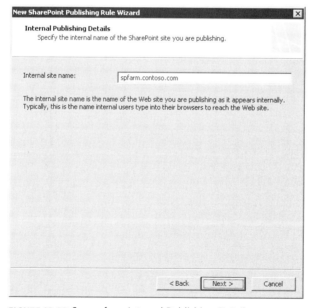

FIGURE 23-29 Server farm Internal Publishing Details page

3. On the Specify Server Farm page, click New as shown in Figure 23-30.

FIGURE 23-30 Specify Server Farm page

4. On the Welcome To The New Server Farm Wizard page, type **SP Farm** in the Server Farm Name field as shown in Figure 23-31 and click Next.

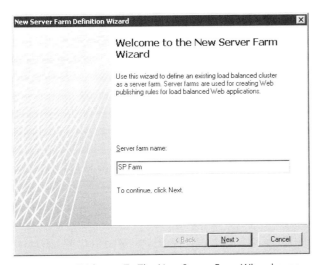

FIGURE 23-31 Welcome To The New Server Farm Wizard page

5. On the Servers page, click Add as shown in Figure 23-32.

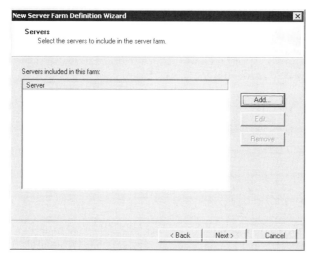

FIGURE 23-32 New Server Farm Definition Wizard Servers page

6. In the Server Details dialog box, type **sydney** as shown in Figure 23-33. Click OK to close the Server Details dialog box.

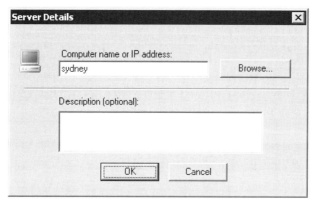

FIGURE 23-33 Server details for the Sydney server

NOTE You may enter simple or qualified names or IP addresses in this field.

7. On the Servers page, click Add.

8. In the Server Details dialog box, type **denver** as shown in Figure 23-34. Click OK to close the Server Details dialog box.

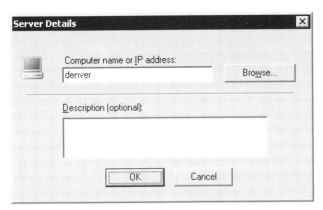

FIGURE 23-34 Server details for the Denver server

9. Verify that the Servers page list appears as shown in Figure 23-35. Click Next.

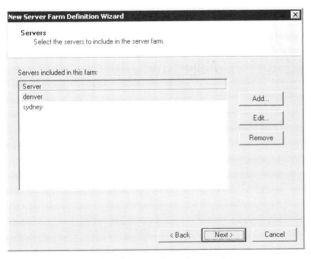

FIGURE 23-35 Completed Server Farm Servers list

10. On the Server Farm Connectivity Monitoring page, leave the defaults as shown in Figure 23-36. Click Next.

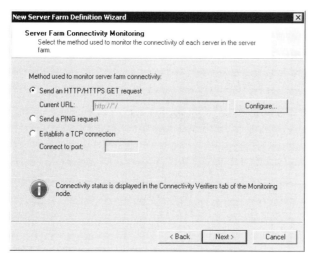

FIGURE 23-36 Server Farm Connectivity Monitoring page

11. On the Completing The New Server Farm Wizard page, verify that the summary appears as shown in Figure 23-37. Click Finish to close the wizard.

FIGURE 23-37 Completing The New Server Farm Wizard page

12. On the Specify Server Farm page, select the new server farm as shown in Figure 23-38. Click Next.

FIGURE 23-38 Completed Server Farm selection

13. On the Public Name Details page, select This Domain Name (Type Below) and type in the FQDN as used by clients in the network where the Web listener will operate. For our scenario, external clients will use **toronto.contoso.com** as shown in Figure 23-39. Click Next.

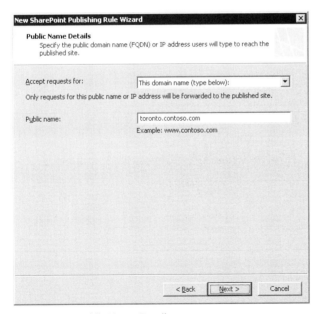

FIGURE 23-39 Public Name Details page

14. On the Select Web Listener Page, select the Web listener that is to accept connections for this publishing rule as shown in Figure 23-40. Click Next.

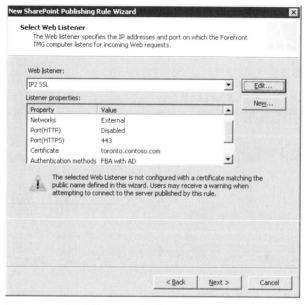

FIGURE 23-40 Web Listener selection page

15. On the Authentication Delegation page, select the authentication method used at the SharePoint site. In this case, we have selected Kerberos Constrained Delegation (KCD) as shown in Figure 23-41. Click Next.

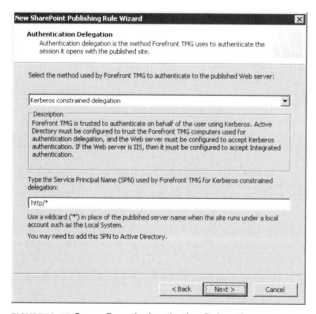

FIGURE 23-41 Server Farm Authentication Delegation page

16. On the Alternate Access Mappings Configuration page, select the choice that best describes your current SharePoint configuration. We know that the Contoso SharePoint site has AAM configured, so select SharePoint AAM Is Already Configured On The SharePoint Server, as shown in Figure 23-42. Click Next.

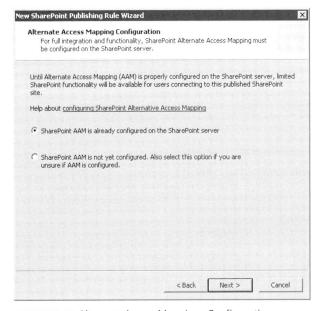

FIGURE 23-42 Alternate Access Mappings Configuration page

17. On the User Sets page, leave the default selection in place as shown in Figure 23-43 and click Next.

18. On the Completing The New SharePoint Publishing Rule Wizard page, verify the summary data as shown in Figure 23-44 and click Finish.

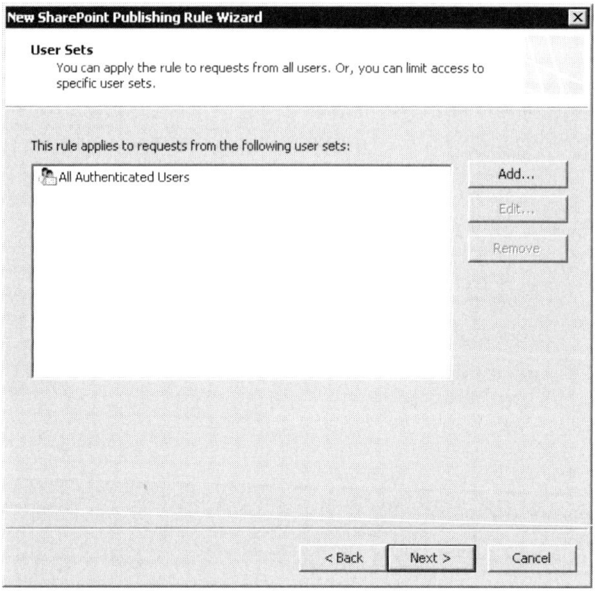

FIGURE 23-43 User Sets page

FIGURE 23-44 Completing the Server Farm Publishing Wizard

Figure 23-45 illustrates the summary information for the server farm rule created.

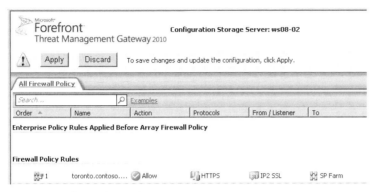

FIGURE 23-45 Server farm rules summary

Troubleshooting

The troubleshooting approach discussed in Chapter 22, "Publishing Servers," is valid for any Web publishing rule and SharePoint publishing rule is no exception. One setting that is very specific to a successful SharePoint publishing rule is the correct configuration of AAM. This is a SharePoint configuration that enables Microsoft Office SharePoint Servers to provide a URL appropriate to the client connection context.

> **MORE INFO** To understand how AAM can affect a publishing rule access read the following ISA/TMG Team Blog posting: *http://blogs.technet.com/isablog/archive/2008/10/02/unable-to-check-out-a-document-in-moss-2007-published-through-isa-server-2006.aspx.*

Review Your Publishing Rule First

Always use the SharePoint Publishing Rule Wizard when you publish SharePoint or MOSS services through TMG. This wizard configures some critical properties that allow the SharePoint publishing rule to work properly, and some areas shouldn't be changed unless you are guided by a Microsoft Support Engineer to do so (such as paths and link translation). For example, you might think that you should change the default paths created by SharePoint Publishing Wizard. Those paths are automatically added by the wizard and should provide proper functionality for your SharePoint site. The default set of paths are shown in Figure 23-46.

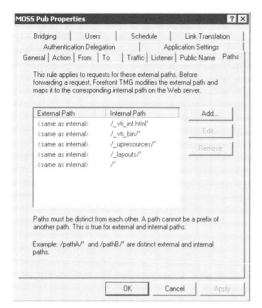

FIGURE 23-46 Default paths created by the SharePoint Publishing Wizard

Another scenario in which you should review a SharePoint publishing rule before collecting data for troubleshooting is if you did not create that rule. As a system administrator, you sometimes inherit a deployment that was already configured by someone else and now you are responsible for maintaining that infrastructure. Reviewing each element of the publishing rule can save you time before you begin your troubleshooting efforts.

Another important element of the SharePoint publishing rule is the TCP port used by the SharePoint site. This is very important because when SharePoint is installed in a Windows Server 2003 it requires Internet Information Services (IIS), which by default uses HTTP on the default port (TCP Port 80) for the default Web site. Because SharePoint Server is installed on top of IIS and the default ports *usually* are already in use, SharePoint will use a random port.

> **NOTE** It is important to note that SharePoint Server will use a random port only in a scenario that the default port is already in use, such as the preceding example. Make sure to review your IIS configuration to identify which ports are in use.

When you finish installing SharePoint on your internal server you will notice, for example, that the Central Administration already uses a custom port randomly chosen during the installation process, as shown Figure 23-47. To make sure that this configuration is working properly review the port that SharePoint site is using and make sure it matches the Bridging tab.

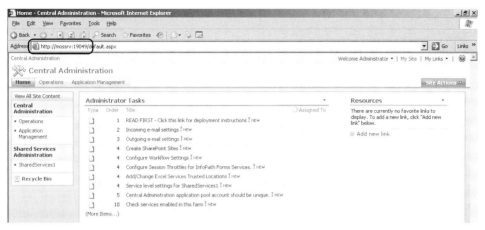

FIGURE 23-47 Central Administration using a custom HTTP port

Another publishing rule configuration that can cause problems is if you have a mismatch between the authentication delegation of the rule and the authentication configuration of the published site. Review the authentication method used by SharePoint site that you are publishing through TMG and make sure to configure the publishing rule authentication delegation option to match this setting. Figure 23-48 shows an example of the authentication provider for the Central Administration site on a SharePoint Server:

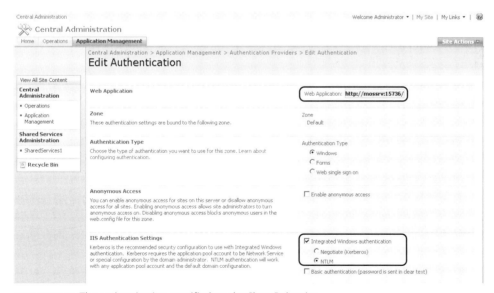

FIGURE 23-48 The authentication specified on the SharePoint site

In this particular example the authentication method used by the SharePoint site is NTLM. Therefore, the authentication delegation method must be NTLM or Direct And The Client May Authenticate Directly.

Useful Tools

One extremely useful tool provided by TMG is the logging query mechanism. The Logging feature allows you to see near real-time access and results, which can point out a possible root cause for the problem. Combining this feature with a network monitor trace obtained during a reproduction of the issue can guide you to faster resolution of the problem.

To allow a better understanding of how those tools combine during the troubleshooting, we will examine a scenario where the external user is unable to access the Contoso SharePoint Web site (moss.contoso.com). In this scenario the external user complains that after entering his credentials in the authentication page, he receives Error Code 403 Forbidden, similar to Figure 23-49.

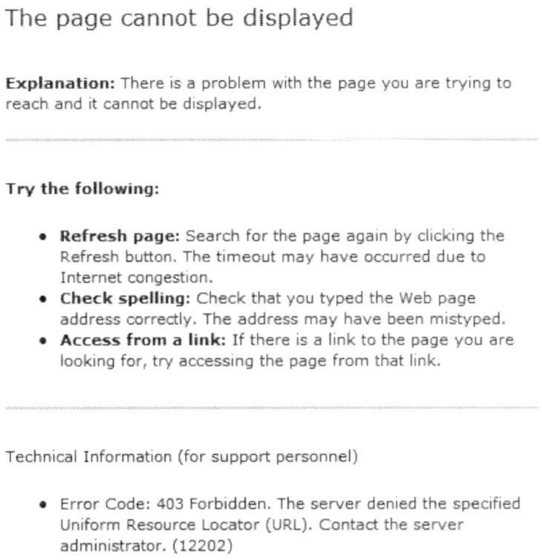

The page cannot be displayed

Explanation: There is a problem with the page you are trying to reach and it cannot be displayed.

Try the following:

- **Refresh page:** Search for the page again by clicking the Refresh button. The timeout may have occurred due to Internet congestion.
- **Check spelling:** Check that you typed the Web page address correctly. The address may have been mistyped.
- **Access from a link:** If there is a link to the page you are looking for, try accessing the page from that link.

Technical Information (for support personnel)

- Error Code: 403 Forbidden. The server denied the specified Uniform Resource Locator (URL). Contact the server administrator. (12202)

FIGURE 23-49 Error message received from external user

To prepare TMG to gather the traffic information at the right moment, follow these steps:

1. On the TMG Server computer (or using remote management console), open the Forefront TMG Management Console.

2. Click Forefront TMG (Array Name) in the left pane.

3. Click the Logs & Reports node in the left pane and click Edit Filter in the task pane, as shown in Figure 23-50.

FIGURE 23-50 The Configuring Logging feature

4. In the Filter By drop-down list, select Client IP.

5. In the Condition drop-down list, select Equals.

6. In the Value field, type in the IP address of your external client.

7. Click Add To List and then click Start Query.

> **NOTE** This is not a mandatory procedure, but it will help you to focus your logging only from traffic originating from that particular IP and also will reduce the amount of information that appears on the Logging screen.

In addition those steps you will need to install Network Monitor on TMG and start a capture from the internal network interface card, which has connectivity with the published server selected for capturing traffic.

> **MORE INFO** For more information on how to use Network Monitor, see Chapter 33, "Using Network Monitor 3 to Troubleshoot TMG."

After you gather the traffic while the external user reproduces the issue, you can analyze it. In this particular case, Figure 23-51 indicates the moment where TMG shows the access denied response for that publishing rule.

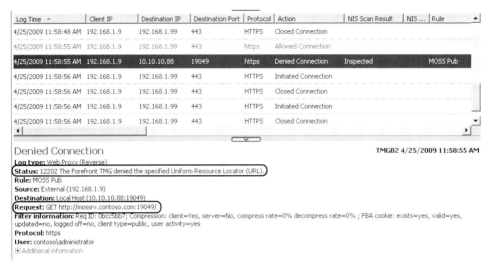

Log Time	Client IP	Destination IP	Destination Port	Protocol	Action	NIS Scan Result	NIS ...	Rule
4/25/2009 11:58:48 AM	192.168.1.9	192.168.1.99	443	HTTPS	Closed Connection			
4/25/2009 11:58:55 AM	192.168.1.9	192.168.1.99	443	https	Allowed Connection			
4/25/2009 11:58:55 AM	192.168.1.9	10.10.10.88	19049	https	Denied Connection	Inspected		MOSS Pub
4/25/2009 11:58:56 AM	192.168.1.9	192.168.1.99	443	HTTPS	Initiated Connection			
4/25/2009 11:58:56 AM	192.168.1.9	192.168.1.99	443	HTTPS	Closed Connection			
4/25/2009 11:58:56 AM	192.168.1.9	192.168.1.99	443	HTTPS	Initiated Connection			
4/25/2009 11:58:56 AM	192.168.1.9	192.168.1.99	443	HTTPS	Closed Connection			

Denied Connection   TMGB2 4/25/2009 11:58:55 AM
Log type: Web Proxy (Reverse)
Status: 12202 The Forefront TMG denied the specified Uniform Resource Locator (URL).
Rule: MOSS Pub
Source: External (192.168.1.9)
Destination: Local Host (10.10.10.88:19049)
Request: GET http://mossrv.contoso.com:19049/
Filter information: Req ID: 0bcc5bb7; Compression: client=Yes, server=No, compress rate=0% decompress rate=0% ; FBA cookie: exists=yes, valid=yes, updated=no, logged off=no, client type=public, user activity=yes
Protocol: https
User: contoso\administrator
⊞ Additional information

FIGURE 23-51 TMG denying the access to the published server

In this case, the Logging feature indicated that TMG was denying the request, but the question of why TMG made that decision remains. This is where Network Monitor can assist you in understanding the underlying cause of a TMG action. Let's follow the traffic between Forefront TMG and SharePoint Server during a request:

1. We observe a successful TCP three-way handshake between TMG and the SharePoint Server:

```
10.10.10.50   10.10.10.88   TCP   TCP:Flags=......S., SrcPort=11839, DstPort=19049
10.10.10.88   10.10.10.50   TCP   TCP:Flags=...A..S., SrcPort=19049, DstPort=11839
10.10.10.50   10.10.10.88   TCP   TCP:Flags=...A...., SrcPort=11839, DstPort=19049
```

2. The client issues the request to TMG, which then forwards it to the SharePoint server, including the credentials supplied by the user. Notice that the request is sending the HTTP GET Request using Basic Authentication:

```
10.10.10.50 10.10.10.88   HTTP   HTTP:Request, GET / , Using Basic Authorization
- Http: Request, GET / , Using Basic Authorization
  Command: GET
  + URI: /
  ProtocolVersion: HTTP/1.1
  Connection: Keep-Alive
  Reverse-Via: TMGB2
  Cookie: MSOWebPartPage_AnonymousAccessCookie=19049;
  Referer: https://moss.contoso.com/CookieAuth.dll?GetLogon?curl=Z2F&reason
          =0&formdir=3
  UserAgent: Mozilla/4.0 (compatible; MSIE 7.0; Windows NT 6.0; WOW64; SLCC1;
          .NET CLR 2.0.50727; Media Center PC 5.0; .NET CLR 3.0.30618)
  Host: mossrv:19049
```

```
Accept: image/gif, image/x-xbitmap, image/jpeg, image/pjpeg, application/
        x-ms-application, application/vnd.ms-xpsdocument, application/
        xaml+xml, application/x-ms-xbap, */*
Accept-Language: en-us
UA-CPU: x86
Cache-Control: no-cache
Front-End-Https: On
X-Experience: Premium
X-LogonType: Public
- Authorization: Basic Y29udG9zb1xhZG1pbmlzdHJhdG9yOlBhc3N3b3JkNQ==
- BasicAuthorization:
Scheme: Basic
- Realm: contoso\Bob:qwer!@#$
+ Realm: contoso\Bob:qwer!@#$
HeaderEnd: CRLF
HeaderEnd: CRLF
```

3. SharePoint Server sends the following packet with HTTP 401 and it specifies NTLM as the authentication method:

```
10.10.10.88  10.10.10.50  HTTP  HTTP:Response, HTTP/1.1, Status Code = 401, URL:
/ , Using NTLM X-Powered-By: Authentication
- Http: Response, HTTP/1.1, Status Code = 401, URL: / , Using NTLM
  X-Powered-By: Authentication
  ProtocolVersion: HTTP/1.1
  StatusCode: 401, Unauthorized
  Reason: Unauthorized
  ContentLength: 1656
  + ContentType: text/html
  Server: Microsoft-IIS/6.0
  + WWWAuthenticate: Negotiate
  WWW-Authenticate:
  + WWWAuthenticate: NTLM
  X-Powered-By:
  XPoweredBy: ASP.NET
  MicrosoftSharePointTeamServices: 12.0.0.6219
  Date: Sat, 25 Apr 2009 18:58:55 GMT
  HeaderEnd: CRLF
  + payload: HttpContentType = text/html
```

As you could see through the packet capture, TMG was configured to delegate Basic authentication while the published server was configured to use NTLM. This is a classical example of authentication delegation mismatch between TMG and the published server.

Summary

In this chapter we discussed how to properly plan a SharePoint server publishing with various security and authentication considerations. We also saw the various options available while publishing a SharePoint server and in the end we saw some troubleshooting techniques in case SharePoint publishing fails. In the next chapter we will discuss Exchange publishing.

## CHAPTER 24

Publishing Exchange Server

- Planning   **697**

- Configuring Exchange Client Access through Forefront TMG   **707**

- Troubleshooting   **719**

- Summary   **730**

M icrosoft Forefront TMG 2010 helps provide secure access to many Microsoft applications and data by providing stateful packet inspection, application layer filtering, and comprehensive publishing tools. Microsoft Exchange Server has been one of the most popular products for messaging to send and receive electronic mail and other forms of interactive communication through computer and mobile devices. TMG and Microsoft Exchange Server are both designed to work closely together in the network to provide a secure messaging environment. In this section we will discuss how to plan for different types of Exchange clients, how to configure publishing rules to allow access for them, and how to troubleshoot issues if access for Exchange clients fails through TMG.

Planning

To ensure that every Exchange deployment published through TMG for access to clients is set up properly, you need to carefully plan and understand the different aspects of this deployment, which includes TMG, Exchange, and the type of Exchange client that is being allowed access. The main aim of planning a deployment is to improve performance for client access and encourage utilization of best practices of Exchange, TMG, and the Exchange clients involved.

Understanding Exchange Server Roles

In Microsoft Exchange 2000 and Exchange 2003, administrators were not given a choice of what features could be installed. The default action was to install all roles on a single server and then disable the undesired features. With Exchange 2007 and Exchange 2010, each Exchange function was broken down into roles so that the administrator could decide which feature to install on a single server. Because every role installs a select logical group of features, the attack surface on the Exchange server is reduced, giving you the ability to configure Exchange for a specific role through a simple installation. Table 24-1 explains the different Exchange roles available.

TABLE 24-1 Exchange Server Roles

SERVER ROLE	DESCRIPTION
Mailbox Server	This is a back-end server that can host mailboxes and public folders.
Client Access Server	The Client Access server role supports Microsoft Outlook Web Access and Microsoft Exchange ActiveSync client applications, and the Post Office Protocol version 3 (POP3) and Internet Message Access Protocol version 4rev1 (IMAP4) protocols. The Client Access server role also supports services such as the Autodiscover service and Web services.
Unified Messaging Server	This is the middle-tier server that connects a Private Branch eXchange (PBX) system to Exchange 2007. This service is removed from Exchange 2010.
Hub Transport Server	This is the mail routing server that routes mail within the Exchange organization.
Edge Transport Server	This is the mail routing server that typically sits at the perimeter of the topology and routes mail into and out of the Exchange organization.

MORE INFO   For more information on Exchange 2007 Server Roles, see *http://technet .microsoft.com/en-us/library/bb124935.aspx*.

Planning Client Access

Many companies need their employees to have access to their mailboxes when they are not in the office. This access provides a company with a competitive business edge by ensuring that employees can respond to important e-mail messages; check calendars; update contacts; and send updates to the organization from a customer's site, hotel, airport, or home—all in a timely fashion. The company can also use this functionality to offer their employees flexible work schedules.

Before allowing client access, you need to understand and plan what client access methods you need to make available on the Internet for your end users. Users with laptops can either use Outlook Web Access (OWA), which is lightweight and available via a Web browser, to access their mailboxes, or they can use RPC over HTTP over the Internet to check e-mail via Microsoft Outlook. Of course users with mobile devices capable of ActiveSync can access their mailboxes using Exchange Active Sync (EAS). When the administrator has decided which client access methods need to be made available, access to certain folders needs to be allowed through TMG. This is done via the Exchange Publishing Wizard, which is discussed in the next section. Table 24-2 shows the default paths configured after running the New Exchange Publishing Wizard.

TABLE 24-2 Default Paths Configured

CLIENT ACCESS METHODS	EXCHANGE 2000	EXCHANGE 2003	EXCHANGE 2007	EXCHANGE 2010
OUTLOOK WEB ACCESS	/public/* /exchweb/* /exchange/*	/public/* /exchweb/* /exchange/*	/owa/* /public/* /exchange/* /exchweb/*	/owa/* /public/* /exchange/* /exchweb/*
RPC OVER HTTP	/rpc/*	/rpc/*	/rpc/*	/rpc/*
OUTLOOK MOBILE ACCESS	Not Supported	/OMA/*	Not Supported	Not Supported
EXCHANGE ACTIVE SYNC	/Microsoft-Server-ActiveSync/*	/Microsoft-Server-ActiveSync/*	/Microsoft-Server-ActiveSync/*	/Microsoft-Server-ActiveSync/*
RPC OVER HTTP WITH PUBLISH ADDITIONAL FOLDERS ON THE EXCHANGE SERVER FOR OUTLOOK 2007 CLIENTS SELECTED	Not Supported	Not Supported	/unifiedmessaging/* /rpc/* /OAB/* /ews/* /AutoDiscover/*	/rpc/* /OAB/* /ews/* /AutoDiscover/*

Certificates

When you publish Exchange client access with TMG, communications from external clients and from TMG itself to the published server can be encrypted using Secure Sockets Layer (SSL). Certain authentication mechanisms, such as Basic Authentication, allow user credentials to be sent in clear text over the wire. This can be potentially unsafe if anyone runs a network sniffer over the wire and can therefore see user names and passwords. Hence it is essential to ensure that traffic is encrypted using SSL. By using certificates, we can analyze the session at TMG before we forward it to the published Exchange Server by terminating the connection at the TMG. This is known as *SSL bridging*. SSL bridging protects against attacks that are hidden in SSL-encrypted connections. For SSL-enabled Web applications, TMG decrypts the client's request, inspects it, and terminates the SSL connection with the client computer. The Web Publishing rules determine how TMG communicates the request for the object to the published Exchange server. If the secure Exchange publishing rule is configured to forward the request using Secure HTTP (HTTPS), TMG initiates a new SSL connection with the published server. Because TMG is now an SSL client, it requires the published Web server to respond with a server-side certificate.

When you choose a certificate, it is essential to keep the following in mind:

- The common name of the certificate or one of the subject alternative names should match the public URL the client is going to request.
- The certificate must be valid and is present on all TMG array members in the case of Enterprise edition.
- The certificate must be trusted to the Root Certificate Authority (CA) on all TMG array members.
- The certificate needs to be trusted to the Root CA on the client computers as well.
- The certificate on the Exchange server should either be of the same name or match the configuration in the publishing rule.
- The certificate must have a private key.
- Enhanced key usage must include Server Authentication.
- Key usage must include Digital Signing and Key Encipherment.

> **MORE INFO** For more details on digital certificates and how to use an Internal Certification Authority, please read *http://technet.microsoft.com/en-us/library/dd547090.aspx*.

Authentication

A major advantage of using Forefront TMG is that TMG can pre-authenticate any request and then delegate those credentials to the Exchange server for validation. The most common form of authentication with Exchange is the use of Forms-Based Authentication (FBA) on TMG. TMG has a custom form for the Outlook Web Access client that is preconfigured when you use the Exchange publishing wizard. Using forms-based authentication, you can enforce required authentication methods, enable two-factor authentication, and provide centralized logging. FBA is also useful in cases where non-browser clients such as Microsoft Outlook, which do not support FBA, can still use the same listener with FBA configured because FBA can fall back to Basic Authentication for non-browser clients.

> **NOTE** When using Basic Authentication or Forms-Based Authentication it is recommended that you should ensure that the traffic is encrypted using SSL.

After a user is authenticated, TMG can then delegate the credentials as per the configuration on the rule to the Exchange Server. It is important to ensure that the credentials being delegated should be in the same form as expected by the Exchange Server. In the event of an authentication mismatch, client access fails and a credential delegation alert is logged by TMG. Remember that TMG cannot delegate credentials to the Exchange server when Exchange Server is using FBA. For this reason, ensure that FBA is not selected on the Exchange server.

TMG also can use Kerberos Constrained Delegation (KCD) to delegate different types of client credentials, such as Client Certificates, but to use KCD, TMG must be a domain member and set to use KCD in the Domain Controller (constrained for the specific Service Principal Name). We will discuss KCD is more depth in the troubleshooting section of this chapter.

It is essential to plan the authentication type that is used on the listener configured in the rule for client access. The delegation options vary depending on the initial authentication type. Table 24-3 lists the most common and recommended client authentication and authentication delegation methods for Exchange 2007 and Exchange 2010.

TABLE 24-3 Common Client Authentication and Authentication Delegation Methods

CLIENT AUTHENTICATION METHOD (CONFIGURED IN THE WEB LISTENER)	AUTHENTICATION VALIDATION METHOD (CONFIGURED IN THE WEB LISTENER)	AUTHENTICATION DELEGATION (CONFIGURED IN THE PUBLISHING RULE)	ACCESS METHODS
HTML forms-based authentication	Windows (Active Directory) LDAP (Active Directory) RADIUS	Basic Negotiate (Kerberos / NTLM)	Outlook Web Access Outlook Anywhere Microsoft ActiveSync (only Basic)
HTML forms-based Authentication	RSA SecurID	RSA SecurID	Outlook Web Access Microsoft ActiveSync (requires RSA SecurID component installed on Exchange servers)
SSL client certificate authentication	Windows (Active Directory)	KCD	Outlook Web Access Microsoft ActiveSync

When choosing the authentication delegation type, you must keep a few considerations in mind:

- If you select Basic for authentication delegation, the following Exchange 2007 features will not function as expected:
  - Outlook Web Access 2007 Web Part requires Integrated Windows authentication configured on the /owa/* directory.
  - Proxying between Exchange Client Access servers in different Active Directory sites fails because it requires the configuration of Integrated Windows authentication on the Exchange Client Access servers.

- If you select Negotiate for Authentication delegation, the following will not work:
  - Access to mailboxes residing on Exchange 2003, through legacy folders, such as /public/*, /exchange/*, and /Exchweb/* requires Basic Authentication.
  - Clients that access the user's mailbox through the legacy folders—such as Microsoft Entourage 2004 for Mac and custom-written applications using WebDAV extensions—require Basic Authentication.

> **MORE INFO**   To read about various authentication mechanisms in TMG, please visit *http://technet.microsoft.com/en-us/library/bb794722.aspx.*

Using the Wizards

TMG provides you with comprehensive wizards to publish Exchange Client Access. It is a simple step-by-step process that guides you through different options for publishing Exchange to the Internet and at the same time provides all security options to ensure that client access is as secure as possible. It is also recommended that you always use the Exchange Publishing Wizard while creating Exchange publishing rules. When you use the Exchange Publishing Wizard, a few options are configured automatically by TMG in the rule set. These options are not available in the user interface but can be seen in the XML. If you obtain an ISAInfo report of an ISA server using the tool Jim Harrison built, called ISA Info Viewer, you will see the following options:

```
Exch / SP Web Publishing Wizard Data
  AddHttpsFrontEndOn: True
  SendLogonOn401 False
  ExchangeVersion Exchange 2003
```

Using the default wizards available is recommended because of the three data points mentioned earlier, which are not available in the user interface.

AddHttpsFrontEndOn tells TMG whether it should add the *HttpsFrontEnd: on* header to the forwarded request so that Exchange can build the URL's properly (which is functionally similar to the SharePoint AAM feature). This is set *True* when the Web listener operates on an SSL port.

SendLogonOn401 tells TMG that if FBA is used for this listener/rule combination and the published server responds to an authentication delegated request with a 401, TMG should redirect the user to the logon page. This is set to *False* for all rules except for OWA-related rules because Exchange Active Sync and Outlook Anywhere (Microsoft Outlook) clients cannot use FBA.

ExchangeVersion tells TMG which Exchange version is in use. This also helps TMG understand the paths that are being used because the paths allowed in Exchange 2003 are different from those in Exchange 2007 and Exchange 2010. This also helps the Forms-Based

Authentication filter (cookieauthfilter.dll) decide which cookie to set, and how to set it, depending on the Exchange version that is published—there is a difference between the cookie types required for each Exchange version.

Capacity Planning

One of the most important aspects of planning an Exchange deployment is capacity planning. Different types of clients put different loads on TMG; hence you need to ensure that TMG does not get overloaded with requests. To understand the type and amount of load that will be generated it is important to first define the following things:

- Type of traffic
- Type of client
- Total number of users
- Total number of concurrent users
- Type of authentication being used

All of these elements help you understand the network profile so that you can take all these factors into consideration during capacity planning and choose the best hardware configuration and the number of servers needed for the given deployment.

Type of Traffic

The most common way to access Exchange is over SSL, which provides secure wrapping, authentication, and encryption for HTTP content. From a performance perspective, SSL encryption and decryption create an additional processing layer beyond regular HTTP processing. This layer includes the following two major CPU intensive phases:

- **SSL handshake**   After establishing a TCP connection, SSL creates a security context between endpoints using Public Key Interchange (PKI). This is known as an *SSL handshake*. In terms of aggregate network traffic, an SSL handshake consumes processing power that is proportional to connection rate (measured in connections per second).

- **Encryption**   After a security context is established, an endpoint uses it to encrypt or decrypt HTTP content, using symmetric encryption. This processing is performed on each byte of HTTP data. Therefore, it consumes processor cycles proportional to aggregate network throughput (measured in megabits per second).

When you deploy TMG with secure Exchange Publishing, the Exchange clients on the external network can connect to the SSL port. SSL bridging is a feature of TMG, which enables you to specify how TMG communicates with the Exchange server that is published. This feature lets you choose between the following two types of bridging:

- **SSL to SSL bridging**   In this type of bridging, TMG accesses the Exchange server with SSL. TMG performs separate SSL handshakes with the back-end server and must use encryption for every packet that it receives from or sends to the back-end server.

- **SSL to HTTP bridging**   In this type of bridging, TMG accesses the Exchange server in clear, unencrypted HTTP.

SSL to SSL bridging strengthens the security on the internal network, but adds the processing cost of double encryption to every packet that is transferred between TMG and the back-end server. SSL to SSL bridging costs about 20 to 30 percent more CPU than SSL to HTTP bridging. Hence when the traffic profile is SSL, you need to keep in mind that this places an additional load on the servers, so proper hardware planning or sizing is necessary.

Type of Client

Every application has its own load characteristics. The ratio between aggregate throughput and connection rate determines the average number of bits that are processed for every connection. This ratio is defined as *bits per connection*, and in practice, every application has a characteristic value for this ratio. Consider the following client types:

- **Outlook Web Access**   When a Web client connects to an Outlook Web Access Exchange Server front-end server, it loads the Outlook Web page that contains the user-interface icons and headers of messages currently in the mailbox. Subsequently, any operation that the user performs (such as Open, Send, or Move To Folder) generates a new HTTP connection that transfers an average of 10 to 20 KB. When accumulating the behavior of Outlook Web Access over many users, the Web client typically creates relatively low bits per connection value (such as 100 kilobits per connection).

- **RPC over HTTP**   RPC over HTTP enables Outlook clients to access an Exchange server in the internal corporate network from the Internet. When connecting to Exchange Server, an Outlook client working in Cached Exchange Mode typically starts with a synchronization of mailbox content with a local cache file by opening up anywhere between 10 to 15 connections to TMG. This behavior is by default. After the synchronization is complete, intermittent connections occur, in which new messages are transferred. The Outlook client would, however, maintain about 10 connections with TMG after it is connected. For a user utilizing Outlook heavily, the synchronization operation transfers many bytes of data over a small number of connections, so the overall characteristic bits per connection value is rather high (such as 500 kilobits per connection).

> **MORE INFO**   To read more about Outlook Anywhere sizing and scalability, please visit *http://technet.microsoft.com/en-us/library/cc540453.aspx.*

- **Exchange Active Sync or Outlook Mobile Access**   This traffic profile is the lightest client of all, with only one TCP connection and very light traffic flow. A new HTTP connection is only made when a user performs an operation such as Open, Send, or Move To Folder.

Total Number of Users

The total number of Exchange front-end and back-end servers would vary depending upon the total number of users. Keep in mind that if you need multiple Exchange servers to host mailboxes, chances are that you need more than one TMG in an array to prevent performance degradation. The best practice is to have at least a one-to-one ratio of TMG to Client Access servers so that in case of full load—all users connecting at peak time—TMG has enough resources to support the load.

Total Number of Concurrent Users

After you have determined the type of traffic, the type of client, and the total number of users, you now should have a rough idea of the load that can be expected. It is generally unexpected that all users will connect at the same time, but a realistic approach is to define or plan an estimate of the total number of concurrent users at any given time. The number of concurrent users needs to be estimated, giving you a rough idea of the number of simultaneous connections that could be open with TMG at any given time. The total number of concurrent connections will not be equal to the total number of concurrent users because this would vary depending on the client type.

The best example is an Outlook Anywhere client or Microsoft Outlook connecting to TMG using RPC over HTTP. The client would make about 10 to 15 initial connections, out of which 10 or so would still remain active. Essentially, you now have about 10 concurrent connections for a given user. If you have about 200 users who use Outlook Anywhere, you are looking at 2,000 to 3,000 connections. You have about 48,000 available ports to use from TMG to the published server (regardless of the number of IP addresses assigned to the system)—out of which about 1,024 are already reserved for applications. Depending on other applications being used on the Windows 2008 server, you may also have other ports in use. Therefore, you do not want to end up exhausting all outbound ports and causing poor performance of the applications being hosted on the Windows 2008 server. That is why you must consider this parameter and do your planning accordingly.

> **MORE INFO**   For more details on capacity planning for ISA server, which can provide some insight on sizing TMG, please visit *http://www.microsoft.com/isaserver/ capacityplanner.swf.*

Type of Authentication

Even though authentication type is considered during general planning to prevent authentication mismatch, you also need to consider it during capacity planning. Many methods of performing Web Authentication are available, and each method has its own performance impact on the deployment. Ideally, an authentication scheme performs best with no per-request overhead and a low per-batch overhead. This means that deciding which authentication scheme to use depends on the strength and infrastructure available for the deployment.

Authentication can be enforced at the listener level as well as at the rule level. If authentication is enforced at the listener level, every request will be authenticated, adding extra overhead on TMG. It is recommended that you enable authentication at the rule level so that requests are only authenticated when required by the rule. This eliminates any extra overhead for rules using the same listener but not requiring authentication. Table 24-4 lists the advantages and disadvantages of different Web Authentication methods available in TMG.

TABLE 24-4 Advantages and Disadvantages of Different Web Authentication Methods

AUTHENTICATION SCHEME	STRENGTH	WHEN AUTHENTICATION IS PERFORMED	OVERHEAD PER REQUEST	OVERHEAD PER BATCH
Basic	Low	Per request	Low	None
Digest	Medium	Per time/count	None	High
NTLM	Medium	Per connection	None	High
NTLMv2	High	Per connection	None	High
Kerberos	High	Per connection	None	Medium
SecurID	High	Per browser session	None	Medium
RADIUS per request	Low RADIUS = Basic to the client	Per request	Medium Not performed per request	None
RADIUS per time out (default)	Low Timeout is not relevant; still Basic to the client	Per time	Low	None

> **MORE INFO** To read more about best practices for performance for ISA server, which can providing some insight on TMG performance, please visit *http://technet.microsoft.com/en-us/library/bb794835.aspx*.

Specific Client Considerations

Apart from capacity planning and other considerations, certain client-specific issues differ in every scenario. However, in certain cases some of the following issues might come up:

- **Direct push for ActiveSync Clients fails to work through TMG** This issue may occur if the firewall has not been configured to let HTTP(S) requests live longer than the minimum heartbeat interval configured on the server running Exchange Server. By default, the minimum heartbeat interval at which the Exchange server triggers this event is nine minutes. To resolve this issue, modify the firewall timeout values for HTTP(S) connections to the Exchange server to be greater than the default timeout limit of nine minutes. You can do this by increasing the Connection-Timeout value on the listener used by the Exchange publishing rule for ActiveSync.

> **MORE INFO**   To read more about Enterprise firewall configuration for Exchange ActiveSync Direct Push Technology, please visit *http://support.microsoft.com/?id=905013*.

- **Outlook Anywhere clients using NTLM authentication over the Internet**   The only way to allow Outlook Anywhere clients using NTLM authentication when TMG pre-authenticates the requests is by delegating the credentials using KCD to the Exchange Server. To use KCD, TMG needs to be a member of the same domain where the Exchange server resides; thus if TMG is in a workgroup, or operates in a different domain, this isn't possible.

- **Outlook Mobile Access isn't working with Exchange 2007**   When you migrate from Exchange 2003 to Exchange 2007, you may find that Outlook Mobile Access (OMA) has stopped working for mobile users. This is because Exchange 2007 does not support OMA.

Configuring Exchange Client Access through Forefront TMG

As explained in the section on planning, OWA and Outlook Anywhere (also known as RPC over HTTP) have different requirements and sizing concerns. The OWA publishing process is similar to publishing any other Web application, except that you must use the Exchange Web Client Access publishing wizard so that TMG can handle the requests properly. This section will guide you through the process of publishing a single Exchange Client Access Server through TMG. See Chapter 23, "Publishing Microsoft Office SharePoint Server," for more information on how to publish a server farm.

For this particular scenario, Contoso wants to achieve the following goals for OWA, ActiveSync, and Outlook Anywhere Publishing:

- Users will use mail.contoso.com to access OWA.

- Users must authenticate using Forms-Based Authentication with their Active Directory credentials for OWA.

- A single Web listener must be used for all client access (OWA, ActiveSync, and Outlook Anywhere) and client configuration (Autodiscovery).

To comply with the last request, a single Web listener should be in use for all types of Exchange client access. Figure 24-1 shows how a single Web listener is shared by those clients and the authentication options.

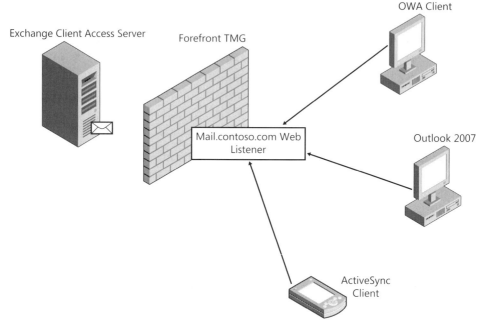

FIGURE 24-1 Sharing a single Web listener for multiple rules

This Web listener is using Forms-Based Authentication (FBA), so when Outlook (2003 or 2007) or Windows Mobile client tries to authenticate against this listener, TMG will offer HTTP-Basic as the alternate authentication method and as long as the Outlook Client is configured to use Basic it will work. Figure 24-2 shows the Outlook 2007 dialog box that defines the authentication method for this configuration.

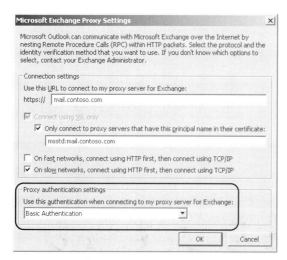

FIGURE 24-2 Authentication method on Outlook 2007

The same process happens with ActiveSync. TMG offers HTTP-Basic because TMG understands which clients don't understand FBA and presents them with alternate authentication according to their capabilities. Note that because Basic Authentication is used for Outlook clients, users will need to provide credentials each time they start the Outlook application. To avoid logging on each time Outlook starts, Kerberos Constrained Delegation must be used.

NOTE For this particular scenario, assume that the certificate for mail.contoso.com is already installed on TMG.

Configuring the OWA Publishing Rule

Follow these steps to configure the Web listener that will be used for the OWA Publishing rule:

1. On the TMG computer (or using remote management console), open the Forefront TMG Management Console.

2. Click Forefront TMG (Array Name) in the left pane and click Firewall Policy.

3. In the right pane, click the Toolbox tab. Under Network Objects, right-click Web Listener and choose New Web Listener as shown in Figure 24-3.

FIGURE 24-3 Creating a new Web listener

4. The Welcome To The New Web Listener Wizard page opens, as shown in Figure 24-4. Type a name for this Web listener and click Next.

FIGURE 24-4 Adding a name for the Web listener

5. For the connection security, leave the default option as shown in Figure 24-5 and click Next.

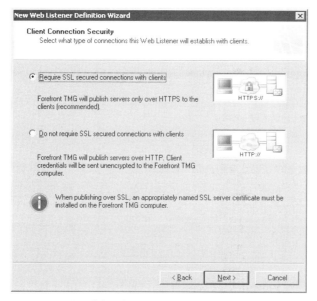

FIGURE 24-5 Specifying the connection type for this Web listener

6. Because the goal is to allow external users to access OWA, select External on the Web Listener IP Addresses page as shown in Figure 24-6. Click Next.

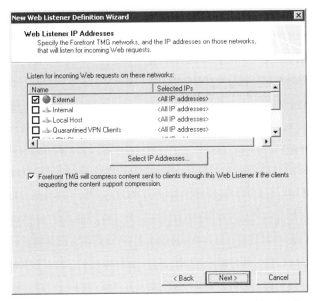

FIGURE 24-6 Choosing the interface that will be used for this listener

7. On the Listener SSL Certificates page, click Use A Single Certificate For This Web Listener, choose the certificate for this listener (mail.contoso.com), click Select, and then click OK.

8. On the Listener SSL Certificates page, confirm that the selected certificate appears as shown in Figure 24-7 and click Next to continue.

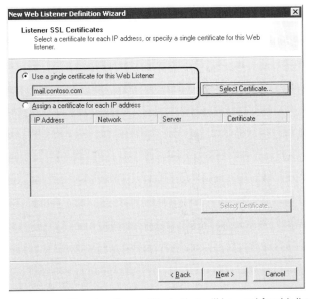

FIGURE 24-7 Choosing the certificate that will be used for this listener

9. Click the drop-down list below the option Select How Clients Will Provide Credentials To Forefront TMG and select HTML Form Authentication, as shown in Figure 24-8. Leave the default client credential validation (Windows) selected. Click Next.

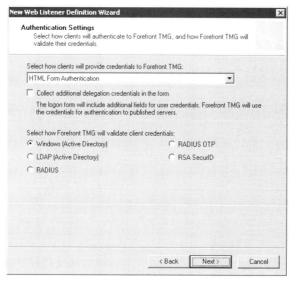

FIGURE 24-8 Choosing the authentication method

10. For the purpose of this example, disable Single Sign On settings as shown in Figure 24-9. Click Next.

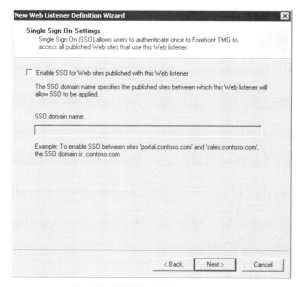

FIGURE 24-9 Disabling SSO for this listener

11. Review the selection on the last page of the wizard. Click Finish and then click Apply to commit the changes.

Now that you've created the Web listener, follow these steps to configure the OWA
Publishing rule:

1. Right-click in Firewall Policy, point to New, and choose Exchange Web Client Access
   Publishing Rule.

2. The Welcome To The New Exchange Publishing Rule Wizard page appears, as shown in
   Figure 24-10. Type a name for this publishing rule and click Next.

FIGURE 24-10 Specifying a name for this publishing rule

3. On the Select Services page, click the Exchange version drop-down list, choose Exchange
   Server 2010, select Outlook Web Access as shown in Figure 24-11, and click Next.

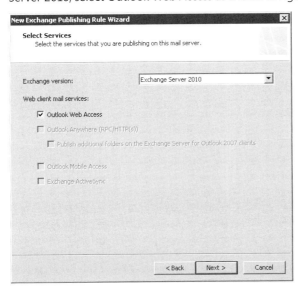

FIGURE 24-11 Choosing the Exchange Web mail service to publish

4. On the Publishing Type page, leave the default option selected as shown in Figure 24-12 and click Next.

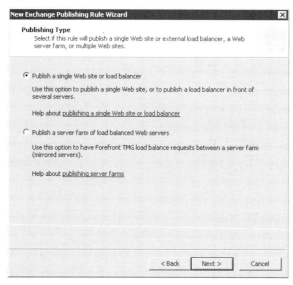

FIGURE 24-12 Choosing the publishing type according to the resource that you need to publish it

5. On the Server Connection Security page, leave the default option selected as shown in Figure 24-13 and click Next.

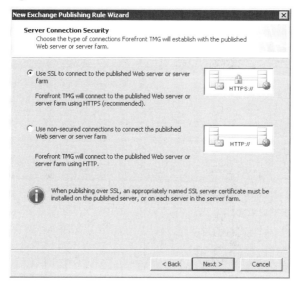

FIGURE 24-13 HTTP connection type that will be used to communicate with the CAS

6. On the Internal Publishing Details page, type the internal site name. This name is part of the subject in the certificate installed in the Exchange CAS. If the CAS has a SAN

certificate, you can use any name that belongs to the certificate subject alternative name list. Add the fully qualified domain name for the Client Access Server server in the Computer Name Or IP Address field, as shown in Figure 24-14, and click Next.

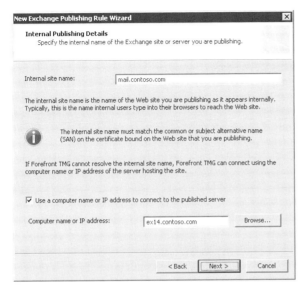

FIGURE 24-14 HTTP connection type that will be used to communicate with the CAS

NOTE   TMG needs to resolve the internal site name to the IP address of the CAS.

7. On the Public Name Details page, type the name that clients will use to connect externally as shown in Figure 24-15 and click Next.

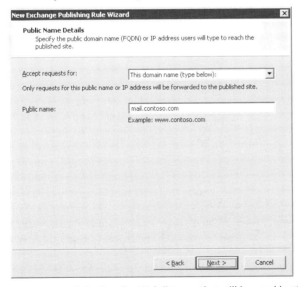

FIGURE 24-15 Selecting the Web listener that will be used by the publishing rule

8. On the Select Web Listener page, choose Exchange Client Access from the Web Listener drop-down list as shown in Figure 24-16 and click Next.

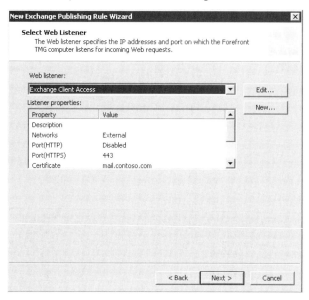

FIGURE 24-16 Selecting the Web listener that will be used for this rule

9. On the Authentication Delegation page, select NTLM Authentication from the drop-down list as shown in Figure 24-17 and click Next.

FIGURE 24-17 Authentication delegation that TMG will use

NOTE The authentication delegation that you select in Figure 24-17 needs to match the authentication on the Exchange CAS (the IIS folder where OWA resides).

10. On the User Sets page, leave the default option as shown in Figure 24-18 and click Next.

FIGURE 24-18 Selecting the Users that are authorized to access this publishing rule

11. Review the selection shown on the last page of the wizard. Click Finish and then click Apply to commit the changes.

Configuring an Outlook Anywhere Publishing Rule

To configure Outlook Anywhere publishing through TMG you can use the same steps that you used to publish OWA. The only difference is that in step 3 (the Select Services page), choose Outlook Anywhere (RPC/HTTP(s)) as shown in Figure 24-19.

FIGURE 24-19 Enabling Outlook Anywhere in the New Exchange Publishing Rule Wizard

As explained in the beginning of this chapter, the work that you do prior to starting the configuration is the most important step for this type of publishing.

Configuring an ActiveSync Publishing Rule

Like the other types of clients, publishing ActiveSync through TMG is another functionality that is ready to be used as long as the configuration matches the publishing rule and Exchange CAS. The steps also are the same as for OWA publishing with the exception of step 3, in which you should choose Exchange ActiveSync on the Select Services page, as shown in Figure 24-20.

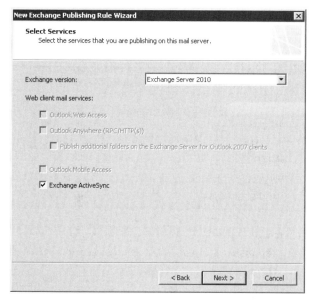

FIGURE 24-20 Enabling ActiveSync during the New Exchange Publishing Rule Wizard

Troubleshooting

Troubleshooting Exchange Web traffic is very much like troubleshooting any other Web-published application. Like Microsoft SharePoint publishing, proper Exchange Web traffic flow is dependent on using rules created by the *proper* Exchange publishing wizards. Until you verify that the rules are created properly, you will have difficulty troubleshooting Exchange Web traffic.

Another critical step you must take is to isolate the traffic scenario you are troubleshooting. To say "I'm trying to make Exchange work through TMG" is the same as saying "I haven't really thought through what I'm trying to do." Always work on one scenario at a time. Although it's true that fixing one problem often resolves others, it's equally true that trying to solve multiple problems simultaneously may lead to cranial follicle freedom.

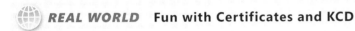 **REAL WORLD** **Fun with Certificates and KCD**

In August of 2007, I was asked to participate with some Microsoft IT teams who were collaborating on a pilot that would require the use of smart-card authentication for OWA publishing. This program was only one aspect of the larger smart-card authentication program under way at the time.

At the time I was brought in, the Active Directory and ISA server configuration had already been defined and testing had proceeded very well until they started adding users from another (trusted) forest. Because I hadn't been involved with the initial design and configuration, I spent quite a bit of time catching up on the configuration and testing that had been performed until then.

They described to me the following problem:

- Smart cards that represented user accounts from the same forest as the ISA server and Exchange servers (Forest 1) successfully authenticated to ISA server and the users could access the published services.

- Smart cards that represented user accounts from a different forest (Forest 2) could not authenticate to ISA server and those users could not access the published services.

Through discussions with the ISA, Exchange, and Active Directory teams, I was able to determine that the proper configurations were in place to allow this scenario to work—at least in theory. We validated the following criteria:

1. The ISA Server array members were trusted for delegation to the Exchange servers.

2. Forest 1 and Forest 2 had a functioning, transitive, bidirectional, forest-level trust.

3. The certificate for the Forest 2 Certificate Authority was included in the Forest 1 Enterprise Trusted Root and NTAuth stores.

4. The Enterprise and Trusted Root certificate stores on the ISA servers matched the contents of the relevant Enterprise stores.

5. The SPN was configured correctly relative to the published servers.

Even though all the right pieces were in place, ISA Server stubbornly refused to authenticate any smart card that represented a user account from Forest 2. To make matters worse, the only error information provided was "make sure the SPN is correct."

Because we knew the SPN configuration was correct, and because Kerberos logging provided no further information, and because I knew that ISA server deferred to Windows Netlogon mechanisms for authenticating users, we engaged the Windows Security team to assist with debugging.

Because of security restrictions in place, we couldn't use any debugging methods that might cause the SSL traffic through the ISA server to become visible to unintended recipients, so I had to build a replica environment in Virtual Server (Hyper-V wasn't available to me yet).

After several days of debugging, testing, configuring, and discussions with some Really Smart Folks in the Windows Security team, we discovered a design limitation in Windows authentication mechanisms that effectively prevented Windows from discovering unqualified account names (domain\user or user@domain).

The Windows team suggested a work-around using the steps described in *http://support.microsoft.com/kb/949015/.* I tested this in my virtual environment and it worked like a charm! Over the next few days, the MSIT teams duplicated those steps and the problem was resolved.

Smart-card authentication for OWA users in all MS forests was achieved!

You can read more about the details of this mechanism at *http://technet.microsoft .com/en-us/library/cc752953.aspx.*

General Troubleshooting Rules

In all cases, you should start with the basics. If you always start from square 1, you probably won't have to return to it later. Likewise, learning to distinguish between the various client requests in the TMG logs is a very valuable skill that is well worth your time. Gaining this skill will help you identify and resolve issues for specific clients in a much shorter time than if you simply wander through the logs chasing "error states" that may actually be normal for that traffic profile. The client profiles that follow are listed in traffic "weight" order. In other words, they're listed according to the amount of effort TMG must expend to manage and process this traffic.

You should be aware that testing your publishing rules using a browser is an invalid test methodology for all except OWA publishing, which is designed for use by browsers. This is especially true if you choose to use a single rule to publish all your Exchange Web services, because OWA works when using a browser, but Outlook Anywhere doesn't.

Exchange ActiveSync (EAS) and Office Mobile Access (OMA)

This traffic profile is the lightest client of all, with only one TCP connection and very light traffic flow. EAS clients are also the primary reason that the default timeout for Web listener sessions was increased to 30 minutes in ISA Server 2006 and this configuration was continued into TMG. This choice was made based on the desire to extend mobile device battery life more than any desire to reduce traffic overhead.

Paths

This client can use the same public name as the rest of the Exchange Web client rules, but the path used by each client is different, as shown in Table 24-5.

TABLE 24-5 EAS and OMA Paths

PRODUCT	VALID PATHS
Exchange 2000	Not supported
Exchange 2003	/Microsoft-Server-ActiveSync/* /OMA/*
Exchange 2007	/Microsoft-Server-ActiveSync/*
Exchange 2010	/Microsoft-Server-ActiveSync/*

Authentication

The authentication methods supported by these clients vary according to the operating system and version they use. Typically, you can achieve the best range of client functionality by using HTTP-Basic at the TMG listener and HTTP-Basic for authentication delegation as well.

Certificates

These clients tend to be very limited in their certificate storage and management capabilities, so using a self-signed certificate or a certificate that imposes a long trust chain in the TMG Web listener can be problematic for these clients.

Outlook Web Access (OWA)

This traffic profile is relatively light and is distinguished by only two TCP connections, with a request rate corresponding to the user's e-mail activity. Because this client is browser-based, it's much less likely to produce error states as a normal course of events as does the Outlook

Anywhere client. Note, however, that when the user closes the browser or the browser tab, the browser resets the connections related to that instance of the browser or tab. This will appear in the Web Proxy logs as error 64, error 10054, or error 995; all of which mean effectively the same thing—that the connection was broken at the TCP layer before TMG expected it to be closed.

Paths

The paths for Exchange OWA clients differ, as shown in Table 24-6.

TABLE 24-6 OWA Paths

PRODUCT	VALID PATHS
Exchange 2000 & 2003	/Exchange/* /ExchWeb/* /Public/*
Exchange 2007	/Exchange/* /ExchWeb/* /Public/* /owa/*
Exchange 2010	/Ecp/* /Exchange/* /Public/* /owa/*

Authentication

The authentication methods supported by this client are limited only by the browser and the authentication delegation you choose. Typically, you can achieve the best range of client functionality by using Forms or HTTP-Basic at the TMG listener and HTTP-Basic for authentication delegation as well.

> **NOTE** You cannot use forms-based authentication at the Client Access server and TMG unless you're willing to impose two separate authentication cycles on your users.

> **MORE INFO** You can read more about troubleshooting OWA clients at *http://blogs.technet.com/isablog/archive/2008/04/29/troubleshooting-owa-2007-publishing-rules-on-isa-server-2006.aspx*.

Certificates

Because these clients have greater certificate storage, they don't impose the same certificate limitations EAS and OMA clients do. Also, because this client is browser-based, the user has the ability to accept an untrusted or invalid certificate via browser prompts. This makes it possible for users to connect to their e-mail even if you use a self-signed certificate at the Web listener.

Exchange Web Services (EWS)

This traffic profile is the most interesting of all because it's completely unpredictable. Any third-party Outlook plug-in or stand-alone application can make use of this functionality, and depending on the business needs, users may be running any number of them in their Outlook client. Office Communicator is one such application that creates HTTP sessions through Exchange Web Services.

> **MORE INFO** You can read more about Exchange Web Services at *http://msdn.microsoft .com/en-us/exchange/default.aspx*.

Paths

The paths for all Exchange Web Services clients are available as part of the Additional Folders option in the publishing wizard, as shown in Table 24-7.

TABLE 24-7 EWS Paths

PRODUCT	VALID PATHS
Exchange 2000 & 2003	Not supported
Exchange 2007 & 2010	/ews/*

Authentication

The authentication methods supported by this client are determined by the client itself. Because the service is provided by a Windows application (Exchange), you may be able to use Windows Integrated (Kerberos, negotiate, NTLM) authentication. Typically, you can achieve the best range of client functionality by using HTTP-Basic at the TMG listener and HTTP-Basic for authentication delegation as well.

Certificates

Because these clients' behavior and functionality vary according to the design goals, certificate support is completely unpredictable.

Outlook Anywhere (OA)

Also known as RPC over HTTP, this traffic profile is the noisiest of all Exchange clients. It imposes a combination of high connection count (can be 20 or more separate TCP connections) with a higher data rate also coincident with the user activity.

Paths

The paths for Outlook Anywhere clients are described in Table 24-8.

TABLE 24-8 OA Paths

PRODUCT	VALID PATHS
Exchange 2000	Not supported
Exchange 2003	/rpc/*
Exchange 2007	/AutoDiscover/*
	/ews/*
	/OAB/*
	/rpc/*
	/unifiedmessaging/*
Exchange 2010	/AutoDiscover/*
	/ews/*
	/OAB/*
	/rpc/*

> **NOTE** The folder set shown for Exchange 2007 and 2010 includes those folders added when you select Additional Folders in the publishing wizard. If you do not choose this option during the wizard, only the /rpc/* folder is used.

Authentication

The authentication methods supported by this client are determined by the client itself. Because the service is provided by a Windows application (Exchange), you may be able to use Windows Integrated (Kerberos, negotiate, NTLM) authentication. Typically, you can achieve the best range of client functionality by using HTTP-Basic at the TMG listener and HTTP-Basic for authentication delegation as well.

Certificates

The OA client is unable to accept any certificate other than that which matches the host name in the Exchange proxy configuration in Outlook. If Outlook encounters any certificate error, the connection simply fails and the user is not afforded the opportunity to accept the certificate error.

Using the Test Rule Button

As with ISA Server 2006 Service Pack 1, Forefront TMG 2010 includes a rule test mechanism designed to help you assess the network connectivity from layer 1 through layer 7 between the TMG computer and the published Web service. Figure 24-21 shows the location of the Test Rule button in our example Web Publishing rule.

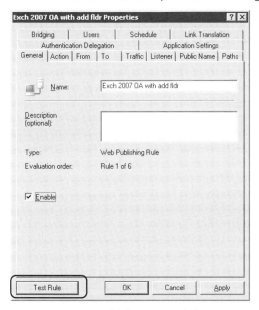

FIGURE 24-21 Web Publishing Test Rule button

Figure 24-22 describes the topology used in the following examples.

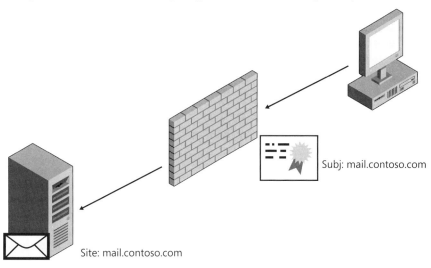

FIGURE 24-22 Example network topology

The rule we will use for the following tests is an Exchange 2007 Outlook Anywhere rule created using the Additional Folders option. This rule is summarized in Table 24-9.

TABLE 24-9 Outlook Anywhere Rule

NAME	EXCH 2007 OA WITH ADD FLDR
Listener	HTTPS on port 443
Public Name	mail.contoso.com
Paths	/AutoDiscover/* /ews/* /OAB/* /rpc/*
To	ws08-05.contoso.com Send original host header
Bridging	HTTP to port 80
Authentication	Forms-based with AD
Delegation	KCD
Service Principle Name	http/ws08-05.contoso.com

Exchange 2010 has been installed on ws08-05 using the typical configuration for a HUB server role.

The Test Rule button may be used at the end of a Web Publishing Rule Wizard or through the property page of any Web Publishing rule. The following steps illustrate the process of using this functionality to work through multiple problems in an Exchange Web Publishing scenario:

1. When you use the Rule Test button, the results received are indicated in Figure 24-23.

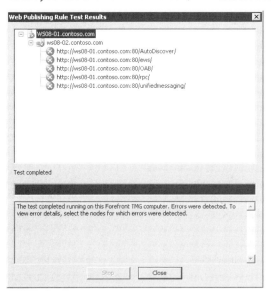

FIGURE 24 23 Published site test button failure

2. When one of the published folders is selected, you are provided with additional details about the failure for the request to the /rpc/ folder as shown in Figure 24-24.

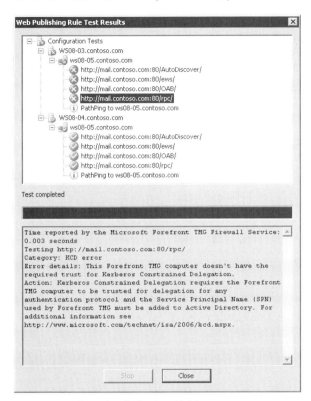

FIGURE 24-24 Error details for /rpc/ folder

The error details for this request clearly indicate a failure to authenticate using Kerberos Constrained Delegation. The message "The Forefront TMG computer doesn't have the required trust for Kerberos Constrained Delegation" provides exactly the information you need to correct the problem; the TMG computer WS08-03 isn't trusted for delegation to the published server using the SPN provided in the rule. Because the test failed before any connection was made to the published server, we're not too interested in the logs just yet. Because the test succeeded for the TMG computer WS08-04, it's clear that whoever configured delegation overlooked WS08-03.

> **MORE INFO** Instructions for configuring constrained delegation can be found at *http://www.isaserver.org/tutorials/Configuring-ISA-Firewalls-ISA-2006-RC-Support-User-Certificate-Authentication-using-Constrained-Delegation-Part1.html.*

3. Now that you've configured constrained delegation for the TMG computer WS08-03, you can return to the publishing rule test button and click it again. Unlike the first test, this time you're rewarded with a successful test result as shown in Figure 24-25.

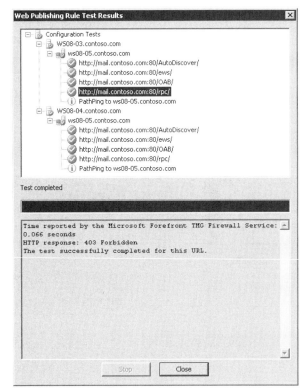

FIGURE 24-25 First successful test

4. You can see from that although the test results indicate success, they also indicate an HTTP 403 (forbidden) response from Exchange.

   What's interesting about this result is that although TMG allowed the request, the published service refused the connection with a 403 (forbidden) response. This is considered a successful test by the rule test mechanism because:

   - DNS resolution for ws08-05.contoso.com produced a valid IP address.

   - Forefront TMG was able to establish a successful TCP connection to WS08-05.contoso.com on port 80.

   - Forefront TMG did not receive an HTTP 404 (not found) response.

   One thing you must always bear in mind about the rule test functionality is that it considers any valid HTTP response other than 404 to be a success state because it cannot authenticate, nor can it evaluate the many HTTP response codes. You need to examine the IIS logs on the Client Access Server to determine why this request was refused.

NOTE By default, IIS maintains the site logs under C:\inetpub\logs\logfiles\ws3svc\ u_exyymmdd.log (yymmdd represents the GMT date as year-month-day). IIS status codes are available at *http://support.microsoft.com/kb/318380*.

In this example, IIS rejected this request with the following codes:

SC-STATUS 403

SC-SUBSTATUS 4

An IIS result code of 403.4 means "SSL Required". What this means is that you (or your Exchange administrator) has not enabled secure channel (SSL) offloading for Outlook Anywhere, or if they don't intend to enable that functionality, you should change the publishing rule so that the bridging is defined as HTTPS on port 443.

> **NOTE** IIS will also respond with 403.4 when the RPC Proxy component was not installed prior to installing Exchange server.

5. Now that the Exchange administrators have enabled SSL offloading, you can re-run the test. When you click the Test Rule button this time, you're rewarded with the results shown in Figures 24-26 and 24-27.

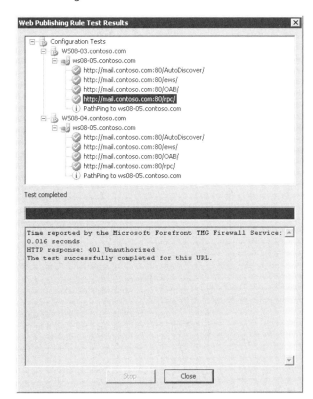

FIGURE 24-26 Successful test results

FIGURE 24-27 Authentication required response

This is as far as the test button can take you, because it can't help you solve authentication errors such as a bad username or password, but as you can see from this example, it can help you solve quite a few common configuration errors very quickly.

Summary

This chapter provided you with an overview of Exchange Web client publishing scenarios, the methods for enabling them, and some basic troubleshooting techniques. You also had the opportunity to walk through the use of the Web Publishing rule Test button and observe how it can help you solve some common configuration problems. In Chapter 25, "Understanding Remote Access," you will read about general VPN concepts and the functionality TMG brings to these scenarios.

PART VIII

Remote Access

CHAPTER 25 Understanding Remote Access   **733**

CHAPTER 26 Implementing Dial-in Client VPN   **747**

CHAPTER 27 Implementing Site-to-Site VPN   **773**

Understanding Remote Access

- Understanding VPN Concepts   **733**

- Planning VPN Access   **737**

- NAP Integration   **743**

- Summary   **745**

I n this chapter, you will become familiar with the basic concepts, planning, and NAP integration related to VPN services as used by Microsoft Forefront Threat Management Gateway (TMG).

Understanding VPN Concepts

Virtual Private Networks (VPNs) provide an encrypted tunnel that carries IP traffic to a remote server that terminates the encrypted tunnel and routes the user's traffic into a remote network. The VPN protocols used vary according to the capabilities of the VPN client and server as well as the functional and security requirements of the organization.

In general, VPN connections are used to provide secure access to a remote network. A common misconception is that VPN tunnels provide unrestricted access to a remote network. Because this statement is a function of the VPN terminator (such as TMG) and because TMG traffic policies can be defined as restrictive or as open as you like, this statement is untrue as a general rule.

Because VPN tunnels are intended to be secure and trusted, they must provide strong encryption and authentication methods. Additionally, they must employ tunnel management to control the traffic flow through the tunnel. Figure 25-1 illustrates the VPN relationship between these functions.

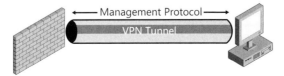

FIGURE 25-1 VPN tunnel protocol relationships

Recent changes in various technologies have led to the emergence of a secure tunnel methodology collectively referred to as *SSL-VPN*. Depending on the vendor's product design, they may provide a limited or complete VPN solution. Because TMG does not provide an SSL-VPN solution, this chapter discusses only those protocols and scenarios that deal with classic VPN technologies.

Tunnel Types

In general, VPN tunnels fall into two operational modes: transport and tunnel. Not all VPN tunnel technologies offer both modes. The primary difference between the modes is the way each is used:

- **Transport mode** This mode operates in the context of the two endpoints only; that is, it cannot be used to route traffic between two remote networks. This is the operational mode generally used for dial-on-demand VPN connections between individual users and a VPN terminator.

- **Tunnel mode** This mode is intended to provide routing between two networks as well as between the two endpoints. This operational mode is typically used for site-to-site VPN connections, where disjoint networks need to communicate. In this mode, the non-VPN hosts in each network must use their VPN endpoint as a route to the remote end of the tunnel if they are to communicate with each other.

Protocols

Windows Server 2008 and TMG support three VPN protocols, which are described in this section.

Point-to-Point Tunneling Protocol (PPTP)

PPTP is defined in RFC 2637 and is made up of two protocols: PPTP, which operates over TCP port 1723, and Generic Routing Encapsulation (GRE) IP protocol 47 (not *port 47*). The PPTP protocol itself serves as the management protocol, whereas GRE provides the secure tunnel between the client and server. NAT traversal requires a PPTP editor in the NAT device between the client and server. PPTP connections begin with the client establishing a PPTP control channel connection to the VPN server. The client authenticates to the server and they negotiate the encryption keys to be used on the GRE tunnel. The client establishes a second connection to the server using GRE. All client traffic except the PPTP control channel is carried within the encrypted GRE tunnel until the session is terminated. PPTP does not provide special functionality for NAT traversal and depends on the intelligence (or lack of it) in the NAT devices between the client and server to handle this properly.

> **MORE INFO** See *http://blogs.technet.com/isablog/archive/2009/01/07/a-pptp-client-might-fail-to-connect-to-a-vpn-server-on-the-internet-through-an-isa-server-2006.aspx* for a description of a case where some PPTP NAT editors have caused problems with PPTP tunnels.

Layer-Two Tunneling Protocol Over IPsec (L2TP/IPsec)

L2TP is described in RFC 2661 and operates together with Internet Key Exchange (IKE) and IPsec to provide a secure tunnel. IPsec provides machine-level authentication and encryption using IP protocol 50 (ESP) or IP protocol 51 (Authentication Header, or AH), whereas L2TP provides the tunnel management over UDP port 1701. IPsec protects the traffic tunnel. NAT traversal is accomplished through the use of IPsec NAT-T, which operates using UDP ports 500 and 4500. For normal (non-NAT) L2TP/IPsec sessions, the client establishes a connection to the server using UDP port 500. The client and server exchange encryption keys using certificates or pre-shared keys. Once this is completed, the client negotiates the L2TP session with the server within the encrypted IPsec tunnel over IP protocol 50 (ESP) or protocol 51 (AH). All traffic between the client and server, including the L2TP management traffic, is carried within the IPsec tunnel. L2TP/IPsec provides special behavior for those times when NAT traversal is required. In this case, the client connects to the VPN server using UDP port 500 to negotiate the encryption, then passes the L2TP and client traffic through UDP port 4500.

Secure Socket Tunneling Protocol (SSTP)

This protocol uses Point-to-Point Protocol (PPP) over HTTP, encrypted by SSL. HTTP provides the tunnel management and traffic tunnel. The biggest advantage SSTP brings is its ability to use a Web proxy to reach the VPN server. It's worth noting that SSTP cannot authenticate to the Web proxy, so if the local Web proxy requires authentication, SSTP cannot function through it. SSTP clients connect to the VPN server by establishing a connection on TCP port 443, negotiating the SSL handshake, then issuing an HTTP request to the VPN server indicating that this is an SSTP connection. All client traffic is passed through this HTTPS tunnel.

Address Assignment

Unlike physical or wireless networks, IP assignment for VPN connections does not employ Dynamic Host Configuration Protocol (DHCP). Instead, VPN connections negotiate IP assignment using Internet Protocol Control Protocol (IPCP). RFC 1332 defines this protocol and its capabilities. RRAS can be configured to obtain IP addresses from a DHCP server or it can assign IP addresses using a static pool defined by the administrator. Unlike DHCP, IPCP provides only the IP address itself. The client self-assigns a 32-bit subnet mask.

Authentication

Authentication for each VPN solution differs, but they generally share a common set of authentication protocols (presented here in increasing order of relative security):

- **Password Authentication Protocol (PAP)**   Available for use in all VPN protocols, PAP is the weakest of all user authentication protocols because the user credentials are sent in plain text, potentially making them available to network sniffers. Of course, if the tunnel is encrypted prior to starting user authentication, this becomes less of a problem.

- **Challenge Handshake Authentication Protocol (CHAP)** CHAP uses an MD5 hashing algorithm to protect the credentials while they're passed between the client and server. Like Digest authentication, this authentication method requires that user passwords in Active Directory are stored using reversible encryption. CHAP shares many of the weaknesses inherent in LAN Manager (LANMAN) and NT LAN Manager (NTLM) v1 authentication protocols.

- **Microsoft Challenge Handshake Authentication Protocol Version 2 (MS-CHAPv2)** MS-CHAPv2 solves many of the security weaknesses in CHAP by adding one-way salted encryption of the credentials using a unique salt value each time so that each time the encryption key is calculated, it produces a different value. This effectively mitigates any hash-based password guessing attacks.

- **Extensible Authentication Protocol (EAP)** This authentication method is actually made up of three different authentication schemes:

  - **MD5-Challenge** This is effectively identical to PPP-CHAP, but is sent as an EAP message.

  - **EAP-TLS** This method uses mutual certificate authentication of the caller and server. The certificate exchange is used to sign the messages. This authentication method is required to use smart cards for VPN.

  - **EAP-RADIUS** This method uses a RADIUS server as the credentials authority. The actual credentials are passed using MD5-Challenge or TLS and are satisfied through a call to the specified RADIUS server.

- **Internet Key Exchange Version 2 (IKEv2)** This authentication protocol provides the means for the caller and server to encrypt the initial connection so that all other communications can be sent without any concern that they may be read off the network. This requires that the caller and server share a common trusted root CA and that their certificates are issued for the purpose of IPsec negotiation.

> **MORE INFO** See *http://technet.microsoft.com/en-us/library/cc737286(WS.10).aspx* for a good summary of VPN authentication methods. IKEv2 scenarios are discussed in *http://blogs.technet.com/rrasblog/archive/2008/12/31/the-mobility-manager-managing-mobility-for-agile-vpn-connections.aspx*.

VPN Technology Comparison

Table 25-1 provides a comparison of the various VPN tunnel technologies supported in Windows Server 2008 and TMG.

TABLE 25-1 VPN protocol comparison

	SSTP	L2TP/IPSEC	PPTP
ENCAPSULATION	PPP over HTTP over TCP over SSL	IPsec	GRE
SITE-TO-SITE CAPABLE	No	Yes	Yes
ENCRYPTION	SSL with RC4 or AES	IPsec ESP with Triple Data Encryption Standard (3DES) or Advanced Encryption Standard (AES)	Microsoft Point-to-Point Encryption (MPPE) with RC4
TUNNEL MAINTENANCE PROTOCOL	SSTP	L2TP	PPTP
NAT TRAVERSAL	Native NAT or Web proxy	IPsec NAT-T	NAT editor on the firewall
USER AUTHENTICATION	After the SSL session is established	After the IPsec encryption occurs	Before PPTP encryption
CERTIFICATES	Server certificate on VPN server, root CA certificate on VPN client	Computer certificates on both the VPN client and VPN server or pre-shared keys	None

Planning VPN Access

In the past when the subject was remote access, many IT professionals imagined dialing in to access their network resources using a Plain Old Telephone System (POTS) line. The security aspect of this type of access was not the main concern. Now companies are making their internal network resources more available for employees to work remotely. In addition to roaming users, now employees who wish to work from home need remote access. Enabling secure remote access to corporate resources presents many challenges. When planning VPN access, consider the following issues:

- **Confidentiality**   Select the most appropriate VPN protocol to use to encrypt VPN traffic end to end.
- **Integrity**   Select the most appropriate authentication protocol and allow access to VPN resources based upon an endpoint integrity health check.
- **Availability**   Make the resources available to the users.

Keeping these core principles in mind can assist you during the planning phase and help you achieve the overall goal of the remote access project that you are about to implement.

Selecting the VPN Protocol

Table 25-1 provided a protocol comparison that can assist you during the planning phase to select the right protocol for your VPN access solution. However, you need to consider other aspects of a VPN protocol.

Client Operating System Support

You need to decide which operating systems you want to support. If you want to support almost all operating systems, you should consider enabling PPTP or L2TP/IPSec, which are supported on almost all versions of Windows. There are also PPTP client applications for Mac and Linux. If you want to be more restrictive, you can enable only L2TP/IPsec. This reduces the range of client operating systems that will be able to connect to your VPN server. However, almost all modern Windows hosts and third-party operating systems such as Mac and Linux can connect using L2TP/IPsec. SSTP is the most restrictive VPN protocol at this time, at least from the perspective of supported operating systems. Only Windows Vista SP1 and above and Windows 7 support the SSTP VPN protocol.

During the planning phase you should not only take into account the operating systems you need to support, but also the level of security you are comfortable with giving to any specific VPN protocol. To achieve this balance, you might need to upgrade client operating systems or allow less secure VPN protocols (such as PPTP).

Security

Which protocol is more secure? Which protocol is better for your network? These questions will come up during the planning phase. You need to take a moment to verify what your expectations are for this VPN access project and balance security needs with implementation costs. PPTP provides the essential security required for most networks and is compatible with a vast majority of the platforms. The overall cost to implement PPTP is lower because it doesn't require certificates or other special settings.

Another point to consider is the availability of using this protocol in a variety of remote locations. One common frustration for VPN users occurs when they are traveling and try to connect to the VPN server from a hotel room. They may get an error because the hotel doesn't allow outbound access for PPTP. Some locations only allow HTTP and HTTPS outbound. This lack of universal support for outbound PPTP is something you need to consider.

LT2P/IPsec offers the highest level of security for VPN protocols and provides data confidentiality, integrity, and origin authentication but has a higher implementation cost. This is because to take full advantage of L2TP/IPsec, you will need to deploy certificates. Although all those elements are built into the Windows operating system, you will need additional planning to support the Public Key Infrastructure (PKI) required to implement IPsec.

SSTP provides the highest level of availability in remote locations because it uses only HTTPS. But because it is the newest VPN protocol, it has the lowest level of compatibility with older operating systems. Thus it increases the implementation cost because you might need to upgrade your old operating system to make use of SSTP.

Performance

IPsec is much more CPU-intensive than PPTP, which means that the same Forefront TMG VPN server will consume more resources using L2TP than PPTP or SSTP. Windows Server 2008 imposes some limitations on the number of allowed and concurrent VPN connections that may be used, depending on the edition:

- **Windows Server 2008 Web Edition**   You may define no more than 1,000 PPTP, 1,000 L2TP, or 1,000 SSTP connections, and no more than one VPN connection may be used at a time.
- **Windows Server 2008 Standard Edition**   You may define no more than 1,000 PPTP, 1,000 L2TP, and 1,000 SSTP connections, and no more than 1,000 total connections of any type may operate at the same time.
- **Windows Server 2008 Enterprise and Data Center Edition**   No specific limits exist for VPN connections beyond what may be imposed by memory and network constraints.

NOTE   TMG is supported on Windows Server 2008 Standard, Enterprise, and Datacenter editions. TMG is not supported on Windows Server 2008 Web edition.

Hardware Requirements

For VPN access, it is important to remember that you have to correctly plan not only for your TMG VPN server, but also for other network components that work to make the VPN connections available. Your Internet connection and your router need to properly accommodate incoming VPN requests and not act as a bottleneck, as shown in Figure 25-2.

In many cases the planning phase focuses more on the VPN server itself for hardware capacity and doesn't address those two core elements, which can turn out to be the culprit in performance capacity issues in the future.

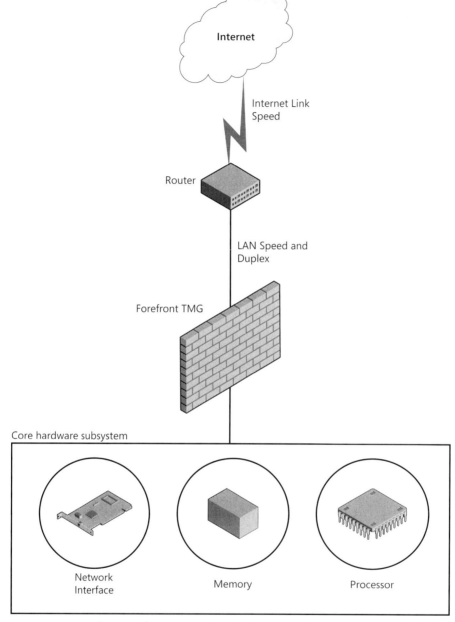

FIGURE 25-2 Core elements of the hardware planning phase

The overall calculation for RAM consumption on a VPN scenario is approximately 40 KB of non-page-pool memory for each active connection. For every 1,000 concurrent connections you should provide an extra 256 MB of RAM (128 MB for 1,000 connections plus 128 MB for RRAS Service itself). The CPU choice and speed will vary according to the protocol that you will use for your VPN access; the general rule of thumb is that for L2TP/IPsec you should plan to have a more powerful processor. For the network subsystem the main recommendations include the following:

- Use a network adapter that is capable of IPsec hardware offload, preferably on the external Network Interface.
- Match the speed and duplex mode between TMG and the switch or router.

MORE INFO The RRAS Team published performance results for different VPN protocols that you can also use as reference for comparison purposes. Access the report at *http://blogs.technet.com/rrasblog/archive/2009/02/09/rras-performance-results.aspx*.

Authentication

Another important part of VPN access is authentication. During the planning phase you need to define whether you will use your current Active Directory infrastructure to authenticate remote users or if you want to use a separate entity to handle authentication. Some companies prefer to unify the authentication process and use the same authentication provider that is used when the user is logged through the local corporate network. The general guideline is to provide the end user with the smoothest experience possible, but stay aligned with the most secure access control.

In other scenarios, authentication is consolidated by using a single protocol for all types of access. For example, internal clients connecting through the wireless access point or wired network will always send the authentication request to the same entity. To take advantage of a single authentication infrastructure you can also use Remote Authentication Dial-In User Service (RADIUS) protocol. TMG is capable of acting as a RADIUS Proxy and will forward RADIUS connection requests and accounting messages between RADIUS clients and RADIUS servers.

MORE INFO For more information on how RADIUS works, review *http://technet.microsoft .com/en-us/library/cc785693.aspx*.

VPN Access Policy

During the planning phase, another element that should be addressed is VPN client access policy. A company that creates a comprehensive access policy in advance has a much greater chance of succeeding during the implementation and maintenance phases. You need to define who will have VPN access and what the requirements are to allow remote users to connect to internal resources.

By planning those requirements in advance, you can go to the implementation phase with a checklist of what the client needs to gain VPN access. This list can be distributed through administrative and technical controls.

- **Administrative Controls**   Requirements that the user must satisfy to be eligible for VPN access. Here are some sample questions that the employee (or the employee's manager) needs to answer:

    1. Does your job require remote access?

    2. How often do you work from home?

    3. Do you use one company's asset (laptop for example) to access VPN remotely?

    4. What resources do you need to access remotely?

    5. Can these resources be accessed via other means (such as Web Publishing or Server Publishing)?

- **Technical Controls**   Here you will take advantage of Forefront TMG firewall policy to allow users to have access only to the resources that they need, implementing the principle of least privilege. In other words, don't give more access than the user needs. Another technology that can be included as a technical control is Network Access Protection (NAP). With NAP you can do endpoint protection by evaluating the health of the client's workstation and verify whether the client satisfies the minimum requirements to gain VPN access.

Supportability

Supportability is a very interesting topic because—depending on the size of the company and its security policy—it can be addressed by very different approaches. In general, all security devices are managed by the IT security department, which includes the VPN server. However, some companies don't have enough resources to implement the concept of separation of duties and they merge computer networking management with IT security management. During the planning phase, it is important to define the roles within the internal teams to identify who will support what and the supportability boundaries among the teams.

VPN Supportability Boundaries within Forefront TMG

Forefront TMG enhances VPN connectivity over that enabled by the native Windows RRAS by adding application inspection and access control through Firewall Policy. Forefront TMG is built upon the core Windows RRAS component, which means that if Windows RRAS is broken, Forefront TMG VPN resource will suffer the pain.

Supportability is an important subject outside and within Microsoft. Because Microsoft has many teams for different products and different components within the product, it is essential that each team knows exactly what functions are performed by their component and how this can affect other components outside the supportability scope of their team. Because TMG includes RRAS to support VPN connections, we have many interesting cases with our folks from the Windows Networking Team and this real-world scenario is based on an interesting collaboration between the Forefront Edge and Windows Networking Teams.

External clients were receiving a 691 error when connecting from home to the VPN server (during that time, ISA Server 2006). Error 691 is "Access denied because username and/or password is invalid on the domain". We knew this was not the case because we knew that the username and password were valid. ISA Server 2006 logging didn't show any error, there was no deny on the request, and everything was looking pretty healthy at that point.

Because ISA Server 2006 didn't seem to be causing the problem, we engaged our Windows Networking Team to review the RRAS component and determine whether anything was wrong there. They identified that the RRAS component was using a wrong server name in the Remote Access Logging feature. Because the RRAS Service couldn't log information on the Microsoft SQL Server computer specified in the properties, it was rejecting the attempt to log on.

This was a great example of an issue on RRAS configuration being exposed by ISA Server 2006, giving the impression that ISA Server 2006 was the culprit.

MORE INFO   For more information on this scenario and a graphical view of the components, see *http://blogs.technet.com/isablog/archive/2009/03/19/clients-receives-error-691-trying-to-connect-to-isa-server-2006-as-vpn-server.aspx*.

NAP Integration

Windows Server 2008 Network Access Protection (NAP) is a platform that enforces compliance with computer health requirements for network access. Forefront TMG integrates with that by acting as a VPN server, as shown in Figure 25-3.

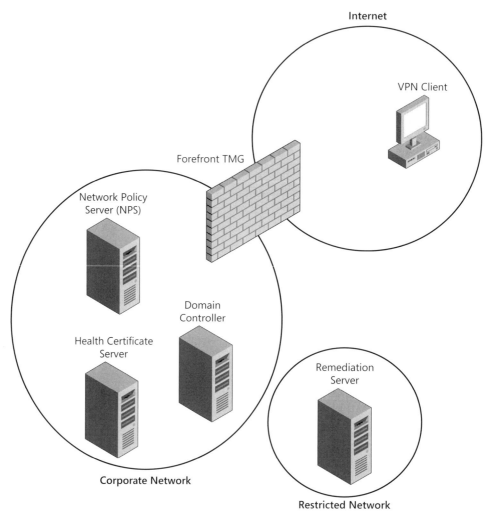

FIGURE 25-3 TMG acting as a VPN server in the NAP infrastructure

TMG's role in the NAP infrastructure is to request credentials from VPN clients and send the authentication request to the Network Policy Server (NPS). If the connection is approved and the client is compliant, NPS instructs TMG to allow the traffic from this host in accordance with existing TMG traffic policies. TMG accepts the connection and forwards the access response to the client computer. The enhancement added by TMG is the capability to inspect VPN traffic and provide access rules to restrict access from remote clients.

Considerations When Planning NAP Integration

When considering implementing NAP integration with TMG it is important to evaluate your current scenario: Are you already using NAP in your local network, or will NAP deployment happen at the same time as TMG integration? This is an important question because the answer will assist you in defining the needs for your environment. If you already have a NAP infrastructure in place, you have more than half the work done—configuring Forefront TMG is smaller compared to the NAP solution as a whole. On the other hand, if you don't have NAP yet, you will need to do more planning before you even start configuring Forefront TMG.

> **MORE INFO**   For more information about the items that need to be covered during the NAP planning phase, use the NAP Deployment Guide at *http://technet.microsoft.com/en-us/library/dd314158.aspx.*

If you are deploying a pristine scenario where Forefront TMG will act as VPN server, you need to address the following tasks:

- Configure Forefront TMG as a RADIUS client.
- Create system health validators.
- Create NAP health policies.
- Create network policies.
- Create connection request policies.

Although you can install the Network Policy Server on the Forefront TMG computer, you should separate those roles for performance reasons.

> **MORE INFO**   For more information about NAP capacity planning, see *http://technet.microsoft.com/en-us/library/dd125353(WS.10).aspx.*

Summary

In this chapter, you learned about the basic concepts behind various VPN scenarios, including the protocols and authentication methods used. You compared the features and failings of each. You also learned how to evaluate your organization's security and business requirements and how to balance the needs of one against the other. Last, you learned how to plan for your expected VPN client load and how to evaluate VPN performance. In Chapter 26, you will learn how to configure TMG for dial-in VPN scenarios.

## CHAPTER 26

Implementing Dial-in Client VPN

- Configuring VPN Client Access   **747**

- Configuring VPN Client Access with NAP Integration   **756**

- Configuring VPN Client Access Using SSTP   **763**

- Summary   **771**

Microsoft Forefront TMG can provide VPN access to clients using the Windows Routing and Remote Access service (RRAS). TMG supports the Point to Point Tunneling Protocol (PPTP), Layer 2 Tunneling Protocol over IP Security (L2TP/IPSec), and Secure Socket Tunneling Protocol (SSTP) VPN connections. You do not need Client Access Licenses (CALs) for remote-access VPN clients. In this chapter we will discuss how to configure VPN client access using PPTP, how to configure VPN Client Access with NAP Integration, and finally how to configure VPN client access using SSTP.

Configuring VPN Client Access

Configuring VPN client access in Forefront TMG is easy. As long as proper planning is done, all you need to do is follow the wizard to set up VPN access for clients. In this section we will configure VPN client access in TMG with the settings shown in Table 26-1.

TABLE 26-1 VPN Client Access settings

SETTING	VALUE
Number of VPN Clients	100
User Group	Domain Users
VPN Type	PPTP
Access Networks	External
Address Assignment	DHCP
Authentication	MS-CHAPv2
Authentication Repository	Windows Active Directory

To configure VPN client access on Forefront TMG, follow these steps:

1. Open the Forefront TMG management console and click Remote Access Policy (VPN) in the left pane. Under General VPN Configuration in the right pane, click Select Access Networks, as shown in Figure 26-1.

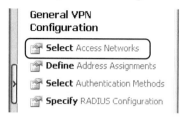

FIGURE 26-1 Selecting access networks

2. The Remote Access Policy (VPN) Properties window opens. On the Access Networks tab you can define from which network the client will be able to initiate a VPN connection to the VPN server. Because the clients will be connecting from the Internet, select the External check box as shown in Figure 26-2. When External is selected, the clients can connect to any IP address on the External network interface. If you would like to limit the clients so that they connect to only specific IP addresses on the External network interface, you can use packet filters in RRAS.

> **MORE INFO**   For more information about packet filters in Routing and Remote Access (RRAS), please visit *http://blogs.technet.com/rrasblog/archive/2006/06/14/435839.aspx*.

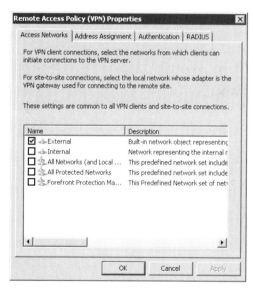

FIGURE 26-2 Access Networks tab

3. Click the Address Assignment tab to select whether the clients will be assigned an IP address from a static IP addresses pool or from a DHCP. In case of an Enterprise array

with more than one array member, you can only use static IP address pools to assign IP addresses to VPN clients. (The DHCP option is disabled.) Also, if you use a static address pool you need to make sure that the address range does not overlap with any other network in TMG. For our example we will select Static IP assignment, as shown in Figure 26-3.

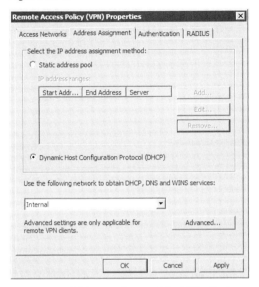

FIGURE 26-3 Address assignment for VPN clients

4. Click the Advanced button shown in Figure 26-3. The Name Resolution dialog box opens, as shown in Figure 26-4. You can use these settings to define manual alternate DNS and WINS servers IP addresses in the event that you want to specify different server addresses for VPN clients. In this example we will leave the settings at their default and click OK to return to the Remote Access Policy (VPN) properties dialog box.

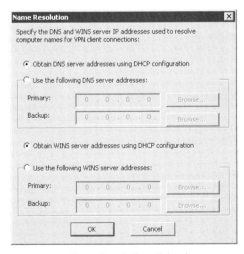

FIGURE 26-4 Name Resolution dialog box

5. Click the Authentication tab, as shown in Figure 26-5, to select the authentication method used when the remote VPN client initiates a connection to Forefront TMG. MS-CHAPv2 is the default setting. For our example we will also use MS-CHAPv2 for authentication so we will leave this setting at its default.

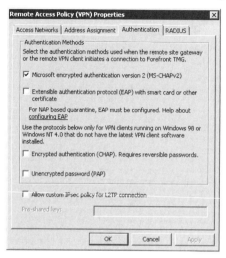

FIGURE 26-5 Authentication tab

> **MORE INFO** For more information about the different authentication types, please visit *http://technet.microsoft.com/en-us/library/cc785072(WS.10).aspx*.

6. Click the RADIUS tab, as shown in Figure 26-6, if you want to specify a RADIUS server to authenticate the VPN clients against a RADIUS server. Because we are using Active Directory for authentication in our example, we will not change any settings on this tab. Click OK to return to the Forefront TMG console.

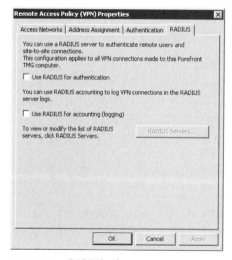

FIGURE 26-6 RADIUS tab

MORE INFO For more information about configuring VPN access using RADIUS Authentication, please visit *http://technet.microsoft.com/en-us/library/cc713343.aspx.*

7. Click Apply to commit the changes.

8. Under Tasks in the TMG management console right pane, click Configure VPN Client Access as shown in Figure 26-7.

FIGURE 26-7 Configure VPN Client Access option

9. The VPN Clients Properties dialog box opens. Select the Enable VPN Client Access check box, as shown in Figure 26-8. As planned previously, type **100** in the Maximum Number Of VPN Clients Allowed text box.

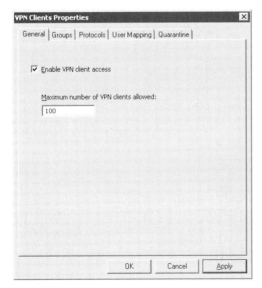

FIGURE 26-8 General tab for VPN Clients Properties

10. Click the Groups tab to select the domain groups for which remote access is allowed. The users to be selected should have dial-in permissions as allowed in Active Directory. Click Add, enter the domain group as **Contoso\Domain Users,** and click OK. Domain Users are now selected and displayed with the namespace and domain, as shown in Figure 26-9.

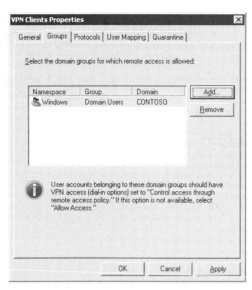

FIGURE 26-9 Domain Groups allowed under the Groups tab

11. Click the Protocols tab to select the VPN tunneling protocol to use for VPN access. Select the Enable PPTP check box to allow clients to connect using PPTP for VPN, as shown in Figure 26-10. If you have multiple protocols enabled on the server, the type of VPN protocol that will be used will depend on the client settings, which we discussed in the section "Configuring a VPN Client."

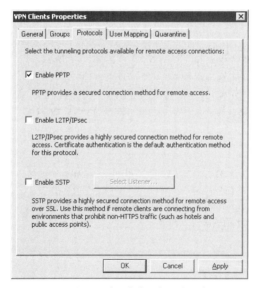

FIGURE 26-10 Protocols tab for choosing the VPN tunneling protocol

12. Click the User Mapping tab, as shown in Figure 26-11. User Mapping is used to map VPN clients from non-Windows namespaces (RADIUS or EAP authenticated users) to the Windows namespace so that access rules applying to Windows user sets can also apply to the users from non-Windows namespaces. Because we are using Active Directory for authentication in our example, and our TMG is a member of the domain, we do not have to take any action on this tab.

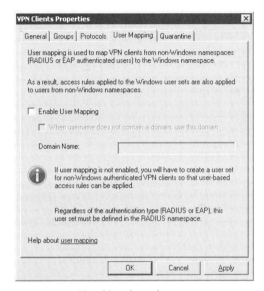

FIGURE 26-11 User Mapping tab

> **NOTE** User Mapping can and should only be enabled when TMG is a member of the domain. User mapping is used to enable TMG to map those users to the Active Directory who do not supply domain information to the TMG itself, such as RADIUS clients who only supply that information to a RADIUS server (the information is not shared with TMG).

13. Click the Quarantine tab, as shown in Figure 26-12. You can enable quarantine control to keep VPN clients in a quarantined network until specific client configuration requirements that you define have been met and verified. For our example we will not enable quarantine control. Click OK to return to the main TMG console.

> **NOTE** To read more about how to set up Quarantine using NAP, please visit *http://technet.microsoft.com/en-us/library/cc995142.aspx*. To read more about Configuring RQS/RQC-based quarantine control, please visit *http://technet.microsoft .com/en-us/library/cc995086.aspx*.

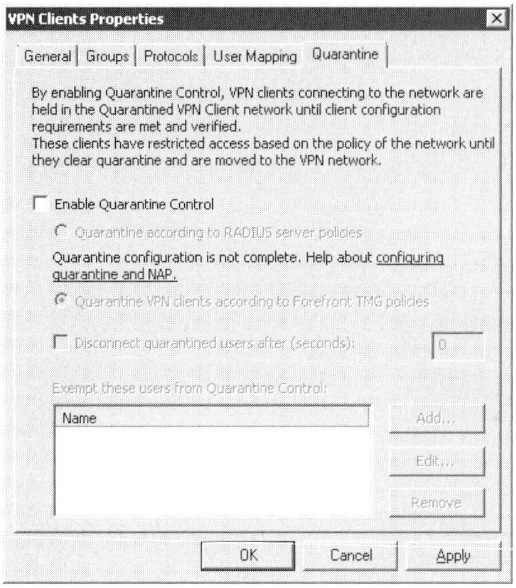

FIGURE 26-12 Quarantine tab

Configuring a VPN Client

After configuring the server-side settings, we now have to create a client-side VPN connection (sometimes called a connectoid) to initiate and connect to the VPN server. To configure a VPN client on a Windows Vista client computer, follow these steps:

1. Click Start, click Control Panel, and then browse to Network And Sharing Center.

2. Under Tasks, click Connect To A Network as shown in Figure 26-13.

Tasks

View computers and devices

Connect to a network

Set up a connection or network

Manage network connections

Diagnose and repair

FIGURE 26-13 Connect to a network

NOTE You may encounter a page indicating that Windows cannot find any other networks. If this occurs, click Set up A Connection Or Network as shown in Figure 26-14.

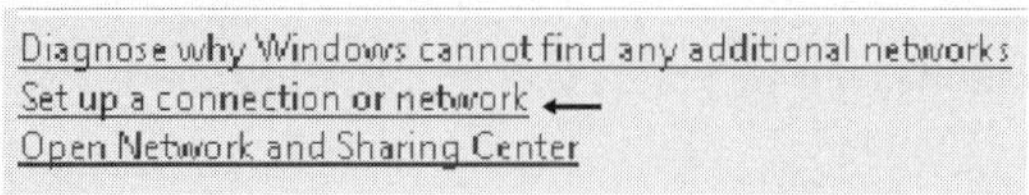

Diagnose why Windows cannot find any additional networks
Set up a connection or network ⟵
Open Network and Sharing Center

FIGURE 26-14 Set Up A Connection Or Network option

3. The Set Up A Connection Or Network Wizard launches. Select Connect To A Workplace, as shown in Figure 26-15, and click Next.

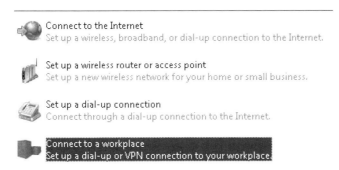

Connect to the Internet
Set up a wireless, broadband, or dial-up connection to the Internet.

Set up a wireless router or access point
Set up a new wireless network for your home or small business.

Set up a dial-up connection
Connect through a dial-up connection to the Internet.

Connect to a workplace
Set up a dial-up or VPN connection to your workplace.

FIGURE 26-15 Set Up A Connection Or Network Wizard

4. In the Connect To A Workplace dialog box, click Use My Internet Connection (VPN) as shown in Figure 26-16.

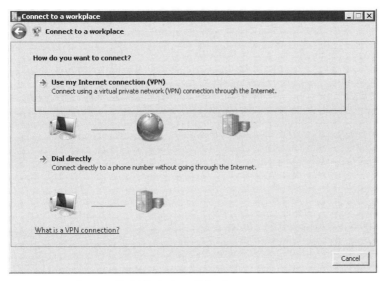

FIGURE 26-16 Connect To A Workplace dialog box

5. In the next dialog box, type in the Internet address that the VPN client will connect to. This can be an IP address or a fully qualified domain name (FQDN) that is resolvable over the Internet. For our example we will connect to **vpn.contoso.com**, which we will type in the Internet Address field. In the Destination Name field specify a friendly name to identify the VPN connectoid, as shown in Figure 26-17, and click Next.

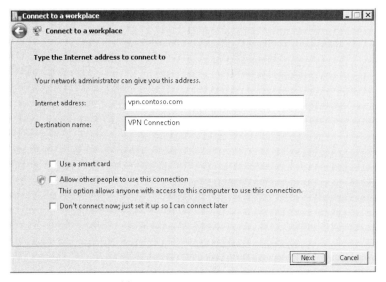

FIGURE 26-17 Internet address to connect to

6. In the dialog box that appears next, type in the username, password, and domain for a user who has been granted dial-in privileges for VPN access. Click Connect. In case the user wants to use the option Log On Via Dial Up Networking available at system logon, we need to enable the option Allow Other People To Use This Connection.

At this point the user should be able to connect without any issues. The VPN when set to Automatic type for VPN will follow the order mentioned in the following steps while connecting to the VPN Server:

1. Connect using IKEv2.

2. If IKEv2 fails, connect using SSTP.

3. If SSTP fails, connect using PPTP.

4. If PPTP fails, connect using L2TP/IPsec.

5. If L2TP/IPSec fails, stop connection establishment and report error.

It is important to note that this order will vary based on the operating system version of the VPN connectoid. The protocol selection method noted here applies to Windows 7, which supports VPN Reconnect (IKEv2). Windows Vista SP1 and earlier do not support VPN Reconnect and therefore begin by negotiating an SSTP connection.

Configure VPN Client Access with NAP Integration

As mentioned in the previous chapter it is necessary to have a NAP infrastructure in place before configuring Forefront TMG to allow VPN client access with NAP Integration. The scenario we'll use for this example has the NAP infrastructure shown in Figure 26-18.

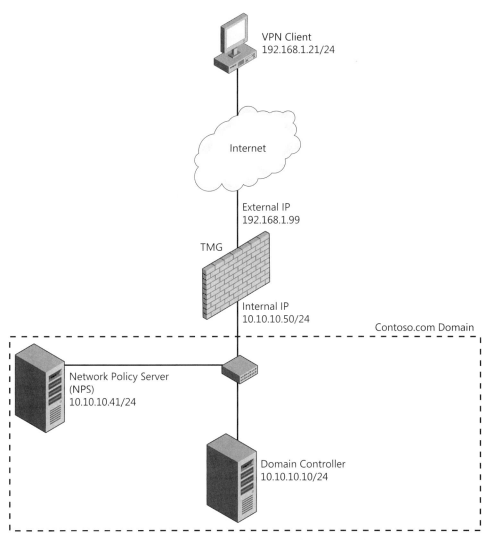

FIGURE 26-18 Topology used in this scenario to configure Forefront TMG with NAP Integration

The process to configure Forefront TMG NAP Integration can be divided into two core phases:

- Enable VPN Access on TMG and configure NAP Integration.
- Configure NPS to use Forefront TMG as a RADIUS Client.

It is important to emphasize that for the purpose of this explanation the current NAP Infrastructure used by Contoso.com already has the following components in place and configured:

- System health validators
- NAP health policies

- Network Policies
- Connection request policies

MORE INFO For more information on how to configure a NAP infrastructure, go to *http://technet.microsoft.com/en-us/library/cc441502.aspx*.

Configuring Forefront TMG for NAP Integration

In the beginning of this chapter you learned how to configure VPN client access on Forefront TMG. Those steps are required for configuring NAP Integration. Follow these steps to change the current configuration to enable NAP Integration:

1. Click Forefront TMG (Array Name) in the left pane.

2. Click Remote Access Policy (VPN) and in the task pane click Specify RADIUS Configuration.

3. Click Use RADIUS For Authentication, and then click RADIUS Servers as shown in Figure 26-19.

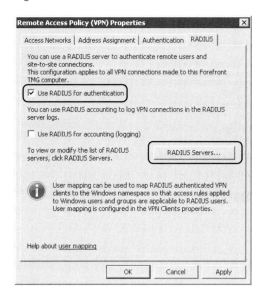

FIGURE 26-19 Selecting RADIUS parameters

4. Click Add in the RADIUS Servers dialog box.

5. Type the RADIUS Server (which is the NPS server name) name (which needs to be resolvable by TMG), as shown in Figure 26-20.

6. Click the Change button next to the Shared Secret field to specify a new secret. You need to enter the same value here and in the configuration on the NPS server. Type a secret and confirm it, as shown in Figure 26-21.

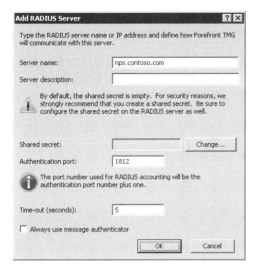

FIGURE 26-20 Specifying RADIUS parameters

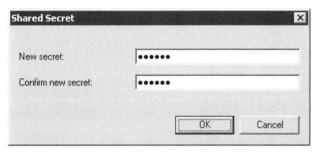

FIGURE 26-21 The secret needs to be shared between NPS and Forefront TMG.

7. Click OK and in the Add RADIUS Server dialog box click OK again. Your RADIUS servers should appear with the NPS name and port, as shown in Figure 26-22.

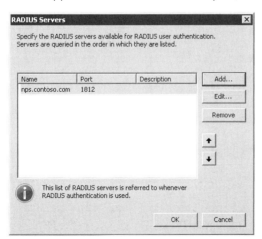

FIGURE 26-22 RADIUS server that will be used for NAP Integration

8. Click OK and then click OK again in the Remote Access Policy (VPN) Properties dialog box. Figure 26-23 shows a dialog box asking for confirmation because the Routing and Remote Access service will be restarted. Click OK to confirm.

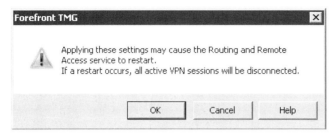

FIGURE 26-23 Warning that the RRAS services will be restarted

9. In the tasks pane, click Select Authentication Methods.

10. Select Extensible Authentication Protocol (EAP) With Smart Card Or Other Certificate. An informational window appears, as shown in Figure 26-24. Click OK.

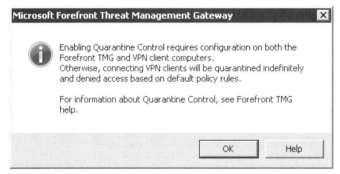

FIGURE 26-24 Informational window about EAP authentication

11. The Authentication tab should appear, as shown in Figure 26-25. Click OK to confirm.

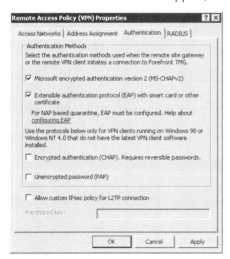

FIGURE 26-25 Authentication methods selected for NAP Integration

12. In the tasks pane, click Configure Quarantine Control.

13. On the Quarantine tab, select Enable Quarantine Control. The dialog box shown in Figure 26-26 opens.

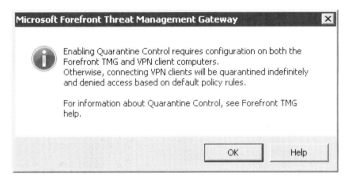

FIGURE 26-26 A reminder that the client also needs to be configured for quarantine control

14. Click OK and select the option Quarantine According To RADIUS Server Policies, as shown in Figure 26-27. Click OK.

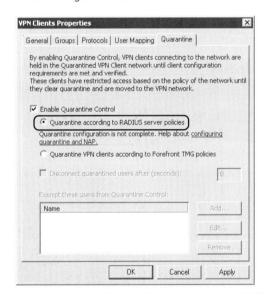

FIGURE 26-27 Enabling Forefront TMG to use RADIUS Server Policy (NPS)

15. Click Apply to commit the changes and then click OK on the Saving Configuration Changes window.

Configuring NPS to Use Forefront TMG as a RADIUS Client

You need to do this part of the configuration on the Network Policy Server, which in this case is nps.contoso.com. Follow these steps to perform this configuration:

1. Click Start, click Run, type **nps.msc** in the Open text box, and press Enter.

2. In the left pane of the Network Policy Server MMC, select and expand RADIUS Clients And Servers.

3. Right-click RADIUS Clients and select New RADIUS Client.

4. Type in the Forefront TMG details information, as shown in Figure 26-28.

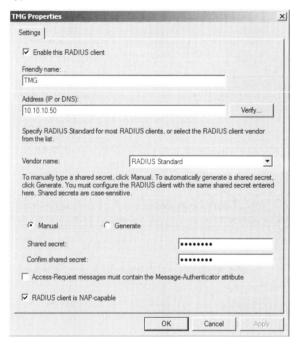

FIGURE 26-28 Specifying parameters used on Forefront TMG

5. Click OK to confirm the changes. The Network Policy Server dialog box appears with TMG as a RADIUS Client, as shown in Figure 26-29.

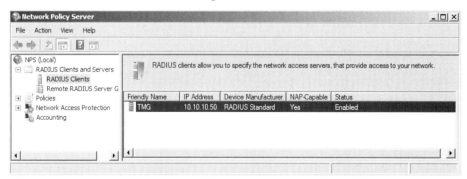

FIGURE 26-29 NPS window with TMG as RADIUS Client

With these steps in place—and assuming that your internal NAP infrastructure is functional—the last step is the client configuration for NAP integration. The steps for the client side will vary according to the operating system that the remote client is using.

> **MORE INFO**   For more details about client configuration for NAP capability, go to *http://technet.microsoft.com/en-us/library/cc441483.aspx*.

Configuring VPN Client Access Using SSTP

Some roaming users face issues when they are located in hotels that don't allow outbound VPN access. It's not that the hotels are against the use of VPN connections, it's due more to the fact that some hotels don't allow outbound connections that use a port other than 80 or 443. To address difficulties like this, a new tunneling protocol called Secure Socket Tunneling Protocol (SSTP) was developed.

Windows Server 2008 was the first Microsoft operating system to include an SSTP server as part of RRAS services. Forefront TMG uses the resources from RRAS and provides SSTP management.

> **MORE INFO**   To learn more about how SSTP works on Windows Server 2008, see the following article: *http://technet.microsoft.com/en-us/library/cc731352.aspx*.

SSTP configuration relies on two main components: RRAS and HTTP.SYS. TMG uses those components in the following way:

- **RRAS Service**   Configures the RRAS service to accept SSTP connections and defines the number of SSTP connections to be allowed.
- **HTTP.SYS**   Configures HTTP.SYS to listen on port 6601. TMG acts as an SSL terminator, forwarding traffic from port 443 to 127.0.0.1 on TCP port 6601. You can see this configuration by looking at the system policy rule number 46, as shown in Figures 26-30 and 26-31.

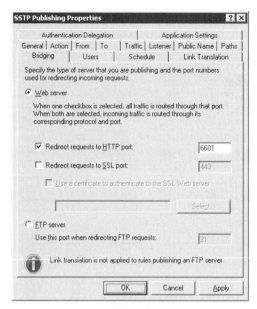

FIGURE 26-30 Port used for HTTP.SYS

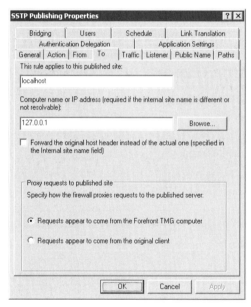

FIGURE 26-31 Configuration of the SSTP system rule

If you try to use the *netstat* command you will not see port 6601 listed because HTTP.SYS is responsible for handling requests on that port.

The path that comes encapsulated in the SSTP request from the VPN client has the following value in the URL: */sra_{BA195980-CD49-458b-9E23-C84EE0ADCD75}/.* You can see this value in the SSTP system policy rule on the Path tab, as shown in Figure 26-32.

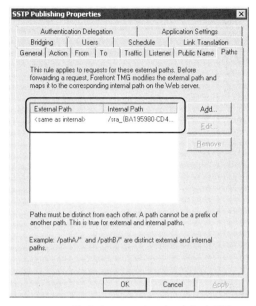

FIGURE 26-32 Path that contains the default URL used by the SSTP request from the VPN client

You can also see this URL by using the command *netsh http show urlacl*, which shows the reserved URLs. The following output shows this entry:

```
C:\>netsh http show URLACL
URL Reservations:
-----------------
    Reserved URL            : https://+:443/sra_{BA195980-CD49-458b-9E23-C84EE0ADCD75}/
        User: NT SERVICE\SstpSvc
            Listen: Yes
            Delegate: Yes
        User: BUILTIN\Administrators
            Listen: No
            Delegate: No
        User: NT AUTHORITY\SYSTEM
            Listen: Yes
            Delegate: Yes
            SDDL: D:(A;;GA;;;S-1-5-80-3435701886-799518250-3791383489-3228296122-
                2938884314)(A;;GR;;;BA)(A;;GA;;;SY)
    Reserved URL            : http://+:6601/sra_{BA195980-CD49-458b-9E23-C84EE0ADCD75}/
        User: NT SERVICE\SstpSvc
            Listen: Yes
            Delegate: Yes
```

```
User: BUILTIN\Administrators
    Listen: No
    Delegate: No
User: NT AUTHORITY\SYSTEM
    Listen: Yes
    Delegate: Yes
    SDDL: D:(A;;GA;;;S-1-5-80-3435701886-799518250-3791383489-3228296122-
        2938884314)(A;;GR;;;BA)(A;;GA;;;SY)
```

> **NOTE**   Port 6601 is registered as mstmg-sstp; 6601/tcp; Microsoft Threat Management Gateway SSTP at IANA. For more information, see *http://www.iana.org/assignments/port-numbers*.

Planning SSTP

Before you enable SSTP on Forefront TMG it is important to plan the configuration of the following three components:

- **Certificate**   SSTP uses HTTP over SSL (TLS), which means that you need a server certificate for the Web listener. You need to ensure that:
  - The name that you use on the server certificate matches the name that remote clients use to connect to the VPN server. For instance, if the clients use *vpn.contoso .com* in the VPN connector configuration, your server certificate must use *vpn.contoso.com*.
  - Clients need to trust the certificate authority that issued the server certificate that you used for the TMG SSTP Web listener. Therefore, if you decide to use an internal root CA, you need to make sure that all remote client workstations have the CA Root Certificate installed locally on each computer in the Trusted Root store.
  - If the certificate is issued by an internal CA, you will need to make the CRL available for external clients to consult; otherwise, the external client will receive the error 0x80092013 saying that the client was unable to check the revocation list.
- **Web Listener**   To use the certificate created for SSTP, you need to create a Web listener and associate the certificate with it.
- **Client Workstation**   The client workstation must use Windows Vista SP1 or later. SSTP-based VPN is not available for earlier Windows versions.
- **IP Address**   Because the Web listener used by SSTP is not going to enforce authentication, it is important to reserve one specific IP address to be dedicated to SSTP.

For the purpose of this configuration, Contoso Security Team has the following requirements:

- Remote clients will connect to the VPN server using the name vpn.contoso.com.
- Preserve the current PPTP configuration and just enable SSTP support.

Enabling SSTP on Forefront TMG

Because the current TMG configuration already has PPTP enabled, the only additional steps are to create a Web listener and then enable SSTP to use this listener. Assuming that the certificate is already installed on TMG, follow these steps to configure the remaining settings:

1. Click Forefront TMG (Array Name) in the left pane.

2. In the task pane, on the Tasks tab, click Remote Access Policy (VPN) and then click Configure VPN Client Access.

3. In the VPN Clients Properties dialog box, click the Protocols tab and select Enable SSTP as shown in Figure 26-33. Then click Configure.

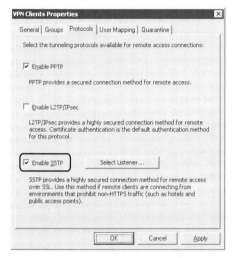

FIGURE 26-33 Enabling SSTP protocol

4. The Choose Web Listener For SSTP dialog box appears, as shown in Figure 26-34. Click New.

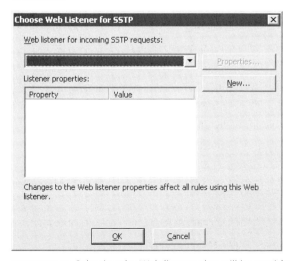

FIGURE 26-34 Selecting the Web listener that will be used for this protocol

5. The Web Listener Wizard launches. This Web listener will be used to accept the inbound SSTP connections to the TMG VPN server. Type the name for this listener, as shown in Figure 26-35.

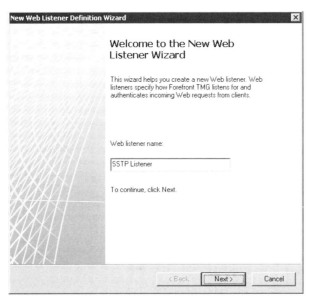

FIGURE 26-35 Web Listener Wizard

6. On the Web Listener IP Addresses page, select the interface that will be listening for this request. In this case it is External, as shown in Figure 26-36. Click Next.

FIGURE 26-36 Selecting the interface that this listener will use

7. In the Listener SSL Certificates dialog box, click Select Certificate beside the Use A Single Certificate For This Web Listener option, select the certificate that will be used for this Web listener, and click Select. Your dialog box should appear, as shown in Figure 26-37. Click Next.

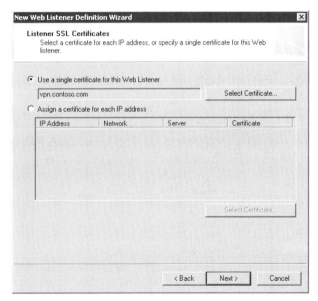

FIGURE 26-37 Choosing the certificate that will be used for this Web listener

8. On the Completing The New Web Listener Wizard page, click Finish.
9. The Choose Web Listener For This SSTP dialog box appears again, but now with the listener properties shown in Figure 26-38.

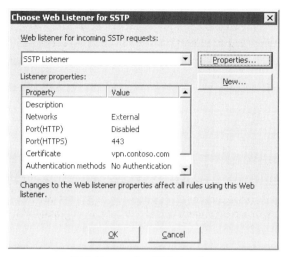

FIGURE 26-38 Web Listener For SSTP details

10. Click OK twice and then click Apply to commit the changes.

As you can see, the Web Listener Wizard for SSTP doesn't offer all the options when creating a regular Web listener using the Toolbox. One item that is not present on this wizard is the authentication portion. SSTP will use the same authentication mechanism as PPTP or L2TP. In other words, the client is not authenticated to the server at the HTTPS layer; SSTP client is authenticated to the server at the PPP layer.

Changing Client Configuration

Now that TMG is ready to use SSTP it is necessary to perform a small change on the VPN Connection properties. Assuming that the current client VPN connection is using PPTP (which was the first scenario in this chapter), you need to change the VPN client settings to use SSTP as shown in Figure 26-39.

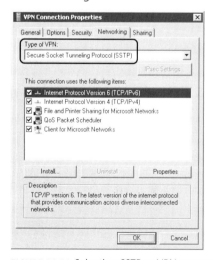

FIGURE 26-39 Selecting SSTP as VPN protocol in the client configuration

Summary

In this chapter, you learned how to configure TMG for VPN client access and how to configure NAP criteria for VPN client access. Finally, you learned about how the TMG-supported VPN protocols behave "on the wire" and how to evaluate their behavior using a network monitoring tool. In Chapter 27, "Implementing Site-to-Site VPN," you will learn how to configure site-to-site VPN.

## CHAPTER 27

Implementing Site-to-Site VPN

■ Configuring L2TP Over IPsec Site-to-Site VPN **774**

■ Configuring PPTP Site-to-Site VPN **782**

■ Troubleshooting VPN Client Connections **788**

■ Summary **794**

A Virtual Private Network (VPN) allows a private network to be extended across other shared networks like the Internet. VPN connections allow users who work at home or are travelling to access their corporate network and access files just as if they were in the office. VPN connections also allow organizations to have routed connections with other organizations over a public network, such as the Internet, while maintaining secure communications (for example, between offices that are geographically separate). A routed VPN connection across the Internet logically operates as a dedicated wide area network (WAN) link.

By using Forefront TMG as a VPN server, you can create and manage site-to-site VPN connections over pubic or shared networks such as the Internet. A site-to-site connection connects two portions of a private network. This site-to-site connection can be made between two TMG VPN gateways, or between TMG and a non-TMG VPN gateway that supports the same tunneling protocol.

There are three VPN protocols for site-to-site connections:

■ Point-to-Point Tunneling Protocol (PPTP)

■ Layer Two Tunneling Protocol (L2TP) over Internet Protocol security (IPsec)

■ Internet Protocol security (IPsec) tunnel mode

Depending on security requirements and type of routers involved, you can decide which VPN protocol to use for site-to-site connections. Table 27-1 summarizes how and when to use these three protocols.

TABLE 27-1 The Three Site-to-Site VPN Protocols

PROTOCOL	WHEN TO USE	SECURITY LEVEL	COMMENTS
IPsec tunnel mode	Connecting to a third-party VPN server	High	This is the only option you can use if you are connecting to a non-Microsoft VPN server.
L2TP over IPsec	Connecting to another TMG, ISA Server 2006, ISA Server 2004, ISA Server 2000 computer, or Windows VPN server	High	Uses Routing and Remote Access. Less complicated than the IPsec tunnel solution, but requires that the remote VPN server be a TMG, ISA server, or Windows VPN server.
PPTP	Connecting to another TMG, ISA Server 2006, ISA Server 2004, ISA Server 2000 computer, or Windows VPN server	Moderate	Uses Routing and Remote Access. Same restrictions as L2TP, but slightly easier to configure. L2TP is considered more secure because it uses IPsec encryption.

MORE INFO For more information about these VPN protocols, please visit *http://technet .microsoft.com/en-us/library/cc302474.aspx.*

In this chapter we will cover how to create a site-to-site VPN tunnel between two TMG VPN gateways using PPTP and L2TP over IPsec and how to troubleshoot VPN connection issues depending upon the type of VPN protocol being used.

Configuring L2TP Over IPsec Site-to-Site VPN

In this scenario, Fabrikam, Inc., has merged with Contoso, Inc., and the network teams have decided that the first goal of the network merge is to provide a site-to-site VPN connection through which users in either domain will be able to access the Web servers located on either location. Eventually the domains will be merged, but until then, a site-to-site VPN is configured to provide access to resources.

For either of the locations to connect to the Web servers and manage them, the protocols HTTP, HTTPS, and RDP must be allowed to pass through. You also need to ensure that site-to-site VPN traffic is encrypted using IP Security (IPsec); hence we will configure a site-to-site VPN tunnel using L2TP (Layer 2 Tunneling Protocol) over IPsec. We can use either a pre-shared key for mutual authentication or digital certificates when choosing L2TP over IPsec. For the sake of simplicity we will use pre-shared keys in our setup because pre-shared key authentication does not require the hardware and configuration investment of a public key infrastructure (PKI), which is necessary for using computer certificates for IPsec authentication. Pre-shared keys are simple to configure on a local VPN server.

NOTE If you want a long-term, strong authentication method, you should consider using a PKI. This requires installation of digital certificates from the same certification authority on both the local and the remote VPN servers. For more information about digital certificates, see *http://technet.microsoft.com/en-us/library/cc302474.aspx*.

Use the following steps to configure the Contoso site to accept and initiate an L2TP over IPsec site-to-site VPN connection with the Fabrikam site. The configuration at the Fabrikam site will be functionally identical, except for specific data points that we will point out along the way.

1. Open the TMG management console and select Remote Access Policy (VPN) in the left pane.

2. In the center pane, click the Remote Sites tab.

3. In the right pane, click Create VPN Site-To-Site Connection as shown in Figure 27-1.

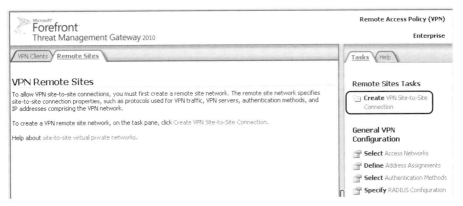

FIGURE 27-1 VPN configuration context

4. On the Welcome To The Create VPN Site-To-Site Connection Wizard page, enter the name of the remote site as shown in Figure 27-2.

NOTE The name you enter here *must* match a user account in the Contoso domain. You may create this account before or after completing the VPN connection configuration at both sites, but this account *must* exist before connection can be established from the Fabrikam site. The only requirement for this account is that it should be an active user account. You should treat this account as you would any other service-level account; in other words, use it only for this purpose.

Type **Fabrikam_Contoso** for the site-to-site network name and click Next.

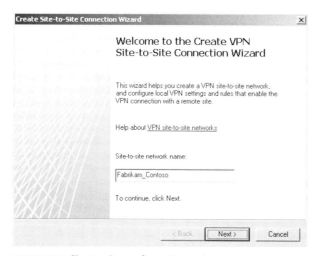

FIGURE 27-2 Site-to-site configuration welcome page

5. On the VPN Protocol page, select Layer Two Tunneling Protocol (L2TP) Over IPsec and click Next. You will see a warning as shown in Figure 27-3. Click OK to close the warning.

FIGURE 27-3 VPN account warning

6. On the Local Network VPN Settings page, click Dynamic Host Configuration Protocol (DHCP) as shown in Figure 27-4. This is used to assign IP addresses dynamically from a DHCP server in Contoso for VPN clients connecting between Contoso and Fabrikam.

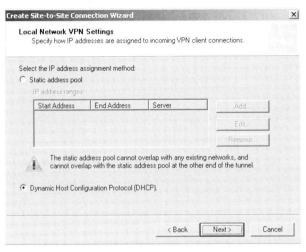

FIGURE 27-4 Local Network VPN Settings page

MORE INFO If you would like to use a Static Address Range, follow the steps used in "Configuring PPTP Site-to-Site VPN."

7. On the Remote Site Gateway settings page, enter the name or IP address of the remote site VPN server as shown in Figure 27-5 and click Next.

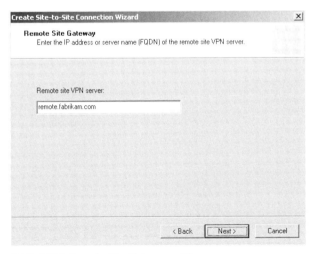

FIGURE 27-5 Remote Site Gateway settings

8. On the Local Network VPN Settings page, click Next.

9. On the Remote Authentication page, enter the account used by the Contoso VPN server to connect to the Fabrikam VPN server; in this case, **Fabrikam_Contoso.** Enter the domain (**Fabrikam**) and the account password, as shown in Figure 27-6, and click Next.

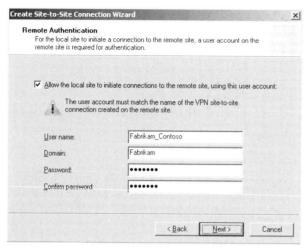

FIGURE 27-6 Fabrikam domain account credentials

NOTE The name of the site-to-site network at the Fabrikam VPN server must match this account name or the VPN connection initiated from the Contoso server will fail.

10. On the L2TP/IPsec Outgoing Authentication settings page, enter a pre-shared key as shown in Figure 27-7. This will be used for mutual authentication between the two VPN Servers at Fabrikam and Contoso.

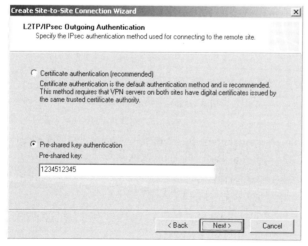

FIGURE 27-7 L2TP/IPsec Outgoing Authentication settings

11. On the Incoming L2TP/IPsec Authentication settings page, enter the same pre-shared key as shown in Figure 27-8. This key is the same one the one used in step 10 and is used for authenticating incoming L2TP over IPsec connections from Fabrikam to Contoso.

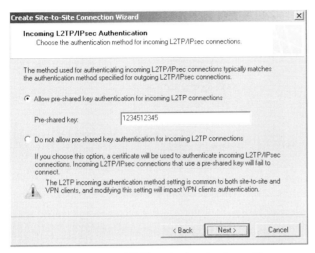

FIGURE 27-8 Incoming L2TP/IPsec Authentication settings

12. On the Network Addresses page, click Add to create an address range that matches the Fabrikam internal network.

13. On the IP Address Range Properties page, type **172.16.100.1 – 172.31.100.250**.

14. On the Network Addresses page, click Next.

15. On the Remote NLB Addresses page, clear the check box The Remote Site Is Enabled For Network Load Balancing and click Next.

> **NOTE** If the remote site uses NLB, *you must always select virtual IPs (VIPs) for site-to-site VPN connections.*

16. On the Site-To-Site Network Rule page, the Contoso and Fabrikam network administrators wish to define a routed relationship, so you must leave the default options selected and click Next.

17. On the Site-To-Site Network Access Rule page, click Add to include the protocols required by the Contoso and Fabrikam Web administrators.

18. On the Add Protocols page, add the HTTP, HTTPS, and RDP protocols by selecting each and clicking Add in turn and then click OK.

19. On the Site-To-Site Network Access Rule page, verify that the protocol selection appears as shown in Figure 27-9 and then click Next.

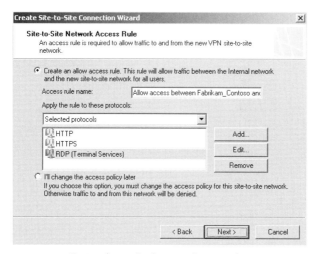

FIGURE 27-9 Protocols required across the tunnel

20. On the Completing The New VPN Site-To-Site Network Wizard page, verify that the summary matches the definition you desire and then click Finish.

21. You will see a warning, as shown in Figure 27-10, describing the possible need to restart the Routing and Remote Access service to complete the configuration and the adverse effect this will have on existing VPN connections. Click OK.

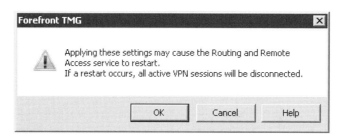

FIGURE 27-10 VPN configuration warning

22. In the TMG management console center pane, click Apply to commit the changes. When you do this, you will see an informational dialog box as shown in Figure 27-11 listing additional steps you may need to take for the VPN connection to work. Take note of these steps and click OK to close the dialog box.

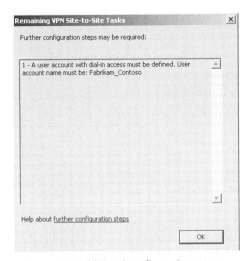

FIGURE 27-11 Additional configuration steps

For the site-to-site VPN connection to work, you must perform similar (though *not* identical) configuration actions at the Fabrikam TMG server. As part of that process, the following steps will change:

- **Step 4**   You must enter **Fabrikam_Contoso** as the network name and also ensure that the Fabrikam domain has a user with the same name and dial-in permissions.

- **Step 6**   You must enter the Internet IP address or URL used to connect to the Contoso TMG server.

- **Step 9**   You must enter an account name of **Fabrikam**, a domain of **contoso.com,** and the password of the fabrikam user account in the contoso.com domain.

- **Step 13**   You must enter the internal address range of the Contoso network.

If the hosts in each site do not use TMG as part of their default route, you will have to create static route entries on any host which is expected to communicate through the VPN tunnel. Assuming that TMG is assigned the first IP address in its Internal network address range, these routing table commands would be entered as shown here:

- **Contoso hosts   route -p add 172.16.100.0 mask 255.240.0.0 "Internal IP of Contoso TMG"**

Similarly, for Fabrikam hosts you will have to add the route for the IP address range of Contoso with the default gateway as the Internal IP of Fabrikam TMG.

After the VPN configuration is completed at each site, the connections should connect automatically and the Web administrators and users on each site should have access to the other's Web services.

Configuring PPTP Site-to-Site VPN

In this scenario, Contoso, Inc., has merged with Litware, LLC, and the network teams have decided that the first goal of the network merge is to provide a site-to-site VPN connection through which they will share e-mail between Contoso and Litware servers. Eventually they will merge their domains, but this is not required now. Figure 27-12 illustrates the desired traffic relationship for this effort.

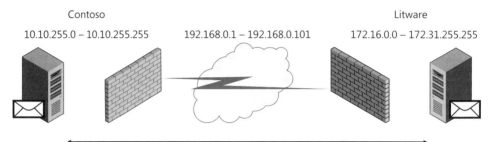

Contoso
10.10.255.0 – 10.10.255.255

192.168.0.1 – 192.168.0.101

Litware
172.16.0.0 – 172.31.255.255

FIGURE 27-12 Contoso and Litware merge scenario

Because each site has an SMTP server, and because each server must be manageable from either end of the tunnel, you must allow SMTP and RDP traffic between the two sites.

Use the following steps to configure the Contoso site to accept and initiate a PPTP site-to-site VPN connection with the Litware site. The configuration at the Litware site will be functionally identical, except for specific data points that we will point out along the way.

1. Open the TMG management console and select Remote Access Policy (VPN) in the left pane.

2. In the center pane, click the Remote Sites tab.

3. In the right pane, click Create VPN Site-To-Site Connection as shown in Figure 27-13.

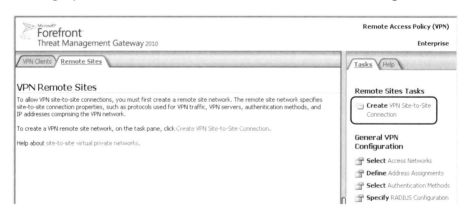

FIGURE 27-13 VPN configuration context

4. On the Welcome To The Create VPN Site-To-Site Connection Wizard page, enter the name of the remote site as shown in Figure 27-14.

Type **Litware** in the Site-To-Site Network Name text box and click Next.

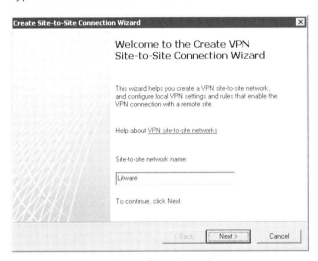

FIGURE 27-14 Site-to-site configuration welcome page

5. On the VPN Protocol page, select Point-To-Point Tunneling Protocol and click Next. You will see a warning, as shown in Figure 27-15, that discusses the same points made in the note about step 4. Click OK to close the warning.

FIGURE 27-15 VPN account warning

6. On the Local Network VPN Settings page, click Add to provide an address range to be used for the VPN connection between Contoso and Litware.

7. In the Server IP Address Range Properties dialog box, select the TMG server name in the Select The Server drop-down list and enter the address range specified earlier in Figure 27-12: **192.168.0.1 – 192.168.0.101** as shown in Figure 27-16, and then click OK.

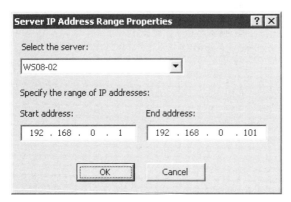

FIGURE 27-16 Local VPN connection address range dialog box

NOTE TMG adds the defined client VPN connections to the number of defined site-to-site VPN connections to determine the total number of required addresses. Because TMG must own at least one address (depending on the type of VPN connection being established), the total addresses defined must be at least one address larger than the total number of dial-in VPN clients plus the total number of site-to-site connections. If you specify an address range that is too small, you will see a warning dialog as shown in Figure 27-17.

FIGURE 27-17 Insufficient address range warning

8. On the Local Network VPN Settings page, click Next.

9. On the Remote Site Gateway page, type in the IP address of the Litware VPN server (**10.10.0.15** in this example), and then click Next.

10. On the Remote Authentication page, type in the account used by the Contoso VPN server to connect to the Litware VPN server (**Contoso** in this case). Type in the domain (**Litware.com**) and the account password, as shown in Figure 27-18, and click Next.

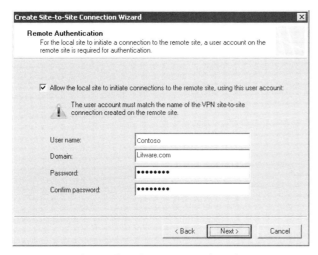

FIGURE 27-18 Litware domain account credentials

NOTE The name of the site-to-site network at the Litware VPN server must match this account name or the VPN connection initiated from the Contoso server will fail.

11. On the Network Addresses page, click Add to create an address range that matches the Litware internal network.

12. In the IP Address Range Properties dialog box, type **172.16.0.0 – 172.31.255.255** as shown in Figure 27-19 and click OK.

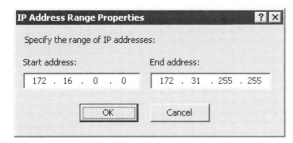

FIGURE 27-19 Litware internal address range

13. On the Network Addresses page, click Next.

14. On the Remote NLB Addresses page, clear the check box The Remote Site Is Enabled For Network Load Balancing and click Next.

NOTE If the remote site uses NLB, you must always select Virtual IPs (VIPs) for site-to-site VPN connections.

15. On the Site-To-Site Network Rule page, the Contoso and Litware network administrators wish to define a routed relationship, so you must leave the default options selected and click Next.

16. On the Site-To-Site Network Access Rule page, click Add to include the protocols required by the Contoso and Litware mail administrators as shown in Figure 27-20.

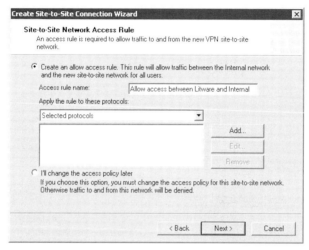

FIGURE 27-20 Site-To-Site Network Access Rule page

17. On the Add Protocols page, add the SMTP and RDP protocols by selecting each and clicking Add in turn. Click OK.

18. On the Site-To-Site Network Access Rule page, verify that the protocol list appears as shown in Figure 27-21 and then click Next.

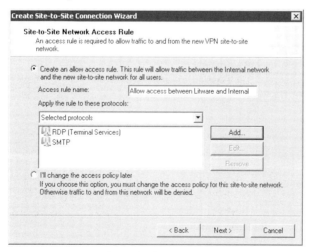

FIGURE 27-21 Protocols required across the tunnel

19. On the Completing The New VPN Site-To-Site Network Wizard page, verify that the summary matches the definition you desire and then click Finish.

20. You will see a warning, as shown in Figure 27-22, describing the possible need to restart the Routing and Remote Access service to complete the configuration and the adverse effect this will have on existing VPN connections. Click OK.

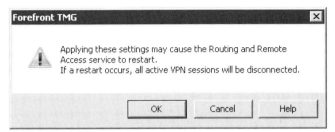

FIGURE 27-22 VPN configuration warning

21. In the TMG management console center pane, click Apply to commit the changes. When you do this, you will see an informational dialog box as shown in Figure 27-23 listing additional steps you may need to take for the VPN connection to work. Take note of these steps and click OK to close the dialog box.

FIGURE 27-23 Additional configuration steps

For the site-to-site VPN connection to work, you must perform similar (though *not* identical) configuration actions at the Litware TMG server. As part of that process, the following steps will change:

- **Step 4** You must type in **Contoso** as the network name.
- **Step 7** You must select a server in the Litware array and enter an IP address range that matches the one defined at the Contoso side of the connection.

- **Step 9** You must enter the Internet IP address or a resolvable fully qualified domain name of the Contoso TMG server.

- **Step 10** You must type in the account name **Litware**, the domain **contoso.com,** and the password of the Litware user account in the contoso.com domain.

- **Step 12** You must type in the internal address range of the Contoso network: **10.10.255.0 – 10.10.255.255**.

If the hosts in each site do not use TMG as part of their default route, you will have to create static route entries on any host that is expected to communicate through the VPN tunnel. Assuming that TMG is assigned the first IP address in its Internal network address range, these routing table commands would be entered as shown here:

- **Contoso hosts**   route -p add 172.16.0.0 mask 255.240.0.0 10.10.255.1

- **Litware hosts**   route -p add 10.10.255.0 mask 255.255.255.0 172.16.0.1

After the VPN configuration is completed at each site, the connections should connect automatically and the SMTP administrators in each site should have access to the other's SMTP services.

Troubleshooting VPN Client Connections

In general, troubleshooting VPN connections is very much like troubleshooting any other client/server traffic path. Troubleshooting VPN connections differs from troubleshooting other traffic flow problems in the negotiated, encrypted nature of the VPN connection. What you must understand before trying to troubleshoot any connection is the way the various protocols are used to establish and manage the VPN tunnel. The following protocol descriptions are intentionally limited to only those behaviors you can observe using a network capture tool such as Network Monitor 3.

PPTP

Unlike L2TP/IPsec and SSTP, PPTP defines an unencrypted control channel that operates using TCP port 1723 separate from the actual VPN tunnel that uses IP protocol 47 (GRE). This makes PPTP a bit easier to troubleshoot than the other VPN protocols because they embed the control channel within the encrypted tunnel.

> **MORE INFO**   The PPTP protocol is defined in RFC 2637. You can read more about this at *http://www.ietf.org/rfc/rfc2637.txt*.

Figure 27-24 shows the network stack relationship for the main protocols involved in a PPTP VPN connection.

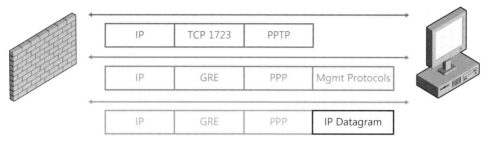

FIGURE 27-24 PPTP protocol stack relationships

Because the control channel is external to the encrypted tunnel, you can observe much of the process that controls tunnel behavior.

The PPTP control channel provides initial authentication, encryption negotiation, and VPN tunnel management. All of the remaining data exchanged between the VPN client and server passes within the GRE tunnel. PPTP connections operate as described in Figure 27-25 and the following list.

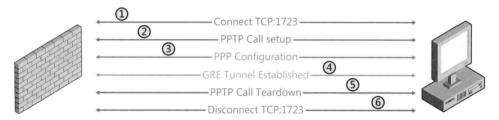

FIGURE 27-25 PPTP session process

1. The client connects to the server on TCP port 1723.

2. The client and server use PPTP messages to negotiate the VPN connection specifics, such as data framing, caller capabilities, and the CallID for each end of the connection.

3. The client and server use the following protocols within PPP over GRE to define the tunnel operating parameters:

   a. Link Configuration Protocol (LCP) to negotiate additional connection specifics, such as the authentication protocol and data compression

   b. Challenge Handshake Protocol (CHAP) to authenticate the user

   c. Callback Configuration Protocol (CBCP) to negotiate callback capabilities

   d. Internet Protocol Configuration Protocol (IPCP) or Internet Protocol v6 Configuration Protocol (IPv6CP) to assign the IP address and DNS servers for the client

   e. Compression Configuration protocol (CCP) to negotiate the tunnel compression algorithm

4. The client and server exchange all other data using PPP over GRE.

5. When the client or server ends the session, they use PPTP and LCP over PPP over GRE to negotiate graceful tunnel teardown.

6. The session ends when the client or server closes the PPTP control channel on TCP port 1723.

L2TP over IPsec

In L2TP/IPsec VPN connections, IPsec is used to authenticate the two hosts through certificates or pre-shared keys and then provide an encrypted tunnel within which the user authenticates to the VPN server using PPP within L2TP. L2TP and PPP provide the tunnel management from that point on. You should be aware that you cannot see beyond the IPsec protocol using a network capture tool.

> **MORE INFO**   L2TP over IPsec is defined in RFC 2661 and RFC 3193. You can read more about this at *http://www.faqs.org/rfcs/rfc2661.html* and *http://www.ietf.org/rfc/rfc3193.txt*.

IPsec ESP

Figure 27-26 shows the network stack relationship for the main protocols involved in an L2TP over native IPsec VPN connection.

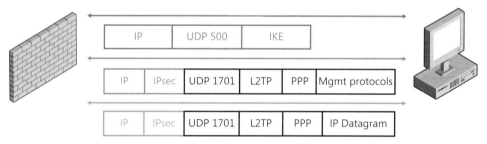

FIGURE 27-26 L2TP over native IPsec protocol stack relationships

L2TP over IPsec ESP connections operate as illustrated in Figure 27-27 and the following list.

FIGURE 27-27 L2TP over IPsec ESP

1. The client initiates Internet Key Exchange (IKE) main mode to the server on UDP port 500. As part of this negotiation, they do the following:

   a. Exchange their encryption keys. The key is derived from the certificate or pre-shared key depending on the configuration chosen.

   b. Perform NAT discovery by exchanging a hash representing their own IP and port for this conversation. If the receiver calculates a different hash for the sender's IP and port, the receiver uses IPsec NAT-T for the remaining communications.

2. The client initiates IKE quick mode over UDP port 500 to finalize the key exchange and negotiate the encryption to be used in the VPN tunnel.

3. The client establishes a VPN tunnel using PPP over L2TP over IPsec ESP.

4. When the client and server end the session, they exchange IKE informational messages over UDP port 500.

IPsec NAT-T

Figure 27-28 shows the network stack relationship for the main protocols involved in an LT2P over IPsec NAT-T VPN connection.

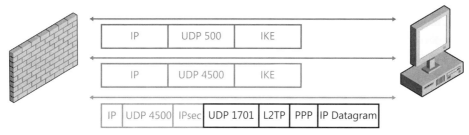

FIGURE 27-28 L2TP over IPsec NAT-T protocol stack relationships

L2TP over IPsec NAT-T connections operate as illustrated in Figure 27-29 and the following list.

FIGURE 27-29 L2TP over IPsec NAT-T

1. The client initiates Internet Key Exchange (IKE) main mode to the server on UDP port 500. As part of this negotiation, they do the following:

   a. Exchange their encryption keys. The key is derived from the certificate or pre-shared key depending on the configuration chosen.

b. Perform NAT discovery by exchanging a hash representing their own IP and port for this conversation. If the receiver calculates a different hash for the sender's IP and port, the receiver uses IPsec NAT-T for the remaining communications.

2. The client initiates IKE quick mode over UDP port 4500 to finalize the key exchange and negotiate the encryption to be used in the VPN tunnel.

3. The client establishes a VPN tunnel using PPP over L2TP over IPsec ESP over UDP port 4500.

4. When the client and server end the session, they exchange IKE informational messages over UDP port 500.

SSTP

In SSTP connections, SSL is used to authenticate the server and user authentication is handled using either user certificate or PPP within the HTTPS tunnel. You should be aware that you cannot see beyond the SSL protocol using a network capture tool.

> **MORE INFO** The SSTP protocol is defined by MS protocol document SSTP 15.2.1.1.12, available at *http://msdn.microsoft.com/en-us/library/cc239916.aspx*.

Figure 27-30 shows the network stack relationship for the main protocols involved in an SSTP VPN connection.

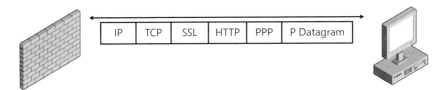

| IP | TCP | SSL | HTTP | PPP | P Datagram |

FIGURE 27-30 SSTP protocol stack relationships

SSTP connections operate as illustrated in Figure 27-31 and the following list.

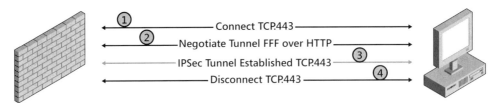

① — Connect TCP.443 →
② — Negotiate Tunnel FFF over HTTP →
③ — IPSec Tunnel Established TCP.443 —
④ — Disconnect TCP.443 →

FIGURE 27-31 L2TP over IPsec NAT-T

1. The client connects to the server on TCP port 443.

2. The client and server use SSL or TLS protocol to authenticate and negotiate the encryption to be used in the VPN tunnel.

3. The client passes all tunnel management and application traffic through the SSL tunnel using PPP frames within HTTP.

4. When the client or server wishes to end the session, it negotiates this within the SSTP tunnel, then gracefully closes the TCP port 443 connection.

Common Errors and Likely Causes

The following list provides some examples of the more common errors encountered for the various VPN protocols supported by TMG:

- PPTP connection fails at "Verifying username and password" (Error 809). The most likely reason for this failure is that something between the client and server is blocking TCP port 1723 or the server is not configured to accept PPTP connections.

- PPTP connection fails at "Verifying username and password" (Error 806). Assuming the user credentials are correct, the most likely reason for this failure is that something between the client and server is blocking the GRE protocol.

- L2TP connection fails with "certificate could not be found" (Error 766). There are multiple potential causes for this error:
  - An IPsec certificate cannot be located on the client.
  - An IPsec certificate was located, but was not issued by a trusted certificate authority.
  - The VPN connection authentication should be defined as using a pre-shared key.

- L2TP connection failed (Error 789). IKE Main mode could not be started. The most likely cause is that something between the client and server is blocking UDP port 500 or the server is not configured to accept L2TP over IPsec connections.

- SSTP connection fails at "Connecting to ..." (Error 809). The most likely reason for this failure is that something between the client and server is blocking TCP port 443 or the server is not configured to accept SSTP connections.

- SSTP connection fails with "The certificate's CN name does not match the passed value" (Error 0x800B010F). There are two likely causes for this:
  - The data entered in the client's VPN connector General tab Host Name Or IP Address field does not match the data contained in the SSTP server's Subject attribute.
  - The wrong server certificate was chosen for the SSTP listener.

- SSTP connection fails with "The server certificate revocation state could not be verified." You should ensure that the Certificate Revocation List (CRL) URL is available to the SSTP clients. If the CRL does not contain a URL that is reachable by the clients, you will have to reissue the certificate with a new CRL.

> **MOREINFO** You can read more about certificate revocation on TechNet at *http://technet.microsoft.com/en-us/library/bb457027.aspx* and about CRL specification at *http://technet.microsoft.com/en-us/library/cc753296.aspx*.

Summary

In this chapter we covered the use of site-to-site VPN and what the different types of VPN protocols are that can be used in a site-to-site VPN. We also covered how to configure a site-to-site VPN using PPTP protocol and using L2TP over IPsec protocol. We ended by looking at how to troubleshoot issues related to VPN connections depending upon the type of protocol being used. In the next chapter we will discuss how logging works and why logging is important for administrators to monitor and troubleshoot various issues on TMG.

## PART IX

Logging and Reporting

CHAPTER 28 Logging **797**

CHAPTER 29 Enhanced NAT **817**

CHAPTER 30 Scripting TMG **829**

Logging

- Why Logging Is Important **797**

- Configuring TMG Logging **800**

- Logging Best Practices **809**

- Summary **815**

L̲ogging is one of the most important firewall functions for network and security management. Logging offers a great deal of information about what is happening on and around the firewall and gives detailed information about who is accessing what through the firewall and possible attacks or probes. In this chapter we will discuss why logging is important, improvements in logging in Forefront TMG, how to configure logging in TMG, various options available for logging in TMG, and the best practices around logging in TMG.

Why Logging Is Important

Logging is one of the most important functions on a firewall for network and security management. As a security and firewall administrator, it is important for you to keep a record of the changes happening on the firewall, keep a detailed record of the end-user activity through the firewall, and monitor any attacks that are happening in the network aimed at or through the firewall. Logging is considered important to security and firewall administrators for the following reasons:

- **Tracking User Activity** A lot of companies need to keep records of all end-user activity passing through the firewall. When user activity through the firewall is tracked, you should be able to provide detailed logs of which sites the user has visited and how long the user remained online for the duration of the day. This information can also treated as evidentiary material. To support the use of log information as evidentiary material, no user should be able to pass through the firewall unless there is a backup logging mechanism that can be used for logging and later merged with the original logs in the event that the primary logging mechanism fails.

- **Troubleshooting** You can use logs to troubleshoot a lot of issues. The simplest way to determine whether any traffic is being blocked by the firewall and what port or IP address is being blocked by the firewall is to see these events in the logs. Custom applications often require custom ports that sometimes aren't documented well enough for firewall administrators to follow. In those cases, you can use logs to easily determine what ports are being blocked and create rules to allow those ports.

- **Network Health** You can use logs to review the health of your network. This means that you can see network utilization and traffic patterns. You can also determine whether any specific host is generating too much traffic and whether there is a DoS attack on the network. Some of the attacks may be short in duration and therefore will never be caught, but by analyzing the logs you can determine a pattern and create policies to block such attacks or isolate compromised hosts.

- **Change Tracking** For security, it is important that any change made on the firewall is tracked, and if needed, there should be a way to revert back to the original configuration extant before the change was made. Although most companies follow strict guidelines around any change made to their firewalls, mistakes are possible. Therefore, change tracking logs should be available to evaluate the nature of any changes to the firewall configuration so that if a configuration error is made, it can be rectified quickly.

New Firewall and Web Proxy Log Fields

In addition to the log fields included with ISA Server, TMG includes a great many new fields to support the new TMG, TMG Client, Forefront Client Security, and UAG functionality. Rather than inundate you with a list all of the log fields, we'll limit the following list to the most interesting in terms of TMG functionality and troubleshooting.

> **MORE INFO** Full details of the TMG Firewall Log fields are available at *http://technet .microsoft.com/en-us/library/cc995278.aspx* and full details of the TMG Web Proxy Log fields are available at *http://technet.microsoft.com/en-us/library/cc995299.aspx*.

TMG Client Fields

The TMG Client (TMGC) offers some new functionality in that it is able to provide much more information about the application, user, and operating environment than the ISA Firewall client was able to. However, this new functionality isn't usable as part of your TMG policies, but it is available in the Firewall log when you choose these fields:

- **Firewall Client Application File Version** This field contains the file version of the Winsock application, as seen on the Details tab of the file properties page.

- **Firewall Client Application Internal Name** This field contains the description of the Winsock application, as seen on the Details tab of the file properties page.

- **Firewall Client Application Original File Name**   This field contains the original file version of the Winsock application, as seen on the Details tab of the file properties page.

- **Firewall Client Application Product Name**   This field contains the product name of the Winsock application, as seen on the Details tab of the file properties page.

- **Firewall Client Application Product Version**   This field contains the product version of the Winsock application, as seen on the Details tab of the file properties page.

- **Firewall Client Application SHA1 Hash**   This field contains the hash value of the Winsock application executable calculated using the SHA1 has algorithm.

- **Firewall Client Application Trust State**   This field provides the trust state of the Winsock application as determined by the TMG client. This state is only relevant when the Forefront Client Security (FCS) client is also installed on the TMGC-enabled computer.

- **Firewall Client FQDN**   This field includes the FQDN of the TMGC-enabled computer.

- **Fwc Application Path**   This field contains the full path of the executable making Winsock calls.

Enhanced Malware Inspection (EMP) Fields

With the introduction of Malware Inspection, TMG introduces new fields in logging that help administrators keep a track of content that was inspected and delivered back to the users.

- **Content Delivery Method**   This field indicates whether fast or slow trickling was used to deliver the content to the user.

- **Malware Inspection Action**   This field provides an indicator of the EMP action taken for the traffic that triggered this log entry. This field should be one of your primary log fields to scan when you're troubleshooting traffic flow.

- **Malware Inspection Duration**   Regardless of the EMP results, this field will contain the amount of time in milliseconds (mS) EMP took to scan the content.

- **Malware Inspection Result**   This field indicates whether EMP was successful in scanning the content. For instance, user cancellation, or Web server connection closure before the content is fully received, will generate an EMP error and this field will contain that result code.

- **Threat Name**   When EMP action is logged, this field will contain the name of the threat as understood by EMP.

- **Threat Level**   When EMP action is logged, this field will contain the severity or level of threat as understood by EMP.

Network Inspection (NIS) Fields

The Network Inspection provides intrusion prevention and intrusion detection capabilities. As a result, new logs that correspond to actions taken by NIS are introduced in TMG, helping administrators keep track of traffic as passed and inspected by NIS.

- **NIS Scan Result**   This field provides an indicator of the NIS action taken for the traffic that triggered this log entry. This field should be one of your primary log fields to scan when you're troubleshooting traffic flow.

- **NIS Signature**   If the NIS Scan Result is blocked or detected, this field will indicate which NIS signature triggered this action.

- **NIS Application Protocol**   When NIS action is logged, this field will contain the application protocol understood by NIS.

Configuring TMG Logging

TMG logging offers several options that you will want to understand so that you can configure them to best suit your needs and environment. Keep in mind that if you choose any logging destination other than SQL Express, you will be presented with a warning dialog as shown in Figure 28-1.

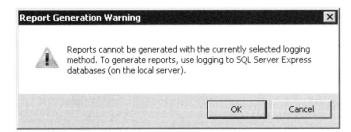

FIGURE 28-1 Report generation warning dialog

   This limitation is due to the fact that the SQL Reporting Services instance used by TMG for report generation only operates against the local SQL Server Express instance.

Common Logging Options

The Firewall and Web Proxy logs share many configuration settings in common, such as the following:

- **Log type**   TMG can be configured to send log data to SQL server or a text file.

- **Log destination**   When TMG writes to SQL, TMG can send log data to a SQL instance on the local computer or a remote SQL instance.

- **Log format**   When TMG writes to text logs, you can configure TMG to write the logs to ISA- or W3C-formatted logs.

- **Log file maintenance**   When TMG is using local-host SQL or text logging, TMG can manage log retention and disk space usage.

- **Enable logging**   TMG can be configured to write no log data at all when this option is disabled.

To configure TMG logging options, follow these steps:

1. Open the TMG management console.

2. Expand Forefront TMG (*ArrayName*).

3. Select Logs And Reports.

4. In the right pane, select Configure Firewall Logging as indicated in Figure 28-2.

> **NOTE** Because the Firewall and Web Proxy logging options are identical except for the log fields, we'll use only the Firewall log for the following process.

FIGURE 28-2 Log configuration options

Figure 28-3 shows the default options for the Firewall and Web Proxy logs.

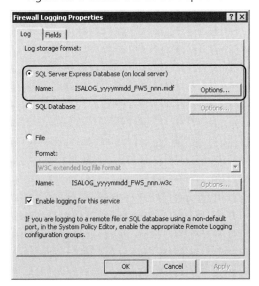

FIGURE 28-3 Default log options

These options define the following functionality:

- **SQL Server Express Database (On Local Server)** This option configures TMG to use a SQL Server 2008 Express instance on the local computer. Functionally, this is identical to logging to a central SQL server except that only the local TMG instance may log into this database. This limitation is due to the SQL Server Express configuration and by TMG policies. SQL Server Express is configured by the TMG installer so that it only accepts shared memory connections, as shown in Figure 28-4. This configuration, along with the TMG default firewall policy that disallows SQL connections to the TMG computer, effectively reduces the attack surface of the TMG computer.

> **NOTE** The configuration shown in Figure 28-3 is accessible through All Programs, Microsoft SQL Server 2008, Configuration Tools, SQL Server Configuration Manager.

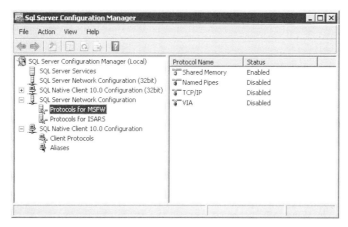

FIGURE 28-4 Default SQL Express network configuration

- **SQL Database** This option configures TMG to log all data to a SQL Server instance on a remote server or the local computer. Functionally, this is identical to logging onto a local SQL Express instance except that TMG no longer manages disk space consumption and the network connection becomes an important factor in logging.

- **File** This option configures TMG to use text-file logging in one of two formats. The primary distinctions for file-based logging vs. SQL-based logging are:
  - Text logs can be compressed
  - Text logs consume the least system resources
  - You cannot perform historical queries in the log viewer

- **Enable Logging For This Service** As you might have guessed, this turns logging on or off for the firewall or Web Proxy service. This is most frequently used to help isolate performance problems.

Log File and Disk Space Controls

Figure 28-5 shows the default options for log file options. With the exception of file compression, the defaults are the same for SQL Express and local text logging. These options are not available for SQL Database logging.

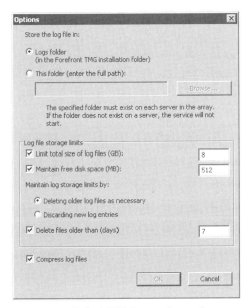

FIGURE 28-5 Default SQL Express log options

These options control TMG logging behavior in the following ways:

- **ISALogs Folder**   This option determines the location of the log files. The default selection of ISALogs folder places the database files in the %ProgramFiles%\Microsoft ISA Server\ISALogs folder, where %ProgramFiles% is typically found as C:\Program Files.

- **This Folder (Enter The Full Path)**   This option allows you to select any location on the TMG computer for the database files.

- **Limit Total Size Of Log Files (GB)**   This option allows you to specify the maximum space in GB that may be consumed by all of the log files used by this service (Firewall or Web proxy). By default, TMG will delete logs starting with the oldest database files when the total size of the active log files exceeds 80 percent of this value. To prevent unexpected log data loss, you should keep a close watch on the logs to understand how your traffic load is reflected in the resulting database log file size.

- **Maintain Free Disk Space (MB)** This option allows you to specify the minimum space available on the drive in MB at which TMG will start to delete old logs related to this service. As with the total log file size limit, it's a good idea to keep a close watch on your logs to understand what limits are appropriate for your environment.

- **Maintain Log Storage Limits By (Deleting Old Log Files As Necessary)** This option instructs TMG to delete log files starting with the oldest active logs.

> **IMPORTANT** Because TMG queries SQL Server Express for the database file list, if any of the database files have been disconnected from SQL Server Express, they are not visible to TMG and will not be deleted. Thus, you should ensure that you delete or reattach any databases you detach so that TMG can manage the disk space properly.

- **Maintain Log Storage Limits By (Discarding New Log Entries)** This option causes TMG to cease logging for this service until the logging control point that triggered this action is corrected.

> **IMPORTANT** If you select this option, TMG will not log *anything* for this service until the trigger state is corrected. The log data lost during this time *is not recoverable*. Therefore, this option should only be used during extreme service outages caused by logging failure.

- **Delete Log Files Older Than (Days)** This option causes TMG to remove log files older than the number of days specified in this field. Even if file and disk space constraints are within specified limits, if a log file date is older than specified in this option TMG will delete the file.

SQL Express

As indicated in Figure 28-4, SQL Express Database is the default configuration for TMG. Unlike ISA Server, this functionality cannot be removed through Control Panel, Programs and Features (Control Panel, Add/Remove Programs in Windows Server 2003). TMG Medium Business edition uses SQL Server 2005 Express for local SQL logging, whereas TMG 2010 uses SQL Server 2008 Express. One of the benefits of using SQL Server 2008 Express is that the SQL 2008 Reporting Services do not require Internet Information Service (IIS) to be installed on the TMG computer. Having one less service to be concerned with is a *good thing*.

If you click the Options button, you are presented with the ability to change several aspects of SQL Express logging. SQL Server 2008 Express imposes limits on the database file sizes and TMG is designed to work within these constraints when monitoring the file size and disk space consumption.

The files created by SQL Server Express are located in the destination folder specified in Figure 28-5 as ISALOG_YYYYMMDD_SVC_###.ldf and ISALOG_YYYYMMDD_SVC_###.mdf, where:

- *YYYYMMDD* is the local system date—for example, 20090606.

- *SVC* is the relevant TMG service log. *FWS* is used for the firewall service log and *WEB* is used for the Web Proxy service log.

- *###* is the file index for the TMG service for that day. This number increments by one for each new logfile created during that day. If the traffic logs reach 80 percent of the maximum size (4 GB for SQL 2008 Express), TMG will instruct SQL Express to create a new logfile.

- *.ldf* is the SQL transaction log file for the log database file.

- *.mdf* is the actual database file.

Because SQL Server 2008 Express limits the size of database files to 4 GB (as opposed to MSDE, which limits database files to 2 GB), the default value of 8 GB for the maximum disk usage control may only allow two active log files if your TMG is tasked with a high daily traffic load. For this reason, you should keep a close watch on your log file sizes until you get a sense of the file sizes created by your traffic profile.

SQL Database

SQL database logging is unique for the following reasons:

- The log file maintenance is left to the SQL Server database administrators (DBA), so the log file controls used for SQL Express and text logging are unavailable.

- It is very dependent on the network and SQL Server responsiveness.

- It presents a different set of options that are unavailable for SQL Express or text logging. Figure 28-6 illustrates these options.

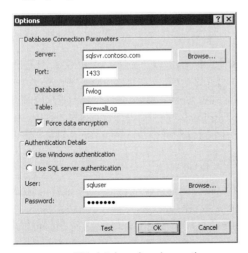

FIGURE 28-6 SQL database logging options

The Database Connection Parameters and Authentication Details sections define the primary criteria for TMG to use when sending log data to the SQL server instance. Similar data is used for SQL Express logging, but because this can be configured during TMG installation, and because TMG uses shared memory logging for SQL Express, there is no need to bother you with these details.

- **Server**   This field must contain the fully qualified name or IP address of the server that is hosting the TMG logging instance. In preference order, this field should be populated using:

  - **IP Address**   To avoid connectivity problems caused by name resolution errors.
  - **Fully Qualified Domain Name (FQDN)**   To reduce name resolution time.
  - **Unqualified Name**   This is the least reliable specification because it relies not only on name resolution, but also may also incur a dependency on domain name suffix devolution to determine the IP address of the SQL server.

- **Port**   Enter the listening port used by the remote SQL instance. Typically, this is 1433, but your database administrator (DBA) may have defined a custom port for various reasons.

- **Database**   Enter the name of the database provided by your DBA for TMG logging.

- **Table**   Enter the table designated for this service log within the selected database.

> **IMPORTANT**   Failure to provide accurate information for any of these fields will result in TMG failing to connect to the SQL instance for logging. TMG will log an alert and a Windows Application event log complaining about this state.

- **Use Windows Authentication**   If the SQL DBA has configured your SQL instance for Windows authentication, you must use this option.
- **Use SQL Server Authentication**   If the SQL DBA has configured your SQL instance for SQL authentication, you must use this option.

> **NOTE**   There is a great deal of disagreement as to whether Windows or SQL authentication represents the more secure authentication method. See *http://www .windowsecurity.com/articles/SQL_Server_2000_Authentication.html* for a fairly detailed discussion on this point. You will have to discuss this with your SQL DBA and come to agreement on this point before SQL Database logging will be usable.

- **Test button**   This allows you to validate the specified connection criteria as well as the network connectivity between TMG and the SQL server. An error encountered as a result of this test will be expressed in an error dialog, such as the one shown in Figure 28-7. You must correct any errors indicated through the test button before attempting to use SQL Database logging.

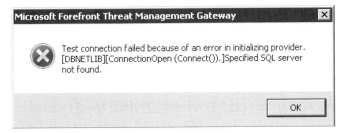

FIGURE 28-7 Name resolution failure error dialog

When you successfully complete the SQL Database configuration test and apply the new settings, you will be presented with a dialog, as shown in Figure 28-8, explaining the need to modify the system policies so that TMG can communicate with the SQL instance you've specified.

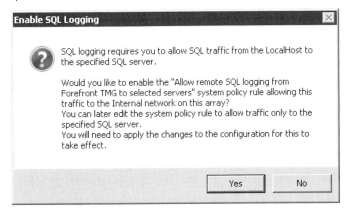

FIGURE 28-8 Initial SQL Database choice dialog

You should allow TMG to enable the default rule so that when the service restarts, the log destination service will be available. As noted in the choice dialog, you can (and should) edit the system policy later to limit the traffic to only the specified SQL server. One thing to consider when defining this limitation is that if you change to another SQL server, you must remember to change the system policy destination to agree with this change or you'll end up working in circles until you correct this state.

Local Text Logging

Text is the logging format that consumes the least resources, but like remote SQL logging, it also removes the option of historical log viewing. Unlike SQL Express and SQL database logs, you have the option of two log formats: Forefront TMG and W3C format. The differences between these two log formats are:

- **W3C** The filename follows the same format as with SQL Express, except that there is only one file per log and the log file extension is .w3c. Each log file begins with a header that is written in accordance with the standard defined by the World Wide Web Consortium (W3C).

```
#Software: Microsoft Forefront Threat Management Gateway Beta
#Version: 2.0
#Date: 2009-06-29 01:50:10
#Fields: computer        date        time        IP protocol        source
destination        original client IP        source network        destination
network        action        status        rule        application protocol
bytes sent        bytes sent intermediate        bytes received        bytes
received intermediate        connection time        connection time intermediate
username        agent        session ID        connection ID        NIS
scan result        NIS signature        NAT address        fwc-app-path
internal-service-info
TMG01        2009-06-29        01:50:10        UDP        10.10.255.127:60921
128.9.0.107:53        10.10.255.127        Internal        External
Denied        0x800704d0        None - see Result Code        DNS        0
0        0        0        -        -        -        -        0        0
-        -        ::        -        0
TMG01        2009-06-29        01:50:10        UDP        10.10.255.127:60921
198.41.0.4:53        10.10.255.127        Internal        External        Denied
0x800704d0        None - see Result Code        DNS        0        0        0
0        -        -        -        -        0        0        -        -
::        -        0
```

The log header identifies the log source, log format version, the GMT date this log file was started, and the log fields that may be seen in this log.

- **Forefront TMG**   The filename follows the same format as W3C, except that the file extension is .iis. TMG-format text logs do not include a header, but are written in a specific format that follows IIS log formatting:

```
TMG01, 6/28/2009, 18:54:01, UDP, 10.10.253.1:137, 10.10.253.255:137,
10.10.253.1, External, Local Host, Denied, 0xc004000d, Default rule, NetBios
Name Service, -, 0, 0, 0, 0, -, -, -, -, -, 0, 0, -, -, -, -, -, -, ::, -, -, -,
-, -, -, -, -, -, 0, -
```

In both formats, any log fields that were disabled through the Fields tab in the log configuration are written to the log as a dash (-) rather than simply leaving them empty. This is done to ensure that each log entry clearly consumes the same number of fields, whether they are used or not. Doing this ensures that any log analysis tools will have a consistent data format regardless of whether a specific field is actually used.

The primary disadvantage to using text logs is that they're a bit more difficult to search for specific data. Fortunately, plenty of tools are available to make this task easier for you. One such tool that will cost you absolutely nothing is LogParser, which is available at *http://www.microsoft.com/downloads/details.aspx?FamilyID=890cd06b-abf8-4c25-91b2-f8d975cf8c07*. This tool was written specifically to ease the task of performing statistical analysis on text logs, but eventually grew to handle much more.

Logging Queue

The new TMG logging queue was created to answer the problems caused when network and SQL server errors caused log failure in ISA Server. This mechanism buffers log batches while the log destination is unavailable. This queue saves each log batch in a binary file until the logging destination becomes available once again.

Log queue configuration is limited to a single factor—where to place the log queue. By default, the log queue is stored in the same place the TMG logs are stored: %ProgramFiles%\Microsoft ISA Server\ISALogs. As shown in Figure 28-9, you can change this and as you'll see in the next section, "Logging Best Practices," you absolutely should change this location.

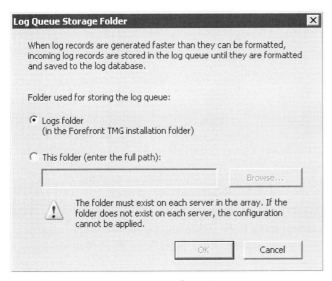

FIGURE 28-9 Log queue location configuration

Logging Best Practices

In general, you need to consider the following rules of thumb when deciding which logging options to choose:

- Local-host SQL logging is more expensive in terms of system resources (CPU, memory, and disk) than local-host text logging or either of the remote logging options.

- Remote logging incurs additional network traffic in direct proportion to the amount of traffic being processed by TMG. If you're thinking this is a circular statement, you're not wrong. The more traffic TMG processes, the more log data it will generate and thus, more log entries will be created.

- Regardless of the logging destination and format, the resources required to satisfy the logging are directly proportional to the log fields selected for each log.

Each logging method available on TMG has advantages and disadvantages, but ultimately the method that you will choose needs to be evaluated based on two core factors: environment needs and performance.

Collecting Information about Your Environment

Logging is an important subject on TMG because it allows you to better understand your traffic and also to perform postmortem analysis when troubleshooting issues such as failed to access some Web sites. To configure TMG logging to best fit the needs of your environment, you need to collect some information prior to starting the configuration:

- Does your company need to use historical or offline log viewer using TMG Console?
- Does your company have a SQL Server computer dedicated for logging?
- What connectivity does TMG have with SQL Server (100 Mbps, 1 Gbps, and so on)?
- Is your SQL Server computer configured for high availability (using clusters, for example)?
- Did you size your TMG to have enough disk space for local logging?
- Does your TMG have a separate disk just for logging?

The answers to these questions will lead you to choose between local logging or remote logging. Let's use the Contoso company as an example. They answered those questions saying: yes, yes, 1 Gbps, yes, no and no. These answers clearly lead the TMG administrator to choose SQL Server as the logging method.

Logging Options

After the initial assessment of your environment the next step is to understand the logging options and what each one can offer to best address your needs. Table 28-1 compares key elements for each logging option.

TABLE 28-1 Logging Comparison

KEY AREA	FILE	SQL SERVER EXPRESS (LOCAL)	SQL SERVER DATABASE
NETWORK CONSUMPTION	If the log is configured to be local there is no network consumption.	Because the log is local there is no network consumption.	It is recommended to have a 1 GB network connectivity between TMG and SQL Server.
LOG SIZE LIMIT	Each file is limited to 1.5 GB and a new file is automatically created in the same location where the logging is configured to be store (either local or remote).	Each file is limited to 1.5 GB and a new file is automatically created.	No limit and it relies on the SQL maintenance policy for data retention.

KEY AREA	FILE	SQL SERVER EXPRESS (LOCAL)	SQL SERVER DATABASE
SECURITY	Data is stored locally and even if the logging fails the TMG Firewall Service doesn't stop because of the LLQ feature.	Data is stored locally and even if the logging fails the TMG Firewall Service doesn't stop because of the LLQ feature.	Data can be encrypted when logging into remote SQL Server and only users with permission on the SQL database will be able to read the data offline. Mutual authentication is also performed between TMG and SQL Server.
PERFORMANCE	Best overall performance and relies on the speed of the local disk.	Good performance and also relies on the speed of the local disk.	Overall performance will rely on two key elements: connectivity speed between TMG - SQL Server and SQL Server overall performance. More planning is necessary in this case.
HISTORICAL AND OFFLINE VIEW	Not supported.	Supported.	Supported.

NOTE TMG uses SSL-encrypted connection to log information to the SQL Server database. For more information about SQL-encrypted connection, see *http://technet .microsoft.com/en-us/library/ms189067.aspx*.

 REAL WORLD **Slow Internet Access**

When the browsing experience is affected and all users start to complain about slow access, the edge device is the first to blame. This real-world scenario is based on a situation where users were having a huge delay when trying to open Internet pages while browsing through ISA Server 2006. The problem was happening for all users and for all Web sites—the interesting part was that ISA Server didn't have any apparently bottleneck. All the core subsystems (disk, memory, network, and CPU) were functioning as expected.

Troubleshooting browsing problems can be tricky because many elements are involved. In this particular case the issue happened right after Windows Server 2003 SP2 was applied on ISA Server 2006, so there was a natural concern about the networking changes that SP2 causes. However, we found out that KB948496 had already been applied.

After intensive troubleshooting that covered elements, such as name resolution, local disk performance, and networking, we decided to get a user mode dump of the process wspsrv.exe while the user was trying to browse the Internet. The result showed that ISA Server 2006 was waiting for the remote SQL Server to answer logging requests and therefore causing browsing delays. As a work-around, we changed the logging method to TXT while the SQL administrator worked to fix the performance issue that SQL Server was having.

This is an example of an external component affecting how ISA Server 2006 behaves and causing delays for users. The SQL Server performance issues directly affected ISA because of the logging options.

> **MORE INFO** For more information on this scenario, read *http://blogs.technet .com/yuridiogenes/archive/2008/08/06/intermittent-performance-problem- while-accessing-internet-through-isa-server-2006.aspx.*

General Guidelines

At this point you should have a good idea of what logging method should best fit your environment. The next step is to follow some general guidelines for the best logging experience.

Disk

Regardless of whether you use local or remote logging, the disk you choose for logging should be planned and some guidelines should be considered, including:

- Log files should be located on a dedicated disk, preferably using RAID for best performance and fault tolerance. See Table 28-2 for a comparison between the RAID levels.
- Use the NTFS file system.
- Have enough space for logging. The recommendation is to have initially at least 8 GB for logging but this value might increase according to your environment. More traffic means more data being logged, which means more disk space may be required for the log files. Additionally, there is also a concern regarding log retention policy that needs to be addressed. If your company wants to keep locally the logs for the last three months and then move to tape, 8 GB might not be enough.

TABLE 28-2 Main RAID Levels

RAID	FEATURES	ADVANTAGES	DISADVANTAGES
0	Also known as *disk striping*, where the data is divided into blocks and spread in a fixed order among all disks that are part of the array.	Improves read and write performance.	Doesn't provide fault tolerance.
1	Also known as *disk mirroring* because all data written in the primary disk is mirrored to the other disk.	Improves read performance and provides fault tolerance.	It is the most expensive RAID solution per byte because one disk is used only as a mirror. It may degrade the writing performance.
5	Also known as *stripe sets with parity*. It provides the same functionality of RAID 0 but it writes the parity across all the disks.	Improves read and writing performance and provides fault tolerance.	Requires at least three disks, and if one disk is lost the read and write performance can be affected.
10	Also known as *mirroring with striping* or RAID 1+0, this level is the combination of RAID 1 plus RAID 0.	It provides the highest read-and-write performance of any one of the other RAID levels and it has an excellent level of redundancy.	Has a higher cost of implementation.

> **MORE INFO** Although those four types of RAID are considered the core ones, other variants of those levels can also be used. For more information on other types of RAID, read *http://en.wikipedia.org/wiki/Redundant_array_of_independent_disks*.

Connectivity

This guideline is specifically for remote logging and doesn't apply to local logging. If you choose SQL Server as a logging option, you need a fast and reliable connection between TMG and the SQL Server. We do not recommended locating the SQL Server locate in a remote location over a WAN because it can cause a delay that will affect the end user's experience. In a scenario where TMG needs to log all access in the database located across a WAN this can cause a bottleneck since this process is highly intensive when your network traffic that crosses TMG is intensive and you have many rules to process.

Large Logging Queue (LLQ) Recommendations

By default, the Log Queue is located in the ISALogs folder (in the same hierarchy that TMG is installed); however, we recommend that you store these files on a separate disk to improve performance and availability in the event that the disk where TMG is installed gets full. You can use Table 28-2 to compare the different RAID levels to store log queue files.

Another important point to mention is that if you have a file-level antivirus installed on the firewall, you should exclude the LLQ folder from the real-time scan and any other scan job that you have the antivirus software configured to run.

Log Retention

If your company already has a log retention policy, TMG will have to adhere to it; if your company doesn't have a log retention policy, now is a great time to think about putting one together. Log retention policies might vary with the logging method you choose. For the logs that are stored locally, TMG allows you to control how big the log file can get and which files will be deleted (by default files older than seven days will be deleted) as shown in the options in Figure 28-10.

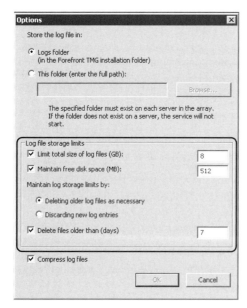

FIGURE 28-10 Log maintenance options for text logging

When planning for log retention locally on TMG you will need to plan disk sizing according to the volume that you store per day. You can calculate the approximate future growth of your logging by creating a baseline for at least one week and then verifying the amount of logging that is created on a daily basis. Then verify the amount of data that you want to keep local and the frequency that you will store the data outside of TMG computer. To reduce contention on the system drive where you are installing, it is highly recommended that you have another disk for logging.

If you use the SQL Server database logging option, you will need to consider whether this SQL Server computer is dedicated to TMG logging or whether there are other databases shared with other applications. The amount of disk required for log retention will vary according to the scenario where SQL Server is being used.

> **MORE INFO**   For SQL Server storage best practices, see *http://technet.microsoft.com/ en-us/library/cc966534.aspx.*

Summary

In this chapter, you learned about the value of Firewall logging, how to configure the various TMG logging options, and some best practices that you should consider when planning your TMG logging. In the next chapter, you will learn how TMG and Forefront Protection Manager operate together to close the gap between malware detection and mitigation.

## CHAPTER 29

Enhanced NAT

■ Understanding Enhanced NAT **817**

■ Configuring Enhanced NAT **820**

■ Troubleshooting Enhanced NAT **826**

■ Summary **828**

M any domains only allow mail from specific IP addresses. One major feature that was missing in ISA Server was the use of an alternate IP address for outbound traffic. If for some reason the Mail Exchange (MX) record of a domain was registered to a different IP address than the default IP address on the external interface of your ISA firewall, the mail would be sent only using the default IP address, causing the remote domain to reject the e-mail. TMG includes a new feature to help solve this problem: Enhanced NAT (ENAT). In this chapter we will discuss how ENAT works, how to configure ENAT, and how to troubleshoot issues related to ENAT.

Understanding Enhanced NAT

In Chapter 11, "Configuring TMG Networks," you learned that you can configure Network Rules that establish either a NAT or a Route relationship between two networks. ENAT changes the fundamental behavior that was present on ISA Server 2006: on outgoing connections where the network relationship is configured as NAT, the traffic seen at the ISA external NIC would be sourced from the default IP address. This means that all outbound connections from ISA Server 2006 always left with the same source address, which was the primary IP address for the TMG network interface card for that network. To better understand this, let's use SMTP traffic flow as an example. Figure 29-1 shows a normal inbound attempt from an external SMTP Server and an internal SMTP published through TMG.

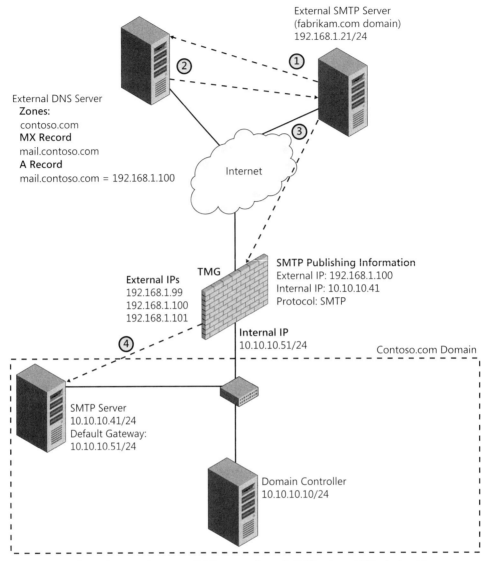

FIGURE 29-1 Inbound connection to an SMTP server through TMG using a NAT relationship

The steps outlined in Figure 29-1 are detailed as follows:

1. Before a message is sent, it is necessary to resolve the name for the destination MX record, which in this case is mail.contoso.com. To do that the external SMTP server verifies whether this name mapping is present on its own DNS cache, Because in this case the name mapping is not present, the SMTP server performs a DNS query against the DNS Server.

2. The DNS Server queries its local zones to see whether it is authoritative for that domain. In this case it is. The DNS server resolves the name: mail.contoso.com is 192.168.1.100.

3. The external SMTP server then starts the TCP handshake with the destination server and starts a connection attempt to TCP Port 25 against 192.168.1.100.

4. TMG verifies that there is a publishing rule to accept incoming SMTP traffic and that this traffic should be redirected using a NAT relationship to the internal SMTP server. When the handshake is finished, the SMTP protocol itself takes place between the source SMTP Server (192.168.1.21) and the destination SMTP server (10.10.10.50), which usually starts with the SMTP HELO or EHLO command.

These steps demonstrate a normal incoming SMTP flow. Let's see what happens when the internal SMTP server tries to send a message outside, as shown in Figure 29-2.

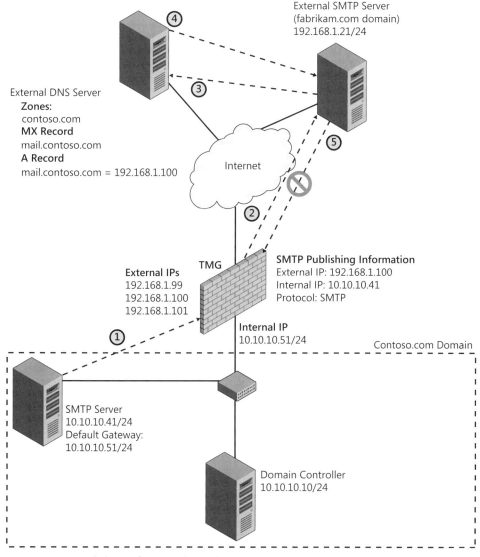

FIGURE 29-2 ENAT behavior for NAT relationship networks

1. The internal SMTP server uses its cache information to resolve the destination MX record (mx.fabrikam.com) and initiates the connection attempt by forwarding the message to TMG.

2. TMG evaluates the request, verifies that there is a rule allowing SMTP traffic from that server, and initiates a TCP handshake to the destination server. After finishing the TCP handshake it initiates an SMTP connection by sending the SMTP HELO or EHLO message.

3. The destination server in this case is using a feature to prevent SPAM that performs a reverse DNS lookup on incoming SMTP connections. Therefore, the destination server will send a reverse DNS lookup query to the DNS Server asking for the name relevant to IP address 192.168.1.99.

4. The DNS server replies saying that 192.168.1.99 is otherhost.contoso.com.

5. The destination SMTP server realizes that "otherhost.contoso.com" does not match "mx.contoso.com" and sends an SMTP 501 error message and drops the connection.

MORE INFO   For more information on reverse DNS lookup for SMTP, see the following article: *http://technet.microsoft.com/en-us/library/aa996903.aspx*. Another e-mail protection resource that applies to this scenario is the Sender ID Evaluation. For more information on this, see *http://technet.microsoft.com/en-us/library/aa996295(EXCHG.140).aspx*.

ENAT essentially adds the capability to map a specific source server to a specific external IP address when traffic is translated through the TMG NAT mechanism. This resolves the problem with mismatched reverse lookups. The traffic matches the network rule specifying a NAT relationship with a manually configured outbound address. The firewall engine uses the specified address as the source address of the packet and creates the appropriate state as required.

Although this is the most common scenario for using ENAT, it is not the only one. In many other situations you might need to make sure that outbound connections from a published server present a specific source IP address to external servers. That is when you'll use the ENAT feature, such as FTP Publishing.

Configuring Enhanced NAT

The scenario shown in Figure 29-3 demonstrates this feature and how it can solve the problem explained in the previous section.

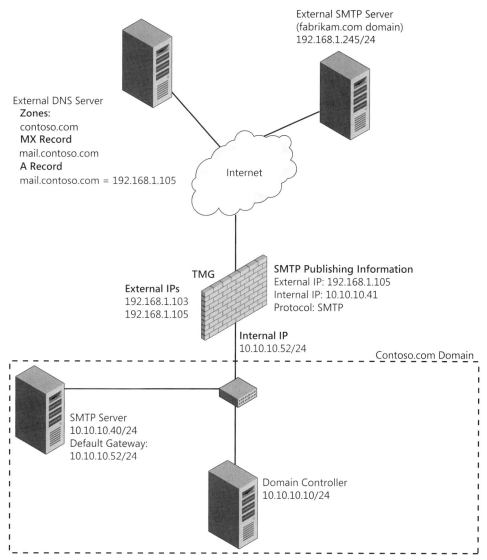

External SMTP Server
(fabrikam.com domain)
192.168.1.245/24

External DNS Server
Zones:
contoso.com
MX Record
mail.contoso.com
A Record
mail.contoso.com = 192.168.1.105

Internet

SMTP Publishing Information
External IP: 192.168.1.105
Internal IP: 10.10.10.41
Protocol: SMTP

TMG

External IPs
192.168.1.103
192.168.1.105

Internal IP
10.10.10.52/24

Contoso.com Domain

SMTP Server
10.10.10.40/24
Default Gateway:
10.10.10.52/24

Domain Controller
10.10.10.10/24

FIGURE 29-3 Scenario for ENAT configuration

This scenario uses the SMTP Server Publishing feature, employing the concepts that you learned in Chapter 22, "Publishing Servers." For the purpose of this demonstration, we won't use the E-mail Protection feature. (For more information on how to configure this feature, see Chapter 19, "Enhancing E-Mail Protection.") The following steps are based on the scenario explained in Figure 29-3 and have the following assumptions:

- The current scenario is already working for outbound SMTP traffic and is having the problem that was presented earlier in this chapter (incoming SMTP traffic).

- The internal SMTP server already has a computer object created that points to its own IP (10.10.10.40).

Now you need to create the ENAT rule to cause originating outbound traffic from the internal SMTP server to use IP 192.168.1.105, which is the same as the MX record.

> **NOTE**   It is very important to emphasize that ENAT does not affect response traffic—it only affects traffic originated from the outside host to the internal published resource.

Follow these steps to start the configuration:

1. Open the Forefront TMG console, Right-click Networking, point to New, and then click Network Rule. The New Network Rule Wizard appears, Type the name of this rule as shown in Figure 29-4 (**SMTP ENAT Network Rule**) and click Next.

FIGURE 29-4 Configuring an ENAT Network Rule

2. On the Network Traffic Source page, click Add. Expand Computers, select the SMTP Server computer object, click Add, and then click Close. The Network Traffic Source page should resemble Figure 29-5. Click Next.

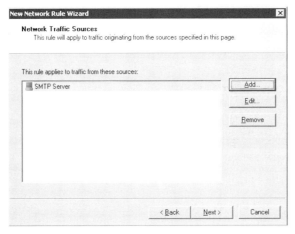

FIGURE 29-5 Selecting the source computer that will use ENAT

3. On the Network Traffic Destination page, click Add, expand Networks, and select External. Click Add and then click Close. The Network Traffic Destination page should resemble Figure 29-6. Click Next.

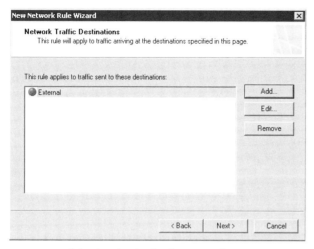

FIGURE 29-6 Selecting the destination network

4. On the Network Relationship page leave the default option (NAT) and click Next.

5. On the NAT Address Selection page, select Use The Specified IP Address and choose the IP address from the drop-down box (192.168.1.105 in this case) as shown in Figure 29-7. Click Next.

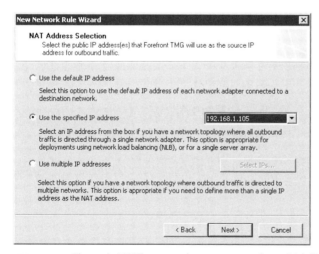

FIGURE 29-7 The main ENAT screen where you can select which IP to use for outbound connections

6. On the Completing The New Network Rule Wizard page, click Finish.

7. Make sure that the Network Rule is above the regular Internet Access default Network Rule, If you don't take this step, the traffic will always leave with the primary IP address on the external interface of the TMG firewall. To change the network rule make sure that the SMTP ENAT Network Rule is selected and click Move Selected Rules Up twice so that this network rule will be processed first and thus avoid conflicts with other rules that you might have. Figure 29-8 shows this operation.

FIGURE 29-8 Adjusting the new Network Rule to precede the default Internet Access network rule

8. After moving the selected network rule to the top of the others and below Local Host Access click Apply to commit the changes.

Now that this feature is configured you can test it to validate that it works as intended. You can take two approaches to test whether this feature is working:

- Logging
- Network Monitor

Follow these steps to configure the Logging feature to log all outbound attempts using the NAT address 192.168.1.105:

1. Expand the Forefront TMG (Server Name) option in the left pane of the TMG management console.

2. Click the Logs & Reports node in the left pane and click Edit Filter in the task pane, as shown in Figure 29-9.

3. Click Filter By and select NAT Address, Choose Equals from the Condition drop-down list. The value will be 192.168.1.105, as shown in Figure 29-10.

4. Go to the internal workstation where you have your SMTP Client and send an e-mail to an outside address. On the Logging tab you should see traffic similar to that shown in the log entries in Figure 29-11.

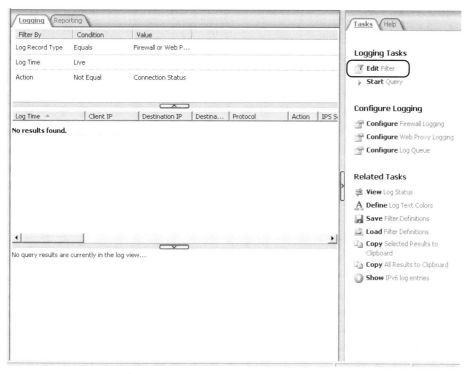

FIGURE 29-9 Configuring the Logging feature

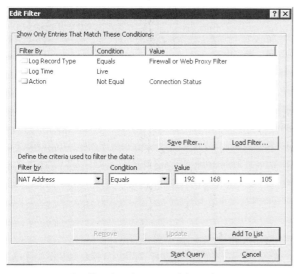

FIGURE 29-10 Configuring the NAT address that you want to monitor

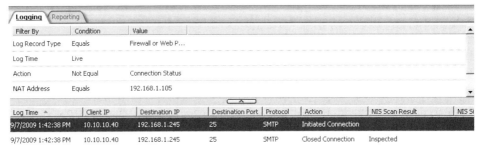

FIGURE 29-11 Using new logging field criteria to monitor ENAT

To use Network Monitor to test whether the traffic is leaving using the correct IP specified in the network rule, you can follow the same guidelines for general data gathering with Network Monitor that are explained in more detail in Chapter 33, "Using Network Monitor 3 for Troubleshooting TMG."

Troubleshooting Enhanced NAT

ENAT is relatively easy to implement, as seen in the previous section. The common issues seen with ENAT configuration are largely dependent upon how a protocol or application is accessed or the limitations associated with either of them. It is important to remember that ENAT is primary targeted for SMTP servers; however, it is not limited to them. The long and short of this feature, as mentioned in the earlier sections, is that you can create network rules that describe special NAT behavior for one or more hosts in the source network. This means that traffic origination from a host meeting the source criteria will be handled according to the configuration specified in that network rule:

- **Default**   Use the default TMG IP address in the destination network.
- **Selected IP**   Use the specified TMG IP address in the destination network.
- **Multiple IPs (arrays only)**   Use one selected TMG IP address in the destination network, depending on which TMG firewall processes the traffic.

You can only choose one IP address per TMG firewall. If you select more than one per TMG firewall, you'll receive a warning alert and TMG will select the lowest-bound IP from the set. However, if you have a specific NAT IP address and you also have the ISP Redundancy (ISP-R) feature in TMG, the ISP-R will not fail over to the alternate IP if the primary link fails for this specific network rule.

Understanding these limitations and requirements is important and can help administrators avoid simple mistakes during the planning or configuration stage. Let's consider a real-life scenario to understand how an administrator can narrow down issues related to ENAT.

REAL WORLD   Unable to Access FTP

A customer recently migrated from ISA 2006 Standard Edition to a TMG Standard Edition. The rules he imported from the ISA 2006 deployment had an internal SMTP server and an internal FTP server published through the ISA server, which now will be published through TMG. The MX record for the SMTP server publicly resolves to an IP address that is not the default IP address on the TMG firewall's external interface. Hence the customer created an ENAT rule as per the configuration discussed in the "Configuring Enhanced NAT" section earlier in the chapter. The FTP server was published using the default IP address on the TMG external interface. Upon testing the setup he found that the SMTP server was working fine. However, users started to complain that even though they could do Passive FTP to the published FTP server they could not use Active FTP to connect to the same published FTP server.

The simplest way to troubleshoot this issue is to get a Network Monitor trace of a successful scenario and a failing scenario. So we installed and started the Network Monitor trace capture on TMG and collected two sets of traces: a successful network monitor trace from a client doing Passive FTP and a failing network monitor trace from a client doing an Active FTP. In the failing scenario we noticed that TMG responded back to the client from the additional IP address on its network interface rather than its default IP address, which the client didn't expect and thus rejected the connection—therefore, Active FTP failed. On a closer examination we found that TMG was doing as it was told to do. As per the ENAT rule set up by the administrator, any traffic originating from the source network of the published servers was being asked to use an additional IP address set by the administrator for the use of SMTP server. This behavior conflicted with the functioning of the FTP server.

To understand why Passive FTP worked and Active FTP failed, you must understand first the difference between the two. In the case of Active FTP, a client initiates a connection to the published FTP server and then waits for the server to make a connection back to it on the control channel port. In the case of Passive FTP, the client makes a connection to the published FTP server and then the client again makes a connection to the server on the data channel port sent by the server. In Passive FTP, both connections are initiated by the client, whereas in Active FTP the second part (the control channel connection) is initiated by the FTP server. In our customer's case, the client made a connection to the FTP server; however, the data channel connection comes from a different IP because ENAT was applied, which wasn't expected by the client. Hence the connection is reset by the client and Active FTP failed.

To resolve this issue, the customer can make a computer object for the SMTP server and then create ENAT rules based on the computer object rather than a network. By doing this, the ENAT rule will only be applied to the SMTP server and not to the other servers in that network.

Summary

The Enhanced NAT feature has definitely been a widely requested feature, and the inclusion of ENAT in TMG provides administrators with a lot of flexibility in creating their rules. In this chapter we discussed how ENAT works and how to configure ENAT rules. We also discussed some common limitations in ENAT and how to troubleshoot common ENAT issues. In the next chapter we will discuss scripting in TMG.

## CHAPTER 30

Scripting TMG

▪ Understanding the TMG Component Object Model (COM) **829**

▪ Administering TMG with VBScript or JScript **834**

▪ Administering TMG with Windows PowerShell **842**

▪ Summary **848**

S cripting is an important tool for a TMG administrator. With the help of scripts, an administrator can use script to automate tasks and create rules based on, alerts, events or even run it at scheduled time intervals. In this section we will discuss what Component Object Model (COM) is and how to use the Forefront TMG administration COM. We will discuss how to create some basic scripts using VBScript and Windows PowerShell.

Understanding the TMG Component Object Model (COM)

The Component Object Model (COM) is a component software architecture that allows applications and systems to be built from components supplied by different software vendors. COM is the underlying architecture that forms the foundation for higher-level software services, such as those provided by Object Linking and Embedding (OLE). OLE services span various aspects of component software, including compound documents, custom controls, inter-application scripting, data transfer, and other software interactions.

These services share a fundamental requirement for a mechanism that allows software components supplied by different software vendors to connect to and communicate with each other in a well-defined manner. This mechanism is supplied by COM. COM is extensible and defines a standard for component interoperability. It is programming language–independent and provides a robust evolution of component-based applications and systems. COM also provides a mechanism for communication between components even across process and network boundaries and for shared memory management between components. It also provides a mechanism for error and status reporting and dynamic loading of components.

Forefront TMG COM Hierarchy

The Forefront TMG administration object model gives developers a mechanism to extend the functionality of Forefront TMG. Scripting allows you to use the Forefront TMG administration COM objects to access and control any Forefront TMG computer within an organization. The administration objects allow for automation of all the tasks performed through Forefront TMG Management. This capability allows administrators to create scripts to automate repetitive and complex tasks requiring the use of Forefront TMG Management. These scripts can then be included in batch files. By programming with the same administration objects that Forefront TMG uses, developers can provide persistent and configurable data storage for their programs, and can have Forefront TMG notify programs when the configuration data has changed.

The Forefront TMG COM has a root object for which the version-independent program identifier is *FPC.Root*. The root object manages the Enterprise object which is identified as *FPCEnterprise* object type and the Arrays object which is identified as the *FPCArrays* object type, which in turn manages the *FPCArray* object type. The *FPC* object is the root of the administration COM object hierarchy, and provides programmatic access to almost all of the other *FPC* objects. The *FPCEnterprise* object defines the centrally managed enterprise and provides access to the configuration settings of the enterprise through its properties. Only enterprise-level configuration settings can be accessed through this object. The *FPCArrays* collection holds a set of *FPCArray* objects. Each Forefront TMG computer is associated with an *FPCArray* object that represents a Forefront TMG array and provides access to the array-level configuration settings of the Forefront TMG computers that are associated with the array. The *FPCArray* object defines a single Forefront TMG array, and its properties provide access to the array-level configuration settings in the hierarchy of administration COM objects for the Forefront TMG computers associated with it. Each Forefront TMG computer is associated with a single array as one of many fpcServer objects within the fpcServers collection. When multiple Forefront TMG computers are associated with the same *FPCArray* object, you can configure these servers at the same time through the array-level properties and methods of the *FPCArray* object. A group of Forefront TMG computers that are associated with the same array can be managed as a single, logical entity and can provide distributed caching, load balancing, and fault tolerance.

The other objects that are managed by the Enterprise object and the Array object are:

- Server object (used by Array object)
- Admin Security object (used by Enterprise and Array objects)
- Extensions object (used by Enterprise and Array objects)
- Policy Rule object (used by Enterprise and Array objects)
- Array Policy object (used by Array object)
- Rule Elements object (used by Enterprise and Array objects)
- Network Configuration object (used by Enterprise and Array objects)
- IP Selection object (used by Array object)
- Cache object (used by Array object)

- Reports object (used by Array object)
- Web Listener Properties object (used by Array object)

To see a complete list of all the COM objects in each branch and their descriptions, please visit Forefront TMG Administration Object Model at *http://msdn.microsoft.com/en-us/library/dd435807.aspx.*

New COM Elements in TMG

Forefront TMG introduces a lot of new features over ISA 2006 or ISA 2004. With the introduction of new features we also have many new objects, methods, properties, and enumerated types which are not available in ISA 2006 or ISA 2004. Table 30-1 lists all the new COM elements that have been introduced in TMG.

TABLE 30-1 New COM Elements in TMG

OBJECTS AND COLLECTIONS	METHODS	PROPERTIES	ENUMERATED TYPES
FPCActivity Statistics (Collection)	*FPCAdapter .EnableAutoDns Detection*	*FPC.ConfigurationMode* *FPCAccessProperties.Custom MessageText*	FpcActivity Statistics PeriodType
FPCActivity StatisticsEntry (Object)	*FPCAdapter .EnableDhcp* *FPCAdapter*	*FPCAccessProperties.Display CustomMessageText*	FpcAdapter ConnectionType
FPCAllAdapters (Collection)	*.GetPrimary DnsServer*	*FPCAdapter.Addresses* *FPCAdapter.AutoDnsServer Detection*	FpcAdapterState FpcConfiguration Mode
FPCContent Delivery Settings (Object)	*FPCAdapter .GetPrimary Gateway*	*FPCAdapter.ConnectionType* *FPCAdapter.DhcpServer*	FpcDayOfWeek FpcDefinition UpdatesStatus
FPCDestinations (Object)	*FPCAdapter .GetPrimary IpAddress*	*FPCAdapter.DnsServers* *FPCAdapter.Gateways*	FpcFast TricklingMode
FPCLicense (Object)	*FPCAdapter .GetPrimary SubnetMask*	*FPCAdapter.State* *FPCAdapter.SubnetMasks*	FpcIpsScanResult FpcMalware
FPCLicenses (Collection)	*FPCAdapter .GetSecondary*	*FPCArray.CreateThreadPer HttpVerifier*	InspectionAction FpcMalware
FPCMalware Inspection Properties (Object)	*DnsServer* *FPCAdapter .SetPrimary DnsServer*	*FPCArray.IsJoinedToEnterprise* *FPCArray.MalwareInspection Settings*	InspectionAction Reason FpcMalware Inspection
		FPCArray.SpyNetLevel *FPCArray.UpdateCenter*	ContentDelivery Method
		FPCClientAutoScript .ConvertUrlToLowerCase	
		FPCConnectionLimit.Client ExtendedStorageLimitInMegs	

OBJECTS AND COLLECTIONS	METHODS	PROPERTIES	ENUMERATED TYPES
FPCMalware Inspection Reports (Object)	*FPCAdapter .SetPrimary Gateway*	*FPCConnectionLimit.Client ExtendedStorageLimitPoolSize*	FpcMalware Inspection ThreatLevel
FPCMalware Inspection Scanner Settings (Object)	*FPCAdapter .SetPrimary IpAddress*	*FPCConnectionLimit.Client StorageLimitInMegs*	FpcMicrosoft UpdateSetting
FPCMalware Inspection Settings (Object)	*FPCAdapter .SetPrimary SubnetMask*	*FPCEnterpriseNetwork .Ipv6RangeSet*	FpcPolicyRule Groups
	FPCAdapter .SetSecondary DnsServer	*FPCLog.LogFieldSelectionString*	FpcProtocol Message
FPCProtocol Message Definition (Collection)	*FPCArray .GetActivity Statistics*	*FPCLogEntry.IpsScanResult*	Definition Transport Protocol
		FPCLogEntry.IpsSignature	
FPCProtocol Message Definition Parameter (Object)	*FPCFilter Expressions .AddMultiple EnumFilter*	*FPCLogEntry.Malware InspectionAction*	FpcSpyNetLevel
		FPCLogEntry.Malware InspectionActionReason	FpcSSL ClientCertificate Claim
FPCProtocol Message Definitions (Collection)	*FPCFilter Expressions .AddMultiple StringFilter*	*FPCLogEntry.Malware InspectionContent DeliveryMethod*	FpcSSL Termination Mode
		FPCLogEntry.Malware InspectionDuration	
FPCRdlReport Definition (Object)	*FPCReportJob .CreateReport*	*FPCLogEntry.Malware InspectionThreatLevel*	FpcUpdate Action
	FPCReportJob .SetAs Immediate ReportJob	*FPCLogEntry.ThreatName*	
FPCRdlReport Definitions (Collection)		*FPCLogEntry.UagArrayId*	
		FPCLogEntry.UagErrorCode	
FPCReporting Services Properties (Object)	*FPCReportJob .SetAsRunOnce*	*FPCLogEntry.UagEventName*	
		FPCLogEntry.UagId	
	FPCServer.Get Adapter Routable IpRangeSet	*FPCLogEntry.UagModuleId*	
		FPCLogEntry.UagServiceName	
FPCReport Summary Definition (Object)		*FPCLogEntry.UagSessionId*	
	FPCServer .JoinDomain	*FPCLogEntry.UagSeverity*	
		FPCLogEntry.UagTrunkName	
	FPCServer .JoinWorkgroup	*FPCLogEntry.UagType*	
		FPCLogEntry.UagVersion	
		FPCLogEntry.URLCategory	
		FPCLogs.IsaDatabaseNumber OfInsertsPerBatch	
		FPCLogs.IsaDatabase QueryTimeout	
		FPCLogs.LogQueueDirectory	

OBJECTS AND COLLECTIONS	METHODS	PROPERTIES	ENUMERATED TYPES
FPCReport Summary Definitions (Collection)	FPCServer .PopulateArray StaticRoutes	FPCLogs.LogQueueDirectoryType	
FPCRoute (Object)	FPCServer .RestartOS	FPCLogViewer.Log ContentIsaDatabase	
FPCRouting Table (Collection)	FPCServer.Set Primary DNSSuffix	FPCLowLevelSettings .TrustedWindows FilteringPlatformCalloutGuids	
FPCService UpdatesState (Object)	FPCServer .SetServer Name	FPCNetwork.Ipv6RangeSet	
FPCService UpdatesStates (Collection)	FPCServer .SetUserName AndPassword	FPCPolicyRule.Group FPCPolicyRule.Malware InspectionProperties	
FPCSoftware UpdatesSettings (Object)	FPCServer .ShutdownOS	FPCRadiusServer.AccountingPort FPCRadiusServer.UsedFor Accounting	
FPC Temporary StorageSettings (Object)	FPCServer .StartIsa Database LogService	FPCRadiusServer.Used ForAuthentication FPCReports.RdlReportDefinitions	
FPC UpdateCenter (Object)	FPCServer .StopIsa Database LogService	FPCReports.Reporting ServicesProperties	
FPC UpdateSchedule (Object)		FPCReports.ReportSummary Definitions	
FPCUpdate Service (Object)		FPCReportsProperties .MalwareInspectionReports	
FPCUpdate Services (Collection)		FPCServer.AllAdapters	
		FPCServer.CurrentUserName	
		FPCServer.DomainOr WorkgroupName	
		FPCServer.IsaDatabaseLog ServiceStatus	
		FPCServer.IsJoinedToDomain	
		FPCServer.MicrosoftUpdateSetting	
		FPCServer.PrimaryDNSSuffix	
		FPCServer.RoutingTable	
		FPCServer.ServiceUpdatesStates	
		FPCServer.WSUSConfigured	
		FPCWebListenerProperties .SSLTerminationMode	
		FPCWebPublishingProperties .SSLClientCertificateClaim	

> **NOTE** A *collection object* refers to a group of objects. When referring to a collection object you can refer to a related group of items as a single object.

To see a complete description of each of these new COM elements in TMG, please visit *http://msdn.microsoft.com/en-us/library/dd447763.aspx.*

Administering TMG with VBScript or JScript

In general, the choice of using JScript versus VBScript to automate your TMG administration is a matter of personal preference. Neither one makes scripting TMG any easier or harder except through your familiarity with either language or your preference for features of one language over those provided by the other.

> **NOTE** Except for the task examples, the code provided in this section is written in what is known as *pseudo-code*. This style offers contextual relevance using non-functional code.

For instance, I prefer using JScript for several reasons:

- JScript imposes a stricter writing style than VBScript does, which helps reduce human error in the script. For example, unlike VBScript, JScript variables are case-sensitive. This means JScript considers variables named *thisvalue* and *ThisValue* to be unique, but VBScript treats them both as a single variable. VBScript also allows you to use a variable without first declaring it. These points invariably (pun intended) lead to "interesting" script errors that are caused by unplanned variable reuse.

- JScript has greater self-awareness than VBScript does. I make liberal use of this functionality in the debugging script component on the companion CD.

- JScript is supported by all browsers as client-side code. This is important if you write Hyper-Text Applications (HTAs); this point isn't quite as interesting for TMG scripting.

VBScript has its own set of advantages over JScript:

- VBScript reads more like a set of English operations and behaviors. This makes VBScript easier for beginners to grasp.

- String parsing (locate "cat" within "the cat in the hat", for example) is more flexible in VBScript than in JScript.

- COM events are easier to handle in VBScript, although this is less interesting in most TMG administration tasks.

TMG Scripting Best Practices

Plenty of articles on the Internet discuss the coding styles and habits of successful developers. Whether you think of yourself as a developer, if you decide that writing TMG scripts will help you manage your TMG deployments, you'll need to acquire some of those skills to be truly successful at automating TMG management. In particular, you must bear in mind the following aspects of TMG automation when designing or executing your scripts:

- Write reusable code. If you find yourself writing the same mechanisms in different scripts, those actions are clear candidates for exporting to a script containing common functions. This habit will make your code easier to maintain (there's only one place to fix a bug or add a feature) and easier to understand for others.

- Execute .Save() only once in your script. When creating multiple changes as part of a larger task, you *must not* save individual changes—especially within a loop. There are two reasons for this:

  - Multiple .Save() operations place a heavy processing load on TMG storage and policy engines because they are forced to manage storage and running policy updates for each and every .Save() operation your script executes. If you call .Save() before one policy update is complete, the previous action must be completed and the new changes merged with the previous changes.

  - Errors encountered after successful .Save() operations that occur before the policy or configuration changes are completed can leave partial changes behind, requiring you to manually revert them or your script will have to recognize them and behave accordingly. If your script delays the .Save() operation until all of the changes are completed, no changes will be made to the running policy if .Save() fails.

- Execute .Save() at the highest reasonable hierarchical level. For instance, even if you are updating Network rules, you should perform the .Save() operation at the .Array level, rather than the .NetworkRules level. If the changes are executed in an Enterprise context, such as an Enterprise policy, perform .Save() at the .Enterprise level. This allows TMG to manage the policy updates more efficiently.

- Avoid loops whenever possible. Most of the TMG objects are accessible through their parent collection .Item() method using their name as seen in the UI or their index within the collection. For instance, if you're looking for a specific array, it's more efficient (not to mention *much* faster) to use FPC.Arrays.Item("ArrayName") than to use a "for," "while," or "do" loop across the FPC.Arrays collection. This is especially true for collections that contain a large number of child objects as would exist in the array policy or rule elements sets.

- Be *generous* with error checking. Better that your script operates slightly slower but more reliably than fails badly and quickly. In general, management scripts are designed to operate only once or very infrequently (such as scheduled daily exports). Performing proper error checking in the script will save you troubleshooting and error correction time later.

- Perform error handling as close to individual actions as possible. This allows you to provide more useful error messaging and makes your scripts more robust.

- Always verify the results of your script action. More than a few CSS cases have been caused by scripts that were written on the basis that "a lack of failure indication is a successful run."

Way back in the dark ages when I first started learning to write scripts for ISA Server 2000, I made several mistakes; some because I was a relative newcomer to scripting in general, but most caused by my lack of understanding of how ISA COM works and how ISA Server itself was designed to operate.

Unlike TMG, ISA Server policy changes were not reflected immediately for existing traffic flow. This meant that if you wanted to see immediate changes in traffic policy, you had to either cycle the ISA services or wait until they decided to refresh the policy state. Choosing to restart the ISA services had the effect of forcing a policy reload as well as stopping all traffic across ISA until the services were ready to accept traffic. To make script testing easier, I started the habit of adding a services restart mechanism at the end of my scripts so that I didn't have to do it manually. This had the desired effect of forcing an immediate policy update so that my post-script behavioral testing was more accurate. Happy-Happy-Joy-Joy! I just reduced my script testing time by several seconds per run!

My script testing had the interesting side effect of repeated service restarts in a short period of time (run script, restart services, test, run scripts, and so on). This behavior also had an unfortunate side effect of causing a race condition between repeated policy updates and service restarts, so that I eventually created a state where the ISA services could not start at all because of storage corruption.

Needless to say, this forced me to do two things:

- Rebuild my ISA server deployment from scratch
- Re-evaluate my scripting and testing habits

Obviously, the time I lost because of script design eventually cost me more time than the time I tried to gain. Much of what I learned from that experience as well as the experience gained from working around some scary-smart ISA and TMG developers forms the basis for the TMG scripting best practices.

TMG Task Automation Example

In this example, you are tasked with updating the firewall policy for all of the arrays associated with the Outbound Proxy Enterprise policy by importing a file that was exported from the Contoso TMG policy test lab. Contoso has deployed TMG in multiple arrays separated into three functional tasks: outbound proxy/firewall, VPN, and publishing. Your task is to update the policy only in arrays that use the Outbound Proxy Enterprise policy.

The final result of this example produces a script that automates a common task in many large enterprises: that of applying a single array-level policy change to specific arrays. In the interest of brevity, only one of the script examples here includes error checking. The scripts available on the companion CD (which include a more flexible version of this script) include much more error checking.

Step 1: Locating Arrays Associated by an Enterprise Policy

In this example, the script will gather a list of TMG arrays that are associated by a common Enterprise policy named Outbound Proxy. You may have noticed that this script example appears to violate the best practice of not using a loop to discover the desired item. This is because the items to be discovered cannot be individually called out based on their relationship to the Enterprise policy.

This step performs multiple subtasks:

1. Discovers the arrays that use the Outbound Proxy Enterprise policy

2. Transfers control to and receive results from the *UpdateArray()* function

3. Saves the policy updates only if *all* changes were successful

VBSCRIPT

```
' force pre-declaration of variables
Option Explicit
Main
Function Main
    ' declare and define the TMG root object
    Dim oFPC: Set oFPC = CreateObject( "FPC.Root" )
    ' declare and define the value that expresses if array work was successful
    Dim bFailed: bFailed = False
    ' declare and define the value that expresses whether any changes occurred
    Dim bChanges: bChanges = False
    ' declare and define the TMG arrays collection
    Dim cArrays: Set cArrays = oFPC.Arrays
    ' declare the Array object variable
    Dim oArray
    ' enumerate (walk through) the array list looking for the ones of interest
    For Each oArray in cArrays
        If "Outbound Proxy" = oArray.PolicyAssignment.EnterprisePolicyUsed.Name Then
            ' if we try to work an array and fail, we want to quit now
            If Not( UpdateArray( oArray ) ) Then
                bFailed = True
                Exit For
            End If
            ' otherwise, we declare that we made changes to at least one array
            bChanges = True
        End If
    Next
    ' if we made any changes without failures, now is the time to save them
    If bChanges And Not( bFailed ) Then SaveChanges( oArray )
End Function
```

```
Function Main
{
    ' declare and define the TMG root object
    var oFPC = new ActiveXObject( "FPC.Root" );
    ' declare and define the value that expresses if array work was successful
    var bFailed = False;
    // declare and define the value that expresses whether any changes occurred
    var bChanges = false;
    // declare and define the TMG arrays collection
    // declare the Array object variable
    var oArray = null;
    // enumerate (walk through) the array list seeking the ones that interest us
    var eArrays = new Enumerator( oFPC.Arrays );
    for( ; !eArrays.atEnd(); eArrays.moveNext() )
    {
        oArray = eArrays.item();
        if( "Outbound Proxy" == oArray.PolicyAssignment.EnterprisePolicyUsed.Name )
        {
            // if we try to work an array and fail, we want to quit now
            if( !UpdateArray( oArray ) )
            {
                bFailed = true;
                break;
            }
            // otherwise, we declare that we made changes to at least one array
            bChanges = true;
        }
    }
    // if we made any changes without failures, now is the time to save them
    if( bChanges && !bFailed )
        SaveChanges( oArray );
}
```

Step 2: Exporting and Importing Using Files

This function performs the following tasks:

1. Exports the current array policy to a file

2. Imports the array policy changes from a file

3. Returns the Boolean status of these actions to the caller

VBSCRIPT

```vbscript
Function UpdateArray( oArray )
    ' define the default return value for this function
    UpdateArray = False
    ' declare and define the TMG export file path
    Dim szOutFilePath: szOutFilePath = "C:\TmgExportFile.xml"
    ' declare and define the optional data for the export method
    Dim iOptionalData: iOptionalData = 0
    ' declare and define the TMG export data password
    Dim szPassword: szPassword = ""
    ' declare and define the TMG export file comment section
    Dim szComment: szComment = "Exported by " & WScript.ScriptName & " at " & Now
    ' enable script error handling
    On Error Resume Next
    ' try to export the current configuration to a file
    oArray.ExportToFile szOutFilePath, iOptionalData, szPassword, szComment
    ' if it fails, tell the user and bail out
    If 0 <> Err.Number Then
        WScript.Echo "Failed to export the current array configuration to " & _
                    szOutFilePath & "; " & Err.Number & "; " & Err.Description
        Exit Function
    End If
    ' disable script error handling
    On Error Goto 0
    ' declare and define the TMG import policy overwrite flag
    Dim bOverwrite: bOverwrite = False
    ' declare and define the TMG import services reset flag
    Dim bReset: bReset = False
    ' declare and define the TMG import policy reload flag
    Dim bReload: bReload = True
    ' declare and define the TMG import file path
    Dim szInFilePath: szInFilePath = "C:\TmgImportFile.xml"
    ' enable script error handling
    On Error Resume Next
    ' try to import the configuration update from a file
    oArray.ImportFromFile szInFilePath, iOptionalData, szPassword, bOverwrite, _
                        bReset, bReload
    ' if it fails, tell the user and bail out
    If 0 <> Err.Number Then
        WScript.Echo "Failed to import the current array configuration from " & _
                    szInFilePath & "; " & Err.Number & "; " & Err.Description
        Exit Function
    End If

    ' no failures, return "true"
    UpdateArray = True
End Function
```

JSCRIPT

```jscript
function UpdateArray( oArray )
{
    // declare and define the TMG export file path
    var szOutFilePath = "C:\TmgExportFile.xml";
    // declare and define the optional data for the export method
    var iOptionalData = 0;
    // declare and define the TMG export data password
    var szPassword = "";
    // declare and define the TMG export file comment section
    var szComment = "Exported by " + WScript.ScriptName + " at " + new
                    Date().toLocaleString();
    // enable script error handling
    try
    {
        // try to export the current configuration to a file
        oArray.ExportToFile( szOutFilePath, iOptionalData, szPassword, szComment );
    }
    catch( err )
    {
        // if it fails, tell the user and bail out
        WScript.Echo( "Failed to export the current array configuration to " +
                      szOutFilePath + "; " + err.Number + "; " + err.Description );
        return false;
    }
    // declare and define the TMG import policy overwrite flag
    Dim bOverwrite: bOverwrite = false;
    // declare and define the TMG import services reset flag
    Dim bReset: bReset = false;
    // declare and define the TMG import policy reload flag
    Dim bReload: bReload = true;
    // declare and define the TMG import file path
    Dim szInFilePath: szInFilePath = "C:\TmgImportFile.xml";
    // enable script error handling
    try
    {
        // try to import the configuration update from a file
        oArray.ImportFromFile( szInFilePath, iOptionalData, szPassword, bOverwrite,
                            bReset, bReload );
    }
```

```
    catch( err )
    {
        // if it fails, tell the user and bail out
        WScript.Echo( "Failed to import the current array configuration from " +
                      szInFilePath + "; " + err.Number + "; " + err.Description );
        return false;
    }


    // no failures, return "true"
    return true;
}
```

Step 3: Saving the Changes

In this step, the script attempts to save the configuration updates to the specified array:

VBSCRIPT

```
Function SaveChanges( oArray )
    ' define the default value of this function
    SaveChanges = False

    On Error Resume Next
    ' try to save the configuration changes
    oArray.Save
    ' if it fails, tell the user and bail out
    If 0 <> Err.Number Then
        WScript.Echo "Failed to save the array configuration changes; " & _
        Err.Number & "; " & Err.Description
        Exit Function
    End If


    ' no failures, return "true"
    SaveChanges = True
End Function
```

JSCRIPT

```
function SaveChanges( oArray )
{
    try
    {
        // try to save the configuration changes
        oArray.Save();
    }
    catch( err )
    {
        // if it fails, tell the user and bail out
        WScript.Echo "Failed to save the array configuration changes; " +
                     err.Number + "; " + err.Description
        return false;
    }

     // no failures, return "true"
    return true;
}
```

You may be wondering why an entire function was created rather than simply adding the .*Save()* action to the *Main* function. The reason for this is as stated in the "TMG Scripting Best Practices" section—reusable code. You will call the .*Save()* method in almost any script you write, and having a pluggable function will save you development and testing time.

This script can be made much more flexible (for example, it could accept command-line options) and robust (it could retry failed actions), but the goal is to illustrate how simple an apparently complex task could be when you understand the relationships within the TMG COM.

> **MORE INFO**   You can read more about the TMG COM methods used in these examples at (ExportTofile) *http://msdn.microsoft.com/en-us/library/dd436299.aspx*, (ImportFromFile) *http://msdn.microsoft.com/en-us/library/dd436301.aspx* and (Save) *http://msdn.microsoft .com/en-us/library/dd436307.aspx*.

Administering TMG with Windows PowerShell

As explained throughout the chapter, Forefront TMG allows scripting automation by using the COM object model. Although TMG doesn't have a built-in Windows PowerShell cmdlet, you can still take advantage of this powerful tool by using COM objects.

COM objects have a unique name also known as a Programmatic Identifier (ProgID) that is stored in the registry. When you have access to the ProgID of a COM component you can use the New-Object command on Windows PowerShell. The following approach is a simple way to view the methods of a COM object (in this case TMG COM Object) :

```
PS C:\Users\administrator.CONTOSO> $TMGRoot = New-Object -comObject FPC.root
```

This command instantiates a COM object using the object's ProgID rather than instantiating a managed object and storing the resulting object into the *$TMGRoot* variable (Windows PowerShell variables are preceded by a $ character). To see the methods for this object, type the following command:

```
PS C:\Users\administrator.CONTOSO> $TMGRoot | Get-Member -memberType *method
   TypeName: System.__ComObject#{8bf0aefa-b4fd-4d81-8046-a069d948d673}

Name                                     MemberType Definition
----                                     ---------- ----------
ApplyChanges                             Method     void ApplyChanges (bool, bool)
ApplyChangesWithDescription              Method     void ApplyChangesWithDescription
                                                    (bool, bool, string)
CanImport                                Method     bool CanImport (IUnknown, bool)
ChangeController                         Method     void ChangeController (string)
ConnectToConfigServerPort                Method     void ConnectToConfigServerPort
                                                    (string, string, string, string, ...
ConnectToConfigurationStorageServer      Method     void ConnectToConfigurationStorage
                                                    Server (string, string, string...
ConnectToLocalStorage                    Method     void ConnectToLocalStorage ()
DiscardChanges                           Method     void DiscardChanges ()
DisconnectFromConfigurationStorageServer Method     void
DisconnectFromConfigurationStorageServer ()
DisconnectFromLocalStorage               Method     void DisconnectFromLocalStorage ()
Export                                   Method     void Export (IUnknown, int,
                                                    string, string)
ExportToFile                             Method     void ExportToFile (string, int,
                                                    string, string)
GetContainingArray                       Method     IFPCArray GetContainingArray ()
GetContainingServer                      Method     IFPCServer GetContainingServer ()
Import                                   Method     void Import (IUnknown, int,
                                                    string, bool, bool, bool)
ImportFromFile                           Method     void ImportFromFile (string, int,
                                                    string, bool, bool, bool)
```

InstallRootCACertificate	Method	void InstallRootCACertificate (string)
InstallStorageServerCertificate	Method	void
InstallStorageServerCertificate (string, string)		
JoinArray	Method	void JoinArray (IFPCArray3)
LeaveArray	Method	void LeaveArray (bool)
LoadDocProperties	Method	void LoadDocProperties (IUnknown, string, int, string)
Refresh	Method	void Refresh (bool)
RestoreToStandalone	Method	void RestoreToStandalone ()
Save	Method	void Save (bool, bool)
SaveWithDescription	Method	void SaveWithDescription (bool, bool, string)
SetAsController	Method	void SetAsController ()t

Notice that the type name for the object has the ProgID that was mentioned earlier:

```
TypeName: System.__ComObject#{8bf0aefa-b4fd-4d81-8046-a069d948d673}
```

To see the properties of the *FPC.Root* object you just need to change the last part of the command and use the *argument* property:

```
PS C:\Users\administrator.CONTOSO> $TMGRoot | Get-Member -memberType *property
   TypeName: System.__ComObject#{8bf0aefa-b4fd-4d81-8046-a069d948d673}
Name                       MemberType Definition
----                       ---------- ----------
Arrays                     Property   IFPCArrays Arrays () {get}
ChangesMade                Property   bool ChangesMade () {get}
ConfigurationMode          Property   FpcConfigurationMode ConfigurationMode () {get}
ConfigurationStorageServer Property   string ConfigurationStorageServer () {get}
Enterprise                 Property   IFPCEEEnterprise Enterprise () {get}
IsaEdition                 Property   FpcIsaEditionType IsaEdition () {get}
RequireApplyChanges        Property   bool RequireApplyChanges () {get} {set}
StorageChangeNumber        Property   int64 StorageChangeNumber () {get}
VendorMode                 Property   bool VendorMode () {get} {set}
```

> **NOTE** You can also use the command *$TMGRoot | get-member | more* to view both methods and properties.

Because this variable is defined you also can use it for other purposes—for example, if you want to find out who is the Configuration Storage Server, you just need to type the variable name—in this case **$TMGRoot**—and you get the following output:

```
PS C:\Users\administrator.CONTOSO> $TMGRoot
Arrays                     : {TMGB3}
Enterprise                 : System.__ComObject
ConfigurationStorageServer : TMGB3.contoso.com
RequireApplyChanges        : False
ChangesMade                : False
StorageChangeNumber        : 20599
IsaEdition                 : 32
VendorMode                 : False
ConfigurationMode          : 0
```

You can also access a property of the *FPC.Root* object (stored on the variable *$TMGRoot*) by typing the variable name plus the property name. If you just want to see who is the Configuration Storage server, type the following command:

```
PS C:\Users\administrator.CONTOSO> $TMGRoot.ConfigurationStorageServer
TMGB3.contoso.com
```

> **IMPORTANT** You can use Windows PowerShell's discover capability for command completion. If you type **$TMGRoot.** and press the Tab key you will see the available options for the command.

Windows PowerShell Automation Examples

The tasks that were automated previously using VBScript and JScript will now be performed by Windows PowerShell. You can use Notepad to write your Windows PowerShell script and then save it with a .ps1 extension. However, some free Windows PowerShell editors have the IntelliSense feature and can help you write your script.

> **MORE INFO** The following post from Taylor Brown, Test Lead for the Windows Core Operating System Division, offers more information about some of these editors: *http://blogs.msdn.com/taylorb/archive/2008/08/22/open-source-free-powershell-editor-powergui.aspx.*

The first step is to locate arrays associated with an Enterprise policy, which can be accomplished with the following Windows PowerShell script:

```
# declare and define the TMG root object
$oFPC = New-Object -comObject FPC.root

# declare and define the value that expresses if array work was successful
$bFailed = $False

# declare and define the value that expresses whether any changes occurred
$bChanges = $False

# declare and define the TMG arrays collection
$cArrays = $oFPC.Arrays

# declare the Array object variable
$oArray

# enumerate (walk through) the array list looking for the ones of interest
$Result = "Outbound Proxy"

Foreach ($oArray in $cArrays)
{
    write-host "Policy name:" $oArray.PolicyAssignment.EnterprisePolicyUsed.Name
    If ( $oArray.PolicyAssignment.EnterprisePolicyUsed.Name -eq $Result){
        write-host "Array Name:" $oArray.name
        # if we try to work an array and fail, we want to quit now
        If ( UpdateArray($oArray) -eq $false )
                {$bFailed = $True}
        # otherwise, we declare that we made changes to at least one array
                else {$bChanges = $True}
                }
    }
    # if we made any changes without failures, now is the time to save them
If ($bChanges -ne ( $bFailed ))
        {SaveChanges( $oArray )}
        {SaveChanges( $oArray )}
```

MORE INFO   To make your transition from VBScript to Windows PowerShell easier, read the VBScript-to-Windows PowerShell Conversion Guide at *http://www.microsoft.com/ technet/scriptcenter/topics/winpsh/convert/default.mspx.*

The second step is to export and import using files:

```
Function UpdateArray( $oArray )
{
    #define the default return value for this function
    $UpdateArray = $False

    #declare and define the TMG export file path
    $szOutFilePath = "C:\TmgExportFile.xml"

    #declare and define the optional data for the export method
    $iOptionalData = 0

    #declare and define the TMG export data password
    $szPassword = ""

    #declare and define the TMG export file comment section
    $szComment = "Exported by ExportArrays.ps1 at "

    #try to export the current configuration to a file
    write-host "Name:" $oArray.Name
    $oArray.ExportToFile($szOutFilePath, $iOptionalData, $szPassword, $szComment)

    #disable script error handling
    $bOverwrite= $False

    #declare and define the TMG import services reset flag
    $bReset = $False

    #declare and define the TMG import policy reload flag
    $bReload = $True

    #declare and define the TMG import file path
    $szInFilePath = "C:\TmgImportFile.xml"

    #try to import the configuration update from a file
    $oArray.ImportFromFile($szInFilePath, $iOptionalData, $szPassword, $bOverwrite,
$bReset, $bReload)
    $UpdateArray = $True
}
```

The third and final step is to save the changes:

```
Function SaveChanges( $oArray )
{
    Trap [Exception]
    {
    write-host "Failed to save the array configuration changes; "
$_.Exception.GetType().FullName "; "  $_.Exception.Message

    # if it fails, tell the user and bail out
    write-host "Failed to save the array configuration changes; "
$_.Exception.GetType().FullName "; "  $_.Exception.Message
    Exit
    }

    # define the default value of this function
    $SaveChanges = $False
    $oArray.Save

    # no failures, return "true"
    $SaveChanges = $True
    write-host "Changes Saved"
}
```

Summary

In this chapter you learned some basics about COM and how to write some sample scripts for TMG using VBScript, JScript, and Windows PowerShell. This helps eliminate the need to use the UI to configure any settings if the administrator wants to provide this information in an automated way. In the next chapter we will discuss how to use Network Monitor to troubleshoot issues in TMG.

PART X

Troubleshooting

CHAPTER 31 Mastering the Art of Troubleshooting **851**

CHAPTER 32 Exploring HTTP Protocol **869**

CHAPTER 33 Using Network Monitor 3
for Troubleshooting TMG **891**

Mastering the Art of Troubleshooting

- General Troubleshooting Methodology   **851**

- Troubleshooting Tools   **855**

- Putting It All Together   **862**

- Summary   **868**

Troubleshooting any issue requires you to understand the different tools and logs available and to decide which ones fit the current scenario. Sometimes, as a result of various constraints, you will only be able to use a subset of logs. However, if you follow a linear, logical troubleshooting methodology, you can easily decide which tools and logs to use and solve the issue quickly. In the chapter you will learn about the different tools and logs available to help you troubleshoot problems with TMG.

General Troubleshooting Methodology

When troubleshooting an issue (not necessarily a computer issue) the very first thing that you need to do is understand and precisely define the problem. Scoping the issue and defining the problem is a great start, because without a definition the problem might not even be solved. You must have a clear understanding of the problem before you can come up with a solution.

When defining the problem, try to answer questions like the following:

- **Define the implementation**   Did this implementation ever work?

- **Continue asking questions about possible changes**   What changes were made since the last time things were correctly working?

- **Take a broad view and determine whether new additions have been made**   If no changes were made, were any new elements introduced in this environment?

- **Verify how often it happens**   What is the frequency of this problem? Is it random or does it happen all the time?

It is normal to sometimes ask questions and find out that the person you are speaking with doesn't have all the answers. The important thing to remember is that when you are dealing with Forefront TMG problems you have tools that can assist you in determining whether changes were made in the system. Using the change tracking tool—introduced in ISA Server 2006 SP1 and included in TMG—is a great example of how to go beyond asking questions about an issue to get concrete data about possible changes. Figure 31-1 shows an example of the Change Tracking indicating changes that were made.

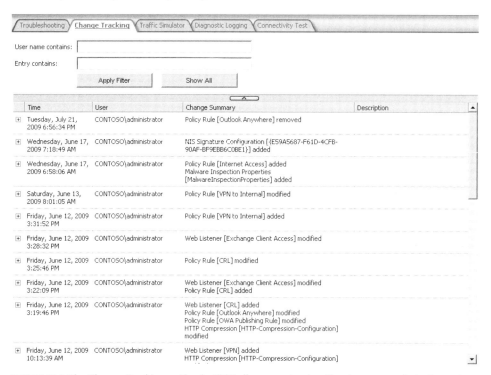

FIGURE 31-1 The Change Tracking option in TMG allows you to view the changes made to the system.

A very common mistake made during problem definition is usually the result of performance-related issues. Administrators commonly tend to mix their terms and create confusion about what is really happening. For example, let's say the person you are speaking with tells you that TMG is hanging and nobody can access Internet when this happens. This is a very broad definition of the problem—you need to refine the problem and dig in to get more information:

- **Clarify the terminology** When you say that TMG is hanging, are you saying that you cannot even log on locally on TMG and open the TMG console?

- **Try to isolate the component (is it the operating system or TMG?)** When the hanging occurs, does the whole computer slow down?

- **Continue narrowing things down to determine whether a visible element is showing excessive resource utilization** Do you have any process that is consuming more CPU at that time?
- **Verify whether a workaround is possible** Is there any procedure you can do to alleviate the problem when this happens?

After defining the problem it is important to restate your understanding of what the problem is. This is important because sometimes you think that you may really understand the problem; however, the person you're talking to might have a completely different expectation of what is going to be solved. By restating the problem definition to the person you are speaking with you can make sure that you are both on the same page—and that you have a formal agreement regarding what is going to be solved.

It is a good practice to try to resolve one issue at the time. Do not create a broad definition of an issue—this makes finding a solution much more difficult. By working with a single, indivisible issue you can better manage expectations and achieve a more realistic result.

You've Defined the Problem—What's Next?

After all parties understand the problem, restate it and agree on what is going to be resolved. The next step is to collect the data you need to resolve the problem. Having a precise definition of the problem will help you to gather the right data. How you approach acquiring the data you need depends on the type of problem you are dealing with.

An issue that is random and not reproducible is more challenging, because you need to set up the environment to get data while the issue is happening and then keep monitoring the results. If the issue is reproducible, the data gathering is much more straightforward. Usually data gathering for TMG problems is done using ISA Data Packager, which is part of the ISA Best Practices Analyzer; you will read more about this tool later in this chapter.

> **MORE INFO** ISA Data Packager can be used in both reactive and proactive scenarios. For some examples of those scenarios, go to *http://blogs.technet.com/yuridiogenes/ archive/2009/03/13/using-isabpa-for-proactively-and-reactively-work-with-isa-server-part-1-of-2.aspx* and *http://blogs.technet.com/yuridiogenes/archive/2009/05/07/using-isabpa-for-proactive-and-reactive-work-with-isa-server-part-2-of-2.aspx*.

Other scenarios for data gathering involve much more than the ISA Data Packager, such as when you are dealing with performance issues. Troubleshooting performance issues is very challenging because often the root cause is not the TMG firewall itself. In this case you will need to use other tools, such as:

- Windows Performance Monitor
- Get user mode dump using ADPLUS or DebugDiag
- Get kernel memory dump using crash control

Data gathering also can be challenging in scenarios where you need to collect data in multiple parts, such as collecting network monitor traces on the domain controller or on TMG. In some companies the firewall administrator and the Directory Service administrator are separate jobs; therefore, you need to make sure that the whole team shares the same goal and is willing to collaborate to get data at the right time.

Time to Analyze the Data

When you receive the data gathered during the problem, you need to be careful not to start looking for other issues. A common mistake that happens during data analysis is losing focus of what you are really looking for. Verify that error you see in Forefront TMG Alerts is relevant to what you are troubleshooting. If it is not, you can skip it.

When dealing with data analysis from multiple sources it is important to verify that all elements are in sync. For example, in a scenario where a client sends a HTTP GET and Forefront TMG needs to authenticate the request and it fails, you will need to get data from three parts and carefully analyze it using the following guidelines:

- When the client sends the HTTP GET and Forefront TMG requests authentication, does the authenticated packet arrive to Forefront TMG?
- If it does not, does it leave the client workstation?
- If it leaves the client workstation and doesn't reach Forefront TMG, is something in the middle dropping this packet?

How can you answer those questions? By having a network monitor trace from the client and from TMG at the same time so that you can verify whether the packet was sent and received correctly. Notice that this type of analysis depends on a good data gathering plan, which means that if you fail to collect the correct set of data you will also fail during the data analysis.

In some scenarios you won't be able to find the root cause of the problem in the first round of data gathering, or you might have already found the cause of the issue but you need more data to confirm it. In this type of scenario you need to go back and elaborate a new data gathering plan to complement what you already have.

Got It, Now I'm Going to Fix It!

Assuming that the data analysis was successful, and you know exactly what to do to fix the problem, the next step is implementing the solution. Sometimes it's not quite that easy because the solution involves changes or additions that might affect the production environment, such as a hotfix that requires a restart. You need to understand the environment's boundaries while proposing the solution—do not implement it without first considering possible side effects the solution might introduce. For example, if the solution for the problem is a hardware upgrade, this might not happen immediately. Although this can be the ultimate solution, you may need to brainstorm ideas about how to temporarily alleviate the problem. Looking for alternative solutions can help during scenarios like that.

Troubleshooting Tools

Among IT administrators, the first thing most of them will think of when they hear the word *tool* is some hardware or software device that helps them define and isolate a problem they're trying to solve. Although this definition is certainly accurate, your primary tool should be the one you carry with you all day—your brain. If this tool is not working at its best or is lacking information you need to accurately discern fault from fantasy, and no collection of peripheral mechanisms can help. To become an effective TMG troubleshooter you need to understand the following:

- **The traffic profile (protocols used) for your deployment**   It's extremely rare that any client/server communication involves a single protocol. For example, the client typically performs name resolution prior to making a connection to the server. If the client does not need to go through TMG to reach the DNS server, this traffic will not be seen by TMG, but the DNS query *must* complete successfully before the connection can be attempted by the client; much less processed by TMG.

- **The traffic profile for the problematic scenario**   Some application protocols (such as RTSP, MMS, and so on) involve the use of multiple transports and protocols in multiple directions. A client making a VPN connection using PPTP is one such example; it must use DNS to resolve the VPN server name to an IP, then use PPTP (TCP port 1723) to create the management channel, then build a connection to the same VPN server using GRE (IP protocol number 47). If you don't have a clear understanding of this process, the data you gather will be of little value to you.

- **How the client/server pair utilizes the traffic profile to build transactions**   In this context, you need to have a slightly more detailed understanding of the traffic profile. For instance, FTP data transactions cannot begin (much less complete) if the FTP control channel is not established. Likewise, if the FTP client cannot use passive FTP and the firewall blocks active FTP, the control channel will succeed, but the data channel cannot be established.

- **Whether TMG is involved in the transactions**   In many cases, the problem is unrelated to TMG. For instance, the WPAD process begins with DHCP or DNS and only then does the WPAD client attempt to communicate with TMG. Until the WPAD client can discover the name or IP address of the TMG computer, it cannot request the WPAD script. In this instance, WPAD script acquisition fails, but TMG was never involved in the process.

- **How TMG affects the transactions**   TMG must modify some of the data passed between the client and server in order to satisfy the requirements of the protocol designers. In many cases, a Web site will use data presented by the client to build the content it presents to the client. This is done to personalize the content for the user based on the choices they make or preferences they've expressed. Although this can provide a richer user experience, if this is performed carelessly, it can produce some unexpected results.

REAL WORLD   Appearances Can Be Deceptive

One of the most common troubleshooting tactics when the proxy is "misbehaving" is to use a computer that can communicate to the Internet without having to use the proxy. This often helps you determine if the problem is at the proxy, but is not deterministic.

One fine day at Microsoft, our proxy users were complaining that when they accessed a particular Web site through ISA Server many of the images and links were broken. One user pointed out that all of the broken links and images indicated a URL that included the proxy server name. For example, when this user rested his mouse pointer over a broken link, the status bar in the browser described the link as *http://<proxyname>/resource* instead of *http://www.contoso.com/resource*. Users pointed out that because this didn't happen from home, it must be the fault of the ISA Server in their path. Indeed, using a computer that did not use the proxy to reach this site produced a page with proper links.

Because I know that ISA Link Translation does not operate on content requested by CERN proxy clients, I realized that this had to be the fault of the Web site, but I wasn't yet clear on how this could happen. Thus, I had to do a bit more sleuthing to discover why these links were displaying the ISA Server name.

I gathered my trusty Network Monitor and obtained a capture on the external network of my test ISA Server while I accessed this Web site. Once I had this captured, I told Network Monitor to search for any instance of my ISA Server name in the capture data. As expected, it located it in the VIA header sent by ISA when it forwarded the request to the Web server.

```
- Http: Request, GET /product/5541270
    Command: GET
  + URI: /product/5541270
    ProtocolVersion: HTTP/1.1
    Via:  1.1 ISASERED-DTAP1
```

Not as expected, Network Monitor also located the ISA Server name in the Web server response, buried in the HTML content as the reference URL in the "base" element.

```
- Http: Response, HTTP/1.1, Status Code = 200, URL: /product/5541270
    ProtocolVersion: HTTP/1.1
    StatusCode: 200, Ok
    Reason: OK
    Date:  Fri, 26 Sep 2008 17:30:24 GMT
    Server:  Apache
    XPoweredBy:  Servlet 2.4; JBoss-4.0.4.GA (build: CVSTag=JBoss_4_0_4_
                 GA date=200605151000)/Tomcat-5.5
    Set-Cookie:  JSESSIONID=qB3MYuKothSTpBZVeUHOuA**.node1; Path=/
    Set-Cookie:  ID_KOT=987123654; Domain=.contoso.com; Path=/
    Connection:  close
    TransferEncoding:  chunked
    ContentType:  text/html;charset=ISO-8859-1
    HeaderEnd: CRLF
  + chunkSize: 8184
  - ChunkPayload: HttpContentType =  text/html;charset=ISO-8859-1
    HtmlElement: <html>
    HtmlElement: <head>
    HtmlElement: <base href="http://ISASERED-DTAP1/">
```

This told me that the Web site was (for whatever reason) building their Web content using the data found in the VIA header sent by all RFC-2616-compliant proxy servers. I contacted the Web site owners, provided the network captures, and explained that this was preventing their customers from browsing beyond the home page (not to mention preventing them from purchasing anything). They thanked me for this information and within a few days, had resolved the problem.

> **NOTE**   The "base" element is used by browsers to build complete URLs from relative URLS. This HTML element is described in *http://msdn.microsoft.com/ en-us/library/ms535191(VS.85).aspx.*

Although this example is a bit extreme, it illustrates my favorite troubleshooting axiom: "Trust your indications and determinations, but validate them anyway." Although the problem seemed to be caused by ISA because "when ISA is not in the path, the problem does not appear," further investigation proved this determination to be false. Remember that especially when under stress (such as when the boss can't reach her favorite research site), we tend to view data through our own expectations. If you validate your test results, you're less likely to fall victim to your own preconceptions.

The reason that you must acquire a functional understanding of these points is that without this information, the data produced by many of the tools described in the following sections will make little sense to you. For example, the TMG log entries or conversation sequence as observed in a traffic capture tool produced by a normal NTLM-over-HTTP authentication cycle may cause you to veer off course in your troubleshooting efforts if you don't understand the traffic patterns that are described by them.

TMG Troubleshooting Tab

Like ISA Server 2006, this section of the management console is designed to provide a one-click source for the most common troubleshooting tools provided with TMG. From this page, you have access to a rich set of troubleshooting tools through which you can resolve the most common problems as reported to Microsoft CSS. Figure 31-2 illustrates this context.

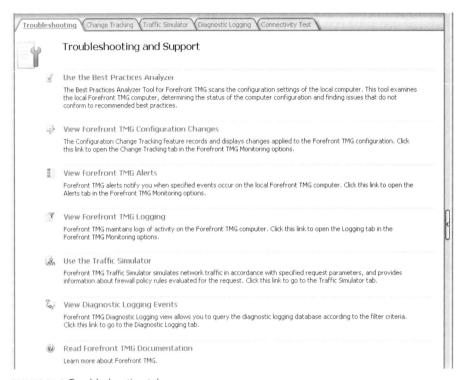

FIGURE 31-2 Troubleshooting tab

- **Use The Best Practices Analyzer** If you have not yet downloaded the Best Practices Analyzer (BPA) tool, this link will take you to the download location from which you can acquire the tool installation package. Once you have downloaded and installed the BPA tool, clicking this link will auto-start the BPA. The BPA is a tool that provides you with the means to quickly validate your TMG installation and configuration against established best practices and will also enumerate any alerts and errors reported by TMG as well as those reported by Windows that may impact TMG functionality.

- **View Forefront TMG Configuration Changes**   This link takes you to the Change Tracking tab on the same TMG management console page. TMG Change Tracking performs exactly the same functions as in ISA Server 2006, except that this feature is enabled by default in TMG. This feature is designed to allow you to "travel back in TMG time" to see what changes were made that might impact TMG behavior relevant to the problem you're currently chasing. This is frequently useful when the problem is stated as "it used to work...."

- **View Forefront TMG Alerts**   This link takes you to the Alerts tab on the Monitoring page of the TMG management console. The Alerts tab is useful when you want to perform a quick search for any recent complaints TMG may have expressed about the traffic, environment, or administrative actions taken. Because TMG is very quick to complain, the Alerts tab is one of the first places you should go when TMG behavior changes unexpectedly.

- **View Forefront TMG Logging**   This link takes you to the Logging tab on the Logs & Reports page of the TMG management console. In this page, you can query the TMG logs or active traffic to determine how TMG handled the traffic presented to it. Once you become familiar with the traffic profile in your environment, this may well become your favorite troubleshooting tool. The traffic log viewer allows you to filter out traffic that doesn't concern you at this time, allowing you to concentrate on the traffic that is relevant to the problem you're chasing.

- **Use The Traffic Simulator**   This link takes you to the Traffic Simulator tab on the Troubleshooting page. Using this tool, you can test TMG behavior in using a simplified context for the traffic as it would be generated by the client without having to use the client itself. This is very useful as it allows you to remove the client application from the equation, thus reducing the number of factors you must consider at one time.

- **View Diagnostic Logging Events**   This link takes you to the Diagnostic Logging tab on the Troubleshooting page. This tab provides filtered visibility into the debug tracing that is created in the ISA Server Diagnostics event log. From within the Diagnostic Logging tab, you can control TMG diagnostic logging and filter the event log data to locate the desired log events. Figure 31-3 illustrates the related event log location within Windows Server Manager MMC.

- **Read Forefront TMG Documentation**   This link takes you the help file installed with TMG.

FIGURE 31-3 ISA Server Diagnostics event log

Best Practices Analyzer

If you are new to TMG, the BPA tool should be your first choice for verifying your TMG deployments. This tool is designed to help you identify and correct most common deployment and installation errors as well as problems in the underlying Windows subsystem that may affect TMG functionality. Figure 31-4 provides an example of a BPA output.

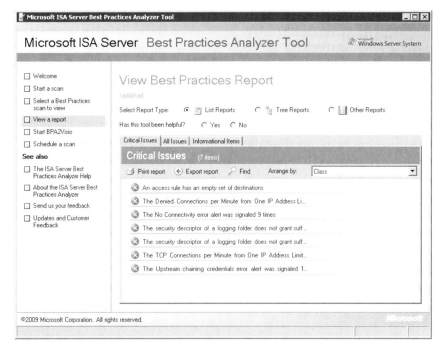

FIGURE 31-4 Example BPA output

BPA was originally created to help CSS engineers gather the data they needed to more quickly understand the environment where ISA Server was operating. It was quickly changed to enable ISA Server administrators to self-solve their own problems, saving them time and money.

BPA includes additional tools that make it easier for you to gather relevant data and describe your TMG configuration:

- **ISA Data Packager (IDP)**   This tool was created to help you more easily and reliably gather the proper data relevant to the scenario you are troubleshooting. This tool was originally designed to assist CSS in their investigation efforts, but was later included in the BPA for customers to use without having to ask a CSS engineer for it.

- **BPA2Visio**   This tool imports the TMG configuration and produces a network map in Microsoft Office Visio format based on the network as described to TMG. This allows you to validate that what you have told TMG about your network structure agrees with how your network is actually constructed.

Network Monitor

Microsoft Network Monitor is designed to gather network traffic and help you discover traffic anomalies. As with any tool, the more time you spend with it, the more proficient you will become at identifying protocol misbehavior. Also, the more time you spend reviewing normal application traffic, the more easily you will identify problems within these protocols. Network Monitor is very useful for discovering the details related to the TMG traffic and diagnostic logging events. The sidebar "Appearances Can Be Deceptive" describes one case where Network Monitor proved to be the best tool for isolating a problem. We will discuss Network Monitor–based troubleshooting in detail in Chapter 33, "Using Network Monitor 3 for Troubleshooting TMG."

Performance Monitor

Windows Performance Monitor (PerfMon) is a tool designed to help you monitor server and application performance in two contexts: establishing a performance baseline and when troubleshooting performance-related problems. If you have not established a performance baseline, you will be hard-pressed to determine whether TMG performance is what should be expected in your environment. The counters you should monitor depend largely on the deployment scenario where TMG operates and the traffic profile it serves. For example, if your TMG operates only as a CERN proxy, the SOCKS and E-mail Hygiene counters will be of no interest to you. Conversely, if your TMG is deployed only for publishing Exchange Web client services, the Enhanced Malware and URL filtering counters will likely provide no useful data. We will discuss TMG performance monitoring in Appendix B, "TMG Performance Counters."

Windows Event Logs

Windows event logs are critical points for analyzing computer behavior, regardless of the computer role. TMG depends on Windows for a great many services, such as user authentication, name resolution, network access, disk services, and so on. It's critically important that whenever TMG misbehaves you verify proper Windows functionality by searching the System, Application, and Security event logs for errors and warnings. Doing this can often save a lot of time. For nearly every event triggered in TMG Monitoring, Alerts, there will be a corresponding Windows Application event log entry that contains amplifying data about the alert. Figure 31-3 shows the location of these event logs.

Putting It All Together

Now that you have learned about the different tools and logs that an administrator can use to troubleshoot an issue, the biggest challenge you face while working on an issue is to decide which logs or what combination of data is needed to effectively resolve the issue. Every issue manifests itself in a different way, yet the solutions may be similar or even identical in many cases. Thus, the thing you need to understand first and foremost is "Do not troubleshoot symptoms, troubleshoot the issue."

Real-Life Case Study

To better understand how you can use different logs to troubleshoot an issue, let's discuss a real-life scenario in which we trace back an issue to its source using simple linear logical troubleshooting techniques.

Scenario

A company reports that Web Proxy clients are randomly being prompted for credentials when going to the Internet through Forefront TMG. Even after entering the proper credentials, the users cannot get to the Internet. The company only allows Internet access to a certain group of users; hence, authentication is required. The problem happens with random users at random times and only lasts for a very short duration (about 10–15 minutes). Eventually the issue goes away on its own and Internet access is restored for the affected users. The company has about 500 Web Proxy users.

Roadblocks

In general the best way to start troubleshooting most of the issues is to start gathering data using ISA Best Practices Analyzer. If the issue is intermittent and only happens for a short duration like in the scenario mentioned here, it might not be possible for you to collect ISA data packager information. Having the ISA data packager logs is always helpful because it collects a variety of different logs pertaining to the issue.

Environment

There are about 500 client computers and three domain controllers in the network. TMG is on the edge and has a direct connection to the Internet. The network is fairly simple without too many devices between the clients and TMG, hence data capturing should be fairly simple except for the roadblocks. Figure 31-5 shows the network diagram.

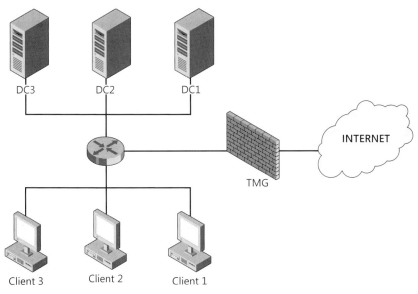

FIGURE 31-5 Network diagram

Troubleshooting

The first thought that may come to mind when users receive random authentication prompts is that some domain controllers may be overloaded with authentication requests or that TMG is not receiving a timely response from the domain controllers. Although the former can be overlooked (mainly because three domain controllers should be enough for 500 users depending upon the traffic generated), the latter could be still highly possible—not because of load but because of other hardware factors.

> **MORE INFO** To understand how Web Proxy authentication works, please refer to *http://technet.microsoft.com/en-us/library/bb984870.aspx*.

In this case, you want to collect the following data if possible:

- ISA Data Packager from TMG
- Network trace from the client computer
- Network trace from the domain controller

- Event logs from TMG, the client computer, and the domain controller
- Netlogon logs from the domain controller

Because there are three domain controllers, you need to locate the domain controller with which TMG has a secure channel. To do so, you can use the NLTEST command. NLTEST is a part of the Windows Support tools; you can find the syntax for the command at *http://technet.microsoft.com/en-us/library/cc786478(WS.10).aspx*.

Running the NLTEST command on TMG reveals that TMG has a secure channel with DC1, as shown in Figure 31-6.

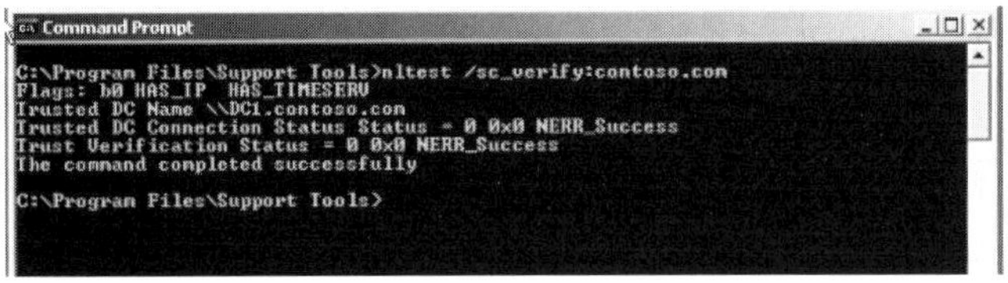

FIGURE 31-6 NLTEST command

Because we know that TMG has a secure channel with DC1, the next task is to enable Netlogon logging on DC1. To enable Netlogon logging you can either use KB 109626 from *http://support.microsoft.com/default.aspx?scid=kb;en-us;109626* or use NLTEST to enable Netlogon logging.

Using **NTLEST /dbflag:0x2080ffff** in the command line on the domain controller, you can enable Netlogon logging. Once Netlogon logging is enabled, a restart of the Netlogon service on the domain controller is required. The Netlogon.Log file is generated in the %Systemroot%\Debug directory.

> **NOTE** Enabling Netlogon logging can reduce the performance of a domain controller and thus should only be enabled for troubleshooting and should be disabled once logs are collected. To disable Netlogon logging use **NLTEST /dbflag: 0x0** from the command prompt.

The following code is a sample of what the Netlogon log looks like:

```
06/10 15:10:01 [LOGON] CONTOSO: SamLogon: Generic logon of CONTOSO.COM\(null)
from (null) (via TESTCLIENT) Package:Kerberos Returns 0x0
06/10 15:10:01 [LOGON] CONTOSO: SamLogon: Generic logon of CONTOSO.COM\(null)
from (null) (via TESTCLIENT) Package:Kerberos Entered
06/10 15:10:01 [LOGON] CONTOSO: SamLogon: Generic logon of CONTOSO.COM\(null)
from (null) (via TESTCLIENT) Package:Kerberos Returns 0x0
06/10 15:10:10 [LOGON] CONTOSO: SamLogon: Generic logon of CONTOSO.COM\(null)
from (null) Package:Kerberos Entered
06/10 15:10:10 [LOGON] CONTOSO: SamLogon: Generic logon of CONTOSO.COM\(null)
from (null) Package:Kerberos Returns 0x0
```

```
06/10 15:10:10 [LOGON] CONTOSO: SamLogon: Generic logon of CONTOSO.COM\(null)
from (null) Package:Kerberos Entered
06/10 15:10:10 [LOGON] CONTOSO: SamLogon: Generic logon of CONTOSO.COM\(null)
from (null) Package:Kerberos Returns 0x0
06/10 15:10:21 [LOGON] CONTOSO: SamLogon: Generic logon of CONTOSO.COM\(null)
from (null) (via TESTCLIENT) Package:Kerberos Entered
06/10 15:10:21 [LOGON] CONTOSO: SamLogon: Generic logon of CONTOSO.COM\(null)
from (null) (via TESTCLIENT) Package:Kerberos Returns 0x0
06/10 15:10:25 [LOGON] CONTOSO: SamLogon: Generic logon of CONTOSO.COM\(null)
from (null) (via TESTCLIENT) Package:Kerberos Entered
06/10 15:10:25 [LOGON] CONTOSO: SamLogon: Generic logon of CONTOSO.COM\(null)
from (null) (via TESTCLIENT) Package:Kerberos Returns 0x0
```

Because the problem happened only for a very short duration, we set up Network Monitor on the TMG with a buffer size of 200 MB so that the administrator has enough time to stop the Network Monitor on TMG once the problem is reported. Netlogon logging is also enabled on the domain controllers.

After we collect the Network Monitor traces from the client we notice the following:

The client makes request to *http://www.fabrikam.com*:

```
GET http://www.fabrikam.com/default.htm HTTP/1.1
Accept: */*
UA-CPU: x86
Accept-Encoding: gzip, deflate
User-Agent: Mozilla/4.0 (compatible; MSIE 7.0; Windows NT 6.0; WOW64; SLCC1;
            .NET CLR 2.0.50727; .NET CLR 3.0.04506; .NET CLR 1.1.4322)
Host: www.fabrikam.com
Proxy-Connection: Keep-Alive
Proxy-Authorization: Negotiate
TlRMTVNTUAABAAAAl4II4gAAAAAAAAAAAAAAAAAAAAAGAHEXAAAADw==
```

TMG replies, saying authorization is needed:

```
HTTP/1.1 407 Proxy Authentication Required ( Access is denied. )
Via: 1.1 TMGServer
Proxy-Authenticate: Negotiate TlRMTVNTUAACAAAACAAIADgAAAAVgoniixZbMGzsm64AAAAAAAAA
JgAmABAAAAAABgBxFwAAAA9DAE8AUgBQAAIACABDAE8AUgBQAAEACABGAFQATQBHAAQAHgBDAG8AcgBwAC4
AVABNAEcATABBAEIALgBOAEUAVAADACgARgBUAE0ARwAuAEMAbwByAHAALgBUAGUAcABWBMAEEAQgAuAE4
ARQBUAAUAUAHgBDAG8AcgBwAC4AVABNAEcATABBAEIALgBOAEUAVAAHAAgAAKmOcrJ8ZygEAAAAA
Connection: Keep-Alive
Proxy-Connection: Keep-Alive
Pragma: no-cache
Cache-Control: no-cache
Content-Type: text/html
Content-Length: 0
```

The client sends the request for *http://www.fabrikam.com* again with user name and credentials:

```
GET http://www.fabrikam.com/default.htm HTTP/1.1
Accept: */*
UA-CPU: x86
Accept-Encoding: gzip, deflate
User-Agent: Mozilla/4.0 (compatible; MSIE 7.0; Windows NT 6.0; WOW64; SLCC1;
            .NET CLR 2.0.50727; .NET CLR 3.0.04506; .NET CLR 1.1.4322)
Host: www.fabrikam.com
Proxy-Connection: Keep-Alive
Proxy-Authorization: Negotiate TlRMTVNTUAADAAAAGAAYAH4AAAAIAQgBlgAAAgACABYAAAACgAKA
GAAAAUABQAagAAABAAEACeAQAAFYKI4gYAcRcAAAAP3PSTXY4idl1mGEdKo75aYWMAbwByAHAAdQBzAGUA
cgBhAFQARQBTAFQAQwBMAEkARQBOAFQAAAAAAAAAAAAAAAAAAAAAAAAAAAAAMGMms7YcOJ9xyuhI/
11rOgEBAAAAAAAAKmOcrJ8ZygGWEj3ubMj25wAAAAACAAgAQwBPAFIAUAABAAgARgBUAEOARwAEAB4AQwBv
AHIAcAAuAFQATQBHBHAEwAQQBCAC4ATgBFAFQAAwAwAoAEYAVABNBNAEcALgBDAG8AcgBwAC4AVABNBNAEcATABBAEIA
LgBOAEUAVAAFAB4AQwBvAHIAcAAuAFQATQBHBHAEwAQQBCAC4ATgBFAFQABwAIACptHKyfGcoBBgAEAAIAAAA
IADAAMAAAAAAAAAAAAAAABAAAIB7I/9XMGigdDKL7aC1uBgzX7C1k2sRE8coizN4QigsAAAAAAAAAAAAAAA
FEQUOwykL/etMpZpUGMjNA==
```

TMG sends the credentials to the domain controller to authorize the request:

```
DCERPC Request: call_id: 12 opnum: 39 ctx_id: 1
```

The domain controller sends the response back to TMG:

```
DCERPC Response: call_id: 12 ctx_id: 1
```

TMG denies the request to the client:

```
HTTP/1.1 407 Proxy Authentication Required ( The Forefront TMG requires authorization
to fulfill the request. Access to the Web Proxy filter is denied. )
Via: 1.1 TMGServer
Proxy-Authenticate: Negotiate
Proxy-Authenticate: Kerberos
Proxy-Authenticate: NTLM
Connection: close
Proxy-Connection: close
Pragma: no-cache
Cache-Control: no-cache
Content-Type: text/html
Content-Length: 4127
```

From the trace, it wasn't clear why the domain controller did not authorize the user's credentials. And because the domain controller did reply, we know that the domain controller was responsive. We check the event logs and did not find any event ID 5783 that is generally logged if the domain controller is unresponsive.

To find out why the domain controller isn't authorizing the user's account, we analyze the Netlogon logs. We use the article "Maintaining and Monitoring Lockouts" from *http://technet .microsoft.com/en-us/library/cc776964(WS.10).aspx* as a reference to better understand the logs. Using this article we can see that the code 0x0 is a successful logon. This log file can get quite large depending on the environment, number of clients, and amount of traffic generated, so it helps to be able to quickly find what you are looking for. Because we know the account name of a user being affected (Contoso\UserA), we can filter this log file and find the information we need. You can use a simple command to help an administrator sort out the entries that we need and to do this by using the command findstr from the command prompt. For our troubleshooting we use the following:

```
findstr /I "contoso\UserA" c:\windows\debug\netlogon.log >> c:\windows\debug\failed.txt
```

A new file by the name of failed.txt is generated, only contains information pertaining to contoso\UserA. From the log file, we find the following:

```
06/10 18:45:07 [LOGON] CONTOSO: SamLogon: Transitive Network logon of CONTOSO\UserA
from TESTCLIENT (via TMGServer) Entered
06/10 18:45:07 [LOGON] CONTOSO: SamLogon: Transitive Network logon of CONTOSO\UserA
from TESTCLIENT (via TMGServer) Returns 0xc0000022
06/10 18:45:07 [LOGON] CONTOSO: SamLogon: Transitive Network logon of CONTOSO\UserA
from TESTCLIENT (via TMGServer) Entered
06/10 18:45:07 [LOGON] CONTOSO: SamLogon: Transitive Network logon of CONTOSO\UserA
from TESTCLIENT (via TMGServer) Returns 0x0
06/10 18:45:21 [LOGON] CONTOSO: SamLogon: Network logon of CONTOSO\UserA from
TESTCLIENT Entered
06/10 18:45:21 [LOGON] CONTOSO: SamLogon: Network logon of CONTOSO\UserA from
TESTCLIENT Returns 0xc0000234
06/10 18:46:27 [LOGON] CONTOSO: SamLogon: Network logon of CONTOSO\UserA from
TESTCLIENT Entered
06/10 18:46:27 [LOGON] CONTOSO: SamLogon: Network logon of CONTOSO\UserA from
TESTCLIENT Returns 0xc0000234
06/10 18:46:45 [LOGON] CONTOSO: SamLogon: Transitive Network logon of CONTOSO\UserA
from TESTCLIENT (via TMGServer) Entered
06/10 18:46:45 [LOGON] CONTOSO: SamLogon: Transitive Network logon of CONTOSO\UserA
from TESTCLIENT (via TMGServer) Returns 0xc0000234
06/10 18:48:01 [LOGON] CONTOSO: SamLogon: Transitive Network logon of CONTOSO\UserA
from TESTCLIENT (via TMGServer) Entered
06/10 18:48:01 [LOGON] CONTOSO: SamLogon: Transitive Network logon of CONTOSO\UserA
from TESTCLIENT (via TMGServer) Returns 0xc0000234
06/10 18:48:30 [LOGON] CONTOSO: SamLogon: Transitive Network logon of CONTOSO\UserA
from TESTCLIENT (via TMGServer) Entered
06/10 18:48:30 [LOGON] CONTOSO: SamLogon: Transitive Network logon of CONTOSO\UserA
from TESTCLIENT (via TMGServer) Returns 0xc0000234
```

Using the article "Maintaining and Monitoring Lockouts" mentioned previously, we find that the code 0xc0000234 corresponds to "The account has been automatically locked." Checking the account in the Active Directory Users and Computers, we find that it was locked for 15 minutes. We find out that the administrator had defined a password policy that allowed for three bad password attempts set in Group Policy for the Domain. The Account Lockout Duration was set to 15 minutes. This explains why the issue only lasted for a short while and then went away.

The main question left unanswered is why the accounts are being locked out. We let the administrator enable debug logging on the domain controllers, who later reported that only a few computers were infected by a virus using a dictionary attack to try and gain access to various accounts.

Conclusion

Although we did not use all the tools as we originally intended to, using a linear logical troubleshooting methodology we were able to use the required tools and logs to find the solution for the authentication issue, which are generally tricky.

Summary

In this chapter we discussed the general troubleshooting methodology, the tools available for solving issues, and a real-life case study where we used different logs and tools to solve an issue. In the next chapter we will discuss the HTTP and HTTPS protocols and how authentication works with HTTP protocol.

## CHAPTER 32

Exploring HTTP Protocol

- Understanding the HTTP Protocol **869**

- How HTTP Authentication Works **874**

- Understanding HTTPS **884**

- Summary **890**

One of the most frequently used application-layer protocols on the Internet is the Hyper Text Transfer Protocol (HTTP). End users usually have no idea what protocol they're using except for the fact that they're using a browser to access Web pages on the Internet. From an administrator's perspective it is important to understand what goes on behind the scenes whenever someone browses to a site on the Internet. In this chapter we will discuss what HTTP is and what actually happens in a HTTP transaction, and we'll help you gain a better understanding of what the HTTP protocol is about.

Understanding the HTTP Protocol

The Internet as we know it today became popular around the 1990s. The dot-com boom and abundance of different kinds of Web sites popping up on the Internet led to the popularity and traffic increase on the Internet that continues even now. All the Web sites on the Internet are mainly accessed over HTTP. For end users, all they are doing is browsing or conducting their business over the Internet. What happens in the background is that the browser is using HTTP, which is carried over TCP/IP to talk to the Web server over the Internet to get to and retrieve the contents of the Web page.

A typical HTTP communication between a client and a Web server follows these steps:

1. The client sends a TCP Synchronization (SYN) to the server.

2. The server responds with a TCP acknowledgment flag (ACK) for the SYN from the client and establishing a reverse connection with a SYN flag of its own.

3. The client acknowledges the SYN sent by the server.

4. The client sends an HTTP Request to the server.

5. The server responds with an HTTP Response to the client.

6. Depending on the connection state negotiated by the client and server, the client may close the connection to the server using TCP Finish (FIN) or a TCP reset (RST), indicating that no more data will be sent on this connection.

7. The server responds with an ACK for the FIN sent by the client.

8. The server then sends a FIN to the client, closing the connection context from the server to the client.

9. The client responds back with an ACK to the FIN sent by the server.

The first three steps in the preceding communication are called the *TCP 3-way handshake*; the last four steps are called the *TCP 4-way closing handshake* and are a part of every communication or protocol transported over TCP. Table 32-1 summarizes the packet flow as seen in a network packet sniffer or Network Monitor capture for the preceding communication.

TABLE 32-1 Detailed Traffic Analysis between a Client and a Web Server

SOURCE	DESTINATION	PROTOCOL	FIELDS
Client	Server	TCP	Syn
Server	Client	TCP	Syn, Ack
Client	Server	TCP	Ack
Client	Server	HTTP	Request
Server	Client	HTTP	Response
Client	Server	TCP	Fin
Server	Client	TCP	Ack
Server	Client	TCP	Fin
Client	Server	TCP	Ack

Table 32-1 should make clear that every HTTP transaction starts with a TCP connection establishment and ends with a TCP connection teardown because HTTP is carried over TCP/IP on the Internet. An important thing to remember is that sometimes while closing the TCP communication, the server might include an RST and ACK or FIN and ACK in a single response. This is normal.

HTTP Transaction

An HTTP transaction is always carried between a client asking for information through a request and a server responding with the information through a response. The default port used by HTTP is port TCP 80 unless specifically set differently by the Web server administrator. Each client-server HTTP transaction, whether an HTTP request or a HTTP response, consists of three main parts:

- A response or a request line
- Header information
- Body

Every HTTP transaction begins with a client request. Depending on the request and the resource availability the server will respond.

The request line from the client in most cases consists of a request method, the location of the resource requested, and the HTTP version number. The address of the resource is specified by the request Uniform Resource Identifier (URI), which identifies the resource upon which the receiving server or proxy should act. The method determines what the server is to do with the supplied location of the resource requested. Table 32-2 shows the most common methods that are used by a client in an HTTP request.

TABLE 32-2 Common HTTP Methods

METHOD	USE
GET	Used when the client is requesting a resource on the Web server
HEAD	Used when the client is requesting some information about a resource but not requesting the resource itself
POST	Used when the client is sending information or data to the server—for example, filling out an online form
PUT	Used when the client is sending a replacement document or uploading a new document to the Web server
DELETE	Used when the client is trying to delete a document from the Web server
TRACE	Used when the client is asking the available proxies or intermediate servers changing the request to announce themselves
OPTIONS	Used when the client wants to determine other available methods to retrieve or process a document on the Web server
CONNECT	Used when the client wants to establish a transparent connection to a remote host, usually to facilitate SSL-encrypted communication (HTTPS) through an HTTP proxy

MORE INFO For complete lists of supported HTTP methods, please visit *http://www.w3.org/Protocols/rfc2616/rfc2616-sec9.html* and *http://www.w3.org/Protocols/HTTP/Methods.html.*

Following the request line is header data, which consists of configuration information about the client and its document viewing preferences. The header is a series of lines or REQUEST fields, each of which contains a specific detail about the client and ends with a blank line. The function of these fields is to modify or clarify a method. Table 32-3 lists the standard REQUEST fields.

TABLE 32-3 Standard REQUEST Fields

FIELD	USE
Accept:	Contains a semicolon-separated list of content types that the browser can accept and format. To save time it is possible to use wildcards in the Accept: field, such as Accept: text.*
Accept-Encoding:	Contains a semicolon-separated list of content types that the browser can handle in the response, such as files that can be received and saved locally. The Accept-encoding field does not necessarily imply the ability to parse or display that content type.
User-Agent:	Contains data identifying the application that originated the query. This may influence the response, depending on how the server application is designed to behave.
Referrer:	If present, contains the URL of the document from which the current query is derived. For example, if you are browsing a document (A) and select a URL (B), the Referrer: field in your browser's HTTP request should be set to the URL of (A).
Authorization:	Used to pass credentials to the server.
Charge-To:	Used for account information; tells the server who to bill the request to.
If-Modified-Since:	This field can be used to make a request conditional. If you are using a caching browser that saves visited files locally, it can use this field to ensure that the file is only re-sent if it has been modified since the last time a local copy was stored.
Pragma:	Primarily used to control cache behavior, this field may be used in a context understood only by the server itself.

Finally, the body of the request contains data that is sent by the client if the request indicates that data follows (such as a POST method) to the server. A sample HTTP Request looks like this:

```
GET /mypage.html HTTP/1.1
Host: www.fabrikam.com
Referrer: http://www.fabrikam.com/default.html?ServerType=IIS2&redir=%2F
User-Agent: Mozilla/4.0 (compatible; MSIE 6.0; Windows NT 5.1; SV1; .NET CLR 1.0.3705;
.NET CLR 1.1.4322; .NET CLR 2.0.50727; .NET CLR 3.0.04506.30; .NET CLR 3.0.04506.648;
.NET CLR 3.5.21022)
Accept: */*
Accept-Language: en-us
Connection: Keep-Alive
```

The server response depends on the client's request. The response also includes three parts. The Response line contains the HTTP version number, a status code that indicates the result of the request from the client, and a description of the status code in English. The status codes define clearly the action to which the server responds with the client's request. Various status codes are available and belong to the 10X, 20X, 30X, 40X, and 50X series. Table 32-4 shows the various status codes available for a HTTP response.

TABLE 32-4 Important Status Codes Sent by Web Server

CODE	DESCRIPTION	CODE	DESCRIPTION
100	Continue	400	Bad Request
101	Switching Protocols	401	Unauthorized
200	OK	402	Payment Required
201	Created	403	Forbidden
202	Accepted	404	Not Found
203	Non-Authoritative Information	405	Method Not Allowed
204	No Content	407	Proxy Authentication Required
205	Reset Content	408	Request Time-out
206	Partial Content	415	Unsupported Media Type
300	Multiple Choices	500	Internal Server Error
301	Moved Permanently	501	Not Implemented
302	Moved Temporarily	502	Bad Gateway
303	See Other	502	Bad Gateway
304	Not Modified	503	Service Unavailable
305	Use Proxy	505	HTTP version not supported

The header fields in an HTTP response from the server contain information about the server software and the status of the document sent to the client. The header set is followed by a blank line that indicates the end of the header information. A sample HTTP response looks like this:

```
HTTP/1.1 200 OK
Server: Microsoft-IIS/5.0
X-Powered-By: ASP.NET
Date: Mon, 18 May 2009 18:36:39 GMT
Content-Type: application/x-javascript
Last-Modified: Wed, 12 Sep 2007 06:29:17 GMT
Content-Length: 22082
```

In the preceding example, the HTTP version used is 1.1 and the status code 200 and *OK* explain the result of the client's request. The server sends JScript of size 22,082 bytes as shown by the *Content-Type* and *Content-Length* lines and the *Server* header provides details about the server software.

> **NOTE** For more information about HTTP status codes and Response Header fields, please visit *http://www.w3.org/Protocols/rfc2616/rfc2616-sec6.html*.

How HTTP Authentication Works

Before we start dissecting the authentication methods used within the HTTP protocol itself, we need to define some terminology:

- **Authentication** The process where user credentials are passed between a client and server and those credentials are validated against a credentials authority
- **Trust** The process where user credentials are assumed to be valid based on their relationship to an entity other than a credentials authority (a Certificate Authority, for instance)
- **Authorization** The process where user credentials are validated against access policies for a given resource

Without authentication, access controls (authorization) are not effective, if even definable. Also, many people make the mistake of assuming that "trusted credentials" is equivalent to authentication; *this is not true*! For instance, Internet Information Services can be configured to accept, deny, or require client certificates, but unless the IIS administrator enables Directory Services certificate mapping within IIS, the credentials represented within the certificate are not validated against any credentials authority and the credentials cannot be used to satisfy authorization. System Center Configuration Manager 2007 is one such server application that does not map certificates to an actual domain machine account. Instead, it satisfies the authentication process by comparing the credentials represented by the certificate to the SSCM machine account database. It does so to support Internet Based Configuration Management, where non-domain members may be configured in its database and managed as if they were domain members.

Rules of the Game

Several documents define the client, proxy, and server behaviors with regard to HTTP authentication and the authentication mechanisms used:

- Request For Comments article 2616 Hypertext Transfer Protocol – HTTP/1.1
- Request For Comments article 2617 HTTP Authentication: Basic and Digest Access Authentication

- Request For Comments article 4559 SPNEGO-based Kerberos and NTLM HTTP Authentication in Microsoft Windows
- Microsoft Developer Network article [MS-NTHT]: NTLM Over HTTP Protocol Specification
- Microsoft Developer Network article [MS-NLMP]: NT LAN Manager (NTLM) Authentication Protocol Specification
- Microsoft Developer Network article [MS-DPSP]: Digest Protocol Extensions
- Microsoft Developer Network article [MS-KILE]: Kerberos Protocol Extensions

Because we'll refer to most of these documents during this discussion, it might be worthwhile to have them handy.

As noted earlier in this chapter, HTTP includes headers that help define the parameters of the conversation between the client and server or the client and proxy. Although many of these headers are unique to each case, a significant number of them are shared between both. RFC 2616 distinguishes these as *end-to-end* and *hop-by-hop* headers:

- End-to-end headers must be carried between the client and server without being modified in any way.
- Hop-by-hop headers are generated by an intermediate entity (such as a proxy, but not necessarily) between the client and server, and should be used only by the entity for which the header is intended.

Because the HTTP client must be able to distinguish between authentication required by the server and that required by a proxy, RFC 2616 defines two HTTP response codes and header pairs for each:

401 – Unauthorized

- **WWW-Authenticate**   This header is sent by the server as part of the 401 response to inform the client of the authentication mechanisms allowed by the server. The server may provide the authentication mechanisms in the data portion of a single header or it may provide each in a separate header.
- **Authorization**   This header is sent by the client in response to a 401 from the server to inform the server that the client wishes to authenticate using the mechanism and credentials provided in the response header data.

407 – Proxy Authentication Required

- **Proxy-Authenticate**   This header is sent by the proxy as part of the 407 response to inform the client of the authentication mechanisms allowed by the proxy. The proxy may provide the authentication mechanisms in the data portion of a single header or it may provide each in a separate header.
- **Proxy-Authorization**   This header is sent by the client in response to a 407 from the proxy to inform the proxy that the client wishes to authenticate using the mechanism and credentials provided in the response header data.

RFC 2617 requires that if the HTTP client is presented with more than one authentication mechanism in a 401 or 407 response, it must choose the strongest authentication mechanism the client can support. In this case, strength is the measure of relative trust afforded by each authentication mechanism. Of the current authentication mechanisms used in HTTP, they can be listed in order from strongest to weakest:

- Kerberos
- Negotiate (may include Kerberos or NTLM)
- NTLM
- Digest (may include Windows WDigest)
- Basic

The "strongest authentication mechanism it supports" is an important point to bear in mind when you're working with HTTP applications. If the client cannot support authentication, or if all of the authentication mechanisms specified by the proxy or server are not supported by the client, the client cannot proceed with the request. You should be aware of any client that fails to follow the "order of strength"; this presents a potential security threat to your environment when a client chooses a weaker authentication mechanism than it can support.

Because all authentication mechanisms provide varying levels of privacy, you should avoid the temptation to require authentication outside of an encrypted session—all authentication mechanisms provide some insight into the credentials being presented by the client. Only Basic authentication makes the full credentials (user name and password) easily available in plain text (Base-64 encoded), but all of the authentication mechanisms make the user context (domain\user name) available to anyone with a packet capture tool and the ability to tap into the network where the authentication is being provided.

HTTP Authentication in Action

Now that we have the basics in place, let's look at how this process happens. HTTP authentication is a challenge-response mechanism, where the server or proxy responds to a client request by issuing a challenge to the client for credentials. If possible, the client responds as appropriate to the authentication request or closes the connection. In most cases, this process begins with the client making a request to the proxy or server without providing credentials in any form. The client does this because in most cases, it's impossible for the client to know that the server or proxy require authentication, much less what mechanism is acceptable to it until the client has issued the initial request.

Anonymous Request

In Chapter 1, "What's New in TMG," we discussed the basics of the HTTP protocol. As a reminder, the core process appears in Microsoft Network Monitor as:

Client request directly to a server:
```
HTTP: Request, GET /default.asp
```

Server response:
```
HTTP: Response, HTTP/1.1, Status Code = 200, URL: /default.asp
```

Client request through a proxy (CERN proxy request):
```
HTTP: Request, GET http://www.contoso.com/default.asp
```

Proxy request to the upstream server:
```
HTTP: Request, GET /default.asp
```

Server response to the proxy:
```
HTTP: Response, HTTP/1.1, Status Code = 200, URL: /default.asp
```

Proxy response to the client:
```
HTTP: Response, HTTP/1.1, Status Code = 200, URL: /default.asp
```

The important points in the preceding examples are:

- There is a difference between a direct-to-server request and a CERN proxy request. In the direct case, the client issues the request including the resource-only part of the URL (*/default.asp*). In the CERN proxy request, the client issues the request using the full URL (*http://www.contoso.com/default.asp*).

- The request format changes as it traverses the proxy. What was issued to the proxy as a full URL is sent to the server as a resource-only request. This occurs because the proxy is acting as a client to the server and so must send the request to the server in this form.

When you're evaluating HTTP authentication, you must keep these points firmly in mind so that you don't mistake one case for the other. Many valuable hours have been wasted by an administrator who started chasing a proxy authentication problem that was actually a server authentication case.

The HTTP authentication rules of thumb can be summarized as follows:

- If the request is formed as */path/resource*, 401 is the only valid authentication response code.

- If the request is formed as *http://www.contoso.com/path/resource*, 407 is the only valid authentication response code.

- The client must use an authentication mechanism specified by the proxy or server.

- The client must choose the strongest authentication mechanism that the client supports from the list of authentication methods provided by the server or proxy.

Authentication Methods

HTTP provides five primary authentication methods: Basic, Digest, NTLM, Negotiate, and Kerberos. As noted in the section on SSL, certificate authentication is part of the SSL protocol and so does not belong with the HTTP authentication methods group. Likewise, Forms-Based authentication, although carried out within the HTTP protocol, is more accurately referred to as an application authentication mechanism, not an HTTP protocol-based authentication.

Because HTTP headers can only contain ASCII-encoded text data and most of the authentication mechanisms require binary data, the authentication data is always provided using Base-64 encoding.

- **Basic authentication**   Provides user credentials by encoding the actual user name and password. Because Base-64 encoding is so easily translated to the original data, Basic authentication is considered the weakest authentication method and should not be used over an unencrypted channel.

- **Digest authentication**   Provides user credentials by combining the URL resource, user name, hashed password, the hash type, and a *nonce*, or one-time key used to validate the user's password. Because a hashed password is not reversible, Digest is considered a stronger authentication method than Basic.

- **NTLM authentication**   A negotiated authentication protocol that enforces another challenge/response process beyond that imposed by HTTP. The user credentials are encoded within the NTLM authentication messages.

- **Negotiate authentication**   Refers to SPNEGO (Simple and Protected Generic Security Service Application Program Interface Negotiation Mechanism), an authentication mechanism that can contain one of three authentication packages: NTLM, SPNEGO, or Kerberos.

- **Kerberos authentication**   An authentication protocol invented by MIT and extended by Microsoft to provide Kerberos Delegation (for Windows 2000) and Kerberos Constrained Delegation (for Windows 2003).

Server Authentication

The following examples and netmon capture examples illustrate the server authentication process over HTTP. As always, this begins with the client issuing an anonymous request to the server.

Client 1st Request:
```
HTTP: Request, GET /basic/default.asp
```

Server Response:
```
HTTP: Response, HTTP/1.1, Status Code = 401, URL: /basic/default.asp
StatusCode: 401, Unauthorized
WWW-Authenticate: Basic realm="www.contoso.com"
```

In this case, the server is informing the client of three things:

- The server requires authentication.
- The only acceptable authentication mechanism is Basic.
- The credentials authority is *www.contoso.com*.

According to RFC 2616, the server is allowed to use two formats when it informs the client of the acceptable authentication methods. Assuming the server is able to support Basic, NTLM, and Negotiate mechanisms, this information is expressed to the client in one of the following two ways:

```
WWW-Authenticate: Basic realm="credentials authority", NTLM, Negotiate
```

or

```
WWW-Authenticate: Basic realm="credentials authority"
WWW-Authenticate: NTLM
WWW-Authenticate: Negotiate
```

> **NOTE** The order of the WWW-Authenticate headers in the server response is not specified by any RFC and is not required to have any relationship to the relative strength of each authentication mechanism. As such, the client application should not expect the headers to indicate this relationship.

Client 2nd request:
```
HTTP: Request, GET /basic/default.asp
  Host: www.contoso.com
  Authorization: Basic d3MwM2RvbVxhZG1pbmlzdHJhdG9yOm1zYXFmZVJvY2tzIQ==
```

Note that the client reissues the original request, but this time it provides an Authorization header that includes the selected authentication mechanism and the credentials in Base-64 format. Because the server only allowed Basic authentication in the 401 response, the client is limited to using this authentication mechanism or failing the request. If the credentials supplied by the client are palatable to the server, the server will provide a 200 response for this request.

Proxy Authentication

As illustrated previously, the primary difference between server and proxy authentication is the response code and headers. The process between the client and proxy is very similar to that observed between a client and server. Note that if the proxy requires authentication, it must not forward the request to the destination server or upstream proxy until the client has satisfied the authentication.

Client Request:

```
HTTP: Request, GET http://www.contoso.com/basic/default.asp
```

Proxy Response:

```
HTTP: Response, HTTP/1.1, Status Code = 407, URL: http://www.contoso.com/default.asp
  StatusCode: 407, Proxy authentication required
  Reason: Proxy Authentication Required ( The ISA Server requires authorization to
          fulfill the request. Access to the Web Proxy filter is denied. )
  Via: 1.1 TMG01
  Proxy-Authenticate: Basic realm="tmg01.contoso.com"
```

In this case, the proxy is informing the client of four things:

1. The proxy requires authentication.

2. The only acceptable authentication mechanism is Basic.

3. The credentials authority is "tmg01.contoso.com".

4. The proxy server name (specified in the via header) is "tmg01".

As with the WWW-Authenticate header, the proxy is allowed to use two formats when it informs the client of the acceptable authentication methods. Assuming the proxy is able to support Basic, NTLM, and Negotiate mechanisms, this information is expressed to the client in one of two ways:

```
Proxy-Authenticate: Basic realm="credentials authority",NTLM,Negotiate
```

or

```
Proxy-Authenticate: Basic realm="credentials authority"
Proxy-Authenticate: NTLM
Proxy-Authenticate: Negotiate
```

> **NOTE** The order of the Proxy-Authenticate headers in the server response is not specified by any RFC and is not required to have any relationship to the relative strength of each authentication mechanism. As such, the client application should not expect them to indicate this relationship.

Note that when you choose Integrated authentication in a Web Listener authentication option, and authentication is required to satisfy the defined policies, TMG responds to anonymous requests with the following headers:

```
Proxy-Authenticate: NTLM
Proxy-Authenticate: Negotiate
Proxy-Authenticate: Kerberos
```

Client 2nd request:

```
HTTP: Request, GET http://www.constoso.com/default.asp
Proxy-Authorization: Basic d3MwM2RvbVxhZG1pbmlzdHJhdG9yOmlzYXFmZVZJvY2tzIQ==
Host: www.constoso.com
```

Proxy request to the upstream server:

```
HTTP: Request, GET /default.asp
```

Server response to the proxy:

```
HTTP: Response, HTTP/1.1, Status Code = 200, URL: /default.asp
```

Proxy response to the client:

```
HTTP: Response, HTTP/1.1, Status Code = 200, URL: http://www.contoso.com/default.asp
```

Dual Authentication (Proxy and Server)

If the client has issued a request for a resource and the server and proxy require authentication, the client will be informed of each requirement separately and the client is expected to handle each case separately. In this case, the client will be presented with two different authentication responses: 401 for server authentication and 407 for proxy authentication. Note that the client never has to respond to the proxy and server authentication requirements simultaneously. Until the client satisfies the proxy authentication requirement, the proxy does not forward the client request to the server and so the client never sees the server's authentication response.

Special Case for NTLM (NT LAN Manager) Authentication

NTLM is a unique authentication mechanism in that it imposes a three-phase challenge-response requirement on the client and server or proxy above and beyond the challenge/response imposed by HTTP. The details of the NTLM authentication mechanism are spelled out in great detail in the MSDN [MSDN-NLMP] specification, so we won't belabor them here. The NTLM authentication messages are what interest us today:

- **Negotiate**   This is the first message, sent from the client to the server or proxy.
- **Challenge**   This is the second message, sent from the server or proxy in response to the Negotiate message sent by the client.
- **Authenticate**   This is the last message, sent from the client to the server or proxy in response to the Challenge message.

The fine details of the NTLM authentication mechanism are not relevant to HTTP authentication itself, but the effect NTLM authentication has on HTTP authentication is significant. A summary example of this process follows.

Client 1st Request:

```
HTTP: Request, GET http://www.contoso.com/default.asp
```

Proxy 1st Response:

```
HTTP: Response, HTTP/1.1, Status Code = 407, URL: http://www.contoso.com/default.asp
  StatusCode: 407, Proxy authentication required
  Reason: Proxy Authentication Required ( The ISA Server requires authorization to
          fulfill the request. Access to the Web Proxy filter is denied. )
  Via: 1.1 TMG01
  ProxyAuthenticate: NTLM
```

The second client request must contain the NTLM Negotiate message. The expected response from the server or proxy at this point is the NTLM Challenge message:

Client 2nd Request:

```
HTTP: Request, GET http://www.contoso.com/default.asp, Using NLMP Authentication
  Command: GET
  URI: http://www.contoso.com/default.asp
  ProtocolVersion: HTTP/1.1
  Accept: */*
  Accept-Language: en-us
  UA-CPU: x86
  Accept-Encoding: gzip, deflate
  User-Agent: Mozilla/4.0 (compatible; MSIE 7.0; Windows NT 6.0; SLCC1;
              .NET CLR 2.0.50727)
  Proxy-Authorization: NTLM TlRMTVNTUAABAAAAl4II4gAAAAAAAAAAAAAAAAAAAAGAHEXAAAADw==
```

> **NOTE** Network Monitor 3 parses NTLM authentication as NLMP in accordance with the protocol definitions on MSDN. These are described in *http://msdn.microsoft.com/en-us/library/cc236621(PROT.13).aspx* and *http://msdn.microsoft.com/en-us/library/cc237488(PROT.13).aspx*.

Proxy 2nd Response:

```
HTTP: Response, HTTP/1.1, Status Code = 407, URL: http://www.contoso.com/default.asp
  ProtocolVersion: HTTP/1.1
  StatusCode: 407, Proxy authentication required
  Reason: Proxy Authentication Required ( The ISA Server requires authorization to
          fulfill the request. Access to the Web Proxy filter is denied. )
  Via: 1.1 TMG01
  Proxy-Authenticate: NTLM TlRMTVNTUAACAAAADgAOADgAAAAVgoniCZzUeva1Oq0AAAAAAAAAK
oAqgBGAAAABQLODgAAAA9XAFMAMAAzAEQATwBNAAIADgBXAFMAMAAzAEQATwBNAAEADgBXAFMAMAAzAC0
AMAAyAAQAIgB3AHMAMAAzAGQAbwBtAC4AaQBzAGEAcwBlAC4AbABhAGIAAwAyAFcAUwAwADMALQAwADIALg
B3AHMAMAAzAGQAbw
```

Client 3rd Request:

```
HTTP: Request, GET http://www.contoso.com/default.asp, Using NLMP Authentication
   Command: GET
   URI: http://www.contoso.com/default.asp
   ProtocolVersion: HTTP/1.1
   Accept: */*
   Accept-Language: en-us
   UA-CPU: x86
   Accept-Encoding: gzip, deflate
   User-Agent: Mozilla/4.0 (compatible; MSIE 7.0; Windows NT 6.0; SLCC1;
            .NET CLR 2.0.50727)
   Proxy-Authorization: NTLM
TRMTVNTUAADAAAAGAAYAI4AAAAOAQ4BpgAAAA4ADgBYAAAAGgAaAGYAAAAOAA4AgAAAABAAEACOAQAAFYKI4g
YAcRcAAAAPuSiyfuW2JcRPe/U6fbIsU1cAUwAwADgALQAwADEAQQBkAGOAaQBuAGkAcwB0AHIAYQB0AG8Acg
BXAFMAMAA4ACOAMAAxAOYOqHdUEEx1ONpOT89K6D1fPH/DRkD47BSAhZo28vzPQ
   Host: www.contoso.com
```

Proxy request to the upstream server:

```
HTTP: Request, GET /default.asp
```

Server response to the proxy:

```
HTTP: Response, HTTP/1.1, Status Code = 200, URL: /default.asp
```

Proxy 3rd response to the client:

```
HTTP: Response, HTTP/1.1, Status Code = 200, URL: http://www.contoso.com/default.asp
```

Authentication Delegation

Unlike the initial requests made by client applications, when TMG is configured to perform authentication delegation, the first request TMG sends to the server contains the Authorization header, including the authentication type and user credentials according to the delegation method chosen. The upstream server processes that authentication as if it had been preceded by an anonymous request and 401 response cycle. This method has the added benefit of eliminating the first request/response cycle that would normally precede this request, effectively reducing the turnaround time.

Understanding HTTPS

When HTTP was designed, concerns about security and privacy were not addressed. As a result, applications that use this protocol need another layer on top of HTTP to provide the desired security. This additional layer of security was first implemented by Netscape, which originally developed the Security Sockets Layer (SSL) protocol that was used to secure HTTP communication. In 1995 Netscape released SSL version 2 (version 1 was never publicly available) and because of the number of flaws present in this version they released SSL version 3 one year later. This version was used as a base for IETF to build the Transport Layer Security (TLS), which is specified in RFC 2246. SSL/TLS implementation was built to target security risks such as message tampering, interception, and forgery.

> **NOTE** For more information on SSL version 3, read *http://www.mozilla.org/projects/security/pki/nss/ssl/draft302.txt* and for more information on RFC 2246, read *http://tools.ietf.org/html/rfc2246*

As shown in Figure 32-1, the core idea is quite simple: get the HTTP protocol and add a layer that can encrypt the payload so that if the communication is intercepted it is not possible to read the content.

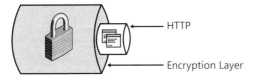

HTTP

Encryption Layer

FIGURE 32-1 HTTP with a secure layer

To establish this encrypted channel, both peers need to establish a TCP connection, which by default (per IANA assignment numbers) uses TCP port 443. After this phase is successfully completed, both peers negotiate a series of parameters related to the algorithm that will be used for encryption, the key exchange, peer authentication, defining the cipher that will be used for symmetric encryption, and the message authentication. This process is called the SSL handshake and although there are quite a few phases involved during this process, not all of them have to be implemented. Figure 32-2 summarizes the SSL handshake phases.

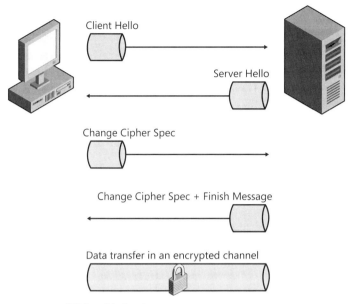

FIGURE 32-2 SSL handshake phases

Negotiation Phase

The first phase within SSL handshake is the negotiation phase. This phase starts when a client workstation initiates a communication with the destination server by sending a Client Hello message, which contains the following main fields:

- **Protocol Version**   Consists of the highest SSL/TLS version protocol supported by the client.

- **Random number**   Composed by client's date and time (4 bytes) plus 28 bytes randomly generated. This number has an important role during the communication because it is used to calculate the master secret that is later used to generate the encrypted keys.

- **Session ID**   (Also known as session identification number) Used to resume a previous session if one exists—hence this is an optional field. In other words, this field is populated only if the client is resuming a prior session with the same destination.

- **Cipher Suite**   A set of cryptographic algorithms that can be used by both peers as long as they support the same cipher suite. Within the Client Hello phase the client includes a list of the cipher suites the client supports.

- **Compression**   This optional field contains the supported compression algorithm by the client.

MORE INFO For more information on Cipher suite for Windows Schannel, read *http://msdn.microsoft.com/en-us/library/aa374757(VS.85).aspx.*

Here is an example of what a Client Hello looks like when captured using Network Monitor:

```
- Ssl: SSLv2RecordLayer, ClientHello(0x01)
  - SslV2RecordLayer:
     Length: 0x804C
     HandShakeMessageType: ClientHello(0x01)
  - Version: TLS 1.0
     Major: 3 (0x3)
     Minor: 1 (0x1)
  - ClientHello:
     CipherSpecLength: 51
     SessionIDLength: 0 (0x0)
     ChallengeLength: 16
   + Ciphers: TLS_RSA_WITH_RC4_128_MD5
   + Ciphers: TLS_RSA_WITH_RC4_128_SHA
   + Ciphers: TLS_RSA_EXPORT_WITH_3DES_EDE_CBC_SHA
   + Ciphers: SSL2_RC4_128_MD5
   + Ciphers: SSL2_DES_192_EDE3_CBC_WITH_MD5
   + Ciphers: SSL2_RC2_CBC_128_CBC_WITH_MD5
   + Ciphers: TLS_RSA_EXPORT_WITH_DES_CBC_SHA
   + Ciphers: SSL2_DES_64_CBC_WITH_MD5
   + Ciphers: TLS_RSA_EXPORT1024_WITH_RC4_56_SHA
   + Ciphers: TLS_RSA_EXPORT1024_WITH_DES_CBC_SHA
   + Ciphers: TLS_RSA_EXPORT_WITH_RC4_40_MD5
   + Ciphers: TLS_RSA_EXPORT_WITH_RC2_CBC_40_MD5
   + Ciphers: SSL2_RC4_EXPORT40_128_MD5
   + Ciphers: SSL2_RC2_CBC_128_CBC_WITH_MD5
   + Ciphers: TLS_DHE_DSS_WITH_3DES_EDE_CBC_SHA
   + Ciphers: TLS_DHE_DSS_WITH_DES_CBC_SHA
   + Ciphers: TLS_DHE_DSS_EXPORT1024_WITH_DES_CBC_SHA
     Challenge: Binary Large Object (16 Bytes)
```

The next step during the negotiation phase is the answer for the Client Hello, which is the Server Hello message. This answer also contains the same fields that are present on Client Hello: protocol version, random number, session ID (also optional), cipher suite, and compression. The only difference is that server now knows what the client supports so it will try to answer with a set of options that can be used by both sides—for example, for the protocol version the server will answer with the highest protocol supported by both peers. In addition to the same set of fields present on the Client Hello, the Server Hello message also contains:

- **Server's Certificate**   The certificate used by the server that contains the public key. Within the server certificate, many other parameters are passed, such as: certificate expiration date, which entity issued the certificate (Root CA), certificate revocation list (CRL), certification purpose, certificate public key, and others. The client uses this public key to authenticate the server and also to generate the premaster secret used later.

- **Server's Key Exchange**   An optional field that can be used by the client to encrypt the client key exchange in case the server's certificate does not have the public key that is capable of key exchange.

- **Client Certificate**   When the server requires that client present it a certificate (also called *client certificate authentication*), this field is present.

Here is an example of what a Server Hello looks like when captured using Network Monitor:

```
- Ssl:    Server Hello. Certificate. Certificate Request.
  - TlsRecordLayer:
      ContentType: HandShake
    - Version: TLS 1.0
        Major: 3 (0x3)
        Minor: 1 (0x1)
      Length: 4593 (0x11F1)
    - SSLHandshake: SSL HandShake TLS 1.0 Certificate Request(0x0D)
        HandShakeType: ServerHello(0x02)
        Length: 70 (0x46)
      - ServerHello: 0x1
        - Version: TLS 1.0
            Major: 3 (0x3)
            Minor: 1 (0x1)
        + RandomBytes:
          SessionIDLength: 32 (0x20)
          SessionID: Binary Large Object (32 Bytes)
          CipherSuite: SSL_RSA_WITH_RC4_128_MD5              { 0x00,0x04 }
          CompressionMethods: 0 (0x0)
        HandShakeType: Certificate(0x0B)
        Length: 1281 (0x501)
      - Cert: 0x1
          CertOffset: 1278 (0x4FE)
        - Certificates:
            CertificateLength: 1275 (0x4FB)
          - X509Cert: Issuer: STAlone Cont,contoso,msft, Subject: DCCONT.contoso.msft
            + SequenceHeader:
            + TbsCertificate: Issuer: STAlone Cont,contoso,msft, Subject:
                              DCCONT.contoso.msft
            + SignatureAlgorithm: Sha1WithRSAEncryption (1.2.840.113549.1.1.5)
            + Signature:
```

```
     HandShakeType: Certificate Request(0x0D)
       Length: 3226 (0xC9A)
    - CertRequest: 0x1
       CertificatesNum: 2 (0x2)
     + CertificateTypes: RSA_SIGN(0x01)
     + CertificateTypes: DSS_SIGN(0x02)
       CertificateAuthorityLength: 3221 (0xC95)
       DistinguishedNameLength: 65 (0x41)
     + DistinguishedName: CTSCA,contoso,msft
       DistinguishedNameLength: 196 (0xC4)
     + DistinguishedName: ,US
```

Client Acknowledgment

After the initial negotiation phase is finished by the Client Hello and Server Hello the next step is having the client agreement upon the parameters that were negotiated. This is done by the client sending a reply with a message that contains the following fields:

- **Client Certificate**   This field is optional (as mentioned previously) and contains the client certificate in case the server requested one.

- **Client Key Exchange Message**   Contains the client key exchange that is generated after calculating the premaster secret by using the two random numbers that were created during the negotiation phase (Client Hello and Server Hello messages). To protect this key, the client encrypts it using the server's public key.

- **Certificate Verify Message**   This is also an optional field and is present only if a client certificate is present during this communication. If it is present it consists of a signature to verify the client certificate.

- **Change Cipher Spec**   This is an acknowledgment to the server that from now on all the messages will be encrypted using the cipher that was negotiated during the negotiation phase (Client Hello and Server Hello messages).

The following example illustrates what the client acknowledgment (change cipher spec) will look like when captured using Network Monitor:

```
 - Ssl:   Certificate. Client Key Exchange. Change Cipher Spec. Encrypted Handshake
          Message.
  - TlsRecordLayer:
      ContentType: HandShake
   - Version: TLS 1.0
       Major: 3 (0x3)
       Minor: 1 (0x1)
     Length: 141 (0x8D)
    - SSLHandshake: SSL HandShake TLS 1.0 Client Key Exchange(0x10)
       HandShakeType: Certificate(0x0B)
```

```
      Length: 3 (0x3)
   - Cert: 0x1
      CertOffset: 0 (0x0)
     HandShakeType: Client Key Exchange(0x10)
     Length: 130 (0x82)
     ClientKeyExchange: Binary Large Object (130 Bytes)
- TlsRecordLayer:
   ContentType: Cipher Change Spec
 - Version: TLS 1.0
   Major: 3 (0x3)
   Minor: 1 (0x1)
   Length: 1 (0x1)
 + ChangeCipherSpec: 0x1
- TlsRecordLayer:
   ContentType: HandShake
 - Version: TLS 1.0
   Major: 3 (0x3)
   Minor: 1 (0x1)
   Length: 32 (0x20)
- SSLHandshake: SSL HandShake TLS 1.0 Encrypted Handshake Message
   HandShakeType: Encrypted Handshake Message
   EncryptedHandshakeMessage: Binary Large Object (31 Bytes)
```

Server Acknowledgment

The last phase is composed of the server's acknowledgment to the client using the change cipher spec message, in which the server says that from now on it will also be encrypting the messages using the keys that were just negotiated. At this point the server and the client already know the session key that will be used. Another field also present on this last message packet is the Finished Message, which is a hash of the complete exchange that was done up to this point using the session and message authentication secret. By sending this message, the server waits to see whether the client can decrypt this message and validate the hashes. If the client can match those computed values, the SSL handshake is considered finished successfully.

Here is an example of what the server acknowledgment (change cipher spec) looks like when captured using Network Monitor:

```
- Ssl:    Change Cipher Spec. Encrypted Handshake Message.
   - TlsRecordLayer:
      ContentType: Cipher Change Spec
    - Version: TLS 1.0
      Major: 3 (0x3)
      Minor: 1 (0x1)
      Length: 1 (0x1)
```

```
  - ChangeCipherSpec: 0x1
    ChangeCipherSpecValue: 1 (0x1)
- TlsRecordLayer:
  ContentType: HandShake
- Version: TLS 1.0
    Major: 3 (0x3)
    Minor: 1 (0x1)
  Length: 32 (0x20)
- SSLHandshake: SSL HandShake TLS 1.0 Encrypted Handshake Message
    HandShakeType: Encrypted Handshake Message
    EncryptedHandshakeMessage: Binary Large Object (31 Bytes)
```

Summary

In this chapter we discussed the most common application protocol used over the Internet—HTTP. Understanding HTTP and understanding how authentication works over HTTP will help any administrator easily troubleshoot Web browsing and authentication over the Web. In this chapter we also discussed what an HTTPS session looks like and what to look for in an HTTPS session to ensure that the session is set up correctly, thereby helping an administrator easily isolate issues that involve a client session over HTTPS. In the next chapter we will discuss Network Monitor and how to use it.

Using Network Monitor 3 for Troubleshooting TMG

- Using Network Monitor to Capture Traffic   **891**

- Reading a Network Monitor Capture   **897**

- Troubleshooting TMG Using Network Monitor   **903**

- Summary   **909**

M icrosoft Forefront TMG includes some built-in tools to assist in troubleshooting various scenarios, such as publishing rules and access rules. However, in some situations you will need to go a step further and analyze what is happening on the wire to better understand TMG behavior. For those scenarios the best tool to use is Network Monitor. This chapter will cover the basics of Network Monitor, including how to capture data and some Network Monitor capture scenarios.

Using Network Monitor to Capture Traffic

As explained in Chapter 4, "Analyzing Network Requirements," the definition and understanding of your network's traffic profile is important so that you can know precisely what TMG should handle as far as protocols are concerned. Perhaps you have proprietary applications that are not using default ports and therefore you need to create a custom protocol definition on the TMG firewall. Commonly, in medium and large network environments not all applications used on the client workstation are precisely documented—the protocol and port the workstation uses are not always described.

> **MORE INFO**   The following blog post offers an example of how Network Monitor can assist you in identifying unknown traffic: *http://blogs.technet.com/yuridiogenes/ archive/2008/10/19/using-Network Monitor-3-2-to-identify-an-unexpected-traffic.aspx.*

Sometimes applications are deployed to client workstations without proper documentation and without you understanding how the application works. These scenarios gain complexity when the application needs to use a server located outside of the internal network and the traffic needs to pass through TMG. Without proper documentation from the application vendor, you will have to investigate what protocols the application requires to create access rules on TMG firewall.

This is only one example of a scenario in which you can use Network Monitor to identify traffic patterns and troubleshoot network connectivity issues. The version that we use in this book is the currently available public version (at least at the time of this writing), which is Network Monitor 3.3.

> **MORE INFO**   Watch for new releases and for articles related to Network Monitor at the Network Monitor Team's blog: *http://blogs.technet.com/netmon*.

Data Gathering with Network Monitor

When using Network Monitor for data gathering it is important to define your primary goal. In other words, what are you looking for? Many times a Network Monitor capture becomes painful to read because whoever is reading it doesn't know what to look for. When you have a clear understanding of the goal of this capture, you can move forward to the next step, which is configuring Network Monitor for data gathering.

Network Monitor allows you to capture data using the Network Monitor Graphical User Interface (GUI) or by using the *nmcap* command-line interface. Troubleshooting scenarios with TMG sometimes require Network Monitor capture plus other logs. This is the nice thing about ISA Data Packager (which is part of the ISABPA): this tool also gathers Network Monitor captures from all TMG firewall network interfaces.

> **MORE INFO**   See the following post for more information on ISA Data Packager: *http://blogs.technet.com/yuridiogenes/archive/2009/05/07/using-isabpa-for-proactive-and-reactive-work-with-isa-server-part-2-of-2.aspx*.

Using Network Monitor GUI

When performing a capture using the Network Monitor console, you need to address some issues before you get started. Figure 33-1 shows the Network Monitor interface, highlighting the main features available.

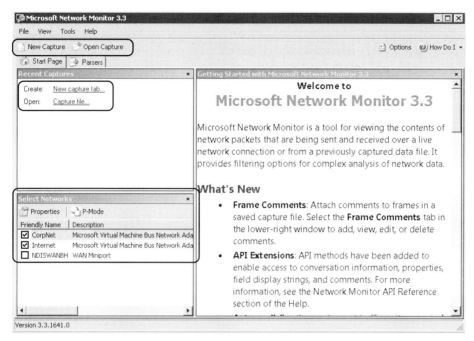

FIGURE 33-1 Network Monitor main screen

By default Network Monitor gathers data only on the following scenarios:

- Traffic generated from the interface that you selected
- Traffic where the selected interface is the destination
- Broadcast traffic

If you want to gather all traffic seen by this interface—including that which has nothing to do with this interface—you need to click the P-Mode (Promiscuous Mode) button on the Select Networks panel. The Select Networks panel also presents the available network interfaces; this is one of the most important options in this dialog box. The majority of the issues that you troubleshoot on TMG will require you to get a Network Monitor capture for all relevant network interfaces on the TMG computer. To do that you need to clear the checkbox for any interfaces (by default both will appear selected) on which you do not wish to capture data and then click the New Capture tab (either on the toolbar or on the Recent Captures panel).

When a new Capture tab is created you will see a dialog box similar to the one shown in Figure 33-2.

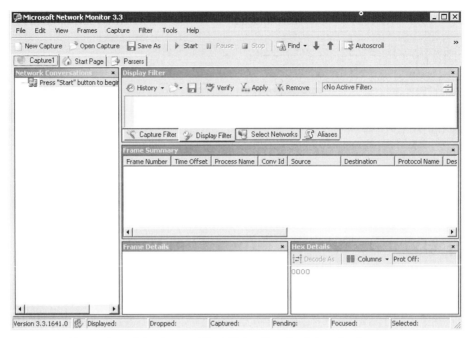

FIGURE 33-2 New capture dialog box and the initial options for data gathering

When you are ready to reproduce the issue that you are troubleshooting, click the Start button located in the toolbar, as shown in Figure 33-2. When Network Monitor captures the traffic it creates a file to temporarily store the captured data. This file has a predefined size determined in the Network Monitor Options dialog box, and after it gets full, Network Monitor starts to overwrite the older packets capture within the capture's temp file. To change the temp file location and the buffer size follow these steps:

1. Click Tools.

2. Click Options.

3. Click the Capture tab. The dialog box shown in Figure 33-3 appears.

4. Change the file location and the buffer size and then click OK.

After you finish reproducing the problem, click the Stop button to stop the capture and save the file by using the option Save As from the File menu. The Save As dialog box appears, as shown in Figure 33-4.

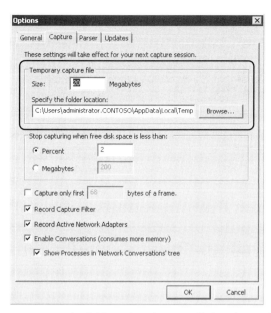

FIGURE 33-3 Available options for temp file location and buffer size

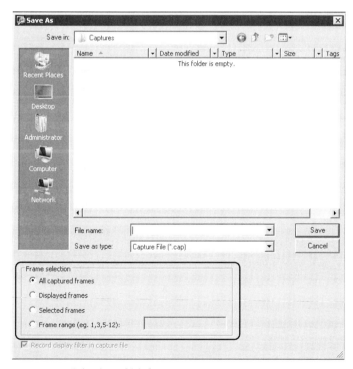

FIGURE 33-4 Selecting which frames you want to save

The following frame selection options are available in the Save As dialog box:

- **All Captured Frames**   Saves all the frames that were captured. Save the temp file with the name that you choose and then delete the temp file.

- **Displayed Frames**   Saves only the frames that are displayed in the capture tab. This option can be interesting if, for example, you want to save only the HTTP traffic from TMG to a specific IP address. You can create and apply a filter and you will only see frames that belong to this filter. This will reduce the final size of the .cap file that you are saving.

- **Selected Frames**   Saves only the frames that you selected (highlighted) in the capture dialog box.

- **Frame Range (e.g., 1,3,5-12)**   Saves only a specific range of frames.

> **NOTE**   Later in this chapter we will explain how to analyze a capture and use the available options within the Capture tab in the Network Monitor interface.

Using Nmcap.exe

The user experience with Network Monitor GUI is much better than Network Monitor 2 for most scenarios. However, in some other scenarios automation and system resource usage are more important than having a nice interface in which to capture and interpret data. To limit the resources consumed by Network Monitor during the capture process, you can use the *Nmcap* command-line interface, which has a rich set of options for data gathering. For the purpose of this example you will capture traffic from all interfaces where the protocol is equal to HTTP (*/capture http*), setting a maximum file size to 40 MB (*/file httptraffic.cap:40M*) and stopping when you press the X key (*/terminatewhen /keypress x*). To accomplish this access follow these steps:

1. Click Start, type **cmd,** and press Enter.

2. Type following the command:

   ```
   Nmcap /network * /capture http /file httptraffic.cap:40M /terminatewhen /keypress x
   ```

3. Press Enter. Open Internet Explorer and browse to *http://www.microsoft.com*. After navigating through the site, go back to the command prompt window and press the X key.

4. A file called httptraffic.cap will be available in the location where you started this command, which is the Network Monitor folder.

To see all the parameters available in the *Nmcap* command-line interface, type the command **nmcap /?**. To see some example scenarios of how to use *Nmcap*, type the command **nmcap /example** and press Enter.

> **NOTE**   A tool called the Network Monitor Wizard was created to assist in the task of configuring the *Nmcap* command-line based on parameters that can be specified by stepping through the wizard. You can download this tool (and the source code) from *http://netwiz.codeplex.com*.

REAL WORLD The Infamous 5783 Event

One of the most challenging scenarios for data gathering is the one that happens intermittently, where there is no immediately discernable pattern and when there is no one available to get data. A classic example is when the ISA or TMG firewall loses connectivity with a domain controller and triggers the event 5783 in the System Log, which says that no domain controllers are available. This problem can be caused by so many issues that a broad data gathering method is required to really understand what is going on.

Nmcap does not have a way to stop a capture if a particular event happens. However, one option you can use in the Windows Server 2008 Event Viewer feature allows you to trigger an action when a specific event occurs. However, this is not an ideal option because when event 5783 appears, it means that the issue already happened—the communication of interest is done, and capturing data from this point will not reveal what happened during that precise time frame. In a scenario like this the goal is really to keep capturing *until* the event happens. In other words, stop Network Monitor capture when event 5783 appears in the event log.

Fortunately, the Network Monitor Team listens to the user community and has developed a helpful tool called NM3EventCap. For this particular case the command line is pretty simple. Just type **NM3EventCap.exe TheEvent.cap 5783**. You can use other parameters, such as the maximum file size, number of adapters to capture, and so on. Download this tool from *http://nm3eventcap.codeplex.com*. This tool was built based on Network Monitor API, which you can also start playing with by downloading the SDK from *http://nmexperts.codeplex.com*.

Reading a Network Monitor Capture

Analyzing network captures is an exercise made up of 50 percent knowledge and 50 percent experience. A dazzling number of digital and print references are available that are intended to help you improve your network analysis skills. Network capture analysis requires at least a basic knowledge of the behavior expected from the application under test as well as some familiarity with the related protocols. The time spent using multiple capture and analysis tools will help you gain these skills.

NOTE Laura Chappell of *http://www.wiresharku.com* offers a vast array of network analysis training. Although the content is Wireshark-focused, the concepts and techniques transfer quite well to Network Monitor. She has presented sessions on network analysis techniques at numerous venues such as Tech Ed and Black Hat.

If you've never used a network analysis tool, you need to understand a few things about how Network Monitor processes network captures:

- All network traffic is divided into data chunks called *packets*.

- The packets contain data relative to one or more protocols.

- The protocols in these packets are identified and analyzed using protocol parsers.

- One parser can call another parser if it has been written to recognize the protocol handled by the next protocol layer parser.

When you open a network capture file, Network Monitor passes the file data through its parser engine, which in turn calls the related protocol parsers as each protocol is identified. The result of this action is displayed to you in the Frame Summary pane of the Network Monitor application window, as shown in Figure 33-5.

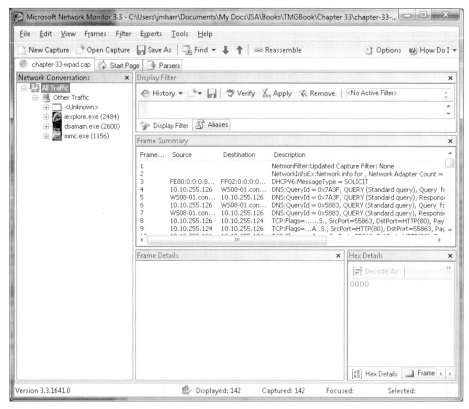

FIGURE 33-5 Network Monitor display example

In the left pane, Network Monitor displays a summary of the IP conversations identified by the parsers that were called by the Network Monitor parsing engine. By default, Network Monitor limits this display to the lowest-layer protocol; in this case, the application process name and process ID are shown because the capture was taken with these options enabled.

Each conversation is assigned a unique number to help you filter the capture so that only the protocols you are interested in are displayed.

You can click the plus sign (+) indicator to expand an IP conversation to display the higher-layer protocols, each of which can be expanded if it contains a higher-layer protocol. If you select one of the conversations in the left pane, the Frame Summary pane is updated to show only those packets that are related to that protocol and conversation. Figure 33-6 illustrates this relationship for one of the conversations.

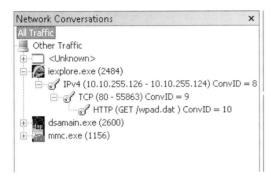

FIGURE 33-6 Conversation summary display

If the data is saved as part of the capture file, Network Monitor organizes the conversation summary so that the relationship between applications and the protocols is clear. If the process information is not part of the capture, Network Monitor only shows the protocol relationships. In the example shown in Figure 33-6, HTTP conversation 10 is part of TCP conversation 9, which in turn is related to IP conversation 8 and was created by iexplore.exe (Internet Explorer) process ID 2484. One thing to remember about Network Monitor conversation identifiers is that they are assigned as each parser tells the parser engine to create a conversation. Because higher-layer protocols are called by lower-layer protocols, the conversation value represents the total number of conversations Network Monitor has identified up to that point in the capture, not the conversation count for a particular protocol. In other words, HTTP conversation 10 represents the tenth conversation Network Monitor was instructed to build, not the tenth HTTP conversation Network Monitor identified.

These values are useful in the display filter pane as values provided in the Conversation. *Protocol*.ID, where *Protocol* is replaced by the name of the protocol of interest, such as TCP, HTTP, and so on. If you wanted to limit the display to HTTP conversation 10, you would type **conversation.http.id==10** in the Display Filter text box and click Apply or press Ctrl+Enter to apply the filter.

Network Monitor also provides the means to filter the capture on any *parsed* aspect of the capture data. Network Monitor depends on the protocol parsers to help with this functionality because it is the parser's responsibility to interpret the data and identify key aspects of the protocol that can be used by you in your analysis efforts. For instance, if you want to limit the display to TCP traffic to and from the TMG Web Proxy listener for a protected network, but you don't yet know the conversation, you can use the display filter statement **tcp.port==8080**. Network Monitor allows you to apply the port number to the source and destination ports simultaneously by using the generic *.port* property. By using this generalization for source and destination ports, the display will show traffic to and from TMG, not just to TMG (as with tcp.dstport==8080) or traffic from the TMG Web Proxy listener (as with tcp.srcport==8080). This applies to UDP as well as TCP because they both utilize source and destination ports as part of the protocol.

This is where having a basic understanding of most common protocols is useful. If you try to apply a display filter to a protocol that doesn't define a property you specify in the display filter, or if you specify an invalid value, Network Monitor will indicate an error and the current Frame Summary display will be unchanged. Figure 33-7 illustrates this behavior.

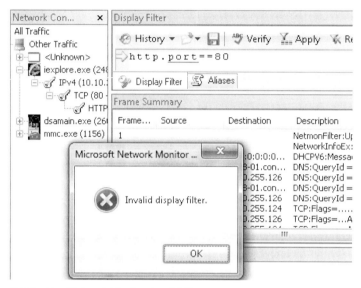

FIGURE 33-7 Network Monitor invalid filter response

The example in Figure 33-7 illustrates a common misunderstanding of protocol relationships. It's generally accepted in the networking community that TCP port 80 is used for HTTP, but a common misunderstanding is that port 80 is part of the HTTP protocol itself.

Recall from Chapter 15, "Web Proxy Auto Discovery for TMG," that the WPAD process is actually made up of three separate protocols:

- DHCP to discover the WPAD URL
- DNS to discover the WPAD host record or resolve the name obtained in the DHCP INFORM response
- HTTP to request the CFILE (configuration file)

If you want to isolate the traffic related to WPAD, you have to use a more complex display filter statement than just ports. There is no way to write a single filter called WPAD, but because you know which protocols are involved, you can write a display filter that includes only the protocols that are part of the WPAD process. The simplest filter would appear as

dhcp or dns or http, instructing Network Monitor to display only the packets that include those three protocols. Unfortunately, it would also display the DNS, DHCP, and HTTP traffic that was not related to WPAD.

You can create a filter that limits the traffic to only the data you want, but it takes a bit of sleuthing to gather the data you need to provide to Network Monitor. Because the Network Monitor team is owned and operated by some very experienced networking folks, they understand the need to make this task as simple as possible. The following steps illustrate how to use Network Monitor to build the query needed to isolate only WPAD-related traffic. The capture file is included on the companion CD as chapter-33-wpad.cap. The example capture doesn't include DHCP traffic, so you get to limit your efforts to DNS and HTTP only.

> **NOTE** To open the example captures, you have to install Network Monitor on your computer. You can obtain the latest version from *http://www.microsoft.com/downloads/ details.aspx?FamilyID=983b941d-06cb-4658-b7f6-3088333d062f* and the latest parsers can be obtained from *http://www.codeplex.com/NMParsers*.

Open Network Monitor

1. Click Start and then click All Programs.
2. Expand Microsoft Network Monitor 3.3 and then click Microsoft Network Monitor 3.3.

Open the Example Capture File

1. In Network Monitor, click Open Capture and navigate to your CD drive.
2. Select chapter-33-wpad.cap and click Open.

Apply the Basic WPAD Display Filter

1. In the Display filter text box, type **dns or http**.
2. Click Apply or press Ctrl+Enter to apply the filter to the Frame Summary display pane.

Your Network Monitor display should appear, as shown in Figure 33-8.

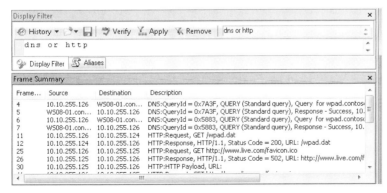

FIGURE 33-8 Initial Frame Summary display

Narrow the DNS Filter Scope

1. In the Frame Summary pane, select Frame 6 (DNS Query for wpad.contoso.com). This is the DNS query for the WPAD record. The Frame Details pane will display the protocol details for this packet.

2. Starting with the DNS protocol in the Frame Details pane, expand each following item until you see QuestionName: wpad.contoso.com.

3. Right-click QuestionName: wpad.contoso.com and select Add Selected Value To Display Filter. The Display Filter text box will change to "dns or http OR DNS.QRecord .QuestionName == "wpad.contoso.com"".

Narrow the HTTP Filter Scope

1. In the Frame Summary pane, select Frame 11. This packet is the WPAD request from the client to TMG. The Frame Details pane will display the protocol details for this packet.

2. In the Frame Details pane, expand the data points within HTTP until you see the host: wpad.contoso.com.

3. Right-click host: wpad.contoso.com and select Add Selected Value To Display Filter. The Display Filter text box will change to "dns or http OR DNS.QRecord .QuestionName == "wpad.contoso.com" OR HTTP.Request.HeaderFields .Host == "wpad.contoso.com"".

4. In the Frame Summary pane, select Frame 12. This packet is the WPAD response from TMG to the client. The Frame Details pane will display the protocol details for this packet.

5. In the Frame Details pane, expand the data points within HTTP until you see MediaType: application/x-ns-proxy-autoconfig.

6. Right-click MediaType: application/x-ns-proxy-autoconfig and select Add Selected Value To Display Filter. The Display Filter text box will change to "dns or http OR DNS.QRecord.QuestionName == "wpad.contoso.com" OR HTTP.Request.HeaderFields .Host == "wpad.contoso.com" OR HTTP.Response.HeaderFields.ContentType .MediaType == "application/x-ns-proxy-autoconfig"."

Narrow the Whole Display Filter

1. In the Display Filter pane, delete "dns or http OR" from the display filter text. The remaining text should read "DNS.QRecord.QuestionName == "wpad.contoso.com" OR HTTP.Request.HeaderFields.Host == "wpad.contoso.com" OR HTTP.Response .HeaderFields.ContentType.MediaType == "application/x-ns-proxy-autoconfig"."

2. In the Display Filter pane, click Apply or press Ctrl+Enter to apply the display filter. The Frame Summary pane contents should resemble Figure 33-9.

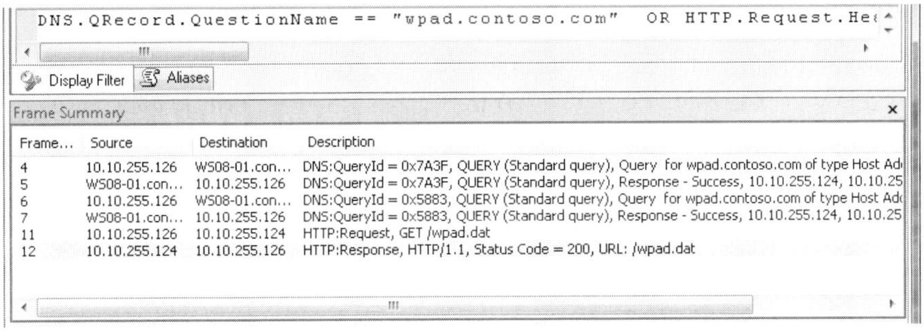

```
DNS.QRecord.QuestionName == "wpad.contoso.com"    OR HTTP.Request.He|
```

Display Filter   Aliases

Frame Summary   ×

Frame...	Source	Destination	Description
4	10.10.255.126	WS08-01.con...	DNS:QueryId = 0x7A3F, QUERY (Standard query), Query for wpad.contoso.com of type Host Ad(
5	WS08-01.con...	10.10.255.126	DNS:QueryId = 0x7A3F, QUERY (Standard query), Response - Success, 10.10.255.124, 10.10.25
6	10.10.255.126	WS08-01.con...	DNS:QueryId = 0x5883, QUERY (Standard query), Query for wpad.contoso.com of type Host Ad(
7	WS08-01.con...	10.10.255.126	DNS:QueryId = 0x5883, QUERY (Standard query), Response - Success, 10.10.255.124, 10.10.25
11	10.10.255.126	10.10.255.124	HTTP:Request, GET /wpad.dat
12	10.10.255.124	10.10.255.126	HTTP:Response, HTTP/1.1, Status Code = 200, URL: /wpad.dat

FIGURE 33-9 WPAD display filter results

Congratulations! You've just defined a filter that will specifically identify the DNS and HTTP portions of the WPAD process used by any host in the Contoso organization. Because Network Monitor also allows you to save filter definitions, you need never be forced to re-create this little gem.

NOTE   If you wanted to further isolate the search in a very large capture to a single client, you need only add that client IP address to the filter definition. If the client in question were operating on IP address 192.168.0.123, that filter would appear as "ipv4.address==192.168.0.123 and (DNS.QRecord.QuestionName == "wpad.contoso.com" OR HTTP.Request.HeaderFields.Host == " wpad.contoso.com" OR HTTP.Response.HeaderFields. ContentType.MediaType == " application/x-ns-proxy-autoconfig")". You need to add the parentheses around the original filter definition so that all of the original filter criteria apply equally to the IP address.

Troubleshooting TMG Using Network Monitor

In this part of the chapter, you'll see how to use various Network Monitor display filters to help evaluate a SOCKS-proxy application's misbehavior. The capture used in this example is contained on the companion CD as socks4_ftp.cap.

In this scenario, a colleague has decided that he wants to test how Internet Explorer (IE) behaves as a SOCKS proxy client when accessing FTP servers. He believes the TMG and IE configurations are correct, but he has two problems that he needs your help to resolve:

1.   His internal DNS structure does not allow clients to resolve public names to IP addresses, yet IE is able to make the connection to the FTP server.

2.   Although IE is apparently able to connect to the FTP server, IE cannot display a directory listing from the FTP server.

At your request, he obtained a Network Monitor capture at the test client during an attempt to use the ftp.3com.com FTP server and sent it to you for analysis. When you open the capture file, Network Monitor initially displays an unfiltered protocol analysis as shown in Figure 33-10.

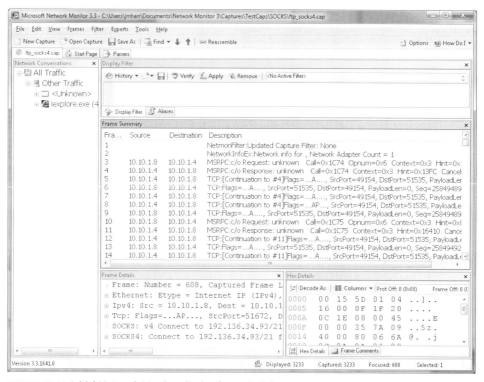

FIGURE 33-10 Initial Network Monitor display for socks4_ftp.cap

You'll notice that because your colleague did not define a filter during the capture, it contains a lot of traffic that appears to be unrelated to the issue you're evaluating—at least right now. You'll see the value of an unfiltered capture as we move through the analysis.

Because you know that your colleague is testing the browser as a SOCKS client, you can apply a display filter to limit the traffic Network Monitor displays to that protocol. You do this by performing the following steps:

1. Enter the name of the protocol (SOCKS) in the Display Filter pane just above the Frame Summary pane, as shown in Figure 33-11.

2. Either click Apply in the Display Filter pane or press Ctrl+Enter to apply the filter to the Frame Summary display.

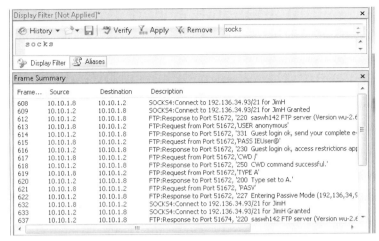

FIGURE 33-11 Frame Summary display filtered for SOCKS protocol

Initially, the capture seems to indicate behavior that is typical of an FTP application configured as a SOCKS proxy client:

1. IE sends a SOCKS CONNECT for IP address 192.136.34.93 and port 21 (FTP control channel). Because IE specified the IP address instead of the FTP server host name, it's clear that IE is indeed resolving the host name to the IP address.

2. The SOCKS proxy replies with GRANTED. This response demonstrates two facts:

   a. The SOCKS proxy rules allow this request.

   b. The connection to the requested destination was successful.

3. Immediately following the SOCKS GRANTED reply, you see the FTP banner in Frame 612. This tells you that the FTP server is functioning at a basic level.

4. The FTP server accepts an anonymous login from IE. You can determine that whatever problem your colleague is having, it's not related to FTP server authentication.

5. The FTP server accepts the IE instruction to change the working directory to the root directory (CWD /).

6. The FTP server accepts the IE command to send ASCII data (TYPE A).

7. The FTP server accepts the PASV command sent by IE and responds with the IP and port that the FTP server has prepared for IE to connect to for use as the FTP data channel. In this case, IE should connect to the FTP server on IP address 192.136.34.93, port 43799.

> **NOTE** FTP commands that describe listeners using addresses and ports are expressed using six-value, comma-separated decimal values. The IP address occupies the first four values and the port is described by the fifth and sixth values. The two port values combine to represent the two bytes of a 16-bit value. The first byte-value is the "high byte" and so represents a multiplier of 256. In this case, the high-byte value is 171,

which produces a literal value of 43776. The second value is 23, which is added to the high byte to produce the actual port: 43799. The FTP response "227 Entering Passive Mode (192,136,34,93,171,23)" literally means "I'm expecting a connection from you on IP address 192.136.34.93, port 43799."

8. IE then issues a SOCKS CONNECT command for IP address 192.136.34.93 and port 21 (FTP control channel).

The process indicated in steps 5 and 6 is typical of an FTP client that is preparing to send a Print Working Directory (PWD) command to an FTP server (similar to the Windows DIR command). What is unusual about this capture is that immediately after the FTP server tells IE how it should establish the FTP data channel connection, IE issues the SOCKS CONNECT request for the *same destination and port as the FTP control channel*. Clearly, this is not what IE should be doing at this point. Because we don't have visibility into the logic IE is using, we have to proceed using reasonable assumptions.

One thing that may have happened is that IE determined that it was unable to establish the FTP data channel connection as directed by the FTP server and decided instead to restart the whole process with the FTP server. Because the capture does not indicate that IE tried to make a SOCKS connection to the FTP server data channel listener, we can see whether IE tried to make a direct connection. To determine whether this is the case, change the display filter to limit the output to the FTP server IP address by following these steps:

1. Type **ipv4.address==192.136.34.93** in the Display Filter pane just above the Frame Summary pane, as shown in Figure 33-12.

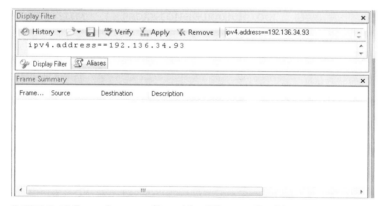

FIGURE 33-12 Frame Summary filtered for FTP server IP address

2. Either click Apply in the Display Filter pane or press Ctrl+Enter to apply the filter to the Frame Summary display.

It seems clear from the Frame Summary display in Figure 33-12 that IE did not try to make a direct connection to the FTP server for the data channel connection. Although this clarifies the scenario for you, it does raise some questions about IE behavior as a SOCKS proxy client.

Now that you can demonstrate why your colleague cannot obtain a directory listing from the FTP server and have the isolated the data required to prove it, you decide to move to the question of name resolution for public names that shouldn't work.

A network capture can't tell you *why* IE is choosing to establish another FTP control channel when it should be establishing an FTP data channel using the parameters provided by the FTP server, but the capture does provide the empirical data your colleague will need when he calls Microsoft Customer Support Services (CSS).

To answer the question of name resolution, your next step would be to filter the capture on the DNS protocol by following these steps:

1. Enter the name of the protocol (DNS in this case) in the Display Filter pane just above the Frame Summary pane, as shown in Figure 33-13.

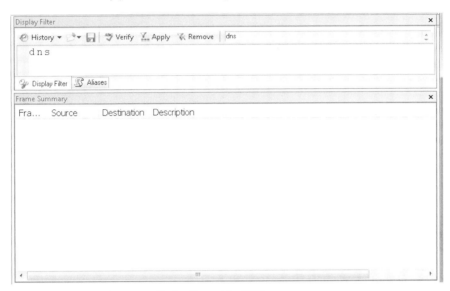

FIGURE 33-13 Frame Summary display filtered for DNS

2. Either click Apply in the Display Filter pane or press Ctrl+Enter to apply the filter to the Frame Summary display.

It seems clear that the client did not issue any DNS queries at all—much less for ftp.3com.com, so the question now is how was IE able to resolve the name "ftp.3com.com" to an IP address?

One thing Network Monitor can do that no other network traffic capture tool does is to include the application process that is generating or accepting network traffic. This provides you with the ability to filter the traffic based on the process that Windows associates with the traffic. Although this is only possible if the capture was taken using Network Monitor 3 or later on a Windows computer, it is nonetheless a very valuable feature, as you'll soon see.

Network Monitor builds the application-to-traffic association in the context of a conversation. To see all the traffic Network Monitor associated with IE while your colleague was taking the capture, follow these steps:

1. Type **Conversation.ProcessName.contains("iexplore")** in the Display Filter pane just above the Frame Summary pane, as shown in Figure 33-14.

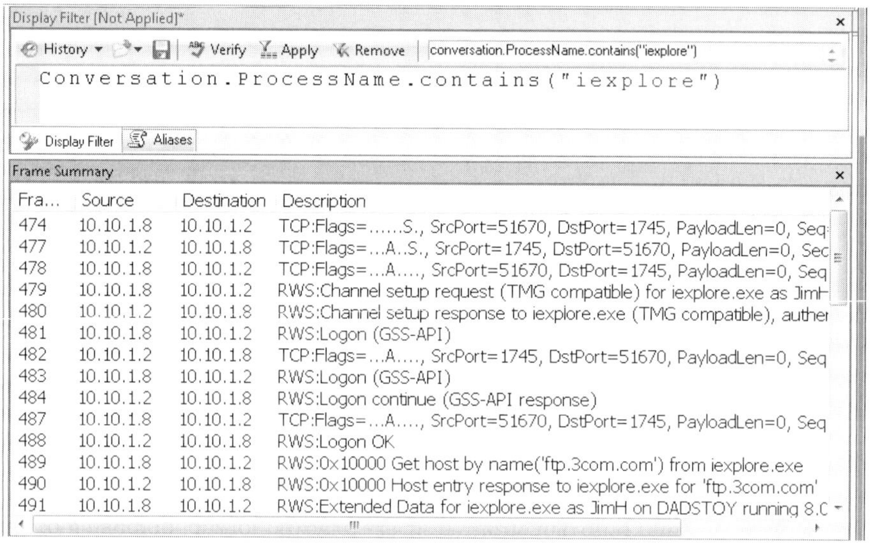

FIGURE 33-14 Frame Summary display filtered for DNS

2. Either click Apply in the Display Filter pane or press Ctrl+Enter to apply the filter to the Frame Summary display.

The first thing you notice is that Network Monitor is displaying a protocol named RWS that includes a reference to TMG. The RWS protocol is one of two protocols used by the TMG Client (TMGC) to communicate with TMG. Therefore, you may surmise that your colleague has the TMGC installed on his test computer.

> **MORE INFO** You can start your TMGC protocol education on TechNet at *http://technet .microsoft.com/en-us/library/ee291341.aspx.*

As you examine the conversation between the TMGC and TMG, you notice that among other things, the TMGC sends a "Get host by name('ftp.3com.com') from iexplore.exe" message to TMG, which responds with a "Host entry response to iexplore.exe for 'ftp.3com. com'" message to the TMGC. Because you learned from the TechNet article that "Get host by name" is related to name resolution, you decide that this part of the conversation merits deeper investigation. You can examine the host entry message in greater detail by selecting the packet in the Frame Summary pane. When you do this, the packet details are displayed in the Frame Details pane. You can view more detail of each protocol by clicking the plus sign on the left side of the display to expand that item. You can continue this process until you find the data that you are seeking. In this case, although you are reasonably sure that IE is resolving the name ftp.3com.com to an IP address via TMG, you want to prove this theory conclusively. You do this by expanding each node in the RWS protocol as it is displayed until you locate the IP address IE used in the SOCKS CONNECT command. Figure 33-15 shows the part of the RWS message that includes this data.

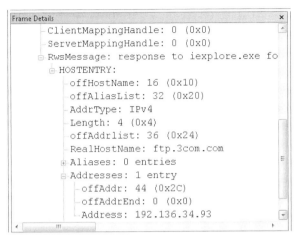

FIGURE 33-15 IP address in the Host Entry response message

Using Network Monitor, you've helped your colleague answer both of his questions—how IE is able to resolve the FTP server name to an IP address and why IE fails to display a directory listing of the FTP server. Although you are unable to explain why IE chooses not to connect to the FTP data channel listener described by the FTP server, you have demonstrated that IE fails to behave as expected based on the conversation with the FTP server. When your colleague contacts Microsoft Customer Support Services (CSS) to inquire about IE misbehavior, he can describe this problem clearly and in great detail. This information goes a long way in helping the CSS engineer determine the proper resources to engage on behalf of the caller.

Summary

In this chapter you learned how important it is to use Network Monitor in order to capture network traffic to troubleshoot TMG related problems. You learned how to configure Network Monitor via GUI and also via command-line interface. To demonstrate the full potential of Network Monitor, two scenarios were covered and there you were able to explore Network Monitor features such as filter syntax, view frame summary, and details. Throughout this exercise you also learned how to perform a step-by-step data analysis using Network Monitor and the correct approach to analyzing captures of different protocols.

From Proxy to TMG

- Understanding the HTTP Protocol **911**

- Understanding Proxy Servers **918**

- The History Behind TMG **923**

The HTTP (Hypertext Transfer Protocol) is an application-level protocol that became very popular with the explosion of the virtual world that we know as the Internet. Almost everything that we do on the Internet is performed using the HTTP, and at the same pace that HTTP became popular it also became a very popular protocol to use maliciously. Without the additional security implemented on top of HTTP, the current online world and the business done over the Internet could not be conducted in a secure manner. Therefore, you need to understand how security is applied to HTTP as well as understand the behavior of common protocols.

Understanding the HTTP Protocol

When HTTP was developed back in the '90s there were few concerns about security. The main goal was to develop a protocol that would allow a type of communication that the existing protocols (mail, news, and file transfer) could not offer. The resultant protocol, HTTP, became more robust and some technologies were added to implement security. Today, HTTP is widely used not only on the Internet, but also on intranets and on corporative environments.

> **MORE INFO** You can review the Internet timeline and milestones from 1945 to 1995 at *http://www.w3.org/History.html*.

The HTTP protocol is an application-layer protocol within the OSI model and uses TCP as the transport layer protocol. By default HTTP protocol uses TCP port 80, but the Web server dictates which port is used. Sometimes the Web server administrator or Web application developer may choose to change the port instead of using the default.

The purpose of a protocol is to allow communication between two or more devices using the same standard language. The HTTP protocol is the same: There is a client and a server and they follow a predefined process in their communication. The client has to use a browser or HTTP-capable application to send this request to the server. To send this request, the client has to type what is called the *Uniform Resource Locator (URL)*. This URL is composed of the components shown in Figure A-1.

protocol://hostname:port/absolute path

URL Components specified in RFC 3986

http://contososrv:81/default.aspx

Common URL used in intranet environments

http://www.microsoft.com

Common URL used in the Internet

FIGURE A-1 URL Components

Although most people talk about URLs, the place where the resource is located is called the *Uniform Resource Identifier (URI)*, which is defined in RFC 3986. Here is an example of a URI:

```
URI: /en/us/default.aspx
```

After you type the URL in the browser, the browser can resolve the host name and connect to the server's IP address. After this, the client sends the request to the destination server, as shown in Figure A-2.

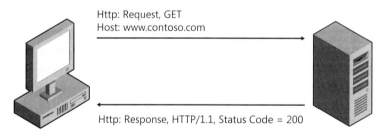

Http: Request, GET
Host: www.contoso.com

Http: Response, HTTP/1.1, Status Code = 200

FIGURE A-2 Basic communication between client and server using HTTP Protocol

As shown in the figure, there is a *simple message request* and a *simple message response*. This two-way communication forms the basis of all HTTP communications—a single request answered by a single response.

HTTP identifies the intended action by means of the *method* that is used in that message. In this message, the client sends the request using the GET *method*. The server answers with the *status code* that indicates the server's ability to serve the request. In this particular case, the status code is 200, indicating that the server successfully performed the requested action. The *host* in this message is obtained from the URL; in this case it is *www.contoso.com*. The client's request and the server's reply contain the HTTP version that is preferred by each end of the communication, which is also called a *conversation*.

The HTTP protocol today works with two major versions: HTTP 1.0 and HTTP 1.1. The HTTP 1.1 protocol enhances and adds features to the original HTTP 1.0 protocol. However, during an HTTP conversation, the peers generally agree on a common version to exchange messages in a standard way. In some cases the client might request HTTP 1.1, but the server replies with HTTP 1.0. In this case, the client should only issue HTTP 1.0 requests to that server.

The HTTP 1.1 version has some advantages when compared to previous versions (0.9 and 1.0). For example the requests now can be *pipelined*, which means that a client can make multiple requests to the server without waiting for a response. As a result, performance is improved, saving CPU in either direction (client and server).

> **MORE INFO**   For more information on the HTTP 1.1 enhancements, check RFC 2616 at *http://www.ietf.org/rfc/rfc2616.txt*.

> **NOTE**   Forefront TMG does not fully support pipelined requests. If a client sends pipelined requests, Forefront TMG will queue any additional requests received from the client until the upstream server responds to the previous requests.

Methods and Status Code

This section describes what happens during the HTTP conversation when the request is sent and the server replies with the response. When a request to access a resource is sent from the client, there is a command—in this case called a *method*—that is used to retrieve that resource or piece of data. There are many methods and you can see an extensive list in RFC 2616 section 9, but this appendix covers the following methods:

- **GET**   Retrieves any data requested by the client.
- **POST**   Sends data from the client to the Web server. This method is sometimes confused with PUT.
- **DELETE**   Sends a delete request from the client to the resource specified in the URI.
- **PUT**   Sends a request to store data on the destination server. This method is sometimes confused with POST.
- **CONNECT**   Sends a request through the proxy server during the tunneling negotiation.

    When the *CONNECT* method is used, the proxy server should not interfere in the transaction. The client will send a HTTP request like the following:

    ```
    CONNECT www.contoso.com:443 HTTP/1.1
    ```

The proxy server tries to resolve *www.contoso.com* to an IP address and establish a connection to that IP address on TCP port 443. If this connection is successful, the proxy responds "200 OK" to the client and passes the following traffic unchanged between the client and destination server.

When an application is using HTTP, it usually sends a single request and waits for the response. The Web server sends the response including a *status code* that informs the client how the server handled the request. As illustrated in Table A-1, the status code is a three-digit number. The first digit is the most significant digit. It indicates the status class, which indicates what is happening during the conversation.

TABLE A-1 HTTP Status Code

STARTS WITH...	MEANS...
1xx	This is an *informational* response from the server. The request from the client was received from the server and it is being processed.
2xx	The request was accepted successfully by the server and the content is included in the body of the response.
3xx	The client should be *redirected* to another place. This server is supplying the URI that the client should use to satisfy this request. The following example is of an HTTP header with the 302 (Redirect) status code: Http: Response, HTTP/1.1, Status Code = 302 StatusCode: 302, Moved temporarily
4xx	There is a problem with the client request. The client sent a request to the server that the server isn't able to satisfy because of the request type.
5xx	Although the client sent a valid request, the server doesn't know how to answer the request. This is generally an error on the server side.

MORE INFO   Within each category of status code, the second and third digits provide additional details about the response. For the complete list of status codes, read section 6 of RFC 2616.

HTTP Content

The purpose of the HTTP protocol is to make Web resources available to the client through a common communication process; the resources offered by the server can be HTML pages, images, and so on. When the client sends a request for a page, the Web server responds with a header indicating the type of content being delivered in the response body. The content-type field tells the client what kind of media will be in the body of the message. It is also necessary for the client to understand how big this content is. To satisfy that requirement, the HTTP protocol has the content-length field. Here is an example of what the fields may look like:

```
ContentType: text/html;
ContentLength: 14587
```

The content type and content length vary from one request to another. Sometimes the body is quite large. The HTTP protocol has a mechanism—the *content-encoding* field—to compress the content while preserving the original value. The most common content encodings are *GZip* (RFC 1952) and *Deflate* (RFC 1951). Here are two examples of the content-encoding field with the encoding type on it:

```
Content-Encoding: gzip
Content-Encoding: deflate
```

IMPORTANT This field is very important when you are dealing with the proxy server. Note that ISA and TMG only support GZip encoding.

Additional Fields

The HTTP protocol has additional header fields that are used to allow more efficient communication between a client and server. RFC 2616 section 14 explains in detail the supported fields for the HTTP protocol. The communication between client and server needs to include fields with defined parameters so it can proceed successfully in both directions and operate within established standards. This section highlights some of the fields that administrators are most likely to encounter in HTTP communications:

- *Accept*
- *User Agent*
- *Connection*
- *Cache-control*

Accept

The parameters of the *Accept* field specify what types of media the client can accept for the request. The following example shows the *Accept* field on a client request message:

```
Http: Request, GET /
Accept: image/gif, image/x-xbitmap, image/jpeg, image/pjpeg,
        application/x-ms-application
```

However, *Accept* itself is not the only type of parameter that makes the client and server accept a determined standard; there are other standards that can or cannot be accepted between client and server communication. The example shows some but not all of the parameters that can be used in the *Accept* header. Another parameter that can be used in the *Accept* header is *language*. Use the *language* parameter to create and customize your Web sites for the region where you are located. Here an example of the *Accept* field with the *language* parameter:

```
Accept-Language: en-us
```

User Agent

Because so many HTTP-aware devices support HTTP and HTML differently, you need to adjust the Web servers to treat each device differently. For example, you can browse a Web site using Microsoft Internet Explorer on your computer or on your Windows Mobile device. The device identification in the HTTP request determines which way the Web page is presented on the browser. The *User-Agent* field tells the server what type of browser the client is using. Here an example of this field:

```
UserAgent: Mozilla/4.0 (compatible; MSIE 7.0; Windows NT 6.0; WOW64; SLCC1;
.NET CLR 2.0.50727; .NET CLR 3.0.04506; Media Center PC 5.0; MS-RTC LM 8; Zune 2.0)
```

Connection

This field allows the client to specify how the connection needs to be handled during a session. For example, if the client is accessing an application that doesn't support persistent connections, this field must include the close command on every single message that is exchanged between the peers. Here an example of this field:

```
Connection: Keep-Alive
```

When this field contains the *Keep-Alive* value, it is also called the *persistent connection*, which means that the same TCP connection is to be used to send and receive multiple HTTP messages. This improves HTTP performance; however, the server and client applications need to support the use of this field.

Cache-Control

This field is used to instruct the client, proxy, and Web servers whether the requested content is to be added to the cache. Here is an example of this field:

```
Cache-Control: public
```

> **IMPORTANT** Many people think that everything is cacheable, but in reality, a great many items are not worth caching. The client that requests the content and server that provides the content will decide whether the content will be cached; it is the proxy's job to read this field and take the proper action.

This field may have the following parameters:

- ■ **Public** The content is cacheable regardless of the proxy type (public or private).
- ■ **Private** The content is not cacheable for public proxy but it could be cacheable for private proxy.
- ■ **No-cache** The content should not be added to the cache.
- ■ **Only-if-cached** The content should be served only from the cache.

BEST PRACTICES The paradigm of caching everything is something that we discourage. As the HTTP protocol defines, some content by definition should not be cached. Understanding the protocol and the fields will help you to better administer the TMG Server and take advantage of the features available on it.

Putting It All Together

Figure A-3 shows an HTTP request and response with all the fields together.

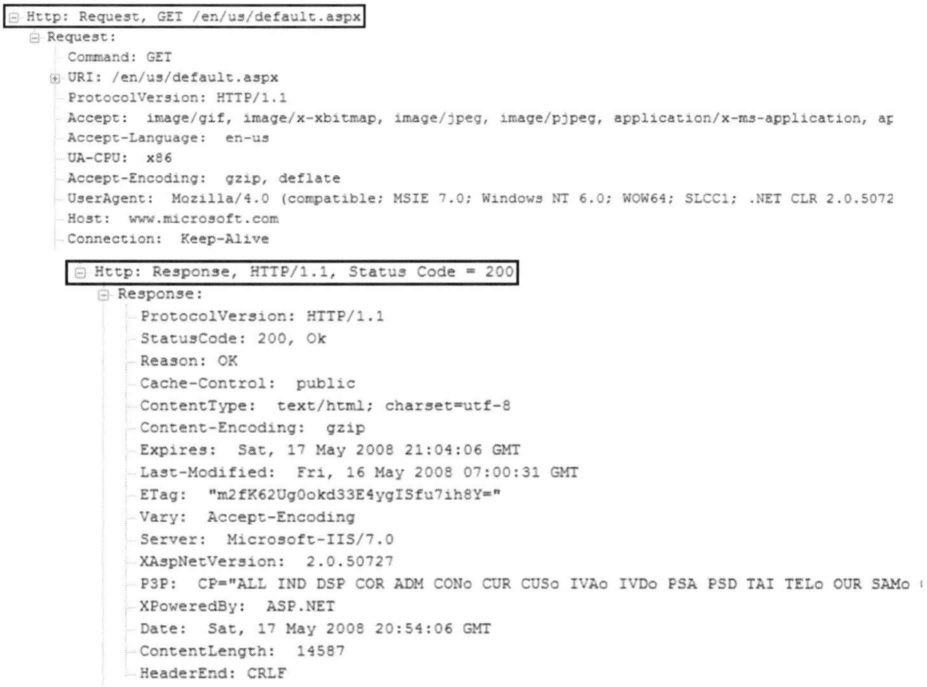

```
⊟ Http: Request, GET /en/us/default.aspx
  ⊟ Request:
      Command: GET
    ⊞ URI: /en/us/default.aspx
      ProtocolVersion: HTTP/1.1
      Accept:  image/gif, image/x-xbitmap, image/jpeg, image/pjpeg, application/x-ms-application, ap
      Accept-Language:  en-us
      UA-CPU:  x86
      Accept-Encoding:  gzip, deflate
      UserAgent:  Mozilla/4.0 (compatible; MSIE 7.0; Windows NT 6.0; WOW64; SLCC1; .NET CLR 2.0.5072
      Host:  www.microsoft.com
      Connection:  Keep-Alive
        ⊟ Http: Response, HTTP/1.1, Status Code = 200
          ⊟ Response:
              ProtocolVersion: HTTP/1.1
              StatusCode: 200, Ok
              Reason: OK
              Cache-Control:  public
              ContentType:  text/html; charset=utf-8
              Content-Encoding:  gzip
              Expires:  Sat, 17 May 2008 21:04:06 GMT
              Last-Modified:  Fri, 16 May 2008 07:00:31 GMT
              ETag:  "m2fK62Ug0okd33E4ygISfu7ih8Y="
              Vary:  Accept-Encoding
              Server:  Microsoft-IIS/7.0
              XAspNetVersion:  2.0.50727
              P3P:  CP="ALL IND DSP COR ADM CONo CUR CUSo IVAo IVDo PSA PSD TAI TELo OUR SAMo (
              XPoweredBy:  ASP.NET
              Date:  Sat, 17 May 2008 20:54:06 GMT
              ContentLength:  14587
              HeaderEnd: CRLF
```

FIGURE A-3 HTTP request and response

In this example, the request goes from the client directly to the server. In a corporate environment where there might be other communication gateways, this communication might not happen so directly.

Understanding Proxy Servers

A *proxy server* is a device that services client requests by forwarding the requests to the destination server and forwarding the reply from the destination server back to the client. Depending on the client, proxy, and network configuration, the proxy server intercepts all requests from the client and sends them to the destination server or servers, as shown in Figure A-4. The requests appear to come from the proxy server and not from the client. Similarly, the response is served to the client by the proxy server. This technology provides a central management point to inspect and filter all incoming and outgoing traffic and provides additional security by isolating the internal clients from the external network.

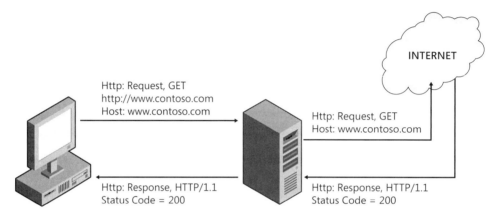

FIGURE A-4 The proxy sends the request to the Internet server on behalf of the client.

The main advantages of using a proxy server are:

- Managing and aggregating IP addresses while hiding internal IP addresses
- Caching HTTP objects, which improves the client application performance
- Access control, which allows more granular control over Internet access

Managing and Aggregating IP Addresses

With each passing day the number of computers and Internet users increases. Each company requests a block of pubic IPv4 addresses for their own consumption on public networks. This introduces a serious problem for the limited number of public IPv4 addresses that are available. The migration to IPv6 solves this problem in theory, but even then it is still not a guaranteed solution in short term because its implementation is not that fast and easy. The proxy technology allows companies that have hundreds of computers to access the Internet using only one public IP address.

The proxy server uses its own IP address to connect to the destination server for all the requests a client makes and does not require the clients to have a public IP addresses. As long as the IP address is valid and routable through the proxy server, the proxy server can handle the request. As per RFC 1918 and RFC 3927, certain IP address ranges are dedicated for private usage. This allows the administrator to use an IP address range within those private addresses offered by IANA. These IP address ranges are used on the internal network and the clients will use one public IP for the proxy server to provide transparent Internet access.

> **NOTE**   Forefront TMG Enhanced NAT provides you the ability to control the "apparent NAT" behavior inherent in Web Proxy functionality. Enhanced NAT is discussed at length in Chapter 29, "Enhanced NAT."

Because the destination server sees the request as originating from the proxy server instead of the client, a proxy server provides additional security by hiding the private network from the public network. The private address ranges mentioned in RFC 1918 and RFC 3927 are non-routable on the Internet even when they go through a proxy server. Therefore, no host using these IP addresses can attempt to bypass the proxy to get access to the Internet. This helps the administrator to make the network less vulnerable to any attack from the Internet where someone could find the physical address of any internal computer.

Caching

On a daily basis, users may browse some Web sites more than the others. For example, a user might browse *http://www.contoso.com*, which is his company's home page, every time he opens a new Web browser. Without caching, the proxy server would create a fresh connection each time to get to the Web site and deliver its contents back to the client. This would generate extra traffic and waste bandwidth usage for the same request over and over. If you have lots of users performing the same procedure, you might create a bottleneck on your WAN. To optimize performance and bandwidth usage, the proxy server offers *caching*, which is a mechanism that works by saving a copy of the resources delivered by the Web site based on actual client requests.

Many proxy servers offer HTTP and FTP caching, and TMG is no exception in this regard. Whenever a user goes to a Web site that is cached on the proxy server, the proxy server first checks the Web server for updated content, and then returns the information from its cache if the content hasn't changed. This "has it changed" request-response process is much cheaper on the wire than an actual resource request-response process because the response includes only the state of the resource, rather than the resource itself. As a result, you have faster response times to the end user and can save network bandwidth for other requests.

To improve security, the proxy server will never cache any content that requires authentication for delivery. When the proxy server communicates with a Web site that requires authentication, the HTTP content from the Web site is marked as non-cacheable. The proxy server reads the cache-control and pragma HTTP headers when it is passed and caches it according to those directives. Some proxies can also cache content on a per-user basis, but that also depends on the headers exchanged between the client and the server. If the client or the servers indicate that the content is non-cacheable, the proxy does not cache the content.

Most proxy servers offer the following types of caching that are beneficial for specific scenarios:

- Passive caching
- Active caching
- Forward caching
- Reverse caching

Passive Caching

With passive caching, the cached content of an object is marked with an expiration time and the content is not renewed until it expires. Only after the content expires and the client requests a particular object again does the proxy server retrieve the newer content from the destination Web site, cache the object, and mark it with the new expiration time.

Active Caching

With active caching, the proxy server keeps track of the expiration time of its cached content and updates the content whenever the content is about to expire. Some proxy servers can go beyond this basic approach and permit you to configure a schedule for downloading content when the network traffic is low or at a specific time of day. This approach allows you to optimize bandwidth and have minimum impact on performance. In the case of some proxy servers, such ISA Server 2000, the administrator can (depending on the Internet connection) set the ISA server to update or refresh the cached content frequently, normally, or less frequently so that there is no load on the network.

Forward Caching

With forward caching, the proxy server caches requests from internal users that are destined for an external server on the Internet. A user can initiate an HTTP, HTTPs, or FTP request for a server on the Internet. When the request reaches the proxy, the proxy services that request by getting the response from the Internet server and caching it; the proxy can service the request from its cache for all subsequent requests to the site for the same content until the content expires.

Reverse Caching

With reverse caching, a proxy server caches requests from Internet users to a published Web server that it proxies. When an Internet user sends a request to the Web server, the proxy server intercepts the request and forwards it to the Web server it has published, gets the response back, caches it for future use, and sends the reply back to the Internet user. Therefore, if an Internet user tries to access a Web server for the same content, the proxy server will respond to the Internet user with the contents from its cache.

Access Control

One of the hardest tasks of an administrator is to keep track of the user's behaviors: what the user is accessing on the Internet or any external network, what time the network is the most congested, and so on. Users can go to a variety of sites and download content that might not be related to their jobs, creating extra traffic and wasting the Internet bandwidth. A proxy server offers a reliable solution in this space by applying access rules or policies. As administrator, you can specify which users can access to the Internet, which Web sites they can access, and when access is allowed. The proxy server can fulfill these functions by applying access rules or policies.

A proxy server can also provide logging features that help administrators to keep track of usage, sites accessed, and which users logged on to the Internet. This information can be retained for future security audits that might be necessary in the environment. The logging features and level of access control can vary, depending on which proxy server is being used.

Functions of a Proxy Server

A proxy server offers four main functions:

- Forward proxy
- Reverse proxy
- Proxy chaining
- Caching

Forward Proxy

A forward proxy server allows client computers in protected networks to connect to the Internet by intercepting their requests and forwarding them to the destination server and relaying the reply back to the client. This is also known as the *Web Proxy* functionality of the proxy server. This is mainly used when users from an internal network with a private address range wants to connect to the Internet.

In a forward proxy mode a proxy server makes use of access rules, which allow certain or all users access to some or all Web sites and, if the content of the site is present in the cache, the reply to the user is returned from the cache. The proxy server also filters requests and responses to make sure they are valid. When the proxy determines that the request is valid and should not be blocked, the request is passed to the destination server if it is not cached on the proxy server. The response is given back to the client and may be cached on the proxy server for future use.

Reverse Proxy

A reverse proxy server passes the request from the Internet to an internal network resource (a Web server, for instance). The most common form of reverse proxy is publishing Web services to the Internet. With the current threats on the Internet, no one wants to publish a Web server directly on the Internet because this increases the attack surface of the Web server. A proxy server offers a convenient solution by publishing this Web server without making Internet clients aware that the requests are being intercepted by a proxy server that is relaying the content from a Web server located on the internal network.

A proxy server can redirect or deny the request based on the policy rule created by the administrator. It can also help reduce response times by serving requests from its cache rather than passing the actual requests to the Web server. A proxy server can also increase performance by load-balancing the requests through the use of a Web server farm, which provides equal distribution and fault tolerance of the service.

Proxy Chaining

In a proxy chaining scenario, a proxy server makes use of one or more proxy servers to handle proxy requests. This helps increase performance and security because it lets a proxy server handle different protocols through a different security layer. The most common example of a chained proxy scenario is the branch office. In this case, the proxy at the branch office would be configured to forward HTTP traffic to the head office proxy for processing and forwarding to the Internet.

In this scenario the first proxy server ensures that the request is valid. If it is denied, the client receives an error or the request is redirected. After the proxy server has confirmed that the request is valid, it checks its cache contents to see if the request object is already cached. If the request object is cached, it is returned from the cache directly to the client. If the request is not found in the cache, the request is forwarded to the next proxy server in the chain. Any proxy server in the chain has the authority to serve, deny, or redirect the request based on the rules it has. This process is repeated until the request reaches the last proxy server in the chain or until it is served.

> **NOTE** When server-side CARP is enabled in a multi-server array, requests that are received by one array member, but (according to the CARP algorithm) should be served by a different array member, effectively creates a chained proxy behavior between the two proxy servers. You can read more about CARP in Chapter 16, "Caching Concepts and Configuration," and in Appendix D, "WPAD Script CARP Operation."

Caching

One of the most important functions of a proxy server is caching. A proxy server can cache requests from Internet users trying to access published Web servers as well as cache requests from internal users trying to access content from the Internet. This provides a faster browsing experience to the clients as well as saving important network bandwidth.

CERN-Proxy Requests

CERN-proxy requests, also known as HTTP-proxy, are the most widely used for HTTP proxy services. The proxy server can proxy HTTP or FTP protocols. However, when the client wants to use a protocol such as FTP, the request to the proxy server is always HTTP. The proxy server then sends the request out to the destination server as FTP and gets the response, but when it sends the response back to the client, it will be HTTP again. Figure A-5 shows how the request is handled.

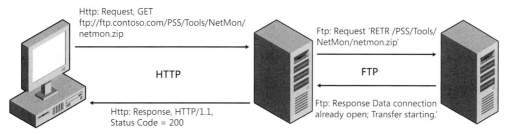

FIGURE A-5 How CERN proxy handles a FTP request

Notice that the request from the client to the proxy server is HTTP even though the command executed by the user is FTP.

The History Behind TMG

More than ten years have passed since Proxy Server 1.0 was released in 1996. As customer requirements and the Internet itself has evolved, so too have the Microsoft offerings evolved to meet those needs and the changing usage and threats. For instance, once considered a "safe haven," the internal LAN is now widely accepted to be the biggest threat of all. As such, the traffic from this source is now treated with at least as much suspicion as traffic received from the Internet. A short history summarizing the evolution of Microsoft proxy/firewall products will help you understand why TMG operates and behaves as it does.

Proxy Server 1.0

Originally code-named Catapult, Proxy Server 1.0 was conceived by members of the Internet Information Services (IIS) team to answer the call for a Microsoft offering in the fledgling Web Proxy product space and was later handed to the Research and Development (R&D) team in Haifa, Israel, for completion.

The Haifa team released Proxy Server 1.0 in October 1996 with the banner "The Only Proxy Server Fully Integrated with Windows NT Server." Although some of the competition (Netscape Proxy server, for instance) were able to run on Windows NT, none of them made as much use of the functionality offered by Windows NT 4.0 or IIS as did Proxy Server 1.0.

This version of proxy server was built around two major components; the Web proxy and the WinSock proxy, as shown in Figure A-6. The Web proxy operated as an Internet Services Application Programming interface (ISAPI) plug-in for IIS, whereas the Winsock Proxy operated as a separate Windows NT service.

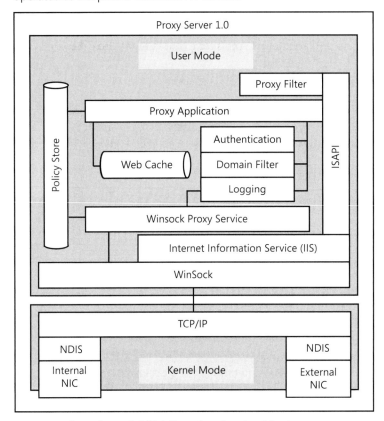

FIGURE A-6 Proxy Server 1,0 Web Proxy functional architecture

The following list summarizes the main product features and baseline installation and operational requirements:

- Requirements:
    - Windows NT version 4.0 (x86 or Alpha) with Service Pack 1
    - Internet Information Services 2.0
    - IPv4 and IPX
- Main features:
    - HTTP 1.0 CERN proxy (HTTP, HTTPS, FTP, Gopher)
    - HTTP 1.0 Web Publishing (local host only)
    - Web content caching
    - WinSock 1.1 Proxy
    - Packet filters

- Winsock Proxy Clients
  - Windows 3.0, 3.1, 3.11
  - Windows NT 4.0
  - Windows 95

Proxy Server 1.0 could be configured to allow Internet-based access to the server-local IIS Web sites, but was unable to publish internal Web sites to the Internet. Proxy Server 1.0 support ended March 2002.

Proxy Server 2.0

Originally code-named Catapult 2, Proxy Server 2.0 was released by the Haifa R&D team in December 1997. Although barely more than a year had passed since the release of Proxy 1.0, the changes included in this new release clearly warranted a full version change for the product. Architecturally similar to Proxy Server 1.0, it nonetheless brought with it several new features and improved performance and security, as shown in Figure A-7.

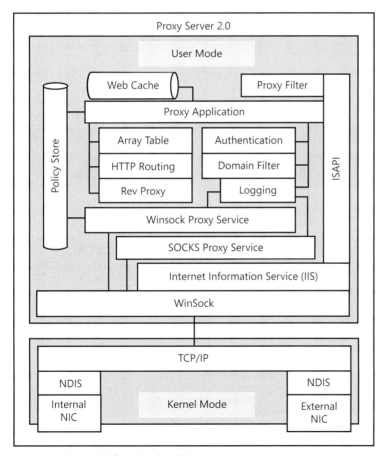

FIGURE A-7 Proxy 2.0 functional architecture

The following list summarizes the main product feature changes since Proxy Server 1.0, baseline installation, and operational requirements:

- Requirements:
  - Windows NT version 4.0 (x86 or Alpha) with Service Pack 3
  - Internet Information Services 3.0
  - IPv4 and IPX
- Changes since Proxy Server 1.0:
  - HTTP 1.1 (RFC 2616)
  - Distributed Web content caching (CARP)
  - Non-local Web Publishing
  - Server Publishing
  - Configuration backup and restore
  - Proxy arrays
  - SOCKS 4.3a Proxy
  - WPAD script
- Supported Winsock Proxy Clients
  - Windows 3.0, 3.1, 3.11
  - Windows NT 4.0
  - Windows 95

Although Proxy Server 2.0 was originally supported only on Windows NT 4.0, an update to enable Proxy Server 2.0 installation on Windows Server 2000 was released in 1999. This update allowed Proxy Server 2.0 deployments to take advantage of the improved security and networking functionality offered by Windows Server 2000. Support for Proxy Server 2.0 ended December 2004.

Internet Security and Acceleration (ISA) Server 2000

Originally code-named Comet, ISA Server 2000 was released by the Haifa R&D team in December 2000. One of the biggest changes from proxy server to ISA Server was the complete departure from the dependence on IIS for Web Proxy functionality. All of the Web Proxy functionality was now completely self-contained in a new service called the *Web proxy*. Often incorrectly referred to as *Proxy 3*, ISA Server 2000 included much more application protocol awareness and so made passing traffic between the Internet and the internal network much safer. Figure A-8 illustrates the core functionality of ISA Server 2000.

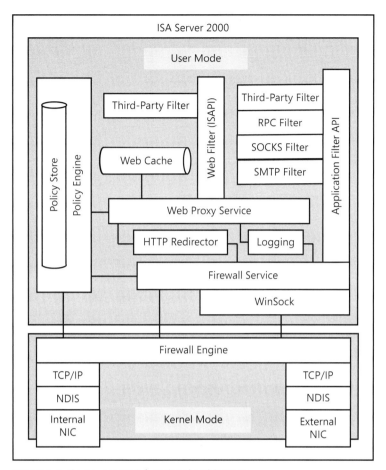

FIGURE A-8 ISA Server 2000 functional architecture

The following list summarizes the product feature changes since Proxy Server, baseline installation, and operational requirements:

- Requirements:
  - Windows Server 2000 (x86 only)
  - IPv4 only
- Changes since Proxy Server 2.0:
  - Two editions: Standard and Enterprise
  - Enterprise edition configuration stored in Active Directory
  - Bandwidth control

- IPX *no longer supported*
- IIS *no longer required*
- H.323 Gatekeeper
- SMTP Message Screener
- application-layer inspection via application and Web filters
- Winsock Proxy client changed to Firewall Client

- Supported Firewall Clients
  - Windows NT 4.0
  - Windows 95, 98, Millennium edition
  - Windows Server 2000
  - Windows XP

ISA Server 2000 was the first proxy/firewall product to be included in Small Business Server 2000 (SBS) Enterprise edition and was included in SBS 2003 Enterprise edition as well. With the delivery of hotfix 255 (MSKB 331062, later included in Service Pack 2), ISA Server 2000 was able to operate on Windows Server 2003, thereby taking advantage of the improved functionality and security it offered. ISA Server 2000 went into extended support in April 2006 and will end support completely in May 2011.

Internet Security and Acceleration (ISA) Server 2000 Feature Pack 1

To provide support for the emerging Internet-based Exchange client deployments such as Outlook Web Access, the ISA Sustained Engineering (SE) team decided to create an ISA 2000 add-on that would increase the security offered by ISA Server and provide Exchange client access policy creation much easier for ISA administrators. This Feature Pack was released In February 2003 and included the following additions to ISA Server functionality:

- **URLScan**   The very same ISAPI plug-in devised for IIS was added to the ISA Web Proxy filter to provide greater HTTP security for ISA Server Web Publishing.

- **SecurID authentication**   Licensed from RSA Security, Inc., this filter provides strong two-factor authentication for Web-published sites that can support this method.

- **Enhanced SMTP Filter**   Developed in collaboration with the Exchange team, this filter gave ISA Server the ability to scan inbound unencrypted e-mail for unwanted content before passing it to the internal mail server.

- **Enhanced RPC Filter**   Also developed in collaboration with the Exchange team, this new filter provided the ISA administrator with the ability to securely publish Exchange RPC (MAPI). This filter later proved to be the only safe method of allowing access to Exchange RPC-based e-mail while simultaneously blocking the Blaster virus. No other firewall was able to make this claim.

- **Outlook Web Access (OWA) Publishing Wizard**   The first of its kind, this wizard made it far easier to provide consistent Web Publishing for Exchange OWA services.
- **Link Translator**   This new filter provided the ISA administrator a means by which to change hyperlinks in Web pages and associated scripts that were not otherwise functional outside of the internal network.

Internet Security and Acceleration (ISA) Server 2004

Code-named Stingray, ISA Server 2004 was released by the Haifa R&D team in two phases: Standard edition in June 2004 and Enterprise edition in January 2005, both of which are shown in Figure A-9. Because the original plan was to support only Windows 2003, the split release was necessary to comply with the requirement to support Windows 2000, a requirement which was dictated late in the product cycle.

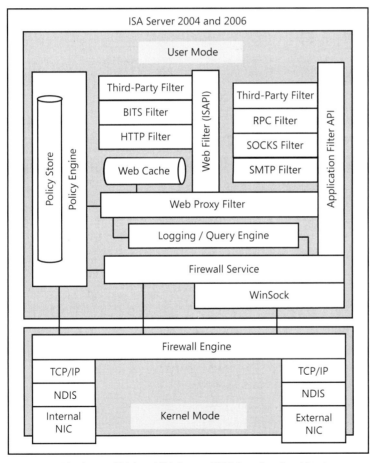

FIGURE A-9 ISA Server 2004 and ISA Server 2006 functional architecture

The following list summarizes the product feature changes since ISA 2000, baseline installation, and operational requirements:

- Requirements:
  - (Standard edition) Windows Server 2000 or 2003
  - (Enterprise edition) Windows Server 2003
  - TCP/IPv4

- Changes since ISA Server 2000:
  - Enterprise edition configuration stored in Active Directory Application Mode (ADAM).
  - Traffic policies are processed in a top-down fashion.
  - Connection limits.
  - Connectivity verifiers for common protocols.
  - Log and session query mechanisms.
  - MSDE logging by default.
  - Multiple protected networks.
  - VPN quarantine.
  - Only one protocol service—all Web and application filters run in the firewall service.
  - Installation and updates are provided by Microsoft Installer (MSI).
  - Gopher was dropped from CERN proxy protocol set.

- Supported Firewall Clients
  - Windows 98 Second edition
  - Windows Millennium edition
  - Windows XP
  - Windows 2000
  - Windows 2003

ISA Server 2004 was made available for SBS 2003 Enterprise edition users as part of SBS 2003 Service Pack 1. This event marked the last ISA Server product release for SBS.

Internet Security and Acceleration (ISA) Server 2004 Service Pack 2

Ordinarily, we wouldn't make a big deal about service packs; after all, they're just a collection of hotfixes, right? On most days, this is true, but this time, the ISA SE team outdid itself. Because the SE team was currently building and testing Service Pack 2, it decided that to make the best use of limited resources and the short delivery schedule for three complex design change requests (DCRs), it should merge the two efforts into a service pack "plus." This service pack was released to the public in February 2006. The primary focus of these changes was to reduce effective bandwidth consumption. All of these additions were built specifically for HTTP traffic handled by the Web proxy.

- **DiffServ-based QoS (RFC 2745)**   Although the bandwidth control mechanism offered in ISA 2000 was dropped with ISA 2004, it was replaced by support for Differentiated Services (DiffServ), a standardized method for traffic prioritization. Because HTTP traffic represents the majority of traffic handled by ISA Server, adding DiffServ prioritization for HTTP traffic handled by the Web Proxy filter meant that ISA could now cooperate with the network in prioritizing traffic according to the designs of the network team.

- **BITS Caching**   Background Intelligent Transfer Service (BITS) is an HTTP transfer management method that allows the client/server pair to exchange large data parcels in small pieces. This was first introduced in Windows 2000, and is used extensively for Windows and Microsoft Updates mechanisms. ISA Server was updated to support these transfer mechanisms and so provide cache extensibility for Windows and Microsoft Updates as well as WSUS and SMS-delivered packages, which also make extensive use of BITS.

- **HTTP Compression**   Because much of the content delivered by HTTP is text-based and text is highly compressible, it stands to reason that bandwidth utilization could be improved by compressing content before placing it "on the wire." ISA Server 2004 Service Pack 2 added GZip-based (an Internet standard) compression to accomplish this goal.

Internet Security and Acceleration (ISA) Server 2004 Service Pack 3

Continuing the service pack plus focus that began in ISA 2004 SP2—and to further support for the goals of making the product easier to manage and troubleshoot—three major enhancements were created for this release:

- **Troubleshooting Context**   The ISA 2004 management console (MMC) was changed to include a new section called *Troubleshooting*. This section made the new additions available from a single place to make this task simpler.

- **Debug logging**   Because the detail level required for troubleshooting is rarely required or desired in the daily logs, a new Windows event log category was added to support detailed logging. When enabled, ISA Server will include step-by-step processing details about every packet being processed while the logging is enabled.

- **ISA Best Practices Analyzer (ISABPA)**   The toughest task for any server administrator is in determining if what they've done falls within the realm of best practices for that product and scenario. To make this task a bit less painful, the ISA SE team took a cue from the Exchange team and built a BPA tool specifically for ISA Server. Freely downloadable—separate from the product or any service pack—this tool provides a few-button method for ISA administrators to quickly identify common configuration errors or behavioral problems in their ISA Server deployments.

Internet Security and Acceleration (ISA) Server 2006

Originally code-named Wolverine and originally intended to be an incremental upgrade to ISA Server 2004, ISA Server 2006 was released by the Haifa R&D team in July 2006. Building on the new model introduced in ISA Server 2004 and including all the functionality created by ISA Server 2004 Service Pack 2, ISA Server 2006 emerged as an even more functional and secure product. We don't include a diagram of ISA 2006 here because it is functionally identical to ISA 2004 with the exception of added Web filters.

The following list summarizes the product feature changes since ISA 2004, baseline installation, and operational requirements:

- Requirements:
  - Windows Server 2003 SP1
  - Active Directory Application Mode (Enterprise edition)
  - TCP/IPv4
- Changes since ISA Server 2004 Service Pack 2:
  - LDAP authentication for Web Publishing
  - Multiple authentication delegation options: NTLM, Kerberos Constrained Delegation (KCD)
  - RADIUS One-Time-Password (OTP) authentication
  - Advanced certificate authentication
  - Multiple protected networks
  - Web farm publishing
- Supported Firewall Clients
  - Windows Millennium edition
  - Windows XP
  - Windows 2000
  - Windows 2003

Internet Security and Acceleration (ISA) Server 2006 Supportability Update

The same updates built for ISA Server 2004 were created for ISA Server 2006 and released shortly afterward. The Supportability Update included the same updates for ISA Server 2006 that were provided in ISA Server 2004 Service Pack 3.

Internet Security and Acceleration (ISA) Server 2006 Service Pack 1

The supportability focus clearly shows in the additions to the product:

- **Web Publishing Test button** Because most errors in ISA Server configuration lie in properly building Web Publishing rules, a new button was added to the properties dialog box for any Web Publishing rule. This button simulates basic HTTP requests to the server as defined in the rule and provides success/failure reports and details of any errors it encounters.

- **Traffic Simulator** Analysis of application traffic is difficult enough when the client and server ends of the application are behaving properly. When they don't, evaluating application-layer firewall behavior becomes a nightmare. Thus was born the traffic simulator. It enables you to test ISA response to traffic as though it came from a real client without actually involving either the client or server.

- **Change Tracking** Change tracking was added to provide the ISA administrator with a tool to see what changes had been made to the ISA configuration near the time when the problem was first observed.

- **Diagnostic Logging Query** The debug logging added to ISA Server 2004 Service Pack 3 provided a tool with which you could query the log for the relevant data. Although this tool was well-crafted, it was—by virtue of not being included in the management console—invisible. This was corrected for ISA Server 2006 in Service Pack 1.

Forefront TMG Medium Business Edition

Originally code-named Nitrogen, Forefront TMG MBE (shown in Figure A-10) continues from the work done for ISA 2006 and adds significant changes to the architecture and the traffic-inspection and traffic-control mechanisms at all layers. New kernel-mode packet filtering mechanisms function in collaboration with Windows Server 2008 Firewall and Network Driver Interface Specification (NDIS) to provide improved packet filtering and traffic management for raw Ethernet frames. HTTP-based application-layer awareness now includes anti-malware inspection and the UI has been reworked to simplify and reorganize the layout to better support task-based usage. As you might expect, the troubleshooting enhancements that were created for ISA 2004 and ISA 2006 have been added to TMG as well. MSDE has been replaced with SQL Server Express 2005 and ISA reports are generated using SQL Reporting Services, providing the administrator with nearly infinite reporting capabilities.

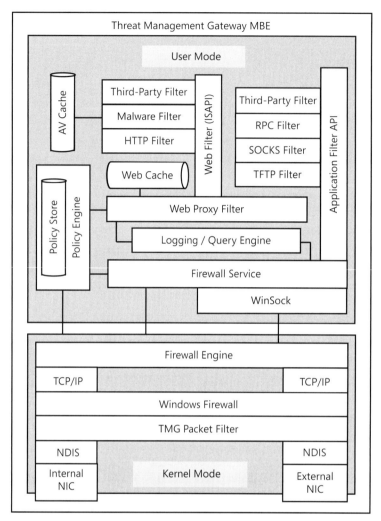

FIGURE A-10 Forefront TMG MBE functional architecture

The following list summarizes the product feature changes since ISA 2006, baseline installation, and operational requirements:

- Requirements:
  - Windows Server 2008 x64 Hosted (SYSWOW64)
  - Active Directory Application Mode (Enterprise edition)
  - IPv4, IPv6

- Changes since ISA Server 2006:
  - Windows Firewall registration.
  - NDIS-level packet filtering.
  - SQL 2005 Express replaces MSDE.
  - Reports are generated through SQL 2005 Reporting Services.
  - HTTP Malware Inspection Filter.
  - Malware signature updates through Microsoft Updates or local WSUS/SMS.
  - SSTP-based VPN via Windows 2008 RRAS.
  - Support for NAP.
- Supported Firewall Clients
  - Windows XP
  - Windows 2003
  - Windows Vista
  - Windows 2008

TMG Performance Counters

- TMG Performance Counters **937**

- How to Use These Counters **964**

- Summary **966**

Throughout the book we have discussed real-life scenarios and best practices to get the best performance from TMG. Another important set of tools often used by TMG administrators is performance counters. In this appendix we will discuss the different performance monitor counters added with a TMG installation.

TMG Performance Counters

The most common question asked by every TMG administrator during the deployment phase is how many TMG servers should be deployed in the array. Other questions that typically come up are, "I have 5,000 users accessing OWA through a single TMG. We'll be adding another 10,000 users to the existing load for OWA traffic. Will my existing TMG be able to handle the load? If I need to scale out, how many more TMG servers need be added to the existing array?" Answering some of these questions is easier for traffic profiles that are easier to predict. When the traffic profile is harder to predict and the load per user might vary, an important tool in the administrator's arsenal is the performance monitor. Using the different performance counters related to TMG, an administrator can view the load on the existing TMG servers in the array and make an informed decision regarding when it is time to scale out. With the installation of TMG, the following performance counters are added to the Windows server:

- Firewall packet engine performance counters
- H.323 filter performance counters
- Cache performance counters
- Microsoft Firewall service performance counters
- SOCKS filter performance counters
- Web Proxy performance counters
- Compression performance counters
- DiffServ performance counters

- Malware protection performance counters
- HTTPS performance counters
- E-mail hygiene performance counters
- URL Filtering performance counters

Each of these performance counter sets has a list of counters that can be added individually to monitor the specific state.

Firewall Packet Engine Performance Counters

Table B-1 shows the performance counters added to the firewall packet engine object along with their descriptions.

TABLE B-1 Firewall packet engine performance counters

PERFORMANCE COUNTER	DESCRIPTION
Active Connections	Shows the total number of active connections currently passing data
Allowed Packets	Shows the total number of packets that TMG allows to pass
Allowed Packets/sec	Shows the number of packets per second that TMG allows to pass
Backlogged Packets	Shows the number of backlogged packets
Bytes	Shows the total number of bytes that passed through TMG
Bytes/sec	Shows the number of bytes passed through TMG per second
Connections/sec	Shows the number of new connections created per second
Dropped Packets	Shows the total number of packets dropped by TMG
Dropped Packets/sec	Shows the number of packets dropped by TMG per second
Log Items enqueued/sec	Shows the number of log items enqueued per second
Packets	Shows the total number of packets inspected by TMG
Packets Blocked by NIS	Shows the number of packets blocked by NIS in kernel mode

PERFORMANCE COUNTER	DESCRIPTION
Packets Blocked by NIS/sec	Shows the number of packets blocked by NIS per second in kernel mode
Packets/sec	Shows the number of packets inspected by TMG per second
TCP Established Connections/sec	Shows the number of TCP connections newly established per second

H.323 Filter Performance Counters

Table B-2 shows the performance counters added to the H.323 filter object along with their descriptions.

TABLE B-2 H.323 filter performance counters

PERFORMANCE COUNTER	DESCRIPTION
Active H.323 Calls	The number of H.323 calls that are currently active
Total H.323 Calls	The total number of H.323 calls handled by the H.323 filter since the Microsoft Firewall service was started

Cache Performance Counters

Table B-3 shows the performance counters added to the *Cache* object along with their descriptions.

TABLE B-3 Cache performance counters

PERFORMANCE COUNTER	DESCRIPTION
Bytes Retrieved Rate from Disk Cache (KB/sec)	Shows the rate at which kilobytes of data are retrieved from the disk cache
Bytes Retrieved Rate from Memory Cache (KB/sec)	Shows the rate at which kilobytes of data are retrieved from the memory cache
Disk Cache Allocated Space (KB)	Shows the amount of space used for the disk cache (from the total disk space allocated for disk caching)
Disk Failure Rate (Fail/sec)	Shows the number of I/O failures per second since the firewall service started. An I/O failure occurs when TMG fails to read from or write to disk cache.

PERFORMANCE COUNTER	DESCRIPTION
Disk Write Rate (writes/sec)	Shows the number of writes to the disk cache per second
Max URLs Cached	Shows the maximum number of URLs stored in the cache simultaneously since the firewall service was started
Max URLs Cached	Measures the maximum number of URLs that have been stored in the cache
Memory Cache Allocated Space (KB)	Shows the amount of space used for the memory cache (from the total memory allocated for memory caching)
Memory Usage Ratio Percent (%)	Shows the amount of fetches from the memory cache in proportion to the total fetches from the cache
Total Bytes Retrieved from Disk Cache (KB)	Shows the cumulative number of kilobytes retrieved from the disk cache
Total Bytes Retrieved from Memory Cache (KB)	Shows the cumulative number of kilobytes retrieved from the memory cache
Total Disk Failures	Shows the number of times since the firewall service started that TMG failed to read from or write to disk cache because of an I/O failure
Total URLs Cached	Shows the cumulative number of URLs stored in the cache
Total URLs Retrieved from Disk Cache	Shows the cumulative number of URLs retrieved from the disk cache
Total URLs Retrieved from Memory Cache	Shows the cumulative number of URLs retrieved from the memory cache
URL Commit Rate (URL/sec)	Shows the rate at which URLs are stored to the cache
URL Retrieve Rate from Disk Cache (URL/sec)	Shows the rate at which URLs are retrieved from the disk cache
URL Retrieve Rate from Memory Cache (URL/sec)	Shows the rate at which URLs are retrieved from the memory cache
URLs in Cache	Shows the current number of URLs stored in the cache

Microsoft Firewall Service Performance Counters

Table B-4 shows the performance counters added to the Microsoft Firewall service object along with their descriptions.

TABLE B-4 Microsoft Firewall service performance counters

PERFORMANCE COUNTER	DESCRIPTION
Accepting TCP Connections	Shows the number of connection objects waiting for a TCP connection from the TMG Client after a successful remote connection. This counter is currently disabled.
Active Sessions	Shows the number of active sessions for the firewall service
Active SIP Registrations	Shows the total number of active SIP registrations
Active SIP Sessions	Shows the total number of active SIP sessions
Active TCP Connections	Shows the number of active TCP connections currently passing data. Connections pending or not yet established are counted elsewhere.
Active UDP Connections	Shows the number of active User Datagram Protocol (UDP) connections
Available UDP Mappings	Shows the number of mappings available for UDP connections
Available Worker Threads	Shows the number of firewall service worker threads that are available or waiting in the completion port queue
Bytes Read/sec	Shows the number of bytes read by the data pump per second
Bytes Written/sec	Shows the number of bytes written by the data pump per second
DNS Cache Entries	Shows the current number of Domain Name System (DNS) domain name entries cached as a result of firewall service activity
DNS Cache Flushes	Shows the number of times that the DNS domain name cache has been flushed or cleared by the firewall service
DNS Cache Hits	Shows the number of times a DNS domain name was found within the DNS cache by the firewall service

PERFORMANCE COUNTER	DESCRIPTION
DNS Cache Hits %	Shows the percentage of DNS domain names serviced by the DNS cache, from the total of all DNS entries that have been retrieved by the firewall service
DNS Retrievals	Shows the number of DNS domain names that have been retrieved by the firewall service
Dropped Connections by IPS	Shows the number of connections dropped by IPS in user mode
Dropped Connections by IPS/sec	Shows the number of connections dropped by IPS per second in user mode
Failed DNS Resolutions	Shows the number of Winsock getaddrinfo() calls that have failed. These are calls used to resolve host DNS domain names and IP addresses for firewall service connections.
Kernel Mode Data Pumps	Shows the number of kernel mode data pump instances created by the firewall service
Listening TCP Connections	Shows the number of connection objects that wait for TCP connections from remote Internet computers
Log Queue Size On Disk	Shows the current size of the TMG log queue on disk
Memory Allocation Failures	Shows the number of memory allocation errors
Pending DNS Resolutions	Shows the number of Winsock gteaddrinfo() calls pending. These are calls used to resolve host DNS domain names and IP addresses for firewall service connections.
Pending TCP Connections	Shows the total number of pending TCP connections. This is the total number of connections that are waiting for a connect call to finish.
SecureNAT Mappings	Shows the number of mappings created by SecureNET.
Successful DNS Resolutions	Shows the number of Winsock getaddrinfo() calls successfully returned. These are calls used to resolve host DNS domain names and IP addresses for firewall service connections.

PERFORMANCE COUNTER	DESCRIPTION
TCP Bytes Transferred/sec by Kernel Mode Data Pump	Shows the number of TCP bytes transferred by the kernel mode data pump per second
TCP Connections Awaiting Inbound Connect Call to Finish	Shows the total number of TCP connections awaiting an inbound connect call to finish. These are connections from the firewall service to a Firewall Client after the firewall service accepted a connection from the Internet on a listening socket.
UDP Bytes Transferred/sec by Kernel Mode Data Pump	Shows the number of UDP bytes transferred by the kernel mode data pump per second
Worker Threads	Shows the total number of firewall service worker threads

SOCKS Filter Performance Counter

Table B-5 shows the performance counters added to the SOCKS filter object along with their descriptions.

TABLE B-5 SOCKS filter performance counter

PERFORMANCE COUNTER	DESCRIPTION
Active Connections	Shows the total number of active connections currently passing data. Connections pending or not yet established are not included. This counter is incremented when a SOCKS connection is established. A SOCKS connection is counted after a successful CONNECT command, when the SOCKS filter begins the data pump stage of the protocol. This counter is decremented when the connection is terminated (for any reason).
Active Sessions	Shows a single SOCKS session; includes the CONNECT and BIND commands for a single client
Bytes Read/sec	Shows the number of bytes read on all SOCKS connections per second. The term *bytes read* refers to the amount of data sent from the client to the server during the data pump stage of the protocol.
Bytes Written/sec	Shows the amount of data sent from the server to the client during the data pump stage of the protocol

PERFORMANCE COUNTER	DESCRIPTION
Connecting Connections	Shows the number of SOCKS connections waiting for a remote computer to accept connections. When a client sends a CONNECT command to the SOCKS filter, the SOCKS filter connects to the specified server on behalf of the client. This counter is incremented immediately before the SOCKS filter starts the connection process to the specified server, and is decremented when the connection (to the specified server) process is completed (successfully or unsuccessfully).
Listening Connections	Shows the number of connection objects waiting for remote computers to connect. When a client sends a BIND command to the SOCKS filter, the SOCKS filter listens for an incoming connection on the specified port. This counter is incremented when the SOCKS filter starts waiting for the incoming connection, and is decremented when the incoming connection is received (or if the connection was terminated).
Pending DNS Resolutions	Shows the number of pending Winsock getaddrinfo() requests. These requests resolve host DNS names and IP addresses for SOCKS connections.
Successful DNS Resolutions	Shows the number of successful Winsock getaddrinfo() calls per second. These requests resolve host DNS names and IP addresses for SOCKS connections.

Web Proxy Performance Counters

Table B-6 shows the performance counters added to the Web Proxy object along with their descriptions.

TABLE B-6 Web Proxy performance counters

PERFORMANCE COUNTER	DESCRIPTIONS
Active Web Sessions	Indicates how many clients are currently being served by the Web Proxy filter. Monitoring this counter at both peak and off-peak times gives a good indication of server usage. The configuration setting for maximum Web request connections influences this value. This counter may also be useful if you need to temporarily stop TMG services. When authentication does not take place, all of the clients from a single IP address are viewed as one session.

PERFORMANCE COUNTER	DESCRIPTIONS
Array Bytes Received/sec (Enterprise)	Shows the rate at which data bytes are received from other TMG computers within the same array
Array Bytes Sent/sec (Enterprise)	Shows the rate at which data bytes are sent to other TMG computers within the same array
Array Bytes Total/sec (Enterprise)	Shows the sum of the Array Bytes Sent/sec and the Array Bytes Received/sec counters. This is the total rate for all data bytes transferred between the TMG computer and other members of the same array.
Average Milliseconds/Request	Shows the mean number of milliseconds required to service a Web Proxy client request, not including requests serviced by the Secure Sockets Layer (SSL) tunnel. This counter can be monitored at peak and off-peak times to get a comprehensive picture of the rate at which client requests are being serviced. A counter with a value that is too high might indicate that the TMG computer is having difficulty in handling all requests and that requests are being delayed.
Average Request Speed	Shows the average speed of the request for all requests in the previous minute. The speed is calculated by dividing the request size by the time needed to serve the request and is provided in bytes per second.
Bytes Actually Requested from Server for Range Requests/ Bytes in Range Requests (%)	Shows the percentage requested from the server for range requests out of the number of bytes in range requests when the cache rule enabled range request caching
Bytes Requested from Server in Ranges	Shows the total number of bytes requested from the server in HTTP requests containing range headers
Bytes Served (Last Hour) from Cache in Ranges	Shows the total number of bytes returned in responses to HTTP requests containing range headers served from cache during the last hour
Bytes Served (Last Hour) in Ranges	Shows the total number of bytes returned in responses to HTTP requests containing range headers during the last hour
Bytes Served from Cache in Ranges	Shows the total number of bytes returned in responses to HTTP requests containing range headers served from cache
Bytes Served in Ranges	Shows the total number of bytes returned in responses to HTTP requests containing range headers

PERFORMANCE COUNTER	DESCRIPTIONS
Cache Hit Percentage for Range Requests	Shows the percentage of bytes served from cache for responses to HTTP requests containing range headers
Cache Hit Ratio (%)	Determines how many Web Proxy client requests have been served using cached data (Total Cache Fetches), as a percentage of the total number of successful Web Proxy client requests to the TMG computer (Total Successful Requests). Its value gives a good indication of the effectiveness of the cache. A high counter value indicates that a high level of requests are being serviced from the cache, meaning faster response times. A zero counter value indicates that caching is not enabled. A low counter value may indicate a configuration problem. The cache size may be too small, or requests may not be cacheable.
Cache Hit Ratio for the Last 10K Requests (%)	Shows the amount of requests served from the cache as a percentage of total successful requests serviced. This ratio is the same as that measured by the Cache Hit Ratio counter. The difference between these two counters is that the Cache Running Hit Ratio counter measures this ratio for the last 10,000 requests serviced, and the Cache Hit Ratio counter measures this ratio since the last time that Web proxy was started. This means that the Cache Running Hit Ratio counter gives a more dynamic evaluation of cache effectiveness.
Client Bytes Received/sec	Shows the rate at which data bytes are received from Web Proxy clients. The value changes according to the volume of Web Proxy client requests, but a consistently slow rate may indicate a delay in servicing requests.
Client Bytes Sent/sec	Shows the rate at which data bytes are sent to Web Proxy clients. The value changes according to the volume of Web Proxy client requests, but a consistently slow rate may indicate a delay in servicing requests.
Client Bytes Total/sec	Shows the sum of the Client Bytes Sent/sec and the Client Bytes Received/sec counters. This is the total rate for all bytes transferred between the TMG computer and Web Proxy clients.

PERFORMANCE COUNTER	DESCRIPTIONS
Connect Errors	Shows the total number of errors that occurred while connecting
Connect Errors/Total Errors (%)	Shows the percentage of errors that occurred while connecting as a ratio of the total number of failed requests during the time shown in the duration field
Current Array Fetches Average (Milliseconds/request)	Shows the average number of milliseconds required to service a Web Proxy client request that is fetched through another array member. This does not include requests for services by the SSL tunnel.
Current Cache Fetches Average (Milliseconds/request)	Shows the average number of milliseconds required to service a Web Proxy client request from the cache. This does not include requests for services by the SSL tunnel.
Current Direct Fetches Average (Milliseconds/request)	Shows the average number of milliseconds required to service a Web Proxy client request directly to the Web server or upstream proxy. This does not include requests for services by the SSL tunnel.
Failing Requests/sec	Shows the rate of Web Proxy client requests that have been completed with some type of error. This counter can be compared with the Requests/sec counter to give an indication of how well TMG is servicing incoming Web requests. A high failure rate, as compared with the rate of incoming requests, suggests that TMG is having difficulty in coping with all incoming requests. Connection settings for incoming Web requests may be incorrectly configured, or connection bandwidth may be insufficient.
Failing Requests/Total Requests (%)	Shows the percentage of failing requests out of the total number of requests during the time shown in the duration field.
FTP Requests	Shows the number of CERN File Transfer Protocol (FTP) requests that have been made to Web proxy. A consistently low counter value may influence the caching policy for FTP objects.
HTTP Requests	Shows the number of HTTP requests that have been made to Web proxy
Incoming Connections/sec	Shows the rate of incoming connections (per second)
IO Errors to Array Member	Shows the total number of input/output errors that occurred during communication with an array member

PERFORMANCE COUNTER	DESCRIPTIONS
IO Errors to Array Member/ Total Errors (%)	Shows the percentage of input/output errors that occurred during communication with an array member out of the total number of failed requests during the time shown in the duration field
IO Errors to Client	Shows the total number of input/output errors that occurred during communication with the client
IO Errors to Client/Total Errors	Shows the percentage of input/output errors that occurred during communication with the client out of the total number of failed requests during the time shown in the duration field
IO Errors to Server	Shows the total number of input/output errors that occurred during communication with the server
IO Errors to Server/Total Errors (%)	Shows the percentage of input/output errors that occurred during communication with the server out of the total number of failed requests during the time shown in the duration field
Maximum Users	Shows the maximum number of users that have connected to Web proxy simultaneously. This counter can be useful for determining load usage and license requirements. *This counter is only valid if Forefront TMG is authenticating user requests.*
Memory Pool for HTTP Requests (%)	Percentage of memory available for HTTP requests. When an HTTP request is made, TMG uses memory from a preallocated pool. You can use the *ProxyVmemAlloc3pSize* registry value in the HKEY_LOCAL_MACHINE\SYSTEM\CurrentControlSet\ Services\W3Proxy\Parameters registry key to modify the size of this pool.
Memory Pool for SSL Requests (%)	Percentage of memory available for SSL requests. When an SSL request is made, TMG uses memory from a pre-allocated pool. You can use the *ProxyVmemAlloc1pSize* registry value in the HKEY_LOCAL_MACHINE\SYSTEM\CurrentControlSet\ Services\W3Proxy\Parameters registry key to modify the size of this pool.
Outgoing Connections/sec	Shows the rate of outgoing connections (per second)
Protocol Anomalies Blocked by NIS in Last Day	Shows the total number of protocol anomalies that the Network Inspection System blocked in the last day

PERFORMANCE COUNTER	DESCRIPTIONS
Protocol Anomalies Detected by NIS in Last Day	Shows the total number of protocol anomalies that the Network Inspection System detected in the last day
Requests from Array Member (Enterprise)	Shows the total number of requests coming from another array member
Requests from Array Member/ Total Errors (%)(Enterprise)	Shows the percentage of requests coming from another array member out of the total number of failed requests during the time shown in the duration field
Requests to Array Member (Enterprise)	Shows the total number of requests going to another array member
Requests to Array Member/ Total Errors (%)(Enterprise)	Shows the percentage of requests going to another array member out of the total number of failed requests during the time shown in the duration field
Requests with Keep Alive to Array Member	Shows the total number of requests that use an existing keep-alive connection between TMG and another array member
Requests with Keep Alive to Array Member/Total Errors (%)	Shows the percentage of requests that use an existing keep-alive connection between TMG and another array member out of the total number of failed requests during the time shown in the duration field
Requests with Keep Alive to Client	Shows the total number of requests that use an existing keep-alive connection between the client and TMG
Requests with Keep Alive to Client/ Total Errors (%)	Shows the percentage of requests that use an existing keep-alive connection between the client and TMG as a ratio of the total number of failed requests during the time shown in the duration field
Requests with Keep Alive to Server	Shows the total number of requests that use an existing keep-alive connection between TMG and the Web server
Requests with Keep Alive to Server/ Total Errors (%)	Shows the percentage of requests that use an existing keep-alive connection between TMG and the Web server as a ratio of the total number of failed requests during the time shown in the duration field
Requests with Multiple Ranges	Shows the number of requests with more than one range in the HTTP Range header

PERFORMANCE COUNTER	DESCRIPTIONS
Requests/sec	Shows the rate of incoming requests that have been made to Web proxy. A higher value means that more TMG resources will be required to service incoming requests.
Reverse Bytes Received/sec	Shows the rate at which data bytes are received by Web proxy from Web Publishing servers in response to incoming requests. This rate can be monitored at peak and off-peak times as an indication of how TMG is performing in servicing incoming Web requests.
Reverse Bytes Sent/sec	Shows the rate at which data bytes are sent by Web proxy to Web Publishing servers in response to incoming requests. This rate can be monitored at peak and off-peak times as an indication of how TMG is performing in servicing incoming Web requests.
Reverse Bytes Total/sec	Shows the total sum of the Reverse Bytes Sent/sec and the Reverse Bytes Received/sec counters. This is the total rate for all bytes transferred between Web proxy and Web Publishing servers in response to incoming requests.
Signatures Blocked by NIS in Last Day	Shows the total number of signatures that the Network Inspection System blocked in the last day
Signatures Detected by NIS in Last Day	Shows the total number of signatures that the Network Inspection System detected in the last day
Sites Allowed	Shows the total number of Internet sites to which Web proxy has denied access. An excessively high number might indicate an access policy that is too restrictive.
Sites Allowed in Last Day	Shows the total number of Web sites to which the Web Proxy filter allowed access in last day
Sites Denied	Shows the total number of Internet sites to which Web proxy has granted access. This can be compared with the Site Access Denied counter to give a numeric summary of the results of access policy configuration.
Sites Denied in Last Day	Shows the total number of Web sites to which the Web Proxy filter denied access in the last day
SNEWS Sessions	Shows the total number of SNEWS sessions serviced by the Web Proxy SSL tunnel

PERFORMANCE COUNTER	DESCRIPTIONS
SSL Client Bytes Received/sec	Shows the rate at which SSL data bytes are received by Web proxy from SSL clients. Similar to the Client Bytes Received/sec counter, but counts only SSL requests.
SSL Client Bytes Sent/sec	Shows the rate at which SSL data bytes are sent by Web proxy to SSL clients. Similar to the Client Bytes Sent/sec counter, but counts only SSL requests.
SSL Client Bytes Total/sec	Shows the sum of the SSL Client Bytes Sent/sec and the SSL Client Bytes Received/sec counters. This is the total rate for all bytes transferred between Web proxy and SSL clients.
Thread Pool Active Sessions	Shows the number of sessions being actively serviced by thread pools
Thread Pool Failures	Shows the number of requests rejected because the thread pool was full
Thread Pool Size	Shows the number of threads in the thread pool. This thread pool represents the resources available to service client requests.
Total Array Fetches (Enterprise)	Shows the total number of Web Proxy client requests that have been served by requesting the data from another TMG computer within this array. These requests are the result of the server-side Cache Array Routing Protocol (CARP) algorithm, which determines which array member should hold this content in its cache. The load factor for each server can also be configured to determine how workload is divided among array members.
Total Cache Fetches	Shows the total number of Web Proxy client requests that have been served by using cached data. A high number indicates a cache being fully exploited.
Total Failing Requests	Shows the total number of requests that have failed to be processed by Web proxy because of errors. Errors can be the result of Web proxy failing to locate a requested server URL on the Internet or because the client did not have authorized access to the requested URL. This counter should be lower than the Total Successful Requests counter. If not, it is an indication that TMG is failing to service requests effectively. This could be a configuration problem, or a connection that is too slow. It could also indicate an access policy that is too restrictive.

PERFORMANCE COUNTER	DESCRIPTIONS
Total Pending Connects	Shows the total number of pending connections to Web proxy. A high value here indicates that TMG may be overtasked or it may be waiting for the upstream servers to accept connections.
Total Requests	Shows the total number of requests that have been made to Web proxy. It is the sum of the Total Successful Requests and the Total Failed Requests counters.
Total Reverse Fetches	Shows the total number of incoming requests that have been served by requesting the data from Web Publishing servers
Total SSL Sessions	Shows the total number of SSL sessions serviced by the SSL tunnel
Total Successful Requests	Shows the total number of requests that have been successfully processed by Web proxy. This counter can be compared with the Total Requests and the Total Failed Requests counters to indicate the effectiveness of TMG in servicing requests.
Total Upstream Fetches	Shows the total number of requests that have been served by using data from the Internet or from a chained proxy computer. This counter can be compared to the Total Cache Fetches counter to determine what proportion of requests are being serviced from remote servers on the Internet or upstream proxies, compared with those being serviced from the cache.
Total Users	Shows the total number of users that have connected to Web proxy. It represents a history of past server usage.
Unknown SSL Sessions	Shows the total number of unknown SSL sessions serviced by the SSL tunnel
Upstream Bytes Received/sec	Shows the rate at which data bytes are received by Web proxy from remote servers on the Internet or from a chained proxy computer in response to requests from Web proxy. The value of this counter depends partially on the connection bandwidth. If the counter value is consistently low, it may indicate a bottleneck caused by a slow connection. Changing the bandwidth priority configuration may help in this situation, or a faster connection may be required.

PERFORMANCE COUNTER	DESCRIPTIONS
Upstream Bytes Sent/sec	Shows the rate at which data bytes are sent by Web proxy to remote servers on the Internet or to a chained proxy computer. The value of this counter depends partially on the connection bandwidth. If the counter value is consistently low, it may indicate a bottleneck caused by a slow connection. Changing the bandwidth priority configuration may help in this situation, or a faster connection may be required.
Upstream Bytes Total/sec	Shows the sum of the Upstream Bytes Sent/sec and the Upstream Bytes Received/sec counters. It represents the total rate for all bytes transferred between Web proxy and remote servers on the Internet or a chained proxy server.

Compression Performance Counters

Table B-7 shows the performance counters added to the Compression object along with their descriptions.

TABLE B-7 Compression performance counters

PERFORMANCE COUNTER	DESCRIPTION
Compression - Current Compression Ratio	For HTTP responses compressed by TMG, the average size reduction of the HTTP response body as a percentage of the uncompressed body size during the sample period
Compression - Current Ratio of Responses Compressed	Shows the percentage of HTTP responses compressed by TMG out of the number of HTTP requests handled by Forefront TMG during the sample period
Compression - Current Ratio of Responses Decompressed	Shows the percentage of HTTP responses decompressed by TMG out of the number of HTTP requests handled by TMG during the sample period
Compression - Ratio of Size Reduction	For HTTP responses compressed by TMG, the average size reduction of the HTTP response body as a percentage of the uncompressed body size
Compression - Responses Compressed: Accumulated Ratio	Shows the percentage of HTTP responses compressed by TMG out of the total number of HTTP requests handled by TMG

PERFORMANCE COUNTER	DESCRIPTION
Compression - Responses Decompressed: Accumulated Ratio	Shows the percentage of HTTP responses decompressed by TMG out of the total number of HTTP requests handled by TMG
Compression - Total Failures	Shows the total number of failures to compress or decompress a response

Diffserv Performance Counters

Table B-8 shows the performance counters added to the Diffserv object along with their descriptions.

TABLE B-8 Diffserv performance counters

PERFORMANCE COUNTER	DESCRIPTION
DiffServ Requests - 1st Priority	The total number of first priority requests since the last performance monitoring sample
DiffServ Requests - 1st Priority Ratio to Total	Shows the ratio of first priority requests to the total number of requests
DiffServ Requests - 2nd Priority	Shows the total number of second priority requests since the last performance monitoring sample
DiffServ Requests - 2nd Priority Ratio to Total	Shows the ratio of second priority requests to the total number of requests
DiffServ Requests - 3rd Priority	Shows the total number of third-priority requests since the last performance monitoring sample
DiffServ Requests - 3rd Priority Ratio to Total	Shows the ratio of third-priority requests to the total number of requests
DiffServ Requests - 4th Priority	Shows the total number of fourth-priority requests since the last performance monitoring sample
DiffServ Requests - 4th Priority Ratio to Total	Shows the ratio of fourth-priority requests to the total number of requests
DiffServ Requests - 5th Priority	Shows the total number of fifth-priority requests since the last performance monitoring sample
DiffServ Requests - 5th Priority Ratio to Total	Shows the ratio of fifth-priority requests to the total number of requests
DiffServ Requests - Low Priority Ratio to Total	Shows the ratio of low-priority requests (sixth priority and lower) to the total number of requests

PERFORMANCE COUNTER	DESCRIPTION
DiffServ Requests - Lower Priority	Shows the total number of low-priority requests (sixth priority and lower) since the last performance monitoring sample
DiffServ Requests - Non-Priority	Shows the total number of requests without an assigned priority since the last performance monitoring sample
DiffServ Requests - Non-Priority Ratio to Total	Shows the ratio of requests without an assigned priority to the total number of requests
DiffServ Requests - Priority Ratio to Total	Shows the ratio of requests with an assigned priority to the total number of requests
DiffServ Requests - Total Priority	Shows the total number of requests with an assigned priority since the last performance monitoring sample
DiffServ Responses - 1st Priority	Shows the total number of first-priority responses since the last performance monitoring sample
DiffServ Responses - 1st Priority Ratio to Total	Shows the ratio of first-priority responses to the total number of responses
DiffServ Responses - 2nd Priority	Shows the total number of second-priority responses since the last performance monitoring sample
DiffServ Responses - 2nd Priority Ratio to Total	Shows the ratio of second-priority responses to the total number of responses
DiffServ Responses - 3rd Priority	Shows the total number of third-priority responses since the last performance monitoring sample
DiffServ Responses - 3rd Priority Ratio to Total	Shows the ratio of third-priority responses to the total number of responses
DiffServ Responses - 4th Priority	Shows the total number of fourth-priority responses since the last performance monitoring sample
DiffServ Responses - 4th Priority Ratio to Total	Shows the ratio of fourth-priority responses to the total number of responses
DiffServ Responses - 5th Priority	Shows the total number of fifth-priority responses since the last performance monitoring sample
DiffServ Responses - 5th Priority Ratio to Total	Shows the ratio of fifth-priority responses to the total number of responses
DiffServ Responses - Lower Priority Ratio to Total	Shows the ratio of low-priority responses (sixth priority and lower) to the total number of responses
DiffServ Responses - Lower Priority	Shows the total number of low-priority responses (sixth priority and lower) since the last performance monitoring sample

PERFORMANCE COUNTER	DESCRIPTION
DiffServ Responses - Non-Priority	Shows the total number of responses without an assigned priority since the last performance monitoring sample
DiffServ Responses - Non-Priority Ratio to Total	Shows the ratio of responses without an assigned priority to the total number of responses
DiffServ Responses - Priority Ratio to Total	Shows the ratio of responses with an assigned priority to the total number of responses
DiffServ Responses - Total Priority	Shows the total number of responses with an assigned priority since the last performance monitoring sample

Malware Protection Performance Counters

Table B-9 shows the performance counters added to the Malware Protection object along with their descriptions.

TABLE B-9 Malware protection performance counters

PERFORMANCE COUNTER	DESCRIPTION
Malware Protection - Items Handled	The number of items currently being handled by the Malware Protection Web filter
Malware Protection - Total Items Handled	The total number of items handled by the Malware Protection Web filter since the service was last started
Malware Inspection - Total Items Handled in Last Day	The total number of items handled by the Malware Inspection Filter in the last day
Malware Protection - Average Accumulation Duration (mSec)	The average amount of time to accumulate each item, in milliseconds
Malware Protection - Average Inspection Duration (mSec)	The average amount of time used to inspect each item, in milliseconds
Malware Protection - Items Trickled (Standard Trickling)	The number of items currently being trickled to clients using standard trickling
Malware Protection - Items Trickled (Fast Trickling)	The number of items currently being trickled to clients using fast trickling
Malware Protection - Total Items Trickled (Standard Trickling)	The total number of items that were trickled to clients using standard trickling since the service was started

PERFORMANCE COUNTER	DESCRIPTION
Malware Protection - Total Items Trickled (Fast Trickling)	The total number of items that were trickled to clients using fast trickling since the service was started
Malware Inspection - Average Trickled Size (Standard Trickling, Bytes)	The average size, in bytes, of content trickled using standard trickling per trickled item
Malware Inspection - Average Trickled Size (Fast Trickling, Bytes)	The average size, in bytes, of content trickled using fast trickling per trickled item
Malware Protection - Items in Progress Page	The number of items for which progress pages are currently being used
Malware Protection - Total Items in Progress Page	The total number of items for which progress pages were used since the service was started
Malware Protection - Average Progress Page Status Requests	The average number of status requests per item for which progress pages were used
Malware Inspection - Streaming Items	The total number of items exempted from inspection because they were identified as streaming content
Malware Inspection - Total Excluded Item	The total number of items exempted from inspection because they were in the exempted destinations list
Malware Inspection - Disk Accumulation (%)	Current percentage of items using disk accumulation out of the total number of items currently being handled
Malware Inspection - Allocated Disk Space (Bytes)	The disk space, in bytes, allocated by the Malware Inspection Filter for accumulation and inspection
Malware Inspection - Disk Errors	The total number of disk errors encountered by the Malware Inspection Filter
Malware Inspection - Total Partial Inspections (Standard Trickling)	The total number of partial inspections (inspection of partial content before it is trickled) for standard trickling
Malware Inspection - Total Partial Inspections (Fast Trickling)	The total number of partial inspections (inspection of partial content before it is trickled) for fast trickling
Malware Inspection - Partial Inspections per Item (Standard Trickling)	The average number of partial inspections (inspection of partial content before it is trickled) for standard trickling per trickled item

PERFORMANCE COUNTER	DESCRIPTION
Malware Inspection - Partial Inspections per Item (Fast Trickling)	The average number of partial inspections (inspection of partial content before it is trickled) for fast trickling per trickled item
Malware Inspection - Inspections Failed	The total number of items that were blocked because of an inspection failure
Malware Inspection - Items Blocked (Size Exceeded)	The total number of items that were blocked because the file size exceeded the configured limit
Malware Inspection - Items Blocked (Unpacked Size Exceeded)	The total number of items that were blocked because the file size after unpacking exceeded the configured limit
Malware Inspection - Items Blocked (Nesting Levels Exceeded)	The total number of items that were blocked because the nesting level limit was exceeded
Malware Inspection - Items Blocked (Corrupted)	The total number of items that were blocked because the file was corrupted
Malware Inspection - Items Blocked (Encrypted)	The total number of items that were blocked because the file was encrypted
Malware Inspection - Items Blocked (Infected)	The total number of items that were blocked because the file was infected
Malware Inspection - Items Blocked (Infected) in the Last 24 Hours	The total number of items that were blocked in the last 24 hours because the file was infected
Malware Inspection - Items Blocked (Policy) in the Last 24 Hours	The total number of items that were blocked in the last 24 hours because of policy restrictions (exceeded size, exceeded nesting level, corrupt file, and so on)
Malware Inspection - Items Blocked (Suspicious)	The total number of items that were blocked because the file was suspicious
Malware Inspection - Items Blocked (Unknown Encoding)	The total number of items that were blocked because the file encoding was unknown
Malware Inspection - Items Blocked (Timeout)	The total number of items that were blocked because the inspection timed out
Malware Inspection - Items Cleaned	The total number of items that were found infected and were successfully cleaned
Malware Inspection - Ping Timeouts	The total number of ping timeouts during progress page processing
Malware Inspection - Download Timeouts	The total number of download timeouts during progress page processing

PERFORMANCE COUNTER	DESCRIPTION
Malware Inspection - Extended Quota Usage (%)	The current percentage of extended quota used out of the total extended quota pool
Malware Inspection - Average Extended Quota Usage Time	The average amount of time, in milliseconds, of extended quota usage, since the service started
Malware Inspection - Extended Quota Exceeded	The total number of times the extended quota was exceeded
Malware Inspection - Extended Quota Unavailable	The total number of times the extended quota was required, but not available
Malware Inspection - Extended Quota Exceeded Delta	The number of times the extended quota was exceeded in the last period
Malware Inspection - Extended Quota Unavailable Delta	The number of times the extended quota was required, but not available, in the last period
Malware Inspection - Queue Length (High Priority)	The number of items waiting in the high-priority malware inspection queue
Malware Inspection - Queue Length (Medium Priority)	The number of items waiting in the medium-priority malware inspection queue
Malware Inspection - Queue Length (Low Priority)	The number of items waiting in the low-priority malware inspection queue
Malware Inspection - Average Time in Queue (High Priority)	The average time, in milliseconds, that an item processed with high priority waits in the malware inspection queue
Malware Inspection - Average Time in Queue (Medium Priority)	The average time, in milliseconds, that an item processed with medium priority waits in the malware inspection queue

HTTPS Performance Counters

Table B-10 shows the performance counters added to the HTTPS object along with their descriptions.

TABLE B-10 HTTPS performance counters

PERFORMANCE COUNTER	DESCRIPTION
HTTPS Connection Inspection/sec	Shows the rate per second at which HTTPS connections are inspected
HTTPS Connections Excluded	Shows the total number of connections excluded by HTTPS inspection

PERFORMANCE COUNTER	DESCRIPTION
HTTPS Connections Excluded/sec	Shows the rate per second of connections excluded by HTTPS inspection
HTTPS Connection Inspected	Shows the total number of HTTPS connections that were inspected
HTTPS Connection Inspected in Last Day	Shows the total number of HTTPS connections that were inspected in the last day
HTTPS Inspection Blocked Certificates	Shows the total number of certificates blocked by HTTPS inspection
HTTPS Inspection Blocked Certificates in Last Day	Shows the total number of certificates blocked by HTTPS inspection in the last day
HTTPS Inspection Blocked Certificates/sec	Shows the rate per second of certificates blocked by HTTPS inspection
HTTPS Inspection Certificate Cache Hit Ratio	Shows the HTTPS inspection certificate cache hit ratio
HTTPS Inspection Certificate Cache Size	Shows the total number of certificates in the HTTPS inspection certificate cache
HTTPS Inspection Certificate Cloning Time	Shows the average time in milliseconds to clone a certificate
HTTPS Inspection Failures	Shows the total number of HTTPS inspection failures
HTTPS Inspection Failures/sec	Shows the rate per second of HTTPS inspection failures
HTTPS Inspection Processing Time	Shows the average time in milliseconds from receiving a request to the establishment of an HTTPS bridge
HTTPS Sessions	Shows the total number of Secure Hypertext Transfer Protocol (HTTPS) secured sessions serviced by the SSL tunnel. This includes only sessions allowed by rules configured to use SSL tunneling publishing mode.

E-mail Hygiene Performance Counters

Table B-11 shows the performance counters added to the E-mail Hygiene object along with their descriptions.

TABLE B-11 E-mail Hygiene performance counters

PERFORMANCE COUNTER	DESCRIPTION
Email Messages Scanned	Shows the total number of messages inspected by TMG in the last 24 hours (a moving window of the last 24 hours)
Infected Messages	Shows the number of messages blocked by AV in the last 24 hours (a moving window of the last 24 hours)
Spam Messages	Shows the number of messages categorized as spam in the last 24 hours (a moving window of the last 24 hours)

URL Filtering Performance Counters

Table B-12 shows the performance counters added to the URL Filtering object along with their descriptions.

TABLE B-12 URL Filtering performance counters

PERFORMANCE COUNTER	DESCRIPTION
URL Filtering - Variant Cache Hit Rate	Shows the number of cache hits out of the total number of cache lookups
URL Filtering - Variant Cache Size	Shows the number of hashed entries in the variant hash
URL Filtering - Categorizations	Shows the total number of categorizations
URL Filtering - Categorizations Delta	Shows the total number of categorizations in the sample period
URL Filtering - % Component Categorizations	Shows the number of categorizations by the MSAS categorizer out of the total number of categorizations
URL Filtering - % Overrides Categorizations	Shows the number of categorization overrides out of the total number of categorizations
URL Filtering - % Categorizations from Cache	Shows the number of categorizations by the MSAS categorizer returned from cache out of the total number of categorizations
URL Filtering - % Categorizations from Web Service	Shows the number of categorizations by the MSAS categorizer were sent to server out of the total number of categorizations
URL Filtering - % Categorizations Unknown	Shows the number of URLs that were not recognized out of the total number of categorizations

PERFORMANCE COUNTER	DESCRIPTION
URL Filtering - % Categorizations from Server Failed	Shows the number of categorizations by the MSAS categorizer server that failed, out of the total number of categorizations
URL Filtering - Avg Categorization Duration	Shows the average online categorization duration in milliseconds
URL Filtering - % Fast Categorizations from Server	Shows the number of online categorizations that took less than 250 milliseconds, out of the total number of online categorizations
URL Filtering - % Moderate Categorizations from Server	Shows the number of online categorizations that took between 250 and 500 milliseconds, out of the total number of online categorizations
URL Filtering - % Slow Categorizations from Server	Shows the number of online categorizations that took between 500 and 1,000 milliseconds, out of the total number of online categorizations
URL Filtering - % Very Slow Categorizations from Server	Shows the number of online categorizations that took more than one second, out of the total number of online categorizations
URL Filtering - Avg Request Entry Count	Shows the average number of entries in a server request
URL Filtering - Avg Response Entry Count	Shows the average number of entries in a server response

TMG Performance Monitor

TMG also installs the TMG Performance Monitor as a part of the installation. The TMG Performance Monitor is a customized view of the Windows System Monitor that only includes TMG-related counters that help the administrator get a quick snapshot of the health of TMG. These performance counters are a small subset of the counters listed in the preceding sections and can be accessed by the administrator by clicking All Programs, then clicking Microsoft Forefront TMG, and then clicking Forefront TMG Performance Monitor. The default counters appear under the Reliability and Performance Monitor. Table B-13 lists these counters and their general usage.

TABLE B-13 Performance Monitor counters

CATEGORY	PERFORMANCE COUNTER	DESCRIPTION
Forefront TMG Firewall Packet Engine	Active Connections	Shows the total number of active connections currently passing data. Use this counter to monitor general performance.
Forefront TMG Firewall Packet Engine	Bytes/sec	Shows the total throughput in bytes per second passing through the firewall. Every byte is counted twice: once when it enters the firewall and once when it leaves the firewall. Use this counter to monitor general performance.
Forefront TMG Firewall Service	Active Sessions	Shows the number of active sessions for the firewall service. Use this counter to monitor general performance. By comparing this counter at both peak and off-peak times, you can construct a good picture of routine usage.
Forefront TMG Web Proxy	Requests/sec	Shows the request rate each second. Use this counter to monitor general performance. Dividing the Client Bytes Sent/sec counter by this counter provides a measure of average response size, which should be no more than approximately 20 KB.
Forefront TMG Firewall Packet Engine	Dropped packets/sec	Shows the number of denied packets per second. Use to monitor general security threats. If numbers are large (more than 100), check for network configuration errors and attacks.
Forefront TMG Firewall Packet Engine	Packets/sec	Shows the number of allowed and denied packets per second. Use to monitor general security threats and performance. This directly impacts CPU utilization.
Forefront TMG Firewall Packet Engine	Connections/sec	Shows the number of TCP and UDP connections created per second. Use to monitor general security threats and performance. This directly impacts CPU utilization.
Forefront TMG Web Proxy	Average Milliseconds/ request	Shows the average response time. Use to monitor general security threats and performance. Use direct fetches and cache fetches to diagnose.

System Performance

Apart from the Reliability and Performance Monitor, TMG also provides you a quick view of the CPU utilization and the available memory per server in the Dashboard under System Performance as shown in Figure B-1.

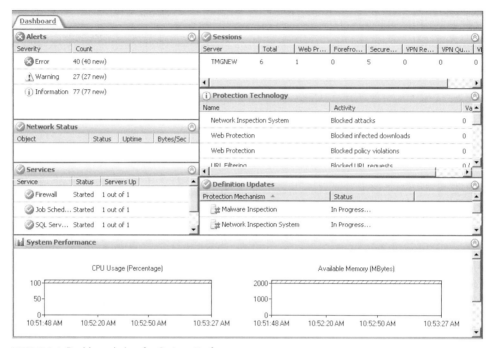

FIGURE B-1 Dashboard view for System Performance

The two counters available are CPU Usage (Percentage) and Available Memory (MBytes). These counters are available per server in the dashboard view.

How to Use These Counters

With the addition of new features in TMG, the number and categories associated with the performance counter objects have increased as well. An administrator has to decide which counters to monitor depending on the issue being troubleshot. To better understand the usage of these counters, consider the following example in which we will use some common counters to see how their pattern and dependencies on other counters can help during analysis. Table B-14 lists the scenario with the counters and analysis based on the patterns.

TABLE B-14 Counters and their analysis based on patterns

PERFORMANCE OBJECT	PERFORMANCE COUNTER	PATTERN IN GRAPH	ANALYSIS
Forefront TMG Firewall Packet Engine	Active Connections	Comparative Baseline	Backlogged packets can impact dropped packets and vice versa: 1. If they rise together or if a rise in backlogged packet precedes the rise in dropped packets, TMG is processing too much traffic
	Backlogged Packets	Drop from High to Low is good	
			2. If this always happens after active connections plateaus, it's time to scale out or resolve other issues
	Dropped Packets	Drop from High to Low is good	
Forefront TMG Firewall Service	Available Worker Threads	Drop from High to Low is bad	1. Available worker threads should never remain near 0 for any length of time; if TMG keeps this at or near 0, it's time to scale out
	Pending DNS Resolutions	Drop from High to Low is good	2. Pending DNS resolutions can impact pending TCP connections; make sure Windows can perform resolutions quickly and reliably, especially for domain-based DNS
	Pending TCP Connections	Drop from High to Low is good	

PERFORMANCE OBJECT	PERFORMANCE COUNTER	PATTERN IN GRAPH	ANALYSIS
Forefront TMG Web Proxy	Failing requests/ Total Requests (%)	Drop from High to Low is good	If the comparative baseline values plateau and the failing or pending counters are rising or the memory pool counters are falling, it's time to scale out
	Memory pool for HTTP Requests (%)	Drop from High to Low is bad	
	Memory pool for SSL Requests (%)	Drop from High to Low is bad	
	Outgoing connections/sec	Comparative Baseline	
	Requests/sec	Comparative Baseline	
	Total Pending Connects	Drop from High to Low is good	

Summary

Performance counters and their analysis help an administrator measure the health of the TMG deployment. Usually counters are collected over a long period of time (a day or two) to get a long-term picture in terms of performance during peak and non-peak hours. In this appendix you learned what the different TMG performance counters are and how they are used.

Windows Internet Libraries

- WinHTTP vs. WinInet **967**

- Autoproxy (WPAD) **968**

- Applications That Use WinHTTP **972**

- Summary **972**

All of the proxy automatic detection in this book and in most of the online content deals with the context of browsers. This appendix will discuss automatic detection in the context of non-browser applications; specifically those that use WinHTTP as their HTTP library.

WinHTTP vs. WinInet

Windows provides two different HTTP libraries: WinInet and WinHTTP. At one time, WinHTTP was intended to replace WinInet, but because so many Web applications had dependencies on WinInet, it has remained.

WinInet and WinHTTP both serve similar purposes: they provide an API designed to simplify the task of writing applications that need to generate and consume HTTP traffic. They both support CERN proxy mechanisms as well as proxy auto-discovery mechanisms. Where these two API differ is in their design.

WinInet

Between WinInet and WinHTTP, WinInet is the older library. It's been around since Internet Explorer was first created and was designed specifically for client applications that needed to use HTTP, FTP, and Gopher protocols. Although WinInet has been used to provide some lightweight HTTP server functionality, it was never designed for this task.

WinInet is able to use CERN proxy and SOCKS proxy to access remote HTTP and FTP servers. In both cases, this requires the user or the domain administrator to define the proxy configuration.

WinHTTP

WinHTTP was originally intended to replace WinInet, but compatibility with legacy applications would have suffered if this had happened. If you're building a client-side application, you can use either WinInet or WinHTTP, but if you need to build a server application, WinHTTP is the only choice if you want to use a Windows-supported library.

WinHTTP also offers access via Windows script (VBScript, Jscript, or Windows PowerShell) or any other script language that support Component Object Model (COM) usage. In fact, the scripting support in WinHTTP is what makes it possible to write tools such as *http://isatools .org/tools/http_tool.zip.*

Autoproxy (WPAD)

One of the most commonly used features of almost all browsers is the ability to automatically use a proxy configuration script. These applications offer varying degrees of Web Proxy Automatic Detection (WPAD) support, but they all allow you to specify a configuration URL or to specify a single proxy server and local destinations. Figure C-1 illustrates these.

FIGURE C-1 Internet Explorer proxy options

- **Automatically Detect Settings**   This option requires you to have built the proper WPAD support processes using DHCP, WINS, or DNS. The WinInet client has to detect the location of the WPAD script and then download and run it.

- **Use Automatic Configuration Script** This option only requires that you provide a valid URL for the WPAD script. This need not necessarily be a Web server; a file share can be specified as file://wpadshare/share/wpad.js.

- **Use A Proxy Server...** This option completely replaces any script intelligence with static data for the proxy connection and the destinations to be considered local. Using this settings effectively disables client-side CARP.

WinInet

WinInet proxy configuration is handled primarily through Internet Explorer or Group Policy for Internet Explorer. Some aspects of WinInet configuration cannot be configured by the user but are available to the domain administrators, such as computer-level settings located in the registry:

- **HKLM\SOFTWARE\Policies\Microsoft\Windows\CurrentVersion\Internet Settings\ProxySettingsPerUser** This is a REG_DWORD value that when set to 0, causes WinInet to ignore the proxy settings specified in the user registry. The related Group Policy location is located in Computer Configuration\Administrative Templates\ Windows Components\Internet Explorer, "Make proxy settings per-machine (rather than per-user)."

- **HKLM\SOFTWARE\Microsoft\Windows\CurrentVersion\Internet Settings** This registry key holds the Internet settings used by applications that run as a system account (LocalSystem, NetworkService, etc.). This registry branch is where WinInet looks for proxy configuration information when *ProxySettingsPerUser* registry value is set to 0. The Group Policy location for this setting is located in Computer Configuration\Administrative Templates\Windows Components\Internet Explorer.

- **HKCU\Software\Microsoft\Windows\CurrentVersion\Internet Settings** This registry key holds many of the same registry values found in the per-user Internet Settings registry tree. This registry branch is where WinInet looks for proxy configuration information when *ProxySettingsPerUser* is missing or set to any non-0 value. The Group Policy location for this setting is located in User Configuration\ Administrative Templates\Windows Components\Internet Explorer.

WinHTTP

In addition to its own proxy configuration, WinHTTP uses most of the proxy options defined for WinInet except for the Automatic Configuration Script option. Figure C-2 illustrates the proxy configuration option that is *not* available to WinHTTP.

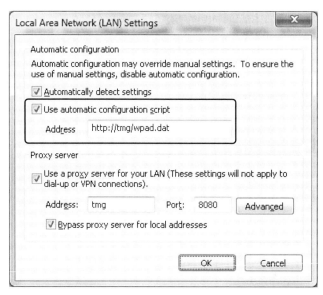

FIGURE C-2 Proxy option not available to WinHTTP

If you configure WinInet to use only the proxy configuration script, WinHTTP can't use the proxy without configuring its own proxy settings. Depending on the operating system, the methods available to configure WinHTTP proxy options differ. Table C-1 lists the relationship between them.

TABLE C-1 WinHTTP proxy configuration tools

OPERATING SYSTEM	PROXY CONFIGURATION TOOL
Windows 2000 Windows XP Windows Server 2003	proxycfg.exe
Windows Vista Windows Server 2008 Windows 7	netsh.exe

Unlike WinInet, WinHTTP proxy settings are only set at the computer level. There is no per-user configuration as is possible with WinInet. The registry location for WinHTTP proxy settings is HKLM\SOFTWARE\Microsoft\Windows\CurrentVersion\Internet Settings\Connections\WinHttpSettings. Remember that even if you set the proxy configuration properly for the environment using the appropriate tool, WinHTTP allows the application to define its proxy usage at run time as well. Needless to say, this can cause you no end of troubleshooting frustration if you don't discover this before you start.

Another limitation imposed by WinHTTP is its use of the proxy configuration script. If the proxy script provides multiple servers in the proxy response list, WinHTTP will only use the first server in the list.

REAL WORLD   WinHTTP AutoProxy Oddity

I run my own Exchange environment at home and, of course, I use RPC over HTTP to access my home e-mail from work. This means that while I'm at work, my Outlook client has to use automatic discovery to acquire the proxy configuration script to find its way through the Microsoft IT (MSIT) proxies.

One day, I discovered that my Outlook client was not able to connect to my e-mail services. Thinking that my home services had failed, I opened my browser and connected to my Outlook Web Access service and was able to access my e-mail easily. Using some of the techniques described in the ISABlog series on troubleshooting RPC over HTTP, I determined that the Internet, Exchange, and ISA Server (TMG wasn't born yet) traffic path was operating just fine. This left only the path between my Outlook client and the MSIT proxies.

I started troubleshooting and noticed that Outlook was behaving oddly. Network Monitor showed me that Outlook followed a very strange pattern:

1. Issue a DNS query for msproxy.domain.sfx.

2. Connect to the first IP address provided in the DNS response. (We use DNS round-robin to help distribute the WPAD and SecureNET client load.)

3. Request the WPAD script.

4. Try to connect to the first proxy in the proxy list.
   (The TCP connection failed.)

5. Connect to the next IP address in the DNS response.

6. Request the WPAD script.

7. Repeat steps 4 through 6 until I close Outlook.

It was clear that the first proxy in the WPAD script response was failing for some reason. What wasn't clear was why Outlook couldn't seem to get past the failing proxy server, so I started doing a bit more sleuthing using Outlook and WinHTTP tracing as well as some MSDN and MSKB searching.

What I finally discovered was that WinHTTP can't use WPAD script results that include more than one proxy. If the first proxy in the list is unresponsive (this one had IPsec problems), WinHTTP will keep trying to use it because the results of the script are the same for a given destination and in this case, the failing server was the first one listed in the script response.

Applications That Use WinHTTP

This is not intended to be an all-inclusive list, but it should help make you aware of those applications that are subject to the behavioral vagaries of WinHTTP:

- RPC over HTTP (Outlook 2003 and later; RDP client 6.1 and later)
- Windows Media Player
- ServerXMLHTTP
- Office Communicator 2007
- .NET HTTP
- Windows Updates (BITS)

Summary

Although hardly all-inclusive, we hope this discussion has helped you appreciate the complexities that come with Internet applications.

> **MORE INFO** You can read more about the various technologies and applications that use them at the following sites:
>
> - Command options for proxycfg.exe: *http://msdn.microsoft.com/en-us/library/aa384069(VS.85).aspx*
> - WinHTTP options for netsh.exe: *http://blogs.msdn.com/wndp/archive/2007/03/21/winhttp-configuration-for-windows-vista.aspx*
> - WinHTTP *http://msdn.microsoft.com/en-us/library/aa382925.aspx*
> - WinHTTP Autoproxy limitations *http://msdn.microsoft.com/en-us/library/aa383157(VS.85).aspx*
> - WinInet *http://msdn.microsoft.com/en-us/library/aa383630(VS.85).aspx*
> - Gopher protocol *http://www.ietf.org/rfc/rfc1436.txt*
> - SOCKSv4 protocol *http://ftp.icm.edu.pl/packages/socks/socks4/SOCKS4.protocol*
> - ServerXmlHttp *http://support.microsoft.com/kb/290761*
> - Troubleshooting RPC over HTTP Part 1: *http://blogs.technet.com/isablog/archive/2007/08/13/testing-rpc-over-http-through-isa-server-2006-part-1-protocols-authentication-and-processing.aspx*
> - Troubleshooting RPC over HTTP Part 2: *http://blogs.technet.com/isablog/archive/2007/08/13/testing-rpc-over-http-through-isa-server-2006-part-2-test-tools-and-strategies.aspx*
> - Troubleshooting RPC over HTTP Part 3: *http://blogs.technet.com/isablog/archive/2007/08/13/testing-rpc-over-http-through-isa-server-2006-part-3-common-failures-and-resolutions.aspx*

WPAD Script CARP Operation

■ CARP Logic **973**

■ CARP Action Examples **975**

■ Summary **980**

As described in Chapter 15, "Web Proxy Auto Discovery for TMG," the WPAD script provides multiple behaviors for the Web Proxy client, depending on the destination host and the Microsoft Forefront TMG configuration options you choose. In this appendix, you'll gain a detailed understanding how the WPAD script CARP algorithm operates and see multiple real-life examples of this functionality.

CARP Logic

In Chapter 15 you learned that there are four paths through the WPAD script: direct, normal CARP, client CARP, and no CARP. Chapter 15 concentrated on the direct connection and introduced the CARP scenarios. Figure D-1 illustrates CARP logical flow.

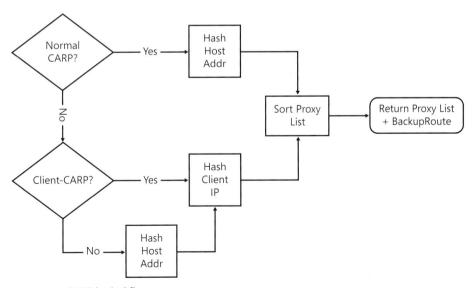

FIGURE D-1 CARP logical flow

To summarize the diagram in Figure D-1: If the request does not meet the criteria defined for normal CARP and client CARP, it must be a no-CARP request. The examples in the following discussions are produced using the script *tmgbook.hash.and.sort.js*, which you'll find on the companion CD.

In all CARP cases, the WPAD script calculates a hash value and produces an ordered proxy list based on that hash value. The Web client uses this list according to how that product team wanted their application to behave. For instance, although Internet Explorer and Windows Media player may use the entire proxy list if circumstances dictate (such as when multiple proxies fail to respond), applications that depend on the default WinHTTP behavior will use only the first proxy provided in the list (see Appendix C for more details on this limitation).

The part of the WPAD script that makes these decisions is listed here:

```
if(cCARPExceptions > 0){
  for(i = 0; i < cCARPExceptions; i++){
   if(ExpMatch(host, CARPExceptions[i])){
    nocarp = true;}
   if(ExpMatch(url, CARPExceptions[i])){
    nocarp = true;
    skiphost = true;
    break;
}}}
if(!skiphost)
 hash = HashString(host,hash);
if(nocarp)
 hash = HashString(pfMyIpAddress(), hash);
```

Five tests are performed within this section:

- ***if(cCARPExceptions > 0)***   "Are there any entries in the CARPExceptions list?" If the answer to this test is "no" (false), the skiphost and nocarp variables remain set to "false" and the script moves to the *if(!skiphost)* test. If this test evaluates as "true", the script moves into a "for" loop that enumerates the list entries and applies the following two tests to each of them in turn.

- ***if(ExpMatch(host, CARPExceptions[i]))***   "Does this entry match the hostname part of the URL?" If the answer to this test is "yes" (true), the script sets the nocarp variable to "true" and moves to the *if(ExpMatch(url, CARPExceptions[i]))* decision point.

- ***if(ExpMatch(url, CARPExceptions[i]))***   "Does this entry match the URL?" If the answer to this test is "yes" (true), the script will set the nocarp and skiphost variables to "true". The "break" statement tells the script to "break out" of the "for" loop. Other than a script runtime error, this is the only case where the CARPExceptions list will not be completely parsed.

- ***if(!skipost)***   "Is the skiphost variable set to "false"?" If the answer to this test is "yes" (true), the script will set the hash variable to a value calculated from the host portion of the URL.

- ***if(nocarp)*** "Is the nocarp variable set to "true"?" If the answer to this test is "yes" (true), the hash variable will be set to a value derived from a combination of the client computer's IP address and the existing value of the hash variable. If the answer to this test is "no" (false), the hash variable will be unchanged.

The *ExpMatch()* function is a WPAD script function that determines whether the URL needs to be converted to lowercase and then calls the *shExpMatch()* function provided by the Web application:

```
function ExpMatch(str, exp){
  if (ConvertUrlToLowerCase)
  {
    str = str.toLowerCase();
  }
  return shExpMatch(str, exp);
}
```

The *shExpMatch()* function compares two values and returns *true* or *false* depending on whether they match. One important aspect of the *shExpMatch()* function is that it interprets the asterisk (*) character as a wildcard. A wildcard character represents "anything else" in a string value. This allows us to use some very creative tricks in the script, as you'll see in the CARP action examples.

> **NOTE** As stated in *http://technet.microsoft.com/en-us/library/dd361918.aspx*, the shExpMatch() function performs the comparison using shell expression patterns. You can read more about this function in *http://support.microsoft.com/kb/274204*.

The *skiphost* and *nocarp* variables are defined as *false* and the hash value is defined as 0 at the beginning of the *ImplementFindProxyForURL()* function. The *nocarp* and *skiphost* values will be changed only when the request matches at least one entry in the CARPExceptions list. The hash variable will be calculated according to the combination of the *nocarp* and *skiphost* values.

The hash variable will never be 0 when the proxy sort begins. By the time the script uses the hash variable to order the proxy list, the hash variable will contain a hash of any one of the following:

- The host name (normal CARP)
- The IP address of the client (client CARP)
- The IP address of the client and the host name (no CARP)

CARP Action Examples

The examples that follow illustrate the CARP algorithm behavior for the three CARP cases in the context of a three-member proxy array for four host names: *contoso.com*, *www.contoso.com*, *margiestravel.com*, and *www.margiestravel.com*.

Normal CARP Destination

For normal CARP destinations, the WPAD script calculates the hash value from the host name in the URL alone. The proxy lists for the host names *contoso.com*, *www.contoso.com*, *margiestravel.com*, and *www.margiestravel.com* are shown in the following selected script results:

```
TMG hashes =
        tmg01 : 2308123914
        tmg02 : 2544688560
        tmg03 : 4133940228

Testing www.contoso.com...
        hash        : 3494183083
        proxy list  : "PROXY tmg02:8080; PROXY tmg01:8080; PROXY tmg03:8080; DIRECT"

Testing contoso.com...
        hash        : 3762751301
        proxy list  : "PROXY tmg02:8080; PROXY tmg03:8080; PROXY tmg01:8080; DIRECT"

Testing www.margiestravel.com...
        hash        : 739486369
        proxy list  : "PROXY tmg03:8080; PROXY tmg02:8080; PROXY tmg01:8080; DIRECT"

Testing margiestravel.com...
        hash        : 4064222820
        proxy list  : "PROXY tmg02:8080; PROXY tmg01:8080; PROXY tmg03:8080; DIRECT"
```

Note that the proxy list order changes for almost every host name passed to the script hash and sorting functions. You may also have noticed that the proxy list for *www.contoso.com* and *margiestravel.com* are identical. This is normal and is due to three factors:

- Statistically unique hash calculations involve very complex algorithms, such as Secure Hash Algorithm Standard 1 (SHA-1).

- These complex hash algorithms depend on extremely random number generation algorithms.

- Windows script uses signed numbers (positive or negative), but the CARP algorithm uses only positive numbers. This design avoids the case where the hash calculation produces a number that is mathematically smaller than all of the hash values assigned to each of the array members, but it also limits the statistical uniqueness of the resulting hash.

> **MORE INFO**   You can read more about Secure Hash algorithms at *http://csrc.nist.gov/ publications/fips/fips180-2/fips180-2withchangenotice.pdf*.

Neither of these requirements is possible in a script without making the script *very* large. Consequently, a comparatively simple hashing algorithm is used, which incurs a greater chance of hash collisions (instances where different input produces identical output).

Also, the fewer members that exist in the proxy list, the greater the chance of duplicate proxy lists for a given URL. Thus, a WPAD script representing an array of twelve proxy servers will produce a greater URL distribution than will a WPAD script that represents an array comprised of only two proxy servers.

Client CARP Destination

For destinations that satisfy client CARP, the WPAD script calculates a hash based on the IP address of the Web client computer. This method produces a more statistically unique distribution across the proxy array, effectively providing a very simplistic form of load-balancing. This mechanism was added to the WPAD script in ISA Server 2004 Service Pack 2 (SP2) and was later refined in ISA Server 2006.

To make use of the client-CARP mechanism, you must enter the destinations in the CARP Exceptions list as ***//contoso.com/*** or ***//www.contoso.com/*** as shown in Figure D-2.

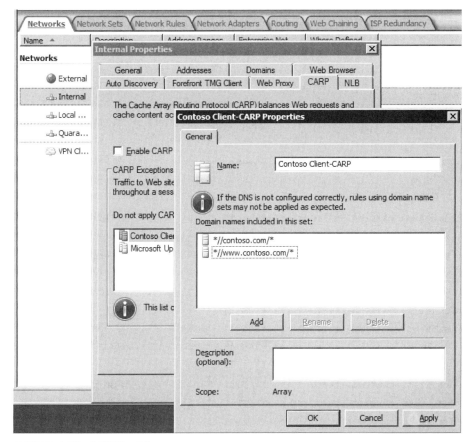

FIGURE D-2 Client CARP entries

This entry causes the WPAD script to evaluate *if(ExpMatch(url, CARPExceptions[i]))* as true. This causes *skiphost* to be set to false; thus the CARP algorithm only uses the local computer IP address in the hash calculation. The following selected examples from tmgbook.hash. and.sort.js illustrate the behavior of this mechanism. You may notice that the proxy server distribution is identical for all requests. This is due to two factors:

- The host name is not part of the hash calculation.
- The IP addresses used in the example are very close in value.

As a result, the output of the hash-based sorting function produces identical proxy server lists for any given request. As with the previous example, the distribution improves as the difference between the IP addresses increases and as more proxy servers are added to the TMG array.

You may also note that the host name hash is missing from the script execution results. Because the script does not use the host name in the calculation, there is no value displaying it.

```
TMG hashes =
        tmg01 : 2308123914
        tmg02 : 2544688560
        tmg03 : 4133940228

Testing www.contoso.com...
        hash for 10.10.0.1     : 2913298145
        proxy list for 10.10.0.1 : "PROXY tmg03:8080; PROXY tmg01:8080;
                                    PROXY tmg02:8080; DIRECT"
        hash for 10.10.0.9     : 592290544
        proxy list for 10.10.0.9 : "PROXY tmg03:8080; PROXY tmg02:8080;
                                    PROXY tmg01:8080; DIRECT"

Testing contoso.com...
        hash for 10.10.0.1     : 2913298145
        proxy list for 10.10.0.1 : "PROXY tmg03:8080; PROXY tmg01:8080;
                                    PROXY tmg02:8080; DIRECT"
        hash for 10.10.0.9     : 592290544
        proxy list for 10.10.0.9 : "PROXY tmg03:8080; PROXY tmg02:8080;
                                    PROXY tmg01:8080; DIRECT"

Testing www.margiestravel.com...
        hash for 10.10.0.1     : 2913298145
        proxy list for 10.10.0.1 : "PROXY tmg03:8080; PROXY tmg01:8080;
                                    PROXY tmg02:8080; DIRECT"
        hash for 10.10.0.9     : 592290544
        proxy list for 10.10.0.9 : "PROXY tmg03:8080; PROXY tmg02:8080;
                                    PROXY tmg01:8080; DIRECT"
```

```
Testing margiestravel.com...
        hash for 10.10.0.1       : 2913298145
        proxy list for 10.10.0.1 : "PROXY tmg03:8080; PROXY tmg01:8080;
                                    PROXY tmg02:8080; DIRECT"
        hash for 10.10.0.9       : 592290544
        proxy list for 10.10.0.9 : "PROXY tmg03:8080; PROXY tmg02:8080;
                                    PROXY tmg01:8080; DIRECT"
```

No-CARP Destination

For destinations that satisfy no-CARP, the WPAD script calculates a hash based on a combination of the Web client computer IP address and the host name in the URL. This method produces a slightly more statistically unique distribution across the proxy array than for client CARP. This mechanism was added to the WPAD script in ISA Server 2004 and modified in ISA Server 2004 Service Pack 2 (SP2). This mechanism has remained unchanged in ISA Server 2006 and TMG.

To make use of the no-CARP mechanism, you must enter the destinations in the CARP Exceptions list using the exact host name or a wildcard such as *.contoso.com. This has the effect of telling the WPAD script to include the host name and the local computer IP address in the hash calculation. The following selected examples from tmgbook.hash.and.sort.js illustrate the behavior of this mechanism. You may notice that the proxy server distribution is more statistically unique than for the client-CARP example. This is because the host name is included in the hash calculation, resulting in more even request distribution across the array.

As with the previous examples, the distribution improves as the difference between the IP addresses increases and as more proxy servers are added to the TMG array.

```
TMG hashes =
        tmg01 : 2308123914
        tmg02 : 2544688560
        tmg03 : 4133940228

Testing www.contoso.com...
    hash for 10.10.0.1       : 4194838421
    proxy list for 10.10.0.1 : "PROXY tmg03:8080; PROXY tmg01:8080;
                                PROXY tmg02:8080; DIRECT"
    hash for 10.10.0.9       : 1960895364
    proxy list for 10.10.0.9 : "PROXY tmg01:8080; PROXY tmg03:8080;
                                PROXY tmg02:8080; DIRECT"

Testing contoso.com...
    hash for 10.10.0.1       : 549571180
    proxy list for 10.10.0.1 : "PROXY tmg03:8080; PROXY tmg01:8080;
                                PROXY tmg02:8080; DIRECT"
```

```
        hash for 10.10.0.9        : 2921926269
        proxy list for 10.10.0.9 : "PROXY tmg03:8080; PROXY tmg02:8080;
                                     PROXY tmg01:8080; DIRECT"

Testing www.margiestravel.com...
        hash for 10.10.0.1        : 3286199586
        proxy list for 10.10.0.1 : "PROXY tmg02:8080; PROXY tmg03:8080;
                                     PROXY tmg01:8080; DIRECT"
        hash for 10.10.0.9        : 1295493427
        proxy list for 10.10.0.9 : "PROXY tmg03:8080; PROXY tmg02:8080;
                                     PROXY tmg01:8080; DIRECT"

Testing margiestravel.com...
        hash for 10.10.0.1        : 1729173564
        proxy list for 10.10.0.1 : "PROXY tmg01:8080; PROXY tmg02:8080;
                                     PROXY tmg03:8080; DIRECT"
        hash for 10.10.0.9        : 3925466157
        proxy list for 10.10.0.9 : "PROXY tmg03:8080; PROXY tmg01:8080;
                                     PROXY tmg02:8080; DIRECT"
```

Summary

You have seen how the WPAD script CARP algorithm works in this appendix. Although the WPAD script uses the same CARP algorithm used by TMG, it offers one feature TMG itself does not: the ability to include the client IP address in the hash calculation. This is because by the time TMG itself is performing CARP, the value of the client IP address as a load-sharing method is lost.

Index

Symbols and Numbers

.iis, logging, 807–08
.NET Framework, 108, 171
.Save(), 835
.vhd files, 25
.w3c, logging, 807–08
32-bit platforms, 5, 36–37, 94
3-Leg Perimeter, 30, 67–68, 223
401-Unauthorized, 875
5-tuple, 72, 209–10
64-bit platforms, 5, 11–12, 36–37, 94

A

A records, DNS, 290–91
AAM (Alternate Access Mapping), 664–65, 689
Accept, HTTP, 915–16
Access control. *See also* Authentication; Filtering;
    Internet; Remote access
  alternate access mapping, 664–65
  CERN proxy HTTP, 242–49
  Configure Client Access, 188
  NAT relationships, 216
  ping requests, 212–15, 242–45
  Policy Reevaluation, 249–53
  proxy servers, 921
  quarantined VPN clients, 31, 91, 223, 753
  server publishing and, 577
  SharePoint Services, 663
  TMG, new features, 17
  traffic policy behavior, 80–81, 241–49, 253–62
  troubleshooting access rules, 253–62
  UAG, security and, 26
  URL filtering, overview, 465–70
  user groups, 663
  Web Access Policy, 185, 188–90, 194, 562–64, 568

Access Rules, network designs for, 80–81, 109
Accumulator, 13
Active caching, 920
Active Directory, 61, 93, 663–64, 741
Active Directory Lightweight Directory Services
    (AD LDS), 147, 165, 171, 186–87
Active Directory Lightweight Directory Services
    Server Role, 37
Active-active mode, 79
Active-passive mode, 78–79
ActiveX, 489–90
AD LDS (Active Directory Lightweight Directory
    Services), 147, 171, 186–87
AddHttpsFrontEndOn, 702
Add-ins, TMG console, 186
Additional Security Policy, 188
Address Range Rule Element, 313
Address Resolution Protocol (ARP), 211–12
Addresses
  DIP (Dedicated IP address), 285, 290
  excluded, Single NIC firewalls, 70
  gethostbyaddress, 121
  installation, TMG 2010, 162–64
  installation, TMG MBE, 149–51
  intra-array addresses, configuring, 415–16
  IP Allow List, 502–03
  IP Allow List Providers, 503–05
  IP Block List, 505–06
  IP Block List Providers, 506
  IP routing, basic, 210–15
  logging, 806
  Malware Inspection configuration, 435
  managing and aggregating, 918–19
  name resolution, 37–39
  NAT relationships, 215–20
  non-Web servers, 640
  preinstallation checklist, 141
  SharePoint Services, 662

TMG networks, configuring, 56
VIP (Virtual IP addresses), 285, 290, 498, 606
VPN connections, 735
Web proxy clients, 108
Alerts
definition updates, 485
flood mitigation, 334, 338–40
Intrusion Detection System (IDS), 324–26
NLB (Network Load Balancing), 303
Policy Enforcement, 252
SharePoint Services, 664–65
spoofed packets, 54
SYN attacks, 338–40
TCP connections, worm attacks, 323
troubleshooting tab, 859
All port scan attack alert, 326
Allow policies, new features, 16
Alternate Access Mapping (AAM), 664–65, 689
AnnaKournikova virus, 488–90
Anonymous public proxy servers, 534–38
Anonymous requests, HTTP, 877
Anti-malware. *See* Malware; Malware protection
Anti-spam. *See* Spam
Antivirus. *See* Virus protection
Application filters. *See also* Filtering
application signatures, 561–70
protocol mapping, 50
publishing and, 573
SecureNET clients, 115, 118
server publishing, 576–77, 590
Session Initiation Protocol (SIP), 18
Single NIC firewalls, 70
TMG console, 191
Application-layer firewalls, 10. *See also* Network
Inspection System (NIS)
Application-layer inspection, 308
Applications. *See also* Application filters
access, TMG, 27
firewall rules, 24
mapping, 49
protocols, traffic profile, 47–51
Session Initiation Protocol (SIP) filtering, 18
TMG deployment options, 52–53
UAG, security and, 26
Winsock API calls, 121–22
Architecture
COM (Component Object Model), 829–34
IAG 2007, 23–24

NLB (Network Load Balancing), 285–88
TMG Setup, 169–72
ARP (Address Resolution Protocol), 210–12
Array Object, 830–31
Arrays
CARP (Cache Array Routing Protocol), 80, 358–60,
362–64, 395–97, 413–17
DNS configuration, 289–91
DNS round-robin, 73, 75, 82, 349
Join Array and Disjoin Array Wizards, 203–04
log files, 812–13
migration, 88
policies, 299
synchronization, 297
Assymetric bridging, 584
Attachment files, 519–22
Attacks. *See also* Malware Inspection; Virus protection
buffer overflow, 489
DNS attack detection, 326
flood mitigation, 330–36
preconfigured attack protection, 337–40
teardrop attacks, 329
Audio streams, new features, 18
Auditing, 373
Authentication. *See also* Certificates; Signatures;
Virtual Private Networks (VPN)
anonymous requests, 877
cache rules, 406
client selection and, 133
downgrade attack, 258
Exchange Server, 699–702, 705–06
failures, 652–53
HTTP
delegation, 883
dual, proxy and server, 881
overview, 874–83
proxy authentication, 879–80
server authentication, 878–79
HTTP Filter
configuring, overview, 550–52
extensions, 555–56
headers, 557–60
inbound access, validating, 560–61
methods, 553–55
signatures, 561–70
HTTPS Inspection
common errors, 548–49
configuring, 534–47

IAS (Internet Authentication Services), 171
L2TP over IPsec, configuring, 775
logging, configuring, 806
migration, 94
NTLM and Exchange Server, 707
Policy Enforcement, 253
preinstallation checklist, 141
protected networks, 233–39
Require All Users To Authenticate, 238–39
requirements, 39–40
SecureNET clients, 118
SharePoint Services, 663–64
smart-cards, 719–20
Test Rule, publishing, 612
TMG Client, 132
troubleshooting access rules, 256–62
UAG, security and, 26
VPN connections, 735–36, 741, 750–51
Web listener, 580, 602–03
Web Proxy Application Filter, 529–32
Web publishing, 584–86
web-proxy requests, 103
Authentication Delegation, 585–86, 609, 635, 653, 669, 676, 686
Authentication Header protocol, 735
Authority, new features, 16
Authorization, 26, 874–83. See also Access control
Automatic Configuration Script, 376, 379
Automatic discovery, 81–82, 93. See also WPAD (Web Proxy Automatic Discovery)
Automatic Proxy Cache, 379–80
Automatic updates, 315. See also Updates
Automation, scripting, 836–42, 845–48. See also Scripting
Auto-negotiation, 145
AutoProxy. See WPAD (Web Proxy Automatic Discovery)
autorun.hta, 171
autorun.inf, 171
Availability. See also Performance; Redundancy
load balancing
configuring, 293–98
enabling, 288–92
ISP redundancy, 263–65, 267–84
link availability testing, 265–67
NLB architecture, 285–88
post-installation best practices, 298–99
troubleshooting, 301–06
virtual environments, 300–01

network design
for Access Rules, 80–81
for publishing rules, 76–80
overview, 71–76
UAG, 26
VPN access, 738–39

B

Back firewalls, 31, 52, 68–69, 223, 335
Back-to-back firewalls, 335
Backup, network mapping, 48
Backward compatibility, 37
Basic authentication, 878. See also Authentication
Basic trunks, 24
BDA (Bidirectional affinity), 74, 288
Behavioral Intrusion Detection, 196–97, 327
Behavioral monitoring. See also Alerts; Logging; Performance
overview, 43–44
Berkeley Sockets. See Winsock
Best Practices Analyzer (BPA), 858–61
Bidirectional affinity (BDA), 74, 288
Bidirectional UDP protocols, 574
bind (), 121
Bing Safe Search, 471, 476
Bits per connection, 704
Block Expired Certificate, 545
BootP clients, 18
BPA (Best Practices Analyzer), 858–61
BPA2Visio, 861
Bridging, 583–84
Broadcast domain, 287
Broadcast protection, 338
Broadcast, name resolution, 58–59
Browsers
Automatic Proxy Cache, 379
client-side CARP, 396–97
embedded scripts, 489
parameters, 233
preinstallation checklist, 145
Web proxy clients, overview, 107–13
Winsock usage, 130–31
worm attacks, 489
WPAD (Web Proxy Auto Discovery) configuration, 364–79, 381

BubbleBoy virus, 489–90. *See also* Virus protection
Buffer overflow attacks, 489
Built-in networks, 222–24

C

Cache Array Routing Protocol (CARP)
  action examples, 949–54
  CARP logic, 947–49
  CARP Name System, 360
  cfile script, 362–64
  configuring, 413–17
  load factor, 359–60, 416–17
  MakeCARPExceptions, 358
  overview, 395–97
Caching
  Automatic Proxy Cache, 379–80
  Cache-Control field, 420, 916–17
  cache-control headers, 248–49
  CacheDir, 420–21
  compressed content, 393–94
  configuring
    add cache rule, 400–07
    add content download job, 407–12
    CARP, 413–17
    Enable Web Caching, 397–400
  DNS (Domain Name Service), 63
  FetchURL, 421
  IIS requests, 24
  internal name, 39
  monitoring, 394–95
  performance counters, 937, 939
  proxy servers, overview, 387–89, 919–20
  rebuilding, 421–22
  reverse caching, 391, 394–95, 920
  rules for, 391–92
  scenarios, 390–91
  settings, 398–400, 407–12
  SharePoint Services, 663
  storage, 389
  temporary disk cache, 429
  TMG console, 185, 190
  troubleshooting, 417–23
  web objects, 392
  Web Proxy Application Filter, 529
Caching Compressed Content Filter, 394
Capacity Planner, 592–93

CAPI (Windows Crypto API), 535
CARP (Cache Array Routing Protocol)
  action examples, 949–54
  CARP Logic, 947–49
  CARPNameSystem, 360
  cfile script, 362–64
  configuring, 413–17
  load factor, 359–60, 416–17
  MakeCARPExceptions, 358
  overview, 395–97
CarpNameSystem, 360
CERN proxy requests, 107–13, 242–49, 384, 649–50,
    877, 923. *See also* WPAD (Web Proxy Automatic
    Discovery)
Certificate Authorities, 535
Certificate Import Wizard, 621–25
Certificate Verify Message, 888
Certificates. *See also* Authentication; Signatures
  authentication, protected networks, 237
  Block Expired Certificate, 545
  cloned, 535
  Exchange Server, 699–700
  file formats, 619
  HTTP Filter
    configuring, overview, 550–52
    extensions, 555–56
    headers, 557–60
    inbound access, validating, 560–61
    methods, 553–55
    signatures, 561–70
  HTTPS Inspection
    common errors, 548–49
    configuring, 534–47
  installing, 619–25
  L2TP over IPsec, configuring, 775
  Listener SSL Certificates, 628
  migration, 91
  proxy migration, 93
  publishing rules, 595
  revocation, 793
  SSTP, 766
  Test Rule, publishing, 612
  TMG, new features, 16
  Web listener errors, 653–56
  Web Proxy Application Filter, 529–32
  Web servers, HTTPS protocol, 618
cfile, 345, 352–64
Chaining, 191, 922

Change tracking, 798, 859

CHAP (Challenge Handshake Authentication Protocol), 736

Checksum offloading settings, 268

Cipher Spec, 888

Cipher Suite, 885–86

Circuit-level firewalls, 10

Class ID (CLSID), 488

Client Access Server, 698

Client certificate, 887–88

Client Certificate Authentication, 663–64

Client hello, 885

Client Key Exchange Message, 888

Clients. *See also* Remote access
  access, 698–99, 747–56
  acknowledgement, 888
  applications
    Automatic Proxy Cache, 379–80
    AutoProxy in managed code, 384–85
    Internet Explorer, 375–79
    TMG Client, 381–82
    Windows Media Player, 353, 382–84
  choosing, 132–34
  client CARP, 363, 396–97
  Configure Client Access, 188
  Exchange Server, 698–99, 704
  Forefront TMG Client (TMGC), 119–32
  HTTP Filter, 533–34
  NLB (Network Load Balancing), 291–92
  requests, single NIC firewalls, 70
  SecureNET client, 113–18
  TMG Client authentication, 132
  VPN access, 738
  Web proxy clients, 107–13, 132

CLSID (Class ID), 488

CNAME, 292–93, 376

CNG (Cryptography Next Generation), 619

Collision domain, 287

COM (Component Object Model), 47–51, 266, 322, 829–34, 842–48

Common Name (CN), 662

Common Vulnerabilities and Exposures (CVE), 310

Compatibility, backward, 37

Component Object Model. *See* COM (Component Object Model)

Compression, 393–94, 529–31, 885, 937, 953

Compression Filter, 393–94

Conditional forwarder, 60–61

Conficker, 316–17, 567–70. *See also* Malware protection

Confidentiality, UAG, 26

Configuration file (cfile), 345, 352–64

Configuration Storage Server (CSS), 289

Configuration Storage Service (CSS), 165

Configuration URL, 81–82

Configure E-mail Policy Wizard, 205

Configure SIP Wizard, 205

Configure Web Access Policy Wizard, 397–400

Configuring
  caching
    add cache rule, 400–07
    add content download job, 407–12
    CARP, 413–17
    enable web caching, 397–400
  Configure Global Link Translation, 190
  Configure Radius Server Settings, 190
  Deployment Wizard, 202–03
  DNS attack detection, 326
  Enhanced NAT (E-NAT), 820–26
  Exchange Server, 707–18
  Firewall Chaining options, 191
  Firewall Client Settings, 191
  flood mitigation, NIS, 330–36
  HTTPS Inspection, 534–47
  IDS (Intrusion Detection System), 324–26
  IP preferences, NIS, 327–30
  LDAP Server Settings, 190
  load-balancing, ISP Redundancy, 276–84
  Malware Inspection, one-time reports, 446–50
  Malware Inspection, recurring reports, 451–55
  networks
    creating networks, 222–31
    network relationships, overview, 209–22
    protected networks, 231–39
  NIS (Network Inspection System), 311–16, 327–36
  NLB (Network Load Balancing), 276, 293–98
  SharePoint Services
    multi-server, 672–79
    overview, 665–66
    server farm, 679–89
    single-server, 667–72
  SMTP protection, overview, 493–94
  spam filtering, 502–18
  TMG console, 185–87
  TMG logging, 800–09
  TMG networks, 54–57

TMG Setup
  architecture, 169–72
  setup options, 172–74
Update Center, 481–85
URL filtering, 470–78
virus and content filtering, 518–27
VPN
  dial-in clients, 747–63
  site-to-site, 774–81
  SSTP, 763–71
  WLBS display, 305
  WPAD (Web Proxy Auto Discovery), 364–79
Conflicts
  IAG, ISA Server, 24
  LSP (Layered Service Providers), 125
  write conflicts, cache and, 389
CONNECT, 871, 913
Connect to Forefront Protection Manager 2010
      Wizard, 204–05
Connection Properties, 281
Connection table, exploitation of, 323
Connection, HTTP, 916
Connectivity. *See also* Access control;
      Intrusion detection
  access, enabling, 22–23
  ISP Redundancy, 264
  logging, 813–14
  SecureNET clients, 115–17
  Web Publishing, availability, 77
ConnectivityRemoteVerificationPort, 267
Content Filtering, 507–11, 515, 518–27
Content for Offline Browsing, cache, 405
Content Requiring User Authentication
      For Retrieval, 406
Content, HTTP, 914–15
Content-encoding, 915
ConvertUrlToLowerCase, 355–56
cookieauthfilter.dll, 702–03
Cookies, 73, 77–78, 587
Coordination, migration and, 94
Counters
  cache, 395, 939
  compression performance, 953
  DiffServ, 954
  e-mail hygiene, 960
  Firewall packet engine, 938
  H.323 filter, 939
  how to use, 964

HTTPS performance, 959
malware protection, 956
Microsoft Firewall service, 941
overview, 937–38
requirements, 41
SOCKS filter, 943
TMG Performance Monitor, 962
URL filtering, 961
Web proxy, 944
CPU load, flood mitigation, 330–36
Create VPN Site-To-Site Connection Wizard, 775–80,
      782–87
Creating
  HTTPS Web listeners, 625–30
  Malware Inspection reports, 446–63
  network rules, 226–31
    networks, 222–31
  Non-Web Server Publishing rule, 637–47
  reports, new features, 15
  Web publishing rule, secure, 630–36
  Web site publishing rules, 558
Credentials. *See also* Authentication; Certificates;
      Signatures
  Exchange Server, 700–02
  HTTP, overview, 874–83
  integrated authentication, 235–36
  requirements, 39–40
  TMG Client, 132
  Web publishing, 585–86
Cryptography Next generation (CNG), 619
CSS (Configuration Storage Server), 289
CSS (Configuration Storage Service), 165
Customer Feedback, 203
CVE (Common Vulnerabilities and Exposures), 310

D

Data transfer, Winsock, 119
DBCS (double-byte character set), 552
DCOM (Distributed Component Object Model),
      47–51
Dedicated IP address (DIP), 285, 290
Dedicated Servers List, ISP, 278, 282
Default gateway, 268
Default internal networks, 54–57
Default IP Address, 219

Deflate algorithms, 393–94
DELETE, 871, 913
Delete wpad command, 93
Demilitarized zone (DMZ), 67–68
Denial of Service (DoS) attack, 323, 333–34
Deny policies, new features, 16
Deployment
    client selection and, 132–33
    network relationships, overview, 209–22
    TMG, 27–28
    TMG option, networks, 51–53
    UAG (Forefront Unified Access Gateway), 25, 27–28
    virtual environments, 44–45
Deployment Wizard, 200, 202–03
DHCP (Dynamic Host Configuration Protocol), 93, 268, 346–50, 366–69
DHCP NFORM request, 369
DhcpRequestParams (), 346–47
Diagnostic Logging Events, 859. See also Logging
Dial-in users, RADIUS, 40, 237–38, 663–64, 751
Dial-in VPN clients, 31, 52–53, 91–92, 663–64, 741, 762–63
DiffServ performance counter, 937, 954
Digest authentication, 234, 878
DIP (Dedicated IP address), 285, 290
Dir1.cdat, 389
Disjoin Array Wizard, 203–04
Disk Write Queue Length, 42
Disks
    caches, 389
    flood mitigation, 330–36
    forward caching, 390
    hardware requirements, 35–36
    log files, 803–04, 812–13
    mirroring, 813
    performance, 41–42
    reverse caching, 391
    striping, 813
    temporary disk cache, 429
Distributed Component Object Model (DCOM), 47–51
DLL (dynamic-linked library), 122–25
DMZ (demilitarized zone), 67–68
DNS (Domain Name System)
    attack detection, 326
    cache, 63
    configuring WPAD, 369
    DNS round-robin, 73, 75, 82, 95, 349
    ISP Redundancy, 78–79
    migration, 92–93, 95
    name resolution, 38, 58–63
    NLB (Network Load Balancing), 289–91
    publishing, 574
    reverse lookup, 516
    Root Servers, 265–67
    SecureNET clients, 115–17
    server publishing, 590
    site-to-site (S2S) VPN migration, 92
    STMP lookup, 820
    WPAD (Web Proxy Auto Discovery), 93, 350–52
DNS Alias, 376
DNS Server, 332
DNS Server Global Query Block List, 374
DNS Server Publishing, 326
DNS System Log, 372
dnscmd command, 371
Domain controllers, 39–40, 701
Domain isolation, 53
Domain membership, migration and, 94
Domain Name System. See DNS (Domain Name System)
Domains, joining to firewalls, 82–84
Double-byte character set (DBCS), 552
Download Job Wizard, 409–12
Downloads
    .vhd files, UAG deployment, 25
    audio and video streams, 18
    cache, content download jobs, 407–12
    TMG, new features, 14, 18
    Trivial File Transfer Protocol (TFTP) filter, 18
    Web proxy client requests, 113
Drivers, preinstallation checklist, 141
Duplex, 78
Dynamic Content, 405
Dynamic Host Configuration Protocol (DHCP), 93, 268, 346–50, 366–69
Dynamic links, alternate access mapping, 664–65
Dynamic load balancing, new features, 19. See also Network Load Balancing (NLB)
Dynamic update, 370–74
Dynamic-linked library (DLL), 122–25

E

EAP (Extensible Authentication Protocol), 736
EAS (Exchange Active Sync), 698–99, 704, 706–07, 718, 721

Echo requests, 212–15, 242–45
ECN (Explicit Congestion Notification), 144
Edge firewalls
    deployment options, 52
    designing, 29–30
    Network Inspection System (NIS), 335
    network rules, 220–22
    network template, 223
    template, 66–67
    tunneling protocols, 22–23
Edge Malware Protection (EMP), 13, 429, 469, 799
Edge Malware Protection (EMP) Scanner, 13
Edge Transport Server, 698
Egress migrations, 90–95
E-mail. *See also* E-NAT (Enhanced NAT)
    alerts, SharePoint Services, 664–65
    E-mail Policy, 192, 194–95, 205
    Exchange Server
        configuring, 707–18
        publishing, planning for, 697–707
        troubleshooting, 719–30
    hygiene performance counter, 938, 960
    protection
        configuring virus and content filtering, 518–27
        SMTP protection, 490–501
        spam filtering, configuring, 502–18
        threat overview, 487–90
    servers, 16–17, 47–51
E-Mail Policy Wizard, 205, 495–501
E-Mail Protection Wizard, 494–501
Embedded scripts, 489–90
EMP (Edge Malware Protection), 13, 429, 469, 799
Enable ISP Redundancy Wizard, 206
E-NAT (Enhanced NAT)
    configuring, 820–26
    ISP Redundancy, 265, 268
    overview, 817–20
    troubleshooting, 826–27
Encryption. *See also* Tunnels, VPNs
    Cipher Spec, 888
    control channel communication, 127
    Exchange Server, 699–700, 703
    SecureNET clients, 115
    SharePoint Services, 662–63
    tunneling protocols, 22–23
Enhanced NAT. *See* E-NAT (Enhanced NAT)
Enterprise policies, locating arrays, 837
Enumerated port scan attack alert, 326

Errors
    691, 743
    766, 793
    789, 793
    806, 793
    809, 793
    reading logs, 177
    scripting practices, 835
    TMG Setup failure, 181–84
Ethernet, IP routing, basic, 210–15
European Institute for Computer Antivirus Research
    (EICAR), 443
Events
    5783 event, 897
    DNS System Log, 372
    flood mitigation, 339–40
    Windows Event Logs, 862
    WLBS display, 305
EWS (Exchange Web Services), 723
Exchange (Anti Spam), 479
Exchange Active Sync (EAS), 698–99, 704, 706–07,
    718, 721
Exchange Hub Transport Server, 523
Exchange Intelligent Message Filter, 490–91
Exchange Outlook Anywhere Services, 77
Exchange Outlook Web Access, 76–78
Exchange Publishing Wizard, 698–700
Exchange Server
    configuring, 707–18
    publishing, planning for, 697–707
    SPAM protection, 491
    troubleshooting, 174, 719–30
Exchange Web Services (EWS), 723
ExchangeVersion, 702–03
Exhange Publishing Wizard, 702–03
Explicit Congestion Notification (ECN), 12, 144
Explicit content, 471
ExpMatch(), 949
Exporting files, 838
Extensible Authentication Protocol (EAP), 736
External Mail Routing Configuration, 498
External networks, 80, 223–24. *See also* Networks

F

Failback, ISP Redundancy, 267
Failed DNS Resolutions counter, 58

Failover. *See also* Availability; Load balancing
  ISP failover, 82, 263–65
  ISP Redundancy, 78–79, 267, 269–76
FailuresToUnavailable, 267
Fast trickling, 438–39
Fault tolerance, new features, 19
FCS (Forefront Client Security), 799
FetchURL, 421
File and Printer Sharing, 144
File Transfer Protocol (FTP), 18, 113. *See also* TFTP
  (Trivial File Transfer Protocol) Filter
File-based antivirus, 440. *See also* Virus protection
Files
  attachments, 519–22
  extensions, 487–90, 519–22, 533–34, 555–56
  filtering, 519–22
  importing and exporting, 838
  logging, 803–04
  Session Initiation Protocol (SIP) filtering, 18
  SharePoint Services
    multi-server, configuring, 672–79
    overview, configuring, 665–66
    planning for publishing, 661–65
    server farm, configuring, 679–89
    single-server, configuring, 667–72
    troubleshooting, 689–95
Filtering. *See also* E-mail protection; HTTP Filter;
  Malware Inspection
  applications, 18, 50, 70, 110, 115, 118, 191, 561–70,
    573, 576–77, 590
  Caching Compressed Content Filter, 394
  Compression Filter, 393–94
  configuring virus and content filtering, 518–27
  Content Filtering, 507–11
  DNS attack detection, 326
  file filtering, 519–22
  Forms-Based Authentication filter, 702–03
  HTTP Malware filter, 12–13
  ISAPI, 23–24
  link translation, 583
  Message Body Filtering, 523–27
  Network Monitor captures, 899–903
  Network Monitor, SOCKS-proxy troubleshooting,
    903–09
  packet filters, RRAS, 748
  performance counters, 937–39, 943
  Recipient Filtering, 512–13
  Sender Filtering, 513–15

server publishing, 590
Session Intiation Protocol (SIP), 18
spam, configuring, 502–18
TMG console, 191
TMG SMTP filter, 491
traffic, overview, 6–8
Trivial File Transfer Protocol (TFTP), 18
URLs
  configuring, 470–78
  new features, 15–16
  overview, 465–70
  Update Center, 478–81
  Update Center, configuring, 481–85
  Web access policy, 194
Virus Filtering, 522–25
Web filters and publishing, 578–80
Web Proxy Application Filter, 529–31
Web proxy filter, 265
FindProxyForUrl, 362–64, 379
FindProxyForURLEx, 362–64
Firewall generation, defined, 10
Firewalls
  chaining, 335
  client considerations, NLB, 293
  Firewall Client, 93, 253, 335, 384
  Firewall Policy, 188, 194
  log fields, 798–800
  packet engine performance counters, 937–38
  policy rules, basics, 242
  types of, 9–10
  URL filtering, 469
Flood attacks, 323, 329–36
Forefront Client Security (FCS), 799
Forefront Protection 2010 for Exchange Server, 491
Forefront Protection Manager 2010 (FPM), 15
Forefront Security for Exchange (FSE), 479
Forefront Threat Management Gateway. *See* Microsoft
  Forefront Threat Management Gateway (TMG)
Forms-Based Authentication, 580, 663–64, 700–03
Forward caching, 390, 394–95, 920. *See also* Caching
Forward proxy, 921
Forwarders, 60–61
FPC.Root, 830
FPCArray, 830
FPM (Forefront Protection Manager 2010), 15
FQDN (Fully Qualified Domain Name), 299, 806
Front Firewall, network templates, 223
FTP (File Transfer Protocol)

commands, 905–06
filters, 50
servers, 583–84, 590
TMG deployment options, 52–53
Web proxy clients, 113
Full-duplex, 78
Fully Qualified Domain Name (FQDN), 299, 806

G

Gates, Bill, 490
Generic Application Protocol Analysis (GAPA), 17, 307
Generic Network Intrusion System (NIS),
    new features, 17
Generic Routing Encapsulation (GRE), 117, 734
GET, 871, 913
getaddrinfo, 121, 125
gethostbyaddress, 121, 125
gethostbyname, 121
GetHostbyName(), 350
Getting Started Wizard, 54–57, 66–67, 69–70, 174,
    200–01
Global HTTP Policy Settings, 190
Global Link Translation, 188, 190
Global Query Block List, 371
Global URL filtering, configuring, 472–75
GRE (Generic Routing Encapsulation), 117, 734
Group policies
    automatic discovery, Internet Explorer, 377–79
    availability, network designs, 81
    SharePoint Services, 663
    traffic, 7
GZIP, 393–94

H

H.323 filter performance counter, 939
H.323 filters, 590
Half open attack, 333
Half-duplex, 78
Handshakes, 870, 884
Hardware
    load balancing, migration and, 95
    preinstallation checklist, 141
    requirements, 35–36
    VPN access requirements, 739–41

HEAD, 871
Headers
    Authentication Header Protocol, 735
    cache-control headers, 248–49
    HTTP, 873
    HTTP Filter, 533–34, 557–60
    malformed, 489
    Maximum Headers Length, 551
    web objects, caching, 392
HELO/EHLO analysis, 516
High Bit Characters, 552
HNode (hybrid node type), 59
Host mismatch, 650–51
HTML e-mail, 489–90
HTML forms-based authentication, 701
HTML progress page, 14
HTTP (Hypertext Transfer Protocol). See also HTTP
    Filter; HTTPS
    anonymous requests, 877
    authentication, 663–64, 874–83
    CERN proxy traffic, 242–49
    compression, caching, 393–94
    dual authentication (proxy and server), 881
    Global HTTP Policy Settings, 190
    header, cache information, 418
    libraries, 353
    NTLM authentication, 881–82
    objects, caching, 392
    overview, 869–74, 911–17
    Policy Reevaluation, 249–53
    proxy authentication, 879–80
    requests, Web proxy clients, 109–11
    resources, client requests for, 110
    server authentication, 878–79
    SharePoint Services, 662–63
    traffic, 22–23, 31, 49, 52–53, 73
    Web listener, 580
    Web Proxy Application Filter, 529–32
    Web proxy clients, 113
    Web publishing, 581, 648
    Web server publishing, 600–18
HTTP 502 Bad Gateway, 549
HTTP Filter, 533–34
    CERN proxy example, 247
    configuring, 550–52
    extensions, 555–56
    headers, 557–60
    methods, 553–55

signatures, 561–70
validating inbound access, 560–61
HTTP Malware filter, 12–13
HTTP.SYS, 763
HTTPS
Exchange Server, 699–700
exclusion list, 469
HTTPS Inspection
common errors, 548–49
configuring, 534–47
new features, 16
outbound traffic, 22–23
overview, 884–89
performance counters, 938, 959
SharePoint Services, 662–63
TMG deployment options, 52–53
Web listener, 580
Web Proxy Application Filter, 529–32
Web proxy clients, 113
Hub Transport Server, 698
Hybrid node type (HNode), 59

I

IAG 2007, 23–24
IANA (Internet Assigned Numbers Authority), 9
IAS (Internet Authentication Services), 171
ICF (Windows Internet Connection Firewall), 7
ICMP Echo Request, 212–15, 242–45
ICS (Internet Connection Sharing), 7
IDP (ISA Data Packager), 861
IDS (Intrusion Detection System)
configuring, 324–26
overview, 323
requirements, 40–41
TMG, new features, 17
IGMP support, 287
IIS (Internet Information Services), 23–24, 690
IKE (Internet Key Exchange), 735–36
ILOVEYOU virus, 488–90. See also Virus protection
ImplementFindProxyForURL, 362–64
Importing files, 838
Inbound traffic, 22–23, 28–32, 264, 560–61.
          See also Traffic
Incoming context, publishing, 573–74
Inetinfo.exe, 24
Ingress migrations, 90–95

Installing
certificates, 619–25
TMG manual installation, 156–68
TMG MBE, manual installation, 145–56
TMG, preinstallation checklist, 141–45
TMG, setup architecture, 169–72
TMG, unattended installation, 168
Integrated authentication, 235–36
Integrated NLB (Network Load Balancing), 288–92
Integration, overview, 8–9
Integrity, UAG, 26
Intelligent Application Gateway (IAG) 2007, 21
Intermediate Certification Authority, 16
Internal Certification Authority, 700
Internal networks, 54–57, 222–24. See also Networks
Internet. See also Internet Explorer
HTTP
anonymous requests, 877
authentication, 878, 883
dual authentication (proxy and server), 881
NTLM authentication, 881–82
overview, 869–74
proxy authentication, 879–80
server authentication, 878–79
HTTPS, overview, 884–89
Malware Inspection, testing, 443–45
preinstallation checklist, 145
timelines and milestones, 911
TMG deployment options, 52–53
traffic management, 48
Windows Libraries, 967
Internet Assigned Numbers Authority (IANA), 9
Internet Authentication Services (IAS), 171
Internet Connection Firewall (ICF), 7
Internet Connection Sharing (ICS), 7
Internet Explorer. See also Internet
Automatic Proxy Cache, 379
client-side CARP, 396–97
embedded scripts, 489–90
parameters, 233
preinstallation checklist, 145
Web proxy clients, overview, 107–13
Winsock, 130–31
worm attacks, 489
WPAD (Web Proxy Auto Discovery),
          364–79, 381
Internet Information Services (IIS), 23–24, 690
Internet Key Exchange (IKE), 735

Internet Key Exchange version 2 (IKEv2), 736
Internet Protocol Control Protocol (IPCP), 735
Internet Protocol security (IPsec), 22–23, 52–53, 330, 735, 773–74, 790–92
Internet Security and Acceleration (ISA) Server 2000, 490–91, 926–29
Internet Security and Acceleration (ISA) Server 2004, 93, 363, 490–91, 929–31
Internet Security and Acceleration (ISA) Server 2006, 93, 99–105, 490–91, 932–33
Internet Server Application Programming Interface (ISAPI), 23–24
Intranet Web publishing, 77
Intrusion detection. See also Intrusion Detection System (IDS); Intrusion Prevention System (IPS)
    requirements, 40–41
    TMG console, 192, 196–97
Intrusion Detection System (IDS)
    configuring, 324–26
    configuring DNS attack detection, 326
    overview, 323
    requirements, 40–41
    TMG, new features, 17
Intrusion Prevention System (IPS), 17, 322
Intrusion prevention, new features, 15. See also Malware protection
IP addresses
    3-Leg Perimeter networks, 68
    5-tuple, 209–10
    basic routing, 210–15
    configuring intra-array addresses, 415–16
    dial-in VPN migration, 91
    DIP (Dedicated IP address), 285
    E-Mail Policy Wizard, 495–501
    IP Allow List, 502–03
    IP Allow List Providers, 503–05
    IP Block List, 505–06
    IP Block List Providers, 506
    load balancing, 587–88
    logging, 806
    lookup performance, 38
    Malware Inspection configuration, 435
    managing and aggregating, 918–19
    NAT relationships, 215–20
    NIS (Network Inspection System), 327–30
    non-Web servers, 640
    server-side CARP, 397
    SharePoint Services, 662

site-to-site (S2S) VPN migration, 92
SSTP, 766
TMGC configuration data, 127
VIP (Virtual IP addresses), 285
Web listener, 580, 602
IP Allow List, 502–03
IP Allow List Providers, 503–05
IP Block List, 505–06
IP Block List Providers, 506
IP fragments, 329
IP half scan, alert, 325
IP protocols
    50 (ESP), 735
    51 (Authenitcation Header), 735
    More Info, 9
    TMGC as name service provider, 125
IP subnet, 268
ipconfig, 305
IPCP (Internet Protocol Control Protocol), 735
IPS (Intrusion Prevention System), 17, 322
IPsec, 22–23, 52–53, 330, 735
IPsec ESP, 790–91
IPsec NAT-T, 735, 791–92
IpSubnet, 362
ISA 2004, 90
ISA 2006, 90
ISA Data Packager (IDP), 861, 892
ISA Info Viewer, 702–03
ISA server
    migration, 88
ISA Server
    IAG 2007 integration, 24
    overview, 10–11
    traffic filtering, 6–8
ISA Server 2000, 490–91, 926–29
ISA Server 2004, 93, 363, 490–91, 929–31
ISA Server 2006, 93, 99–105, 490–91, 932–33
ISA Server 2006 Supportability Update, 3
ISA Setup files, 156
ISA_GettingStarted_XXX.log, 175
ISA_IpsUpdateInstall.log, 175
ISAADAM_IMPORTSCHEMA_XXX.log, 175
ISAADAM_INSTALL_XXX.log, 175
ISAFWSV_XXX.log, 175, 177, 181
ISAFWUI_XXX.log, 175
ISAPI (Internet Server Application Programming Interface)
    filtering, 23–24

ISAPI Extension
  IAG 2007, 23–24
ISASCHED Service, 481
isatap queries, 371
ISATools.org rule, 406
IsaUpdateAgent.log, 175
ISAWRAP_XXX.log, 175–76
isIpv6, 362
ISP 1 Dedicated Servers List, 278
ISP 2 Dedicated Servers list, 282
ISP connections
  Enable ISP Redundancy Wizard, 206
  failover, 82, 263–65, 267
  load balancing, 264, 267
  TMG, new features, 19
ISP Link 1 Connection Properties, 278
ISP Redundancy
  Enable ISP Redundancy Wizard, 206
  hardware requirements, 35–36
  overview, 78–79, 263–65
  rule basics, 242
  TMG console, 197–98
  UAG, security, 26
ISP Redundancy Configuration Wizard, 269–74,
    276–84
ISPredundancyConfig, 266

J

Join Array Wizard, 203–04
JScript
  containers, 359
  importing and exporting files, 838
  locating arrays, 837
  objects, 357–59, 361
  overview, 834
  WPAD, cfile, 352–64
JScript Regular Expressions, 362

K

KaK worm, 489–90
Keep-Alive, 916
Kerberos authentication, 39–40, 878
Kerberos Constrained Delegation (KCD),
    669–70, 701

Kernel mode, IIS requests, 24
Keyword list, 527

L

L2TP (Layer 2 Tunneling Protocol), 22–23, 52–53,
    330, 736–37
L2TP/IPsec (Layer 2 Tunneling Protocol)
  configuring, 774–81
  overview, 735
  site-to-site VPN connections, 773–74
  troubleshooting, 790–93
LAN (Local Area Network), 56, 143, 592–93.
    See also Networks
Land, alert, 325
Large logging queue (LLQ), 814
Latin 1 characters, 552
Layer 2 Tunneling Protocol (L2TP), 22–23, 52–53, 330,
    736–37
Layer 2 Tunneling Protocol over IPsec (L2TP/IPsec), 735,
    773–81, 790–93
Layered Service Providers (LSPs), 122–25
LDAP server, 40, 190
Legacy settings, Internet Explorer and WPAD, 381
Libraries, Windows Internet, 967
Licenses
  Malware Inspection, 441
  Update Center, 481
Lightweight Directory Services (LDS), 37, 147, 165,
    171, 186–87
Link translation, 583, 664–65
listen, 121
Listener SSL Certificates, 628
Listeners
  HTTPS Web listeners, 625–30
  migration, 90–91
  Network Listener, 589
  server publishing, 574–76
  Web listeners, 580, 600–01, 766
  Web Proxy Application Filter, 529
  Web publishing, 578–80
LMHOSTS, 59
Load balancing. See also Availability
  CARP load factor, 416–17
  DNS Round-Robin, 349
  enabling, 288–92
  flood mitigation, 336

ISP Redundancy, 78–79, 263–65, 267–84
link availability testing, 265–67
migration and, 95
new features, 19
NLB architecture, 285–88
NLB, configuring, 293–98
post-installation best practices, 298–99
publishing rules, 595–96
troubleshooting, 301–06
virtual environments, 300–01
Web farms, 26, 587–88
Web Publishing Load Balancing (WPLB), 72
Web server publishing, 606
Load Balancing Factor, 282
Local Area Network (LAN), 56, 143, 592–93.
        See also Networks
Local Host Access, 77
Local Host networks, 222–24
Local storage, 481. *See also* Storage
Log Traffic Blocked By Flood
        Mitigation, 339–40
Logging
  best practices, 809–15
  cache behavior, 417–20
  configuring, 800–09
  DNS System Log, 372
  file and disk space controls, 803–04
  firewall fields, new, 798–800
  flood mitigation, 339–40
  hardware requirements, 36
  HTTP Filter, 566
  importance of, 797–98
  Intrusion Detection System (IDS), 324–26
  local text, 807–08
  Malware Inspection, 429–30, 446–63
  queue, 809
  reports, 446–63, 859
  SharePoint Services, 692–95
  storage, 41–42
  TMG console, 192–93, 199
  TMG Setup, 174–75
  traffic simulator, 261–62
  Web proxy fields, new, 798–800
LogParser, 808
Loopback, SecureNET clients, 116–17
Loops, scripts, 835
Loose Source Routing, 329
LSPs (Layered Service Providers), 122–25

M

MAC (Media Access Control), 210–15
MAC-addresses, 8, 286
Mail. *See* E-Mail; SMTP (Simple Mail Transfer Protocol)
Mailbox Server, 698
MakeCARPExceptions, 358
MakeIPs, 357, 362
MakeIps(), 362
MakeNames, 358, 362
MakeProxies(), 359
Malware Inspection. *See also* Malware protection
  configuring
    content delivery, 438–39
    environment considerations, 431–36
    settings, 437–38
    storage, 439–40
  Internet access, testing, 443–45
  license, 441
  logging, 799
  overview, 427–31
  per-rule, defining, 442
  reports, creating, 446–63
  updates, 440, 478
Malware protection. *See also* Malware Inspection
  Conficker, 567–70
  e-mail threats, overview, 487–90
  MMPC (Microsoft Malware Protection Center), 308
  MS08-067, 316–17
  new features, 11–17, 27
  performance counters, 938, 956
  TMG console, 187
  Update Center, 478–81
  Web Access Policy, 188–90
Management
  applications, 49
  disks, hardware requirements, 36
  Forefront TMG Management Console, 5
  new features, 14–16
  NLB (Network Load Balancing), 288, 302–04
  remote, setup options, 172–74
Media Access Control (MAC), 210–15
Media Player, 353, 382–84
Melissa virus, 488–90. *See also* Virus protection
Memory
  caching, 389–91
  flood mitigation, 330–36
  log files, 803–04, 812–13

requirements, 35–36
TMG requirements, 12
VPN access, requirements, 740–41
Message Body Filtering, 523–27
Message Queuing, 171
Messaging. *See also* E-mail
Exchange Server
  configuring, 707–18
  publishing, planning for, 697–707
  troubleshooting, 719–30
Microsoft .NET Framework, 108, 384–85
Microsoft Challenge Handshake Authentication
    Protocol version 2 (MS-CHAPv2), 736
Microsoft Essential Business Server, 4
Microsoft Exchange Edge Transport Role, 174
Microsoft Exchange Server
  configuring Exchange Client access, 707–18
  publishing, planning for, 697–707
  troubleshooting, 719–30
Microsoft Firewall Service (wspsrv.exe), 469, 941
Microsoft Forefront Threat Management Gateway
    (TMG)
  Capacity Planner, 592–93
  clients, features of, 135
  Console, 5
  deployment, overview, 5–6
  feature comparision, 4
  Firewall Packet Engine, 42
  Firewall Service, 42
  high availability, 79–80
  installation, manual, 156–68
  Management Console, 5
  Medium Business Edition (MBE)
    console, 185–91
    deployment, 5
    installation, manual, 145–56
    migration, 90
    new features, 11–14
    new wizards, 199–206
    overview, 933–35
  MPEngine (Malware Protection Engine), 12–13
  new features
    e-mail, anti-malware, anti-spam support, 16–17
    firewall integration, 8–9
    firewall types, 9–10
    HTTPS inspection, 16
    network functionality, 18–19
    network intrusion prevention, 17

Session Initiation Protocol (SIP) filter, 18
    summary of, 19
    TFTP filter, 18
    URL filtering, 16
    user interface, management and reporting, 14–16
    Windows Server 2008 and 64-bit support, 11–14
  overview, 3–4
  Performance Monitor, 962
Microsoft Forefront Unified Access Gateway
    (UAG), 25–26
Microsoft Hyper-V, 25
Microsoft Malware Protection Center (MMPC),
    308, 316–17
Microsoft Malware Protection Engine
    (TMG MPEngine), 12–13
Microsoft Management Console (MMC), 51
Microsoft Office 2003 Web Components, 37
Microsoft Office Outlook, 353, 698–700, 705
Microsoft Office Outlook Anywhere, 73
Microsoft Office SharePoint Services
  configuring
    multi-server, 672–79
    overview, 665–66
    server farm, 679–89
    single-server, 667–72
  publishing, planning for, 661–65
  troubleshooting, 689–95
Microsoft Reputation Service (MRS). *See also* URL
    filtering
  Bing safe search, 471
  URL filtering, overview, 465–70
Microsoft SmartScreen technology, 511
Microsoft SQL Express, 37
Microsoft SQL Server Native Client, 37
Microsoft SQL Server Setup Support Files, 37
Microsoft SQL Server Volume Shadow Copy Service
    (VSS) Writer, 37
Microsoft Telemetry Service, 203
Microsoft Update, 13, 465, 479–81, 484
Microsoft Update Setup, 202
Microsoft.Isa.ManagedPerfCounters.dll.log, 175
Migration
  checklists, 96–99
  ISA 2006 SE to TMG 2010 EE Forward Proxy, 99–105
  overview, 87–89
  publishing scenarios, 90–91
  scenarios for, 90–95
MIME (Multipurpose Internet Mail Extension), 489

MinimalResumeTime, 267
Mirroring with striping, 813
Mixed node types (MNode), 59
MMC (Microsoft Management Console), 51
MMPC (Microsoft Malware Protection Center), 308,
    316–17
MMS, 50, 382
MNode (mixed node type), 59
Mobile users, 27
Monitoring, 186–87, 193, 319–21, 394–95.
    See also Logging
More Info
  A records, creating, 291
  Active Directory and Group Policy administration, 7
  ActiveSync in Exchange Server, 718
  Alternate Access Mapping, 665, 689
  application signatures, 561
  ARP (Address Resolution Protocol), 210
  attacks, 326
  authentication methods, 806
  authentication, downgrade attack, 258
  authentication, Exchange Server, 702
  authentication, mechanisms and delegations, 586
  authentication, SharePoint Services, 664
  authentication, web-proxy requests, 103
  Automatic Proxy Result Cache, 380
  auto-negotiation, 145
  AutoProxy, 385
  BadTrans, 490
  bidirectional affinity, 288
  Bing safe search, 471
  cache counters, 395
  cache file usage, 421
  cache rules, 401
  Cache-Control field, 420
  certificate errors, troubleshooting, 656
  certificate file format, 619
  certificate requirements, 663
  certificate revocation, 793
  cfile extensions, Web proxy, 354
  Cipher Suite, 886
  client configuration, NAP, 763
  CNAME as proxy server, 292
  Conficker, 567
  connectivity, SQL Server Database, 814
  constrained delegation, configuring, 727
  Content Filtering, 508, 516
  Cryptography Next Generation (CNG), 619

CVE (Common Vulnerabilities and Exposures), 310
DHCP configuration, 368
DhcpRequestParams(), 347
digital certificates, 775
DNS lookup for STMP, 820
DNS Round-Robin, 349
DNS Server Global Query Block List, 374
domain isolation, 53
double encoding, 552
EdgeSync traffic, 500
Enterprise firewall and Exchange Active Sync Direct
    Push, 707
Exchange 2010 client services, 718
Exchange Server 2007, 494
Exchange Server 2007 mail filtering, 491
Exchange Server 2007 Server Role, 698
Exchange Server capacity planning, 705
Exchange Setup Logs, 174
Exchange Web Services, 723
FetchURL, 421
file names, matching patterns, 521
Firewall Client, migration, 93
Forefront Edge Virtual Deployments, 301
Forefront Protection 2010 for Exchange Server, 491
Forefront Protection Manager 2010, 205
Forefront Server Security for Exchange sizing, 523
Forefront TMG, migration, 93
GAPA (Generic Application-Level Protocol
    Analyzer), 307
hardware requirements, 36
HELO/EHLO, 516
HRESULT format, 177
HTTP 1.1 enhancements, 913
HTTP headers, 392, 874
HTTP methods, 871
HTTP Protocol, 109, 245
ICMP messages, 242
Internal Certification Authority, 700
Internet timeline and milestones, 911
IP protocols, 9
ISA Data Packager, 892
ISA Server, 93, 706
ISA Server 2006 Supportability Update, 3
ISA Server Common Criteria, 11
ISA Server Message Screener, 491
Jscript Regular Expressions, 362
Kerberos Constrained Delegation, 669–70
keyword list, 527

L2TP over IPsec, 790
link aggregation, 288
locallat.txt, 129
lockouts, 867
Malware Inspection, 442
Microsoft Essential Business Server, 4
name resolution, 59, 259
NAP planning, 745, 758
NAT (Network Address Translation), 216
Netscape, 352
Network Monitor, 305, 891–92
network templates, choosing, 32
Nimda worm, 489
NLB (Network Load Balancing), 285, 287
NLB in VMWare ESX Server, 301
Outlook Anywhere, 704, 718
Outlook buffer overflow, 489
Outlook Web Access, troubleshooting, 722
phishing, 490
port 6601, 766
PowerShell, 845–46
PPTP NAT editors, 734
PPTP protocol, 788
quarantine, NAP, 753
RADIUS, 741, 751
RAID, 813
Root DNS Servers, 265–67
Routing and Remote Access (RRAS), 748
S4U2Proxy request, 687
secure hash algorithms, 950
security by obscurity, 558
Sender Policy Framework, 218, 515
SMTP command and response, 512
spam, 490
SQL encrypted connections, 811
SQL Server storage, 815
SSL version 3, 884
SSTP, 763, 771, 792
SVVP (Server Virtualization Validation Program), 25
TMG Client, 93, 908
TMG COM methods, 842
TMG Firewall Log fields, 798–800
UAG functionaltiy, 28
virtual deployments, 45
VLAN, 286
VPN authentication, 736, 750–51
VPN connections, 743
VPN protocols and performance, 741, 774

Web site publishing rules, 558
Windows Filtering Platform, 7
Windows Internet libraries, 969–72
WinHTTP, 469
WinINET, 108, 353
WinINET API, proxy settings, 108
Winsock Service Providers, 124
WPAD, 345, 371, 381
WUA COM API, 322
WWSAPI, 469
MRS (Microsoft Reputation Service).
    See also URL filtering
    Bing safe search, 471
    URL filtering, overview, 465–70
MS08-067 associated malware, 316–17
MS-CHAPv2, 736
MSN Messenger, 562–64
Multicast, 285–87
Multicast with IGMP, 285–87
Multipurpose Internet Mail Extension (MIME), 489
Music, streaming, 353, 382–84

N

Name resolution
    CERN proxy traffic, 246
    DNS configuration, 289–91
    migration and, 95
    Name Service Provider (NSP), 122, 125–32
    network configurations, 58–63
    overview, 37–39
    preinstallation checklist, 141
    SecureNET clients, 115–17
    TMGC as name service provider, 125–32
    troubleshooting, 259
    Winsock, 119
    WPAD, configuring, 369
Name Service Provider (NSP), 122, 125–32
Name services, 39, 92
NAP (Network Access Protection)
    dial-in VPN migration, 91
    UAG integration, 26
    VPN integration, 743–45
    VPN integration, configuring, 756–63
NAT (Network Address Translation)
    E-NAT (Enhanced NAT), 265
        configuring, 820–26

overview, 817–20
  troubleshooting, 826–27
flood mitigation, 334
L2TP/IPsec, 735
network rules, creating, 226–31
new features, 18–19
relationships, 215–20
server publishing rules, 576, 590–91
web proxy filter, troubleshooting, 532
NDIS (network driver interface specification), 8
Negotiate authentications, 878
NetBIOS, 38, 51, 58–59, 384
Netmask ordering, 73
Netscape, 352
Network Access Protection. *See* NAP (Network Access Protection)
Network Adaptor properties, 276
Network Address Translation. *See* NAT (Network Address Translation)
Network cards, requirements, 35–36
Network driver interface specification (NDIS), 8
Network Inspection System (NIS)
  configuring, 311–16
  customizing, 316–19
  flood mitigation, configuring, 330–36
  IDS and, 322, 326
  implementing, 309–10
  intrusion detection, 196–97, 324–26
  IP preferences, configuring, 327–30
  logging, 799–800
  Malware Inspection, 429
  monitoring, 319–21
  new features, 17
  overview, 307–09
  preconfigured attack protection, 337–40
  Update Center configuration, 483
  updates, 322, 478
Network Interface, counters, 42–43
Network intrusion, new features, 17
Network Listener, 589
Network Listener IP Addresses, 640
Network Load Balancing (NLB)
  architecture, 285–88
  E-Mail Policy Wizard, 498
  enabling, 288–92
  migration and, 95
  publishing rules, 76–80
  site-to-site VPN connections, 786

TMG Setup architecture, 171
traffic flow, 74
Web server publishing, 606
Network Load Balancing Integration Wizard, 293
Network Monitor
  reading captures, 897–903
  SharePoint Services, troubleshooting, 693–95
  SOCKS- proxy troubleshooting, 903–09
  trace, 371
  trace, cache information, 418
  traffic capture, 891–97
Network Policy and Access Services Server Role, 37
Network Rule Wizard, 221
Network Rules, 77
Network Setup Wizard, 30, 200–02
Network Template Wizard, 201
Network Time Protocol (NTP), 590–91
Network Trace, 419
Networks
  3-Leg Perimeter template, 67–68
  access, enabling, 22–23
  Back Firewall template, 68–69
  bandwidth consumption, 330–36
  configuring
    creating networks, 222–31
    network relationships, 209–22
    protected networks, 231–39
    rules, 220–22
  deploying, virtual environments, 44–45
  Edge Firewall, 66–67
  entities, 279–80, 314
  high availability
    designing for Access Rules, 80–81
    for publishing rules, 76–80
    overview, 71–76
  infrastructure requirements, 37–41
  installation, TMG 2010, 162–64
  installation, TMG MBE, 149
  ISP Redundancy, 268
  joining firewall to domain or workgroup, 82–84
  logging, 798
  migration, 91–93
  NAT relationships, 215–20
  network rules, creating, 220–22, 226–31
  new features, 18–19
  NLB considerations, 286–88
  preinstallation checklist, 141–45
  protection, UAG, 27–32

requirements
  complex networks, 53
  configuring TMG networks, 54–57
  name resolution, 58–63
  TMG deployment options, 51–53
  traffic profile, determining, 47–51
route relationships, 215
rules, 241
server publishing relationships, 576–77
templates, 65–71
TMG console, 185, 191, 197–98
troubleshooting, 892
Web proxy client requirements, 112
New Cache Rule Wizards, 401–07
New Content Download Job Wizard, 409–12
New Network Rule Wizard, 18, 227–31, 822–23
New Network Wizard, 224–26
New Server Farm Wizard, 681–84
New Server Publishing Rule Wizard, 638, 642
New SharePoint Publishing Rule Wizard, 672–89
New URL Category Set Wizard, 475
New Web Listener Wizard, 601, 626–30, 709
New Web Publishing Rule Wizard, 604, 631–36
Next Generation TCP/IP stack, 12
NIC, 268, 288
Nimda worm, 489. *See also* Malware protection
NIS (Network Inspection System)
  configuring, 311–16
  customizing, 316–19
  flood mitigation, configuring, 330–36
  IDS and, 322, 326
  implementing, 309–10
  intrusion detection, 196–97, 324–26
  IP preferences, configuring, 327–30
  logging, 799–800
  Malware Inspection, 429
  monitoring, 319–21
  new features, 17
  overview, 307–09
  preconfigured attack protection, 337–40
  Update Center configuration, 483
  updates, 322, 478
NLB (Network Load Balancing)
  architecture, 285–88
  E-Mail Policy Wizard, 498
  enabling, 288–92
  migration and, 95
  publishing rules, 76–80

site-to-site VPN connections, 786
TMG Setup architecture, 171
traffic flow, 74
Web server publishing, 606
Nmcap.exe, 892, 896
nocarp, 949
Node types, 58–59
Node, JScript, 361
Non-HTTP protocols, 78
Non-integrated NLB (Network Load
    Balancing), 288–92
Non-TCP/UDP protocols, 117
Non-TMG Firewall, 336
Non-Windows authentication, 40
Normalization, 552
nslookup, 371
NSP (Name Service Provider), 122, 125–32
NTFS partition, 389
NTLM authentication, 39–40, 707, 878, 881–82
NTP (Network Time Protocol), 590–91

O

Object Linking and Embedding (OLE), 829
OEM (Original Equipment Manufacturers), 21
Office SharePoint Services. *See* Microsoft Office
    SharePoint Services
Offline servers, 587
OLE (Object Linking and Embedding), 829
One-Time Report Wizard, 446–50
Operating systems
  32-bit, 5, 36–37, 94
  64-bit, 5, 11–12, 36–37, 94
  client selection and, 133
  migration, 88
  preinstallation checklist, 141
  TMG 2010 deployment, 5
  VPN access, client support, 738
OPTIONS, 871
Original Equipment Manufacturers (OEM), 21
Outbound protocols, publishing, 573
Outbound traffic, 22–23, 264, 538–47. *See also* Traffic
Outlook, 120, 489–90, 705
Outlook Anywhere (OA), 724
Outlook Anywhere Publishing, 717–18
Outlook Anywhere Services, 77, 705, 707
Outlook Express, 489

Outlook Mobile Access, 704, 707
Outlook Web Access (OWA), 16, 76–78, 587, 698–702, 704, 709–17, 721–23
Ownership relationships, 96–99

P

Packets, 9–10, 50, 938
Partitions, 35–36, 389
Passive caching, 920
Password Authentication Protocol (PAP), 735
Passwords, 235
Path mismatch, 651
Payload length, 552
Peer node type (PNode), 59
Performance. *See also* Behavioral monitoring;
    Load balancing
  authentication, 39–40
  cache, 394–95, 421–22
  CARP (Cache Array Routing Protocol), 395–97
  counters
    cache, 395, 939
    compression performance, 953
    DiffServ, 954
    e-mail hygiene, 960
    Firewall packet engine, 938
    H.323 filter, 939
    how to use, 964
    HTTPS performance, 959
    malware protection, 956
    Microsoft Firewall service, 941
    overview, 937–38
    requirements, 41
    SOCKS filter, 943
    TMG Performance Monitor, 962
    URL filtering, 961
    Web proxy, 944
  Exchange Server, 705–06
  logging options, 811
  Malware Inspection, 437–39
  migration, 94
  monitoring, requirements, 41–43
  name resolution, 37–39, 62, 246
  networks, requirements, 42–43
  preinstallation checklist, 143–45
  proxy cache, 387–89
  proxy redundancy, 380

  System Performance, 964
  virtual environments, deploying in, 44–45
  Virus Filtering, 523
  VPN access, 739
Performance Monitor, 58, 861, 962
Perimeter networks, 223
Persistent connection, 916
Phishing, 469, 487–90
PICNIC, 88
Ping of death, 325
Ping requests, 212–15, 242–45
ping.exe, 125–26
Pipelined requests, 913
PKI (Public Key Infrastructure), 593
PNode (peer node type), 59
Point-to-Point Tunneling (PPTP)
  access, enabling, 22–23
  over HTTP, 735
  overview, 734
  protocol mapping, 50
  site-to-site VPN connections, 773–74, 782–88
  technology comparison, 736–37
  TMG deployment options, 52–53
  troubleshooting VPN connections, 788–90, 793
Policies. *See also* Access control; Filtering
  Active Directory Lightweight Directory Services
    (LDS), 147
  Additional Security Policy, 188
  arrays, 299, 837
  authentication, 39–40
  CERN proxy HTTP traffic, 242–49
  E-mail Policy, 194–95, 205
  firewall policy, 188, 194
  HTTP policy, 581
  migration and, 87
  name resolution, 37–39
  ping requests, 242–45
  Policy Enforcement, 249–53
  Policy Reevaluation, 249–53
  Protocol Anomalies, 315
  server publishing, 574–76
  system policy, 172
  TMG deployment options, 52–53
  traffic, 7, 241–49
  troubleshooting access rules, 253–62
  UAG, 26
  URL filtering, new features, 16

VPN (Virtual Private Networks), 733–36,
  741–42
Web Access Policy, 188–90, 194, 562–64, 568
Policy engine, rule basics, 241–49
Polling, 265–66, 481
POP Intrusion Detection, 326
POP3 Intrusion Detection filter, 590
Pornographic content, 471
Portal trunks, 24
Ports
  firewall rules, 24
  HTTP, 870
  HTTP.SYS, 763
  logging, SQL listeners, 806
  non-Web servers, 642–47
  PPTP, port 1723, 734, 788–90
  protocol mapping, 50–51
  redirect requests, 617
  redirection, 583–84
  server publishing, 590–91
  SharePoint Services, 690
  source port affinity, 72
  SSTP, 766
  TCP port 80, 900
  UAG, security and, 26
  Web listener, 580
POST, 871, 913
Post Office Protocol (POP), 326, 590
PowerShell, 171, 842–48
PPTP (Point-to-Point Tunneling)
  access, enabling, 22–23
  overview, 734
  protocol mapping, 50
  site-to-site VPN connections, 773–74, 782–88
  technology comparison, 736–37
  TMG deployment options, 52–53
  troubleshooting VPN connections, 788–90, 793
PrerequisiteInstaller.DATE-TIME.log, 175
Printer Sharing, 144
Private keys, 91, 662
Processors, 5, 35–37, 94, 523
Productivity, new features, 16. *See also* Performance
Protected networks, Access Rules, 80–82. *See also* Access control
Protocol Anomalies Policy, 315
Protocol filters, 308
Protocols
  client selection, 133

HTTP
  anonymous requests, 877
  authentication delegation, 883
  authentication methods, 878
  dual authentication (proxy and server), 881
  More Info, 109
  NTLM authentication, 881–82
  overview, 869–74, 911–17
  proxy authentication, 879–80
  server authentication, 878–79
HTTPS, overview, 884–89
mapping, 50–51
non-TCP/UDP, 117
Point-to-Point Tunneling (PPTP), 734
publishing consideration, 593–95
redirection, 583–84
server publishing, 78, 589
SMTP (Simple Mail Transfer Protocol), 47–51
SSTP, 23
TMG deployment options, 52–53
tunneling, 22–23
Web Listener, 77
Proxy authentication, 875–76, 879–80
Proxy cache, overview, 387–89
Proxy chaining, 922
Proxy Server, history of, 923–35
Proxy servers
  overview, 918–23
  public, 534–38
  WPAD (Web Proxy Auto Discovery), 353
Proxy sorting, 361
Proxy traffic, migration and, 94
Proxy, migration, 92–93
ProxyEnable, 108
ProxyOverride, 108
ProxyServer, 108
Public Key Infrastructure (PKI), 593, 703
Publishing
  availability, rules, 76–80, 216, 218
  Exchange Server
    configuring, 707–18
    planning for, 697–707
    troubleshooting, 719–30
  migration, 90–91, 94
  non-Web servers, 637–47
  planning rules, 591–97
  published servers, 117
  scenarios, 573–80

server publishing, 574–77, 588–91
servers, troubleshooting, 647–56
SharePoint Services
    configuring, multi-server, 672–79
    configuring, overview, 665–66
    configuring, server farm, 679–89
    configuring, single-server, 667–72
    planning for, 661–65
    troubleshooting, 689–95
SMTP, configuring, 820–26
Test Button, 656–57
troubleshooting, 657–60
Web publishing, 578–88
Web servers
    HTTP, 600–18
    HTTP protocol, 600–18
    HTTPS, 599–636
    overview, 599–600
Web site publishing rules, creating, 558
PUT, 871, 913

Q

Quarantined VPN clients, 31, 91, 223, 753
Query Length, 552
querystring, 405
Queues, 24, 42, 809, 814

R

RADIUS, 40, 237–38, 663–64, 741, 751, 762–63
Radius Server Settings, Configure, 190
RAID hardware mirroring, 35, 812–13
RAM
    caching, 389–91
    flood mitigation, 330–36
    hardware requirements, 35–36
    log files, 803–04, 812–13
    TMG requirements, 12
    VPN access, requirements, 740–41
RDP client, 353
Reading, log files, 176
Receive Auto Tuning, 12
Recipient Filtering, 512–13
Recurring Report Job Wizard, 451–55
recv, 121

Redirect requests, 617
Redundancy
    Enable ISP Redundancy Wizard, 206
    hardware requirements, 35–36
    ISP Redundancy, 78–79, 263–65
    UAG, security and, 26
Registry, 481
    WinINet updates, 108
Reliability
    best practices, 298–99
    configuring, 293–98
    enabling, 288–92
    ISP redundancy, 263–65, 267–84
    ISP Redundancy Configuration Wizard, 269–74,
        276–84
    ISPRedundancyConfig, 266
    link availability testing, 265–67
    NLB architecture, 285–88
    rule basics, 242
    TMG console, 197–98
    troubleshooting, 301–06
    virtual environments, 300–01
Remote access
    hardware requirements, 36
    management, 147, 172–74, 299
    protocol mapping, 51
    single-NIC, 31
    TMG console, 192
    TMG deployment options, 52–53
    TMGC, Winsock requests, 129
    UAG, security, 26
    VPN
        dial-in clients, 747–56
        L2TP over IPsec, configuring, 774–81
        NAP integration, 743–45
        NAP integration, configuring, 756–63
        overview, 733–36
        planning access, 737–43
        site-to-site, 773–74, 782–93
        SSTP configuration, 763–71
        technology comparisons, 736–37
Remote Authentication Dial-In User Service (RADIUS),
        40, 237–38, 663–64, 741, 751, 762–63
Remote Desktop
    installation, TMG 2010, 165
    installation, TMG MBE, 152
Remote Procedure Call (RPC), 47–51, 77, 120,
        590, 704

Report Generation Warning, 800
Reporting
  Active Directory Lightweight Directory Services
    (LDS), 147
  cache behavior, 417–20
  IIS, default links, 37
  logging options, 800–03
  Malware Inspection, 429–30, 446–63
  new features, 14–16
  TMG console, 192–93
Reputation Service. *See* Microsoft Reputation
  Service (MRS)
REQUEST fields, 871
Require All Users To Authenticate, 238–39
Requirements
  client selection, 134
  deploying in virtual environments, 44–45
  hardware, 35–36
  network infrastructure, 37–41
    complex networks, 53
    configuring TMG networks, 54–57
    name resolution, 58–63
    TMG deployment options, 51–53
    traffic profile, determining, 47–51
  performance monitoring, 41–43
  SecureNET clients, 113–14
  software, 36–37
  Web proxy clients, 112
Resource consumption, flood mitigation, 330–36
Reverse caching, 391, 394–95, 920
Reverse proxy, 921–22
Reverse-lookups, 38–39, 516
Rolling upgrades, 88
Root Certification Authority, new features, 16
Root DNS servers, 265–67
Routing. *See also* CARP (Cache Array Routing Protocol)
  IP routing, basic, 210–15
  network structure, migrating, 91
  networks rules, creating, 226–31
  route relationships, 215
  source routing, 329
  split routing infrastructure, 48
Routing and Remote Access Service (RRAS), 171,
  748, 763
RPC (Remote Procedure Call), 47–51, 77, 120,
  590, 704
RTSP, 50, 382–84
Rule-based URL filtering, configuring, 475–76

S

S4U2Proxy requests, 687
Safe list services, 503–05
Safe Search, Bing, 471
SANs (Subject Alternate Names), 662
Scenarios
  caching, 390–91
  migration, 90–95
  publishing, 573–80
Schedules, 96, 582, 663
SCL (Spam Confidence Level), 511–12
Scripting
  best practices, 834–36
  JScript
    importing and exporting files, 838
    JScript Regular Expressions, 362
    locating arrays, 837
    objects, 357–59, 361
    overview, 834
    WPAD, cfile, 352–64
  task automation, 836–42, 845–48
  TMG Component Object Model (COM), 829–34
  VBScript
    importing and exporting files, 838
    locating arrays, 837
    overview, 834
    PowerShell conversions, 846
    save changes, 841
  Windows PowerShell, 37, 171, 842–48
  WPAD script CARP operation, 947–54
Search, Bing, 471
Secure Socket Tunneling Protocol (SSTP)
  configuring, 763–71
  overview, 735
  TMG deployment options, 52–53
  troubleshooting, 771, 792–93
  VPN protocol, 23, 736–37
Secure Sockets Layer (SSL)
  authentication, protected networks, 237
  cache rules, 392
  connection requests, 110
  Exchange Server, 699–700, 703–04
  handshake, 703, 884
  HTTPS, overview, 884–89
  new features, 16
  SharePoint Services, 662, 665
  SSL-ID affinity, 73–75

tunnels, ports for, 111
web proxy client calls, 534
SecureNET clients
authentication, 239
client considerations, 293
features of, 135
firewall chaining, 335
migration, 93
overview, 113–18
traffic management, 81–82
SecureNETSecureNET, 70
SecurID, 664
Security
client selection and, 133–34
logging, importance of, 797–98
preinstallation checklist, 141
SharePoint Services, 661–63
site-to-site VPN connections, 774
UAG, aligning, 26
updates, 173–74
URL filtering, new features, 16
virtual environments, deploying in, 45
VPN access, 738–39
Security Alert, 15
Security by obscurity, 558
send, 121
Sender Filtering, 513–15
Sender ID, 515–16
Sender open proxy test, 517
Sender Policy Framework (SPF), 218, 515–16
Sender Reputation Level (SRL), 515–18
SendLogonOn401, 702
Server Acknowlegement, 889
Server Certificate errors, 549
Server Connection Security, 606
Server farms, 587–88, 606, 679–89
Server hello, 886
Server Key Exchange, 887
Server Message Block (SMB), 51
Server publishing
access rules and, 577
network relationships and, 576–77
non-Web, 78, 637–47
overview, 574–76
rule, 588–91
Single NIC firewalls, 70
Server Virtualization Validation Program (SVVP), 25
ServerManagerCmdInstallLogDATE-TIME, 175

Servers, dedicated servers list, 278, 282
Server-side CARP, 397
Server-side configurations, Web proxy, 111
Service packs, TMG Setup options, 173–74
Service Principal Name, 669, 677
Service Provider Interface (SPI), 122–25
Session Affinity, 587
Session ID, 885
Session Initiation Protocol (SIP) filter, 18, 50, 205, 336, 590
Settings
authentication, Web listener, 602–03
cache, 397–400, 407–12
flood mitigation, 339–40
Intrustion Detection System (IDS), 324
Malware Inspection, 437–38
NIC configuration, 268
Setup, TMG
architecture, 169–72
options, 172–74
troubleshooting, 174
Sharepoint, 587
SharePoint Services
configuring
multi-server, 672–79
overview, 665–66
server farm, 679–89
single-server, 667–72
publishing, planning for, 661–65
troubleshooting, 689–95
SharePoint Web Publishing Wizard, 665–72
shExpMatch(), 949
Signatures
HTTP Filter, 561–70
new features, 13
NIS (Network Inspection System)
configuring, 311–16
implementing, 309–10
IP preferences, configuring, 327–30
monitoring, 319–21
overview, 308–09
updates, 322
Update Center, 478–81
Simple Mail Transfer Protocol. See SMTP (Simple Mail Transfer Protocol)
Simplex, 78
Single network adapter, 52–53, 223
Single NIC, 62, 69–71

Single-NIC, 31–32
Single-Sign-On (SSO), 580
SIP (Session Intiation Protocol) filter, 18, 50, 205, 336, 590
SirCam virus, 488–90
Site-to-site (S2S) VPN
    migration, 92
    Network Inspection System (NIS), 336
    overview, 773–74
    PPTP, configuring, 782–88
    troubleshooting connections, 788–93
skiphost, 949, 952
Smart-card authentication, 719–20
SMB (Server Message Block), 51
SMTP (Simple Mail Transfer Protocol)
    configuring, 493–501, 518–27
    E-Mail Protection Wizard, 494–501
    Enhanced NAT (E-NAT), 817–20
    new features, 16–17
    protection, overview, 490–92
    publishing rules, 658–60
    route relationships, 215
    server publishing, 590
    SMTP Message Screener, 490–91
    SMTP Protection, 174
    SMTP Publishing, configuring, 820–26
    spam filtering, configuring, 502–18
    traffic profile, 47–51
socket, 121
SOCKS filter, 937, 943
SOCKS-proxy, troubleshooting, 903–09
Software requirements, 36–37, 88
Source IP affinity, 72, 74–75
Source port affinity, 72
Source routing, 329
Spam
    e-mail threats, overview, 487–90
    Exchange (Anti Spam), 479
    filtering, configuring, 502–18
    new features, 16–18
    overview, 490
    policies, 194–95
Spam Confidence Level (SCL), 511–12
spash.hta, 171
SPF (Sender Policy Framework), 218, 515–16
SPI (Service Provider Interface), 122–25
Spindle, 429
Split routing infrastructure, 48

SPNEGO, 878
Spoof detection, 337–38
Spyware. See Malware protection
SQL Express, 804–05
SQL Server 2008, 171, 802–07
SQL Server Express Database, 802
SQL Server Reporting Services (SRS), 14–16
SQL Server, best practices, 815
SRL (Sender Reputation Level), 515–18
SSL (Secure Sockets Layer)
    authentication, protected networks, 237
    cache rules, 392
    connection requests, 110
    Exchange Server, 699–700, 703–04
    HTTPS, overview, 884–89
    new features, 16
    SharePoint Services, 662, 665
    SSL-ID affinity, 73–75
    tunnels, ports for, 111
    web proxy client calls, 534
SSL (Secure Sockets Layer) handshake, 703, 884
SSO (Single-Sign-On), 580
SSTP (Secure Socket Tunneling Protocol)
    configuring, 763–71
    overview, 735
    TMG deployment options, 52–53
    troubleshooting, 771, 792–93
    VPN protocol, 23, 736–37
Stateful failover, 264
Stateful inspection, 10
Static Proxy, 81–82
Status codes, 873, 914
Storage, 389, 395, 439–40, 803–04, 812–13.
        See also Memory
Streaming media, 50, 330, 353, 382–84, 590
Strict Source Routing, 329
Stripe sets with parity, 813
Subject Alternate Names (SANs), 662
SuccessesToAvailable, 267
Supportability, VPN access, 742
SVCHOST.EXE (Windows Server service), 567
SVVP (Server Virtualization Validation
        Program), 25
Switch flooding, 286–87
Symmetric bridging, 584
SYN attack protection, 337–40
System Center Operations Manager, 44
System Configuration Wizard, 200, 202

System node, TMG console, 191
System Performance, 964
System policy, 172

T

Task automation, 836–42
TCP 3-way handshake, 870
TCP 4-way closing handshake, 870
TCP connections
  attacks against, 323
  flood mitigation, 330–36
  non-Web servers, 637–47
  port 1723, PPTP, 734
  ports
    135, 50
    1743, 117
    443 (HTTPS), 28, 111
    593, 111
    80, 15
    8008, 15, 37
    8080, 109
    route relationships, 215
    source port affinity, 72
  PPTP, port 1723, 788–90
  SharePoint Services, 690
  WPAD, Internet Explorer configuration, 376
TCP handshake, 884
TCP sequence protection, 338–40
Teardrop attack, 329
Templates
  3-Leg Perimeter, 67–68
  Back Firewall, 68–69
  Edge Firewall, 66–67
  Single NIC firewall, 69–71
Terminal Services Gateway, 73, 77
Test Rule, 612, 725–30
Testing. See also Troubleshooting
  ISP-Redundancy, 265
  Test Button, Web publishing, 656–57
  URL filtering, 476
TestIntervalLinkAvailable, 267
TestIntervalLinkUnavailable, 267
Text logs, 807–08
TFTP (Trivial File Transfer Protocol) Filter, 18, 50
Third-party platforms, 301
Third-party solutions, high-availability, 74, 76

Timeout values, HTTP(S) connections, 706–07, 721
Time-To-Live (TTL), 78–79, 95, 392
TMCG Control Channel, 127
TMG. See Microsoft Forefront Threat Management Gateway (TMG)
TMG MBE. See Microsoft Forefront Threat Management Gateway (TMG), Medium Business Edition (MBE)
tmgbook.hash.and.sort.js, 947–48
TRACE, 871
Traffic. See also Network Inspection System (NIS)
  buffering, requirements, 37–41
  captures, Network Monitor, 891–97
  captures, reading captures, 897–903
  CERN proxy HTTP, 242–49
  control, requirements, 40–41
  Exchange Server, performance, 703–06
  filtering, 6–8, 22–23
  ISP Redundanccy, 268
  load, authentication, 40
  NAT relationships, 215–20
  network design
    availability, for publishing rules, 76–80
    availability, overview, 71–76
    for Access Rules, 80–81
    protected networks, 231–39
  network relationships, overview, 209–22
  network rules, creating, 226–31
  ping requests, 242–45
  policy behavior, 241–49
  Policy Reevaluation, 249–53
  profile, determining, 47–51
  proxy traffic, migration and, 94
  route relationships, 215
  TMG Setup options, 172–74
  troubleshooting access rules, 253–62
Traffic Simulator, 259–62, 859
Transactions, HTTP, 870–74
Transparent proxy requests, 649–50
Transport mode, VPN tunnels, 734
Transport Service Provider (TSP), 122, 125–32
Trickling, 431, 438–39
Trihomed perimeter network, 30
Trivial File Transfer Protocol (TFTP) Filter, 18, 50
Troubleshooting. See also Performance, counters
  access rules, 253–62
  availability, 80
  Best Practices Analyzer (BPA), 860–61
  cache, 417–23

case study, 862–68
client types, 136
Enhanced NAT (E-NAT), 826–27
Exchange Server, 719–30
general methodology, 851–55
Internet Explorer and WPAD, 381
load balancing, 286, 301–06
logging, 798–800
Network Monitor
  overview, 861
  reading captures, 897–903
  SOCKS-proxy, 903–09
  traffic capture, 891–97
Performance Monitor, 861
PICNIC, 88
publishing rules, 647–56
SharePoint Services, 689–95
SSTP connectivity, 771
tab, Management Console, 858–59
TMG console, 186
TMG Setup
  architecture, 169–72
  failure of, 174
  setup options, 172–74
tools for, 855–58
VPN client connections, 788–93
web proxy traffic, 532
Windows Event Logs, 862
Trunks, types, 24
Trust, HTTP, 874–83
Trusted Root certificate store, 535
TSP (Transport Service Provider), 122
TTL (Time-To-Live), 78–79, 392
Tunnel-based publishing, 588–91
Tunneling protocols, 22–23
Tunnels, VPNs
  dial-in clients, configuring, 747–56
  NAP integration, 743–45
  NAP integration, configuring, 756–63
  overview, 733–36
  planning access, 737–43
  site-to-site
    L2TP over IPsec, configuring, 774–81
    overview, 773–74
    PPTP, configuring, 782–88
    troubleshooting, 788–93
    TP configuration, 763–71
  chnology comparisions, 736–37

U

UAG. *See* Unified Access Gateway (UAG)
UDP. *See* User Datagram Protocol (UDP)
Unattended installations, TMG, 168, 171–72
Unicast, 285–86
Unified Access Gateway (UAG)
  access, enabling, 22–23
  deployment, 27–28
  future release, 21
  IAG 2007, 23–24
  ISA Server, 24
  network protection, designing, 27–32
  new features, 25–26
  security needs, aligning, 26
Unified Messaging Server, 698
Uniform Resource Identifier (URI), 912
Unihomed network, 31–32
Update Center. *See also* Updates
  configuring, 481–85
  Medium Business Edition (MBE), 185
  NIS (Network Inspection System), 322
  overview, 199, 478–81
  TMG console, 187
Update Configuration, 440
Updates. *See also* Update Center
  dynamic update, 370–74
  hotfix, Hyper-V, 301
  migration, preparation for, 88
  NIS (Network Inspection System), 315, 322
  TMG console, 192–93
  TMG Setup options, 173–74
Upgrades, rolling, 88
URI (Uniform Resource Identifier), 912
URL correction, 664–65
URL filtering
  category overrides, 477–78
  configuring, 470–78
  HTTP Filter, 533–34
  manual, 429
  maximum URL length, 552
  overview, 465–70
  performance counter, 938, 961
  TMG Setup architecture, 171
  TMG, new features, 15–16, 194
  Update Center, 478–81
    configuring, 481–85
URL Filtering Updates, 479

URLs
  CARP (Cache Array Routing Protocol), 395–97
  ConvertUrlToLowerCase, 355–56
  FetchURL, 421
User Agent, HTTP, 916
User Datagram Protocol (UDP)
  bidirectional protocols, 574
  flood mitigation, 334
  non-Web servers, 637–47
  route relationships, 215
  source port affinity, 72
  UDP bomb alert, 326
  UDP port 1701, 735
  UDP port 500, 735
User Groups, 663
User interface, new features, 14–16
Users
  authentication, WDigest, 235
  Exchange Server planning, 705
  IIS requests, 24
  logging, 797
  mobile, 27
  Require All Users To Authenticate, 238–39
  Web proxy client, 354
  Web publishing rules, 610
  Web server rules, 635

V

Validation
  HTTP Filter, 550, 564–67
  HTTPS Inspection, 538–47
  requirements, 39–40
  Server Virtualization Validation Program (SVVP), 25
  SharePoint Services, 663–64
  Test Rule, publishing, 612
Variants, URL, 468
VBScript, 834
  importing and exporting files, 838
  locating arrays, 837
  PowerShell conversions, 846
  save changes, 841
verbose mode, 176
Version control, 315
Video streams, 18, 382–84
VIP (Virtual IP addresses), 285, 290, 498, 606
Virtual environments

deployment requirements, 44–45
hardware requirements, 36
load balancing, 300–01
TMG deployment options, 52–53
UAG deployment, 25
Virtual IP addresses (VIPs), 285, 290, 498, 606
Virtual Private Networks (VPN)
  access, enabling, 22–23
  creating, 222–24
  dial-in clients
    configuring, 747–56
  migration, 91–92
  NAP integration, 756–65
  overview, 733–36
  planning access, 737–43
  quarantined clients, 31
  Single NIC firewalls, 69–70
  site-to-site
    L2TP over IPsec, configuring, 774–81
    overview, 773–74
    PPTP, configuring, 782–88
    troubleshooting, 788–93
  SSTP configuration, 763–71
  technology comparisons, 736–37
  TMGC, Winsock requests, 129
  VPN Clients Network, 222–24
Virus Filtering, 522–25
Virus protection
  AnnaKournikova, 488–89
  BadTrans, 489–90
  BubbleBoy, 489–90
  configuring, 518–27
  e-mail threats, overview, 487–90
  ILOVEYOU, 488–89
  Malware Inspection
    content delivery, 438–39
    environment considerations, 431–36
    Internet access, testing, 443–45
    overview, 427–31
    per-rule, defining, 442
    reports, creating, 446–63
    settings, configuring, 437–38
    storage, 439–40
    Update Configuration, 440
  Melissa, 488–89
  new features, 11–14
  SirCam, 488–89
  Update Center, 478–81

VLAN, 286
VLAN tagging, 288
VMWare, 301
VMWare ESX Server, 301
Voice Over IP (VoIP)
  Configure SIP Wizard, 205
  route relationships, 215
  TMG, new features, 18
VPN Clients Network, 222–24
VPNs. *See* Virtual Private Networks (VPN)

W

WAN (wide area networks), 48, 592–93, 773
Waveform audio format (.wav), 489
WDigest, 235
Web Access Policy, 185, 188–90, 194, 562–64, 568
Web Access Policy Wizard, 200, 203, 431, 536
Web Access Wizard, 16, 473
Web Antivirus, new features, 11–14
Web caching, 36, 69–70
Web chaining, 77, 91, 93, 242, 335
Web client requests, 650
Web farms, load-balancing, 26
Web filters, 191, 578–80. *See also* Malware Inspection
Web Listener Wizard, 768–69
Web listeners, 77, 91, 618, 625–30, 653–54, 766
Web objects, caching, 392
Web Proxy
  cache, overview, 387–89
  clients
    availability, 81–82
    cfile, 354
    features of, 135
    NLB, 293
    overview, 107–13
    preinstallation checklist, 142
    with TMGC, 132
  logging options, 800–03
  performance counters, 937, 944
  requests, authentication, 103
  requests, troubleshooting, 649–50
  ervers
    authentication, 40
    vailability, 80–81
    ardware requirements, 36
    ngle NIC firewalls, 69–70

TMG deployment options, 52–53
  SSTP protocol, 735
Web Proxy Automatic Discovery (WPAD)
  client applications
    Automatic Proxy Cache, 379–80
    AutoProxy in managed code, 384–85
    Internet Explorer, configuring, 375–79
    overview, 374
    TMG Client, 381–82
    Windows Media Player, 382–84
  configuring, 364–74
  overview, 968
  protocol, 345–52
  script, 352–64
  script CARP operation, 947–54
  troubleshooting, Internet Explorer, 381
Web Proxy Filter, 265, 429, 573, 580
Web Proxy Log, 469
Web Publishing. *See also* Microsoft Office SharePoint
    Services
  NAT relationships, 218
  network design for, 76–78
  overview, 578–80
  rules, 91, 580–88
  SharePoint Services, 662
  Test Button, 656–57
  troubleshooting, 647–56
Web Publishing Load Balancing (WPLB), 72, 78–80
Web Server (IIS) Server Role, 37
Web servers
  HTTP protocol, 600–18
  HTTPS protocol, 618–36
  publishing, overview, 599–600
  server farm, 587–88
Web site publishing rules, 558
Web-based applications, mapping, 49
Web-based e-mail, new features, 16, 24. *See also* E-mail
WebRequest, 108
Welcome Screen, TMG MBE, 185–86
WFP (Windows Filtering Platform), 6–7
Whale, 24
Whiteboards, 18
Wide area networks (WAN), 48, 592–93, 773
Windows 2000, 374
Windows 2003, 374
Windows 2004, 374
Windows authentication, 39–40, 663–64, 806
Windows Automatic Updates, 479–81

Windows Crypto API (CAPI), 535
Windows DHCP Client API, 346
Windows DNS resolver, 63
Windows Essential Business Server (EBS), 11–12
Windows Event Logs, 862. *See also* Logging
Windows Executable Content, 552
Windows Filtering Platform (WFP), 6–7
Windows Firewall, traffic policies, 7
Windows Internet Connection Firewall (ICF), 7
Windows Internet Libraries, 967
Windows Internet Name Service (WINS), 58–59
Windows Media Player, 353, 382–84
Windows Out-of-Band (WinNuke), 325
Windows Performance Monitor. *See* Performance
    Monitor
Windows PowerShell, 37, 171, 842–48
Windows Security Support (SSP), 235–36
Windows Server 2003, 7, 94, 287, 690
Windows Server 2008, 5, 11–12, 36, 94, 370–74,
    739, 763
Windows Server 2008 Hyper-V RTM, 301
Windows Server service (SVCHOST.EXE), 567
Windows Server Update Services (WSUS),
    479–81, 484
Windows Sockets. *See* Winsock
Windows Temp folder, 174
Windows Update Agent (WUA) API, 322
Windows Web Services API (WWSAPI), 469
Windows XP, 374
WinHTTP, 353, 384–85, 469, 967–72
WinHTTP API, 107
WinHttpGetProxyForUrl, 384
WinInet, 969
WinINet, 108, 353, 967
WinNuke, 325
WINS (Windows Internet Name Service), 38, 58–59,
    92–93
Winsock
    logging, 798–99
    overview, 119–22
    providers, 122–25
    TMGC as layered service provider, 125–32
    Web proxy clients, 113
Wizards
    Certificate Import Wizard, 621–25
    Configure E-mail Policy Wizard, 205
    Configure SIP Wizard, 205
    Configure Web Access Policy Wizard, 397–400

Connect to Forefront Protection Manager 2010
    Wizard, 204–05
Create VPN Site-To-Site Connection Wizard, 775–80,
    782–87
Deployment Wizard, 200, 202–03
E-Mail Policy Wizard, 495–501
E-Mail Protection Wizard, 494–501
Enable ISP Redundancy Wizard, 206
Exchange Publishing Wizard, 698–700
Exchange Server, 702–03
Getting Started Wizard, 54–57, 66–67, 69–70, 174,
    200–01
ISP Redundancy Configuration Wizard, 269–74,
    276–84
Join Array and Disjoin Array, 203–04
Network Load Balancing Integration Wizard, 293
Network Rule Wizard, 221
Network Setup Wizard, 30, 200–02
New Cache Rule Wizards, 401–07
New Content Download Job Wizard, 409–12
New Network Rule Wizard, 18, 227–31, 822–23
New Network Wizard, 224–26
New Server Farm Wizard, 681–84
New Server Publishing Rule Wizard, 638, 642
New SharePoint Publishing Rule Wizard,
    672–89
New URL Category Set Wizard, 475
New Web Listener Wizard, 601, 709
New Web Publishing Rule Wizard, 604
new, overview, 199–200
One-Time Report Wizard, 446–50
Recurring Report Job Wizard, 451–55
SharePoint Web Publishing Wizard, 665–72
System Configuration Wizard, 200, 202
TMG Installation Wizard, 147, 152, 160, 170
Web Access Policy Wizard, 200, 203, 536
Web Access Wizard, 16, 473
Web Listener Wizard, 768–69
WLBS display, 305–06
WLBS IP2MAC, 305
WLBS query, 304
wlbs.exe, 304–06
Workgroups, 60–61, 82–84, 94
Worms. *See also* Malware protection
    BadTrans, 490
    Conficker, 567–70
    e-mail threats, overview, 487–90
    flood mitigation, 333

intrusion detection, 323
KaK, 489–90
Update Center, 478–81
WPAD (Web Proxy Automatic Discovery), 968
  client applications
    Automatic Proxy Cache, 379–80
    AutoProxy in managed code, 384–85
    Internet Explorer, configuring, 375–79
    overview, 374
    TMG Client, 381–82
    Windows Media Player, 382–84
  configuring, 364–74
  migration, 93

protocol, 345–52
script, 352–64
script CARP operation, 947–54
troubleshooting, Internet Explorer, 381
wpad queries, 371
wpad.dat, 375
WPLB (Web Publishing Load Balancing), 72, 78–80
Write conflicts, 389
wspad.dat, 126, 128
wspsrv.exe, 469
WSUS (Windows Server Update Services), 479–81, 484
WWSAPI (Windows Web Services API), 469
WWW-Authenticate, 875

About the Authors

The guys that wrote this book spent a year working together on this one project. What follows offers some insight into how they were able to tolerate each other for so long.

About Jim Harrison

I'm a retired U.S. Navy ET1(SW) who spent my Navy time on three ships: the U.S.S. Proteus (AS-19), the U.S.S. Nimitz (CVN-68), and the U.S.S. California (CGN-36) as well as NAS Corpus Christi, Texas, Naval Station San Diego, and Naval Station Bremerton, Washington. It was during this time that I learned the fine art of complex system troubleshooting on various radar, radio, GPS, depth-finding, and computer equipment.

I began working at Microsoft in 1999 as a Volt contractor in the Windows Media division, helping to create a product called Digital Broadcast Manager (DBM). I joined Microsoft full-time in 2000. Later that year, I moved to the NetDocs team as a network deployment tester. During this time, I was encouraged to familiarize myself with ISA Server 2000. As they say, the rest is history.

I joined the ISA SE team in 2003 as a test engineer helping to test and ship updates and managing customer cases escalated from CSS to the product team. I present on ISA Server and TMG twice a year at Tech Ed US and Black Hat LV. I also enjoy writing a few ISA blogs, answering the rare forum posting, and producing an occasional Tales from the Edge article.

I fill my copious spare time with my wife and two cats, wandering in the woodlands of western Washington, playing guitar, woodworking, and general home handyman activities (OK—honey-dos). When I get the chance, I run around the backyard with my two-year-old grandson until he wears me out.

About Yuri Diogenes

 I started working in the IT field as a computer operator back in 1993 using MS-DOS and Windows 3.1. In 1998 I moved to a Microsoft partner and worked as an instructor for computer classes; I also wrote internal training materials such as NT 4 and Networking. In 1999 I moved to another Microsoft partner as part of a team responsible for maintaining the network of a major Brazilian telecommunications company. There I was responsible for administering the core servers running NT 4.

In December 2003, I moved to the United States to work for Microsoft as a Compcontech contractor in the CSS for the Latin America messaging division, where I supported Exchange. In 2004 I moved to Dell Computers in Round Rock, Texas, to initially work as Server Advisor in the Network Operating System Team, dealing primarily with Windows, Exchange, and ISA. I came back to Microsoft as a full-time employee in 2006 to work again on CSS for LATAM, but this time I was focused on the platform division (Networking and ISA Server).

I joined the CSS ISA Team in 2007 as a Security Support Engineer and started to be fully dedicated to ISA. In 2008 my friend Nathan Bigman had the idea to create the Tales from the Edge. Jim Harrison and I started leading this project; eventually many other engineers started to contribute as well. In 2009 I became Senior Security Support Escalation Engineer on the ISA Team, which gave me some new responsibilities.

I like to spend my spare time with my wife, Alexsandra, and my two daughters, Yanne and Ysis. We enjoy traveling, watching movies, and playing on our Xbox 360.

About Mohit Saxena

 Right after my graduation from college in 2002, I started working for Dell computers in New Delhi. The whole concept of phone support was new to me and I believe this is where I learned the basics of troubleshooting and customer handling. After spending a year with Dell I moved to Convergys India Services, where I joined the Microsoft Enterprise Platform Support on the Networking Team. In 2004, when the Enterprise Platform Support teams were being formed at Microsoft GTSC in Bangalore, I was hired by Microsoft as a full-time engineer on the Networking Team and I became a Technical Lead for the same team in 2005. I moved to Seattle in 2007 and since then I've been working solely on ISA. In 2008 I became a Technical Lead for the ISA Team and a few months later became a lead for the IAG Team as well. As a lead I mainly work on helping the engineers in my team with escalations. I also work with escalation engineers to collaborate with the ISA development team to resolve bugs and design change requests.

I generally spend my spare time with my wife, Anusha, and our little puppy, Mojo, who is a highly energetic springer spaniel. Much of my time is spent making sure that Mojo doesn't chew up the walls or my socks. However, he can make me smile anytime with his antics and he completes my family. I like to read a lot and whenever I can find some free time from work, wife, and the dog (not in that order), I generally try and read novels.

What do you think of this book?

We want to hear from you!

To participate in a brief online survey, please visit:

microsoft.com/learning/booksurvey

Tell us how well this book meets your needs—what works effectively, and what we can do better. Your feedback will help us continually improve our books and learning resources for you.

Thank you in advance for your input!

Stay in touch!

To subscribe to the *Microsoft Press® Book Connection Newsletter*—for news on upcoming books, events, and special offers—please visit:

microsoft.com/learning/books/newsle